A HISTORY OF ENGLAND

IN EIGHT VOLUMES

GENERAL EDITOR: SIR CHARLES OMAN, K.B.E.

VOLUME V

ENGLAND UNDER THE STUARTS

A HISTORY OF ENGLAND

IN EIGHT VOLUMES

EDITED BY SIR CHARLES OMAN

I. ENGLAND BEFORE THE NORMAN CONQUEST. By SIR CHARLES OMAN, K.B.E., M.A. F.B.A., All Souls College, Oxford. [*Eighth Edition.*

II. ENGLAND UNDER THE NORMANS AND ANGEVINS. By H. W. C. DAVIS, M.A., LL.D., C.B.E., late Regius Professor of Modern History in the University of Oxford. [*Twelfth Edition.*

III. ENGLAND IN THE LATER MIDDLE AGES. By KENNETH H. VICKERS, M.A., Principal of University College Southampton. [*Sixth Edition.*

IV. ENGLAND UNDER THE TUDORS. By ARTHUR D. INNES, sometime Scholar of Oriel College, Oxford. Revised by J. M. HENDERSON, M.A., Lecturer in British History in the University of Aberdeen [*Eleventh Edition.*

V. ENGLAND UNDER THE STUARTS. By G. M. TREVELYAN, O.M., Regius Professor of Modern History in the University of Cambridge. [*Nineteenth Edition.*

VI. ENGLAND UNDER THE HANOVERIANS. By Sir CHARLES GRANT ROBERTSON, M.A., LL.D., Fellow of All Souls College, Oxford. [*Thirteenth Edition.*

VII. ENGLAND SINCE WATERLOO. By Sir J. A. R. MARRIOTT, M.A., Honorary Fellow, formerly Fellow, Lecturer and Tutor in Modern History, of Worcester College, Oxford. [*Thirteenth Edition.*

VIII. MODERN ENGLAND. 1885-1945 By Sir J. A. R. MARRIOTT [*Third Edition, Revised and Enlarged.*

ENGLAND UNDER THE STUARTS

BY

GEORGE MACAULAY TREVELYAN

MASTER OF TRINITY COLLEGE, CAMBRIDGE

WITH FOUR MAPS

TWENTIETH EDITION

METHUEN & CO. LTD. LONDON
36 Essex Street, Strand, W.C.2

First Published		.	November	1904
Second Edition	.	.	September	1905
Third Edition	.	.	February	1908
Fourth Edition	.	.	August	1910
Fifth Edition	.	.	March	1912
Sixth Edition	.	.	April	1914
Seventh Edition	.	.	February	1917
Eighth Edition	.	.	February	1919
Ninth Edition	.	.	October	1920
Tenth Edition	.	.	April	1922
Eleventh Edition .		.	January	1924
Twelfth Edition, Revised		.	June	1925
Thirteenth Edition	.	.	Augus	1926
Fourteenth Edition	.	.	May	1929
Fifteenth Edition	.	.	April	1930
Sixteenth Edition	.	.	October	1933
Seventeenth Edition	.	.	May	1938
Eighteenth Edition	.	.	March	1942
Nineteenth Edition, Revised	.		February	1946
Twentieth Edition	.	.		1947

CATALOGUE NO. 3375/U

PRINTED IN GREAT BRITAIN

PREFACE TO REVISED EDITION (1925)

SINCE this book comes of age in 1925 and still remains in considerable demand, revision is perhaps overdue. I have endeavoured to excise some of the more glaring crudities of youthful style and opinion, and I have made additions and corrections suggested by important publications on the period that have appeared since 1904, which are named in the Bibliography or notes of this edition. In addition to Sir Charles Firth's continued elucidation of the period, the chief contribution of new fact and opinion has, perhaps, been made by Mr. W. A. Shaw in his *Calendar of State Papers, Treasury Books*. I have used and discussed some of his findings on pp. 281, 303-5 below, and in Appendix E. Mr. Feiling's *History of the Tory Party, 1640–1714*, also throws new light on the last years of William. But it is difficult for a revision to embody new material satisfactorily. I therefore call the student's special attention to these works, and for the same reason to Vol. V. of Professor Holdsworth's *History of English Law*, particularly the last chapter on Coke.

G. M. TREVELYAN

PREFACE TO THE REVISED EDITION OF 1946

SINCE I revised this volume largely in 1925, I have now only made a few further alterations. I have added to the Bibliography the names of a score of valuable books, mostly published since 1925.

G. M. TREVELYAN

TRINITY COLLEGE,
CAMBRIDGE

CONTENTS

APPENDIX C

APPENDIX D

APPENDIX E

LIST OF MAPS

PRINCIPAL ABBREVIATIONS USED IN FOOTNOTES

G. = Gardiner's *History of England*, 1603-42 (ed. 1893).

G. (*C. W.*) = Gardiner's *Civil War* (ed. 1894).

G. (*C. & P.*) = Gardiner's *Commonwealth and Protectorate* (ed. 1901).

G. (*Const. Docs.*) = *Constitutional Documents*, 1625-60. Gardiner. 1899.

Ranke = Ranke's *History of England*. Clarendon Press Translation. 1875.

Ludlow = *Ludlow's Memoirs*. Ed. by C. H. Firth. 1894.

Hutchinson = *Life of Col. Hutchinson by his Widow* (ed. 1846).

Clar. = Clarendon's *History of the Great Rebellion* (ed. 1843). (*Life = Life of* Clarendon, same edition.)

Carl.'s *Crom.* = *Cromwell's Letters and Speeches.* Carlyle.

Firth's *C. A.* = *Cromwell's Army.* C. H. Firth. 1902.

Firth's *Crom.* = *Oliver Cromwell.* C. H. Firth. (*Heroes of the Nations Series.*)

Cunningham = Cunningham's *Growth of English Industry and Commerce. Modern Times* (ed. 1903).

Verney = *Memoirs of the Verney Family*, 1892-94.

Oppenheim = *History of the Administration of the Royal Navy.* M. Oppenheim. 1896.

Dowell = Dowell's *History of Taxation* (ed. 1888).

Harl. Misc. = *Harleian Miscellany* (ed. 1808-13). 4to ed.

Gooch = *English Democratic Ideas in the Seventeenth Century.* G. P. Gooch. 1898 (*Cambridge Historical Essays*, No. x).

Shaw = *History of the English Church*, 1640-60. W. A. Shaw. 1900.

Sprigge = *Anglia Rediviva* (*England's Recovery*). By Joshua Sprigge, M.A. 1647.

Barclay = *Inner Life of the Religious Societies of the Commonwealth.* R. Barclay. 1876.

Prothero = *Statutes and Constitutional Documents*, 1559-1625. G. W. Prothero. 1894.

Rushworth = Rushworth's *Historical Collections*.

Leonard = *Early History of English Poor Relief.* Miss Leonard. 1900.

Taunton = *History of the Jesuits in England.* E. L. Taunton. 1901.

Lord Herbert = *The Life of Lord Herbert of Cherbury. Written by himself* (ed. 1893).

Stephen = *History of the Criminal Law of England.* 1883.

Rous = *Diary of John Rous* (Camden Society, 1856).

Stats. of Realm = *Statutes of Realm.*

Parl. Hist. = *Parliamentary History* (ed. 1806 *et seq.*).

Hamilton = *Quarter Sessions from Elizabeth to Anne.* A. H. Hamilton. 1878.

D. of Stettin = Diary of the Duke of Stettin, *R. H. S.*, 1892, pp. 1-67.

Einstein = *Italian Renaissance in England.* L. Einstein (Columbia University Press, 1902).

Hewins = *English Trade and Finance.* W. A. S. Hewins.

C. M. H. = *Cambridge Modern History.*

E. H. R. = *English Historical Review.*

H. M. C. R. = *Historical MSS. Commission Report.*

R. H. S. = *Royal Historical Society, Transactions of.*

Thurloe = *State Papers.* John Thurloe. 1742.

Corbett = *England in the Mediterranean.* Julian Corbett. 1904.

Stanhope = *Reign of Queen Anne* (ed. 1872). Earl Stanhope.

Lecky = *History of England in the Eighteenth Century* (ed. 1892).

Burnet = *History of His Own Times*, vols. i., ii. (ed. 1897, Airy) ; vols. iii.-vi. (ed. 1833).

Coxe = W. Coxe. *Life of Marlborough* (ed. 1818).

Airy = *Charles II.* Osmund Airy. 1901.

Pollock = *The Popish Plot.* John Pollock. 1903.

Grey = *Debates of the House of Commons*, 1667-94. Anchitel Grey. 1769.

First Whig = *The First Whig* (= William Sacheverell). 1894. Sir George Sitwell (unpublished).

Christie = *Life of Shaftesbury.* 1871.

Marvell = *Works of Andrew Marvell.* 1776.

Ailesbury = *Memoirs of Thomas Bruce, Earl of Ailesbury (Roxburgh Club).* 1890.

Bol. = *Letters of Bolingbroke.* 4 vols. 1798.

Wentworth = *The Wentworth Papers*, 1705-39. 1883.

INTRODUCTION

ENGLAND has contributed many things, good and bad, to the history of the world. But of all her achievements there is one, the most insular in origin and yet the most universal in effect. While Germany boasts her Reformation and France her Revolution, England can point to her dealings with the House of Stuart. Our Tudor Reformation, although it affected greater changes in the structure of English society and the evolution of English intellect, was but one part of a movement general throughout Europe. But the transference of sovereignty from Crown to Parliament was effected in direct antagonism to all continental tendencies. During the seventeenth century a despotic scheme of society and government was so firmly established in Europe, that but for the course of events in England it would have been the sole successor of the mediæval system. Everywhere on the ruins of the old privileges and powers of city, Church and baronage, arose the monarchy, firmly based on a standing army and a service of bureaucrats. In the latter half of the century this result was apparent and the theory of it accepted. The Spaniards had long surrendered their ancient liberties to their Catholic King ; Italy had forgotten even the name of freedom ; in France Louis XIV. wielded to admiration the sceptre set in his hand by the cunning Cardinals ; the nobles and the heretics of Bohemia had bowed, after a bloody contest, to their Imperial lord ; throughout Germany scores of petty princes, each within his own estate, aped the Grand Monarch. The Swiss cantons retained their liberty and were no longer of any account in Europe ; the provinces of Holland, which had so long shown that freedom means power, at length were sinking before the advance of the French monarchy ; they hesitated in painful choice between native despotism and foreign conquest. For other choice there was none, as all nations were beginning to agree. Military despotism was the price to be paid for national unity and power. Thus the white races of Europe and America, in whom the hope of mankind lay, were developing a political structure and a fashion of public sentiment akin to those of Czarist Russia. But at this moment the English, unaware of their destiny and of their service, tenacious only of their rights, their religion and their interests, evolved a system of government which differed as completely from the new continental model as it did from the chartered anarchy of the Middle Ages. This system, unlike that of the Swiss and Dutch confederacies of the day, was proved, in the

1

final struggle of Marlborough with Louis, to combine freedom with efficiency, and local rights with national union. It showed the world, by the example of a great nation that was fast becoming a great Empire, how liberty could mean not weakness but strength.

It is, then, to the history of England within her own borders that we must look for the origin of this departure ; we must trace the island struggle ; the rapid changes in methods and ideals ; the contribution of short-lived parties and men to the final result ; and not least of all the " magic hand of chance," in deeds that after generations attribute to inevitable cause.

But first, before we gaze into these events, the admired branches of the noblest tree of all English history, we must search for the spreading of its obscurer roots. We must examine the social, economic and religious life of classes in England, contrast these with the societies ruled by the continental monarchs, and mark how deep was the difference underlying the superficial tie of a common civilisation. Such an inquiry will be rewarded, not only because the general conditions of English life are the root of English political history, but also because those conditions deserve to be studied for their own sake. For the England created by the Elizabethans lasted with considerable development, but with little change, down to the industrial and social revolution that ushered in our own world a hundred years ago. It was a state of society and economics, of thought and emotion, far from ideal, but so healthy in its general influence that it made life strong and good for large masses of men and women, and produced out of a small population a proportion of great men, unmatched either in the earlier ages, or in our own generation as at present ordered.

Perhaps the period during which the conditions of life underwent least observable change is to be found in the years 1603-40. During this time no great alteration took place in institutions, in ideas or in religion, comparable to the changes of the preceding and of the following age. The English whom James came from Edinburgh to rule were the same English as those whom Pym, thirty-seven years later, took upon himself to lead ; the England which, resting from the great Elizabethan labour of State construction and State defence, produced during a few brief years a literature of human life perfect in unity as in vigour, was the same England which, when presented with different problems, flew into fratricidal factions. In the long intervening years a deep change of temper had indeed taken place, due to great political events. But in society, in economics, in the religious convictions of the people, it is difficult to name any great differences between the England of Shakespeare and the England of Pym.

CHAPTER I

ENGLAND, 1603-40.—THE UPPER CLASS; ITS LIFE, CULTURE AND
SOCIAL FUNCTIONS—LAW, POLICE AND HUMANITARIANISM

England, bound in with the triumphant sea.—*Richard II.*

THE division in English society most nearly corresponding to The
    that chasm which on the continent divided the nobles from English
the remainder of mankind, was not nobleman and commoner, but gentry
gentle and simple. For the English Lords were little more than a
section of the gentry enjoying certain political privileges ; they were,
for all purposes of life and intercourse, still part of the larger society
which they claimed to lead.[1] The laws of duel, and the other obligations of *noblesse,* belonged in England to all families of landowners
who could show their coat-of-arms. Thus the class who wore swords
and had the right to demand satisfaction of an Earl, included persons
who differed from each other greatly in income and in manner of
life. There exist to-day several widely different popular concep-
tions of the English country gentleman in the Stuart epoch, whether
it be a vision of the high-souled and cultivated Puritan squire of
the type of Hampden and Hutchinson, or of his brother the Cavalier,
or Macaulay's portrait of the bucolic Tory squire of the period after
the Restoration, growling over his ale at the foreign proclivities of
James II. or William III., in the broadest accent of the country-side.
The truth is that throughout the whole Stuart epoch essential differences of wealth and manners divided the gentry into not a few distinctive kinds.[2]

In respect of religion and politics there was indeed a greater
variety among the landowners under James and Charles I. than was
to be found after 1660. It was only the events of the Great Rebellion
that created a standard type of squirearchical opinion. The country
gentleman, if he did not belong to the strong minority of Catholic
squires, adhered to no separate party in Church or State ; the
Englishman was not yet a creature of politics and denominations.
The leaders and representatives of the landed class, and therefore
presumably a large section of that class itself, were more concerned
to resist the encroachments of the Crown than to support its

---

[1] This close relation of classes was accentuated by the policy of James I. and
his favourites in raising so many of their creatures to sit beside the haughty Tudor
Peers, who had forgotten how they themselves had been raised by the Henries to
a level with the yet more haughty Plantagenet nobles.

[2] The unlettered country gentleman described by Macaulay, and the cultivated
country gentleman described by Sir George Sitwell (*Old Country Life*), probably
existed side by side, both in the early and in the later part of the Stuart period. I
take the first opportunity of acknowledging the kindness of Sir George Sitwell in
lending me that book and *The First Whig,* neither of which he has published.

sovereignty, which had not then been called in question ; and the Puritan temper, which inspired many of their own number, alarmed and disgusted them less than the novelties which Laud was introducing into their Church.

County society was not a close caste. A poor gentleman was sometimes glad to save his estate by marrying his sons to the dowries which a wealthy yeoman could provide for his daughters.[1] The descendants of clothiers, who purchased old lands with new money, or of the richer yeomen who " gentleised " their sons, were sooner or later accepted into the circle of families, many of whom had risen in the same way after the Black Death or the fall of the monasteries. But the period of social probation was irritating to such aspirants while it lasted, and is said to have been a frequent cause of Roundhead proclivities in the Great War.[2]

Residence in the country The Court was a strictly limited circle, and beyond the precincts of the Court there was, in the earlier part of the seventeenth century, no such thing as a " London season ". In the reign of Charles I. an attempt was made on the part of some ladies, who were tired of the country, to take up their residence in the capital and parade in fine dresses in Hyde Park, while their husbands disported themselves at the play-houses across the river ; but a royal proclamation from the most paternal of governments, enforced by some shrewd fines in the Star Chamber, soon drove back these pioneers of fashion to their rural duties. In times of " scarcity and want " James I. had sent back even his courtiers to their places in the country-side. The Bourbons encouraged the French noble to leave his rural home and assert his place in society by living at Paris or Versailles ; but the Stuarts, like all their English subjects, regarded the status of country gentleman as a profession in itself. The Privy Council looked to every squire to keep open house, relieve want, give employment, and so aid the working of the Poor Law, whose administration was in the hands of justices selected from the same useful class.[3]

Under the first two Stuarts the provincial capitals were social centres frequently visited by the richer gentry of the neighbourhood, according to a custom dating from time immemorial. But it was chiefly in the country house life, in the round of visits paid in the family coach or pillioned behind their brothers through the muddy lanes, that young ladies became acquainted with the bridegrooms selected by their parents. The small choice within a thirty-mile radius was no doubt unfortunate, but there were corresponding

---

[1] See the very amusing scene, Act. 1., sc. 2, of Dekker's *Witch of Edmonton*, a play which illustrates more than most the social and other aspects of rural life.

[2] Clar., p. 290. Hutchinson, p. 130. Cunningham, p. 542, note 2.

[3] Leonard, pp. 145, 146. On the other hand, many dissolute young gentlemen came up from country without their families and squandered their estates in London brothels and gaming-houses, affording a regular source of income to the professional sharps and money-lenders of the capital. See old plays *passim*, e.g., *The Enforced Marriage*.

advantages in this confinement to rural society : for there both the
ladies and the gentlemen found the duties and realities of life thick
around them, in daily contact with other classes. As yet they had
not been attracted to an isolated life of fashion in London, and the
country house was still the scene, not merely of relaxation, but of
business. On the other hand, military barbarism in castle and
moat-house was already a thing of the past, and the Renaissance
civilisation introduced at the Elizabethan Court had penetrated to
the seats of the better sort of gentry.

These mansions were of every variety of size and style ; there The
were modest halls and manors, such as now serve as farm-houses or manor
even as barns ; and lofty rural palaces of red brick and carved stone, house
decorating wooded parks and retired valleys. The increased profits
from land newly enclosed went chiefly to the pocket of the landlord ;
and at this period he was more ready to employ money in raising
a great Jacobean mansion than in further improving his estate. In
these halcyon days of pride in new prosperity, when the final success
of the Tudor rule seemed to have secured the island from all chance
of again becoming the scene of military operations, houses were
built for peace that were yet to taste of war ; mullions and gables
rose from which the sentinel would soon look forth ; garden walks
were laid out across which the iron shot would tear ; and carved
oak adorned the staircase, on whose broad landings the pikes of the
last defenders would go down before the roar and the tramp of the
rush that ends the day.

The high vaulted dining-halls were hung with tapestry, armour, Its
weapons and relics of the chase ; the long, well-lighted galleries, pictures
which were then built for resort and conversation, were decorated
with the family portraits—dismal lines of black-painted boards from
which angular maidens and blanched youths looked down out of
their ruffs, relieved here and there by some great ancestor standing
as Holbein saw him, or by the heir in the style of Vandyke. The
only pictures in these English homes were the portraits. In the
great days of Dutch art our writers found fault with Holland, because there " every man's house is full of pictures, a vanity that
draweth on a charge." Diaries and guide-books of travel in Italy,
written by scholars and men of cultivation, describe the treasures
of palaces and churches, and above all the monuments of antiquity ;
but scarcely a word is wasted on the pictures, even in detailed accounts of Florence or the Campo Santo of Pisa. At Rome, Raphael
passes as unnoticed as his predecessors, though in the Sistine a
passing word may be spared to " that excellent artificial painter
called Michael Angelo Buonaretto ". But in spite of the fortunate
demand for family portraits which was filling the mansions in every
part of England with masterpieces of the Dutch and Flemish schools,
and in spite of the influence of King Charles. who was a true

connoisseur, and of the Earl of Arundel, called " the father of *vertu* in England," it cannot be maintained that painting was intelligently appreciated even by the upper class. On the other hand, good taste in architecture, gardening, carving in wood, engraving in metal and other arts that minister to the uses of life, was then natural and widely spread.[1]

Hunting

After the mansion itself, the chief object of pride was the park, where the deer were shut in by high palings, cut from the old oaks of the glades in which they browsed. Sometimes they were hunted slowly round the inside of this enclosure ; the ladies and their cavaliers caught glimpses of the sport from some point of vantage, and listened critically to the cry of the hounds, whose notes of different pitch were meant to harmonise like a peal of bells.[2] But a nobler form of the chase was to hunt " at force " over the whole country-side. Although deer-hunting and deer-poaching were at this time the ambition of all English sportsmen, some of the smaller gentry had to be content with forms of the chase more within their means. The otter was speared, the badger trapped, the hare coursed, and the fox hunted by squires who each led out his own little pack, and confined the chase within the borders of his own estate and to the company of his own family and guests. County hunts and long runs were unusual.[3] Some landowners recognised no other function in life save the daily hunt, followed by the nightly carouse at the ale-house whither they repaired after dinner with the ladies of the family ; a scheme varied by little else than the statutory church service on Sunday. The round of earthy amusements and besotted pleasures wasted the lives and fortunes of many

---

[1] *Harl. Misc.*, v., p. 18. Fynes Moryson's *Itinerary*, ed. 1617, *passim ;* in his fourth part (ed. 1902, *Shakespeare's Europe*), p. 106, he gives it as his opinion that " we may indeed the Italians some pre-eminence of glory in fountains, aqueducts, gardens, jewels, and some such permanent goods,"—not a word of pictures. Arber's *Reprints*, viii., Howell's *Instructions. Somers' Tracts*, iii., p. 635. Nor does Dudley North, in 1661, or the guide in *Harl. Misc.*, v., pp. 1-42, show any advance on this view of painting. Evelyn, who travelled in Italy during our first Civil War, took with him an appreciation of pictures quite exceptional in his day, though the Court of Charles I. had by then done something to cultivate that taste. See also Einstein, pp. 148, 149, 202-7, and *Life of the Earl of Arundel*, by Mary Hervey, Cam. Press, 1921.

[2] This is the meaning of the lines in *A Midsummer-Night's Dream* :—

> " Slow in pursuit, but matched in mouth like bells.
> Each unto each. A cry more tunable
> Was never halloo'd to, nor cheered with horn
> In Crete, in Sparta, nor in Thessaly."

See *Stuart Tracts* (Firth), p. 61, and *Diary of Master Will. Silence*, 1897.

[3] In the excellent old song, *The Old and Young Courtier*, in Percy's *Reliques*, the old gentleman who had a great estate, " never hawked or hunted but in his own grounds ". It is perhaps implied, though not stated, that the " young courtier " of King James who succeeds him, begins the modern habit of hunting over other people's ground.

gentlemen not really above the common people in their habits, who if they had but been classed as yeomen would have worked hard upon their estates.[1]

Fowling stood in the same position of honourable rivalry to hunt- Fowling ing that it holds to-day. But fowling was then conducted, not with gun, but with hawk or net. The art of netting and luring birds by innumerable devices, was then much practised by gentlemen ; but the ride along the brook or across the meadows, watching the professional movements of the hawk overhead, was at once the most fashionable and popular mode of taking fowl. The use of the shotgun, which was destined to displace all other methods of fowling, was still forbidden by an old law, of which the penalties were sometimes exacted under King James. The two birds principally mentioned in the game laws are partridge and pheasant, then about equally wild. For the pheasant was not in those days cross bred and reared by the keeper ; its remote ancestor, the eastern bird of plumage, introduced by the Romans to adorn their villas, had taken refuge during the lawless centuries that followed the departure of the legions, in the depth of the mediæval forest. When Elizabeth died, game was so plentiful in the wastes and woods of England that no great jealousy was felt of the sporting instincts of " mean tenants and freeholders," so that foreigners noted with surprise that " peasants " were " permitted to hunt " with big dogs. But the game laws of James's Parliaments began that series of squirearchical enactments, which before the century ended had in effect taken from the small yeoman the right of sporting over his own land,

---

[1] See *Assheton's Journal* (Chetham Soc., 1848) *passim* and note (3) on p. 1.

(1617) " May. 2. Hunting the otter : killed one : taken another, quick, at Salley. Spent VId.
May. 12. Father Greenacres, mother, aunt Besse, John, wyffe, self, at ale. Sp. IVd.

. . . .

June. 11. Tryed for a fox, found none ; rayne ; wet thorough. Home agayne.
June. 15. Sunday Trin. Parson preached ; to Church. Aft. sermon ; sp. VId. Home. To Church pson. preached.
June. 16. Fox-hunting.
June. 17. I and brother Greenacres to Portfield (rayne), then to Whalley ; fox-hunting. To the pond : a duck and a dogg. To the Abbey : drunk there. Home . . .
June. 24. Tryed for ye fox ; found nothing. Towler lay at a rabbit, and wee stayed and wrought and took her."

Fox-hunting in the reign of James I. was sometimes a sport for the smaller gentry, sometimes a necessity for the countryside. It already had its own professional rules and phraseology among sportsmen ; yet often a whole village turned out with clubs, nets and dogs to a general massacre in the woods. By the end of the century this intermediate stage was past, and the fox was no longer regarded as vermin but only as a beast of the chase (*Assheton's Journal*, p. 14, note 1. *Return from Parnassus*, pt. ii., Act II., sc. 5, *circa* 1606 (Clar. Press, 1886). *Gentleman's Recreation*, 1686, " Hunting," p. 87).

and had made the taking of game a privilege of the larger land-owners.[1]

Duelling   The duel was then beginning to come into prominence with all its well-known modern characteristics. Offensive as it has now become to common-sense, it was then a step in the direction of humanity and law, for it took the place of the "killing affray". In the fifteenth century, that golden age of bravoes, feuds begun in the law-court or the dining-hall were brought to an issue outside by open and murderous assaults. The hand of royal justice, becoming somewhat heavier under the Tudors, suppressed much of this private war and "bridled such stout noblemen or gentlemen". But the work was still incomplete, and the law alone would have been unable to suppress these butcheries, so long as they were still condoned by public opinion. It was the new code of honour, which insisted that man should stand up alone against man, with equal weapons, that was now superseding that odious power of the grandee to set upon a poor neighbour with a host of bullies and retainers. But many characteristic stories of both town and country in the reign of James I., show how long the old ideas lingered. A fencing-master in London accidentally put out an eye of one of his patrons, the Scottish Lord Sanquhar ; after brooding over it for seven years, his lordship thought it essential to his dignity to hire assassins, who wiped out the score in the blood of the man who had maimed him, while he himself tried to conceal his share in the deed.[2] The memoirs of the reign are rife with stories of assassination as a point of honour. One of the most remarkable is recorded in the autobiography of the philosopher, Lord Herbert of Cherbury. One day, as he was riding through Scotland Yard behind the King's own residence of Whitehall, the safest place one would think in the island, a gentleman, suffering from Othello's complaint, rushed out at the head of four retainers from behind a corner, and let drive at his adversary. Lord Herbert, though worsted for a moment by the sudden and cowardly assault, continued to defend himself against his five assailants, before the eyes of a score of hostile spectators who had come to see the husband take his revenge. The four

[1] The restriction on the right of small landowners to kill game on their ground was made because gentlemen complained that "mean tenants and freeholders destroy game of partridges and pheasants". The property qualification for taking game was raised step by step in a succession of statutes beginning from 1 J. I., xxvii. See 7 J. I., xi. ; 22-3 C. II., xxv. ; 4 W. and M., xxiii. For illustrations of statements in this paragraph, see *Worc. County Records*, i., pp. lxvii-x., 50 (44), 195 (44). Hamilton, 89, 162. D. of Stettin, p. 47. Addison's *Spectator*, No. 122. See p. 393 below.

[2] G., ii., pp. 131-33. He was partly instigated by Henry IV. of France, who expressed surprise at hearing that the fencing-master "still lived". As Sanquhar was executed for the murder by English justice, we may suppose that his idea of honour was more Scottish and French than English. Still, such a story throws light on the reason why Laertes, "a very noble youth," hopes to clear his honour by treacherously murdering Hamlet with poison.

retainers, who were probably afraid of being hung for murder, pressed the attack so feebly that their master was finally dragged away in pitiable plight from under the knees of the redoubtable sage. Such at least is the account, perhaps too favourable to himself, which he gives of the matter. Public opinion at Court, which had progressed since the days of York and Lancaster, condemned the assault as murderous and dishonourable ; but the attitude of the spectators who had come to see Lord Herbert stabbed, shows that the " killing affray " was not yet held in universal abhorrence ; so the stricter customs of the duel were likely to do more good than harm.[1] Systematised duelling never reached the excess of popularity which it enjoyed in France, where ladies so encouraged it as the proper vocation of nobility, that there was " scarce any man thought worth looking at that had not killed some other man in a duel ". If it was never so in England, the secret of the difference lay in this ; the only business of the French *noblesse* under the Bourbons was soldiering ; but as the English gentry pursued peaceable callings, their social ideas were eminently civilian. In contrast to the " swordsmen " who swaggered about London streets, quarrelled on the " second cause " of a point of honour, and ran each other through the body by the rules of Italian fence, there were many country squires who could give and take the lie direct in broad upland dialect, without feeling bound in courtesy to kill one another.[2]

As there was more than one type of English gentleman, so there were many types of lady, ranging from the heroines of allegories and sonnets, from Mrs. Hutchinson, whose learning, taste and intellect would have met the marital requirements of John Milton himself, down to the housewife who dozed with the squire over his ale, or the titled wanton and murderess who dominated over the factions at Court. The ladies of that day were forced to give a large part of their lives to household duties, and had less to spare for society and culture. In the absence of country doctors, it was the women of the house who practised the quaint lore of the art of healing— in part medicine, in part charms and white magic. Almost all the food, drink and delicacies of the landlord's family came off the estate, and in small manors the brewing of the beer, the salting of the Martinmas beef and the daily cooking were the province of the wife and daughters : even in fine houses it was their business to preserve the garden fruit, and to sew for household use or ornament during long hours that would now either be devoted to more

(margin note: Ladies and their occupations)

---

[1] How desirable stricter custom was, and how much wanting at this period even among the honourably disposed who met singly man to man, can be seen in the horrible Sackville and Bruce duel, 1613. See *Guardian* (1713), Nos. 129, 133, and Carlyle's *Historical Sketches*, pt. i., chap. xii.

[2] Hutchinson, p. 38. Rous, p. 23. Lord Herbert, pp. 19, 72, 77, 92-96. Einstein, pp. 68-76.

intellectual or more athletic pursuits, or else dissipated in conventionalities and distractions.[1]

While the daughters of the well-to-do classes were not yet divorced from the active business of life, nor relegated to the drawing-rooms to which Miss Austen's heroines were confined, on the other hand no professions or trades higher than manual were open to women, and scarcely any education was provided for them save that which each home could give. A very few clever women were classical scholars ; a somewhat larger number were Puritan theologians, or students of English and even Italian poetry.

Besides verses and plays there were but few other books to amuse their leisure. Imaginative writing found its chief outlet in the drama. There were indeed a few romances, in prose, very popular among ladies. In the time of the civil troubles the old-established monarchy of Lyly's *Euphues* and Sidney's *Arcadia* yielded to the more intolerable usurpation of Mlle. Scudéri's French romance, Under the Commonwealth, even the witty and unaffected Dorothy Osborne enjoyed the " tomes " of the *Grand Cyrus* as light literature.[2]

Since painting was not yet practised by amateurs, ladies' artistic skill was exercised on the domestic arts of tapestry, embroidery and gardening. But they carried music, especially in the sense of singing to stringed instruments, to a high perfection ; the art was encouraged by the fashionable habit of writing masques, verses and love songs, and the extraordinary power of writing them well, which was then so profusely spread among a generation of unpretentious and unprofessional poets.[3]

Marriages The usual age for the marriage of ladies was thirteen to eighteen, and of gentlemen from fifteen to twenty-eight. Sometimes, for one or two years after the ceremony, the husband travelled abroad with a tutor, or resided at the University, to complete his education.[4] Since many men and nearly all women were married

---

[1] It is difficult to ascertain how much exercise ladies took. In the higher circles of society they hunted and hawked so much that the deer-hunting parties " were usually arranged in honour of the ladies " (Duke of Stettin, p. 47). Yet I find little evidence that in the average squire's household they took part in the field-sports. There is no means of ascertaining how much they walked and rode merely for health or enjoyment, but in days when roads were bad for carriages, riding was a very common means of locomotion for both men and women.

[2] The publication of " vain books of Amadis de Gaul and of comedies " was frowned on by the stricter Puritans, who thought Laud could have better exercised his censorship in that direction, instead of against evangelical literature (*Somers' Tracts*, v., p. 17. Jusserand's *English Novel in the Time of Shakespeare*, 1899, pp. 140, 141, 262. *The English Novel*, Walter Raleigh, 1894, pp. 86-88. *Dorothy Osborne's Letters, passim*).

[3] *Comus* was set to music by Lawes ; indeed, the poem was written partly at the instigation of the musician.

[4] Lord Herbert, pp. 38, 39. It was solely by way of " family treaty," and in order to acquire estates, that he was married at the age o. fifteen to a woman of twenty-one. He records it as a thing by no means out of the way.

before they had reached an age when the soul is mistress of her choice, parents were generally able to arrange matches without incurring resistance. It was considered the business of a good father to find husbands and wives for his children, by negotiating family treaties in which portion was carefully weighed against income. After the preliminaries were settled, the young man was sent to pay his addresses, often to a lady whom he had not yet seen ; and it was but seldom that the affair was broken off at this stage. One good result of this bad system was that a very small proportion of eligible men and women remained unmarried. It may also be argued that when barbarous social custom required people to be married for life while they were still boys and girls, a wise parental choice was likely to lead to the least unhappy results possible under such conditions. The memoirs and letters of the time show that some, at least, of these arranged marriages resulted in real affection. But it is significant that much of the love poetry, in which the period was so prolific, bore no more relation to marriage than did the sonnets of that accepted model to the age, Sir Philip Sidney. Moralists were already beginning to denounce the miseries of " enforced marriages " ; it is clear from the memoirs, letters and stage-plays of the time that love matches were sometimes tolerated by the parents ; that in many families the daughter had the right, not of choice, but at least of veto ; and that the secret love marriage and runaway match were not uncommon. In this epoch, if not indeed in earlier times, the great battle of Gretna Green had already been joined, which after long generations of strife secured the liberty of youth. Of the habits of the middle and lower classes in these matters we have less information. But it is probable that in grades of society where portions and income were less considered and the sons looked for support more to what they could earn than to what they could inherit, marriages, though equally early, were more often made by free choice. Thus the honest yeoman in the *Witch of Edmonton* [1] declares that his daughters " shall choose for themselves by my consent."

England was already ahead of other countries in the liberty allowed to women, and the freedom of social intercourse between the sexes, on which both Germans and Italians remarked with surprise. [2]

The education of gentlemen's sons varied more according to their intended profession than in these days when all are found together in the " public school ". Many a younger son destined to the apprentice's apron, many an heir destined to hunt the coverts and exact the rentals of a small patrimony, were taught little beyond their letters. But a good education was attainable in more

Schools: mixture of classes

[1] Act 1., sc. 2.   [2] Duke of Stettin, p. 65.   Einstein, pp. 223, 224.

than one class of academy. In those frugal days, the sons of leading county families were sometimes sent first to the village school
and afterwards to the grammar school of the neighbouring market-
town, as John Hampden was sent to Thame. There, sitting on the
bench with the cleverest sons of farmers and townspeople, the young
gentlemen learnt many things more useful to the future governors
of a country than the aristocratic tone and exclusive ideas of a
Victorian public school. In this way the middle and upper classes
came to understand each other, with great mutual advantage, and
the gentry were fitted to take part in municipal, magisterial and
Parliamentary life. The belief that higher education can only be
bought at a heavy price, and is therefore the monopoly of the rich,
had not yet penetrated the English mind ; it was therefore the custom of parents in more than one class to send the clever boy of the
family at the smallest possible charge to school and college, where,
as he well understood, he was to prepare for his future profession.
In education, as in after life, the rich were less cut off from personal
contact with other classes than they afterwards became.[1]

Education in great houses
But besides these grammar schools, the more exclusive Westminster, Winchester and Eton, existed then as now. Also persons
born to high position were sometimes brought up in their own
homes by private tutors ; and often, by a tradition coming down
from the Middle Ages, the households of Lords and county magnates
received specially favoured sons of neighbouring gentry into their
homes, partly as scholars, partly as pages or companions. In these
lordly mansions the young men unconsciously imbibed the Cavalier
ideal of life, in all its folly and in all its charm. It was in this way
that the manners and literature, and as the Puritans observed, the
profligacy and extravagance of the Court, spread to families that
never saw London.[2] This kind of school, involving intimate connection with the great, attracted the ambitious, the greedy and the
imaginative ; for it was only through patrons that unknown men
were introduced into Court or Parliament. Every great Lord who
played with Raleigh, Somerset or Bacon for the prizes of the world,
brought with him to flaunt in the corridors of Whitehall a train of
his country gallants glittering in unwonted pearls and gold ; and
the understanding that the patron would finally provide for each of
these clients out of his own or out of the public purse, ruined many
noble houses, embittered the scramble for pensions and places, and
made the government of the country, as long as it was seated in
the Court, an affair of personal factions.

Old Country Life, Sir G. Sitwell, pp. 49, 50. The foundation of endowed
schools was going on more rapidly between 1600 and 1650 than between 1500 and
1600, though the Tudor period has been wrongly accredited with an educational
advance more properly due to the first half of the seventeenth century (English
Schools at the Reformation. Leach.   E. H. R., xv., pp. 58-72 (Watson)).
    Hutchinson, p. 78.

Oxford and Cambridge, inferior to what they have since become Univer-
as seats of learning, already discharged as places of education much sities
the same functions as in the nineteenth century.   They were a
national institution, a training for the ideas, manners and character.
Their degrees gave the world assurance of a class of man rather than
of a scholar.   From the great country houses the younger son was
sent up to obtain, not a learned, but a liberal education ; while
his elder brother, who was to inherit the estate, had no thought of
fitting himself for a profession, but regarded his undergraduate
career, either as a preparation for public life, or as a pleasant means
of throwing away time and money among his equals.   These types,
encouraged by the college authorities as " future benefactors,"
became under the later Tudors a much larger proportion of the
students than they had been in the Middle Ages.[1]   The idea if not
of scholarship, at least of residence at a University, had become
connected with the Elizabethan idea of gentleman and courtier.
This change, stimulated by the frequent residence of King James's
Court in the colleges, probably helped to decrease the learned and
to increase the literary and political, character of Oxford and Cambridge.

But the Universities also afforded training to persons of lower Class dis-
rank, whose facility at Latin grammar or clumsiness at handling tinctions
the plough had marked them out for masters or clergymen in the at college
eyes of discerning parents.   The teaching and clerical professions
were largely recruited from the middle class, though no longer from
the lower grades of peasantry, who had often filled the parsonage in
the days of the Plantagenets.   During the Stuart period, the sons of
yeomen, farmers and tradesmen, chosen out for these careers, had
somehow to be forced through the portals of the University on insufficient means ; they were often engaged as " servitors " to their
fellow-students, who there as at home stood upon their rank.   The
life of the sevitor and sizar was often hard as well as degrading.
" Bed-making, chamber-sweeping and water-fetching " were " doubt-
less great preservatives against too much vain philosophy ".[2]   Yet
this custom of observing ranks, though often abused, was not in
itself considered an abuse, for it enabled many to live at college on
the only financial and social footing that was possible for them.   So
long as society was based not on competition but on patronage,

[1] One reason why the learning of the Dons was scarcely worthy of so great a
nation in so great an age, was the custom of giving fellowships, etc., largely to the
sons of patrons, rich men, and lawyers who worked for the college ; this nepotism
was openly pursued as a necessary policy in that age of patronage (*Harl. Misc.*,
i., p. 495.   W. Harrison's *Description of England*, ed. Furnivall, p. 253).

[2] Eachard's *Contempt of the Clergy*.   The distance between fellow-commoner
and pensioner was observed, as well as the distance between pensioner and sizar.
Thus as late as 1667, Roger North, though in straitened circumstances and not
himself heir to the family peerage, was " tied up by quality from mixing " with
the " common scholars " at football (*Autobiography*, sec. 20).

social distinctions that have now vanished from the Universities were a necessary condition of their existence. And it seems that in those days a large proportion of poor men were to be found at Oxford and Cambridge.

Prospects of poor scholars   The college career of the poor scholar, generally dependent on the whim of some private person, was often cut short. In any case he was liable at the end to be turned out upon the world, the most helpless and despised of the unemployed, if no living, private chaplaincy, tutorship or grammar school had fallen to him in the indecent jostle for the favour of hard and venal patrons. The prizes were indeed but poor rewards for devotion to learning : yet they might by good fortune be secured, though not always, by the worthiest. Every year youthful clergy and schoolmasters, knowing little besides Latin grammar, and whether they were Puritan or Laudian, were sent down from the Alma Mater on the top of the carrier's waggon to take up life-long residence in remote country hamlets. Yet it is probable that the education, abilities and number of University men in training for these professions, however insufficient, had improved since the days of Edward VI., when Hugh Latimer had told his fellow-Protestants some home truths on the subject, in his famous sermon *On the Plough.* And although the person of the parish priest was no longer, as in Catholic times, fenced about by superstitious awe, his social position was more distinctly above that of the peasant than it had been before the Reformation, and it perhaps continued to rise during the seventeenth century, as it certainly rose with much increased rapidity in the eighteenth.

There was no organised athleticism among the students. But exercise was recognised as necessary for health in the " beastly air of Cambridge " ; so the ordinary undergraduate who was not a sporting man, diverted himself in the afternoon with " walking in the fields," bathing in the river, bell pulling, jumping, running, bowls, pitching the bar and football, which last was little better than an excuse for a fight between the general body of two or more colleges.[1]

Classical learning   The progress of study at the English Universities since the time of their foundation has been a series of rapid advances followed by long and sometimes untimely halts. The first sixty years of the century were not a period of change. Bacon's work scarcely affected the schools. The crabbed systems of logic, philosophy and physical science had not yet been inspired with new life by the genius of Descartes and Newton, or by the academical activity of Barrow. The classical teaching, though based on the reforms effected a hundred years back by the Renaissance scholars, was as much below the notice of Casaubon when he visited the Universities, as the old mediæval classics had been below the notice of Erasmus in former days. The undergraduates in the reign of James I. learnt a mere

[1] See D'Ewes' *College Life.*

smattering of the Greek tongue and nothing of Greek literature, except when individual zeal supplied the defects of teaching. But the Latin course was most thorough. Latin was still the medium of ordinary instruction and often of friendly conversation; Latin was the language of oratory and of original compositions in prose and verse, by which eager rivals for the favour of the Muse cultivated scholarship, ingenuity and taste more than by any other academical exercise. There were, however, at Cambridge cliques of poetical undergraduates who composed verses and wrote and acted whole dramas in the mother-tongue, aspiring to become playwrights at the capital, or literary hangers-on to some great Lord at the Court. But the taste even of these modern aspirants was, in the opinion of London stage managers, too much soaked in the phraseology of the Latin poets.

Under James I. classics had almost a monopoly of attention at Its value the Universities. Law and medicine flourished elsewhere, at the Inns of Court and the College of Physicians. Controversial theology, however, was not neglected by the academicians at a time when the theological views which they inculcated decided the fate of Churches, dynasties and realms. But the classical studies reacted even on politics and religion. When Milton was an undergraduate, just as again when Mazzini was a schoolboy, familiarity with the great pagan names and stories suggested to young patriots, as Royalist writers observed with regret, the civic ideals of the ancient republics. Classics saved young theologians, who had in them any spark of poetry latent, from complete absorption in controversial divinity. Although the Arts course was well constructed to draw off the mind into less heated channels, theology, neglected in the lecture-room, was none the less the atmosphere breathed by the sons of learning. The doctrines of Papist, Arminian and Calvinist, the best sermon that Sunday, the views of the new Dean, were the talk of all serious-minded students. Most of those who came up to the Universities had some kind of patronage to beg or to bestow; and the bestowal of patronage was largely guided by the politico-religious controversies of the day. The quarrel deeply affected the society of the undergraduates, among whom the Puritans of a stricter way condemned their profligate comrades as " atheists," a catchword of party abuse transferred to the whole Cavalier side at the outbreak of the war.[1]

[1] For what has been said in the preceding paragraphs, see Wordsworth's *Scholæ Academicæ*. Mark Pattison's *Casaubon*. *English Universities*, Huber and Newman, vol. i., pp. 315-68 ; ii., pp. 1-74. Burton's *Anatomy*, i., 2, 3, 15, " Why the Muses are Melancholy ". Hobbes' *Behemoth* (1889), p. 3. Babington, *Mr. Macaulay's Character of the Clergy* (1849), pp. 40, 41, 51, 52. *Royal Hist. Soc.*, xvi., pp. 164, 187. Masson's *Life of Milton. Visitation of Oxford* (Camden Soc., 1881), Mr. Burrows' introd., pp. xi-xxx. And lastly, the *Pilgrimage to and Return from Parnassus* (Clar. Press, 1886), the most intimate account of University men in the days of Shakespeare that we possess.

Its mono-
poly

The curriculum of the schools necessarily followed the requirements of Oxford and Cambridge. Classical scholarship enjoyed a
monopoly that was not even questioned. For it was as yet the
most intelligent and humane part of the education of an age slowly
emerging out of mediæval ideas. It was only in the rationalistic
epoch of Charles II. that critics ventured to inquire whether a little
reading " of innocent English authors," the writing of " English
exercises," and " the principles of arithmetic, geometry and such
alluring parts of learning," might not be made part of a boy's school
education.

> But if instead hereof, you diet him with nothing but with rules and exceptions ;
> with tiresome repititions of *Amo's* and τύπτώ's setting a day also apart to recite
> *verbatim* all the burdensome task of the foregoing week (which I am confident is
> usually as dreadful as an old Parliament Fast) we must needs believe, that such
> a one thus managed, will scarce think to prove immortal by such performances
> and accomplishments as these.   You know very well, sir, that lads in the general,
> have but a kind of ugly and odd conception of learning ; and look upon it as such
> a starving thing, and unnecessary perfection, (especially as it is usually dispence'd
> out unto them) that Nine-pins and Span-counter are judged much more heavenly
> employments ; and therefore what pleasure, do we think, can such a one take,
> in being bound to get against breakfast two or three hundred Rumblers out of
> Homer, in commendation of Achilles's toes, or the Grecians' boots ?   Or, to have
> measured out unto him, very early in the morning, fifteen or twenty well laid-on
> lashes, for letting a syllable slip too soon, or hanging too long upon it ?   Doubtless,
> instant execution upon such grand miscarriages as these, will eternally engage
> him to a most admirable opinion of the Muses.   (EACHARD.)

Such questions were raised ten years after the Restoration only
by the eccentric Eachard, afterwards Master of St. Catherine's,
Cambridge, and in Queen Anne's reign by the unpopular Bishop
Burnet : but they have since excited more general attention.[1]

Younger
sons of
gentry in
commerce

While the English custom of primogeniture forbade the younger
sons to live on the family estate, they were not forbidden, like the
children of noble houses on the continent, to seek their fortunes in
commerce.   Large families were brought up in the country houses
of the gentry, in spite of the terrible death-rate among the children
of the upper classes, much greater than the death-rate among the
children of the poorest to-day ; and the numerous cadets of the
family were sent to swell the river of national life with a stream of
high-spirited adventurers.   The boy who was sent as prentice to the
city, had before him the prospect of new activity leading to plebeian
honours ; while behind him lay the memory of days spent afield
round the manor house, carrying the nets or the falcon for his elder
brother.   Some of these gentlemen prentices " did affect to go in
costly apparel and wear weapons ".   When we read of the proud
spirit in which the shopkeepers of London claimed to be heard in
Church and State, and faced the royal soldiers in street riot and on

[1] Eachard's *Contempt of the Clergy*, 1670   Burnet, vi., p. 213.

battlefield, it must be remembered that there was a leaven among them of the sons of gentlemen brought up in the country-side.[1] The English townsfolk were in blood and temper a blend of the two classes. Accordingly, the squires regarded neighbouring cities, where they watched their sons rising to wealth and fame, with none of that jealousy which in other lands divided a nobility, proud in arms, from a rival plutocracy of pure burgher blood. If such a feud had existed in England, the Civil War, however begun, would have resolved itself into a strife between town and country, from which the Prince would have emerged, as from the revolt of the Spanish Communeros and the Knights' War in Germany, an umpire with powers supreme.

But other roads besides the lowly path by which the prentice rose to civic honours were open to the " younger son ". Many went to the Bar, or obtained the best preferments of the Church. The adventurous sought the German wars. Although the officering of the militia, the only armed force in England, was left to very civilian magistrates, there were Englishmen renowned in foreign camps for long service in the van of Protestant war. The Dutch service always, and later the Swedish and Palatine, attracted a continuous flight of island volunteers ; some were noblemen seeking the experience of a year's service under a famous chief, but more were landless men following the profession of arms. *Service in foreign wars*

While his brethren were carrying the colours by the Scheldt and the Danube, or building up their fortunes in the city, the heir of the estate was fitting himself for his future place. After the University a short course of legal training was the fashion, both to prepare a man for his duties as Justice of Peace, and to give him a sight of London from the good society of the Inns of Court. The more wealthy finished their education with the grand tour, which often brought with it knowledge of the language, and acquaintance with the courtiers and sages, of Italy, or of France, or even of Spain. It was largely by this custom of travelling in Italy and corresponding with friends made there, very common under Henry VIII., that the Renaissance culture had been introduced into England. In the reign of James I. the peace with Philip III. caused a revival of English travel in Spain and the Italian states under Spanish and Papal government, where in Elizabeth's reign even a clever linguist from our island dared scarcely ride in disguise for fear of the Inquisition. The noble societies and learned academies that were then to be found in every Italian capital, gladly welcomed young Englishmen of high fortune and promise, who quarrelled among themselves as to whether it were treason to kiss the Pope's toe and to visit one's Popish cousin at the Jesuit College ; stared through Galileo's " optic glass " , in- *The elder brother* *Foreign travel*

---

[1] Cunningham, p. 126. See also, for apprenticing sons of gentry, many old plays and ballads, *e.g.*, *Eastward Ho !*, and the *Bailiff's Daughter of Islington.* and *Verney Papers* (Camb. Soc., 1853), pp. 6, 12

2

quired how the Duke of Tuscany raised his " Dutch guard " ; sung
midnight canzonettes in the gardens of Siena ; and at last returned
home to their several duties in England, never again to leave her
shores save as old and sorrowful exiles for Parliament or King.[1]

Though the landlords of this period did little to help their tenants,
many small squires farmed their own estates ; and many great
proprietors kept a portion in their own hands, interesting themselves
in new methods of tillage, or, like Sir John Harrington, in their
" *oves* and *boves* " ; others were content to discharge the ordinary
duties of a landlord, or to neglect them in favour of drinking, hunting and gambling.

Justices
of Peace

Another task to which many devoted their lives was local government. The administration of each district was conducted by certain
of the local gentry, selected by the Crown as unpaid Justices of
Peace. The rural districts were therefore governed, neither by the
feudal rule of the landowner in his own estate and in his own right,
nor by royal bureaucrats sent down from the capital. The magistrate's authority derived from the Crown, and yet it was in effect
local government and squirearchal power. This mutual dependence
of the central and provincial administrations is the key to the history
of the Stuart epoch. The institution of unpaid local magistrates
ensured both the ill-success of the republican propaganda and the
failure of the Stuart Kings to establish a despotism without possessing
a bureaucracy. For while the majority of the squires always rallied
to preserve the sovereignty of the Crown, whose service had been
from father to son the chief pride of many ancient families, on the
other hand the same class was able in 1640 and in 1688 to maintain
views of policy and religion against the will of kings from whom
they derived neither income, lands, nor social esteem. The policy
of the Crown depended for its execution on the active consent of
magistrates, who again depended for their own social position on
the good-will of the neighbouring squires, and were on such friendly
terms with the middle class in town and country, that magisterial
resistance to the Crown might at moments become one with the
resistance of the whole nation : and it was these moments which
decided the fate of England.

Adminis-
tration of
the poor-
law

During the early years of James I. the Justices of Peace were
the willing instruments of Government in continuing the home
policy of the great Queen. As administrators they were chiefly

[1] Fynes Moryson, and other travels of period. See note, p. 6 above. Einstein,
pp. 115-75. *Harl. Misc.*, v., p. 12. Sir H. Unton, who travelled in Venetian
territory in Elizabeth's reign, rode through the wooded spurs of the sub-Alpine
country, carrying an umbrella as he rode to keep off the sun, and preceded by a
mounted attendant blowing a horn ; see the curious picture of the events of his
life in the Elizabethan room, National Portrait Gallery, which gives a lively
portraiture of the typical education and career of a rich gentleman : Oxford,
continental travel, low country wars, etc., and some minor customs of the age,
such as the elaborate marriage masque and funeral.

engaged in executing the poor-law scheme by which the Elizabethan
legislators had propped up the tottering foundations of economic
society, and rendered them stable for two centuries of political
progress and colonial expansion.   In the reigns of the first two Tudor
Kings, owing to a variety of economic, social and political causes,
unemployment was rife and " sturdy beggars " were a danger.
England was like a kingdom terrorised by disbanding armies, and
the chronic disease might at any moment come to a head in social
revolt.   To meet this danger, Elizabeth's Parliaments had erected
a system of charity and control of which the poor-law was the central
provision.   To replace the doubtful benefits of promiscuous relief at
the Abbey Gate, they instituted the legal obligation of every parish
to maintain its own poor.   This great principle saved society, though
it could not abolish pauperism.   But the principle would have stood
as vainly on the statute-book as did the penal laws of that day
against swearing oaths and tippling ale, if it had not been rigorously
enforced on recalcitrant, selfish and impoverished parishes by an
elaborate system of checks.   The Justices of Peace in the shire were
held responsible by the Privy Council in London for the levy of the
hated poor-rate, and the Judges on circuit acted for the central
government as inspectors of the magistrates' conduct.

The assizes were at this time more than a mere gaol delivery. Assizes
They were made the occasion for an informal meeting of the shire
for every imaginable purpose.   The fashionable young squire came
to air his new doublet, and the cut-purse to relieve him of its rich
trimmings ; the magistrates to make their reports ; the yeomen to
form the juries, and at times of political crisis to present petitions ;
all to hear and discuss the news of the great world.   It was on these
high occasions that the Judge made solemn inquiry into the administration of the county, lectured the awe-struck assembly, explained the policy of the nation and the large interests of society
to those whose ideas were bounded by the petty interests of the
parish and the local prejudice of the shire.   If the magistrates had
through fear or favour neglected of late to search the houses of their
Catholic neighbours for arms, if the ale-houses had been allowed to
become dens of disorder, if the wool trade had declined owing to
the state of the roads, if two parishes had a point in dispute about
the assessment of the rate, the Judge had words of reproof, command and advice for all.   Under the stimulus of this inquisition,
the local magistrates learnt to carry out in detail the general policy
of the State.

Private vested interests, other than land, had then little chance Various
of defying society so armed in its own defence.   Ale-houses, in magis-
which no one had interest except the ale-wife or publican, who functions
brewed what they sold, were often suppressed without pity or compensation.   Corners in wheat were broken up by fixing a maximum

price, an expedient then found practicable, at least in time of famine.[1] Youths without employment, save that of wandering round the palings of the deer-park, or camping out on the common with a cow, were forcibly apprenticed to some honest tradesman, or compelled to take service with some farmer who had applied to the magistrates to find him in hands. The sturdy beggar was flogged at the whipping-post of every town on the road till he was glad to return to his native parish, as the only place where the law ordered persecution to be stayed and public charity to be extended. Such squirearchy must have seemed rich man's law to many a " rogue forlorn," as he lay hungry and bleeding by the roadside, cursing the Quarter Sessions in the spirit of Lear. None the less squirearchy still had its uses in the era of the Stuarts. It preserved society from confusion and the poor from death by hunger, while at the same time it saved England's local liberties, and thereby in the long run her Parliamentary institutions.

The Justices of Peace were not only administrators but judges and police magistrates. The State depended on their willingness to execute the harsh laws that kept the Catholics down, and maintained the fabric of Elizabethan England secure. But the greatest amount of their magisterial work consisted in the enforcement of the law against ordinary criminals, the management of the police, the examination of prisoners, the drawing up of indictments for the Judges of Assize, the dispensing of petty justice at their own sessions and the control of prisons.

Miscarriage of justice The clumsy machine of English police, judicature and punishment maintained social order through the political convulsions of the century, but at the expense of the continual escape of the guilty, and in all probability of the condemnation of the innocent, besides horrible sufferings that the law inflicted confessedly on the merely unfortunate. Men of that less sensitive generation were more indifferent to the fate of others, partly because they were more ready themselves to endure pain and injustice. These they regarded as irremediable evils of human life. The natural right of " Fortune " to dispense death or ruin, shame or reward, with blinded eyes and wanton favour, was the constant theme of poets ; who, when they were not contemplating " Mortality," were railing at " Fortune," to an audience only too familiar with the fickleness of " the jade," in the vagaries of the law. These defects of justice were left unaltered, partly from want of the humanitarian, but still more from want of

---

[1] Even in ordinary times, one of the many duties of the J.P.'s was to fix the price at which wheat was to be sold and the wages which each kind of labourer should receive. How far their decisions were enforced, or how far they influenced wages and prices, will probably always be a matter of dispute among historians.

the scientific spirit, a defect which showed itself alike in the organisation of police, in the treatment of evidence, and in the system of
punishment.

The severity of the judicial and penal systems was partly caused Police
by the defects of the police. Only a small proportion of criminals
were caught, and even when arrests were made, but little evidence
was collected. The officers, so far from being scientific, were not
even properly professional. For although the constable of each
village and the watchman of each town were paid to guard peace and
property, they were yet neither specially fitted nor trained for that
employment. In the towns, men superannuated from other trades
were chosen to play the part of Dogberry and Verges. In a country
village the case was even worse. For there the magistrates could
only afford to hire the part-service of a farmer-constable, who spent
his day in agriculture, and left the plough to lead the hue-and-cry
as far as the parish bounds. When the chase reached those limits,
Master Constable was as like as not to sit down and thank God they
were well rid of a thief, while the criminal pursued his way, feebly
followed by officers of other parishes, ever less interested in his arrest
as he drew farther from the scene of his crime. Under such conditions, when a district became notoriously infested by thieves, and
the magistrates, after a severe lecture from the Judge, were aware
that more men must somehow be hung at the next Assizes, the
village constable too often made haste to seize the innocent on
general rumour or manufactured evidence. But it was yet more
common that the guilty thief remained unprosecuted, spared by the
charity of his poor neighbours, " who would not procure any man's
death for all the goods in the world " ; such was one result of capital
punishment for theft. There was no public prosecutor, no county
police, and no national detective force, except Cecil's political spies.
The inefficient character of the constabulary was due, like so much
else in the infancy of the rating system, to want of money to hire
a professional staff ; and the badness of its organisation to the want
of a larger police area.[1]

The energy of Elizabeth's magistrates, helped by improved economic conditions, had at last got the upper hand of the sturdy beggars
who in her father's day rendered high roads and lonely farms unsafe ;
but law-breakers more formidably armed had still little to fear.
The watchmen and constables, diligent in harrying the plague-
stricken and the vagrant, shrank aside before the companies of
sword-wearing ruffians and broken gallants—the Roaring Boys,
Tityre Tues and Bravadors, who made night unsafe in many an
English street.

---

[1] There was a High Constable for the Hundred or the Franchise (areas midway
in size between parish and county). But the High Constables do not appear to
have been very different from the Parish Constables as regards efficiency.

The improbability of arrest was not the sole encouragement to crime. The English judicial system, like a lottery where tickets were drawn for life or death, let a certain proportion of the arrested slip through its clutches, irrespective of their guilt or innocence. If the indictment was wrongly drawn by a word, the accused went free as Barabbas. All who, being able to read, claimed " benefit of clergy," for the first offence escaped punishment in the case of many common crimes such as petty larceny. When the prisoner had friends among the jury, or when from corruption, ignorance or prejudice the countrymen were in the mood to thwart the law, he was acquitted in spite of protests from the Bench. The English jury system, while it protected our liberties, by no means always increased the fairness of trials ; and verdicts inspired by terrorism, favour and folly would have been even more frequent, but for the wholesome fear now felt for the Judge. A proper respect for the Bench had been strengthened under the Tudors by the backing it had received from the Privy Council and the Star Chamber.

The great number of criminals, who, owing to the faults of the police, the law, or the juries, were never brought to a genuine trial, made men unwilling to try other prisoners fairly. Anxious lest the law should lose its terrors, the courts, with the approval of society, retained rules framed to secure the conviction of the guilty rather than the safety of the innocent. The prisoner had no counsel either before or during the trial ; the nature of the evidence for the prosecution was concealed from him till he came into court ; he could not arrange beforehand that the proper witnesses should appear in his defence ; he had no books or notes before him, but spoke from memory or on the spur of the moment ; if, not being a lawyer, he ventured to quote Bracton, the prosecutor denounced him for surreptitiously receiving counsel in prison. While any hearsay evidence was listened to with attention, he could not claim to have the real witnesses brought into court, or the original documents produced. In an age when scientific methods of valuing evidence were quite unknown, the prejudice of the court against the prisoner led to results like the condemnation of Raleigh for a crime he would have abhorred to commit, and of hundreds of witches for crimes no one can commit at all.[1]

---

[1] One custom was perhaps in favour of the accused, if innocent. In the early Stuart period trials were decided more by examination of the prisoner than by evidence of witnesses. The prisoner was compelled to answer any question put to him, first, at the preliminary examination before the J.P., or in cases of treason before the Privy Council ; afterwards, if he had been unable to satisfy those authorities of his innocence, he wrangled in court with his prosecutors. These examinations, though they helped to convict the guilty, gave the innocent their best chance of escape in days of unscientific methods of taking evidence. Helpless as an unlearned prisoner was in altercation with a well-primed magistrate or a couple of lawyers, innocence would have been still more helpless if the verdict

The net results of these methods of judicature was that, while **Penal** the proportion of unjust convictions was probably large, the pro- **Code** portion of convictions to crimes was certainly small.   Hence the severity of the penal system : for if there were several hundred thieves in a county, of whom only fifty could be caught and thirty convicted in a year, it seemed good to the wisdom of our ancestors that the gallows should rid the world of at least a score.   The rate-payers could not then afford the money, either for the employment of highly-trained officers to watch, catch, imprison and release the same person twenty times over ; or for the maintenance of gaols large enough to lodge the criminal population.   The prison was regarded neither as a reformatory nor as a place of vindictive punish-ment, but as a house of detention for political prisoners, debtors, accused awaiting trial, and persons of these classes who had been unable on the order for their release to pay the gaoler his fees. When a large number of condemned felons had their capital sentence commuted to imprisonment, the gaol was overcrowded, starvation and pestilence afflicted its regular occupants, the debtors, and complaint was made that the prisons were being put to an im-proper use.[1]

The prison was the house of misery and misfortune, not of crime. **Prisons** But the misery of the unfortunate was then greater than the misery which we now think right to inflict on the criminal.   For the magis-trates, being bound to maintain the prisons out of the rates, yet wishing to diminish this charge on the community, in effect farmed out the business to gaolers, who not only covered the expenses of the public by exacting the legalised fees, but extorted fortunes for themselves out of their victims, under penalty of blows, starvation and foul lodging.   When one of these bad men retired, he often sold his lucrative post to another wretch equally prepared to specu-late in the woes of mankind.   If the ordinary punishment for theft had been imprisonment, these gaols would have become a heavy charge on the rates, since they must needs have been greatly enlarged. But the punishment was hanging or flogging ; and so the gallows or the whipping-post saved the thief from the worse fate of the penniless prisoner.   He, poor wretch, rotted in dungeon for the remainder of a life which was seldom long, if once it put the gaoler to a charge.

In this period, when there was still no effective police, the security **General** of life and goods and the maintenance of public order would still **effects of** have been as bad as in the Middle Ages but for the sound adminis- **the poor-law**

had depended solely on evidence heard, when that evidence was chiefly at second-hand, and nearly all against the accused.

The best authorities on police and judicature of the period are Mr. Lee's *History of Police*, 1901, and Stephen's *History of Criminal Law*.   See also Hamilton's *Quarter Sessions from Elizabeth to Anne.*

[1] *Court and Times of Charles I.*, ii., p. 244.

tration of the poor-law. The householder, unwillingly forced to contribute to the poor-rate, got back more than his money's worth. The panic terror that in Plantagenet and Tudor days rushed through every room in the lonely farmstead and every house in the hamlet when the growling of the watchdogs proclaimed that " the beggars were coming to town," had become a memory and a nursery tale. In this century of civic and religious feuds, the law-abiding character of the English survived, not entirely by reason of our racial temperament, but also because the community had secured itself by making provision for the destitute.

Upon the whole, as compared with other periods of our history, this was an age when the poor were well treated by the public action of the community, because in the preceding age the " sturdy beggars " had frightened society into active and beneficial measures for their relief. In dealing with the problems of poverty, the reign of Elizabeth was the period of creative legislation and the reigns of her two successors was the period of effective administration. Now administration was nine points of the poor-law ; the same principle of poor relief was proclaimed by law in France and Scotland, but remained a dead letter for want of a proper combination of central and local machinery, and for lack of public spirit in the upper and middle class. In England alone the King's Council supervised and the magistrates under that supervision executed the unpopular legislation. The early Stuart monarchy did one great and good thing for England ; it secured that the provisions for the relief of the impotent poor should never again fall into disuse; and in its own day it even did a little to alleviate the lot of the unemployed.[1] But without the active and intelligent co-operation of the gentry and Justices of Peace in each shire, the central government could have done nothing.

No accusation is more petulantly bandied about between rival races and rival generations than that of inhumanity. Each considers itself humane, because its anger is easily aroused against the cruelty of other places or times ; yet the circumstances in every case must be carefully examined before this feeling of self-satisfied superiority can be rightly indulged. A few facts relating to our ancestors' humanity, in the sense of unwillingness to inflict physical pain and discomfort, may interest the speculator in the inexact science of comparative morals.

[1] The legal responsibility of each parish had some bad economical effects. It prevented the fluidity of labour, because each parish refused to admit fresh hands to settle in its boundaries, lest they should become fresh mouths. And it prevented the increase of population, because, from the same fear of an increased poor-rate, parish authorities often forbade the erection of new cottages. On the whole subject of the poor-law, see Miss Leonard's excellent book, *English Poor Relief*, and App. B. below.

In the early disuse of torture as a means of extracting confession, Disuse of English law and custom led the world.[1] Torture for this purpose torture in England was unknown in our common law, and the Tower rack was regarded as the special political privilege of the Crown, whereby the Privy Council alone might extort information for want of which the State might be imperilled. Yet even the butcher's last plea of *Salus Publici* became obsolete in the reign of James I. The torture from which Guy Fawkes had been lifted up to die, shattered in all save his Promethean spirit, was twenty years later pronounced illegal and was not used to compel the murderer of Buckingham to incriminate the King's Parliamentary enemies. Nor in the utmost height of Royal or Roundhead despotism was it again employed. It is impossible to account for this definite change except by the growth of humanitarian sentiment.

In other lands, torture to extract evidence was an important part of the judicial system swept away by the French Revolution, and torture as an accompaniment of capital punishment held a high place in continental codes. The common criminal was broken on the wheel, the witch and the Socinian were burned alive. In Spain, the roasting of the victims of superstition, though necessarily rarer since the extinction of Protestantism, was regarded by the populace as a special delight, and by the priests as an offering to their Pantheon, among whose principal attributes were those of Moloch. But in England ordinary criminals were never put to death by torture. In the reign of James I. two heretics, who denied the doctrine of the Trinity, closed the fiery roll of Smithfield martyrdom. These two brave men, braver than Ridley and Latimer in that no great party pitied their fate or embraced their creed, were the last persons to die for heresy in England. Our statesmanship was at once too humane and too timid to put Catholics to death for their religion even at the block, much less at the stake. " English people," says Sir James Stephen, " were reckless about taking life, but they have been usually averse to the infliction of death by torture ".[2]

---

[1] The torture of *peine forte et dure* (namely, pressing to death) was still used in the seventeenth century to force a man to plead. But this was a comparatively rare incident. The disuse of torture as a means of extracting evidence had taken place in English common law in the Middle Ages, partly perhaps because the English of that period did not require evidence of guilt before hanging a man, but were content with the belief prevalent among his neighbours (Stephen. i., p. 222).

[2] See also Harrison's *Description of England*, ed. Furnivall, pp. 237, 238, for contemporary opinion and practice. Although the punishment for treason was hanging and disembowelling, those who investigate the hideous subject will be thankful to find that the Jesuit and the regicide scarcely suffered pain for more than a few seconds. The legal punishment of women for treason was the more painful death at the stake ; but they were in practice usually, though not always, strangled before the straw was lit. Petty treason, punishable thus, included then the murder of a husband, master or mistress. The execution of women for political treason had long fallen into disuse with English Governments and

English
humanity
in war

When Civil War at last broke out in the midst of our peaceful island, its conduct contrasted well in every point of humanity with the uncontrolled destruction that was laying waste the continent. For the English were not a military population ; the state of war was rare and unpopular ; the combatants were men of the same race, and the religious animosity less intense than in Holland, France and Germany ; the violence of armed Episcopalian and Puritan was as much milder than the devilries of Alva and Tilly, as the Bishops of the High Commission Court were more mild than the Inquisitors of Spain.

Cruelty in
some
other re-
spects

But while the English, by their very insularity, drew ahead of others in their methods of conducting war, and in the disuse of torture as a means of extracting evidence or inflicting capital punishment, there were several respects in which their humanity was low. In their treatment of coloured races, and of white peoples whom they reckoned inferior in civilisation, the English were no better than the Dutch and French, or, except for the Inquisition, than the Spaniard. Of the state of our prisons, and of the use of torture as a means of punishment other than capital, we have already spoken. Since corporal punishments were the only alternative to the gallows or the living death of the prison,[1] they were perhaps less abominable for their cruelty to the victim than for their brutalising effect on others as everyday spectacles. But while we condemn our ancestors for flocking to see the thief faint in the pillory under the shower of filthy missiles, and women suffer agonies under the lash, we must remember that we are ignorant what proportion of the populace went to these sights and in what spirit.

The witch
hunt

But the most scandalous blot in English humanity was witch-finding. The inhabitants of continental Europe, brutalised by the continual presence of war, torture and murder, which rival priesthoods blessed, frenzied by doubt as to the true escape from the lively vision of hell, and taught to see powers of evil in every common event, fell with maniac cruelty upon a class of persons whom old tradition pointed out as the devil's servants. In countries of either faith, old and solitary women perished by thousands amid agonies of torture. Across the guardian waters that divided England from the atmosphere of religious wars, this loathsome infection of the mind was wafted like a plague-blast ; but since the material and intellectual causes were less marked, the vile panic was never here

parties, when James II. revived it to put down the sheltering of fugitives. Hanging, before the principle of the drop was adopted, unavoidably lasted many minutes. Though it was not meant as a torture, a more humane generation would have found means of making death instantaneous.

[1] Some few convicts, but not those of the worst kind, were transported to Virginia as " servants ". The custom was resisted, with partial success, by the colonists. Between 1649 and 1685 a much greater number of political offenders were transported to Virginia and the West Indies (*Economic Hist. of Virginia*, Bruce, 1896, i., pp. 596-612).

quite so horrible or so extensive. The sceptical Elizabeth, perhaps with some pity for her sex, had refused to yield when the pamphlet press called on the Government to enact fiercer laws " not suffering a witch to live ". The outburst came with the accession of a Scottish King, who, though he rejected the best part of the spirit of Knox, was crazed beyond his English subjects with the witch-mania of Scotland and the continent. His first Parliament enacted new death-laws ; at once the Judges and magistrates, the constables and the mob, began to hunt up the oldest and ugliest spinster who lived with her geese in the hut on the common, or tottered about the village street muttering the inaudible soliloquies of second childhood. Many pleaded guilty, and described the covenants they had formed with black dogs and " goblins called Tibb " : some had undoubtedly taken to what they believed to be black arts, to repel or requite the malevolence of their neighbours, or to win money and reputation from their credulity ; but many were beaten or terrified into fictitious confessions, or perished denying their guilt to the last. Educated men soon perceived that not a few of these unfortunate creatures were innocent, but this acuteness of perception in no way disturbed the belief of any such observers in the general prevalence of witch-craft.[1] This black business culminated during the Civil War under the rule of Presbyterianism, when systematic though illegal tortures were successfully applied by scoundrels like Matthew Hopkins to obtain the death of scores of women. A reaction took place about the time of the rise of the Independents to power, and the practice disappeared during the Rationalist movement which found refuge under the banner of the Anglican Restoration.[2] But in its origin the witch-hunt was stirred up by no section ; it arose out of a profound and universal belief. Learning, headed by the pedant King, was master of the hounds ; science with Bacon, and law with Coke pointed the trail ; imagination and poetry blew the horn with Shakespeare and his brother play-wrights ; religion blessed the chase that she had set on foot ; while the discordant pack of vulgar beliefs, fears and hatreds came yelling on their prey. Still it is worth remark that in England the witches were nearly always hung and not

---

[1] " Many are unjustly accused for witches. Sometimes out of ignorance of natural and misapplying of supernatural causes ; sometimes out of their neighbours mere malice, and the suspicion is increased if the party accused be notoriously ill-favoured ; . . . sometimes out of their own causeless confessions, being brought before a magistrate they acknowledge themselves to be witches, being themselves rather bewildered with fear or deluded with phancy " (*The Profane State*, bk. v. chap. iii.). But Fuller goes on to show that he believed the charges in many cases to be true.

It is right to say that there was a real witchcraft in the line of poisoning and drugs (though not nearly so common as on the continent) ; perhaps also attempts were made to injure by mesmerism or hypnotic suggestion.

[2] Lecky's *Rationalism*, chap. i. Article on Matthew Hopkins in *Twelve Bad Men*. Mr. Firth thinks, judging from the actual records, the numbers of witches killed have been exaggerated.

burnt, and that while confession was in too many cases extorted by cruelty which amounted to torture, such use was at least illegal.

Not an age of humanitarianism

Unwillingness to take life or to inflict physical pain is so far from being the whole of morality that it is only one part of human kindness. Thus the Scots of that epoch burnt, tortured and slew more readily than the English; but they were still a kindly race, and perhaps had stronger affections than their more humane neighbours. Neither does it condemn our English ancestors for a lack of the higher emotions, to admit that the Stuart epoch in England was unmarked by any public movement of a philanthropic nature. The state of the prisons, the treatment of inferior races, passed without protest from any section.[1] The causes of this apathy are not far to seek. Other great principles and noble aspirations absorbed the attention of parties and men. And there had not yet begun that Rationalist movement, which, as Lecky has pointed out, was in no small degree a cause of modern humanitarian activity.[2] Religion was in that age almost the sole intellectual and moral influence, and while the nobility of thought and conduct which it then breathed into some of its chosen has hardly since been equalled, humanity was no part of its special teaching. It must indeed be allowed that religion was then associated with the rack, the stake, the burning town, the massacre of women and children, the hate that never dies, the wrongs that

An age of religion

can never be avenged. The greatest mass of mental suffering and physical pain that Europe had undergone since the barbaric ages . was brought about by the partially successful struggle of the Catholic reaction to recover revolted Christendom. In England the worst horrors were spared; but here, too, religion meant the ransacking of Catholic houses, the haling of Puritans to gaol, the rabbling of Anglican curates, the shouts of the crowd as demented women, who were persuaded they had sold themselves to eternal fire, were dragged screaming to the gallows. If in that age there had existed a man whose prime motive and sole object had been humanitarian, he would have shuddered at the name of religion, and regarded its omnipotence with despair. Our second Puritanism, the Evangelical revival, in many ways a weakly imitation of the first, had this great merit of its own—humanitarian activity. For in the interval the Rationalist movement had shaken the persecutor's sword from the hand of Faith, and Religion had been to school with her rival, Reason. From Cromwell to Wilberforce the road lay through Voltaire.

---

[1] The crusade of the Independents of the Commonwealth period against the "tortuous ungodly jungle" of the English law, was rather utilitarian than humanitarian. While they proposed to abolish *peine forte et dure* and the burning of women for treason, they allowed the number of capital crimes to be increased by one. Cromwell, indeed, who was ahead of his own and all other parties in this matter, took steps to abolish hanging for all offences except murder. "To hang a man for six-and-eightpence," "to see men lose their lives for petty matters is a thing God will reckon" (Firth's *Cromwell*, p. 349).

[2] *History of Rationalism.*

CHAPTER II

THE MIDDLE AND LOWER CLASSES IN COUNTRY AND TOWN— INDUSTRY AND COMMERCE—THE CONDITIONS FAVOURABLE TO POETRY AND TO RELIGION

Well, Your Majesty, is not this world a catholic kind of place ?   The Puritan Gospel and Shakespeare's plays : such a pair of facts I have rarely seen saved out of one chimerical generation.—Historical Sketches, CARLYLE.

AT the opening of the twentieth century England may be com- pared to a garden, a ground cut up for purposes of cultivation by hedgerows and lines of trees.   The regularity of this garden is pleasantly broken by woods and coppices artificially maintained by man for his use or pleasure.   But through this fertile territory, the new economy of industrialism is pushing out its iron claws, changing vast tracts of garden into town, and altering the character and appearance of the rest by introducing, even in agricultural districts, materials and houses of uniform type.   That part of the population which lives permanently under the influence of industrial sights and sounds, is larger than that which lives in the garden ; and even the inhabitants of the rural districts have lost their own characteristic ideals of life under the all-pervading influence of the towns.   One condition of modern times is, that what pays best is generally ugly, and that whatever man now touches for a purely economic reason, he mars.

Aspect of modern England; what pays best is ugly

At the beginning of the seventeenth century the reverse of every one of these conditions prevailed.   The bulk of the acreage of England was not a garden but an open country ; one part wilderness of heath, turf or marsh ; the other part unenclosed plough-fields like those of France and Germany to-day.   But the bleakness of this open land was broken by great tracts of brushwood and tall trees, wrecks of the old English forest that the hand of man had never planted.   Over this wide surface, in every direction, the new economy of enclosure was pushing out its green regularity of hedge-row and planted tree ; the garden of England was slowly being made ; this work of enclosing the open fields began under the Tudors and was completed only in the nineteenth century.   When James I. ascended the throne, the little population of England (somewhere on its rise from two and a half to five millions) was scattered through-out the cultivated country in fairly even distribution.   The most marked variations in thickness of inhabitants were caused, not by congestion in great cities, but by vast tracts of wilderness in all the Northern and several of the Southern shires.   The cities, though they drew to themselves the busiest and best tithe of English

Aspect of England under the Stuarts

humanity, and led the nation in its noblest undertakings, were so small in size and so isolated by the imperfect means of communication, that town influence scarcely affected the lives of the great majority of Englishmen.

What paid best was beautiful

It happened, too, that economic progress in that day unconsciously involved æsthetic improvement. The garden of England, created by the new system of enclosure, was more beautiful than the wilderness or the bare plough-lands to which it succeeded. Land could then be most cheaply enclosed, not by barbed wire, but by planted hedgerows ; cowsheds and barns could be erected most quickly, not with corrugated iron, but with timber from the forest and thatch from the field. Even the habitations of man improved the appearance of nature, for hedges and orchards rose round new houses, and the buildings themselves were pleasing to the eye. This was not because every village mason was a born artist, but because the materials with which he had to work were beautiful, and the structural forms that were most suited to his limited resources and knowledge were more picturesque than regular. The gable and lattice window were adopted at least as much for economic as for æsthetic reasons. But there was no one monotonous type of structure or of material. Manor house and cottage varied pleasantly in every district. Some were of oak-beam and plaster, others of stone or red brick ; some were roofed with thatch, others with stone-slab, according to the natural products and the immemorial tradition of each country-side.

Enclosure of fields

The appearance of the country was being gradually changed from open landscape to enclosed fields by the substitution of modern for mediæval tillage. The evolution of all villeins and serfs into freemen of the status of farmers, yeomen or agricultural labourers, had in the Tudor epoch been completed without strife and almost without notice. Side by side with this great legal and social evolution, a corresponding change in methods of agriculture had begun to take place, more slowly, more painfully and with more noise and rumour. This was the enclosure of the land.

In mediæval England the corn land of every township consisted of an immense open field, neither divided nor enclosed by hedges ; it was cultivated by the common labour, implements and cattle of the whole village. At harvest each man took the crop off that part of the field which belonged to him. During the Tudor period many of these open fields were broken up and surrounded by hedges, suffering conversion into arable or pasture farms of the modern type. Yet it is probable that in the reign of the first two Stuarts more than half the acreage under corn was still open land, cultivated by the common efforts of the villagers, after the methods pursued by their ancestors in the days of Wat Tyler. The great corn growing districts of the midlands were still unenclosed. And the whole acreage of pasture and corn, enclosed and unenclosed, scarcely equalled the wilderness still unreclaimed.[1]

The change from the common cultivation of open strips of field to individual responsibility for pieces of enclosed ground, brought to the front two figures characteristic of English agricultural history —the tenant-farmer and the yeoman. These two classes existed under the old system, but wherever the new order was established they gained a new importance. For on the farmer and the yeoman rested the first opportunity for initiative in those improvements which compact farms and hedges had at last rendered possible. Individual farmers could do nothing to introduce new methods of agriculture on that half of the corn land of England which was still unenclosed, and cultivated by the common efforts of the whole village. On the newly enclosed lands the farmers of the seventeenth century had some power of improvement, but not on a large scale. For it was not yet the fashion, as it became in the next century, for landlords to sink great sums of capital in scientific improvements, and the farmers, left to themselves, had little capital and less education. The great day of the tenant-farmer was yet to come ; and in the Stuart epoch he was neither wealthy, independent nor interesting.

The tenant-farmers

The yeomen, who were computed to be more numerous than the tenant-farmers,[2] were at least their match in agricultural enterprise, and were not, like their rivals, discouraged by the prospect of raised rents and fines on their improvements. What little advance in methods was made at this period was due either to the wealthier members of the yeoman class, or to gentlemen who, like Cromwell, worked their own land. But the want of capital and the want of education delayed any such general improvement in methods as might have been expected to follow at once, wherever the system of common tillage was abandoned.[3]

The yeomen

[1] Gregory King calculated that in the reign of William III., out of thirty-nine million acres in England, one million was water and road or roadside, ten millions were " heaths, moors, mountains and barren lands," three " woods and coppices," three " forests, parks and commons " (*Political Observations*, 1696, Chalmers' ed., 1810, p. 52). The comment of his friend Davenant (*Balance of Trade*, 1699), that " *anno* 1600 " " there were *more* forests, woods, commons, coppices and waste ground " than in their own day, is correct (see Nisbet's *Our Forests and Woodlands,* 1900, pp. 72-80). Indeed as early as 1662 the spread of tillage, and of manufacture by furnaces, had excited the alarm of the Dockyard Authorities and of the Royal Society, and Evelyn wrote his *Sylva* to recommend them to make plantations by way of supplying the ground lately lost by natural forest. On the whole subject see Gonner, *Common Land and Enclosure*, 1912.

[2] Gregory King estimated the yeomen, at the end of the Stuart period, when their decline had already begun, at 180,000 families, or one-sixth of the total number of families in the country ; the farmers at 150,000 families. His table calculating the numbers of each class can be found in his own *Observations*, 1696, and in Davenant's *Balance of Trade*, 1699, p. 23, where the number of yeomen families is placed at 160,000.

[3] Methods of cattle-breeding were improved, and root crops introduced to feed the cattle. But turnips were only introduced in some places, and even then

But while in the eye of the pure economist the yeoman was scarcely in advance of the farmer, his social standing was far more enviable. In an age when no one even pretended to think it wrong for a man to enforce political and religious conformity among those over whose fortunes he had control, the yeoman reaping his own field enjoyed an independence denied to many pursuing more lucrative and more cultivated professions. To be counted as a yeoman a man must be able to spend 40s. a year derived from his own freehold land.[1] This was also the qualification for the Parliamentary franchise in the counties, a privilege which the yeoman exercised with more complete freedom than some tenant farmers and field labourers in our own day. So far from desiring the protection of secrecy at the poll, the yeomen took a jolly pride in voting, as eventually in fighting, on the opposite side to the neighbouring squire.

The yeomanry (wrote Fuller in the reign of Charles I.), is an estate of people almost peculiar to England. France and Italy are like a die which hath no points between sink and ace, nobility and peasantry. . . . The yeoman wears russet clothes, but makes golden payment, having tin in his buttons and silver in his pocket. . . . In his own country he is a main man in Juries. He seldom goes far abroad, and his credit stretches further than his travel. He goes not to London, but *se-defendendo*, to save himself a fine, being returned of a Jury, where seeing the King once, he prays for him ever afterwards.[2]

Such pious and simple yeomen were the backbone of Charles's cause in the Western shires when the hour of need came ; but in East Anglia the prayers of the yeomen were sent up less often for the King's health than for the King's conversion.

Abeyance of agitation among the peasantry There are few things in the history of Europe so unaccountable as the ebb and flow of political agitation among the peasantry. At the close of the Middle Ages the tillers of the soil rose in revolt against feudal society, first in France and England during the Hundred Years' War, then towards the beginning of the Lutheran movement in Germany and in the Hungarian Kingdom. Yet after these strange outbreaks, the peasantry of the continent relapsed into a long quiescence under wrongs which they had once refused to endure, until the great Revolution in French society aroused in the ancient villages of many distant lands, hopes and passions that had been buried for centuries in the soil. Nor was there in England any agitation among the peasantry during the Stuart epoch. In the reign of Edward VI. the enclosures had caused local assemblies of armed peasants, not wholly unlike, in theory and in spirit, to the

were badly cultivated. Artificial grasses were discussed but not introduced. Little was done to improve the cultivation of cereals, partly perhaps because the Dutch, whose methods were most studied and imitated, knew more about cattle, roots and grasses than about corn (Cunningham, pp. 545, 546, 549, 550).

[1] And yet some of the more privileged copyholders of the North of England, like the Cumberland " statesmen," must be counted in the yeomen class.

[2] *The Holy State*, bk. ii., chap. xviii.

more general rising of 1381 ; but from these last stirrings of mediæval revolt down to the time of Cobbett, the social agitator was almost unknown on the village green. Even during the Commonwealth, when 30,000 political pamphlets were issued, and all men were invited by the spirit of the age to question the very basis of social conventions, there was no important movement among the peasantry on their own behalf.[1] But although these centuries of social peace in England corresponded in time with the same phenomenon on the continent, the English peasant was not resting in the same status as his brother across the channel. The French and German peasant was a serf ; the English peasant was now, by law, a freeman. The French peasant was preparing a bright future for his descendants by acquiring land, but for the present his own position was unenviable : the wars of religion in France and Germany, followed by the endless campaigns dictated by the proud policy of the House of Bourbon, reduced the tillers of the soil to a state of misery such as in a former age had caused the terrible outbreak of the Jacquerie to interrupt the wars of Froissart. But in peaceful England the economic effect of the brief war between Charles and his Parliament was to raise the wage of the agricultural labourer. English travellers were shocked at the " wooden shoes and straw hats " of the foreign peasantry, and the " grass herbs and roots " which was too often their only food.[2]

But though the English field labourer was ahead of the German and French in economic and legal position, we must not ascribe the abeyance of rural agitation so much to the absence of rural grievances, as to the division of class interests and the want of leadership from above. The farmers and yeomen were now more divided off from the agricultural labourer and more contented with their own economic and social position than in the days of Wat Tyler. These two classes, thus already ranged on the side of social conservatism, formed in the Stuart epoch a far larger proportion of the whole agricultural community than they form to-day. Society in England was based on the stable and prosperous foundation of a very large number of small farms and small estates. The evils inseparable from private property in land, the loss of liberty which it too often inflicts on those who have to live and work on the land of others, were in those days limited by the high proportion of landowners to the total population.

But even then the agricultural labourer for hire represented the

---

[1] The score of " diggers on St. George's Hill " initiated an interesting but wholly powerless communistic movement in 1649 (see Gooch, pp. 214-25, and p. 233, note, below). The only other stirring of peasant revolt throughout the Stuart period was some unimportant rioting in 1607 in Warwickshire and Leicestershire, where enclosure for pasturage was still in progress after it had ceased elsewhere and where the fashionable rage for deer-parks made further inroads on agricultural land. But though the peasants pulled down some fences, the affair scarcely amounted to a rising.

[2] Arber's *Reprints*, viii, Howell's *Instructions*, p. 74.

The agri-
cultural
labourers
most numerous class. The English peasant, though badly paid, was in some cases well fed by his employer. The " servant in husbandry " only went into a separate cottage when he married. Until then he boarded in the farm-house, and partook freely at the family table of the staple dish of meat, though not always of the puddings and delicacies. There was a closer contact between master and men than now ; most of the farmers and yeomen were small and unpretentious people, living on intimate terms with their servants, whose families had often been on the same farm for generations.

Seasons
and
feasts
The food of the farm-house, which the unmarried " servant in husbandry " shared, varied according to each season of the year, with its traditional fasts and feasts. In Lent all ate fish—fresh, if near seas and rivers, but salted, if in dry and upland districts. For meat was prohibited, both by immemorial custom, which must in many places have still been in part religious, and by the statutes of Protestant Parliaments. Those shrewd legislators continued to enforce the observance of Lent, not, as they were careful to state, for superstitious reasons, but to encourage the fisheries as the great school of seamanship and national defence. But the chief reason why the Lenten fast was still observed was because the ordinary rural [1] household had no meat to hand at that time of year except the flitch of bacon and the beef that had been slaughtered and salted last Martinmas Day (11th November). At midsummer fresh beef and mutton was killed amid general rejoicings, and continued to grace the tables until winter. At Christmas, during " the twelve days " of the year when least was to be gained by labour in the fields, the agricultural world made holiday, feasting on collars of brawn, fowls, turkeys, mince-pies and plum-pottage, besides nameless dishes which the park-forester was not invited to share unless he came to court the honest yeoman's daughter ; the roasting piece of beef was stuck with rosemary, and though Jeremiah Carpenter standing by the spit testified concerning meats offered to idols, yet notwithstanding surely he ate thereof. Compared to other sorts of food, there was

Abun-
dance of
meat food
abundance of meat to be had in old England, for besides flocks of sheep, and herds of cattle and pigs, the country-side swarmed with rabbits, hares and birds of all kinds, which, as the game laws then stood, were the legitimate prey of the yeomen over whose land they strayed. The farm, which had to supply all the food of its inmates except perhaps a little bad fish during Lent, could boast of a few vegetables in the garden but none in the fields. Fruit was more common ; strawberries, raspberries and gooseberries had been grown in farm-gardens fifty years before James came to the throne.[2]

[1] Town butchers sometimes killed by stealth in the forbidden season (*Ct. and Times of C. I.*, ii., p. 72.)

[2] Cunningham (ed. 1892), p. 193. Hewins, pp. 88-96. Hamilton, p. 14. Also see Tusser's rhymes in *Somers' Tracts*, iii., for an intimate account of farm life in the middle of the Tudor period. Meat was so common that foreigners in the year 1602 remarked with surprise that the English rejected the entrails and feet for the table (Duke of Stettin, p. 47).

But the abundance of meat food procurable off the farm is not Village rights
the only reason why it is unsafe to judge of the real condition of
the agricultural labourer solely from the statistics of wages and
prices.[1] Common land for pasturage of cows, pigs and poultry,
common rights of collecting fuel and fowling on moor and waste,
were an important part of the cottagers' livelihood, though already
encroached upon by deer-parks and destined to extinction in the
great era of enclosure for arable at the close of the eighteenth century.
Moreover, the wages of the head of the cottar family might be aug- Employ-
mented by those of his wife and children, who were often separately ment of
employed and paid by the farmers. In hay-time and harvest the women
whole population turned out ; and the mothers worked, putting
their babies to play together in a corner of the busy field. At most
other times throughout the year the unmarried girls were employed,
as now, at certain kinds of agricultural labour, but not at the more
severe ditching and carrying. That last sacrifice of poverty was
spared. English gentlemen going out to join Prince Charles at
Madrid, were shocked at the sight of the Spanish women staggering
under loads and going through that round of labour which brought
the women of some of the most beautiful races of Europe to premature
old age.[2]

But besides their work in the fields, country women were largely
employed in industry. The cloth manufacture was organised by
the. " clothiers " of the towns ; but much labour was carried on in
distant cottages, each of which was visited by the clothier on his
periodic rounds. The old wool-pack inns of England recall the time
when it was common to meet, round the turning of a country lane,
a train of horses laden with sacks of wool hanging to the ground on
either side, or a clothier riding into market with pieces of cloth upon
his saddle-bow. In this and other employments boys and girls were
set to work at an early age. Although the state of things among
the families of the continental peasantry was perhaps worse, yet
English women and children were overworked long before the era of
the factory system.

Under the first two Stuarts all classes who lived on the land and Sanitary
yet more those who were gathered in the towns, were in perpetual conditions
terror of plague. Disease and infant mortality prevented the rapid
increase of the population. Medicine, as commonly practised, was
a formulated superstition rather than a science ; rules of health were
little understood ; sanitary habits were free and filthy among rich

---

[1] Agricultural wages were generally somewhere between 3s. and 5s. a week
(when food was not given), but rose slowly throughout the century. Wheat,
varying very greatly from year to year and county to county, was generally between 20s. and 50s., the average price, 1600-10, being 34s. 9½d. ; and 1620-30
being 43s. 0¾d. (Leonard, pp. 145, 301, 198, 199. Hamilton, pp. 12-14, 163
Hewins, p. 86. Thorold Rogers, *Six Centuries*, pp. 391-94, 426, 427).
[2] Verney, i., p. 78.

as well as poor. Our ancestors washed little, and their standard of
public decency in trivialities was that of some modern nations which
we now readily condemn. Prudery was rare even among Puritans;
and cleanliness even among courtiers, who compounded by free use
of oils and scents. Drinking-water was often contaminated, and
the danger seldom recognised. Little value was set on fresh air
indoors. The population, though thinly scattered on the soil, was
closely packed in the houses. Servants and apprentices generally
slept in holes among the rafters, and industry was often conducted
in the crowded dwelling-rooms of the family. Many of the worst
conditions of slum life existed in a small and chiefly rural population,
who had, however, the supreme advantage of open air and the beauties
of nature outside their door. It is not possible to know whether the
general standard of physique was higher or lower than it is in the
present day under conditions so much better and so much worse.

The towns   Although the cities of England contained in the seventeenth
century but a small part of the population, they were destined in
that epoch to take the lead in almost every branch of national
activity. And the services rendered by the English towns to arts
and crafts, reason, literature, politics and science, were fortunately
not accompanied by the open feud between town and country, by
the war of municipal privilege against central power, which had
been the price paid for the yet greater contributions of Italian and
German burgherdom towards human progress.

The
prentice
laws
Few as were the inhabitants of the towns, they were on the
whole select. A rigorous limit was set to the influx from the country
of wastrels and untrained hands, while every craftsman who worked
within the city bounds had received a technical education. The
Statute of Apprentices forbade any one to set up trade, or even
to work for wages as a journeyman artisan, until he had served
seven years of apprenticeship; and it was not easy to evade this
law, enforced as it was by craft-guilds and municipalities, who saw
their own interest both in limiting the number and in maintaining
the quality of craftsmen within the bounds of their jurisdiction.
Another provision of this famous statute forbade any one withdrawn
from agricultural pursuits to be apprenticed to an ordinary craft in
any town; this prevented the field labourer from changing his employment, and in effect made the country districts instead of the
cities the receptacle of surplus population. Another clause, which
forbade merchants and shopkeepers in towns to take as apprentice
any one under the rank of yeoman's son, shows the high standard
of blood and breeding maintained among even the employees of
commerce, which must have exalted the general average of life and
intelligence in the towns.

Such laws had manifest disadvantages. As administered by

jealous corporations they checked the fluidity of labour and the growth of population ; [1] they hindered adventurous men from embarking in trade, or drove them to set up business in rural districts where the apprentice laws only partially applied. Seven years was a needlessly long period for a universal rule, since many occupations could be learnt in half the time. Yet for all its faults the apprentice system maintained the best trade traditions, supplied domestic discipline at an age when it is usually most wanting, trained the hand, the eye and the mind, and afforded a technical education on a natural economic basis which no diminution of the revenue or of the rates, and no lapse of educational enthusiasm, could in the slightest degree affect.

In the Middle Ages the inhabitants of each town regarded themselves as a separate community, almost a separate race, at commercial war with the rest of the world. Only a freeman of the city could be bound apprentice ; and the freedom of the city was but grudgingly bestowed on " foreigners " or " aliens," as the people of the neighbouring towns and villages were called. This idea of the civic community was now gradually yielding to the idea of the national community, and to the broader aspects of economic and racial policy introduced by the discovery of America and the struggle with Spain. But the old ideas still lingered. Throughout the seventeenth century York refused to admit " foreigners," English or Dutch. The cathedral city, starved of new blood, gradually yielded its old supremacy in the northern cloth trade to Hull and to the western dales. But in many other towns a more liberal policy brought its due reward. In London and Norwich, the first and second cities of England, the sons of gentry and yeomen from all parts of the island were welcomed as apprentices. Even race hatred was often overcome by religious sympathy. The Huguenots of France, Flanders and Holland were made welcome in Puritan towns, for their sufferings and for their skill. The Tudor and Stuart Governments generally allowed these strangers the privilege of separate religious organisation, for which pure-born Englishmen clamoured in vain ; though Laud, in his narrow jealousy, would fain have put a stop to the freedom of worship for which they or their fathers had come to our island. By adopting a more liberal policy, England, from the reign of Elizabeth to the reign of Anne, shared with Holland the advantages which the Most Catholic and the Most Christian

Municipal and national policy towards immigration

---

[1] No doubt these apprentice laws greatly increased the difficulty of the rural parishes in disposing of their poor, and drove them to those efforts, not wholly unsuccessful, to prevent the growth of the population (see Appendix B.).

Also the apprentice laws caused great distress by preventing men thrown out of their own trade from obtaining employment in any other. " In our own time a sudden falling off in trade causes great hardship to the workmen and in the seventeenth century the hardship was thus far greater " (Leonard, p. 155).

The domestic system

Kings threw away by the expulsion of the Jews and Moriscoes from Spain, and the Protestants from Flanders and France.[1]

Industry was conducted under what is now known as the "domestic" as distinguished from the "factory" system. In the country clothing trade the employee worked in his own cottage. In town his master's house served for all purposes,—residence, factory, warehouse and retail shop. The apprentices, when the seven years of board and service under their master's roof had come to an end, either continued there for wages as common journeymen, or left to set up in business on their own account. In favoured cases they were admitted into partnership with their master, often under seal of marriage with the daughter of the house; this transaction, which in rude, popular rhymes made an unfailing appeal to the sentiment of the street audience, in many actual cases contained as much of business as of romance. The conditions of life and work in these shops varied according to the circumstances and character of the head of the house. The jolly pictures of friendship between masters and men, the humours and freedom of apprentice life, which were continually put on the stage of the Southwark theatres to draw the city groundlings across London Bridge, had reality at least in the houses of many prosperous craftsmen. But the personal relation could have been little more than personal bondage under an ill-tempered master trying to check the decline of his small business by truck payments, long hours, hard words and cruel blows. For the employer had complete control, legally of his apprentices, economically of his journeymen. Under the domestic system there was no Government inspection of conditions of employment, and combinations of workmen were not easily carried out. This human and personal relation between employer and employed, living and working in the same house, was sometimes better and sometimes worse than the modern "cash nexus" of formal treaty between the employer in his villa residence and the workmen in their street. In old England there was more distinction of class; but on the other hand all classes lived more together.

The coal and iron trades

Industry, under these conditions, was making rapid progress; but as yet, with the great exception of the cloth trade, it was almost entirely for home consumption. The slow unconscious advance of our ancestors along the path that led towards the modern industrial revolution, may be measured by the condition and mutual relation of the coal and iron trades. Caldrons from the famous Tyne pits were the common domestic fuel in London and other towns where the "sea-coal," as it was called, could arrive by barge. But coal had not yet replaced wood in manufacture. The smelting furnaces of the Sussex and Kentish weald that made iron for the capital,

[1] Dr. Cunningham, *C. M. H.*, i., pp. 494-581   *E. H. R.*, xii., pp. 437-47. Lecky, i., pp. 235-40.   G., viii., pp. 120, 121.

and of the Forest of Dean that supplied raw material for the hardware trades of Warwickshire, Worcestershire and Staffordshire, were growing fast, fed on the primeval forest, where glades that had harboured the stags and the outlaws of twelve centuries rang to the sounds of axe and forge.[1]

The English cloth manufacture, unlike our other trades, depended on the foreign market.   The clothiers were said to provide our commercial men with far the greater part of the goods which they exported.   The weaving industry, which had sprung up during the Middle Ages in East Anglia, had in Elizabeth's reign been greatly improved and stimulated by the influx of skilled Flemish and French weavers flying from the sword of Alva and Guise.   Yet now, in spite of the great wealth of Colchester and Norwich, the Eastern clothing counties were slowly yielding to the competition of Western rivals. The clothiers of Yorkshire, shut off in their steep dales from contact with the manners and social history of the South, were inaugurating, on a model of life and custom all their own, the slow transmutation of North England from a barbarous and feudal border province, to the land of industrial enterprise and democracy ; while in the plain to west of the Cotswold sheep-runs, and in the valleys of Devon and Somerset, village-looms supplied the great merchant-cities of Gloucester, Bristol, Exeter and Plymouth with the sinews of trade beyond the sea. *The cloth trade*

Our maritime commerce was conducted by companies, each holding by charter from the Crown the exclusive right of trading to some particular part of the world.   The system derived from the privileges of the Merchant Adventurers' Company, who had pushed our cloth trade by monopoly in North Europe during the Middle Ages.   But when, in the reigns of Elizabeth and James, new markets and new continents were opened out beyond the Indian Ocean, the Baltic and the Atlantic, new companies, with corresponding monopolies, sent out ship after ship to explore, fight and trade in the snows of Archangel, the forests of Virginia, and the treacherous waters where Turk and Spaniard, Dutch and Portuguese guarded the treasures of the East.   The danger of these enterprises, the loss of ships in storm and battle, the expense of maintaining consuls and provisioning forts, all fell upon the traders themselves, in days when Government made little pretence of protecting British subjects beyond the ocean.   Indeed, from the death of Elizabeth to the time when the Long Parliament assumed control of the navy, the royal ships failed to protect commerce even in the Channel against pirates from the Turkish ports.   A well-managed company whose doors *Trading companies and Inter-lopers*

---

[1] In James I.'s reign Dudley attempted to use coal for smelting furnaces, but was ruined rather by the jealousy of other iron-masters than by real economic causes.   After this attempt the use of coal in manufacture remained slight until the eighteenth century—until, in fact, the great forests had been used up (Ashley, pp. 12-17. Cunningham, pp. 522-30).

were open to all merchants wishing to invest in the trade, protected Englishmen in a particular part of the world at its own cost of blood and money, and so fulfilled the functions of a state : such a company claimed in return that no Interloper should drive an independent trade in those waters. But unfortunately many of the monopolist concerns were ill-managed and many refused to admit new members. The most energetic merchants, the young blood of commerce, would have been shut out from commercial venture if they had not found vent in illicit trade. The debt of English commerce to the Interlopers of the seventeenth century is scarcely less than its debt to the great companies which they defied. From the beginning to the end of the Stuart epoch, remote seas and shores resounded to obscure and unreported conflicts, not only of English with Dutch, Spaniards and natives, but of English traders with each other ; while at home the partisans of old and new companies, of Monopolists and Interlopers, disturbed the public with rival clamours for its gratitude, and passed shares and gold into the hands of lords and statesmen, at first in the galleries of Whitehall, and at the close of the century, when the control of commerce passed to Parliament, in the walks and lobbies of Westminster.[1]

East Indian trade

The East Indian Company, chartered in 1600 to carry on all our commerce in the Far East, discovered by painful experiment that the ports most favourable to English trade were neither among the Spice Islands of the Indian Archipelago, nor in the fabled China seas, but along the coasts of Hindoostan, where the Mogul Emperors welcomed white merchants with the lordly patronage of secure power, and protected those of the weaker nations from the malevolence of their rivals. The chief event which decided our settlement on the mainland of India, was the massacre of Amboyna in 1623, when the Dutch freed themselves from the presence of the English on the principal Spice Islands by the most summary of all methods. So short was the arm of the State, so strict the line drawn between international relations in Europe and in Asia, that the event scarcely disturbed the friendly relations of London and the Hague, and no compensation was extorted till in the next generation the Protector made it his policy to wipe out all scores left standing by the kings.[2]

Contact with the Spaniards

But other tales of cruel outrage committed by Spanish priests, admirals and custom-house officials on our merchants in the Peninsula and Mediterranean, reached England more quickly and more

---

[1] Cunningham, pp. 214-84. Hewins, pp. 24-73. Oppenheim, pp. 198, 199, 274-78, 345.

[2] The expulsion of the Portuguese from their trade and settlements in the East by the Dutch and English cannon, was one of the chief features of this period of English peace with the Spanish Empire, of which Portugal was then a part. For a fine page of writing on this episode of our history, see Carlyle's *Historical Sketches*, pt. i., chap. ix., pp. 90, 91.

often than news from beyond the Malacca Strait, affected a larger number of traders than the select shareholders of the East Indian Company, and so kept alive the deadly national animosities of the Elizabethan war, by means of that very renewal of commercial intercourse whereby James had hoped to see them allayed. The Protestant zeal of the sea-going population, which during the struggle with Philip had grown into the most constant political sentiment upon which English statesmen could calculate, in no way diminished during the forty years of peace that preceded the Civil War. Along the coasts of Europe and America there was still a freemasonry for defence and offence between all Protestant sailors, whether they hailed from Plymouth, Amsterdam or Rochelle, a fellow-feeling kept alive by forecastle yarns illustrating the pride and extortion of corrupt Spanish officials, and by stories that stirred the blood, of comrades mysteriously disappearing in the streets of Spanish towns. Drake's *Pelican* still lay in the Thames, like Nelson's *Victory* at Portsmouth, the symbol of a great past and the hope of a like future. Adventurers, setting out on long voyages, had their farewell " supper brought aboard Sir Francis Drake's ship that hath compassed the world," since " some good spirits of the waters should haunt the desert ribs of her." [1] These simple and wholesome traditions were the creed of the seafaring men, who at once protected the isolation and enlarged the outlook of England. The short life of danger and hardship that was the mariner's lot in those days of piracy and battle, scurvy and starvation on board frail sailing ships that had no strength against the tempest, gave the seaman a peculiar character which reacted powerfully on the whole people, to whom he now stood in the place of the soldier as the type of national hero. To the commercial and maritime population of the new age, pride of race, pursuit of gain, love of adventure, and a sturdy personal independence were all associated with the idea of the Protestant religion.

By taking to the sea, the English fell under the influence of the Dutch. As friends or as enemies, as partners or as rivals, men of the two nations were now in perpetual contact. Holland affected every department of English life, more, perhaps, than any other nation has ever done by the mere force of example. The little republic, which from 1600 to 1650 maintained its territory as a safe and prosperous oasis in the midst of the wilderness of fire and destruction around, was during those years the leader of mankind in most of the sciences and arts. She was the school of scientific war, agriculture, gardening, finance and trade, and of numberless arts and crafts ; the academy of painting ; the home of theology whence Calvinist and Arminian alike drew their theories ; the asylum for philosophy and free speculation ; and last but not least, the example to our merchants and our politicians of a community

Contact with the Dutch

[1] Chapman's *Eastward Ho !* Act III., sc. 2.

which had attained prosperity, enlightenment and power by rebellion against a legitimate Prince.

Municipal self-government

But of all the conditions which formed the political character of the English merchant class, the most important was self-government. None of the monarchs of England before Charles II. attempted to interfere with the management of the towns by freely elected Mayors, Aldermen and Bailiffs. The Kings of France and Spain had lately replaced the old burgher magistrates by Royal Commissioners. But in the English towns the system of autonomy survived in a great variety of forms from the Middle Ages. The municipal bodies were sometimes close, co-optive corporations ; sometimes they were elected by all the burgesses. In some towns the burgesses themselves were a small minority of the inhabitants ; in others, a system almost of household suffrage prevailed. Civic freedom was secure because the formidable militia of each great city was in the hands, not of the king, but of the municipality itself.

The causes that produce genius in individual men, and outbursts of activity in nations, are mysteries which only become more impenetrable as one theory after another is flung out to account for that which is beyond knowledge. But though he may make no pretence of having penetrated the laws of the spiritual world, the historian is bound to describe the manner of life and the intellectual atmosphere which shaped and coloured, whether or not they occasioned, greatness of deed and mind. Something has been said above on the manner of life in England under the early Stuarts, but little yet of certain general conditions of life which may have had influence upon imagination. The most obvious of these was the perpetual contact of man, in the ordinary course of his work and recreation, with the force and beauty of nature.

Direct contact with nature

With the single exception of London, the largest cities were still country towns, where the central market cross was never a mile from the orchards and fruit gardens that clustered outside the grey stone battlements, filled the empty moat, encompassed the new white suburb beyond, and led down by pleasant paths to the open cornfield country.[1] The recreation of the city dweller was by the hedgerows and river banks, riding and hunting if he were rich, if poor, walking in the fields, fishing, or joining in games

See maps of the cities of the time, *e.g.*, those of the county capitals, in *Speed's Atlas*. There is no exact calculation of the town population in James I.'s reign, but at the Restoration London contained over 400,000 ; Bristol and Norwich under 30,000, and no other city over 10,000. Creighton (*History of Epidemics*, i., p. 660 ; ii., pp. 42-43) estimates London in 1603 at 250,000. Unlike the other cities of England, it was surrounded by extensive slum districts outside its walls known as the " liberties," where vast multitudes not only of respectable workmen but of the broken population that collects round a great capital, were herded in conditions of squalor, misery and disease that made London famous for its plagues and terrible in riot and revolution. See p. 298 below.

and sports. The ungarnished streets, noisome with plague-breeding smells, and vexed with petty discomforts to the passenger, were yet neither ugly nor monotonous to the eye, but were varied with every kind of gable and projection, decorated on the house fronts with oak carving, and over the doors with quaint signs, such as the Black Swan, the Three Pigeons and the Cross Keys, which then distinguished each shop of every trade. And the inhabitants of these towns, though

> Long in populous city pent
> Where houses thick and sewers annoy the air,

had the country ever near at hand for them

> Forth issuing on a summer's morn to breathe
> Among the pleasant villages and farms
> Adjoined.   (*Par. Lost.* ix., l. 445.)

But the country was the actual home of the great majority of men. The south English feared, as strangers fear, the mountainous districts which they seldom visited ; but they have recorded their delight in their own land of hedgerow, lawn and copse, song of bird and fall of mill-stream. The love of nature received conscious and reiterated expression in the verses of pastoral, dramatic, epic and lyrical poets, of whom the most notable are Spenser, Shakespeare, Herrick, Marvell and Milton. Nor did the rural Pan breathe only on those who speak of his power and acknowledge his influence. Nursed on the breast of nature, the Cavaliers drew their charm from the fields, and the Puritans their strength from the earth.

A love of beauty, since disappeared, was native to the English of every class. In each village, oak furniture for farm and cottage was carved into pleasing forms, which now win the admiration of connoisseurs. The commonest objects—the family-coach, the beer-jug, the lintel of the door, or the sign that hung over it—had the touch of natural taste, and often of true artistic effort. But the sense of beauty was perhaps best shown in the pleasure taken by all classes in a native music. Songs and airs, composed all over the country by persons in every walk of life, were constantly sung, whether by Bunyan's Pilgrim or Shakespeare's Autolycus, in roads, lanes and streets which their descendants traverse in noisy silence. Foreigners noted the " beautiful music of violas and pandoras, for in all England it is the custom that even in small villages the musicians wait on you for a small fee. In the morning about wakening time they stand outside the chamber playing religious hymns." Minstrels wandering through the land with their pipes and fiddles, were welcomed in ale-houses, farms and rich men's mansions, and maintained in all classes a wholesome and natural taste, enshrined in sweet old songs, both sad and merry. Since bell-ringing was regarded with great favour by the youth, both as

Songs and music

an art and an exercise, parishes " spent much money in harmoniously sounding bells, that one being preferred which has the best bells ".[1]

The way for the high triumphs of imagination that marked this age, was left open by the exclusion of science from all the ordinary affairs and occupations of life. There were some learned but no scientific professions. Though good work was being done by a few *savants* of the College of Physicians in London, there was no large body of medical men at practice in the ordinary towns and villages of England. Engineers there were none, except those who used petards for military purposes. Most of the ways and means by which ordinary business was conducted—manufacture, building, navigation—were learned not as sciences but as arts and crafts. The study of political and other statistics, like so much of exact knowledge, hardly began before the Restoration. The idea of regular law guiding the universe was unfamiliar to the contemporaries of Francis Bacon. The fields around town and hamlet were filled, as soon as the day-labourers had left them, by goblins and will-o'-the-wisps ; and the woods, as soon as the forester had closed the door of his hut, became the haunt of fairies ; the ghosts could be heard gibbering all night under the yew-tree of the churchyard ; the witch, a well-known figure in the village, was in the pay of lovers whose mistresses were hard to win, and of gentlemen-farmers, whose cattle had sickened. If a criminal was detected and punished, the astonishing event was set down as God's revenge against murder ; if a dry summer threatened the harvest, the parson was expected to draw down rain by prayer. The charms that ward off disease, the stars of birth that rule fortune, the comet that foretold the wars in Germany, the mystic laws that govern the fall of the dice, were the common interest of ordinary men and women. In a soil that imagination had so prepared, poetry and Puritanism were likely to flourish loftily among lofty men, basely among the base. The better kind of men were full of ardour, fancy and reverence. The ignoble were superstitious, ignorant and coarse.[2] The world was still a mystery, of which the wonder was not dispelled in foolish minds by

[1] Duke of Stettin, pp. 7, 63. For the wandering minstrels, see old plays, pictures and records *passim*.

[2] Our ancestors, when the century opened, were still in some respects the " primitive, vigorous sons " of mother-earth. They were nearer to her than we, for evil as well as for good. The barbarous primeval superstitions even of the upper class, only two generations before Newton and the Royal Society, are sometimes startling. Thus, on 18th January, 1604-5, the Master of Requests, noted in his journal that " Mr. Harley my host at Huntingdon told me this night, supping with me, that he being before a farmer and 24 horses for plows 12 horses and 30 cattle were bewitched and died in 2 days, suddenly sick, crying and grinning and staring ; in the end was advised to burn a sick horse alive and so did, and after had no more died ; another did so by his sheep by Harley's advice : none after died. And Harley said a known witch advised him to burn the heart by roasting on a spit, and the witch would come to the door before the heart was roasted " (*Camden Misc.*, x., p. 69).

a daily stream of facts and cheap explanations. He who, comparing the types of mind produced by different ages, studies the commonest and the lowest records of old English life, will find much that is coarse and brutal, but will search in vain for what is vulgar. The ale-house songs, the hedgerow and the street ballads, were often exquisite literature, sung now in drawing-rooms by the cultured classes ; and even those that were worthless or lewd, were simple and natural, innocent of the knowing leer and artificial pretentiousness of the modern musical comedy.

Since thought among common people had now reached a mo- The mentary perfection for the purposes of religious and imaginative English literature, the English language was for those purposes perfect. language Whether in the Bible, the play-book, the street ballad, the broadsheet or report of the commonest dialogue of daily life, it was always the same language, ignorant of scientific terms and instinct with a poetical feeling about life that was native to the whole generation of those who used it. Its fault, corresponding to the state of thought in that age, is want of exactness and of complexity in ideas, that renders it unfit for psychology or for close analysis of things either material or spiritual.[1]

The great religious writers and the yet greater poets who ex- Condi-ploited the English language in the short day when for their ends it tions of was perfect, worked under conditions favourable to the fullest and author-purest employment of what genius each possessed. The difficulties ship of locomotion that isolated men for months together, the absence of distractions and mental luxuries to dissipate thought, long days without company and long weeks without news, gave the individual time and freedom to be himself, called up the powers of fancy and contemplation, and induced the undertaking of works loftily conceived and leisurely fulfilled. The writers of books could not then hope to make a livelihood by their sale. Some authors were also engaged in more lucrative professions ; some were men of independent means ; and those who wrote to gain a subsistence speculated not on the sale but on the reputation of their works, seeking less to please the public than to attract the notice of the Court when the King was a man of learning, of the Bishops when religious controversy was the key to high preferment, or of some lord of fashion when poetry was fashionable. But the reading public, in the bookseller's sense, was but a small fraction of a small population ; the number of great writers was in inverse ratio to the number of readers.[2]

[1] If Mill or Darwin, Browning or Meredith had tried to express their ideas in the English of the seventeenth century they would have failed. The extreme simplicity of Hamlet's thought is only concealed by the obscurity of his motives and the richness of his poetical diction.
[2] Some idea of the solid reading of an ordinary man, not specially literary or poetical, but anxious to instruct himself, may be gathered from the following list.

The writing of plays for the theatre was influenced by conditions not wholly dissimilar from those of writing books for the press. The theatre depended in part on a keen-witted but ill-educated popular audience, and in part on patrons of the most refined taste and exalted position. It was saved from falling either into silly coarseness or into artificial preciosity, by the need to place popular comedy side by side with choice poetry, without exciting disgust by the one or derision by the other.[1]

The conditions of theatrical patronage were governed by the local history of the capital, where three societies formed, together and in rivalry, the heart of the body politic. These were, first the commercial population resident within the gates of London ; secondly the officials, lords and fine gentlemen of the Court who lived in mansions or lodgings in the city of Westminster ; and lastly the lawyers of the Inns of Court who formed, geographically, socially, and politically a link between the other two. The most adventurous and the most talented young men came up from the country to complete their education or to seek their fortune in one or other of these three social camps. But besides the busy politicians of Whitehall, the industrious merchants of Cheapside, and the keen-eyed lawyers who drove daily from the Temple to Westminster Hall at four for a shilling in the new hackney-coaches, each of these societies had its drones. Foppish courtiers and idle law students who set the fashion, and apprentices too good for their trades who aped it, all regarded the capital as a place in which to see life. A common ground where these runagates of the different classes could assemble, admiring and admired, was afforded by the playhouses on the Southwark bank of the Thames, where they found the freedom, the entertainment, and the female society which they desired. The theatres were under the ban not only of Puritan pulpits, but of the city fathers. Indeed, the municipal authorities would have stamped out the drama from England, for the purposes of police as much as for the salvation of souls, had not the courtiers intervened.

Great lords and ladies were accustomed to the drama both at the King's Court and in their own country houses, where strolling players were made as welcome as at Elsinore, and where marriages were celebrated and winter nights enlivened by pageants and masques

recommended by an old gentleman (born 1580) to his grandson, as having formed the library of his youth (*Harl. Misc.*, ix., p. 592). After the Bible he recommends Hooker's *Ecclesiastical Polity*, Sir W. Raleigh's *History of the World*, Plutarch's *Lives*, Camden's *Brittania*, " my friend Sir Richard Baker's *Chronicle*," Xenophon's *Cyrus*, Tully's *Offices*, James I.'s *Basilicon Doron*. Lastly, he adds : " When I was young it was a defect not to be versed in Sir Philip Sidney ". Indeed while Shakespeare and even Spenser are not mentioned, the old gentleman says : " To refresh yourself with poetical stories you may take Sir Philip Sidney instead of all ".

[1] The difficulty felt by playwrights in catering for a popular audience with a classical subject is treated by Ben Jonson in the puppet play of Hero and Leander at the end of *Bartholomew Fair*.

—a form of drama in which it was easy for amateur actors to hide their want of histrionic skill beneath the splendour of allegorical costumes and aristocratic dignity of carriage. Nor was this passion for private theatricals the only cause predisposing the leaders of society to patronise the Southwark plays. Poetry as well as drama had a home in the court of Elizabeth and the early Stuarts. The English renaissance had at last taken up the work of continental grammarians and artists, and converted it freely to the use of English literature. " The pageant of renascent humanity to which the English were invited by Italians, Spaniards and Frenchmen, our predecessors in the arts and studies of two centuries, stimulated the poets of the race to their dramatic triumphs."[1] The leaders of the renaissance in its English literary form were courtiers and noble- men attached to the corrupt official world of Whitehall, who loved to be rowed across the Thames for a breath of human life among the poets and players in the tiring-room, and to sit in all their mag- nificence on the stage, the admiration or the jest of the sixpenny mechanics in the yard below. The would-be courtier and gallant, trying to pass himself off as the Sidney of his day, misquoted *Romeo and Juliet* to his mistress, slept with " *Venus and Adonis* under his pillow," and hung up " sweet Mr. Shakespeare's " picture in " his study at the Court ".[2]

Thus it came about that the success of authors, managers and players depended on their ability to interest two kinds of audiences in one play. An unlettered crowd paid the bulk of the gate-money ; but Court lords and Temple gallants, proud of their taste and learn- ing, shielded the theatres from invectives of the clergy and the official action of the respectable middle class, and relieved with liberal gifts the hard life of the actor and playwright. It is possible to trace the effects of this dual patronage in the very various kinds of drama introduced into one play and even into one scene, and in the frequent appearance of such characters as the spendthrift law student, the sweaty-capped artisan, the close-fisted merchant, the scented fop, the politician with his smirk and curtsey to his " sweet lord " ; alternating with the honest citizen, the jolly prentice, the gallant gentleman and the polished courtier : these topical portraits seem drawn sometimes to set one part of the house laughing at the other, sometimes to flatter the class pride of the groundlings or of the stools on the stage. In this strange scene and company, amid jewelled silks and leather aprons, there met together the best and worst, the wisest and most foolish of the land ; and hither, to this fortunate isle of space and time, came the greatest of all mankind ; small wonder, then, that the world of his creation was as various

The London theatres

---

[1] Symond's *Shakespere's Predecessors*, pp. 26, 27. For the influence of the *Italian Renaissance in England*, see Lewis Einstein's scholarly work on that subject (1902).

[2] *Return from Parnassus*, pt. i., Act III., sc. 1, and Act IV., sc. 1.

and as free from rule as the crowds that laughed and clamoured about the old playhouse for a while, had their brief, glad day there, and departed.

Puritanism and the stage   The excellence of the English theatre was as short-lived as other great literary movements. Some twenty years before the Puritans closed the theatre doors at the outbreak of the Civil War, our plays had been deserted by the genius of poetry, and had for the most part become bad prose drama cut up into halting blank verse.[1] The Puritans did more harm by permanently fixing the stigma of frivolity upon the stage than by temporarily closing its doors. By teaching so many serious and respectable families in England to avoid the playhouse as they would avoid a brothel, they brought it about that the Anglo-Saxons do not take that serious and religious interest in the drama that is due to the first of arts.

Puritanism and literature   Dramatic authorship in the days of Shakespeare only escaped destruction because the triumph of its enemies was deferred until the silver age ; poetry, on the other hand, obtained from the Puritans themselves that force of spiritual imagination, without which the most ingenious art parades but futile elegance. The genius and the reality which had ennobled the English literary renaissance in the days of Sidney and Spenser was already cold, when a young Puritan breathed into the learned service of English verse, perpetually chanted round the shrine of the classical pantheon, his own enthusiasm for active virtue—that saving grace common to all Puritan sects. The masques and minor poems of Milton, written before the Civil War had divided all things excellent into hostile camps, and taught Cromwell's secretary to treat the gods of Greece with the distance proper to disguised demons,—those few hundred verses, scarcely influential in their own day, have proved of the highest importance in the history of the English race. The literary tradition which they inaugurated, associating the deepest and most religious feelings with lyrical verse and unfettered fancy, survived the long triumph of the French school from Dryden to Dr. Johnson, and from the days of Coleridge and Wordsworth have had no small share in the revival of English poetry.

Not an age of religious doubt   While the unscientific character of the age perhaps stimulated men's poetical instincts, their religious beliefs were not yet modified by the conception of regular law guiding the universe. No serious attack was directed against the doctrines of orthodox Christianity. From the time when Marlowe's death in a tavern brawl had illustrated God's judgment on the impious, till the rise of " Mr. Hobbes

---

[1] It is a matter of opinion whether there was very high value in the plays written between 1620 and 1640. I am glad to be able to shelter my own view of that question behind the authority of Symonds, Prof. Dowden, Prof. Raleigh, and Gardiner (see *Shakespere's Predecessors*, pp. 2-7. *Puritan and Anglican*, p. 2. Prof. Raleigh's *Milton*, pp. 189, 190. G., vii., pp. 327-38.)

the Atheist " to notoriety, there was scarcely one known sceptic in the island. No rationalistic analysis was directed against faith by the literary men ; though Raleigh was falsely accused of atheism, and Shakespeare wavered, according to the poetical impulse of the moment, between the imagery of religion and the suggestions of a contemplative humour curiously eyeing the lot of man. These children of fancy and freedom might sometimes wander into fairy-lands, where truth was not disguised in creeds, but if recalled to earth by an accusation of unorthodoxy they were well able to deny the charge.

Nevertheless, the popular conception of the sphere of the miracu-lous was becoming more limited. The partisans of the old and of the new religion held in common the belief in witchcraft, fairy-circles and other manifest activities of evil or indifferent spirits, but the miraculous working of the power of good was less universally acknowledged. The Catholics indeed, whose numbers and influence had long been on the wane, upheld the credit of relics and sacred places, and comforted themselves in the hour of oppression with stories of miracles vouchsafed on behalf of the Jesuit martyrs ; but the adherents of the incoming religion of Protestantism laughed at these stories, not only as politically treasonous but as naturally improbable, and believed little in the special sacredness of one material object more than another, or in visible interference by God in the course of nature. Instead of the mediæval miracle, the Puritan believed in the secret management of human affairs by Providence, in ways that the godless might lightly attribute to chance. Angels did not visit his house, but he recognised a judgment if he fell off his horse, and a " mercy " if his ship returned safe from Ternate. God no longer divided the waters of the Red Sea for Israel to go over dryshod, but it was expected of Him to send a fair wind to take the Swedish army across the Baltic. Cromwell would have been much astonished if the sun had stood still over Marston while he completed the rout upon the Moor, but he wrote to tell the Speaker how his retreat to Dunbar had been covered, when " the Lord by His good Providence put a cloud over the moon ".[1] The Puritan, in fact, applied logically, continually and imaginatively the belief that prayer is effective ; but he did not believe in miracles.

Thus rationalism had achieved an advance on the old concep-tion of the miraculous. But as no materialist view of the universe existed even in germ, and as no idealist philosophy had yet learnt to deny revelation or to dispense with a personal God, all that minority of mankind who thought seriously about life was genuinely Christian. Under these conditions, the type of thought and feeling that most frequently had attraction to men of strong character or of deep emotions was that which we know as Puritanism.

Limitation of the sphere of the miraculous

[1] Carl.'s *Crom.*, Letter cxl.

Puritans
not of one
type That word, so variously and often inaccurately defined, will be used throughout this book to signify, according to its original meaning, the religion of all those who wished either to " purify " the usages of the Established Church from taint of Popery, or to worship separately by forms so " purified ".[1] The many various sects and persons who fall under this definition, were usually characterised both by an aversion from gaiety and by a passionate love of civic freedom. But they had little else in common. While some of them were more inclined to persecution than Laud himself, others were the first of all Englishmen who objected to the theory of a State Church, and who desired to give as well as to receive religious freedom. Some again were far more dogmatic than the Anglicans, but others regarded the system of Calvin as a barrier created between the human spirit and the Divine light. Prynne and Milton, Cartwright and Cromwell, Baxter and George Fox, the Covenanters and the Unitarians were all products of the Puritan movement.

Bible reading Before the rise of the Quakers, the vitality of Puritanism in all its branches was derived from the imaginative study of the Bible. While other literary movements, however noble in quality, affected only a few, the study of the Bible was becoming the national education. Recommended by the King, translated by the Bishops, yet in chief request with the Puritans, without the rivalry of books or newspapers, the Bible told to the unscholarly the story of another age and race, not in bald generalisation and doctrinal harangue, but with such wealth of simple narrative and lyrical force that each man recognised his own dim strivings after a new spirit, written clear in words two thousand years old. A deep and splendid effect was wrought by the monopoly of this book as the sole reading of common households, in an age when men's minds were instinct with natural poetry and open to receive the light of imagination. A new religion arose, of which the mythus was the Bible stories, and the pervading spirit the direct relations of man with God, exemplified in human life.

And while the imagination was kindled, the intellect was freed by this private study of the Bible. For its private study involved its private interpretation. Each reader, even if a Churchman, became in some sort a Church to himself. Hence the hundred sects and thousand doctrines that astonished foreigners, and opened England's strange path to intellectual liberty. The Bible cultivated here, more than in any other land, the growth of individual thought and practice.

Puritans not agreed on Church government Puritanism was not an ecclasiastical system. From the reign of Elizabeth onwards. it covered at least three rival views on Church

[1] See this, the proper definition and meaning of the word, in Prof. Maitland's article (*C. M. H.*, ii., p. 590)—the finest and most authoritative account of the origins of the English Church settlement.

government. There were, first, those Puritans who wished only to modify the usages of the Established Church, preserving government by Bishops, subject to some measure of lay control. Secondly, there were those who wished for Puritan coercion under a Presbyterian *régime*. When James ascended the throne the first class was more numerous than the second. Cartwright's Presbyterian agitation under Elizabeth had failed for want of support among the Puritans. Throughout the reign of James I. the bulk of them stood by the principles of their Millenary Petition of 1603, desiring to modify, but ready to accept, Episcopate and Prayer-book as the background of their own domestic worship and daily life. It was only the severity of Laud's persecution and the Catholicising tendency of Charles I.'s Bishops which turned the majority against Episcopal government in 1641 : and it was only the Scottish military alliance which forced them two years later to adopt a strict Presbyterian system.[1] But there was also a third class of Puritans. Ever since the early years of Elizabeth there had been sectaries persecuted by the Bishops and hated by all strict followers of Calvin : men who desired to abolish the coercive power of the Church, whether Anglican or Presbyterian, and to leave individuals free to form congregations at will. These Free Churchmen, who increased in power as time went on, especially after the outbreak of the Civil War, were themselves divided ; there were those who, like Cromwell, would tolerate all sorts of Puritans, and there were those who, like Baptists and Quakers, would tolerate all sorts of men.[2]

Puritanism can not be defined by a creed. It was not divided *Puritans* from Anglicanism by any shibboleth like the belief in predestination. *not* *agreed on* All English Protestants, including King James and his High Church *dogma* Bishops, were Calvinists on that point of doctrine, until Laud's school adopted the contrary theories of the Dutchman Arminius, for no reason apparently relative to the religious controversy in our island. Meanwhile, the orthodoxy of Calvin had been rejected by many of the Baptist and other sects, and their revolt was followed in a later generation by that of the Quakers and Unitarians. Those indeed—and they were at first the majority—who laid great store on Puritan dogma, had to be satisfied with dark tomes of theology unlighted by the literary genius that saves the Anglican doctors from oblivion. The power of the Puritan writers lay elsewhere than in theology. *Pilgrim's Progress* and George Fox's *Journal* tell of the immediate experience of the soul. For indeed the peculiarity of the Puritans, in the lowest and in the highest rank of life, lay in the intensity with which they felt that " God is a Spirit," and must be worshipped neither by ritual nor by doctrine, but by feeling and

[1] Shaw, *History of English Church, passim,* and *Manchester Classis* (Chetham Soc., 1890), pp. xiii-xvii.
[2] See Shaw, Barclay and Gooch *passim.*

conduct. Cromwell expressed the motive of his life when he said, "The true knowledge is not literal or speculative; but inward and transforming the mind to it".

The history of the leadership of the Commons from 1600 to 1640 presents, in an era when public life was specially corrupt and unprincipled, the spectacle of prolonged, heroic, unselfish and well-advised action by the representatives of the English country gentlemen, such as is rare in the politics of any age and was wholly wanting in the struggle of the Whig Parliaments against Charles II. But Eliot, Hampden, Pym and their colleagues were Puritans.

At this time when Puritanism was eminent as the religion that inspired the leaders of the landlord class, it was already pervading those humbler ranks where its strength survived the Restoration. Its influence brought seriousness of thought to thousands, and induced them to put that restraint on their luxuries and that vigour into the performance of their duties, which all religions enjoin, but which few enforce against the dead weight of social custom. It is not likely that the influence of Hooker, or of Laud, could have done as much as the Puritans did to thin the ranks of the thoughtless, the gross and the indifferent.

Need for the Puritan propaganda　The conversion of the people to an intelligent Protestantism, which alone could secure and excuse the violent overthrow of Romanism effected by the Tudors, had already taken place in the great towns, in the home counties and among the sea-going population; but no substitute for proscribed Catholicism had yet been established, except in name, in the country districts of the North and West. The parish clergy, who two generations before had passed from Catholic to Protestant, or from Protestant to Catholic, with every change of Government, were still very generally of the same type of careless shepherds, anxious only to retain their seats at the shearer's feast, devoid of learning or enthusiasm to fulfil their duties, which they often relegated to substitutes too like themselves. The Church service was read on Sunday as a State test; attendance proved loyalty, and non-attendance involved fine. Sermons were rare; house visitation and religious instruction were neglected. The country people, deprived by law and police of the Catholic ministry, still retained memories of ancestral rhymes of which the sense was becoming obscure. In 1608 a clergyman, who was more alive to his duties than most of his fellow-labourers, complained that his flock " superstitiously refuse to pray in their own language with understanding," and contented themselves with such wreckage of the old religion as the following :—

Creezum zuum patrum onitentem creatorum ejus amicum, Dominum nostrum qui sum sops, virgini Mariae, crixus fixus, Ponchi Pilati audubitiers, morti by Sunday, father a furnes, scerest ut judicarum, finis a mortibus.

or again—

> White Pater-noster, St. Peter's brother,
> What hast i' th t' one hand ? white book leaves.
> What hast i' th t' other hand ? heaven gate keys.

Such ignorance could never have been dispelled by the neglectful methods of tithe-loving parsons, but offered a fine field of useful labour for the zeal of the Puritan, who, whether cleric or layman, made it his business to preach the Gospel in his own household and among his neighbours, and, as far as in him lay, to make the Protestantism of London and the seaports the religion of all England. The upland English considered the religious duties of the day fulfilled if they muttered the Creed or Hail Mary as they tumbled into bed, and showed no more natural desire to study the Bible than to make any other effort of an intellectual order. It was only by the sustained personal effort of Puritans in every part of the island, during the period when they were still within the official Church, that family prayers and Bible reading became at all customary. These habits, which remained as the staple of English education for generations after official Puritanism had been crushed out of the Church, were being slowly established during the reigns of James and Charles I. by the patient work of exhortation and instruction carried on by thousands of zealous men, each in his own sphere of life.[1]

Another side of Puritan activity inseparable from the invitation to prayer and study was the reproving of sin. From some contemporary accounts it might be supposed that the time of the early Stuarts was the most immoral of all ages, but it is never easy to tell in such cases whether abnormal licence caused the denunciation of the reformer, or whether an unusual movement of reform drew special attention to a degree of vice common to all epochs. But certainly vice was not in those days compelled to dissimulate its popularity and prevalence. The Court of James I. was notoriously corrupt in morals, and the country houses of many great lords, the pattern to the gentry of whole districts, were little better. Many noble families, as Clarendon remarked, had desperately compromised their finances by luxury and ostentation when the Civil War came to complete or repair their ruin. If we add to this that the coarseness of ordinary language was as yet unrestrained by conventions of propriety, that drunkenness was the acknowledged national fault, and that the upper classes had no shame on that score, it will appear that the Puritans were at least not without provocation to the combat with vice which finally cost them so dear.

Common men, finding their habits assailed, turned against the precisians the talk round the market cross and the laugh on the

Puritan censorship of morals

---

[1] Baxter, *Life*, and *True History of Church Councils.*   G., i., pp. 148-50 : viii. pp. 124-62. *Notes and Queries*, I., viii., pp. 613, 614.

ale-house bench. Baxter thus describes the experiences of his boyhood in a western village about the time of the death of James I. :—

When I heard them speak scornfully of others as Puritans whom I never knew, I was at first apt to believe all the Lies and Slanders wherewith they loaded them. But when I heard my own Father so reproached, and perceived the Drunkards were the forwardest in the reproach, I perceived that it was mere Malice. For my Father never scrupled Common-Prayer or Cermonies, nor spake against Bishops, nor ever so much as prayed but by a Book or Form, being not ever acquainted then with any who did otherwise. But only for reading Scripture when the rest were Dancing on the Lord's Day, and for praying (by a Form out of the end of the Common Prayer Book) in his House, and for reproving Drunkards and Swearers, and for talking sometimes a few words of Scripture and the Life to come, he was reviled commonly by the Name of Puritan, Precisian and Hypocrite : and so were the Godly conformable Ministers that lived any where in the Country near us, not only by our Neighbours, but by the common talk of the Vulgar Rabble of all around us. By this experience I was fully convinc'd that Godly People were the best, and those that despised them and lived in Sin and Pleasure, were a malignant unhappy sort of People : and this kept me out of their Company, except now and then when the Love of Sports and Play enticed me.[1]

Puritan coteries   Many Puritans were more offensive people than the Baxter family, although most were no less " conformable " to the Church service. In the towns they sometimes lived in exclusive coteries of mutual admiration, speaking of each other as " brother This " and " sister That," and directed by some favourite clergyman who dispensed the common funds for charitable objects. We gather from the descriptions left by playwrights and satirists, that these societies were not wholly unlike the Evangelical cliques of the early nineteenth century, in the relations of the members to each other, to the Established Church and to the world.

The talk of the godly ran into cant phrases, of which the most pronounced were " surely," " verily " and " yea verily ". " Very likely," says Ben Jonson's Puritan, " exceeding likely, very exceeding likely ". Their dress was studiously out of the fashion ; when ruffs were superseded by the beautiful lace collar, the wives of Puritan citizens were still known by their " little ruffs ". Many of the men wore sad-coloured and simply cut clothes, which were as much more tasteful than the gaudy and ill-shaped caricatures of finery which were the rage under James I., as they were less elegant than the exquisite grace of fashion under his son. Brethren of the stricter discipline cut their hair short, but left " so many little peaks as was ridiculous to behold," with the sole object of making hideous protest against the " unloveliness of love-locks ". But such eccentricities were chiefly confined to the merchant and industrial classes, who felt a touch of pride in condemning the habits and appearance of ranks to which they could not aspire. In higher

[1] Baxter, *Life* (ed. 1696), pp. 2, 3.

circles it is not easy to distinguish by dress the portraits of Cavalier
from those of Puritan leaders. Eliot, Hampden, Cromwell, Milton
wore their hair falling over their shoulders ; and the Puritan lady,
Mrs. Hutchinson, was never tired of casting ridicule on the personal
appearance of her allies, the Presbyterian bourgeois. When fortunes were being sunk and estates mortgaged in order that men
should wear jewels and dress in coloured silks, some protest against
fashion was required ; yet few need agree with

> Mistress Scruple and her husband, who
> Do verily ascribe the German war
> And the late persecutions to curling,
> False teeth, and oil of talc.[1]

The Puritans, while they abhorred the confessional, encouraged, **Puritan self-discipline**
as their private journals disclose, the more virile practice of self-
examination ; and while they regarded with suspicion the fasts on
Fridays and at stated Church seasons, they had fasts of their own,
on occasions selected from time to time by Parliament, congregation or individual. By self-imposed discipline, they endeavoured,
in the very thick of worldly business, to preserve self-control and
unquenchable devotion to the ideal of duty.

The call on men to abandon drunkenness and immorality, and **Puritanism and the customs of the age**
devote their hours of leisure to religious study, raised the question
of public sports and festivities, which, even when innocent in their
own nature, were rendered incompatible with the new life, by the
day of the week chosen for their celebration and by the circumstances which attended them. But the religious idealists did not
stand alone in this question. During the first forty years of the
century, Parliamentary statutes, royal ordinances, and administrative acts of municipalities and of Quarter Session benches, again
and again interfered with popular customs in the supposed interests
of decency and public order. The controversies relating to the control of popular amusements, on which Puritanism took up so decided
an attitude, involved other aspects of life besides religion, and were
so various that each has to be considered on its own merits.

The two national vices that were classed together in the denunciations of moralists were " drunkenness and swearing ". The
latter sin was held in abhorrence, not as a vulgar but as a blasphemous habit, likely to compromise the nation with the powers of the
other world, and to draw down heavy reprisals. The third Parliament of James I. passed an Act to " prevent swearing and cursing " ;
it was drafted in a spirit of decided optimism with regard to its
effect, for we read that, *If any person or persons shall hereinafter
offend,* he shall pay twelve pence to the poor for each offence. The
Act was not essentially Puritan, for in 1635, at the height of the

---

Mayne's *City Match* (Dodsley), Act II., sc. 1.   Hutchinson, pp. 120, 121.

Laudian supremacy, Charles I. endeavoured to enforce its provisions by royal ordinance. But fines for swearing were seldom actually levied until the rule of the Saints began. A similar Act of the same Parliament of James I. to prevent " tippling " was probably less effectual than the suppression of riotous ale-houses, which was then a constant and excellent feature of local administration.

Drinking habits Before the introduction of tea and coffee, strong drink was in a very different relation to human life from that which it occupies to-day. In an age when there were few other luxuries and no other stimulants, it was regarded as the staff of life from the cradle to the grave. Even in sober households, where the children's drinking tastes were not encouraged by invitation to share the wines, they " were indulged full liberty of drinking small beer," and even took their medicine concealed or diluted in the " stone bottle " of the nursery.[1] For adults the need for something in the course of each day to stimulate bodily and mental vigour, rendered total abstinence an ideal necessarily foreign even to the temperate and censorious Puritans. But while they never thought of demanding the suppression of the ordinary sale of liquor, they had no tolerance for the public feasts and village merry-makings at Church Ales, Bride Ales and Wakes, where custom prescribed and religion sanctified assemblies generally ending in drunkenness and often in grosser forms of debauchery.

Village games and customs Besides those junketings there were many more delectable customs, which, in illiterate and isolated communities had stood for unrecorded generations in place of other interests and amusements ; these also were regarded by the Puritan as obstacles to the new life of prayer and Bible study. Christmas and Twelfthnight had their holiday and feast. Marriage was the occasion for

> Pomp, and feast, and revelry,
> With masque and antique pageantry.

St. Valentine's Day, had quaint privileges and customs ; and on May Day, before the earliest light, the young men and maidens rose up in town and village and went into the woods, returning as the sun rose with the spoils of the forest, to hang the doors and windows with garlands—a mode of worshipping mother-earth as pagan in its charm and licence as if Christianity had not for so many hundred years been proclaiming other gods. Even from the vast labyrinth of narrow streets that composed the City and Liberties of London, the apprentices escaped into the country to celebrate May Day with full rural rites. In other towns the country lay at men's doors. On holidays, or in honour of the arrival of a distinguished stranger, rude masques and allegorical processions were fitted out,

[1] Roger North, *Autobiography*, secs. 2, 3.

with weeks of preparation, such as the wealth and wit of each village or city could supply. Bell-pulling, at which men often fell fainting, wrestling, where limb and even life were at stake, jumping, pitching the bar, dancing and nine-pins were sports of which one variety or another was native custom in every village. But the acknowledged king of games was football, at this time far more general than it afterwards became. The husbandmen, when the fat swine were killed on the approach of winter, " got the bladder and blew it great and thin," and " tried it out at football with the shins ". The simplest of all games, it was played with local rules suited to the nature of the ground, often across the stream and up the length of the village street. An officious magistrate occasionally tried to revive the moribund archery laws, which forbade husbandmen and labourers to play at football ; and King James forbade it at Court as " meeter for the laming than the making able " of his liege subjects. But all classes commonly joined in the scrimmage, to the good old cry of " all fellows at football ".

The commonest popular spectacles were bull and bear-baiting. These were regarded with particular aversion by authority, as being the centres of disorder, and for this reason stood among the very few pastimes declared unlawful on Sunday by the Book of Sports, although the royal author of that declaration himself loved to see Sackerson tear up his chain and break with a roar among the scattering dogs. But the sport was in some quarters arraigned on higher grounds. A few of the more sensitive divines, Anglican as well as Puritan, without raising strictly humanitarian objections, pronounced it unworthy of man's high calling to be " a common barrator to set the animals at discord ".

The fact that these various entertainments were usually arranged Sabba-for the first day of the week, when alone most hands were free, in- tarianism creased whatever objection the Puritans might otherwise have taken to the influence of plays, ales, dances and sports ; and on the other hand, the offensive nature of some of these pastimes assisted the rapid spread in respectable circles of the new doctrine that all amusement on Sunday was sinful. The fathers of continental Protestantism had held no strict Sabbatarian views. Calvin, it is said, was found by John Knox playing bowls on Sunday ; and Knox in his turn had allowed the cold light of his countenance to shine upon festivities on the Lord's Day, holding that what little was right on week days was not wrong on Sundays. But the English and Scottish Puritans had since evolved a new doctrine of the first day of the week, which they called the Sabbath, in order to take advantage by a name of the commandment delivered on Sinai. For the claim of the Sabbatarians was fortunately extended to the prohibition of work as well as of play, and here there was much need for their new doctrine. One of Elizabeth's Injunctions had urged people to work after the service on Sunday, as on other holidays, if they wished.[1] Business men used Sunday to clear off arrears of clerical work left over from the week ; the King's Council chose it as their day of meeting ; waggoners, drovers and carriers continued their slow journeys along the roads, and held markets where they came ; much regular buying and selling was done even in London, and in western towns less subject to Puritan influence shops were regularly open and men at work ; the temptation to gather the harvest on a fine Sunday was nowhere resisted, until these habits were materially altered by the new Sabbatarian ideas, which taught the British, above all other peoples, to regard work on that day as a sin.[2]

But the change effected by Sabbatarians in old custom was greatest, perhaps, in regard to sports. At the period of James I.'s accession, the inhabitants of each parish, having satisfied the law by hearing the Common Prayer read on Sunday morning, streamed out from church eager for the ale to flow and the rebecks to sound on the green, and spent the rest of the day and much of the night in roaring and dancing through the village in wanton revels ; to the envy of the " married man " condemned by a jealous wife to " sigh away Sundays ". This noisy method of spending Sunday was as unfavourable to religious study and meditation, as the Puritan system, which so rapidly superseded it, was unfavourable to healthy life of body and mind. When the Long Parliament met, public opinion had already in many places enforced the discipline of what is now known as the " English Sunday " ; after the Restoration the Sabbatarian idea was hardly challenged. It is extraordinary with what success the religious minority imposed their view of the matter on the worldly majority. But in this question at least, the Puritans, though they were fighting against the love of pleasure, had time and change on their side ; for as the generations came and went, improved means of intercourse stole their ancient sanctity from the peculiar sports, festivals and rites of each parish ; while the printing press gradually drew away from the common merry-making the increasing number of those who could read, to the study of religious and political controversy, and of literature good and bad. The hard-pressed economic unit in the modern world of Anglo-Saxon industrialism, owes the secure enjoyment of his Sabbath—that humane charter which even commercial greed dare seldom violate— to the same stern influence which long forbade him to make his day of rest a day of physical exercise or of honest " schooling in the pleasures ".

---

[1] Hessey, *Bampton Lectures*, 1860, pp. 268-70, and lectures vi., vii. *passim*.

[2] On the other hand, Puritan influence helped to make people work on great Saints' days occurring in the middle of the week. They regarded respite from labour on those occasions as encouraging a mythology which they were trying to eradicate.

Such was Puritanism as a social and spiritual influence inside Import-
the pale of the Church, before persecution made it a sect in religion ance of
and a party in politics.   How would the royal government regard govern-
these aspirations towards social and spiritual reformation ?   Would tude to
it favour, tolerate or try to suppress them ?   On the relations of Puritan-
the monarchy to Puritanism depended not only the religion but, ism
by a coincidence in time, the liberty and institutions of the English,
and the future supremacy of our race in the Western Hemisphere.
The policy, though strongly indicated by Elizabeth, was not when
she died irrevocably fixed by the course of past history or by any
general prejudice of the governing class, and the decision, so vast
in its ulterior consequences, rested entirely on the caprices and theories
of a stranger from Scotland, who had been bred a Presbyterian, had
married a Catholic, but was in heart and mind a scholar.

We have now given some account of those features which, at Summary
the opening of the seventeenth century, differentiated England from
the other countries of Europe.   Owing to these characteristics, it
was still possible that, if our island could for a while remain isolated
from continental affairs, we might evolve some new kind of state,
more free but not less highly organised than the military and
bureaucratic depotism, which otherwise bade fair to become the
one type of civilised government.   For England was a land of local
government, local armaments, local feeling, where the life of the
shire, the parish and the city was vigorous, yet where no feud existed
between country and town ;   where ranks were for ever mingling ;
where the gentry intermarried with the middle class, and shared
with them the commercial and professional careers.   Bureaucrats
and soldiers were almost unknown ;   the King depended for the execution of his mandates on an unpaid magistracy, and for his defence
on the loyalty of his subjects.   The religion which most inspired the
best and ablest men, did not depend, like the Protestantism of
Germany or the Catholicism of France, on a State Church or a Church
State, but referred the individual to his own intellect and his own
conscience, and inspired him to defend his spiritual liberties.   And
this country, when Elizabeth died, was entering on a period of peace
and isolation favourable to internal activities, while the nations on
the continent again embarked on a series of gigantic wars.   Whether
in such a land, liberty had still a chance of survival ;   or whether the
universal tide of monarchy in Europe would not after all prove
irresistible even in England, now that feudal traditions were lost
and no republican ideals had taken their place, was soon to be decided by the hazard of events, and by the prejudice and passion of
men whom fortune would raise above their fellows, not to guide the
world whither they themselves would, but blindly to impel it down
courses which neither themselves not any other had foreseen.

CHAPTER III

JAMES I.—PURITANS AND CATHOLICS

He feels himself as an immense brood-fowl set over this England, and would so fain gather it all under his wings.—Historical Sketches, CARLYLE.

Death of
Elizabeth

IN the grey hours of morning, 24th March, 1603, watch and ward was kept in London streets ; and in all the neighbouring counties men who had much at stake in time of crisis, dreamed uncertainly of the thousand chances that day might bring. For the last and greatest of the Tudor race had at length turned away to die, leaving to its own devices the world which her patient valour had led into the forward path. Her death would bring about one of those rare occasions when the platitudes of national loyalty and unity, which have imposed on secure men for a whole generation, are put to the test of the event. It would now be seen whether all was really as officials asserted it to be ; whether the new England had been built to stand for ages ; or whether, after all, the party of the old religion and society was large, united, and determined enough to throw all once more into confusion.

Accession
of
James I.

When day broke two horsemen were far on the northern road, each spurring to forestall the other at Holyrood with homage impatiently expected by the first ruler of the British isles. At a more leisurely pace the Elizabethan statesmen were riding in from Richmond, where their mistress lay dead, to Whitehall gate, where at ten in the morning they proclaimed King James I. By employing as their spokesman Robert Cecil, who personified the late Queen's system in Church and State, the Lords of the Council showed themselves agreed that there should be no revolution. The decision was silently endorsed by a grateful nation. In city and manor house men laid aside their arms and breathed again. Fast as the news spread, all consented and most rejoiced. The Puritan sailors, who had taken out their ships to guard against Popish invasion from the Flemish coast, put back to port ; and the borderers who kept watch on Naworth turrets, learned from their mild Catholic Lord, Belted Will Howard, that, since England and Scotland had one King, the northern sky-line was no longer the territory of a foe. So the work of Elizabeth stood the test of real consent, and the English people invited the royal line of Scotland to come and fill her place.

Royal
progress
from
Scotland

The first of these four Stuarts, who have left their indelible negative impression upon England, ushered in the tragedy of King and people with a pageant of royal progress from Berwick to London, which then excited to ecstasies the loyalty and curiosity of a simple nation, and has since, in the reflex light of all that followed, become

a theme for the irony of historians.   For a month of spring weather
James rode south.   The land seemed bursting into bud to welcome
him, growing greener each day as the ever-increasing train of courtiers
wound slowly down out of the north country into the midland valleys;
through shouting market-places where the masque of welcome and
the corporation with its address were lost in the press of men ; by
ancient steeples rocking with the clash of bells ; along open roads
hedged with countrymen who had come on pilgrimage across whole
counties.   There was hunting of the stag through the neighbouring
parks, when His Majesty might learnedly discourse to the foresters
on the art of venery, and show how your Scotchman will blow a
mort ; while at night, in private mansions, the regal entertainment
witnessed to the solid magnificence and free loyalty of England.

The man on whom the English thus first set eyes was by no
means contemptible in person, in spite of grossly coarse manners.
In the prime of life, over middle height, a good horseman, devoted
to the chase, drinking hugely but never overcome by his liquor :
he employed a pithy wit and a wealth of homely images and learned
conceits in free and familiar discourse with all.   Nor during the
progress did he dispel the prejudice in his favour.

Above all he gave satisfaction by keeping Robert Cecil as his Ideas and
chief counsellor.   He had, in fact, determined to maintain the system character
of Elizabeth, with this good change—that henceforth the royal of James
policy should display an acuteness and a largeness of mind worthy
of a man of uncommon penetration and learning, who knew by
theory how to outwit the Pope, manage the King of Spain, convert
the English Catholics by proclamations, and guide his other subjects
on the path of unity and wisdom.   The English people having been
loyal even to Elizabeth, probably from their sense of the obedience
due by right divine to all rulers, would be doubly loyal to one like
himself, the living symbol of justice and reconciliation, the " Re-
storer," as he loved to hear, " of perpetual peace in Church and
Commonwealth ".

His naturally authoritative temper in politics was flattered both
by his theories and his experience.   His dogma of the divine right
of Kings was gleaned from the new theory of State now in favour
among the monarchies of the continent, better known to him than
to his more ignorant and insular English subjects ; while his experience of Scottish kingship had led him, during the years of life
when opinions are formed, to see how necessary is royal authority
to tame a fierce baronage and a frantic clergy.   But he had devoted
none of his studious hours to the department of learning that now
most concerned him.   He knew nothing of the peculiar laws and
liberties of England, either in the spirit or the letter ; he began by
ordering a cut-purse, who had been caught preying on the crowd as
he passed through Newark, to be hanged without trial.   When, too

late in life to profit by new knowledge, he discovered the existence of constitutional custom and Parliamentary privilege, he set them down in his logical mind as tiresome anomalies hampering government in its benevolent course. Nor would he consider local sentiment and English national jealousy, except to despise them as forces disintegrating his plans of peace and union.

As a man, James was one whom it is easy to love or to despise, but impossible to hate. Though every inch a pedant, he was human —far more human than his more noble and reserved successor. His instinct to sympathise warmly, except when annoyed or prejudiced, with any one who spoke to him, led to rapid and unconscious vacillations in his conduct. The more intimate friendships which were a necessity to his life, counteracted yet more disastrously his excellent intentions as a ruler. Choosing his favourites for no other merit but their charm as companions, he was too fond to deny them anything. Their power for evil was the greater, because he himself hated the details of administration, and loved to live in the abstract heights of a general scheme, oblivious of the monstrous distortions to which a plan is liable in action, and the terrible wrongs for which even a love of justice, if it despises diligence, can easily be made the cloak.

Beneath all his carelessness as to the ordering of his Court, and in seeing to the execution of his commands, lay a will stubbornly adherent to a main course of a policy through years of ominous failure, when once he had persuaded himself that king-craft required a certain attitude, whether towards Spain, towards the Puritans or towards Parliament. Opposition, even if couched in reverent terms, aroused neither his admiration nor his curiosity, but only his spleen. Of cruelty, indeed, he had none. An opponent, especially if a subject, was a pitiable thing to be lectured and set aside. If, as in the case of his later Parliaments, opposition became too strong, he would resort to concession, but not to conciliation or to a change of front.

His most fatal defect was that, in spite of great acuteness and some originality in discovering points of vantage for himself and detecting weakness in his adversaries' position, he could never tell a good man from a rogue, or a wise man from a fool ; still less could he distinguish the great currents of opinion and the main tide of political force, from the bright, shallow eddies that catch and please a monarch's eye. The patriotism of Eliot repelled him ; the large political wisdom of Bacon appeared to him a rushlight rival to his own royal beam ; the daring and unquiet genius of Raleigh was opposed alike to his peaceful instincts and his pedestrian intellect. Turning from all this varied wealth of excellence, he deliberately chose Carr and Villiers. One who thus judged of persons, was not likely to understand the real problems with which his king-craft had in fact to deal ; to penetrate the soul of Puritanism, or to recognise any purpose beyond that of thwarting good government, in the turbulent faction of the House of Commons.

In the first three years of James's English rule, each of the great problems of the coming century took an irrevocable turn. Against Puritans and against Parliament the King adopted in 1604 a position from which his stubborn character afterwards forbade him to retreat, and, by the time his son succeeded him, the continuous traditions of a long reign had established this principle as the very first of royal policy. In the same year, 1604, by making a wise peace with Spain,[1] he prepared the way for his foolish friendship with Catholic powers which soon alienated nationalist feeling from the throne. In the winter of 1605 his attempt to secure the loyalty of the Papists by holding out alternately the olive-branch and the sword ended in the Gunpowder treason ; the event gave only a momentary impulse to the ever-vacillating conduct of the Stuart monarchs towards their Catholic subjects, but it excited popular imagination to a panic that lasted with slight intermissions for more than a century. Thus all the main causes that twice combined to drive the Stuarts from the throne. were in three fatal years set in motion by an overwise King.

Fatal consequences of the first acts of the reign

Already during his·progress from Scotland the new King had been met by the " Millenary Petition," [2] presented by several hundred conformist Puritan clergy, in the hope that the doubtful toleration afforded them within the Elizabethan establishment, might under the new *régime* be changed for a secure and legalised comprehension. They were serving the Episcopal Church with sufficient loyalty to her form of government and her Prayer-book service, and with a missionary zeal and a pastoral energy to which no other section could pretend. In return they now asked, not for supremacy, but for security. The petitioners suggested that a clergyman should be allowed to choose for himself whether he would wear cap and surplice, and that he should not be required to declare his belief in the absolute truth of the whole Prayer-book, provided he signed the Articles and used the service. The royal reply would be a test of much besides : if the new King was ready to tolerate Puritanism within the pale of the National Church. he would be ready to leave these points optional.

The Millenary Petition. 1603

Other items of the Millenary Petition—the disuse of the sign of the cross in baptism and the bowing at the name of Jesus, the abridgement of the service, the simplification of music and chanting, the

---

[1] See p. 94 below, note.
[2] The " Millenary " Petition was so called because it pretended to express the opinion of a thousand clergy of the Established Church.

encouragement of preaching and sermons, the prevention of ecclesiastical pluralities and sinecures, the observance of Sunday, the
non-observance of saints' days—were such as a wise monarch might
have refused or left unanswered, on the ground that any strict order
favouring the Puritans on these points would give offence to many
clergy and to many congregations. But the moderation of even
these requests, so different from the demand for the abolition of the
episcopate haughtily advanced thirty years before, show the humble
and conformist spirit of Puritanism at this auspicious moment, which
James the peacemaker was fated to throw away.

The
Hampton
Court
Confer-
ence,
Jan., 1604
In January, 1604, the King presided at Hampton Court over a
conference summoned to consider the Petition. The Bishops came
up determined to oppose all compromise. As the death struggle
against Catholicism gave ever more apparent promise of triumph,
the Protestant zeal originally shown by Elizabeth's Bishops had
begun to cool ; and when Cartwright had made his Presbyterian
attack on their authority, they had grafted on to their Erastian
pride of Church office under the Crown the yet loftier pretension
that episcopal government is of Divine origin. Bancroft, Bishop of
London, the champion of the new theory, took the lead at Hampton
Court. On the second day of the session, when the principal demands of the Millenary Petition were to be discussed, he began by
asking James to silence the Puritan divines on the high ground that
Canon Law forbade schismatics to be heard against their Bishops,
and then tried to raise a silly laugh against the " Turkey gowns "
in which the good men had thought fit to appear at the conference.
But James was not going to lose the chance of a disputation. Re-
buking Bancroft's unfairness, he assumed the part of the good-
humoured and talkative umpire of debate, hearing all in full, but
deciding point after point against the Puritan spokesman, Dr.
Reynolds. The session, however, came to a more stormy close.
Reynold's proposed that the lower clergy should have the right of
meeting in conference, and that the Bishop should consult the Synod
of his diocese. At the word " Synod," redolent to James of the
daily humiliations of his youth among the rude lieutenants of Knox,
the petulance which was always chafing under the crust of his learning and wisdom, burst out in loose native fury. " If you aim at
a Scottish Presbytery," he cried, " it agreeth as well with a monarchy, as God and the Devil." Seizing up his hat to dismiss the
assembly, he poured out, in a strain of colloquial epigram, the secret
of the personal passion that dictated his policy. " How they used
the poor lady, my mother, is not unknown, and how they dealt
with me in my minority. I thus apply it. . . . No Bishop, no
King. . . . Well, Doctor, have you anything more to say ? " " No
more, if it please your Majesty." " If this be all your party hath
to say, I will make them conform themselves, or else will harry

them out of the land."   " In two minutes," as Gardiner says, " he
had sealed his own fate and that of England for ever."

On many points James was not out of sympathy with the James's
Puritans.   Unlike Charles I., he was not brought up in the atmos- ecclesias-
phere of Anglicanism ; he cared nothing for ritual, he was a Calvinist views
in doctrine ; and when he first entered England he was anxious to
promote in his half-Catholic kingdom the pastoral and missionary
propaganda which the Puritans alone carried on, in spite of episcopal
discouragement.   He had wished to settle endowments for the
maintenance of preachers, until Archbishop Whitgift persuaded
him that much preaching was a dangerous innovation.[1] But the
one point on which he differed completely from the Puritans, was
the relative authority of the bishops and their clergy.   It was in
fact not for speculative or religious, but for political, reasons that he
disliked the Puritans.   He saw in them the sect that in Scotland
had made his youth one long humiliation, his manhood one long
struggle—men who would take the Lord's Anointed by the sleeve
and call him " God's silly vassal ".   The English Puritans were at
this stage of their career of a milder temper : but the policy of
suppression by which James thought to " harry them out of the
land " served to arouse in them the instincts which he most feared,
and led them indeed to abolish Bishops and to put his son to death.

When his first Parliament met in the spring of 1604, the House
of Commons supported the Millenary Petition and the arguments
of Dr. Reynolds.   It escaped the King how ominous was the alliance ; Effect on
how considerable the fact that the flustered divines who had picked Puritan-
up their Turkey gowns and scurried from his presence amid the King's
laughter of Bishops, represented the religion of the gentry and the hostility
towns of England.   Such considerations gave him no pause.   It
was enough for him to lecture Parliament on " Puritans and
Novelists," [2] " which I call a sect rather than a religion," " who do
not so far differ from us in points of religion as in their confused
form of policy and parity ".   In that sentence James summed up
the mistake of his life.   Because the Puritan leaders of the previous
generation had desired a Presbyterian " policy " of Church government, and a " parity " of clergy with their Bishops, therefore the
services and merits of all Puritans were to be overlooked, they were
at once to be deprived of their benefices, and finally, together with
all their lay adherents, " harried out of the land ".   James did not

---

[1] This was in 1603 (see G., i., p. 151). But in 1604, at Hampton Court, James
had already adopted the opinion expressed by Bancroft that there ought to be a
" praying," not a " preaching ministry " : because, although " in a Church
newly to be planted, preaching is most necessary, not so in one long established,"
like the Church of England, which Bancroft regarded as having already completely
converted the Catholic population.   That was the Anglican, as opposed to the
Puritan, view of the religious situation in England and of the duties attaching
to the cure of souls.

[2] Novelists, *i.e.*, Innovators.

5

perceive that if they were allowed to continue their work in the Church and to take their fair place on the episcopal Bench, the desire for " parity " would be kept in the background ; while on the other hand, if they were driven out by the Bishops, the Presbyterian " policy " would revive, with the arm of the House of Commons for its support.

Three hundred Puritan clergy ejected, 1604

As soon as Parliament had risen in July, the King informed the clergy by proclamation that unless before December they were ready to conform to all existing rules of Church service, they would then be deprived of their livings. When the fatal month came round, Bancroft himself, elevated to the See of Canterbury as a new broom to sweep the Church clean, eagerly set himself to carry out the orders of the King's Council. All curates and unbeneficed preachers were required to sign a statement that the Prayer-book contained nothing contrary to the Word of God ; and the beneficed clergy, while excused this severer test, were required to obey the rubric in every detail. Three hundred refused and were ejected. Many of the most influential and conscientious of the servants of the Church were driven into the position of Sectarians. Till then, the only schism from the English Church had been the voluntary secession of the Brownists and a few other proto-martyrs of the Congregational system, who were hated by the average Puritan almost as much as by the Bishops. But now an important group of Churchmen, forcibly expelled, gathered round them large congregations of admirers. The " silenced brethren," as they were called, became a living reproach to the numerous Puritan clergy who remained in the Church, a witness of the honours of martyrdom and the injustice of episcopal government. This, the first of the great ejections for conscience' sake that mark the history of the reformed English Church, began a cycle of revolutionary tests, which, after weeding out in turn the more scrupulous champions of Puritanism and of Anglicanism, at the end of a hundred years left the Vicar of Bray as the type of an English clergyman in the eighteenth century.

Bacon in favour of comprehension

Although the Bishops had applauded and fostered the royal design, the ejections of 1604 were as much the act and choice of James as the Revocation of the Edict of Nantes was the act and choice of Louis XIV. The English monarch's responsibility is, however, the less of the two, because intolerance was in his day not a retrogression, but the accepted theory of religion and of statecraft. Among his political advisers, Robert Cecil, who hated the Catholics and in no way shared Bancroft's high Anglican views, considered the expulsion of the silenced ministers as a necessary act, conservative of the Elizabethan tradition. Men did not recognise that there were vigorous variations in English religion ; that either the Church must be widely comprehensive, or else cease to be the

National Church of all English Protestants. Bacon, alone of statesmen, favoured the comprehension of the Puritans without being
himself of their persuasion ; for he alone, with his broad philosophic
scope, could foresee the results of breaking up the unity of the Protestant national life. Vainly he presented his scheme to a King
whom he thought wise, in the hope that it might at once save the
nation and bring to himself favour and high employment. When
his advice had been scorned and the fatal proclamation issued, the
philosopher sadly watched the chemical elements of opinion, disturbed by the new injection, fermenting and suffering change into
new and ominous combinations and gathering into heads of explosive
matter. What if the first discharge should blow sky-high none
other than this wary and keen-eyed chemist, so quick to mark the
mistakes and dangers of all except himself ? [1]

The threat of the Catholic reaction to destroy in every country
of Europe all governments and institutions, whose existence guaranteed the future development of the human intellect, was at that
time the gravest of all perils. Again and again the shout of Catholic
victory rose throughout the world, when great princes were converted, brave populations silenced, and old established churches
overthrown. Everywhere on the ruins of the reformed faiths rose
a machinery of persuasion and repression, never since shaken off
by any religious community on which it was then imposed. And
again and again the boast was heard that this island would be neither
the least nor the last victim. Meanwhile, among the English dwelt
a Catholic population whose real numbers and common purpose
were a mystery to themselves and to their countrymen then, and
remain a mystery to us now. But as the organisers of universal
reaction always appealed confidently to these English Catholics to
stand in readiness " until that time," men's hearts were set hard as
flint against their papist neighbours, through constant apprehension
of an hour which might always strike, and of a domestic foe who
could never be numbered. However much the strength and intentions of this mysterious and intangible body of English Catholics
may have secretly altered in the course of long years, however much
their condition and prospects ostensibly fluctuated from time to
time, yet during the Stuart epoch they underwent no essential
change in regard to the classes and districts where their strength
lay, the parties and policies which divided them internally, and the
kinds of persecution to which they were subjected. An account of
how these matters stood at the time of the Gunpowder Plot will
serve to throw light on each successive crisis of English history in
which the Catholic question reappears, down to the year 1688, when
it decided the wavering balance of many vast destinies.

When Elizabeth died, Protestantism was so firmly rooted in

The
Catholic
reaction

---

[1] See p. 101 below.

the intelligence and the passions of the city populace that there
was not an important town in England where a Catholic priest
could prudently have shown himself in the streets ; but the English
rustics, especially north of Trent and west of Avon, had as yet
little prejudice and less understanding on the great religious question
that divided Europe, and were ready to swallow any opinion provided for them by their betters. The translated Bible, the Church
service and the Puritan propaganda had not had time to do their
work, and if now the Catholics had been able to neutralise the towns,
the gentry and the machinery of law, they might perhaps have
drawn back the rural population into the ancestral forms of piety,
which still lingered in the memory and the love of simple men.
But under the arrangements of the Protestant *régime*, these indifferent classes, being just those which could least afford to pay
for the expensive privilege of " recusancy," [1] year by year imbibed
the atmosphere and association of the new Church to whose services they had at first to be driven like schoolboys. Even those
among the yeoman farmers and labourers who decidedly preferred
the old forms of worship, were deprived of their rites and their
ministers, and ruined by spies, pursuivants and bad neighbours,
who carried off their goods under cover of collecting recusancy fines,
till one by one they gave up the struggle and conformed. Some,
indeed, sought refuge in areas specially protected by a Catholic
squire or nobleman. The influence of the landlord, as yet unchallenged on social grounds, could easily have eliminated Protestant tenants from all lands owned by Catholics, if the State
had not interfered on behalf of the religion which it favoured. To
save England from forcible recovery by Rome, the only alternative
to Penal Laws would have been the confiscation of Catholic estates.
In spite of all legislation, there could be found scattered throughout
the island whole villages adhering to the old religion, under the
protective and coercive influence of the neighbouring manor house.
In some of the counties of the North, where the feudal relation and
the Catholic faith still flourished, half the landowners secretly attended Mass, and, in the day when war made each man free to
confess his heart's allegiance, half the rural population of Lancashire
marched to storm the Puritan clothing towns. arrayed under the
banners of their lords as open recusants.

The ancient halls which the Catholic squires maintained as
asylums of the faith, were each filled with a great " family " of
serving-men and dependants, who, in their enforced isolation from
the pursuits and prizes of the great world, cherished an intense
devotion for the religion that held the household together. It was

---

[1] Recusant meant a Catholic who refused to attend church. I have always
used it in this, its proper sense. But it was sometimes used to denote any kind
of Roman Catholic.

not without reason that their Protestant neighbours, armed with writs from vigilant magistrates, came again and again to burst open cupboards and tap wainscoats in the search for arms. But the pistols and corselets were safely stowed with the pyx and chasuble in the passage between the great chimney and the outer wall. Thither the priests also retired until the search party had clattered off down the avenue, and he could again walk freely through the house, honoured of all the inmates, and welcome by night under the thatch of the cottages around. The head of such a house was often, as the Jesuits themselves reported, " either by his own position or by the good esteem of his neighbours, superior to the action of the laws ". But in seasons when persecution was more severe, as after the Gunpowder Plot, the breaking of the Spanish match, or the meeting of the Long Parliament, the freedom of such households was curtailed, the priest walked at night and vanished at cock-crow, and the old serving-men who could be trusted to sleep through a Protestant homily were sent to Church on Sunday morning.

In other families, where the neighbourhood was more hostile, or where part of the servants were heretics, such precautions were the standing rule even at times when the enemy was least vigilant. The presence of the priest in a remote garret of the great house among the chimneys and gables, was kept a secret from several score of persons whom he could hear moving through the courts and chambers beneath, as he pored over Parsons' *Apologia* and the *Life of Mary of Scots*, gazed wistfully at the tree tops and the flying clouds, or paced delicately along the great beam in the floor that he could trust not to betray his existence by a creak. At night he could use no lamp, lest the forester should see that the garret was inhabited. For months, though in his friend's house, he lived alone, except for that hour when, each day, hasty steps were heard and figures slid silently in as he celebrated Mass at the altar behind his bed. More fortunate were those Jesuits who moved from house to house, mixing disguised with the world, at the price of increased danger of imprisonment or death.[1]

The system of persecution, which prevented the recovery of power by the Catholic party, was remarkably irregular in its working. As embodied in the letter of the Penal Code, it was at no moment in the century completely enforced : nor was it ever before the Great Rebellion in complete abeyance. The degree of its enforcement varied continually in respect to persons, places and times ; Catholicism meant for one man ruin ; for another a certain picturesque distinction. In one district it was the pass to the highest county society : in another it was the butt of intolerable injuries

Priests in hiding

Persecution irregular

[1] For these details, see the Jesuit report, 1616, printed in Taunton, pp. 362-64.

and insults. One year it brought social infamy and political proscription ; the next, Court favour and the attentions of all the time-servers of the land.

The Penal Laws   The object of the loosely administered Penal Code, passed by Elizabeth's Parliaments, was three-fold. First, in order to prevent the papal party from seizing political power, or spreading the personal authority of Catholics in the country, recusants were made to confine their activity and influence to their own estates, by laws which excluded them from any post in national or local government, and even forbade them to travel five miles from their place of residence without licenses signed by neighbouring magistrates.[1]

The second object was to penalise even those Catholics who stayed quietly at home, by fines for not attending church. The desire to avoid these ruinous tolls was calculated to outweigh with many the influence of their landlord and the exhortations of their priest. The fines were collected in different ways from different classes. A dozen of the richest men in England were liable to pay £20 a month for the privilege of staying away from church on Sunday ; lesser Catholic landowners, who would be ruined by such a charge, could purchase the same immunity by giving up two-thirds of their yearly rental ; but heavy fines were also collected from farmers and cottagers, by pursuivants who broke into the house, carried off the spoils from barn and kitchen at a scandalously low valuation and often indulged in wanton uproar, insult and destruction. And yet the levy of these fines was very irregular and in many districts quite unusual. Even in 1606, a year of panic when persecution was at its height, only 162 gentlemen paid the two-thirds of their rental, and less than £5,000 from all classes together reached the treasury. In other years Government realised scarcely a quarter of this sum. The fines actually fell only on a small proportion of those who absented themselves from church, for the lists returned by the authorities as the basis of the levy were always incomplete and often, through fear, favour or negligence, scarcely one recusant in five was named.[2]

The third method by which the spread of Catholic principles was checked, was the proscription of the Mass and priesthood. But here the laws served nominally for one purpose and were actually used for another. While every priest who exercised his functions in England and every layman who abetted him, were doomed by the statute to die the death of traitors, in practice these bloody laws were kept suspended over the heads of the priests and their congregations, serving only to check the boldness of their propaganda and the publicity of their worship. While no Catholic

---

[1] The latter rule was sometimes, though seldom, enforced see *Trevelyan Papers* (Camden Soc.), iii., pp. 231, 232).

[2] G., i., pp. 228, 229. *Worcester County Records*, vol. i., pp. ccxv-xviii.

service was openly held, except in the chapels of the foreign ambassadors at the capital, every day Mass was heard in garrets and libraries by hundreds of little congregations, none of whom had to fear the penalties incurred, as long as they did not parade their breach of the law. Similarly, no systematic attempt was made to hunt the priests out of England. When in 1604 King James heard that his Judges had taken upon themselves to hang several priests and their abettors in Western counties, where the Catholics had seemed to them too prominent, he at once put a stop to these legalised atrocities, and would not allow them to be renewed even after the Gunpowder Plot. But as long as the laws themselves remained unrepealed, every zealous Catholic, holding his life and property at the mercy of the Government, felt the restraint implied ; and a mission, that might otherwise have competed with the Puritan propaganda and the Established Church, was deprived of publicity and vigour.

The numerical strength of the Catholics, often and variously *Real* estimated, was quite unknown. The returns of " recusants " were *strength* well understood to represent those whom their neighbours thought *of the* *Catholics* it necessary to persecute and not the whole body of those who *unknown* refused to attend church. The lists themselves were incomplete and in any case the " recusants " were only one part of the Catholic body. The " Church Papists," as those were called who consented to attend the national worship, could not legally be distinguished from the Protestants, and were therefore a wholly incalculable force. Some, like the Howards, prominent in the King's service and deep in his counsels, might in an hour of need betray the new religion as readily as they had deserted the old ; while others made no pretence of loyalty to the established order, attended church merely to avoid the fines, walked out ostentatiously before the sermon and alarmed their Protestant gossips with blood-curdling announcements that the good times of Queen Mary were coming back, when " faggotts should be deere " yet.[1] On the other hand, many of these " Church Papists " were slowly adapting themselves to the English communion.

The political strength of the Catholics as a danger to the State *Catholic* was even more hard to calculate than their numbers as a religious *divisions,* body. For on the question of loyalty to the State they were *Jesuits* divided between two parties and policies, and none knew to which *and* side the bulk of the laity, recusant and conformist alike, would *Seculars* in the hour of trial adhere. The two parties were the Jesuits and the secular clergy. Although their quarrel was, in one aspect, a selfish struggle for the privilege of governing the Catholic body in England, their rival claims to authority coincided with rival policies of State. In the middle of Elizabeth's reign, the secular

---

[1] *Trevelyan Papers* (Camden Soc.), ii., p. 118 , iii., p. xxii.

priests, then in sole charge of the English flock, had bowed to the
storm and sought safety in diminished vigour ; but it was then that
the Jesuits had landed in England and imposed themselves on
clergy and laity alike, by their zeal as missionaries, and their authority as the Pope's messengers ; their influence was further enhanced
by their connection with the Spanish political conspiracies, and the
reputation they consequently won as the Tyburn martyrs, famous
throughout the whole Catholic world.   When their policy of rebellion, assassination and foreign conquest brought down the Penal
Laws upon the whole Catholic body, increased persecution supplied a fresh argument to the Jesuits for the need to overthrow
the heretic State ; while on the other hand it served to convince
the seculars of the folly of political agitation.

At the moment of James I.'s accession, this struggle for authority
was at its height.   The nominal head of the English Catholics was
the so-called " Archpriest," Blackwell, who stood in matters of policy
half-way between the two parties, but who owed his position to the
Jesuits.   Their influence at Rome had obtained the establishment
of his strange office, as an alternative to the episcopal control for
which the secular clergy petitioned as a means of emancipating
themselves from the Jesuit yoke.   Appeals to Rome were in these
years frequent on both sides, but as yet Parsons, the founder of
the Jesuit power in England, had the oracle on his side and secured
the discomfiture of his rivals.   The animosity with which this man
of iron pursued the adherents of his own faith, matched the steady
determination with which he assailed the independence of his own
country.[1]   When he died in 1610, he had, by thirty years of un-
tiring effort, imposed on the English Catholics an internal feud
between two embittered factions and an external system of reliance on the armed enemies of England, that resulted in the final
catastrophe of 1688, when Petre completed what Parsons had begun.

The
Jesuit
point of
view

Historians, looking rather to the results than the motives of
action, take the part of the loyal English Catholics, who having
abandoned the attempt to convert the island, only asked to be left
in peace, but who were forced to undergo two centuries of un-
merited persecution because the foreign-hearted Jesuits pursued
desperate counsels, doomed after all to failure.   Yet the Jesuits'
plan was both politic and right, if once their premise be granted
that the Catholic is infinitely preferable to the Protestant religion.

[1] *E.g.*, in a tract called *A Manifestation of Great Folly and Bad Spirit of
certain in England calling themselves Secular Priests* (1602), Parsons thus gently
admonishes them : " And here now the very multitude of these outrageous libels,
with the immensity of hatred, hellish spite and poisoned entrails, discovered
therein, do force us against our former purpose to cut off and stay all further
passage and proceeding, in this horrible puddle of lies, slanderous invectives, and
devilish detraction " (Taunton, pp. 493, 494).   Such was the unity of spirit in
the Catholic Church at the time of James's accession.

How should the peace of a few small and ever-dwindling Catholic congregations be compared to the least chance of converting the island, of saving the souls of innumerable millions of Englishmen to come ? That conversion could be effected in no other way than by the overthrow of the State and the use of war and persecution. The final choice between the two religions, made by every nation of the old Latin communion, was in many cases dictated, as none knew better than the Jesuits, not by a nation's preference for the religion most suited to its genius, but by the chance turns of politics and war. If their native religion would involve all the English in damnation, was it unpatriotic to save them by introducing Spanish spearmen into their homes, and driving James from the throne in favour of a Catholic Prince ?

Similarly, from the point of view either of Protestantism or of English national life, it would have been suicide to allow the Catholic propaganda to continue unchecked, when so many land-owners were ready to force it upon their tenants, and so many foreign enemies to assist them in a civil war. For the Jesuits had connected the Catholic reaction on the continent with Catholicism in this island. It was unsafe for Government to rely on the loyalty of the secular priests, for though their leaders opposed the Jesuit schemes, nearly all the rank and file who had now replaced the old Marian priesthood had been educated within King Philip's territories, in seminaries controlled by the Jesuits, had forgotten all native sympathies and learned the Spanish theory of propaganda by sword and stake.[1] The results that followed Catholic victory over a Protestant people could be seen in other lands, and no pretence was made that England would be more gently treated. The development of intellectual and of political life would both be crushed. Parsons thus describes the double use that would be made of victory. First.

The Protestant point of view

> Public and private libraries must be searched and examined for books, as also bookbinders', stationers' and booksellers' shops, and severe order and punishment appointed for such as shall conceal these kind of writings ; and like order set down for printing of good things for the time to come. What form or manner of inquisition to bring in, whether that of Spain (whose rigour is misliked by some) or that which is used in divers parts of Italy (where coldness is reprehended by more) . . . is not so easy to determine ; but the time itself will speak, when the day shall come, and perhaps some mixture of all will not be amiss for England.

As to politics, the restored Catholic Bishops were to have the power to negative or confirm elections to the House of Commons.[2]

> The Church (says Gardiner) which these men joined was pledged to change the moral and intellectual atmosphere in which Englishmen moved and breathed.

[1] Soon after the Gunpowder Plot the Benedictines began to compete with the Jesuits as educators of the English secular priesthood. This blow at the Jesuit monopoly restored the balance and embittered the strife of the two parties.

[2] Taunton, pp. 485, 486.

Neither freedom of thought nor political liberty had as yet reached their perfect development in England, but it was beyond doubt that the victory of the Papacy would extinguish both. Even the received maxims of the nineteenth century would hardly be proof against a demand for toleration put forward by a community which itself refused toleration to all those principles on which our society is based, if it had any chance of acquiring sufficient strength to employ against others that persecution which in its own case it deprecated.[1]

A vicious circle Here was a vicious circle. The Jesuit policy induced statesmen to prevent the spread of Catholicism by the Penal Laws ; but the Penal Laws, because they prevented the spread of Catholicism, could well justify to any whole-hearted Catholic the Jesuit policy. So strong was this chain of necessity, that until Protestantism was either overthrown or irremovably established, premature attempts at toleration would defeat their own ends. The first of these attempts was coincident in time with the accession of the House of Stuart.

Catholic hopes of the new King During the years when Elizabeth was known to be sinking to the grave, the conduct of James had not been wanting in dignity and common-sense, for Robert Cecil, in a correspondence kept secret from his jealous mistress, had indicated the attitude proper to assume at Edinburgh towards men and parties in England. But there was one party whom the secretary knew not how to approach. James, perceiving that his new friend had no dealings with the Catholics, saw in that direction a fair field open for himself to exercise his own broader philosophy and more adaptable methods of king-craft. He renewed diplomatic relations with the Pope. He was heard to utter promises of relief to the Catholics. Strictly interpreted his words can be reduced to a promise of toleration and State preferment for " Church Papists," but they were reported in Catholic households as a pledge to remit the fines for recusancy. This rumour secured for him, during his progress to London, an enthusiastic welcome from the moderates and seculars. The Jesuits acquiesced for a very different reason. Garnet, the provincial head of the society in England, had shortly before the Queen's death received breves from the Pope directing him if possible to oppose James's accession, and the Spanish King had promised military aid to the English Jesuit envoys sent to Madrid in 1602. But Philip III. drew back, in the hope, soon afterwards justified, of obtaining international peace from the unwarlike James. So Garnet burnt the breves and joined in the national acclamations.

Watson's plot, 1603 The new King had scarcely reached London before the eyes of the seculars were opened to their delusion. The fines were still to be collected from the recusants. A secular priest named Watson, who had preached acquiescence as the sure high road to a toleration, was so enraged to find himself deluded, that he organised a plot among his own friends to seize the person of James and force

[1] G., i., p. 231.

him to carry out his promise. The plot was in every way characteristic of the seculars. It was not bloody or treacherous in its means ; it did not propose the total overthrow of Protestantism and English institutions as its end ; and it was wholly impracticable. The Jesuit party, who had never been so foolish as to expect toleration from a heretic King, laughed to see their disappointed adversaries take refuge in the unfamiliar mazes of conspiracy, and scored a point for their own faction by undermining the whole plot and betraying it to Cecil. The result of this comedy, with all the parts so strangely inverted, was a *rapprochement* between James and the High Catholics. It was a moment propitious for his schemes of toleration. The recusancy fines were almost entirely remitted, and the priests went about their work without fear of the gallows.

But though the moment was propitious for toleration, the age was still hostile to its success. The plan conceived by James was to tolerate the private exercise of religion, on condition, first that all the Catholics should transfer their loyalty from Pope to King ; secondly that there should be no increase in their numbers. This ideal solution was far superior to anything aimed at by the Elizabethan statesmen, but it could not be realised. The two proposed conditions were alike impossible. For though the Jesuits had amused themselves by betraying Watson, they had not the least intention of becoming loyal ; and from the moment that toleration was granted, the skeleton army of Catholicism resumed an appearance of its full strength. As soon as the recusancy fines were remitted, familiar figures were missed from the back benches in many a Parish Church, and now that the laws against the Mass were no longer enforced, whole neighbourhoods were alarmed by great gatherings of Catholic devotees. These avowals of long concealed opinion were denounced by the Protestant party as recent conversions due to the renewed activity of the priests. James, terrified at the phantoms his first stroke of king-craft had conjured up, rushed back into Cecil's arms. In February, 1604, a proclamation appeared ordering all priests to quit the country ; in August several were hanged by the Judges on Circuit, though without instructions from Government ; in November the levy of fines from lay recusants was vigorously resumed ; in December five men were mining a tunnel from a neighbouring cellar to the wall of Parliament House.

The Gunpowder Treason was conceived by Robert Catesby. That form of assassination was then a familiar idea : the Kirk o' Field had been blown up on the mysterious night that Darnley lay under its roof ; and in a book written shortly before the death of Elizabeth, the Jesuit author, illustrating a point of casuistry, takes the case that a criminal has placed gunpowder " under a certain house and that unless it be removed the house will be burnt, the sovereign killed and as many as go in or out of the city destroyed ".

Toleration extended and withdrawn, 1603-4

Gunpowder Plot, 1604-5

Catesby saw that the method was peculiarly suited to the large needs of the English Catholics. To destroy the King would be useless if the heads of the Protestant party survived to assemble in their Parliament, an institution spoken of by the plotters as the true source and security of the Protestant *regime*. But the disorganisation that would follow the death of King, Lords and Commons together, would create a moment during which the Catholics could rebel with some chance of success. Nor would the most backward be able to let that moment go by, since the rage and panic of the Protestants would compel all to defend themselves from massacre by resort to arms. No one who is acquainted with the national rejoicings at the assassination of Buckingham, or with the plots of the Cavaliers and Royal family to murder Cromwell and the regieides, will suppose that horror at the deed would have prevented the Catholics from seizing their advantage. Catesby knew that if Parliament could be blown up, as fast as the news spread the men of the two religions would mount and ride to cut each other's throats, without leaders and without law.

The con-   It was no group of obscure fanatics who laid so terrible a plot
spirators to force the hands of their co-religionists. Catesby and the friends to whom he dictated his resolves, were already known men, as the agents of the Jesuit party. In 1602 they had consulted with Garnet, the head of the society in England, as to the desirability of a foreign invasion, and one of their number had been sent, together with the Jesuit Greenway, on embassy to the Spanish King. But unlike their clerical chiefs, they were pure from self-interest and love of power. It is difficult to detect any stain upon their conduct, except the one monstrous illusion that murder is right, which put all their virtues at the devil's service. Courage cold as steel, self-sacrifice untainted by jealousy or ambition, readiness when all was lost to endure all, raises the Gunpowder Plot into a story of which the ungarnished facts might well be read by those of every faith, not with shame or anger, but with enlarged admiration and pity for the things which men can do.

The cellar They hired no cut-throats to do their work. All who laboured at the mine " were gentlemen of name and blood." Guy Fawkes, the professional soldier whom they brought back from Flanders out of the ranks of the English Catholic legion, was a man who had enlisted in the Spanish service after selling his Yorkshire property for religion's sake, and soon proved himself a conspirator equal even to Catesby in all the sterner virtues. This man, who had learnt the sieger's art in mines and countermines where Dutch and Spaniards wrought like moles after each other's lives, could show his friends how to drive a tunnel safely through the earth, from the cellar of the building which they had hired as the basis of operations, to the foundation wall of the Parliament House. But when they began to attack that nine feet of stone wall the labour became excessive. One day in March, 1605, as they plied their noiseless daily task, they heard a " rushing " rather above their heads. A dreadful fear of discovery struck them all still. But Fawkes, who in the part of serving-man to Percy went everywhere and did everything, strolled round to examine the unknown danger, and returned with joyful news that it was a woman moving her sea-coals in the long lumber-room immediately under the House of Lords, and that the use of the room might perhaps be had for money. In these new premises, obtained on lease by Percy, Fawkes stored thirty-six barrels of gunpowder, strewed them with great bars of iron to break the roof in pieces and concealed the whole under piles of firewood. The useless mine below was left unfinished, and the conspirators dispersed for six months.

If the half-dozen men who placed the materials for the explosion had kept the secret to themselves, their part of the design might have proved successful. But, thinking it wise that some of the Catholic chiefs should be prepared for the coming death struggle, they enlisted two classes of persons as accessories to the great crime.

First, as a matter partly of conscience, partly of policy, they consulted their friends the Jesuit leaders, both in and out of confession.[1] The fathers were much perturbed. It was not their plot in origin, but it derived from their teaching and influence, and now, much against their will, they were required to pronounce whether it was right or wrong. Father Greenway, who was the first to learn the details of the design, probably encouraged it, for he afterwards joined the conspirators in their abortive rising, as one " that would live and die with them ". But Garnet himself adopted a middle course. Even according to his own account, he made but feeble protestations when Catesby informed him that some violence was intended, and when he learnt the whole terrible truth from Greenway he made no serious efforts to dissuade his friends, avoided their company, gradually retired from the neighbourhood of London as the fatal autumn session drew near, and during the week when he knew the matter was to be put to the touch, lay concealed in a remote manor house on the borders of Worcestershire. Thus the Provincial of the English Jesuits acted like a coward. Either he half-approved of the design, or else the prospect of withstanding Catesby to the face terrified from his duty the one man who could successfully have forbidden the conspirators to proceed.

Although by informing their spiritual advisers the assassins were preparing a grave scandal for the Catholic religion, their resolve to

The Jesuit fathers informed

---

[1] Garnet states, first, that he had obtained " a general knowledge of Mr. Catesby's intention," *not* in confession, and acknowledges himself " highly guilty and to have offended God " in not revealing it. Secondly, that he learnt the full details of the plot from Greenway, " not in confession but by way of confession ".

Other ac-
cessories;
prepara-
tions in
the
country

disclose their design to another class of persons proved yet more disastrous. They determined that there must be arms, horses and men ready on the day of the destruction of Parliament, in order that the truceless war might open with some notable advantage to their cause. It was easy to make general preparations for a rebellion among many large households, threatened with economic ruin by the reinforcement of the Penal Code in the summer of 1605, and only restrained from flying to arms on their own account by the pacific injunctions which the Pope at this time transmitted to them through the Jesuit Fathers. But some link was needed to connect the general discontent with the Gunpowder Plot. For this purpose, three rich men—Rookwood, who owned a stud of horses famous throughout the midlands, Sir Everard Digby and Tresham—were admitted as accessories, not to handle the gunpowder, but to prepare a rising to coincide with the explosion. Rookwood and Digby answered to the call. Through their agency numerous mansions lying between the Avon and the Severn were converted into places of arms, the resort of mysterious horsemen by day and night.

Shake-
speare's
neigh-
bourhood
to the
conspir-
ators

Within an easy ride of several of these centres of treason, Clopton House lay on the edge of the broken dingles and low hills that look down from the north over Stratford town. This convenient station was hired shortly before Michaelmas, at Rookwood's expense, and here Catesby, himself a native of that district, and other arch-conspirators met to concert their plots. Adjoining Clopton were the Welcombe lands, where Shakespeare had lately formed for himself a freehold estate, among the unforgotten hills of his boyhood. That very summer he had been investing yet more of his London winnings in the purchase of part of the Welcombe tithes.[1] In the autumn, in his passage to and fro upon the London road, in Stratford streets, or even among his own fields adjoining the very house of conspiracy, he might well have had speech with these new neighbours, greeted young Rookwood in his " Hungarian riding cloak, lined all in velvet exceeding costly," wondered what business or pleasure brought so many gallants to Clopton, and so passed on—

> For every man hath business and desire,
> Such as it is.

Tresham
mars the
plot

But the last of the three accessories admitted to the secret lacked the spirit of Digby or Rookwood. Tresham, who had a few years back been as deep as any in the treasonable counsels of the Jesuits, had lately succeeded to great wealth, he was related to several peers in the doomed House of Lords, and he lacked the pure zeal to con-template undismayed so horrid a massacre. He entered into con-spiracy with his Catholic brother-in-law, Lord Monteagle, to prevent

---

[1] For the full details of this curious coincidence in time and place, see *Fraser's Mag.*, April, 1878. See also Sidney Lee, *Shakespeare's Life and Work* (ed. 1900), pp. 103, 143, for Shakespeare's purchases.

the whole design without sacrificing the lives of those who had trusted him. A letter, carefully composed for this purpose, was conveyed to Monteagle and by him passed on to the Government, after a little preliminary farce which successfully notified to the conspirators that the plot was being revealed.[1] It is probable that Cecil, now Earl of Salisbury, received his first warning from this famous letter. It is certain that he had no source of detailed information as to who the traitors were, for he made no attempt to arrest them. They lingered safely in the capital till the 5th of November ; then fled unquestioned into the conntry ; and if they had not there betrayed themselves by raising open insurrection, the whole gang would have escaped, except their devoted sentinel, Guy Fawkes.

At three in the afternoon of the 4th of November, the eve of the day on which Parliament was to meet and be destroyed, the Earl of Suffolk looked in for a moment upon the solitary watchman, and asked him to whom the faggots belonged. After such an interview, any man of human mould would have fled. But Fawkes, though he knew that Government had received the warning letter, that the lumber-room was not the usual promenade for members of the Privy Council, and that the name of Percy as the owner of the faggots would scarcely allay any suspicions that might have prompted so strange a visit, chose rather to face the nine chances that he would be seized and tortured, than to lose the one chance that he might still be left to do the deed. At ten o'clock one of his friends stole in, to bid him Godspeed, and left him a watch to tell the fateful hours. At eleven o'clock he was standing outside. Strange men came round him. Some went in to examine the faggots. When they came out again he was knocked down, fiercely struggling, and bound with his own garters.

Early the next morning the other conspirators could have been seen galloping into the country, at top speed, to raise the now desperate rebellion. A few score of rebels joined their cavalcade, but they found that the ardour of many, who a few days back had been eager for the fray, was chilled by the news that a murderous

Arrest of Guy Fawkes, 4th Nov., 1605

Flight of the conspirators, 5th Nov.

---

[1] Monteagle had the letter brought to him while he was at supper and caused it to be read aloud before all the attendants by a gentleman in his service, who was intimately connected with the conspirators and who, in fact, immediately informed them. The important part of the letter was as follows : " I would advise you as you tender your life, to devise some excuse to shift your attendance at this Parliament ; for God and man hath concurred to punish the wickedness of this time. And think not slightly of this advertisement but retire yourself into the country, where you may expect the event in safety, for though there be no appearance of any stir, yet I say they shall receive a terrible blow this Parliament, and they shall not see who hurts them." Whether James or Salisbury guessed that the last sentence meant a gunpowder plot, or whether Monteagle dropped some hint of it when he handed over the letter, is immaterial to the fact that the Government was still left in absolute ignorance of the names and whereabouts of the conspirators.

plot had failed. Catholics closed their doors upon them ; Protestants swarmed out to hunt them down. From house to house they fled before the sheriffs and men of the western shires. At Holbeche House in Staffordshire, wearied with their furious ride through the island, broken with despair, wounded by an avenging accident with their own gunpowder, they sank down, crying that their plot had all the while been a great sin, which they must now expiate by staying to die in that place. In a few hours the chase came up and men fired into the house as into a den of wild beasts. Catesby and others were killed on the spot. The survivors were carried off, several bleeding from mortal wounds, to trial and death in London.

Meantime, in the Tower, when silence could no longer save his friends, Fawkes under repeated tortures was day by day yielding up to the Council the story of the Plot, while around, from every wharf and labyrinth of the great city, rose the hum of terror and rage and triumph.

Trials and executions On the 1st of February, 1606, Fawkes was carried up the steps of the scaffold. In the spring, Garnet, dragged after many days from his lair behind the chimney in Hindlip House, was brought up to his famous trial at Guildhall. In an age when the rules of evidence were the rules of probability interpreted by prejudice, Government was able to persuade itself, and all good Protestants, that the Provincial of the English Jesuits had himself fostered the plot ; modern historians confine his fault to misprision of treason and acquiescence in that which it was his duty to prevent. Greenway, the Jesuit, who had taken a more active part, escaped oversea. The Catholic world, by a plausible though strained interpretation of a doubtful case, raised the cry that Garnet suffered death for concealing what he had learnt in confession, and rejoiced in the story of an image miraculously imprinted by his blood upon a straw of the scaffold.

Consequences of Gunpowder Plot If Watson's Plot had drawn the Government into better relations with the Jesuits, the Gunpowder Plot, traced to their influence and punished by the execution of their English Provincial, revived the feud beyond all healing. Together with new Penal Laws, an attempt was made to distinguish between the adherents of the Jesuits and of the seculars, with a view to relieving the latter from the savage penalties enacted against disloyal Catholics. All were required to take a new Oath of Supremacy, renouncing the doctrine that the Pope could depose Kings. The test did in fact very nicely distinguish the two factions, for while Paul V., instigated by the Jesuits, charged men, on the safety of their souls, to refuse an oath so contrary to his pretensions, the party of the seculars, led on this occasion by the Archpriest Blackwell himself, were in favour of swallowing the test to secure peace and good-will. This bitter quarrel, added to all the former causes of division, rendered Catholicism powerless for years to come.

Those who took the oath became, not legally but practically, exempt from the recusant fines. But those whose conscience forbade them to disregard the Pope's express order, were for the next dozen years subjected to an active though always irregular persecution. Some escaped by favour or obscurity ; more by paying blackmail to the rascally courtiers of King James ; others from time to time were cast into prison, were driven from their houses for months together, or suffered temporary sequestration of their lands, About the year 1619 a new era of relief began for the English Catholics. when the advanced stage of the Spanish match put the whole body under royal protection. But ere that day they had suffered irreparable loss. The cruel but somewhat idle threatenings of the statute book for 1606 and 1610, were not the only outcome of the Gunpowder Plot : its more important consequences were that for a dozen years the King allowed some of the Penal Laws to be partially enforced ; that Popery became at last unfashionable in the hall and more than ever unpopular in the street ; that for a hundred years to come the religion of Guy Fawkes and the Jesuits was regarded as a creed so dark and murderous that any man who made political alliance with the Catholics, imperilled the adhesion of his supporters, or even the loyalty of his subjects. Such was the issue of the new state-craft, by which James had calculated to reconcile the English of all religions in common devotion to the throne.[1]

[1] For this account of Gunpowder Plot, see chiefly Rev. J. Gerard's *What was Gunpowder Plot ?* (1897), and Gardiner's conclusive reply, *What Gunpowder Plot was* (1897). Father Gerard's rejoinder, *The Gunpowder Plot and the Gunpowder Plotters* (1897), carries the controversy very little further.

CHAPTER IV

JAMES I.—PARLIAMENTS AND COURTIERS

" Le Roy s'avisera, the King will take thought of it " : really he should !
—*Historical Sketches*, CARLYLE.

Origins
and de-
velop-
ment of
the two
Houses

THE forms and functions of the English Parliament derived
from mediæval origins. The baron, able, when he chose, to
let war loose over the land from his castle-yard, consented to spare
his country so long as he was compensated with an hereditary share
in the counsels of State. The gentleman, the burgess and the yeoman, in days when the central power could do little to strengthen
the hands of the tax-collector against the passive resistance of a
scattered population, consented to fill the royal treasury, so long
as they were consulted as to the amount and reassured as to the
necessity of the royal demands. Such was the original meaning of
the House of Lords and of the House of Commons.

The Tudors retained the forms but altered the significance of our
Parliamentary institutions. By destroying the barons and their
armies, the King removed the only political power that could pre-
sume to name his Ministers or dictate his policy. Having thus
enslaved the Lords, he could safely make use of the Lower House.
Urged and directed by the Tudor monarchs, the Commons entered
into a career of legislative activity for which there had been no
scope in the more conservative ages gone by. As the royal instrument of religious and social reconstruction, they gained prestige
more than they lost independence. At a time when the Hapsburgs
and Valois were jealously trenching on the ancient liberties of their
Cortez and Etats Généraux, the English Parliament preserved its
privileges and increased its functions by becoming part of the new
English Monarchy. " The Crown in Parliament " became omnipotent
in the State.

In the days of the Plantagenet and Lancastrian dynasties,
Parliament often acted as opposition. But in those days it had
been the Peers who stirred up the Commons to criticise the King's
finance, and protected them when they impeached his servants.
When, therefore, the military power of the Lords had been destroyed
in the Wars of the Roses, the element of opposition disappeared
from both Houses together. During the century that divided the
battle of Bosworth from the defeat of the Armada, the Commons,
while they forgot how to resist the King, learnt to be independent
of the Lords. In the last years of Elizabeth, signs of a revival of
opposition came not from the Upper but from the Lower House ;
under the management of James, the Commons developed a new

tradition of political resistance, under a new class of leaders, and
created constitutional precedents more novel in reality than they
were in law.

The House of Commons represented all the independent classes, Classes
not as separate and jealous " estates," but as friendly partners in a repre-
common political heritage. The farmer and agricultural labourer, the Com-
since they enjoyed no social independence, exercised no political mons
franchise. But yeomen freeholders, though they seldom if ever
aspired to sit in Parliament, decided by their votes between the
knights, squires and baronets, who courted them hat in hand on
market days, when the writs were travelling down from London.
The yeomen were devotedly attached to the privileges of Parliament,
and the principle of no taxation without representation : these
watchwords were specially associated with their class pride as freeholders. As Fuller quaintly expresses it, the yeoman

hath a great stroke in making a Knight of the shire. Good reason, for he makes
a whole line in the Subsidy book,[1] not caring how much his purse is let blood, so
it be done by the advice of the physicians of State.[2]

But the feature most distinctive of the English Parliament was Borough
the method of mutual accommodation by which the gentry and the and
burgesses shared between them the anomalous representative County
system. The life and the wealth of England was to be found chiefly sentatives
in the farm and the manor house, yet the Chamber that represented
her opinion contained only 92 members for the counties, and some
400 members for the towns.[3] And yet, in practice, the country
gentlemen were well represented, for it was they who sat for the
boroughs. In the official returns of each Parliament we only find
the names of a score of " merchants," " aldermen," " recorders "
and " mayors " ; the remaining 350 and odd borough members,
with the exception of a few " sergeants-at-law," are entitled
" baronets," " knights," " esquires " and " gentlemen ". Although
a certain number of the boroughs were Cornish villages in the hands
of the Crown or of private landowners, the proportion was not in
the seventeenth century large ; the bulk of the elections were genuine
contests. Corruption of voters by money was not so general as it
afterwards became, but the power of great neighbouring families
was felt in the smaller towns, sometimes, probably in a very sinister
manner. But in many cases the English burghers deliberately preferred to look outside their own class for a member. Except the
men of London, Bristol and Plymouth, who usually chose one of
their merchant princes, the shopkeepers considered that the privileges
of Parliament were treated with more respect, and their own interests
with more attention, when the market-towns of Buckinghamshire

---

[1] The tax-collector's book.   [2] *The Holy State*, bk. ii., chap. xviii.
[3] The English shires and boroughs sent up two members each, and the Welsh
one. The numbers of the House rose during James's reign.

sent up such neighbours as the Verneys and the Hampdens, and the cities of Yorkshire spoke through a Wentworth or a Beaumont, a Cholmeley or a Fairfax. Nor did the English gentleman, like the French noble, scorn the political alliance of the "third estate"; but rather, in the pursuit of social estimation among his own equals, valued, next to representing the yeomen as county member, the scarcely inferior honour of sitting for the capital of the shire. So long as this mutual accommodation prevailed, the English chambers would not perish, like those of continental states, by the division of classes.

Character of the members of Parliament

The pick of the country gentlemen, sent by far-distant communities to act together for a few weeks in St. Stephen's Chapel, came up uncorrupted by previous contact with Vanity Fair. Except the lawyers resident at the Inns of Court, the members knew no more of London than that the merchants were honest men, and no more of Whitehall than that the courtiers were false knaves. The character and public spirit of the Commons under James and Charles I. were higher than in those subsequent periods of our history, when the Parliament men began to reside for a large part of each year on the scene of their more protracted labours, instituted a "London Season," haunted the Court and aspired to posts under the Crown. Until the Long Parliament the members had no thought of obtaining office. The edge was not taken off their patriotism by fear of losing favour at Court, nor was the spirit of inquiry smothered by that indifference to scandals and to blunders which is fostered by fashionable society and by official routine. As an opposition, no assembly of men at once so shrewd and so stalwart ever met to resist the abuse of power. But this homely ignorance of the great world, while it fortified their character as men, limited their outlook as politicians. They knew so little of the details of foreign affairs, of the cost of wars, of the preparation of armaments, that while they justly condemned they were unable to correct the *haute politique* of Buckingham. Fortunately, what the time required of them was not an alternative national policy, but the protection of national liberties; for that task the English squires were fitted by their birth, their traditions and the freshness of mind with which they came to each new Parliament from hunting deer, interviewing bailiffs and assessing poor-rates. Hundreds of forgotten men, who during the Parliaments of forty years, succeeded each other on the benches beside Coke, Eliot, Wentworth, Hyde and Pym, brought to the help of England a type of character that never reappeared in our history, marked by directness of intention and simplicity of mind, the inheritance of modest generations of active and hearty rural life, but informed by Elizabethan culture and inspired by Puritan religion.

English local life was the source and safeguard of English liberty, which Parliament only concentrated and expressed. During the

abeyance of Parliamentary opposition, the caprice of the Tudor Parlia-
monarchs had been restrained by the knowledge that any one shire ment leads
could assert its cause by a rebellion, and that, since no standing opinion in
army existed, such a rebellion could only be suppressed if the other the
districts were in a temper to march to the aid of the central Govern- country
ment. In the reign of James I. the House of Commons again became
the focus of local opinions, which otherwise would never have united
into a national policy. The isolated communities of England, divided
from each other by days of riding on steep and muddy roads, uninformed by newspapers, and perplexed by strange tales about
poisoners and papists at the Court, could only rely, for credible information and sober opinion, on the men whom they sent up to
Parliament to inquire into these matters on the spot. The Norfolk
parson, who distrusted " light scoffing wits not apt to deeper search,"
records in his diary that he would have been " free from all harder
censure " of the Duke of Buckingham, " but that the Parliament did
so oppose him ".[1] The Commons knowing their speeches to be the
sole voice and their resolutions the sole instruction of a politically
minded nation, would not even compromise on the greatest of the
privileges of Parliament—free speech within the walls of the House.
And very free speech it was. Foreigners, accustomed to the secret
intrigues of Paris and the silent obedience of Madrid, censured the
boldness but envied the impunity of the Opposition, when some
country gentleman, who had ridden up a few days before from his
home beyond the Dorset Downs, rose in his seat to abuse the highest
Minister of State, and was suffered to walk back unmolested through
the darkening streets to his lodgings in Holborn. It was only when
the session had ended that the King dared to lay by the heels a few
of the boldest speakers.

The Commons well knew what had happened to representative The Com-
bodies in other lands. Foreign ambassadors lodged complaints of mons con-
the abuse showered upon their masters, who were described in the scious of their his-
House as " overthrowing the Parliaments throughout Christendom," torical
and reducing their subjects by arbitrary taxation to " wear only position.
wooden shoes on their feet ".[2] " England," cried the member for
Somerset, " is the last monarchy that yet retains her liberties. Let
them not perish now ! " The Commons therefore knew that they
must look, not to the " rights of nations " or to any theories of
government prevalent in that age, but to definite laws and customs
peculiar to England. As historians they unearthed a period in
English history from the thirteenth to the fifteenth century, when
Parliament had controlled the counsels of the Crown ; and as lawyers
they pleaded statutes of the same period, which forbade the encroachments of royal power in specific matters, such as the imposi-
tion of particular kinds of taxation. Thus an antiquarian revival,

---

[1] Rous, p. 30.   [2] Rushworth, i., p. 573.

instituted by several hundred of the most hard-headed men in the country, decided the future of our island. The partisans of absolutism pleaded the equally valid Tudor precedents, and demonstrated that even in the Middle Ages the custom of the Constitution had by no means always followed the statutes, in which the Parliaments had but recorded claims never heartily allowed by the King.

The theoretical basis and the legal limits of Parliamentary privilege and royal prerogative, questions wisely left to sleep by the late Queen and her loving subjects, occupied the full attention of James's first Parliament, which after sitting for four sessions over a space of six years, was " broken " in 1610 to make way for the first long period of unparliamentary Stuart despotism.

The Commons challenge the theory of Divine Right, 1604-10

The King was the first to open the high debate. The light head of the scholar was turned by the new wine of an absolutist theory of government, as alien to the mediæval English Constitution, as were the later theories of " King Pym " and " Freeborn John Lilburne ". The claim of the Pope as Vicar of Christ to depose sovereigns had driven the champions of Protestant monarchies to invent a rival dogma. A Divine Right was asserted to be inherent in Kings : not acquired, as the Jesuits taught, by clerical or by popular consent, but by heredity. James, as Divine hereditary sovereign, made haste to state his claims to an authority that would have flattered the pride of the Castilian monarch.

The state of monarchy (he told his first Parliament) is the supremest thing upon earth : for Kings are not only God's lieutenants upon earth and sit upon God's throne, but even by God Himself they are called gods.

Hence there was no place for constitutional discussion of a prerogative that had no limits.

As to dispute what God may do is blasphemy, so it is sedition in subjects to dispute what a King may do in height of his power. I will not be content that my power be disputed on.

The House of Commons, so he told its members, " derived all matters of privilege from him " ; it sat, not in its own right, but of his grace.

The sudden challenge was taken up at once and by the whole House. There was no Royalist party in St. Stephen's before the Long Parliament ; nor, beyond the King's own servants, did any section of any class in the country believe in the theory of Divine Right as applied by James. The members of his first House of Commons, with unanimity recorded their solemn dissent from the royal utterances. When in the first session His Majesty asserted that Parliamentary privilege was not of right but of grace, they told him that he had been " misinformed," and when in the last he challenged their right to discuss the limits of his prerogative, they replied :—

We hold it an ancient, general and undoubted right of Parliament to debate freely all matters which properly concern the subject and his right or state ; which freedom of debate being once foreclosed, the essence of the liberty of Parliament is withal dissolved.

The new claims of personal authority advanced by the Stuarts Efficiency were connected with new plans for national efficiency. Their best and freeservants, Salisbury, Bacon and Strafford, saw, like Richelieu, that dom a country must be equipped with the machinery of centralised government and of productive taxation if she was to keep her place in the modern world. James and Charles I. aimed at union with Scotland, a good army, and a new system of finance. In every one of these objects they were defeated, partly by their own lack of economy and administrative talent, partly by the resistance of the Commons, who opposed the strengthening of the central power as dangerous to local and Parliamentary rights. That danger passed away as soon as the central power became representative. In the reigns of William III. and Anne the Whig Ministers carried out the schemes of James I.—united, taxed and armed Great Britain, and so enabled her in the eighteenth century to take a place in the world's politics higher than that of countries which had purchased a brief period of efficiency by a lasting sacrifice of their freedom.

The issue came up under various forms in the Parliament of Question 1604-10. A Royal Commission appointed to consider James's of Union favourite project—the closer union of England and Scotland—had Scotland, recommended free-trade in commerce, and the naturalisation of all 1604-7 Scots born after their King's accession to the English throne. The House of Commons rejected both proposals, though the latter came into effect in spite of them, by the workings of the common law.[1]

Commercial fears of free-trade, national ignorance and hatred of Scotchmen, were combated in vain by the wisest man in the House. When Sir Francis Bacon assured his brother members that the Scots were " in their capacities and understandings a people ingenious, in labour industrious, in courage valiant," the members listened with an incredulous smile to praises lavished by the Court aspirant on barbarians as poor, and therefore as despicable, as the wild tribes of Ireland. The Puritan House of Commons had yet to learn, in an hour of dire need, the true qualities of their " brother Scots ". None the less, Parliament had good reasons for its decision. The innocent proposals which they rejected were steps towards such a fusion of the laws and Governments of the two nations as would have rendered the King independent alike of Scottish nobles and of English Parliaments. James by a characteristic figure expressed his desire for this further union :—

I am the husband and all the whole Isle is my wife. I hope, therefore, that no man will be so unreasonable as to think that I, that am a Christian King under the Gospel, should be the Polygamist and husband to two wives.

[1] The naturalisation of the " post-nati " (Scottish subjects of James born after his accession to the English throne) was effected by a decision of the English law courts in the case of the infant Colvill (born at Edinburgh, 1605), or " Calvin " as he is called in the English law books. Thus the judges, rightly interpreting the common law, overrode the policy of the Commons, who wished to keep the Scots as aliens.

But the members of the House of Commons, fearing for British freedom, refused in 1607 to countenance an Union, which in 1707 their successors passed under changed conditions, as the surest guarantee of those very liberties.

Finance

But it was impossible to neglect for a hundred years the need for a more productive system of taxation, a problem which, after the death of the parsimonious Queen, continually returned to vex and embroil Kings with their Parliaments. Elizabeth had waged the most serious of England's wars with a revenue no larger than that which James exhausted in time of peace.[1] At slight expense to herself and her subjects, she had presided over a Court, corrupt indeed, but famous to all ages for wisdom in politics and for excellence in literature ; James, at a vast charge to the nation, maintained a Court no less corrupt, but notorious for folly and lack of taste. When the King realised that he was spending at the rate of from £500,000 to £600,000 a year, and thereby incurring an annual deficit of from £50,000 to £150,000, he was the more willing to exert to the utmost all the prerogative rights of the Crown which could bring in a revenue.

Imposi-
tions,
Bate's
case,
1606-10

The regulation of trade with foreign countries, by Impositions of duties at the ports, and by the grant or sale of trading monopolies, was a power that rested, by the custom of the Tudor Queens, not with Parliament but with the Crown. It had hitherto been regarded rather as an administrative function than as a financial advantage, but the increasing volume of English trade enabled the needy James to find in it a source of large and independent revenue. The Book of Rates which he issued, was an attempt to systematise the import duties on many various articles ; and the commercial and financial policy involved in the tariff was determined by the Privy Council Commissioners of Trade, afterwards turned by Charles I. into a Council of Trade.[2] In 1606 the resistance of a merchant named Bate to a new form of these duties, brought the whole question of impositions before the Judges, who decided that the King had acted within his legal rights. The Commons, not yet aware of all the points at issue between themselves and the Crown, paid no attention to the matter in the following session of 1608 ; but in the two sessions of 1610 they realised that the power of the purse, the chief safeguard of their liberties, would slip from them as trade increased, unless this right to lay Impositions was at once challenged. A vigorous controversy ensued. Statutes of Edward I. clearly prohibiting the levy of duties without consent of Parliament, were quoted in the House ; while the Crown lawyers advanced Tudor precedent and Tudor statutes

---

[1] Elizabeth's receipts Mich. 30 Eliz. to Mich. 31 Eliz. (1588-89) were £344,931 19s. 8¼d. (*Pell's Declarations*). In 1597-98 they were £414,311 7s. 11½d. James's revenue was between £400,000 and £500,000 (see G., i., pp. 294, 295 ; G., ii., pp. 113, 114).

[2] Cunningham, i., pp. 200, 201, 221 note, 289 ; ii., pp. 900-12.

that implied the existence of the right.[1] The question, still undecided, became merged in all the other questions at issue between
Parliament and King.

Side by side with the controversy over Impositions, a friendly The
negotiation was being conducted to put the whole financial system Great
on a new footing. The Great Contract, which Salisbury attempted Contract,
to make with Parliament, was to commute the antiquated and 1610
vexatious feudal rights of the Crown for a permanent settlement of
£200,000 a year, which together with the other sources of income
should have met the annual expenditure of £600,000. Both sides
were desirous of coming to such terms as would at once supply the
financial needs of England, and put an end to the use of prerogative
powers to raise money without Parliament : for James would on
these terms forego his right to Impositions.

But at the last moment religious and political misunderstanding
prevented financial agreement. As early as 1604 the Commons
had protested against the deprivation of their favourite clergy, the
300 silenced Puritan pastors. As the sessions came and went, the
complaints on this head were strengthened by others, touching all
the points of the religious question—the imperfect enforcement of
the Penal Laws ; non-residence, so common with the inefficient
type of incumbents favoured by the Bishops ; and the swelling
pride shown by those prelates to all classes of men in their ecclesiastical
courts. James, always in arms to defend the episcopal power, was
still more indignant to find his Parliaments seeking to interfere in
his own management of the Church. The Great Contract was broken
off through mutual suspicion, the dispute on Impositions was left
undecided, and finally, in February, 1611, the Houses were dissolved.
The King determined henceforth to carry on affairs free from the
vexatious cavilling of a Parliament.

The dissolution of James's first Parliament marks the moment Breach
when the " establisher of perpetual peace in Church and Common- with
wealth " had fairly set on foot the three great feuds of Stuart England Parlia-
—the Constitutional, the Catholic, the Puritan. The first nine years dissolu-
of King James, the seed-time of our politics, had proved the harvest tion,
season of our literature, the fruitful autumn of the Elizabethan age. 1610-11
The production of *Hamlet* fitly honoured the last year of the great
Queen, but *Othello*, *Macbeth* and *Lear* ushered in the new reign ;
and only in the year 1611, when James broke the Parliament, did Retire-
Shakespeare retire to Stratford and to the silence that he maintained ment of
till his death (1616).   Shake-
                                                                    speare,
                                                                    1611

From February, 1611, to January, 1621, no Parliament met, except during the two months of 1614, when the " Addled " Parliament

---

[1] Prothero, lxxiii-vi. He thinks the Commons were technically on doubtful
ground. Gardiner (ii., p. 79) holds the opposite view.

expressed the anger, but demonstrated the impotence of the
electoral classes. For a whole decade public affairs were abandoned
to the chance intrigues of a Court, so managed as to exclude from its
precincts the many able and conscientious men whom England then
contained. As there was no organised Civil Service, and, during the
abeyance of Parliament, no political life outside the circle of the
Palace, the public servant had to purchase his position by a life of
bribery and sycophancy. Bacon, with his eye fixed on lofty public
ends, overlooked the baseness of the means. Archbishop Abbot,
after long trying, like William Penn in later days, to combine influence
at a bad Court with the conscience of a good man, fell into honourable
disgrace. The more self-respecting of the Lords preferred the retirement of their mansions, or the society of famous men in Italy,
France and Spain, to Court masques, in which ladies were too drunk
to perform their parts,[1] divorce cases and adulteries favoured by the
sovereign, and the whisper, scarcely hushed, of scandals yet more
vile. Others, who might have served the country well, were kept
at home by the lavish expenses fashionable at the Court of Elizabeth's
successor, when political aspirants were expected to give feasts at
£1,000 apiece, present costly hangings, horses and jewellery to all
officers and favourites according to their degree, and sit down to
dicing-tables where parks and manors were thrown away. Only the
rich were able, and only the mean were willing to seek State employment on such terms. English politics were then more a matter of
personal relations than they have ever been before or since. A time
had been when hereditary prestige and military power had secured
for each baron his place by the throne ; a time was to come when,
under the supremacy of Parliament, great principles and great interests
involved the fortunes of statesmen. But at this epoch the royal
government, not even systematised as a bureaucracy, was a chaos
of personal intrigue. The change from a wise Queen to a foolish
King removed all the good, and brought out all the bad which this
most elastic type of polity rendered possible.

Salisbury   Until 1612 the worst influences at Court were kept in partial
restraint by the presence at the head of affairs of Robert Cecil,
become Earl of Salisbury and Lord Treasurer. He owed nothing
to favourites, but held office by his own prestige as chief minister to
the late Queen, and prime negotiator of the peaceful accession.
Though far from a great, he was by no means an unworthy man ; he
continued to regard the Puritan and Parliamentary questions with
the eyes of an Elizabethan official, but he would never, like the
impatient doctrinaire whom he served, have willingly brought the
quarrel to a head. Though far from scrupulous, he was alsolutely
honest to his cause : like most of his colleagues he received a secret
pension from the King of Spain, but his policy remained firmly

[1] G., i., p. 300.

anti-Spanish. So long as he lived, the Stuart House was never caught in the fatal net of alliance with Catholic powers ; and even the domestic government, though less under his control, was more respectable and cautious than it became when he was no longer there to restrain the favourites. In everything he maintained the Elizabethan tradition, hostile to Spain without and to the Catholics within, but desirous of peace and unfavourable to the Puritans. This had been the school founded by his father, William Cecil, and to this the son would still have adhered though he had lived to be a hundred.

The other and less orthodox school of Elizabethan statesman- **Raleigh** ship, the war party that desired to seize the Spanish colonies, was represented by Sir Walter Raleigh. James from the first moment of his accession turned to the safer policy and the less brilliant man. Raleigh, warned from the royal presence, lost all footing in the heartless Court ; his froward genius had made for him many enemies, and few admirers outside the taverns, where seafaring men celebrated the epic of the Spanish main. The conduct of the disgraced and angry courtier aroused false suspicions : his friend, Lord Cobham, no less disgusted with the distribution of favours at the new Court, had trifled criminally with the idea of placing James's cousin, Arabella Stuart,[1] on the throne. Cobham's plot had gone little further than **Cobham's** abortive negotiations with Spanish agents ; Raleigh, though he may **plot, 1603** have heard more than was safe from his dangerous friend, was certainly not implicated. When the story came before the Privy Council, Cobham, contradicting and retracting his own evidence at every turn, accused Raleigh of having led him into the mischief. So little was the hero whom posterity celebrates understood by his contemporaries, that he was brought to trial on the charge of concocting this treason with his life-long foe, the Spaniard. " Thou hast a Spanish heart, and thyself art a viper of hell," cried Coke, the most brutal Attorney-General who ever served the Stuarts, though afterwards the proudest Judge who ever withstood their usurpations. The friendless prisoner, entrapped in the meshes of a legal procedure that required him to prove his innocence alone

---

[1] This poor lady, who resembled Lady Jane Grey in her gentle character, her claims upon the English throne and her sad resulting fate, had not, like her predecessor in misfortune, any party of her own. Her fate was as undeserved and as unnecessary as it was pitiful and romantic. She refused to head the Catholics, who at first had looked towards her ; and Cecil acknowledged that she had given Cobham no encouragement in his folly. She therefore escaped, for six years, the jealousy of her royal cousin, and lived quietly and innocently at his Court, until she had the unique misfortune to love and to be loved by the one man in all his kingdoms whom James would not allow her to marry. This was William Seymour, also a claimant to the throne. In 1610 they married secretly, were imprisoned by the King, escaped severally, and tried to fly to the continent to meet there and live beyond the range of Courts and politicians. William reached Ostend. Arabella lingered for news of him and was taken at sea. She died in prison after four years' misery.

against a hostile tribunal, was mewed up, a condemned traitor, in the Tower of London. Cecil had taken little part in the persecution of his rival. It was not till after the Lord Treasurer's death, and after the triumph of the Spanish party, abhorrent to all schools of Elizabethan statesmanship alike, that Raleigh, let out like a bird from the trap to soar towards the sun, was struck down dead out of the sky.

Death of Prince Henry, 1612   The Elizabethan tradition, which could' not wholly pass away while Salisbury still lived, seemed likely to renew its youth whenever Prince Henry should succeed to his father's throne. There was every reason to expect that the monarchy would then again be vigorous, popular, actively Protestant in foreign affairs, perhaps even warlike. But a game of tennis and a fever changed the fate of England and removed Henry Stuart from the scene before he had begun to play his part. The same year, 1612, saw the death of the old counsellor and the young Prince who would both have checked James in his unseemly attachment to favourites and in his unfortunate alliance abroad.

Government by favourites   When Salisbury and Prince Henry were dead, the King entered without restraint on a course of conduct and policy towards which he had long been drifting. He deprived the Privy Council Board of its functions as a consultative body ; and left the great Lords who sat round it to discover, with increasing chagrin, that they were confined to the mechanical details of administration. Meanwhile, at some country seat within a day's ride of London, under the trees after the deer had been pulled down, or at the table after the last bottle had been emptied, James arranged the outline of high policy in familiar discourse with a single favourite, whose claim to advancement was neither birth nor wisdom, but beauty of face and graceful though discourteous manners. Consequences followed of grave import to the system of monarchy in England. The House of Lords was alienated from the Crown by the affront to the dignity of birth, which was only made worse when the upstarts became Earls and Dukes. Individual Peers, no less affronted in their dignity as men, nursed the feelings, and one day espoused the cause, of political revolt. The common subjects of the land lost that respect for the " Lords of the Council " and for the whole system of monarchical administration, which no mere difference with the religious or foreign policy of their sovereign had ever shaken under the virile rule of the Tudors.

Carr and the Essex divorce, 1613   This new system of government was soon implicated in a scandal such as often precedes the fall of dynasties. The Howards were the most worthless of the political nobility of that day. While the fit representative of their great name, Belted Will, the watchman of Naworth, was guiding the Border through the generation of anarchy that intervened between the centuries of unbroken war

and the centuries of final peace, the Howards of the Court, deserting
in public the old religion to which they still adhered, served King
James with sycophancy and evil counsel.   Though they held among
them many of the highest offices of State, they saw that, to secure
their position with the fond King, they must enter into a treaty
with the young Scotchman, Robert Carr.   The favourite himself,
anxious to cement an alliance of such great mutual advantage,
cast about to marry Lady Francis Howard, daughter of the Earl
of Suffolk.   Since the lady loved Carr as intensely as she hated her
husband, the Earl of Essex, the confederates determined, without
blasting her character, to secure her divorce.   The King, in whom
the sense of personal dignity was weaker than the sense of personal
obligation, took a gracious interest in the unedifying details of the
case.   The divorce was obtained by royal influence, in spite of the
stand made by Abbot, the Puritan Primate.   Essex retired, not for
ever, into private life.   Carr, created Earl of Somerset, to celebrate
the occasion, led his hard-won bride to the altar, in the smile of
royalty and amid the congratulations of an envious Court.   Seldom
had a triumph, so shamefully won, been so openly celebrated.   But
worse remained behind, such as even James could not stomach.
After leading the Court for two years, the Countess of Somerset was **Fall of**
cast headlong by the appalling revelation that she had secured her **the**
divorce by the murder of Sir Thomas Overbury.   James, who was **Somer-**
not a wicked man, insisted that the trial of his ill-chosen friends **sets,**
should be a spectacle no less public than their marriage.   Husband **1615-16**
and wife were both condemned, the latter justly, the former with
less certain justice.   The lives of both were spared.   The revealing
flood of these events did much to disgust common men with the
royal government ; yet more it filled Puritan households in remote
halls and farmsteads with the dark indignation of the righteous
suppressed.   Such, they saw, were the men whom the King delighted
to honour ; these were they who, concealed papists themselves, were
permitted to trouble Israel and cast out the godly preaching pastors.

On the ruins of Carr's fortune rose a more splendid and stable **Rise of**
edifice.   Though it was solely by charm, wit and beauty that George **George**
Villiers, afterwards Earl and Duke of Buckingham, first found favour **Villiers**
with the King, a certain magnanimity, combined with some talent
for administration, soon fixed his power at a point far above that
reached by his predecessor.   As early as 1619 he was more than
favourite, he was sole ruler of the land ; he did not need to seek the
alliance of great families, but taught the highest to come to him as
the sole fount of honour.   The Howards made a last attempt to
attract the attention of James to another youth, whom they prepared by washing " his face every day with posset curd ".   But
every device failed, and they were driven from all the offices of State.
This change of ministry rendered the public service less bad and

wasteful, for Buckingham could conduct the ordinary routine of domestic affairs. His talents rendered his monopoly of power more absolute, and drove further from all hope of advancement every man who would not come, cap in hand, to flatter his strongest passion, vanity. Efficient as an administrator, as a statesman he was below contempt. Without one political conviction beyond the belief in his own right to supreme power, he moved in a perpetual atmosphere of excitement and change, adopting with equal passion each side of a question in turn, as pique or ennui dictated.

Relations with Spain

The peace with Spain, negotiated by James and Cecil in 1604,[1] was the first condition of English development in the seventeenth century. A great war, for which Parliament and the Puritans often clamoured without counting the cost, would have swallowed up all the resources, all the attention, and all the enthusiasm of the English ; would perhaps have strengthened monarchy here, as did the wars of Gustavus in Sweden ; and would certainly have drawn away the meagre flow of our colonisation far from the yet uninhabited shores of Virginia and New England, to South American conquests, where climate, gold mines and coloured labour would have prevented the healthy and vigorous development of our race. Unfortunately, from the death of Salisbury, the last of the orthodox Elizabethans, to the death of his master twelve years later, there was no middle party at Court between those who wished to wage war on Spain, and those who were willing to conduct our foreign policy in close concert with advices from Madrid. The fall of Carr, who had been hand in glove not only with the Catholic Howards but with the Spanish Ambassador himself, was the signal for a great effort by the war party to consummate their purpose. The first step was to persuade the King to loose Raleigh upon Spanish America on some ostensibly neutral mission, as in days of old Drake had been loosed, in peace the harbinger of war. Villiers, the rising hope of the war party, at first supported the scheme. But the light wind of his favour had shifted round to the Spanish quarter, even before Raleigh had set sail.

Raleigh's expedition, 1617-18

Never did an expedition set out under worse auspices. The prisoner from the Tower had nothing but splendid memories and utter desperation to drive him on. Hatred and treachery waited for him at home, and sailed with him in his fleet. Even the mariners

[1] This peace was one of Cecil's best strokes of statesmanship, and one of the few cases in which James's practice of king-craft was not worse than his theory. We refused to admit the illegality of our trade with Spanish America ; and we refused to give over carrying Dutch goods in our capacity as neutrals, or to prevent the Dutch from paying English subjects to fight for them against Spain. Thus, while securing in permanence all the advantages of peace, we gave up nothing of our own interests, or of those of our allies the Dutch, who chose to go on fighting for a few years longer, until they realised that they could not conquer the Spanish Netherlands. The final truce between Holland and Spain was in 1609.

he was able to enlist were a " scum of men " ; the right breed shrank
from so hopeless an enterprise. He had pledged himself to the King
to find and work a gold mine in Spanish Guiana without fighting the
Spaniards. He ended by fighting the Spaniards without finding the
gold mine. While he remained in the ships, watching against the
coming of the Spanish fleet, a party of his men went up the Orinoco
to explore. The first thing they came across was a Spanish settlement barring their progress up the river. They were soon overpowered in the dense forest by the Spanish marksmen, and fell back
in rout to the coast, bringing back to Raleigh the dead body of his
son. He sailed home to meet his fate. He had disappointed the
war party ; the favourite was against him ; the Spanish Ambassador
demanded his head. Even Elizabeth would only have forgiven his
attack on a friendly power if he had brought back plunder to share
with her ; and he was coming back empty-handed to James. He
was executed under the unjust sentence of treason passed on him a
dozen years back. Raleigh died a victim, not so much to the sacred
cause of international peace, as to the King's now fixed resolve to
divert the whole policy of England to the hard task of propitiating
Spain. From this moment forward, until the crisis of 1624, James, by
the advice of Buckingham, adhered to the policy of the Spanish match.

To marry the heir to the throne with a princess from the Escurial, The
would involve an immediate revolution in the existing system of Spanish
Church and State. Our foreign policy, the essence of which was match
that we should be regarded as the reserve champion of Protestantism
if all others were beaten to their knees, would be abandoned, and
perhaps reversed. At home the establishment of the Spanish
Infanta as the English Queen would convert the most privileged and
not the least influential wing of the Palace into an office for the
Jesuit emissaries, an asylum for the great English Catholics, and a
school where future Ministers and favourites would learn that
Catholicism was fashionable in society and profitable in politics.
The terms of the Queen's residence would lift the threat of the
Penal Laws from her co-religionists in every corner of the land ;
and both the House of Commons and the Spanish Ambassador
expressed the opinion that a free Catholic propaganda would render
possible, in course of time, the re-establishment of Catholic supremacy.
Last, but not least, there would be every prospect of a long succession
of Catholic kings. The influence of the Catholic mother, Mary of
Medici, over her children had, on the death of Henry IV., ruined the
Protestant cause in France ; the influence of Henrietta Maria over
her children was destined, after the death of Charles I., to endanger
it in England. In the age before the Great Rebellion had set limits
to the royal prerogative, it was regarded as certain that the heir to
an unbounded sovereignty, if brought up in the atmosphere of
Spanish Catholicism, would attempt in England the reaction which

the sword of Tilly and Wallenstein effected in equally Protestant countries abroad.

National
feeling
hostile
For such reasons, rightly or wrongly, our ancestors estimated that the Spanish match might some day bring down in ruin, long prepared, our national life and institutions, which were wholly incompatible with the Catholic system. England was threatened by her kings with the establishment of an alien influence that might undermine both public rights and private property. More than any other part of James's schemes, more than his ejection of the Puritan pastors, far more than his desertion of the continental Protestants in their hour of need, this project of the Spanish match made the ordinary man a Puritan at least in his politics. Selfish as well as generous passions were enlisted. The holders of Abbey lands were alarmed. Over this matter concurred those who feared for their estates, those who feared for their country, and those who feared for their religion.

The sentiment of nationalism has in its nature no political affinities either with liberty on the one hand or with tyranny on the other ; it can be turned by some chance current of events, or by the cunning or clumsiness of statesmen, to run in any channel and to work any wheel. In the course of the world's history it has lent to many different causes, some good and some bad, a power which they would never otherwise have obtained. For a hundred years the foreign policy of the Stuarts drove the forces of nationalism to aid the cause of Protestant enthusiasm and civic freedom.

Prince Henry had grasped the objections to a Catholic marriage as firmly as if he had foreseen the ruin it was destined to bring upon his House. When James proposed to marry him to a French Catholic, he was so " resolved that two religions should not lie in his bed," that he prepared to fly to the continent and marry a German Protestant. But he was dead now, and his brother Charles was not of the same mould.

Position
of English
Catholics
improved,
1619
When the Spanish match, so often before contemplated and laid aside, became, after Raleigh's execution, the principal motive of policy, toleration had to be extended to the English Catholics. The twelve black years which had brought such miseries on those who refused to take the oath prescribed after the Gunpowder Plot, were succeeded by twenty years white in the annals of English Catholicism. The evil race of pursuivants were warned off the victims on whose fears and miseries they fed ; the unwilling judges were commanded to release the Catholics from every prison in England ; the recusancy fines dwindled to an insignificant part of the revenue. The persecution continued only in districts where the Justices of Peace were indifferent or hostile to the influence of the central Government. From 1619 until the meeting of the Long Parliament. except during a brief period of reaction in 1625, the

great majority of Catholics remained in comfort on condition of seeking obscurity, while a few obtained an ostentatious influence which brought jealousy on all.

This new phase of royal policy permanently altered the relations Gondo- of the Catholics to the Crown. The memories of 1605-6 were ob- mar literated, and the Stuarts henceforth had no more faithful servants than the party which they shielded from so much rage. But the new policy of toleration alienated the Catholics yet further from their fellow-subjects. It was recommended to the nation in the first instance, not as mercy shown to Englishmen, but as a favour done to Spain. Spanish pride was incarnate in her Ambassador, Gondomar. This man, at once the terror and delight of James, acquired, next to Buckingham, the most powerful voice in English affairs. But above all he was lord and champion of the English recusants. On his visit to Spain in 1618, he made a triumphal procession from London to Dover, with a train of a hundred priests whom James liberated from prison to do him honour. When he returned, the great English Catholics waited upon him in the ante- rooms and worshipped in the chapel of the Spanish embassy, till the French Ambassador, who maintained a rival asylum of the faith, jealously complained of their neglect. Caricatures, lampoons and sermons directed against Spain were, at Gondomar's instigation, punished by the Privy Council.

The sight of England ruled by the advice of a Spaniard aroused Popular the coarse brutality of the London mob. The cruelty of their feeling against feelings towards the Catholics were regulated by the rise and fall of Catholics the royal clemency. At the time of the final crisis of the marriage in negotiation (1623), the quiet of Puritan Sunday in London was London disturbed by the crashing fall of an upper storey, in which a hundred devotees had secretly met to listen to the exhortations of a Jesuit ; a crowd at once assembled round the ruins, but not to relieve those who still suffered or to disentangle the heaps of dead ; the prentices stood raising angry cries at the discovery of this nest of Jesuits, while their masters went home to cheer the Sabbath evening with pious discourse on the clear judgment of God. Bickerings in the streets with Gondomar's servants led to serious riots. Once the embassy was assaulted, and the inmates only saved from massacre by the strength of the doors and the timely arrival of the popular Lord Mayor (1618). James was compelled to override the magis- trates in order to secure punishment of the offenders. Three years later, on a similar provocation, he came down in person to Guildhall to champion the honour of Spain, threatening to put a garrison in the city and suspend its charter. For sixty years London had been the home of anti-Spanish and of anti-Catholic feeling, but it was a new thing that those two fiercest passions of Cheapside, so long the test of loyalty, should now be directed against the Crown.

7

The Bo-
hemian
and
Palatin-
ate
questions,
1620

In 1620 events took place in the upland countries of continental Europe which complicated the relations of maritime Spain and England, altered the significance of the proposed marriage treaty, brought to a head English discontent with the King's policy, and forced him at last to summon a Parliament in which that discontent could find voice. Bohemia was occupied by the Austrians and the Rhenish Palatinate by the Spaniards. Both these territories were seized in the interest of Catholicism, and at the expense of Frederic, Elector Palatine, husband of James's daughter Elizabeth. The claim of the Palatinate Prince to the throne of Bohemia had been the invitation of its rebellious nobles and people, who called him across Europe to defend feudal anarchy against Imperial despotism, and religious rights, won long ago by Ziska's dreaded sword, against the oncoming tide of Jesuit reaction. At this summons, the uncounselled Frederic had left his safe patrimony on the banks of the Rhine to become the leader of an outlandish people in a cause which was only injured by his championship, and which was to involve his family and his heritage on the Rhine, the Protestant religion and the German people, in the irrecoverable disasters of the Thirty Years' War. James correctly refused to support his son-in-law in Eastern Europe. The conquest of Bohemia by the Austrians, and the suppression of Protestantism within its ancient mountain barriers, could not deeply concern our island people, who knew no reason to smile when seamen were represented at the London theatres as landing in the " deserts of Bohemia ".[1] But it concerned us more nearly that the Spaniards, from their base in the Netherlands, had overrun the Rhenish Palatinate. James, who had a Scotchman's sense of duty to his kindred, would not let the rightful heritage of his grandchildren be taken from them, least of all by the chiefs of a victorious Catholic confederacy. To obtain a restoration, it was necessary to make Spain and Austria believe that England would. in the last resort, send great armies on to the Rhine ; but unfortunately, the Cabinet of Madrid, informed by the astute observation of Gondomar, regarded James's character as sufficient security against effective intervention. The impression that James was not in earnest, was confirmed when he attempted to persuade Philip voluntarily to evacuate the Palatinate as a condition of the proposed marriage of Prince Charles to the Infanta. So long as they could lead James astray in the vain pursuit of his own marriage project, the Spaniards felt perfectly secure of their position in the Palatinate ; while the English were enraged to see the disasters of continental Protestantism, which should at least have delivered them from the hated " Spanish match," only serve to bind their ruler more obstinately than ever to his projected outrage on their national independence.

James
and his
kindred

[1] *The Winter's Tale*, Act III., sc. 3.

But James was sufficiently alive to the necessity of preparing war, to feel bound to summon Parliament. For ten years he had governed without its help, and during all that time had been in want of money even for his peace establishment. After " breaking " the Addled Parliament of 1614, before it had either passed laws or voted taxes, he had attempted to fill the exchequer by raising " Benevolences," or free gifts of money from his subjects. Although the judges on circuit were employed to solicit contribution, the smallness of the sum collected in the towns and shires even by those formidable missionaries of the central power, shows how universally the rustic English, ignorant as they were of so much else, understood the constitutional issue. Passive resistance had its reward, for seven years later the occupation of the Palatinate rendered the King's needs imperative ; he had no choice but to summon Parliament to meet in January, 1621.

During the period of unparliamentary government (1611-21), the rights of the subject had been defended by a lawyer. What Parliament could not assert on behalf of the nation, a single Judge had asserted on behalf of himself and of the law of England. Sir Edward Coke, one of the most disagreeable figures in our history, is one of the most important champions of our liberties. At a dangerous period in the development of the constitutional struggle, it was he who first revived the theory that the law was not the instrument but the boundary of royal prerogative, and that the Judges were not, as his rival Bacon declared : " lions under the throne," but umpires between King and subject. His ferocious power of self-assertion, working through the medium of a legal learning, memory and intellect seldom equalled even on the English Bench, caused his brethren, who were almost equally afraid of Chief Justice Coke and of King James, to break for a season with the Tudor traditions of their office. At this time the law of the Constitution was not yet interpreted by an established custom of the Constitution, and it lay with the courts to decide many questions arising between King and Parliament, or between King and subject. As the law was often obscure and the precedents contradictory, a very slight political bias could, without scandal, be decisive of grave issues. Hitherto the bias of the Judges had been Royalist. They had pronounced for the King in the question of Impositions, in the year that Coke became Chief Justice of the Common Pleas (1606). Under his influence their decisions soon began to take a different colour. In 1613 Coke was punished by being moved, much against his wishes, to preside over the King's Bench. But still in one question after another James met with attempts to thwart his authority from the quarter where his predecessors had found the most ready support. At last the exasperated King claimed the right to interview the Judges in his own chamber, whenever they were called to decide a

question affecting his prerogative. Coke, knowing that this concession would destroy both the independence of his brethren as a
body and his own power to dictate their decisions, refused to give
way, even when all the rest had capitulated. His obstinacy cost him
his seat on the Bench, and even at the Council Board. In the course
of the whole reign, no measure that James took to strengthen his
authority succeeded half so well as the dismissal of Coke. The
Judges at once relapsed into servants removable at the King's
pleasure, and sure defenders of his prerogative. But Coke had not
striven in vain. He had enlisted the professional pride of the students
of the common law against the rival systems of law specially favoured
by the Crown in the Star Chamber, the admiralty and the Ecclesiastical Courts. He had turned the minds of the young gentlemen
of the Inns of Court, who watched him from afar with fear and
reverence, to contemplate a new idea of the constitutional function
and of the political affinities of their profession, which they were
destined in their generation to develop in a hundred ways, as counsel
for England gone to law with her King.

Dismissal of Coke, 1616

Coke had scarcely ceased to be Chief Justice when his enemy
Bacon received the Great Seal. The fortunes of these two men,
like everything else in England, were in the hands of Buckingham.
In 1617 the fallen Judge, who had in him much of the antique
Roman, consented to repurchase, by the sacrifice of his daughter,
the favour which he had deliberately forfeited to preserve his own
self-respect. Coke offered up his child, together with a large dowry,
over which he haggled longer, to Sir John Villiers, the idiotic and
weakly brother of the favourite. Although the girl shrank from a
forced union, which was indeed destined to be her ruin, she could
not, under the social laws of the time, have made resistance herself,
but for the interference of her mother, who hated old Sir Edward
as he deserved. My lady carried off her daughter to a house in the
country. But no place could afford refuge from the coming storm.
Followed by his son, " fighting Clem Coke," and a train of armed
serving-men, the ex-Chief Justice illustrated the *patria potestas* by
seizing up a log, breaking in the door with his own hand, and dragging
his daughter into the coach. Bacon, uninformed as to the wishes
of James and Buckingham, who were absent in Scotland, concluded
that it would be safe to take sides against the fallen patriot, and
agreed with the rest of the Council to summon Coke before the Star
Chamber for riot. But they soon learnt their error. The favourite,
it appeared, only regarded the affair as the means of making a settlement for his brother. The loathsome marriage was performed ;
Coke was recalled, not indeed to the Bench, but to the Council Board ;
and Bacon, marked out for sacrifice by the cowardly whisperers of
Whitehall, was in grave danger of losing his newly won honours.
Complete submission, however, at length appeased the wrath of
Buckingham.

Coke and his family

After this breeze had blown over, for four years Bacon enjoyed Bacon and Buckingham
the worship of the world, subject to Buckingham's good-will. Yet
all the while he was but mocked with the semblance of power. His
political wisdom, which might have saved the State, was not consulted. He judged, he administered, but did not advise. The
King's ear was for Buckingham alone. For these four years Coke
was silenced ; and Bacon, perhaps, was satisfied. Then, in January,
1621, the Parliament met.

At first, a reconciliation rather than a struggle seemed impending. Meeting of Parliament, 1621
The members did not come up in the angry temper usual to a Parlia-
ment long postponed, for they knew that James was prepared cheerfully to admit their interference as domestic reformers, and they
wrongly supposed that by a similar change of foreign policy, he had
at last determined to lead them on a Protestant crusade. They
little suspected that, three days after the opening of Parliament,
while they were still busy making acquaintance with each other,
and asking what could be done for the Protestant cause throughout
the world, James, with his usual unconscious duplicity, was pouring
into the ear of the polite but incredulous Gondomar protestations of
lifelong attachment to Philip, and plans to reunite Christendom by
admitting the Pope as spiritual head of the Church.

The Commons, almost encouraged by the King, fell fiercely on Monopolies
the courtier tribe. " Monopolies " were the first object of attack.
It was the undoubted right of the Crown, challenged by Parliament
rather as inexpedient than as illegal, to grant by patent to any
company or person the monopoly of selling a particular class of
goods by retail. These monopoly patents were employed for a
variety of purposes ; sometimes to reward invention ; sometimes to
supervise the quality of wares, or to control in the public interest
the distribution of special kinds, such as gunpowder ; sometimes to
enrich a favourite or his *clientèle* out of the purse of the general
consumer ; and afterwards, in the reign of the needy and ingenious
Charles I., as a kind of indirect excise to raise a revenue for the
Crown. But whatever the purpose of the grant, the monopolist
always enhanced the price. Though the public had no feeling
against the reward of inventors by patent, the strongest passions
were aroused against a tax placed on articles of common necessity,
such as glass or soap, to reward a knight for his handsome face, or
a nobleman for his Scottish accent ; nor, when the monopolies were
made an important part of the royal revenue, did indignation subside
among a people who regarded every form of " gabelle " or excise
as the special badge of slavery among nations less fortunate than
themselves.[1] Parliament now fell on the patentees who had most

---

[1] Arber's *Reprints*, viii, Howell's *Instructions*, p. 74. Such are the " gabels of
Italy," that " one cannot bring an egg or root to the market but the Prince his
part lies thereinna ".

obviously abused their privileges ; they were lodged in prison or fled oversea. But when the Houses proceeded to inquire who had recommended them for patents and what forces had been at work behind the throne, the King apologetically interfered and after an ostentatious declaration against the system of monopolies had been mouthed by the favourite himself, further proceedings against individuals on this score were abandoned by consent.

Impeach-
ment and
fall of
Bacon,
1621

The man to whom the stifled inquiry had seemed to point was Chancellor Bacon. The Houses had met with no desire to call him to account, but his mean-spirited master, Buckingham, had offered to thrust him forward as the scapegoat in the matter of monopolies, and his lifelong enemy, Coke, as member for Liskeard, had assumed the leadership of the delighted Commons in a work of general and particular vengeance which he well knew how to direct. It is not therefore surprising that, when the attack on patentees had been diverted, men boldly came forward to accuse the Chancellor of receiving bribes in the administration of justice. No political interference was available, and no legal defence possible. Bacon, impeached by the Commons before the Lords, confessed himself " guilty of corruption," and was condemned to financial ruin and public disgrace. The severity of the sentence was ere long remitted. With characteristic pettiness he continued for the last four years of his life to keep up a great retinue and to petition Buckingham for fresh public employment ; and with magnanimity yet more characteristic, to bring forth the fruits of philosophy and science by the exercise of that divine diligence, which neither the toils of office nor the self-inflicted tortures of his retirement could ever compel him to forgo.

Corrupt
customs
of the day

In England during the Elizabethan age, as in some countries at this day, the transaction of business in almost every department of life was sealed, either before or after conclusion, by gifts from the favoured party. At the Court and at the Bar, in houses of business and in the domestic circle, in the camp and even in the school-room, favours, appointments and the adjustment of personal relations were accompanied by the giving and taking, not merely of the recognised fees, but of presents ; of these some were secret and others open, some known to be wrong and others regarded as right. Whether the gift had the effect of a bribe probably depended more on the relations and character of the individuals concerned, than on the nature, pretext and time of the present. One gift, though made secretly before the event. might yet prove of no avail ; while another, though openly made after the decision, might none the less be part of a corrupt bargain. If this custom of receiving bribe, commission, gratuity or present has in England been eliminated from several departments of life, the change has been largely due to a long series of public protests, of which the impeachment of

Chancellor Bacon was one of the earliest and most famous. Such acts of reformation have often been effected by the genuine indignation of one corrupt class against the form of corruption usual in another. Thus many of Bacon's accusers were accustomed with a good conscience to accept very questionable gifts in their own administration of county business. When Herbert of Cherbury, more nice than Bacon in his sense of those things to which philosophy obliges her servants, refused, as sheriff of Montgomeryshire, to accept thankofferings from the under officers whom he appointed, he was going against established local custom.[1] But the country gentlemen, when they came up to Parliament, having no connection with the Court, had no familiarity with such practices in central Government and genuinely desired to purify the fountainhead of that stream of justice, which some of them at least sullied in its lower channels.

Though it did not concern Bacon's judges to inquire, it is a pleasure to posterity to believe, that his decisions were not affected by the bribes which he too often received while the cases were pending. Attempts were in vain made to overset his decrees in Chancery, even after his own condemnation had made them most obnoxious to attack. He had taken money without scruple, but he had not put up justice to sale. His fault in this, as in all his public career, was not wickedness, but the absence of any lofty ideal of personal conduct. Having conceived a national policy too broad for acceptance either by Parliament or King, he never practised that which alone can give reality to the scheme of the theorist—the courage and self-sacrifice of the politician. The advancer of human learning could not read in the book of human life ; love, friendship and virtue were little more than names to him ; so he turned the abundant energies of his mind to pursue the obvious ends of gold and pomp and honours. Yet, bruised and wearied by the strain of that lifelong shadow-hunt, he never deigned to taste of rest or pleasure, lest time should fail for his other enormous task of discovering knowledge, which no mean-minded man, however great his genius, would on such terms have undertaken and in such a spirit have fulfilled. *Bacon's fault*

In domestic affairs the Commons had won a victory all the more important because it had been uncontested. They had revived the ancient right of ruining ministers by impeachment before the Lords and the whole Court had learnt once more, as in the days of John of Gaunt and Piers Gaveston, to fear Parliament as the nation's watch-dog.[2] But could it, besides avenging the wrongs, dictate the *Parliamentary interference in foreign affairs*

[1] Lord Herbert, p. 65.
[2] There had been no Impeachment between 1459 and 1621. Its place had been taken in Tudor times by Bills of Attainder, which were a handier method of political proscription when King and Houses were agreed. But now that the Houses once more wished to act independently of the King, the old judicial method of Impeachment before the Lords, which did not require the King's participation, was revived.

policy of the State ? Had it the same control over foreign as over domestic affairs ? This more doubtful constitutional issue was now forced on by the immediate necessity of choosing between war and alliance with Spain. The three years' struggle that ensued between nation and King on the Palatinate and marriage questions, came also to involve the power of Parliament in foreign affairs and thereby its freedom of debate.

James wished, by alarming Philip with a display of the warlike ardour of Parliament, to obtain a marriage treaty, of which the restoration of the Palatinate was to be one condition. Parliament wished to break off all alliance with Spain and to recover the Palatinate by war, or by the severe threat of war. James had so wrought that the only apparent alternative to the Spanish match and the disasters in which it would involve the English for generations to come, was war with Spain. And apart from all insular motives, the desire for war to rescue the Protestants of Europe from cruel oppression was the dominant passion both in Parliament and in the city. Common men of that hard but imaginative generation, though they would have scorned a humanitarian appeal to abandon the slave-trade or to interfere with the atrocities of the Turk, were deeply moved by the spectacle of true religion, in town after town and province after province oversea, extinguished for ever by the children of darkness. The new Puritanism of the upper and middle classes gave rise, for the first time in England, to a sense of moral responsibility in foreign affairs, which was neither sentimental nor hypocritical. Impelled by their own and by the national enthusiasm, the Commons, fresh from their triumph in domestic politics, urged the cause of war. The King was treated in their speeches with the deep respect that Englishmen still felt for his office, but his foreign friends learnt what could be said of them in a free country. Coke raved at Spain and the Spaniards as if they had been prisoners up for trial and he once again Attorney-General. Gondomar haughtily complained. James ordered the House not to debate foreign affairs. The members urged in reply the privilege of free speech within the walls. It was true that this right was theirs beyond all question, but it was equally true that it had not formerly been exercised to impose a reversal of foreign policy upon the sovereign. The Commons put themselves on their strongest ground, when they entered in the journals of the House a just and sober Protestation of their privilege to speak freely on all subjects. James put himself as much as possible in the wrong when he sent for the book and tore out the page with his own hand. It was decided at the next Council Board to dissolve

Dissolu-　Parliament. Buckingham, with unnecessary baseness, hastened to
tion of　salute the Spanish Ambassador with the joyful tidings. There was
Parlia-
ment,　good cause to congratulate the enemies of England and of the
Jan., 1622 reformed religion, for all hope of alliance between King and people

had perished and with it all hope of our interference abroad. " It is the best thing," wrote Gondomar to his master, " that has happened in the interests of Spain and the Catholic religion since Luther began to preach heresy, a hundred years ago."

In the next two years the marriage project, to which James had sacrificed the fortunes of his kinsfolk and the love of his subjects, was diplomatically demonstrated to be absurd. Buckingham and young Prince Charles, to whose affections the favourite was laying careful siege, grew weary of delay, and wrung leave from the King to go themselves to fetch the Infanta from Spain. They took ship secretly, galloped in disguise across France, and presented themselves in the astonished streets of Madrid. Charles, though he was not permitted by Spanish ideas of decorum to speak to the poor Princess, imagined that he had fallen in love at first sight. Without a thought for the public welfare, he offered to make every concession to English Catholicism, to repeal the Penal Laws, and to allow the education of his children in their mother's faith. The Spaniards, however, still lacked a guarantee that these promises would really be fulfilled and still refused to evacuate the Palatinate. Meanwhile a personal quarrel arose between Buckingham and the Spanish nation. The favourite, who in his manners was a caricature of the proverbial Englishman abroad, observed neither Spanish etiquette nor common decency. The lordly hidalgos could not endure the liberties he took. " We would rather," they declared, " put the Infanta headlong into a well than into his hands." The English gentlemen, who soon came out to join their runaway rulers, laughed at the barren lands, the beggarly populations and the bad inns through which they passed and boasted of their England. They were not made welcome to Madrid and fancied themselves pestered by the priests. Even Sir Edmund Verney, the good knight without fear and without reproach, from whose dead hand the royal standard was wrenched at Edgehill, struck in the face a Jesuit who attempted to reconcile one of them to Rome. They began to hate the Spaniards and to dread the match. Buckingham was sensitive to the emotions of those immediately around him and he soon imparted the change of his own feelings about Spain to the silent and sullen Prince.

For some time after their departure, James delighted himself with the thought of Steenie and Baby Charles sallying forth like " dear adventurous knights worthy to be put in a new romanso ". He sent after them the robes proper to be worn on the feast of St. George, " if they come in time, which I pray God they may, for it will be a goodly sight for the Spaniards to see my two boys dine in them ". But as the months wore on he began to feel uneasy. The " romanso " rivalled Amadis De Gaul for tediousness and Don Quixote for realism ; the presence of the Fairy Prince had failed to release the Lady, and the Magician was quarrelling with the

The journey to Spain, Feb., 1623

Dragons. Opinion at home was divided as to whether Charles would be murdered or converted. Meanwhile, James was separated from the two beings without whom he could not accustom himself to live. At last, still hoping to complete the treaty over here, he called them back to England. What an England it was to welcome home men who had had more than enough of foreign

The return to London, Oct., 1623 ways ! When it was known that the Prince had come back from Spain, a live man, a Protestant and a bachelor, London broke out into rejoicings that could scarcely have been more hearty if he had been bringing the whole Spanish fleet up the Thames as prize of war. Debtors were released, thieves were set free from the Tyburn death-cart, each steeple vied with its neighbour in that city of bells, mobs roared round the Prince's coach and at night the bonfires made one continuous line down the middle of the winding streets. The outburst was a monster demonstration against the Spanish policy, yet in a form that could not fail to please the Prince and the favourite. The object-lesson, on which those two ill-fated men looked out that day from the windows of their coach, was not entirely lost upon Buckingham. He had had enough of the people's hate, and he found this popularity, which had fallen to him by accident, too sweet to be thrown away ; rather he would abandon the scheme to secure which he had, a few months back, been promising foreigners to alter the politico-religious system of England. He rushed, headlong as ever, in the new direction. He caused the King to summon Parliament, and appeared before it as the champion of English nationality and the appointed hero of a war with Spain.

Failure of James I. When the Houses met in February, 1624, the personal rule of James was over. Too old to struggle for peace against his favourite, his son and his Parliament, yet unwilling to put himself at the head of the war which he detested, he practically made over the government to Buckingham. For four years the Duke, as he was now called, was King in all but name. For the first of these years James lingered on, little regarded. The buoyant self-conceit of his busy brain could not hide from him how completely he had failed to make England the peaceful arbiter of the continent. But it was not given him to see how, by his failure in foreign policy, he had deprived the English king-ship of its ancient " right divine ". As his subjects watched him year after year dragging England and the Protestant interest through the mud, they forgot their pride in the throne that Elizabeth had filled and began to contemplate with other feelings the estate of kings upon earth. The doctrine of the sovereignty of Parliament was still unknown, even to Mr. Pym, whose reasoned harangues against the Catholics were already favourite hearing with the House ; but the old glad confidence in royal sovereignty was gone for ever. A scurrilous popular writer. assuming the name and functions of " Tom Tell-Troath," impudently assures James that his name is a jest in all companies, even of dicers ; that ten healths are drunk to his son-in-law before one to him ; that

they make a mock of your word " Great Britain," and offer to prove that it is a great deal less than little England was wont to be, less in reputation, less in strength less in riches, less in all manner of virtue.

For a whole generation before the Civil War, common men were accustomed in every ale-house, where the news of the capital was retailed, to take their tobacco over such half-treasonable talk ; and accordingly, when at last the Puritan idealists rode out to battle against the King, they were followed by neighbours Pliable and Worldly-wiseman, who had come to imagine by force of long political sympathy that they themselves were Puritans.

CHAPTER V

THE RULE OF BUCKINGHAM—WARS AND PARLIAMENTS, 1624-28

The man whom the King delighteth to honour.—Book of Esther.

Prospect
of
national
unity,
1624

THE last Parliament of King James was the only Parliament, held between the death of Elizabeth and the Civil War, in which the programme laid by the Court before the Houses was identical with that laid by the Houses before the Court. The first of a rapid succession of four Parliaments, to which Charles and Buckingham appealed for support in their wars, it was the only one whose members took the two young men at their own valuation. Every good design was imputed to a silent Prince, of whom nothing was known, and a specious favourite, who gave an account of himself that was radically false. Summoning Lords and Commons to wait on him at Whitehall, as if he were King, the Duke unrolled to them the story of what he now imagined to have been his motives and conduct in the Spanish journey. Parliament, unwilling to compromise the prospect of a fair future by prying too closely into a doubtful past, accepted the tale, laid hold of his proffered alliance, which a single offence to his vanity would shatter, and therewith smote off from England the chains of Spanish diplomacy. Both Houses petitioned James to tear up the treaties still on foot. Their recommendations were carried by the Duke into the royal closet, where they received an assent no more voluntary than that which Walpole long afterwards gave to another breach with Spain.

Death of
James,
27th
March,
1625.
Forecast
of the
years
1625-28

The old King was the only co-operator who was not also an enthusiast in the movement of national revival ; and after another year he was removed by death. England might well have expected a period of unity within and success without. Yet in four years of war with Catholic powers nothing was achieved abroad, while at home the quarrel between Crown and Parliament broke out more fiercely than in the days when Gondomar was dictating the policy of James. The causes of our failure abroad were the military inefficiency usual with England after a long peace, the ignorance of the Parliament men about foreign affairs, but above all else the incompetence displayed by Buckingham. Six times in these four years English fleets or armies were sent out on expeditions, diplomatically ill-conceived and militarily unsound, and six times they returned home with shame. After the first disaster, the Commons refused to throw away money on the war until it was taken out of the Duke's hands. Charles, refusing to part with his friend, was reduced to carry on the war by insufficient and unconstitutional taxation. At the same time the Puritan Parliaments discovered with horror that King and favourite were under the influence of a new school of High Churchmen, whom even James had kept at arm's length. Fear and indignation on both sides flamed up in a crisis, ending with the murder of the Duke and the resolve of Charles to abolish Parliaments in England.

After the readiness to use Buckingham as national leader, which had characterised the last Parliament of James, the determination to drive him from power, with which the first Parliament of Charles assembled, needs to be explained by two intervening events—the loss of Mansfeld's army and the French marriage. The first in the series of disasters which constitute the history of our arms at this period, sufficed to warn the civilian islanders how unfit they were to take the field and how regardless of the clearest principles of diplomacy and war was the man whom they had accepted as their chief. Under command of the foreign soldier Mansfeld, twelve thousand English foot, or rather, " a rabble of raw and poor rascals," torn straight from civil employments by the press-gang, were landed on the coast of Holland with five days' provisions, without money or credit and with orders to march on the Palatinate and defeat the veteran armies that had been mustered for its defence from beyond the Alps, the Pyrenees and the Bohemian Forest. Not only did Buckingham neglect to plan the co-operation of a sufficient force from France, Denmark or any other of the powers friendly to our object, but he disregarded till too late the expressed wishes of the Dutch at a moment when we were landing on their shore an armament so strangely dependent on their generosity for equipment and even for subsistence. Cast away, like their descendants on the Isle of Walcheren, the army perished of cold, starvation and plague. " All day," wrote one of the colonels, " we go about for victuals and bury our dead." The survivors, too few to venture out against the enemy, lingered in Holland till nine-tenths of their number had deserted or died. *English army under Mansfeld lost, Feb.-March, 1625*

Our men had been sacrificed to the Duke's latest fancy to marry Charles to a Princess of France. Fearing that the Houses, if they met before the ceremony had taken place, would declare against it as effectually as they had declared against the match with Spain, he had persuaded James not to hold the intended autumn session of 1624. Rather than go to Parliament for supply at the crisis of the new marriage treaty, Buckingham thought it a light thing to wage war without money and to fling twelve thousand Englishmen naked on the shores of Holland, as a gambler flings dice upon the board. Thus when England was about to strike her first blow in the battle, he wrenched from her uplifted hand the magic sword, without which it was decreed that she could not conquer—the union of Crown *Fatal marriage of Charles I., May, 1625* and Parliament. The fatal marriage of Charles I. with Henrietta Maria, sister of the King of France, celebrated by proxy in front of the doors of Notre Dame de Paris, before his first Parliament could meet to forbid the banns, ensured that this severance of Crown and Commons would be perpetuated from generation to generation. Buckingham, the evil match-maker, had prepared twofold ruin for the House of his friend. For as soon as Charles had ceased to mourn for the murdered Duke and learnt to love his wife, she led him in silken bands the straight way to the scaffold. Nor could the Spanish match itself have been more fatal in the end ; for when the children born of this French union were called back to sit on their father's throne, it was not any longer Spain, but France under Louis XIV. that persecuted Protestantism and threatened England ; and so because the second Charles and the second James clave to their mother's people and to their mother's gods, the House of Stuart forfeited a second time the allegiance of the English.

The girl of fifteen who landed in June as Queen of England, gossipping to her French women of the dances and duels of their land, and aglow with virtuous recollections of her confessor's precepts for conduct among heretics, looked or felt no more like a Queen of tragedy than did Marie Antoinette on her way from Vienna to Versailles. Yet Henrietta Maria was bringing into England the feud of parties yet unformed, the wild terrors of the Popish Plot, the furies of the Exclusion Bill and the wrath that should unite bitter foes to drive back her son James II. to the land whence now she came.

Charles's first Parliament, June-Aug.,1625 In the first Parliament of the new reign, the old quarrel broke out afresh. Charles had some cause to feel incensed ; under the leadership of Sir Robert Phelips, the Commons refused supplies for a war which they had demanded fifteen months back and named as unfit for his post the man whom they had then hailed as " saviour ". Such inconsistency Charles could only attribute to the spirit of faction. But the members saw good reason for a change of attitude : last autumn, when Parliament was most needed, its summons had been postponed, in order that the nation might be tricked into a Catholic marriage, which it was now disloyal openly to assail, but unpatriotic not secretly to resent. The first fruits of this alliance had been, not the recovery of the Palatinate by French aid, but the loan of English ships to reduce the Huguenots of Rochelle, the port where for fifty years, in peace or war, English sailors had been welcomed as brothers in arms. And meanwhile Mansfeld's regiments had perished of want. All these disasters were the work of the Duke, from whom, therefore, the Commons were right to withdraw their misplaced confidence.

Their conduct in curtailing supplies for a war which they had instigated is less easy to judge. It was indeed not without reason Refusal of that they refused supply, until some check was put upon the power supplies of the incompetent Duke and until the King and his Minister consented to give some general indication of the purposes for which they intended to use the grant. But one motive that prompted the Commons to close their purses was less reasonable. They complained that they were drawn into a general war on the continent, when they had contemplated a maritime duel with Spain. Far from indifferent to the fate of the German Protestants, they were so ill-informed as to imagine Spain the only bar to the restoration of the Palatinate Prince. Ignoring Austria, they supposed that a blow to the Spanish shipping on the Atlantic coasts would be seriously felt on the Rhine. It was a mistake natural to country gentlemen whose instruction in current foreign affairs was confined to conversations with merchants of the seaports and whose stock of general history was limited to the Elizabethan epic of how England had saved Europe on the sea. The minister whose duty it was to instruct them from the level of an informed and responsible diplomacy, would lay no plans or explanations before Parliament and was himself as deeply ignorant as its members of the real conditions of success abroad. Charles, seeing that he could not obtain Dissolu-supplies without first giving security for their employment, only tion, Aug., waited till Buckingham was named in debate, to dissolve the Houses 1625 for interfering with his choice of servants.

The six months that intervened between his first and second The Cadiz Parliament were marked by fresh follies in diplomacy and fresh expedi-disasters in war. An expedition which was sent to capture Cadiz, 1625 tion, Oct., the emporium of Spain and America, would, if successful, have gratified the desires of England, but not have effected the relief of the Palatinate. The city had thirty years before been carried at a rush by the sea-dogs who sailed with Raleigh into its harbour, and the hardened veterans who followed Essex and Vere over its walls. But on this occasion it was perfectly safe when assailed by crews prostrated by sickness and starvation, mismanaging rotten ships under the orders of captains ignorant of the sea, and by ploughmen and footpads suddenly collected according to the principles of Sir John Falstaff to do duty as English soldiers. The expedition was perhaps the lowest point ever reached by our warfare on sea and land.[1]

Meanwhile, the Duke, not content to wage unsuccessful war on Breach Spain, deliberately sacrificed the friendship of France, to purchase with which he had already by the royal marriage paid away the good-France will of Parliament and mortgaged the future of England. An understanding with Richelieu, if steadily cultivated, would have led to active alliance and the recovery of the Palatinate. But

[1] Oppenheim, pp. 219-21. Firth's *C. A.*, pp. 3, 4.

because the Cardinal refused to commit France instantly to a war dependent on two such weather-cocks as Charles and Buckingham, the Duke conceived the same personal grievance that had led him two years before to break with Spain.   It is said that he marked his change of attitude by making love openly to the French King's wife.   The quarrel between Buckingham and Louis XIII. was enhanced by a coolness between Charles and Henrietta Maria. A short-lived rivival of persecution against the Catholics, in direct contravention of the terms of the marriage treaty which the husband insisted on regarding as an insignificant formality, gave large scope for conjugal recrimination.   Louis, incensed as a man at Charles's breach of faith to his sister and perhaps also by the addresses of Buckingham to his wife, was called upon as King to protect the shipping of his subjects, still neutral towards Spain, from confiscation by English searchers.   England and France drifted into a war that stultified the general European policy of both combatants. The moment that we began hostilities with the French, all hope that either country could effect anything against Spain or Austria was at an end ; this fact was so patent that the Duke could not blind Parliament to the truth, even by undertaking, with huge Protestant bluster, the relief of those very Huguenots whom he had been helping Richelieu to suppress.

Charles's second Parliament, Feb.-June, 1626

The quarrel with France had not reached the stage of war when Charles convoked his second Parliament.   The Duke's attitude to our Parliamentary institutions was more friendly than the implacable sullenness of the King, or the far-sighted hostility of Strafford.   The first prolonged attempt to govern without summoning the estates of the realm had been adopted as a policy by James before Buckingham's rise to power, and the second was only instituted after his assassination.   The Duke's vanity and love of applause made him a constant victim to the delusion that he could yet, by some great stroke of diplomacy or war, convert the Commons to acclaim him as the greatest of warrior statesmen. In this hope, bright to the very last, lived and died the most incompetent of all English war ministers.   Instead of imprisoning the leaders who had thwarted him in 1625, he had them pricked as sheriffs, so that they were disqualified for the House in 1626. This device, which kept Coke and Sir Robert Phelips from their accustomed seats, thereby brought to the front a patriot of loftier mind than the old dragon of the law, and of even higher ability than the knight of Somerset who had led the last Parliament.

Sir John Eliot

Sir John Eliot, the squire of St. Germans and Vice-Admiral of Devon, had watched the Cadiz armament leave and return to Plymouth ; he had seen the bad food, the rotten ships, the tackle, some of which had been used in the chase after the Armada, the English sailors starving in port and the English soldiers robbing

from farm to farm in their own country. Bound though he was
to Buckingham by old service and friendship, Eliot determined
that it would be his duty, if he were sent up to Parliament, to
remove that man from his place.   By undertaking this task, which
he conceived specially incumbent on him as a private member.
he stepped at once into the informal leadership left vacant by
Coke and Phelips. He instituted the impeachment of the Duke
before the Lords, this being then the only means of obtaining a
change of minister.   The Commons showed, by frequent advances,
that they would be satisfied if the Duke retired from office ; but
when Charles refused to consider their resolutions, they could only
enforce their complaint of incompetence by converting it into a
charge of crime.   Yet Buckingham could not be proved guilty,
unless folly becomes criminal through excess.   The confusion of
the royal accounts baffled inquiry into the charges of peculation :
but it is probable that he was innocent, for the favourite had no
need to acquire money by stealth.   Charles, who loved Buckingham
as he never loved Strafford, took up his cause with passion.   To
save the Duke he dissolved the Parliament.

*Impeach-
ment of
Bucking-
ham and
dissolu-
tion of
Parlia-
ment,
June,
1626*

After the dissolution England continued to drift rapidly into war
with France.   If Buckingham was to blame for the first set of the
current in that direction, Charles was chiefly responsible for the final
catastrophe.   He claimed that France should recognise him as the
official Protector of Louis' armed Huguenot subjects ; he refused to
consider a compromise on the shipping dispute, which Richelieu
would willingly have found ; so little did he think apology due to
his wife and his brother-in-law for ignoring the terms of the marriage
treaty, that he embittered their resentment by chasing out of the
country the French attendants of the Queen.   In all this he gave
not a thought to the feelings of his wife, or the pride of the French
King, nor yet did he consider the consequences of war between the
two countries, or the expectations which his written undertaking
to relieve the English Catholics, had of course aroused.   He tried
the situation solely by the touchstone of his own honour.   This
honour, as he conceived, lay not in the strict observation of his
faith as a man, still less in the fulfilment of his duties as a King,
but in the exaction of all to which, as King or as man, he felt himself entitled.   Faithful and just only to the very few who won his
personal affection, he pursued through long years this ideal of a
selfish honour, utterly regardless of the rights, the wishes or the
resisting force of those with whom he dealt ; till at the end of his
life, surprised and indignant to the last, he was brought face to
face with the failure that is almost invariably the lot of one who
judges others solely by their relation to himself.

*Charles,
his wife
and the
French
King*

When the war finally broke out in 1627, an expedition was
sent to seize the Island of Rhé off Rochelle as a basis for English

Expedi-
tion to
Rochelle,
1627

commerce and privateering at the expense of France, secured by the neighbourhood and alliance of the great Huguenot port. Bucking-ham himself went in command. He showed personal courage, vigour, industry and fair talents as a commander, but he had already prepared ruin for his generalship by his folly as a diplo-matist, a war minister and a politician. The engagement in hostilities at once with France, with Spain and with the Catholics of Germany, rendered success in any quarter impossible ; the troops he had prepared for himself to lead to Rhé were beggarly, untrained and mutinous ; England, that should have volunteered to support his efforts, was alienated by his politics and torn by a fierce struggle with the King's officers over the Forced Loan. As the whole system of government was out of gear, the fleet that should have reinforced the Duke on the Isle of Rhé never arrived ; the French army came across from the mainland, attacked the English as they attempted to re-embark, and slaughtered them without resistance. Forty English flags were hung up in Notre Dame de Paris. With less than half the eight thousand who had sailed, Buckingham came home from a disgrace which stung to fury a proud nation, already in conflict with its governors.

The
Forced
Loan,
1626-27

Since the dissolution of 1626, Charles had been driven, by the cost of so many wars, into a measure which brought violence and misery into the homes of all classes of his subjects, and taught them by personal experience to dread the approach of a despotic system. The refusal of a Free Gift led to the extraction of a Forced Loan. It differed from taxation in nothing but name ; the payments were assessed like a subsidy, and enforced by severe punishment. In the preamble of the Commission for its levy, Charles urged the state of the continent ; the destruction at Lutter of the last hope of Protestantism, the Danish Army ; the impending advance of Wallenstein to plant the banners of the Catholic Alliance along the shores of the Baltic and the Northern Sea ; the need of immediate interference, if we would not see the whole continent closed to our goods and armed for our destruction. But the appeal to religion and to commerce was made in vain. Merchants saw their interests in no other war save the maritime attack on Spain ; Puritans were agreed that Buckingham could not, even if he would, save the German Protestants ; all detested the French war, to which in fact every other object was being sacrificed. The future was to show that our ancestors better served the Protestant cause, whose present need the Swedish champion would supply, by preserving England from despotism and bringing the central government under the control of popular feeling, than they would have done by waging futile war such as a nation, in bonds but not yet reconciled to des-potism, is likely to wage under incompetent masters.

Commissioners for the Forced Loan were appointed in each

county, with power to summon their neighbours, assess them man by man, and send each case of resistance before the Privy Council. Many, to escape ruin, paid with wrath in their hearts ; but others preferred to suffer. Some eighty gentlemen were imprisoned ; poor men, to whom the laws of England were no less dear, were pressed into the army, that their families might beg in the streets, while French and Austrian did execution on their bodies. The agitation and resistance specially convulsed East Anglia, London and its neighbourhood and the south-western shires.

Meanwhile, the condition and conduct of the troops newly levied for the foreign expeditions, added to the general suspicion and distress. In the reign of terror that followed in every district on the establishment of the Loan Commission, men saw a new and sinister meaning in the mutiny law by which the new recruits were held together, they resented as a despot's revenge the licence of the starving soldiers and detected a design to enslave the country in the system of billeting which a pennilesss and incompetent war ministry had no alternative but to adopt. Thus the question of the Forced Loan became closely connected in the popular mind with the question of Martial Law. *Martial Law*

Charles struggled for more than a year to carry on war by continental methods of despotism, but without the continental conditions for success. He employed no trained bureaucracy and his subjects were without traditions of obedience. The Commissioners of his Loans, suddenly chosen out to oppress neighbours whose interests they shared and whose friendship they valued, had in many cases themselves refused to pay : they were very different men from Richelieu's Intendants. The gentry who bearded the Privy Council and marched off indignantly to prison, bore little resemblance to the nobles of the Fronde. The common people who refused the loan at the risk of being sent to die oversea, were not the " taillables," or " taxables," as the peasantry were called who for century after century paid with their blood and sweat for all the follies of France. Even Charles and Buckingham began to realise that it was hardly with such material so managed that they could conquer at the same instant, France and Spain, the Baltic and the Palatinate. The attempt had only produced anarchy at home. Charles had two alternatives : either to wage war by constitutional methods, or to make peace as a preliminary to despotism ; to summon Parliament, or to change his foreign policy. In 1628 he chose the first alternative, though it was not to be long before he adopted the second. So in March the Parliament met that was to pass the Petition of Right. *Failure of Charles's first attempt at despotism, 1626-27*

The English were now roused to lay claim to that privilege which for so long afterwards distinguished them from other nations— the right of the individual to free enjoyment of person and property, up to limits fixed by known law. Under James I. rulers and ruled *Charles's third Parliament, March, 1628-March, 1629*

Temper of the nation

had confined their quarrel to religion, finance, and foreign affairs. Occasional arbitrary imprisonments had escaped the censure of men who had seen the popular Elizabethan system secure itself against suspected traitors by like acts of authority. But now the practice of arbitary imprisonment had been abused : it was being applied on a far more extensive scale, not in defence of the State but in an attack on the property of all classes. These measures had indeed failed as part of a war policy, but they might succeed in time of peace, unless they were at once branded with an official stigma of national disapproval, and unless the existing laws, protecting a man from restraint and violence at the pleasure of his rulers, were interpreted beyond all doubt by a new statute. The passage of such a law through Parliament would be neither easy nor safe. The leaders well knew that their privileges would protect them from Charles's vengeance only until the dissolution, which might well be as sudden as those of 1625 and 1626. So long as the Commons had no voice in the selection of the King's Ministers—and until 1640 they had no voice whatever—every man who spoke against the Government on the floor of the House was not talking himself into office but into prison. The Petition of Right could only be carried if the House were led by men who had neither private ambitions nor private fears, who were prepared to sacrifice liberty, happiness and life, for the freedom of others. Fortunately, at the elections of 1628 the constituencies had very generally at their command a type of candidate now long vanished from the world—the Puritan squire.

The men of 1628   When the gentlemen who had refused the Loan were released from prison, they and their like were carried to the head of the poll as representatives of the townsmen and of the yeomen, no less than of their own class. They were accustomed to mix in daily converse with all and had at heart the interests and passions of all ranks save the agricultural labourer. Yet they themselves were aristocrats.

> The House of Commons (writes a contemporary) was both yesterday and to-day as full as one could sit by another. And they say it is the most noble, magnanimous assembly that ever those walls contained ; and I heard a lord estimate they were able to buy the Upper House (His Majesty alone excepted) thrice over, notwithstanding there be of lords temporal the number of 118. And what lord in England would be followed by so many freeholders as some of those are ? [1]

The House of Lords was composed partly of the unpopular *nouveaux riches* who had risen by sycophancy at James's Court and partly of the heirs to great old houses ruined by the prodigal expense which custom then imposed for the maintenance of their dignity : they let the initiative pass to the Commons Chamber,

---

[1] *Court and Times of Charles I.*, i., p. 331.

which was filled with men of wealth and prestige who yet possessed the popular sympathies, the refinement and the self-control of that generation of our Puritans. These were not the fierce partisans who in 1643 tried to force Presbyterianism on England. But, being themselves Puritan, they maintained the Puritan influence in the Church of England and the Puritan spirit in the State ; while their enemies, the High Churchmen, were already preaching the absolute power of the King and the sinfulness of refusing the Forced Loan. In this Parliament the issue of slavery and freedom was treated by men whose speeches combined culture with simplicity, religion with common-sense and democratic leanings with aristocratic dignity of sentiment and utterance. Even Coke, in such an atmosphere, forgot to hope or fear for himself, forgot all save his great love of the laws of England. In the stately, simple, poetical English of the time, Wentworth, Seymour and Selden, Phelips, Eliot and Pym pleaded the cause of posterity, while Hampden, Cromwell and hundreds more listened with a passion that sometimes broke forth in tears.[1]

To secure the rights of the individual to person and property, the Commons left aside all questions of State which might confuse the issue or imperil the result and drew up a Petition of Right, in terms as brief and expressive as those of Magna Carta, on the four cardinal points—Billeting, Martial Law, Arbitrary Taxation and Arbitary Imprisonment.

Billeting and Martial Law had perhaps caused the greatest

[1] Examples of their oratory may not be uninteresting to a posterity which owes them such a debt.

Eliot, speaking of the importance of the question of the Forced Loan, says : " Yes it is of more ; more than is pretended ; more than can be uttered. Upon this dispute not alone our lands and goods are engaged, but all that we call ours. These rights, these privileges, which made our fathers freemen, are in question. If they bo not tho moro carefully preserved, they will I fear render us to posterity less free, less worthy than our fathers. For this particular admits a power to antiquate the laws " (G., vi., p. 233).

Phelips, speaking of the decision of the Judges in favour of arbitrary imprisonment, says : " I can live, although another without title be put to live with me (*viz.*, *billeted on me*) ; nay I can live though I pay excises and impositions more than I do ; but to have the liberty which is the soul of my life taken from me by power, and to be pent up in a gaol without remedy by law, and to be so adjudged to perish in gaol ; O improvident ancestors ! O unwise forefathers ! To be so curious in providing for the quiet possession of our lands and liberties of Parliament, and to neglect our persons and bodies, and to let them die in prison, and that *durante beneplacito*, remediless. If this be law, why do we talk of our liberties ? " And again : " Let the House consider to prepare our grievances fit for His Majesty's view—not to make a law to give us new liberties but declaration with respective penalties ; so that those which violate them, if they would be vile, they should fear infamy with men. And then we shall think of such a supply as never Prince received, and with our moneys we shall give him our hearts and give him a new people raised from the dead. Then I hope this Parliament will be entituled the Parliament of Wonders, and God's judgments diverted, and these beams of goodness shall give us life, and we shall go home to our Countries (*Counties*), and leave our Posterities as free as our Ancestors left us " (Rushworth, i., pp. 504, 505).

quantity of actual distress. Unable to feed and control the raw
levies at the ports of embarkation, Buckingham had left them
scattered about through the inland counties ; and having no money
to pay inn-keepers, had made them chargeable on the inhabitants.
The soldiers not only robbed and insulted the hosts on whom they
were quartered, but broke loose in companies upon the country-
side to pillage, rape and murder ; in some parts the highways and
markets were deserted, and men durst not venture to church on
Sunday, lest in their absence their homes should become a prey to
bandits, armed at the King's expense and clothed in something
of the King's authority. The attempt to restrain these rascals by
Martial Law only incensed the jealous population. Men heard
with alarm that the soldiers who had robbed them had been hanged
by Courts Martial, which might next be employed to punish all who
resisted the Government ; for the jurisdiction of these courts was
not confined to the military, but had already been extended to cases
lying between soldier and civilian. In these cases the officers were
accused of partiality. When a countryman, who had seen his
thatch fired and his horses carried off by a company of pikemen,
appeared before the Court Martial with the tale of his wrongs and
was dismissed with scant courtesy by a harassed colonel whose
troops had disappeared and who did not understand his dialect,
he went home in no humour to regard Martial Law as a necessity,
or Billeting as a privilege. The sound prejudice of the English
against militarism, silently grown up during a hundred years of
peace and civil life under the Tudors, now caused an outbreak of
public feeling, which found voice at Westminster. The members
recalled in their speeches how Rome had perished through the
" insolency of the soldiers," and what the Turkey merchants reported of the Janissaries. And so the charter of the most civilian
nation of Europe was laid down in the Petition of Right. Statutory
form was given to the principles that no man can be punished except
by the ordinary civil tribunals of the land, and that " no man is
forced to take soldiers, but inns and they to be paid for them ".
By this great Act not only was arbitrary Government deprived of
powers which it would soon have learnt to use as a political weapon,
but the civilian nature of life under the British flag was secured till
the present day. The Stuarts never obtained leave to become
military despots ; Cromwell, who insisted, thereby ruined his cause.
When at last a standing army was found imperative, the annual
mutiny bill secured control by Parliament, and the countryman saw
without alarm the inns crowded with the red-coats of King William
or King George, paying their bills like common travellers. Best of
all, the King could not empower military commissions to put his
subjects to trial.[1]

[1] In 1569 Queen Elizabeth had allowed 600 of her rebel subjects to be executed by military commissions (Stephen, i., p. 210).

But if Billeting and Martial Law had caused most distress, Arbitrary Taxation and Arbitrary Imprisonment had aroused most agitation. For while grievances under the first head might be accounted the act of an incompetent war ministry struggling with its difficulties, those under the second were clearly the act of a Government feeling its way to a system of despotism. Therefore the Petition of Right, after recalling the statutes and precedents of Plantagenet times, prayed that—

no man hereafter be compelled to make or yield any gift, loan, benevolence, tax, or such like charge, without common consent by Act of Parliament.

But most of all had feeling been stirred by the imprisonment without trial of the eighty gentlemen for refusing the loan. It was Richelieu's system of *lettres de cachet*. The Petition exposed how

divers of your subjects have of late been imprisoned without any cause showed, and when for their deliverance they were brought before your Justices, by your Majesty's writs of Habeas Corpus, there to undergo and receive as the court should order, and their keepers commanded to certify the causes of their detainer ; no cause was certified, but that they were detained by your Majesty's special command, signified by the Lords of your Privy Council, and yet were returned back to their several prisons, without being charged with anything to which they might make answer according to the law.

Wherefore the Petition prays that

no freeman, in any such manner as before mentioned, be imprisoned or detained.

Such were the four points of the Petition—Martial Law, Billeting, Arbitrary Taxation, Arbitrary Imprisonment. It is remarkable that, though one of the chief grievances was compulsory enlistment in the army of men who had refused the Loan, nothing was said in the Petition to forbid pressing. For all knew that, so long as no standing army was allowed, the press-gang must be used in emergencies to fill the ranks of the hasty levies by which England then waged war.

The Lords, after one attempt to make the meaning of the terms less clear, endorsed the Petition as it stood. There was a Court party among the newer peers ; but the old families of England regarded the supremacy of Villiers as an insult to themselves ; and it was neither their social nor political interest to allow a system of despotism to be established, which would reduce the hereditary influence of all whom it did not admit into its counsels. The Petition, together with a bribe of five subsidies, was offered by both Houses to the King. He had to choose between accepting the terms and dissolving Parliament ; between money for a constitutional war policy and a beggared despotism of peace. For a week he hesitated and on one day seemed to have decided for a breach. But the attitude of the Lords and his own desire to avenge his honour on France, outweighed his resentment. He made the Petition a

Charles
accepts it,
7th June,
1628
statute of the realm. London and all England broke into rejoicings which recalled the night of the return from Spain. For men believed that the King's heart was softened, or his reason convinced ; on the night of the bonfires it was believed that he had sent the Duke to the Tower. But that heart was never softened, that reason was never convinced ; and the blood of his friend was soon to flow, a dividing stream, between the King and his people. England was at the beginning, not at the end, of the struggle for the principles of the Petition of Right. But its acceptance had put law on the side of personal freedom, and in those days the law was, next to the Bible, the learning of Englishmen.

Remon-
strance
against
Bucking-
ham, 11th
June
The apparent reconciliation did not last a week. The Commons, who regarded the Petition of Right as a digression that ought never to have been made necessary, proceeded at once to deal with all the current questions of Church and State. Of these the most pressing was the continuance of the Duke's rule over a nation that detested him. In their Remonstrance of 11th June, the Commons enumerated his shortcomings and prayed for his removal. Charles replied by proroguing Parliament and sending down Buckingham to Portsmouth, with every mark of honour, to put himself at the head of a last expedition to relieve Rochelle. But the Remonstrance was not without effect : for the terms in which it denounced the Duke had suggested to a fearless mind the terrible error of Brutus and of Ravaillac.

Murder of
Bucking-
ham, 23rd
Aug.,1628
Waggoners, wending through the August harvests in the dust of the Portsmouth road, gave friendly lifts to a needy and impatient pedestrian, lieutenant of the late army of Rhé, but unpromoted, unpaid and starving, and seemingly oppressed with melancholy. In this way Felton reached the city where our ships rode waiting for the wind for France, found the Duke, and stabbed him dead at a blow.

England burst into rejoicings. Men drank the murderer's health in the London streets. Popular songs were composed and sung in his honour.[1] To avoid outrage from the mob, the Duke's body received secret interment in the Abbey ; at the false funeral next day, the city train-bands, who protected the hearse, shouldered arms and beat up their drums, as if they were marching to a Coronation.

Obvious causes can be assigned for this shameless approval of

[1] *E.g.*, Awake, sadde Britaine, and advance at last
Thy drooping heade ; let all thy sorrows past
Be drownde and sunke with theire owne teares, and nowe
O'erlooke thy foes with a triumphant browe.
Thy foe, Spaine's agent, Holland's bane, Rome's frend,
By a victorious hand receivde his ende.
Live ever Felton, thou hast turned to dust
Treason, ambition, murther, pride, and lust.—(Rous, p. 29.)

murder. Buckingham had been saddled on England, and her repeated efforts to throw him had been defeated ; the honours with which the men of Athens perpetuated the memory of Harmodius and Aristogiton, are always liable to find a counterpart in modern civilisation when a proud people is governed against its will by one whom it detests. Moreover, though the long Tudor peace had tamed, it had not eradicated the murderous instincts of the Middle Ages. The Englishman already had less frequent recourse to sword and knife than the men of more military nations, but there still lurked in him something of the savage. Even in the later part of the century, one side plotted the murder of the regicides and of William III., and the other undertook the assassination of Charles II.

The echo of these brutal rejoicings penetrated to the Palace, where the King was struggling with the greatest sorrow of his life. With that dignity wherein his real virtue lay, he dissembled the violence of grief and rage ; but it cannot be that he ever forgave or forgot the joy of his people at the murder of his friend. After Buckingham he never loved any man ; he had many good servants, but never again one that was dear to him.

So the fleet sailed without the Duke. When they arrived off Rochelle and saw the mole that the war-like Cardinal had piled across the harbour guarded by the gallant gentlemen and disciplined mercenaries of France, the pressed merchantmen, of which the English armament chiefly consisted, refused to go into action. The surrender of Rochelle within sight of our mutinous fleet was a fit ending to the most disgraceful period of our military annals. Charles, anxious to lay aside all weights in his contest with Parliament, hastened to make peace with France, Spain and the German Catholics. He was beginning to feel the wounds to his honour at home even more acutely than the wounds to his honour abroad. His subjects were on their side not unwilling that he should make peace. The war-fever had died down. Men felt what they scarcely liked to confess, that long years of apprenticeship would be needed before England recovered her ancient mastery of the craft of war. In four years articled to Buckingham she had learnt nothing.

England paid by occasional periods of inefficiency for the high social and political privilege of being the most civilian country in Europe. She had no continuous school of military traditions, not even the nucleus of a standing army, no gentry or burgherdom proud in arms and trained in private wars. When a force was needed to cross the seas, martial ardour was so faint that the regiments had to be created by the press-gang ; nor would public opinion suffer any but rogues and weaklings, whom their neighbourhood could well spare, to be carried off on ill-managed expeditions on which it was usual for the greater part to perish. This system,

Second failure before Rochelle, Sep.-Oct., 1628

Causes of military inefficiency

which Shakespeare ridiculed and Cromwell reformed, Buckingham could only accept.

Nor could England make up in quantity what was lacking in quality. She resembled all countries of that age in being poor ; but she differed from France and Spain in not being large and populous. Like every one else, the English were agriculturists, whose wealth could not easily be realised in money ; but unlike the French and Spaniards, they were extremely jealous of paying a moderate proportion of their money in taxes to the King. For these reasons the size of our force in war, under Elizabeth and the first Stuarts, was ludicrously small. But in Elizabeth's day it had been unequalled in quality, because, in time of nominal peace, a decade of piracy at sea and volunteering in the Netherlands had prepared a large navy and a very small army for the death struggle with Spain.[1] To the civilian English such a training was indispensable ; and so, because James had given us twenty years of real peace (1604-24), at the outbreak of the second Spanish war the island that contained the best material for an army, sent out what was actually the worst military force in Europe. The generation whose fathers had served under Drake, Raleigh and Vere, whose sons were to follow Blake, Rupert and Cromwell, were themselves the jest of Spanish cloisters and French guard-rooms.[2]

Book of Sports, 1618   The final rupture of Charles with Parliamentary institutions, which took place when the Houses reassembled after the murder of Buckingham, was largely due to the religious situation. James I., after the fatal expulsion of the 300 Puritan clergy with which he inaugurated his reign, had made no further assault on Protestantism within the Church. His issue of the *Book of Sports*, the Declaration in which he authorised but did not command the continuance of the old English Sunday games, was in no sense a persecution. He published it only in one diocese ; and even there, he did not, like Charles and Laud in 1633, force recalcitrant clergy to read it under pain of deprivation.[3] Meanwhile, the Puritan Abbot had succeeded

---

[1] The English regiments in Dutch service, borrowed by Elizabeth for the famous expedition to Cadiz, were the only first-rate soldiers whom she had at her disposal (see *Vere's Commentaries*, 1657). She was no more able than willing to dismember the Spanish Empire.

[2] Firth's *C. A.*, chap. i. Oppenheim, pp. 184-301.

[3] For the general aspect of the question, see p. 58 above, and L. A. Govett's *The King's Book of Sports* (1890). A genuine common-sense breathes in the quaint phrases and quainter provisions of that Declaration. James there ascribes two evils to the Puritan Sabbath—" the one, the hindering of the conversion of many (*Catholics*), whom their priests will take occasion hereby to vex, persuading that no honest mirth or recreation is lawful or tolerable in our Religion.

The other inconvenience is, that this prohibition barreth the common and meaner sort of people from using such exercises as may make their bodies more able to war, when we or our successors have occasion to use them. And in place thereof sets up filthy tipplings and drunkenness, and breeds a number of idle and discontented speeches in their Ale-houses."

Bancroft as Primate. The doctrinal part of Calvin's system was taught, universally at Cambridge and still very generally at Oxford, to the rising generation of parish clergy ; and before the time of Laud, alienation from foreign Protestants was no part of the teaching of the English Church, whose representatives were sent over by James to the Calvinistic Synod of Dort.

Besides this official sanction of the dogmas of continental Calvinism, the spirit and practice of English Puritanism was making its own way without any such encouragement. In many villages and in every town a few zealous men, of whom the parson was sometimes but not always one, were gradually training their neighbours in the habits of Bible reading and private prayer. As the law and the Bishops prohibited conventicles and meetings outside the regular service, these practices the more readily assumed a domestic or individual nature ; the Englishman's house became his church and his family the congregation. These customs and the accompanying habits of thought and imagination, which were for long the heart of English religion, more even than the sacramental system, were fixed during this period by the efforts of " conformist Puritans ". These men did a work which the sacramentalists were never afterwards able, as many of them have never been willing to eradicate. Thus an active propaganda, indifferent rather than hostile to Episcopacy, began to secure England against the possibility of Roman reaction, by creating in a large proportion of the population a genuine zeal for Protestant religion. Meanwhile, the pressure of the Penal Laws from 1605-20, drove to church all but the richer or the more determined Catholics ; the forced recruits found no attraction in the domestic worship of their Puritan neighbours ; but in the antique glamour of the village church, where for generations uncounted their ancestors had bowed to Host and Rood, they listened with mingled feelings to the piety of early and mediæval Christendom revealed in the stately English of the Book of Common Prayer.

Thus while there was no toleration there was a fairly wide comprehension. James's reign was a " peace of the Church," and brought forth the fruits of peace. But he had already sown the seeds of future disruption. The 300 " silenced brethren," the stalwarts of Puritanism expelled in 1604, remained in the eyes of the gentlemen of the Lower House a grievance unredressed, and formed a nucleus round which dissent and rebellion would surely gather, if any further attack were made on the position of the conformist Puritans who remained in the Episcopalian Church.

About the year 1620 the storm began to brew. Strong Protestants of all sections were drawn together by a vague sense of approaching peril, which thenceforward inspired every word and action of the House of Commons. Domestic persecution had not yet actually arisen, but the Catholic victories on the continent, the threatened Spanish match, the relaxation of the Penal Laws as an earnest of that policy, tended to identify nationalist with Puritan feeling. So James I., when he died, left Protestants angry and suspicious and bold in the consciousness of representing general opinion.

Attack on Puritanism in the new reign In the first years of Charles's reign, while the Catholic reaction still gathered force on the continent and rolled daily nearer to our shores, an internal danger suddenly arose to threaten the position of Protestants in the Church of England. The most advanced leaders of the High Church school obtained the ear of favourite and King, and established at Whitehall their personal influence, which had long dominated certain Colleges at Oxford. Both sides perceived that the truce observed by James was at an end, that an attempt would at last be made to drive out of the Church the distinctively Protestant element. But to expel from the Church was in those days to expel from England, for no one contemplated the recognition of Nonconformist bodies. Charles, if he listened to Laud's views of Anglicanism, would have to fulfil his father's threat against the Puritans, and " harry them out of the land ". The Parliaments determined to strike before they were struck, and in the sessions of 1625-29 attacked individually the High Church *protégés* of the Court. Both sides entered on a war of extermination in self-defence, which ended in 1689 with the nobler victory of toleration.

What, then, were the tenets of the small band of High Anglican divines who, weak in popular sympathy, but strong in their control of the executive power in Church and State, undertook the destruction of Puritanism in England ?

The High Churchmen are Erastians and Absolutists In the first place they were Erastian in Church affairs, and Absolutist in politics. They tried to realise their conception of the English branch of the Catholic Church, not by apostolical methods, but by inviting the personal interference of the King in the details of ecclesiastical government. In return, they maintained his authority, even in matters purely political. The High Churchmen whom Charles's early Parliaments attacked, had used the pulpit and the religious press to urge the payment of the Forced Loan as a Christian duty, and to vindicate anti-legal theories of prerogative.

If (wrote Manwaring) any King shall command that which stand not in any opposition to the original laws of God, nature, nations, and the Gospel (though it be not correspondent in every circumstance to laws national and municipal), no subject may, without hazard of his own damnation in rebelling against God, question or disobey the will and pleasure of his sovereign.

Laud, with more moderation, was content always to interpret statute and custom favourably to the King. So, too, it followed that, because Archbishop Abbot was a Puritan, he refused in spite of Charles's repeated command to license the publication of a treatise on royal power, utterly subversive of the laws. He was suspended from his jurisdiction, which passed, through the contrivance of a commission, chiefly into the hands of Laud, Bishop of London.

The High Churchmen cared no more for the spiritual inde-pendence of the Church, than for the political liberty of the State. The King was their factotum. To him they applied for advice on all questions, and for support in every act of power. Laud, writes Creighton, "took no other view of his right to exercise his office, either of power or jurisdiction, than as derived from the Crown, and exercisable according to law". The discipline over morals, which he exercised in the ecclesiastical courts with a vigour worthy of the Scottish Kirk, he regarded so little as a spiritual function that he sometimes consulted Charles about the punishments he should award for sin. In the curious document entitled the "Annual Account" of his Province, rendered to the King after his elevation to the Archbishopric, he asks and obtains orders on details of Church government. The royal will is expressed in notes running along the margin, signed C. R. Sometimes they signify mere assent, as "Do so." Sometimes they go further, as "Let me see those ex-emptions and then I shall declare my further pleasure"; or, "So that the Catechising be first duly performed, let them have a Sermon after that if they desire it". When the distressed Primate relates his difficulties in the suppression of Puritan pamphlets, "what the High Commission cannot do in this," answers the royal commentator, "I shall supply, as I shall find cause, in a more powerful way".

Laud's Annual Account of his Province to Charles

If the King was not Head of the Church in Anglican theory, he was so in Anglican practice. Had High Churchmen succeeded, they would have crushed out the right of the individual conscience, only to substitute a mundane Church State; they would have taken the heart out of English religion, and reduced it to the like-ness of French or German State religion under Louis XIV., or the Lutheran Electors.[1]

In the second place these men were Catholics as well as Protes-tants. True religion, to them, involved inclusion in the Catholic Church, which they conceived not as a vague Communion of Saints, but as a visible and law-established body, of which the English Church was one branch, the Roman another. But this theory did not prevent Laud from glorying in the name of Protestant in his frequent and whole-hearted controversies with Roman antagonists. To the Catholic the Laudians called themselves Protestants, to the Protestant they called themselves Catholics. Closely connected

The High Church-men are Sacra-menta-lists and Sacer-dotalists

[1] *Library of Anglo-Catholic Theology, Laud's Works*, vol. v., pt. ii., pp. 323-70. *Archbishop Laud Commemoration*, 1895, pp. 21-64, essays of Creighton and Professor Collins.

with the importance they attached to the Church was their reverence for her Sacraments. And from their sacramental conception of religion followed their love of ritual and their view of the nature and position of the altar. So also the priest was exalted by virtue not of his personality but of his office. The habit of private confession to priests was encouraged. Laud undertook the duty of confessor to Buckingham. Unstable in religion as in politics, the Duke kept his friends in perpetual fear of his conversion to Rome, and only remained in the English communion on condition of enjoying there the substantial comforts which such minds require.

Bases of Anglican and Puritan theory In the first half of the seventeenth century, a few lovers of truth, of whom Descartes was the most favoured, indifferent rather than hostile, to the dogmatists whom they were in no position to provoke, were obscurely preparing paths by which many have since made exodus into healthier regions of rational philosophy and religion. But except these few, no man dared openly seek truth by his own instinct or reason ; each believed that he accepted his premises from some external authority and drew his conclusions from some written system of theology. While the Catholic took his premises from the Church, and his conclusions from the long and imposing array of her doctrinal pronouncements, the Protestant had for authority the Bible, and for exposition two rival systems, laboriously manufactured by dull Germans out of Luther's word, and out of Calvin's logic by his Dutch disciples. In the reign of James I. it might have seemed that the Calvinistic system of theology, patronised by Crown and Parliament alike, would stifle thought in England. Yet nothing was in reality less probable. For hidden in the brave heart of English Puritanism was germinating a principle not to be found in the books of continental pedants, the right of individual interpretation, which shattered the Puritan Church in the hour of her victory into a hundred sects and destroyed the whole system of Protestant dogmatics. But in so far as there would have been danger to free-thought in the unchallenged triumph, of Puritan theology that danger was now removed by the increased prominence of a rival system. The Anglican doctors honoured the Bible as one authority and the Church as another ; they looked for exposition of the ecclesiastical polity to the acts of Elizabeth and the writings of Hooker and for a dogmatic system to the early fathers. They thereby rejected not only the government of Presbyter and of Pope, but all modern systems of theology, the cumbrous output of Trent, Geneva and Wittenberg. They looked for Church government to the Crown and for truth to antiquarian research.[1]

---

[1] The earning of the Anglicans is much praised, but it was not so much their antiquarian learning as their freedom from the doctrine of exclusive salvation, that saved them from some of the Puritan vices. To the Anglican, the jaws of

James had upheld the ecclesiastical polity of the High Church-men; Charles took under his protection their doctrinal system. About the time of his accession, the Anglicans, whose defence of English insularity was based upon a profound study of the early fathers, adopted the theories of a contemporary Dutchman. The doctrine of Free Will promulgated by Arminius was encouraged by Laud, Charles and Buckingham, because to reject Predestination was to ruin Calvin's whole logical structure. The excitement produced seems now almost incredible. A generation that was theological as well as religious supposed that all their deepest beliefs and feelings depended on the dispute. The problem which in every age baffles or divides the acutest metaphysicians, supplied the catchwords of the two parties in Church and State. Prentices hooted down the street after the Arminian rogues ; courtiers damned the Predestinate crew. Our ancestors might understand even less of what they were disputing than did the mobs who massacred one another for the doctrine of the Homoousion in the cities of the Eastern Empire ; yet much that every Englishman could appreciate was for the time involved in the fate of the rival dogmas. The victory of Free Will would establish a coercive and despotic government, a sacramental and priestly religion ; while Predestination implied privilege of Parliament, liberty of person, Protestant ascendancy, and the agreeable doctrine of exclusive salvation.

So long as Parliament was continually meeting, it was impossible to begin a vigorous persecution of Puritanism, but every preparation for such an attempt was being made at Court. Manwaring and Montague, the clergymen whom the Commons had attacked by name for their Arminian and absolutist utterances, were rewarded, the one with a rich living, the other with a Bishopric. Laud, perpetually closeted with King and favourite, drew up at their request a list of the leading clergy, marking each name " P " or " O," (Puritan or Orthodox), as a guide to the exercise of royal patronage. The Commons were rightly convinced that the High Churchmen were striving to acquire not a share but a monopoly. Indeed, neither side contemplated either a comprehension within, or a toleration without the Church. If the sovereign power of the Crown remained untouched for another generation, the Puritans would have to leave England ; if Parliament became sovereign, the High Anglicans would no less certainly be crushed out. Thus the desire for liberty of conscience, then hopelessly involved with the right to persecute, drove Laud to become Erastian, and changed the gentlemen of the House of Commons into unconscious revolutionists. In the brief session of 1629, after the Duke's murder,

hell were less wide, and breathed perhaps less material fire, than to the Puritan. Puritanism and Anglicanism each contained a principle superior to contemporary theologies of the continent. The one encouraged individual judgment, the other a certain breadth of mind.

Session,
20th Jan.-
2nd
March,
1629
the members attempted to dictate an ecclesiastical policy for the kingdom, and thereby proposed in effect, though not yet in name, the sovereignty of Parliament—a doctrine as strange to the Constitution as the prerogative theories of Charles.

Tonnage
and Pre-
destina-
tion
Tonnage and Poundage were closely, connected in their minds with Predestination and Free Will. If the King was not to have his way in Church and State, he must depend for supply upon the Houses. He was already prevented from waging war without their consent, for the Petition of Right forbade him to levy direct taxation—" any gift, loan, benevolence, tax or such like charge without common consent by Act of Parliament ". They now proposed, by granting him Tonnage and Poundage for one year only, to make him dependent on them for indirect taxation also ; he would then be unable to carry on prerogative government even in time of peace. But Charles refused to accept the grant unless it was given him for life, as it had been given to his father. Meanwhile he continued to levy the duties, relying on the decision which the Judges had made in Bate's case, that indirect taxation was within the power of the Crown.[1] The House of Commons fell back upon the doubtful argument that indirect taxation was covered by the terms of the Petition of Right.

The business of the session of January to March, 1629, can be read in the famous Three Resolutions :—

The
Three Re-
solutions,
2nd
March,
1629
Whosoever shall bring in innovation in religion, or by favour seek to extend or introduce Popery or Arminianism, or other opinions disagreeing from the true and orthodox Church, shall be reputed a capital enemy to this kingdom and the commonwealth.

Whosoever shall counsel or advise the taking and levying of the subsidies of tonnage and poundage not being granted by Parliament, or shall be an actor or instrument therein, shall be likewise reputed an innovator in the government, and a capital enemy to this kingdom and commonwealth.

If any merchant or other person whatsoever shall voluntarily yield or pay the said subsidies of tonnage and poundage, not being granted by Parliament, he shall likewise be reputed a betrayer of the liberty of England, and an enemy to the same.

Such were the Three Resolutions of the last and greatest day of Eliot's Parliamentary career, passed by the shouts of the angry members, thronging and swaying round the chair into which they had forced back the frightened Speaker, whilst the blows of the King's officers without resounded on the fastened door. When they had so voted, they flung all open and poured out flushed into the cold air of heaven, freemen still and already almost rebels.

[1] See p. 88 above.

CHAPTER VI

THE PERSONAL GOVERNMENT OF CHARLES I., 1629-40

> Precurse of fierce events,—
> As harbingers preceding still the fates,
> And prologue to the omen coming on.—*Hamlet.*

EVER since the accession of James, the Commons had been fighting to recover that indirect influence on the Government which they had enjoyed under the House of Lancaster and to wring from the Crown the dismissal of Ministers odious to themselves and to the nation. But at last they had wearied of the useless struggle and made a bid for direct power. The Lower House on its own authority had issued ordinances politically though not legally binding on the nation ; for such in effect were the Three Resolutions. They were declarations of constitutional revolt. Conservative Puritans like D'Ewes shrank from participation in the new policy ; Wentworth, who though no Puritan, had opposed Buckingham and supported the Petition of Right, was a convinced adherent of the King on the question of sovereignty ; while others who had actually shouted for the Resolutions on that morning of hot blood, were glad to get safe home and felt little obligation to abide by what they had done.

On his side, Charles was ready to have Parliament as counsellor, not as master. But the House of Commons had declared that it would no longer be contented with the part of a counsellor whose counsels were always neglected and as the King was unwilling to take any part of their advice, he had no alternative but to govern without Parliaments, until some far distant day when the nation and its representatives should have come round to his views. Such was his intention when he dissolved the Houses in March, 1629, expressed in his memorable proclamation :— *No Parliament, 1629-40*

> Whereas for several ill ends the calling again of a Parliament is divulged, however we have showed by our frequent meeting with our people our love to the use of Parliaments ; yet the late abuse having for the present driven us unwillingly out of that course, we shall account it presumption for any to prescribe any time unto us for Parliaments, the calling and continuing of which is always in our own power, and we shall be more inclinable to meet in Parliament again, when our people shall see more clearly into our intents and actions, when such as have bred this interruption shall have received their condign punishment, and those who are misled by them and by such ill reports as are raised in this occasion, shall come to a better understanding of us and themselves.

As these words foreshadowed, the State had entered on a period of probation ; at the end of it one of three things would occur. Either Parliament would meet again in unchanged humour and win the disputed sovereignty; or the King would so far modify his politics as to conciliate a conservative people and obtain a friendly consultative Parliament on the Elizabethan model; or lastly, he would, like the monarchs of Spain and France, levy a permanent and well-disciplined army, override all law and custom, and never again summon the Estates.

Charles's policy of half measures Charles might, with considerable chance of success, have directed his policy during the eleven years of probation to bring about one or other of the two last-named results. He might have conciliated opinion, or he might have prepared absolutism. But he preferred to adhere to a policy which alienated all the doubtful and the conservative, while he still tried to keep within the letter of the old laws and made only belated and feeble efforts to establish the army on which Wentworth designed to build the new State. The origin of this error is indicated by the proclamation itself, where Charles confidently anticipates the day when his opponents shall voluntarily come round to his side without any change of attitude on his own part. None but a self-centred and unobservant man would have expected such a day to arrive.

The Petition of Right circumvented Charles, determined as ever to retain the right of punishing his political opponents at will, wished to enjoy that despot's luxury within the apparent forms of English law. His recent consent to the Petition of Right made it difficult to continue the system of prolonged imprisonment without trial. And why should he override a law which he could easily, by the help of the Judges, circumvent? *Lettres de cachet* were no longer necessary to the monarch whose father had got rid of Coke and who had himself twice dismissed a Judge for political reasons. Nine members of the late Parliament were called to account before the Privy Council for their conduct in the House of Commons. Most of them, after a considerable period of imprisonment, dissembled their real convictions, apologised and were sent home. The remainder, among whom was Eliot, were after infinite delays and hardships brought up before the Judges of the King's Bench. But that Court could not rightfully take cognisance of words spoken within the walls of the House **Members imprisoned** of Commons. The prisoners, standing firm for the privileges of Parliament, refused to plead before an unlawful jurisdiction. They were condemned to pay fines and to lie in prison till they chose to apologise to the King for their conduct in the House. Eliot, Strode and Valentine, refusing to make any submission, were consigned to prison without any hope of release. These proceedings showed that even should the letter of the Petition of Right be always observed, it could not vindicate personal liberty, which nothing but a revolution in the State could secure.

Meanwhile, the Council had to deal with the financial problem created by the last Resolution of the House of Commons, by which

any one voluntarily paying Tonnage and Poundage was branded as Resist-
" a betrayer of the liberty of England ". In strict obedience to this ance of
unauthorised injunction, the whole body of London merchants the
mer-
preferred to give up buying and selling goods, rather than submit chants,
to duties which it was illegal to impose and unpatriotic to pay. March,
" The obstinacy," as a contemporary observed, " lies not only in the 1629
merchant's breast, but moves in every small vein through the kingdom ". Indeed, if a man attempted to move his goods into the
custom-house, the city mob hooted him as a traitor and threatened
him with the fate of the Duke's astrologer, Dr. Lambe, whom they
had a short while before knocked on the head as he was passing
home down the street.[1] For nearly six months the trade of the
capital was almost suspended. The Council rightly foresaw that
this extraordinary protest could not be indefinitely maintained,
but wiser men would have considered that, when all classes of a
great emporium where the trade of the country is concentrated,
deliberately forgo the profits of commerce for several months,
solely to vindicate their reading of the laws, a great political party
has proved its existence and solidarity and given warning of its
spirit and intentions.

The merchants of London were not going permanently to sus- Chambers
pend their trade, any more than the members of the House of
Commons were going to rot for life in prison rather than make lip
submission. During the summer business was gradually resumed.
But just as Eliot, Valentine and Strode suffered for the whole body
of gentry, a man named Chambers suffered for the merchants ;
he was reduced to beggary and lay six years in prison rather than
once retract his expressed opinion about the tax. It is not the
function of whole classes to suffer ruin and extinction in mere passive
resistance, but to preserve their strength together with their opinions
against the hour of fight, when sacrifice will lead to immediate
victory. Martyrdom is for individuals. But the class which cannot
produce a few martyrs will never produce many fighters.

Eliot knew this well. When he heard in prison that the land Eliot dies
seemed sinking to its rest, he was neither shaken in his own purpose in the
Tower,
nor chagrined by the different course followed by his friends. His 1632
letters, speeches and actions in the Tower reveal a spirit of cheerfulness and even of humour, admirable in one who knows that he
has chosen to die in prison in the hands of victorious enemies. In
1632 he contracted consumption from his cold and unhealthy
quarters. He in vain petitioned the King for a change of air.
Charles had determined that if he would not retract he might die.
A month later he was dead. His son asked to be allowed to con-
vey his body to Port Eliot. " Let Sir John Eliot be buried in the

---

[1] Hence the still surviving schoolboy expression " to lamb " a person, meaning " to hit " him.

church of that parish where he died," answered the pitiless man, who was one day himself to appeal for pity to all peoples and ages.

But though the church by the Cornish estuary does not hold Sir John Eliot, the manor house that stands beside it contains a worthy and curious memento of his last hours. A few days before he died, he sent for an artist to the Tower to paint his picture. He stands in a white frilled dressing-gown, with a comb in his hand and hair falling over his eyes, a cheerful invalid not asking for our pity. He left to his descendants that one patient, humorous appeal against the tyranny that took away his life.

Legal methods of raising revenue ; their unfairness
The financial policy of the new *régime* was to raise money by all ways and means, which could with some show of reason be pronounced legal by the biassed but learned opinion of the royal Judges. The resistance to the Forced Loan had made it clear that manifestly illegal taxes could not be levied, until a well-disciplined standing army was present to coerce the subject. But the new legal taxes soon caused discontent more deep, if less widespread, than the old illegal methods. For owing to their necessarily narrow scope, the legal taxes fell heavily, unfairly and unexpectedly on individuals and on small classes. In order to keep within the law, it was necessary to distort it. If the whole community was to escape assessment, those few who could be brought within the fiscal net would be despoiled without any assessment at all. Now those individuals who were put under contribution for the rest, were the haughtiest leaders of society ; the very class whom Charles might have hoped to attract to the ideals of anti-popular despotism ; from whom he would have most to fear if they became the heads of a democratic rebellion.

He revived obsolete mediæval laws so as to tax or fine certain of the gentry. First he exacted heavy fines from all persons holding estates by military tenure who had neglected to receive knighthood. Then he revived claims long ago dropped or commuted by his Plantagenet ancestors on old forest land which had now for generations borne corn-fields instead of oak-copses and populous villages instead of the ranger's lonely lodge. Several of the greatest nobles and richest commoners in the kingdom were fined at some ten or twenty thousand pounds apiece before they could recover lands which their predecessors had held without challenge through all the stormy revolutions of the Tudor epoch. If these proceedings were technically more legal than the Forced Loan, they were less equitable and more dangerous to property. Their operation was less wide, but they were more keenly felt by the aristocratic class. When the Long Parliament met, there was no Cavalier party and even after one had been formed at the outbreak of the war it did not contain all the nobility or much more than half the gentry of England.

The professional courtiers alone were at all times Royalist, for Revival of monopolies as corporations they had their reward. The financial policy that drove Charles to such hard dealings with some of his most powerful subjects, put him in collusion with the favourites of Whitehall. For his own as well as for their benefit, he revived the system of granting monopolies of trade in particular articles after the manner of King James. But the more thrifty son sold these favours at a higher price and so turned them into an important source of revenue. The last Parliament of James had, during its brief alliance with Buckingham, succeeded in passing an Act to prevent the grant of trading monopolies to individuals other than inventors. This law was evaded by forming the purchasers of royal favour into corporations. These Court bargains always aroused commercial, and sometimes religious, opposition. When in 1633 a new Soap Company, patronised principally by the Roman Catholic party, now fully restored to favour at Court, was given the right to test and condemn the commodities offered by all rivals, the " Popish Soap " became the terror of the country ; it was agreed that its use would certainly corrupt the body and perhaps the soul.

Every age has methods of its own peculiarly attractive to those who prefer to intrigue for a fortune rather than to work for a living. In those days a young man of more wit than modesty had only to attach himself to some Lord at the Palace, be found by the King in raptures in his picture gallery and by the Queen in thoughtful attendance in her antechapel and he might soon look for shares in a monopoly that was the hope of the Treasurer and the despair of the City. A Parliament man, speaking the mind of the nation in the day of reckoning, thus describes the patentees of this period :—

It is a nest of wasps, or swarm of vermin, which have overcrept the land, I mean the monopolers and polers of the people. These, like the frogs of Egypt, have got possession of our dwellings, and we have scarce a room free from them : they sip in our cup, they dip in our dish, they sit by our fire ; we find them in the dye-vat, wash-bowl and powdering-tub ; they share with the butler in his box, they have marked and sealed us from head to foot. . . . They have a vizard to hide the brand made by that good law in the last Parliament of King James ; they shelter themselves under the name of Corporation.[1]

Such ways and means were legal but not popular. The Compositions for Knighthood, the Forest Courts, the Monopolies, were all causes why Charles's personal government became obnoxious to those many men who, without real religious or political preference, strenuously took sides according as they conceived that they themselves had been fairly or unfairly used. Britain has always boasted such sturdy citizens, who have often served her in avenging themselves ; but they are not always deserving of the praise accorded them by history as " thoughtful men " and " restorers of the constitutional balance ".

[1] *Parl. Hist.*, ii., p. 656.

Insignifi-
cance of
Charles in
Europe Until the adoption of the expedient of Ship Money, which was itself merely an extension of the same antiquarian and petty-fogging finance, these methods staved off bankruptcy and Parliament. But they did not suffice to maintain an army or to give the Crown weight in the counsels of Europe. England was doomed to international insignificance until Parliament had either gained control of her policy, or given place to a despotic machinery wholly independent of popular opinion. It was fortunate for our interests abroad and for our liberties at home, that there was no call for vigorous action oversea such as could not safely be postponed. It was the period that lay between the decline of the empire of Philip and the rise of the power of Louis XIV. In that interval, when the House of Austria was the tyrant, Europe, not England, felt the danger ; and for Europe another champion was now at hand. While Sir John Eliot was still alive in the Tower, his fellow-countrymen were watching, with even more attention than they accorded to the despotic proceedings of their own Government, the march of Gustavus and his Swedes through the cities of Germany. For many years past Englishmen had witnessed the gradual extinction of Protestantism from the face of the earth : every effort made to withstand the armies of Rome had seemed under a curse. Well might our ancestors exult on behalf of their brethren so long oppressed,

> When God into the hands of their deliverer
> Puts invincible might.

Charles had no share in these feelings. He had no interest in the survival of Protestantism. He saw in the last agonies of Europe only a series of situations by means of which the Palatinate might be recovered for his kinsfolk. For this end, he hawked his unvalued friendship round the Courts of Europe. Now he negotiated with France, now with Gustavus, who knew the worthlessness of the English alliance, as well as he knew the value of English volunteers. Next, without any sense of inconsistency, Charles sought the friendship of Spain, and proposed to that power the partition of the Dutch Charles
proposes
to parti-
tion Hol-
land, 1634 Republic. Sixty years after Alva's repulse, he proposed to open the gates of the cities of Holland to the spearmen of the Catholic King ; to destroy what was then the centre of political, intellectual and industrial progress in Europe, reversing the central idea of British policy and outraging every aspiration of the people whose sole leader and representative he declared himself to be. Fortunately the Spaniards would not trust him.[1]

Discon-
tent has
no means
of expres-
sion,
1629-40 During the decade when Government policy at home and abroad continued in exact contradiction to the general sentiment, the absence of all forms of agitation is most remarkable, if we consider the violence of the storm when once it broke. A hundred years

[1] G., vii., pp. 367-60.

back such discontent would have caused armed risings like the
Pilgrimage of Grace or Wyatt's rebellion. But the Tudor peace
had done its work. The inhabitants of an island where there was
neither an army nor a police force capable of quelling a single mob,
were now, by custom, civil and obedient to law. Until Parliament
met again, and again gave the semblance of authority to the national
cause, there seems to have been no rioting against the unpopular
taxation and the yet more unpopular ecclesiastical courts. And
when Parliament was not sitting, there was no method of constitutional protest possible, except the merely passive resistance of
Hampden. There was no party organisation, no right of public
meeting, no freedom of the press. If meetings had been held, they
would have been suppressed as seditious riots ; when political
writings by chance escaped the censor, their authors were punished
for libel. Words against the royal policy spoken at the ale-house,
the market-place or the dinner-table would be punished if spies
reported them at Whitehall ; the only practical safeguard for
private conversation was that the hand of the central Government
was short and that the local magistrates were unwilling to become
busybodies on its behalf. Since the last of the fighting Barons
had perished, no subject who happened to disagree with his King
had the right of free speech, either in theory or in custom. Liberty
of speech within the walls of Parliament, unknown in other countries
and now violated here by the imprisonment of Eliot, was the limit
of an Englishman's right to talk against his rulers. The methods
of espionage and repression, to which Pitt reverted at the height
of the anti-Jacobin panic, were indisputable Government rights in **Right of**
the time of Charles, and were frequently exercised against indi- **free**
viduals without causing general surprise or offence. For example, **speech**
when Buckingham returned with his routed army from the Isle of **unknown**
Rhé and the whole nation was seething with suppressed rage at
the disaster, a grocer's prentice was laid by the heels for having
in his pocket a " Prophecy of Evil to befal the Kingdom," and a
woman for saying that the Isle of Rhé was now the Isle of Rue.[1]

This state of things, which would now seem quite intolerable,
would probably never have been altered if the people as a whole
had not quarrelled with the Government on general policy. Until
that quarrel came to a head under King Charles, there was no
personal sympathy for the victims of authority, unless they were
champions of the popular cause. Even in much later times it has
been shown how little freedom of speech, in press and person, is
valued, in cases where popular opinion is on the side of central
power. In time of excitement there are few who will go about to
defend the rights of political opponents. It is therefore highly probable that, if Parliament had peacefully and imperceptibly succeeded

[1] *Court and Times of Charles I.*, i., pp. 305, 317.

to the functions of the Crown, the Parliamentary leaders would have inherited from the King the customary ideas of administrative rights in these matters and might even have continued the Star Chamber as the weapon of the national will. It was during the eleven years of unparliamentary government that this famous tribunal and the whole system of repression connected with it, came, fortunately for the progress of the world, into conflict with popular feeling.

The Star Chamber ; its two capacities
The Petition of Right had not aimed at securing freedom of speech, nor succeeded in securing freedom of person. The royal Judges could still use the ordinary courts to condemn the King's opponents ; while the Star Chamber was an engine even more expressly fashioned and more formidably armed for the same purpose. That court consisted of the whole body of Privy Councillors, aided by the two Chief Justices ; they had the power to summon before them any subject whom they chose and to judge him without observing the rules of procedure and evidence which protected the prisoner in ordinary courts ; their punishments were fine, imprisonment or mutilation, without any reference to customary or statutory limitations. The very men in whom the political power of the State resided, sat as judges and gave decisions solely by their own sense of what was just and expedient. So powerful a court could not fail to do great good or great harm. It sat in two capacities, practically though not technically distinct : as a high-handed court of equity and as the sword of political power. In Tudor times it had been indispensable in both capacities. As a court supervising all other tribunals, it had made law and justice strong in an age of social disruption and had tamed the manners of quasi-military barbarism. As the Revolutionary Tribunal of royalty, it had again and again saved the tottering State from murderous plots and armed rebels.

In the reign of Charles I. society had changed, but the Star Chamber had not moved with the times. As a court of equity it was still useful but no longer indispensable. The ordinary tribunals were now strong enough to execute justice, so far as any court was capable of so doing when there was no detective force and no understanding of the laws of evidence. Juries were no longer overawed. or corrupted wholesale by great lords. Judges no longer sat in fear of riot or resistance. Indeed, throughout the seventeenth century, the courts erred much more on the side of bureaucratic tyranny than of subservience to local interests. The Star Chamber of the Tudors had secured respect for the Assize Court of the Stuarts. A careful study of the non-political cases in the Star Chamber in the time of Charles I. shows good work being done by an unnecessarily powerful instrument of State. We do not find cases of the defiance of ordinary justice, nor generally of violence, and scarcely ever of such violence as the ordinary tribunals would have feared to correct ; the Star Chamber in its latter years dealt principally with libel actions, challenges and poaching disputes between silly gentlemen, forgery, perjury, fraud in commercial or domestic life, petty acts of malice or violence among the middle orders of society.[1] If there was little reason why such a jurisdiction should be abolished, there was less why it should be prolonged.

The Star Chamber fell, not because of its work as a court of equity, in which nine-tenths of its time was engaged, but because of its more rarely exercised but far more important political functions, the abolition of which was the first step towards free speech. There could indeed be no more complete and dangerous example of merging the judiciary with the executive. The Privy Councillors were themselves the judges of their political antagonists. Such a jurisdiction becomes hurtful the moment it ceases to be indispensable. Yet the English were so well accustomed to the control of the Government over the expression of political views, that the Star Chamber would quite possibly have survived the Great Rebellion, if it had not interfered in ecclesiastical matters and become the instrument of the Erastian Bishops for the punishment of their libellers, at a moment when all England would have been glad to have a hand in the libels.

To all ephemeral discontents, popular humours and infant Laud aspirations towards political liberty, was added the grand passion for freedom of conscience. That which called the noblest men into public life and the contemplative into the world of action, which made Cromwell a soldier and Milton a pamphleteer, was not the intrigue of priest or presbyter to gain some petty advantage over other creeds, but the last struggle of the individual to maintain his own spiritual existence, and to prevent the extinction upon earth of the lights by which he reads her meaning. This passion, the only one that ever drove the English into the paths of revolution, was aroused by William Laud.

[1] *E.g.*, among the thirty-one cases that came before the Star Chamber from the Easter Term, 1631, to the Trinity Term, 1632, as many as twenty-nine could clearly have been left to the ordinary courts of the land. In only two cases is there any question of force or influence such as might have intimidated or corrupted the Judge and Jury. One concerns the riotous resistance of the fen population to the draining of the fens. The other case, where Lord Saville with a great company and drawn swords interrupted the sport of Sir John Jackson on land where the Free Warren was in dispute, is the only case which approaches to the violence of an armed and riotous aristocrat. Nor is it by any means certain that the ordinary courts could not have dealt even with this case (see *Cases in the Courts of Star Chamber and High Commission* (Camden Soc., 1886)). The exception that proves the rule is the necessary and warrantable interference of the Star Chamber in the ordinary course of Irish justice ; in Ireland society still resembled English society in the fifteenth century, and the courts were subject to violence and corruption (see Rushworth. ii. pp 203. 204).

During the years when his opinions and character were formed, Laud's experience of life was confined to a University and all his knowledge of religion was gathered from theologians. In the narrow hot-bed of college personalities he learned to hate a set of men who were not improbably odious—the Puritan divines then dominant in Oxford. For many years they tried to suppress him; but in 1611 he rose in spite of them to be the President of St. John's. A reaction set in and he was able to purify Oxford, largely by the help of that college discipline and influence, which had, two hundred years before, weeded out Lollardry from its ancient home. A few colleges alone retained their Puritan character; in the cloisters and river walks of Magdalen, Hampden and his Buckinghamshire neighbours imbibed those principles which they afterwards maintained in arms, when they held the Chiltern Hills as the outwork of London against the Oxford Cavaliers.

As a middle-aged man Laud was called into a larger sphere to take part in the government of Church and State; and when at last he became Primate in 1633, he still conceived that all Puritans were like the clerical pedants over whom his first victory had been won. England was to him another Oxford, a place whence Puritanism, at first blustering and assertive, could soon be driven out by methodical application of college discipline.

Discipline indeed and order were to him not only a large part of the essence of religion, but the only means by which it could outwardly be expressed. Thus because he did not find " order " in the churches on his northern journey, he concluded that there was " no religion " among the Scots and proceeded to manufacture one for the use of that nation. The religion that dictated every action of his own modest, unselfish and conscientious life, was genuine, but cold, orderly and formal.

If he is called upon (writes Gardiner) to defend his practice of bowing towards the altar upon entering a church, he founds his arguments not on any high religious theme, but upon the custom of the Order of the Garter. To him a church was not so much the Temple of a living Spirit, as the palace of an invisible King.

The spirit that cries and tears itself and goes out into the wilderness to pray; the mind that, rapt and silent under the sense of the eternal mystery, rejects as trivial impertinences all forms and shows of worship; the free, strong, self-dependent and self-controlling life of a practical and simple religion, were all alike to be " harried out of the land " by this excellent man.[1]

Laud was not cruel. He put no one to death, and corporal punishment was not his favourite method. Systematic and universal inquiry, deprivation, exile, imprisonment, were his regular weapons;

[1] See G., ii., p. 126 ; vii., pp. 125-28, 301, 340, 341 ; viii., pp. 106-29. Though Carlyle did not understand Laud, he understood the real effect of Laud's action admirably (see his *Historical Sketches*, pt. ii., chaps. xiv., xvi.).

and they would have been used with equal readiness by most of the Puritans. But Laud and not his enemies had the power to put an end to that comprehension which had so long held English Protestants together in one Church. And he, more than any other Anglican leader of that day, was ready to use the power to the full. By strict inquiry and coercion he abolished a working system of local variations in religion and imposed the will of the Bishop on that of the congregation. But neither he nor the bitter generation of enemies whom persecution raised up to defy him, could perceive that if there is no comprehension within the Church there must be toleration without. Though many would have wished to continue the practice of comprehension, no one even stated the theory of toleration : that great doctrine, in which expediency and mercy triumph over logic and passion, was taught to England, during fifty years of war and faction and terror, by the miseries with which the justice of events is wont to punish the stupid intolerance of creed or race.

The plan adopted by Laud was to stop up every hole through which Puritan feeling could find vent in the press, the pulpit, the influence of the clergyman, the legal services of the Church, or the illegal worship of conventicles. He was able almost single-handed to accomplish his work of universal repression, because of the prestige he enjoyed and the fear he inspired as the King's confidant ; and because the parish system and the Church Courts gave the Primate much more authority to interfere in local religion than the King possessed in local government. But no other one of the High Churchmen of that day would have been at the pains to use those powers with such unwonted stringency. His two chief instruments were the High Commission Court and the Metropolitical Visitation.

The Court of High Commission was a mixed body of clergy and laity to whom the King delegated the ecclesiastical power of the Crown. Though the bishops swayed its decisions, it was Erastian not only in origin but in spirit. Its members were in close touch with the politicians and the Court. It had long been well and deservedly hated. Even under Elizabeth it " savoured of the Roman Inquisition," as the sage and moderate Burghley declared. Under James, Coke questioned the legality of its jurisdiction, and Parliament exposed its abuses.[1] The unpopularity of the Star Chamber was a late reflex of this old-established feeling against the High Commission. The secular tribunal only fell into disgrace under Charles, and then chiefly because it undertook the rough work of the ecclesiastical court by punishing the Bishops' libellers. The Star Chamber seldom dealt with political cases, but the High Commission in its ordinary daily work dealt with matters in the highest degree controversial. Authors and printers, lecturers and

The Court of High Commission

---

[1] Prothero, pp. xl-xlvii, 302-7, 404-7.

clergymen, congregations of churches and conventicles, were coerced or punished at its bar. The trials [1] were often cut short by the refusal of the prisoners to take the " *ex officio* oath," by which the court compelled its victim to bear witness against himself. This odious power with which the royal prerogative had endowed the Commission, was resented not only by individual prisoners, but by the lawyers of the lay courts and by all Englishmen.

The Metropolitical Visitation   The other chief weapon of Laud's reform, the Metropolitical Visitation, was of his own device. He revived a claim of his mediæval predecessors to visit, in person or by deputy, every parish not only in the diocese, but in the whole province, of Canterbury. He thus established his personal authority throughout the greater part of England and was enabled to make his inquiries and to enforce his own rules in the territories of less busy Bishops. Nothing could now escape the eye of the master. A supervisory system, such as the State could not boast, was established for the Church by this Richelieu of religion.[2]

Armed with these powerful weapons, the fearless and energetic man set to work to silence the religious voices of England. As early as 1628 men had been forbidden to discuss Free Will and Predestination. Free Will had not yet enough supporters, even among the Anglicans, to claim the monopoly in a Church whose Thirty-nine Articles had been drawn up by men of the opposite party. But Laud, who had a natural antipathy to speculation, had seized on the plan which James had initiated, of prohibiting the whole discussion.[3] The Predestinarians, as had been declared on their behalf by the House of Commons, wished to close the mouths of their adversaries ; Laud imposed silence on both sides. It is difficult to say which plan would have proved most fatal to free-thought.

Episcopal censorship of the press   But on other matters, for which they cared far more than for dogmatic speculation, the Anglicans were encouraged to talk, while the Puritans were silenced. The censorship of the press was then not in civil, but in episcopal, hands. A decree of the Star Chamber in Elizabeth's reign had decided that no book might be printed without the leave of an Archbishop or of the Bishop of London. Under this rule Laud diligently prevented the Puritans from speaking in print. The High Commission maintained the rights of episcopal censorship by severe punishments, and even prevented the importation of Calvinist theology from abroad.[4] In proportion as open controversy was suppressed, the libels put secretly into circulation grew more violent and at the same time more popular

---

[1] See Camden Soc., 1886, for full reports.
[2] G., viii., chap. lxxviii. *Laud's Works*, v., pp. 419-35.
[3] G., vii., pp. 20-22, 48. Rushworth, ii pp. 140-42.
[4] Camden Soc., 1886, p. 274.

with an angry people. The channels of genuine political and religious speculation were choked, until the Great Rebellion loosed the pent flood of books and pamphlets which covered the land for twenty years, cutting far and wide new river-beds in which the thought and practice of our own day now run, and leaving when it subsided not a little of pure gold on the sands of the spent deluge. Laud's system of episcopal censorship would, if it had survived to afflict later ages, have distorted the development of English literature and poetry, of which one essential excellence lies in the profundity and freedom of treatment given to historical, speculative and spiritual truth.

In those times the press was scarcely of greater importance than the pulpit. The Sunday sermon, afterwards the chief means of Tory propaganda, was in the days of the first Charles used with most vigour by the Puritans. Those Anglican clergy who were genuine disciples of Laud and Andrews, preferred catechising to preaching, and ritual to dogmatics ; while the great body of indifferent and old-fashioned parsons, with whom Laud was forced to be content for want of better, the " blind mouths " of Milton's *Lycidas*, could only spell out the Prayer-book service and then dismiss their congregations to keep Sunday round the May-pole. The English Bishops, in their jealousy of Puritan influence, had even in the reign of Elizabeth been anxious to restrain long and frequent sermons, not considering how necessary it was to preach, if a Catholic population was to be converted to a vital and intelligent Protestantism. But it was only under Laud's primacy that this long meditated design was put into effect. Deprivations of the clergy for Puritanism had been few since the great " outing of the ministers " in 1604. In 1633 King James's *Book of Sports* was reissued, and on this occasion the clergy who refused to read it were turned out of their livings.[1] Thus a manifesto which under James had been an act of toleration for the laity, became under Charles a persecution of the clergy. Others, challenged on points of ritual or of teaching, were forced to choose between ruin or submission. In the Eastern Counties, Wren, Bishop of Norwich, carried on a vigorous campaign of visitations and suspensions, independent of Laud's activity. On one charge or another, some of the most enthusiastic preachers were either deprived or put to silence. The great majority, against whom no proceedings were taken, dared no longer preach freely for fear of some inquiry by their Bishop, a visitation of their parish, or a summons before the High Commission. /

In trading and market towns, when the incumbent was unwilling to preach or his Puritan audience to listen, the municipality hired unbeneficed clergymen to " lecture " after the service had been read. The profession of lecturer, though practised within

Chaplains and Lecturers forbidden

[1] G., vii., p. 322. Govett's *Book of Sports*, pp. 117-24.

the walls of the church, was a near approach to Nonconformity ; but when powerful classes were unanimous, such a plan was the only alternative to disruption. Gentlemen often employed private chaplains for a similar purpose. But Laud now made it almost impossible for corporations to engage Puritan " lecturers " and forbade private gentlemen to keep chaplains at all. Two proud classes were wounded in their liberties and self-respect and all strong Protestants saw disappear the last means by which their religious feelings could find expression within the pale of the Church, which thereby lost for one eventful generation the loyalty of moderate men.[1]

Ritualism enforced

The manner in which the Prayer-book services were conducted was also made the subject of inquiry in every parish. The table was moved into the east end and treated as an altar, often against the expressed wishes of the people. The Puritan clergy were being gradually superseded by ardent ritualists, or by time-servers who took the ritual path to promotion. The worst grievance was not that in a few churches a native ceremonialism sprouted into gorgeous excess, but that in many churches a moderate ceremonial was being forced on unwilling congregations, who were not permitted to meet for worship elsewhere. The only legal form of worship, beautiful and orderly as it had now become, appeared an intolerable triviality to many of the most imaginative and intellectual and, as events proved, the most forcible men of every class. Such conditions were, in the phrase of the day, " too hot to last ".

Conventiclers persecuted

On these terms the service to which, ever since the accession of Elizabeth, the Government had succeeded in driving four-fifths of the nation, became in many parishes as unedifying to Protestants as it had long been to Catholics. Many indeed who afterwards attested their Puritanism in council and in war, continued to attend church in sullen discontent. Some twenty thousand fled to America. Others met secretly in woods and in garrets to preach and pray. The frequenters of these conventicles were men of mean station ; for the Puritan squires and merchants before the Civil War preferred either to conform or to leave England altogether. The trials for active dissent under Laud are the records of the poor, seized at their worship and confronted with the might of Church and State in the High Commission. Their love of English liberty and their steadfast adherence to the light within them, more than atone for the want of that learning which had never been within their reach.[2] Men and women such as these—more than Bastwick, Burton and Prynne, more than Hampden himself—are worthy to stand with Eliot as pure confessors of liberty and religion. The

---

[1] G., vii., pp. 130-32, 304, 305. *Book of Sports*, chap. vi. Rushworth, ii., p. 7. *Laud's Works*, v., pp. 328, 329, 349, 350.

[2] See Camden Soc., 1886, *passim*, for the verbatim reports of the dialogues between the Bishops and the conventiclers.

apologists of Laud argue now, as the Bishops urged then, that persons so poor and ignorant as the conventiclers could have had no real capacity to make religion for themselves. Even if such an argument could ever be true, it was certainly false when applied to men of that period, when the lower classes of society had high imagination and opportunity for the noblest spiritual life. The meanest of English trades then produced John Bunyan; and George Fox was a shoemaker's man. But if Laud's war on Puritanism as the religion of the poor and ignorant had met with success, the tinker could never have given his *Pilgrim's Progress* to the world ; and the founder of the Friends could never have left his master's shop to revive in the most spiritual of its thousand forms the religions of the Carpenter's Son.

If proof were needed that Laud's rule was a persecution, it would be found in the fact that many thousand religious refugees of all classes abandoned good prospects and loved homes in England, to camp out between the shore of a lonely ocean and forests swarming with savage tribes. Laud was the founder of Anglo-Saxon supremacy in the new world. Previous to the nineteenth century, the exodus from Britain due to purely economic reasons was limited, though by no means negligible. The island as a whole was underpopulated, although there was congestion in some centres of population like London and in some rural parishes, relieved by organised emigration.[1] The colonists sent out to Ireland and to the tobacco plantations, were drawn from both town and country districts. Some were emigrants escaping from overcrowded parishes, while others were attracted to Virginia by the ease of the climate and soil and to Ireland by the opportunities for rapid money-making and for advance in social status afforded by political and racial conditions.[2]

[margin note: Puritan emigration to America]

But it was with the New England colonies that the future of American institutions was mainly to lie. Religion was indeed the main, but it was not the only, motive of emigration to New England under Charles I. Even in Massachusetts only a minority of the colonists were " church members ". With many the desire to have land of their own was as strong a motive as the desire to exercise their own religion. Hard times in East Anglia appear to have been one cause of the determination to emigrate on the part of the yeomen and small squire class in that peculiarly Puritan district. Yet we can safely argue, from the records of the emigration

---

[1] Cunningham, pp. 345-47. Leonard, p. 229. *Economic Hist. of Virginia*, Bruce, i., pp. 578-96.
[2] Maryland, founded 1633 for the benefit of Catholics, became mainly Puritan. Pennsylvania, founded after the Restoration for the Quakers, became a home for religious refugees of all countries and all sects. These two were " Middle Colonies " as opposed to New England in the North and Virginia in the South. They approximated more to the northern type of society, economics and religion. See Map of American Colonies, p. 297 below.

and its English patrons, that without the religious motive and the Puritan leadership and organisation the inhospitable climate and thin soil of New England would never have been the scene of successful colonisation on a large scale.[1]   In 1620 a few score of emigrants in the *May Flower* had shown the way.   To this new home, suggested rather than prepared by these original Pilgrim Fathers, 20,000 Englishmen fled from Laud's persecution between 1628 and 1640. With the triumph of the Puritans the stream of emigration was stopped, and even began to turn back, till 1660.   If chance had directed the course of religious strife differently, New England would not have been peopled by our race.   Canada would then probably have remained French, and the Middle Colonies Dutch, in language and institutions.   For our Virginia tobacco-growers, who from the first established a system of " indentured servants " that prevented all social equality, and who became negro slave-owners in the eighteenth century, could never have made their form of society and politics supreme throughout North America. Economic emigration from Great Britain in the nineteenth century, if it had then turned to the West at all, would not have found it ready prepared with Anglo-Saxon institutions.[2]

Charles, less fanatical than Louis XIV. when he revoked the Edict of Nantes, put no serious bar on the emigration of the Puritans, though he sometimes tried feebly to restrain it ; in spite of a protest from Laud, he allowed them to establish their own religion as the exclusive faith of their new settlements.   The rulers of England consented that a new world should be called into existence, if they might have the fashioning of the old ; they did not forsee that by this arrangement the balance would ever be redressed.

Religious persecution was not the only means by which Laud contributed to his master's downfall.   Immersed in mediæval precedents and in Canon Law, regarding the Tudor reform not as the Creation but only as the Deluge, the successor of Anselm and Becket ignored the social and political revolution of Henry VIII. and attempted to revive the power of the priest over laymen.   A return to clerical government in society and politics alienated some who regarded alteration in doctrine and worship with indifference.

Jurisdiction over morals revived   The Church courts, which had for a hundred years been cowed by fear of the emancipated laity and the prospect of further confiscations, were inspired once more with a conceit of their authority and traditions.   Laud, who feared the anger of the rich as little as he respected the feelings of the poor, used the same tribunals which punished the conventiclers to chastise the adultery of influential men, who might otherwise have been his powerful friends.

---

[1] Truslow Adams, *Founding of New England*, chap. vi.
[2] See Appendix A., " How America was Peopled by the English ".

The Church courts still retained the power to punish sin. In the last two centuries of Catholicism this jurisdiction had been odious and venal ; under the Tudors the terrified clergy had let it fall into abeyance ; and now a few honest men tried to revive what no large body of people were willing again to tolerate. The only result was to unite the loose-liver with the precisian in common hatred of the ecclesiastical courts ; until, on the eve of the Civil War, fear of the approaching rule of the saints drove back Comus and his crew into the arms of mother Church. Both religious parties in this epoch made a fearless effort to put down immorality by force and both paid dearly for the error. But whereas the rule of the saints was an inquisition of laymen over laymen through the agency of Puritan magistrates and Major-Generals, Laud's method was the jurisdiction of the priest.

By another piece of clerical interference, very unpopular at the time, Laud prohibited the secular use to which customs of immemorial antiquity had put the House of God. Within striking distance of the Scottish border squat church towers had been constructed for defence in war, while in the South the body of the church had served a hundred needs of peace. These habits survived the Reformation. In the Gothic nave of old St. Paul's, well known as " Paul's Walk," friends made and kept appointments ; merchants drove and sealed bargains ; serving men waited by a certain pillar for offers of employment ; courtiers strolled for an hour before the midday meal ; the news of the continent, the ocean and the town was brought fresh to Paul's and canvassed with a din of voices ; while through this noisy crowd of business and pleasure, a stream of burdened porters fought their way across the transepts, a recognised short cut through the heart of London. Rural villages, seldom furnished with any other public buildings, transacted parish business in the church. Laud reformed this altogether. Breaking with both mediæval and Protestant tradition, he originated a new view as to the use of sacred buildings, which was imposed in his own day by order and coercion alone, but which won its way into popular custom after his death, as public halls, clubs and secular institutions of every kind rose to serve instead of the church as places of assembly. *Secular use of churches prohibited*

By every form of patronage and encouragement Laud brought to the front a small school of ritualists,[1] who in zeal and learning *The new Laudian clergy and the squires*

---

[1] " The times' new Churchman " is thus described by a Puritan parodist of the year 1635 (Rous, pp. 78, 79).

> A ceremonious, light-timbred scholler,
> With a little dam-mee * peeping over his collar;
> With a Cardinal's cap, broad as a carte wheele,
> With a long coate and cassocke down to his heele.
> See a newe Churchman of the times,
> O the times, the times' newe Churchman

10

were very different from the old-fashioned Anglican incumbent. The new Laudian clergy had high notions of the respect due to them and of the powers which they ought to enjoy in the parish ; but these the gentry were unwilling to concede. Previously to the rise in the value of tithe in the eighteenth century, the clergyman was often of a lower class, a fact which even a higher education could not always efface. The squire was thus accustomed to admit no copartner in his rule and had not yet formed with the parson the Holy Alliance against Dissent, which ever since the Restoration has been the one almost certain factor in English politics. The village quarrel, which in ever-fresh forms of class rivalry or personal pique, has been going on in every English hamlet since before *Domesday Book* was compiled, often assumed under Laud the form of bad blood between parson and squire ; the landlord, constrained by fear of the ecclesiastical courts to dissemble his anger for years together, was heartily willing to vote for Mr. Pym's friend at the elections of 1640 ; and two years later it was lucky if he did not turn the unhappy clergyman out of the vicarage and arm his own serving-men for the Parliament, under the curious delusion that he had adopted Presbyterian principles.

The clergy and the lawyers
   While the parson was driving the squire to radicalism, the Bishops were performing the same office for the lawyers. The increasing pretensions of the Church courts, no less than the absolutist doctrines of the High Church party, aroused the jealousy of a profession which always loves the laws, though not always the liberties of England. The rising generation at the Temple, nursed on the principles and precedents of Coke, were observed to be growing steadily more hostile to the royal prerogative. Their resistance to the Ship Money and the vigour with which they threw themselves into popular politics after the Long Parliament met, was due in part to the jealousy which they felt as lay lawyers to the revived activity of clerical jurisdiction.

Bishops in offices of State
   Fears that priestly power would recover its old position in society and in law, were borne out by the sudden elevation of Bishops to leadership of the Privy Council and to high secular offices, which their order had not enjoyed since the breach with

> His gravity rides up and downe,
> In a long coate or a short gowne ;
> And sweares, by the halfe football on his pate,
> That no man is predestinate.   See, etc.
>
> His divinity is trust up with five points,
> He dops, ducks, bowes, as made all of joints
> But when his Roman nose standes full East,
> He fears neither God nor beast.   See, etc.

* Dammy, from the soldier's band, who usually sweareth God dam me.
                                                        —*Marginal note.*

Rome. When in 1636 Juxon, Bishop of London, was put at the head of the Treasury, Laud noted in his diary that no churchman had held the post since the days of Henry VII. The Archbishop himself had his hand deep in the details of secular administration and more than any other Councillor could influence Charles on the larger questions of State. The laity were alarmed at this revival of priestly rule; while lords-in-waiting and would-be successors of Buckingham murmured that the avenues of promotion were choked up by lawn-sleeves.[1]

The King's party was neither intelligent, zealous, nor united. Although the patron of Rubens and Vandyke made the Court, for the last time in English history, a true school for the nation in art, culture and manners, he took no better pains than his father that it should be " replenished with choice of excellent men ". While he saw nothing of the future Roundheads, he did not introduce into his Council the better sort of Royalists. His Cottingtons, Westons and Windebanks were an ignoble tribe, very different from the Hydes and Falklands, the Verneys and Langdales who rallied in the hour of danger to a cause of which they only half approved. When Laud wrote to Wentworth in Ireland, " I am alone in those things that draw not profit after them," he was scarcely exaggerating the truth ; and the old Oxford tutor had not the courtier's art to conceal from his selfish and venal coadjutors his dislike of their proceedings. Laud and Wentworth were almost the only honest men at the head of affairs, though they were also the two most earnest contrivers of despotism in Church and State. The courtiers hated them for their virtues and the people for their faults. They had no party. They held their ground only by the King's favour. This they were able to enjoy, but were compelled to share it with men and women who were not of their confidence.

Laud did nothing to secure himself by feminine influence against masculine dislike. In personal intercourse he was unable and un-willing to please. His religion, calculated rather to control Protes-tant than to stimulate Catholic ardour, was too little imaginative to become the inspiration of England, too little sensational to be-come the toy of Whitehall. Throughout the country the women of England, whether Puritan or Anglican, were Protestant and not Ritualist.[2] The ladies of the Palace were given over to frivolity and those who wanted ritual as a pastime, went straight to the more splendid and ancient source of those delights. In his dealings with the strong Roman Catholic ring at Court, Laud came to grief, be-cause his influence over Charles, greater than that of any other man, was incomplete. Henrietta Maria was against him.

Laud's position at Court

---

[1] Bishop Williams had held the Great Seal 1621-25, but he was not Laudian, and as Gardiner says (iv., p. 135), he " was a clergyman only in name ".

[2] G., vii., pp. 340, 341.

The
Catholics
again
favoured

Since the death of Buckingham, Charles had fallen in love with his Catholic Queen. He now treated her as much too well as he had formerly treated her too ill. In 1626 he had destroyed his foreign policy by the fatal French war, because he chose, in violation of his marriage treaty, to persecute his Catholic subjects ; after 1629 he destroyed his home policy, because he chose to please his wife by showing those subjects dangerous favour. The period of the Spanish match seemed to have returned. Again in the country the Penal Laws fell into general, though never into complete, disuse ; again at the Palace Catholicism became the fashionable if not the dominant creed. Residence under his uncle's roof had the effect of very nearly making the young Prince Rupert a Catholic, to the intense indignation of his mother, the Electress Palatine.[1] Such was the atmosphere of the house from which England was governed. Papal legates came over, were received with every mark of welcome and concluded from what met their eyes at Court that the country was on the way back to Rome.

Laud
and the
Catholics

Laud was in a difficult position. He had no antipathy to Roman Catholics, whose company he sought while he avoided that of Puritans. Both parties misconstrued this simple preference. When he became Primate, the Pope seriously offered him a Cardinal's hat ; when he persecuted conventiclers, his victims supposed that their sacrifice was designed to prepare the Roman triumph. Indeed, when avowed conversions became numerous, especially among the rich and most of all among the courtiers, and when the strongest Protestants were sailing in thousands for America, the danger was not fanciful that the Catholics might regain social and political power. If the Elizabethan settlement was to be maintained, either the Puritans must be tolerated, or the statutes against the Romanists must be enforced. In 1637 Laud made an honest but insufficient effort to enforce the Penal Laws. The Queen was too strong for him and he gave up the attempt. He had not the wisdom to see that he must therefore give up that other part of his policy which drove the chief opponents of Catholicism across the sea.

As Laud was known to be the King's adviser in the treatment of the Puritans, it was naturally supposed that he was equally responsible for the treatment of the Catholics. All men saw that the enemies of Rome were being crushed, and that her friends were daily growing in wealth, power and self-assertion. Though his contemporaries were in part mistaken as to the motives of Laud's policy, they were by no means mistaken as to the results that must have ensued from its indefinite continuance.

Charles
and
Laud at
Oxford,
Aug.,
1636

In August, 1636, Charles I. held high festival at Oxford. It was the culminating triumph of Laud, who received his royal friends, as Chancellor of the University which he had conquered and re-

[1] Eva Scott, *Rupert. Prince Palatine*, p. 30.

formed. Lords and Ladies partook of magnificent feasts in the
college halls ; they admired in the chapels the new decorations,
and in the gardens the new architecture, which were in no small
degree the work of Laud. A new play was given in Christ Church
Hall, where the Puritan with his short cloak and Prynne with his
short ears, were caricatured on the boards before the rulers of
England. That was how the King knew the Puritans. If he had
had eyes for men in the flesh half so keen as for men on canvas, he
would have looked first at the real Puritans, in the streets even of
loyal Oxford, through which he had just passed without a cheer ;
he would have seen the sad faces and closed lips of many who were
neither cowards nor hypocrites. That autumn festival was the last
careless hour of the old English monarchy. The troubles began
before another year was out. Seven times the trees were to bud
on the banks of Cherwell and again these Lords and Ladies would
inhabit these same colleges of Oxford, acting plays, composing
sonnets, aiming epigrams, fighting duels and making love. But in
1643 the Puritans were no longer the fools upon the stage, but
myriads of armed and angry men weaving far and wide over England the net of destruction for Oxford and its inhabitants.

The year 1637 is the first of the revolutionary epoch. The
demonstrations round the pillory in Palace Yard, the universal
interest in Hampden's Ship Money case and the rising of Scotland
against the Prayer-book, form in an ascending scale of importance
the first three steps of the popular movement which brought Charles
to the scaffold.

Prynne a lawyer, Burton a clergyman, and Bastwick a doctor,
had composed and secretly put into circulation violent attacks on
the Bishops. They were condemned by the Star Chamber to be
pilloried, to lose their ears, and to suffer solitary confinement for
life. The cruel mangling and branding, which idle crowds watched
with cheerful interest when inflicted on cheating tradesmen or
sturdy beggars, were on this occasion resented as an indecent outrage on the three liberal professions to which the victims belonged.
Prynne, indeed, had once before bled unpitied in the pillory for a
fanatical attack on stage plays called *Histriomastix ;* but three
years had passed since then and the libeller of Laud was now the
hero of the nation. London poured out to Palace Yard, and held
round the scaffold a monster reform meeting which Government
had no soldiers to disperse. The orators, with their heads through
the pillory, spoke much of their faith in Jesus, of legal precedents
and of the ancient liberties of Englishmen. In the great crowd
below many wept aloud and the rudest were moved to honest
English anger at cruelty inflicted on the brave. When the hangman sawed off Prynne's ears a yell arose to which Charles should

Prynne,
Burton
and Bast-
wick in
the
pillory,
June,
1637

have listened in Whitehall, while yet it was heard there for the first time. It was a new sound even in old riotous England, for it was not the voice of faction or of plunder, but the cry of deeper mutiny from brain and heart. Often in the coming years that sound would roll through the trembling Palace, across galleries where courtiers stood in silent groups and secret chambers where ladies knelt in terror before the crucifix.

John Lilburne, Dec., 1637 It was many years since a political demonstration had been held, and it is for this reason that the story of these libellers is great in history. The incident must be read not as the cause, but as the result, of the unpopularity of the Church.

The State, too, met its Prynne in the more attractive personality of John Lilburne. " Freeborn John " now began at about the age of twenty-one his life-long confession of liberty ; before he died in the last years of the Protectorate, he had defied, in the same interest of English law and personal freedom, four arbitrary Governments of widely different political complexions. But the first was the most cruel. Six months after Prynne's sentence, he refused, as a prisoner before the Star Chamber, to take the oath to answer all questions put to him by the court. For this offence, though he was a gentleman born, Lilburne was whipped at the cart's tail from the Fleet to Palace Yard, pilloried, gagged and deliberately starved almost to death in prison. Again, men observed with indignation that classes hitherto exempt from corporal punishment were being degraded by a jealous absolutism. Peers and apprentices alike felt, not that democracy was being vindicated by even justice, but that honourable custom was being trodden in the mud by an encroaching and un-English tyranny.[1]

Inefficient state of the navy By ingenious expedients, which were perhaps good law but certainly bad custom, Charles had collected enough revenue for the small wants of his happy island. But forest courts, monopolies and fines for knighthood, even when added to the rapid automatic increase of the Customs duties in a time of growing trade, would not suffice if England desired to recover that supremacy of the ocean which she had held under Elizabeth, in whose reign the monstrous but declining Spanish power alone challenged our supremacy on the waters. Since then, two more antagonists had come into the field. France was obtaining at the hand of her cardinal a royal navy and a commercial policy, which her wars of religion had long postponed. Holland had outstripped us already. The merchantmen of the little Republic carried more than half our trade in and out of our own English ports. In 1620 it was said that owing to Dutch competition London-owned shipping was only half its former tonnage. The Dutch merchants not only carried goods at the cheapest rates, but enjoyed, on every coast to which the white man

traded, the protection of the finest war navy and the best admirals
afloat. The Dutch State existed by commerce and for the protection of commerce. But the English Government, between the
death of Elizabeth and the seizure of power by Parliament in 1642,
was out of touch with merchants and their needs. Though our
armed trading ships showed stout fight against pirates of every
nation, the royal navy did almost nothing to protect them even
in the Channel. Between 1609 and 1616 Turkish pirates from
Algiers, guided by English renegades, took 466 of our merchant
vessels ; in 1625 they carried off 1,000 of our seamen as slaves, and
took twenty-seven vessels in ten days. Even the shore itself was
not safe from insult. Pirates rode, ravaging and kidnapping, up
the wooded creeks of Devon and Cornwall, where Drake and Raleigh
had prepared the death of Spain. Trinity House had the light on
the Lizard extinguished, because it guided the pirates of Sallee,
one of whom was captured in the Thames itself. Nor was the
" Turkish enemy " the only danger of our merchantmen in home
waters. The pirates of Dunkirk, from the coast of Spanish Flanders,
were scarcely less dreaded.[1]

James and Charles were responsible for this state of affairs.
James had permitted Mansell's official peculation to ruin the navy
left by Elizabeth, although after 1617 the worst sort of abuses were
remedied by Cranfield's vigilance in the public service. But the
personnel of the navy continued in a most miserable condition,
chiefly owing to the poverty of kings who had quarrelled with their
Parliaments. The sailors, famished when they were not poisoned,
seldom clothed and hardly ever paid, were kept together by flogging,
keelhauling and other sea tortures, on men-of-war which were often
little better than ill-managed convict hulks and ill-supplied plague
hospitals. Charles never attempted to remedy this, the true source
of the weakness of our wooden walls. But he rightly determined
at least to keep up the number of the royal ships.[2]

For this end he revived and extended an obsolete power, by Ship
which the Plantagenet monarchs had in times of need called out Money
the merchantmen in the English ports to war. In Tudor times,
also, merchant-ships had been pressed into the service, but in small
numbers and at irregular intervals. Yet in 1634 Charles exacted,
not ships, but money to build a royal fleet ; and in the two following years he extended the demand from the seaports to all the shires
of England. The exigencies of a by-gone system of marine defence were transformed into a new method of direct taxation, by
which the Petition of Right would be evaded, if not violated, the
King would be made independent of Parliament and the existing

[1] Oppenheim, pp. 198, 199, 274-78., G., iii., pp. 64-68 ; v., pp. 79, 428. D'Ewes'
College Life, pp. 91, 92. Rushworth, i., p. 176. Stats. of Real., 16 Car. I., xxiv.
[2] Oppenheim, pp. 184-301 passim. Corbett, i., pp. 66-80.

system of Church and State would become perpetual. It was certainly necessary that England should control the sea. But she could never hope to do so under a Government deprived of the popular support which gave strength to Elizabeth and not possessed of the machinery which enabled Richelieu to despise opinion. The present form of monarchy could never be efficient. If only for the sake of external power, choice must ere long be made between popular Government and despotism absolved from law. Fortunately, there was no need hurriedly to decide in favour of absolute monarchy, for the fear of immediate invasion, which might have necessitated the payment of Ship Money, could not be pleaded in time of peace with all European powers.

Hampden's case, 1637-38   John Hampden was therefore consulting the greatness as well as the liberty of his country when he refused to pay Ship Money. His case was brought before the Exchequer Court, and argued out at full length in its antiquarian aspects before an expectant people. The Judges decided for the King by seven voices to five. But the nation had been persuaded by St. John, Hampden's counsel. The pronouncement of Finch, one of the Royalist Judges, was still more injurious to his master's cause. He had the audacity to declare that

Acts of Parliament to take away his Royal power in the defence of his kingdom are void. They are void Acts of Parliament to bind the King not to command the subjects, their persons and goods and I say their money too, for no Acts of Parliament make any difference.

These words, everywhere bruited and everywhere discussed, convinced the most unwilling that, by a strained interpretation of the laws, the laws were being overthrown ; and that nothing but a restoration of the power of Parliament could preserve the individual in his person and goods.

The English unwilling to rebel   As yet the antagonism of the many found no expression beyond the passive resistance of the few. Some went to prison and more fled oversea, but no one headed a riot or plotted a rebellion. No collector of the unpopular taxes met with violence ; no ecclesiastical court was stormed by the mob ; no country gentleman assembled his friends with arms and horses to raise the shire. Such things had happened in the barbarous centuries gone by ; they were to happen again during the hundred factious years dividing the Short Parliament from the battle of Culloden. But the peaceful endurance of Charles's tyranny showed that the Tudor rule had completed its work of civilisation. The English in 1637 did not know how to move against Government, because the custom of raising war had gone out and the art of political agitation had not come in. The last of the fighting nobles had been executed by Elizabeth, but the first of the party leaders had not yet discovered their calling. Harry Percy's spur was cold, but the more politic methods of Pym and Shaftesbury had yet to be invented. So the hour belonged to Charles and his counsellors.

But if men were unwilling to overturn the Government, they would not raise a hand to prevent its ruin. Would Wentworth find time to build for monarchy a foundation independent of the subjects' support ? Or would it fall too soon, at a touch from a little nation, less tender of law and more accustomed in daily life to the primitive methods of self-defence ?

In the days of Elizabeth of England and Mary of Scotland, a England common religious policy had drawn the two peoples together in and Scotland friendship after a blood-feud of three centuries. But since the Union of 1603 their relation had been less intimate. The real leaders of Scotland, who refused to leave their country to serve as favourites to King James, were no longer, as in the days of Elizabeth, courted by embassies and messages from English statesmen. In the border country itself, the chivalric relations so long fostered by a romantic and traditional warfare, disappeared, without at once giving place to any larger intercourse of trade or intellect. The heart of English civilisation, then lying south of the Trent, was separated by 150 miles of high moors and bad roads from a country of which less was known on Paul's Walk, during the wars of Gustavus, than of Sweden or Brandenburg. So the English Puritans forgot for a while, that beyond the Catholics of the north country dales, lay a nation as Calvinist as Holland or Rochelle. But now, in the last years of Charles's personal government, England and Scotland again began to work out their religious and political destiny in common.

The two countries were well fitted to supplement each other. The Scots could boast no great representative institutions, no spirit of obedience to good laws ; the English were so fondly attached to their laws and institutions that they feared to draw sword on their behalf. England knew neither democracy nor feudalism ; Scotland presented a formidable interfusion of both those fighting spirits. The English peasant took his religion from his betters and knew neither learning nor politics ; the Scottish peasant, nominally less free, actually worse fed and housed, had yet acquired an active spirit of equality in thought, religion and even social practice. England was led by squires, a peaceful class, slow to violent courses, though capable when aroused of producing great statesmen and warriors. Scotland was led by nobles and lairds, ready on good occasion to fight their Stuart King, like the Douglas of old. That nobility, which the Crown had never crushed, it now ventured to provoke.

Laud was encouraged by his master to reconstitute the mediæval Scotland society of Scotland, so far as the relations of Church and State were and Laud concerned. Now the Scottish nobles, much as they feared a revival of the power of the Presbytery, were yet more jealous to preserve the wealth and influence which they had won at the Reformation. They suspected Charles of intending to restore the Church lands which their grandfathers had seized ; they saw him place the Bishops on the Council at Edinburgh, and hand over to these interlopers much of the secular administration. In large questions of national policy, the new King of Scotland never deigned to consult the nobles, who could if they wished call out against him the fighting power of the land. The English people knew nothing of Scottish affairs, but the English Government was, after James's death, scarcely better informed. For if Charles had not been grossly ignorant, how could he have expected that, in consequence of an order from London, the whole population of Scotland would troop to the Kirks one Sabbath morning, eager to take part in a service which until that moment had been regarded by them as the Mass was regarded by the English ?

Laud's Prayer-book, 1637 James, who shrewdly declared that Laud " knew not the stomach of that people," " if he hoped to make that stubborn Kirk stoop more to the English platform," had used the episcopal system in Scotland to limit the power of the clergy in the State, and to protect moderate men in the Church against the fanatical party ; but episcopacy under James VI. had been consistent with Calvinist doctrine and ritual, and with democratic government of the village kirks. But in 1637 Charles and Laud ordered the universal adoption of a Prayer-book based on that of the English Church, in place of Knox's Book of Common Order. Neither nobles, people nor clergy had been consulted in the destruction of their national worship. The new ritual, drawn out by the help of four Scottish Bishops, had received the finishing touches at Lambeth and been sent down ready-made for use, like a sack of English goods. It was an order in no veiled terms that Scotland should be Scotland no more.

The new service could nowhere be read. The few attempts made were signals for riot which there was no force in the kingdom to suppress. In the winter of 1637-38 the Scots entered into a Covenant for defence of their religion. Nobles, lairds, clergy, burghers, peasants, all took part in this national act, as active and intelligent co-operators. There was no division yet either of party or of class. Montrose was shoulder to shoulder with Baillie and Argyle. There were no Episcopalians and no Royalists south of the Highland glens where wild tribesmen still bowed their heads before the Host. After spending the year 1638 in vain negotiations to bring back the revolted nation to its duty, Charles determined to conquer Scotland by arms.

First Bishops' War, 1639 The immediate cause of the fall of Charles's tyranny was the want of a military system. If Wentworth had been the King's English adviser from 1632-39 he might have formed the nucleus of a standing army, or at least have made such provision as would have ensured the levy of a few trustworthy regiments in the day of need.   But during all those precious years he had been struggling with the chimera of races and religions in Ireland and there alone was such a force to be found when his master's troubles began. In England the only two means of warfare available to the sovereign were still, as in the days of Elizabeth and Buckingham, militia train-bands which had not been trained, or pressed recruits whose first object would be to escape.   In the spring of 1639 Charles tried to form an army out of the train-bands of the northern counties. The peasants of those parts were not Puritans ; but they had neither experience, discipline nor enthusiasm.   To lead this army and to give counsel in war and politics, Charles summoned the nobles of England round him as he advanced through Yorkshire.   Many of them had long avoided Court, or had appeared there without being able to acquire influence.   They now assembled, fearing the success of the expedition to Scotland which they were called to conduct : for it would lead to the establishment of despotism in England and to the further reduction of their own rapidly diminishing power in the State.   Meanwhile, across the border, a nation in arms, officered in part by the feudal chiefs of each district, in part by veteran Scots returned from the armies of Sweden and Holland, was laagered on Dunse Law under a discipline which would have borne inspection by Gustavus, and with a zeal which would have won the approval of Knox.   Below them, in the meadows of the Tweed, among un-trained, ill-provisioned husbandmen, only longing to be back at the plough with whole skins, lay a foolish King, separated from his few faithful servants and surrounded by a draft of unwilling nobles. The Scots, who could, by attacking, have avenged Flodden within sight of its haunted hills, chose more wisely not to provoke against themselves the fighting spirit of the larger kingdom.   In the negoti-ations that were soon opened between the camps (June, 1639), the Covenanters showed a moderation and loyalty in their demands which favourably impressed the conservative English nobles ; while a closer knowledge of their objects and ideals prepared the way for that understanding, not yet formed, between the Puritans of North and South Britain.   Charles was forced to concede for the time the wishes of the Scots, to disband the militia and to return home.

So ended the First Bishops' War.   By adopting the daydreams of the priesthood as the policy of the State, Charles had suffered a reverse, from the consequences of which he could only be delivered by a stronger man than Laud.   In September, Wentworth hastened over from Ireland, and was at last installed as the chief counsellor of the King.   In January next he was created Earl and first assumed the immortal name of Strafford.   In the fourteen months that elapsed between his arrival in London and his arrest by the Long Parliament, he was, for the first and last time, the brain of

Strafford comes to the rescue Sep., 1639

the monarchy. The fear which in that short while he inspired among the defenders of freedom, was greater than the hate which in a dozen years Laud had gathered round his own less impressive personality.

Strafford was essentially " the man from Ireland ". It was by stories of the imperious conduct of the great Deputy towards Irish juries, councillors and parliaments, that the English knew what to expect when he returned to their own shores. In Ireland, though Pym never understood it, there was indeed some use for the policy of " thorough ". A state of society so backward and so distracted could be best ruled as India was afterwards ruled by its English governors. Wentworth cleared his way through the opposition of self-seeking officials such as Mountnorris and Loftus, crushing them by methods akin to those used by Hastings against Nuncomar and Francis. He saw the impracticability of a free jury system, where the English never did justice to the natives and where the natives, in terror of their chieftains' vendettas, would never do justice to each other. He often made light of the letter of the law, where the law was an organised chicanery to help the powerful in schemes of spoliation. At Council-board and in Parliament he overrode all opposition by sheer force of his character and will.

Upon such acts were founded the charges afterwards brought against him by Pym at the impeachment. But no one in England made it a crime against him that he had ill-used the Catholic Irish. Former Deputies had tried to drive them to the services of the English Church, by levying, from rich and poor, ruinous fines for recusancy. Wentworth recognised that the policy had failed. For the churches which the inhabitants were to attend, were lying in ruins ; the parsons who were to preach and pray, did not know the language of the people and were not unusually absentees ; the Bishops and their officers spent their time, not in converting the recusants, but in amassing fortunes from them by the laws of the State and the machinery of ecclesiastical courts. Celtic Ireland would have gone back to heathendom but for the illegal ministrations of the wandering Catholic priests. Yet though Wentworth did something to mitigate the lot of the recusants, he continued the general anti-Catholic policy of his predecessors. He encouraged the Dublin lawyers to cheat the native Irish of ancient lands and tribal rights for the benefit of the Crown and the Protestants. In 1609 a great seizure of land from the natives, known as the Plantation of Ulster, had taken place, when Scottish and English colonists had settled on the lands of the Catholic tribes in the North. But in Wentworth's day there was still a Catholic merchant class in the port towns of the East, and Catholic landowners still possessed the greater part of the island. Pestered, persecuted and uncertain of the future, they regarded the English law as a machine designed

to deprive them of their property.   Strafford did nothing to alter
this state of feeling or to remove the causes for a great rebellion, which
the fear inspired by his presence still relegated to the future.[1]

Strafford's object, on his return to England, was to establish Straf-
the absolute sovereignty of the Crown, by partisan interpretations ford's
of law and custom, enforced by swift punishment and backed by policy,
armed power.   Thus Ship Money would be preferred to subsidies 1640
as a means of taxation, because its legality could be maintained
with better face ; but Hampden, according to Wentworth's written
advice, unheeded at that earlier time, ought to have been " well
whipt into his right senses " for going to law against the royal claims.
Strafford's love of despotism derived from no theory of Divine
Right, but from the desire to see England strongly governed.   His
Irish experience had taught him to regard all resistance to the
Crown as factious or corrupt and to see the only hope for public
peace and prosperity in an unquestioned absolutism, coercing all
sects, races and persons into obedience.   Blinded in part by his own
ambition and in part by the false analogy of Ireland, he did not
remember, as the old antagonist of Buckingham should have done,
that in England the royal administration had for forty years been
so weak and foolish, that even the material interests of the country
could no longer be trusted to such a system.   It was a more pardonable error that he did not understand how a debating assembly of
500 uninstructed squires could ably conduct the policy of a kingdom
and succeed where the Court had failed.   He was too proud to perceive in his compatriots the political genius of the English race ;
and he could not foresee the reconciliation which the Cabinet system
would afford to the rival claims of executive and representative.
But his worst error lay in this—that to perfect the mere machine of
government, he purposed to abandon for ever the noblest aim of all
rule and all society, the freedom of individual men in speech and act.

The problem with which Strafford's year of power began and
ended, was how to raise a force for the conquest of Scotland.   It
was his design to create for this purpose two armies, one in Ireland
and one in England, raised by the Parliaments of the two kingdoms.
In March, 1640, he went over to deal with the Irish politicians.
The official vote in the Dublin Parliament held the balance between
Catholics and Protestants.   Reversing his previous policy, Strafford
threw it on to the side of the Catholics, preached a crusade against
Presbyterians and so obtained a vote of four subsidies, whereby he
proceeded to raise an Irish army for the suppression of the Scots
in Ulster and in Scotland.[2]   Returning in haste to England, he
was in time for the meeting of the " Short Parliament ".   That

[1] G., i., pp. 358-441 ; viii., pp. 1-66, 183-98 ; ix., pp. 71, 72 ; x., pp. 43, 44.
[2] G., ix., pp. 95, 96.

The Short Parliament, 13th April-5th May, 1640 assembly had been called by his advice. So little did he know his own countrymen, that he thought it possible to obtain in England, as he had obtained in Ireland, an obedient assembly ready to arm the King against his Scottish subjects. As soon as the Houses met, bargaining was begun ; it was proposed to sell to the nation the royal claim to Ship Money. But the more fundamental issues were not long avoided. Pym, in a great speech of the unusual length of two hours, exposed all the grievances of Church and State and proclaimed that " the powers of Parliament are to the body politic as the rational faculty of the soul to man ". He was about to organise a petition against the Scottish war, when the King dissolved the Houses. They had been summoned not to dispute, but to support, the royal policy. They had raised, though in moderate and loyal language, the question of sovereign power.

Its effect upon the situation Strafford had failed to establish absolute monarchy through Parliament. He now turned to establish it, " loose and absolved from all rules of government ". But that task had been made more difficult by the fact that the Short Parliament had come and gone. The Scots had learnt that they were fighting, not a united nation, but a divided Court. The popular party in England had discovered its strength, brought together its leaders, and proclaimed its policy. For eleven years there had been no popular party, but only private discontent in every locality and every class. There had been no newspapers, no knowledge of what men thought in other parishes and shires. The secret circulation of scurrilous pamphlets, the rhymes posted at night on doors in the street and on trees by the wayside, had fostered but not revealed the strength of opinion. Hence Strafford had been deceived and his opponents left uncertain as to the general temper of the nation, till the Short Parliament exposed the facts. After its dissolution, riots, unknown for years, broke out in various parts of England. Round London, mobs of prentices went about seeking the life of the Archbishop. Government punished the ringleaders with death and for a few months drove these manifestations underground.

Absolutism again, May-Oct. During the summer of 1640 undisguised absolutism tried its strength against a nation now thoroughly aroused. Members of the late Parliament were arrested and flung into gaol. Convocation issued a new set of High Church Canons and proposed, on the model of the Covenant, an oath to defend the existing establishment of the Church ; it was a false step, a sign of fear that encouraged the Puritans and of hostility that irritated them. But the real business of the hour was the attempt of Strafford to raise an English army, by force, since he could not by consent. Ship Money and its military equivalent Coat and Conduct Money, though proclaimed illegal in the late House of Commons, were again extorted. A Forced Loan was set on foot in the city and four aldermen who refused to subscribe were thrown into prison. But the passive resistance of the tax-payer, and the fear of provoking local outbreaks before the intended army was in being, rendered all these expedients useless. Though he knew that failure meant ruin, Strafford was unable, by all the efforts of his will and genius, to extort enough money to pay for one army, from a nation which soon afterwards bore, without falling under the burden, the cost of a score of Roundhead and Cavalier armaments, besides all the loss which their ravages could inflict.

If there was no money, the men at least were being mustered to fight the Second Bishops' War. In 1639 the militia had been called out in the North; but in 1640 a regular army was raised by the press-gang in the South. The northern train-bands had proved harmless to the Scots; the southern recruits now proved dangerous to the King. Though drawn from a rural class too low to have much knowledge of politics, many were Puritans and all deeply resented their forced enlistment. In East Anglia they broke into churches and pulled down the altar rails; in the West they chased away Catholics who had been set over them for want of Protestants whom the King could trust and at least one officer was murdered. A Gloucestershire captain thus describes how he managed to preserve discipline :— *Second Bishops' War. Scots occupy Northumberland, Aug.,1640*

> The Puritan rascals of the country had strongly possessed the soldiers that all the commanders of our regiments were Papists, so I was forced for two or three days to sing psalms all the day I marched, for all their religion lies in a psalm. . . . Every morning when I first come amongst them they shake me so heartily by the hand that I was once in doubt I should have my arm shook off in courtesy.

In all parts of England whole companies deserted and could not safely be dragged back to the colours, from the midst of a population itself on the verge of revolt.[1]

As the wrecks of the army which was to have subdued two kingdoms moved mutinously northwards, the Scots, now under-standing the English people to be on their side, boldly crossed the Border, cut up a small Royalist vanguard at the ford across the Tyne at Newburn, seized Newcastle as their headquarters and sat down in occupation of Durham and Northumberland. The military situation invited them to advance on the capital. But they wisely preferred to sell their advantage for all it was worth. Halting at the Tees, they sent Commissioners to negotiate at Ripon.

Meanwhile, Strafford's lieutenants in Ireland had failed to levy the army which the Dublin Parliament had voted him for use against the Scots. The eye of the master was wanting; and in that poverty-stricken island less enthusiasm was shown in paying than in voting subsidies for the extirpation of heresy. In October Strafford pro-posed to revive the warlike ardour of the Irish Catholics by letting *Strafford suggests the up-rooting of the Ulster planta-tion*

---

[1] *Treaty of Ripon* (Camden Soc., 1869), pp. xx-xxiii. G., ix., pp. 159, 160.

them loose at once upon the Scots in Ulster. He was willing to do what James II. afterwards did in the campaign of Londonderry—to associate the royal with the Catholic cause, and kindle the flames of racial and religious war. When we remember that Strafford had no sympathy with Irish nationality or religion, and that he considered the Protestant interest to be the true interest of Ireland, his sudden proposal to uproot the Ulster plantation can only be regarded as a proof of his fierce determination to establish despotism in the British Islands at all costs.[1]

Treaty of Ripon and summons of Parliament, Oct., 1640   As this evil scheme did not meet with support, Charles had no other choice than to surrender to the Scottish Commissioners at Ripon. He had not only to concede all their political and religious claims, but to buy them out of England at the price of a high indemnity and a daily allowance for their soldiers, who were to occupy the northern counties until the lump sum was paid down. The extortion was a policy not of avarice but of state-craft, for there was only one way in which the English Government could meet a demand for gold. After long weeks of debate and confusion at York, surrounded by a divided Court and a mutinous soldiery, Charles, at the instance of popular petitions organised by Pym and his friends and at the advice of the Great Council of Peers, consented to save England from bankruptcy and invasion by summoning her Lords and Commons to the rescue.

The Short Parliament had been called to pay for the conquest of the Scots, but its more famous successor was called to buy them out of England. As regards both English and Scottish politics, the summons of the Long Parliament was a surrender.

Arrest of Strafford, 11th Nov. 1640   But one man was not prepared to lay down arms. Strafford's first instinct, while the members were assembling in London, was to remain in Yorkshire, carefully nursing Royalism and discipline in the army and waiting till time and chance should bring round an occasion which his genius might snatch to recover what was now lost. But Charles, with light promises of safety, summoned him unwilling to London. The Parliamentary leaders began, at first fairly and cautiously, to take measures against him. A committee, on which one of his intimate friends was placed, was appointed to inquire into the late government of Ireland ; a long preliminary investigation was meditated. But events suddenly swept aside all fairness and all caution. For Strafford, seeing that if he sat still he would be caught before long in the toils, persuaded Charles to arrest the Parliamentary leaders on a charge of plotting treason with the Scottish rebels. The King was to review a body of troops in the Tower on the day fixed for the arrest and overawe resistance by force. At the last moment the plan was abandoned, but not before the fatal rumour of it was abroad. The Commons, meeting

[1] G., ix., pp. 155-57, 213, 214.

in terror on the day of the intended blow, listened behind locked doors to Pym's urgent counsels of self-defence, drew up an improvised impeachment and carried it up then and there, in hasty procession, to the Lords.   Strafford, hearing what was done, hurried to the same spot a little after his accusers had arrived.   At that supreme moment, as Strafford moved scowling up the floor of their House, the Lords were judge between two systems of government for England.   In that hour all the personal and class insults which the House of Stuart had heaped on the nobility, all the ungracious manners of Laud and Strafford, all the social ties and national sentiment which bound the English nobles to the class whence their families had risen, stood our country in good stead.   He whom no man had yet safely withstood to the face, was stopped before he reached his seat by the cry of his angry peers—" Withdraw, withdraw ".   He obeyed and was soon called back to kneel a prisoner before the risen majesty of England.

CHAPTER VII

THE FORMATION OF PARTIES, NOV., 1640—AUG., 1642.

When civil dudgeon first grew high.—Hudibras.

Character of the approaching revolution

REVOLUTION is the historian's touchstone, by which to try the quality of a race or age. It may succeed or fail, pass or stay ; but it will in any case reveal the worth or vileness of the soil whence it springs. That most rare of human events, a revolution loftily enacting lofty ideals, can occur only in a State where wealth is well distributed, classes fairly balanced and kindly related, the common intellectual food wholesome, the imagination alive and the moral standard high. It is seldom that all these conditions are fulfilled ; it is yet more seldom that the politics of so fortunate an era demand a revolution. Yet for this once in history all causes for the unique event were found together. It has been shown in the first two chapters that when Charles and Laud began to play the tyrant in England, she was rich in native excellence. The character and function of the various classes, gentleman and yeoman, merchant and apprentice ; the sports, traditions, customs and character of every shire and village, which gave even to the poor a part and a joy in life ; the conditions of labour and leisure in country and town ; the charm of our mother-tongue as then written and spoken by common men ; the Elizabethan culture distilled in life and manners ; the Protestant religion expressed in life and conduct ; all these things together, when warmed by the breath of revolutionary ardour, gave us our Cavaliers and Roundheads. Excepting the Reformation in Holland and in some continental cities, history perhaps records no revolution so noble as this, because no other nation in time of revolt was sound in its material and social fabric, yet alive to the appeals of intellect and quick to hear the restraining voice of conscience. At the overthrow of the decayed society of France, ideals served as ensigns borne along before an army of material hungers. Hence the dark story of their savage vindication ; hence, too, the victory of ideals and hungers together, in modern France of the equal laws. The French revolution appealed to the needs as well as to the aspirations of mankind. But in England the revolutionary passions were stirred by no class in its own material interest. Our patriots were prosperous men, enamoured of liberty, or of religion, or of loyalty, each for her own sake, not as the handmaid of class greed. This was the secret of the moral splendour of our Great Rebellion and our Civil War.

In the first weeks of the Long Parliament, the policy of those who fought the battle of Protestant supremacy and political freedom underwent a change, sudden as when the wind shifts, but permanent as when the flood leaps down into lands below its former level. From the accession of the House of Stuart to the breaking of the Short Parliament the patriots had studied no art but the legal definition of rights, and the fearless presentation of grievances. But from the meeting of the Long Parliament to the accession of the House of Hanover, through all changes of men and measures, of high and low ideals, the first thought alike of Roundhead and Whig was the manipulation of forces. Former Parliaments had spoken for the people, but never called upon the people to protect them. Hence the purity and charm of Eliot's life and death ; he registered the claims. Pym was the master of another art,—to seize the power. Pym first called in clubs and broadswords to protect this Parliament from the fate to which all its predecessors had submitted. At his word, ignorant fanaticism and mob force came to guard religion and liberty, whose cause had looked so fair when only the chivalrous gentlemen of England were its long-suffering champions. And yet the gain was great, for in this way English liberty and religion survived. And in this way English liberty came to include more than the narrow legalism of the Parliament men, English religion more than the stiff gentlemanly Protestantism of the earlier patriots. For the inhabitants of street, and farm, and village, called in the hour of need to acting partnership with the Puritans of the manor house, added not only to the fighting power, but to the spiritual and intellectual content of the cause. Behind the mobs who hooted the King's half-pay captains in Palace Yard and knocked down papists at the street corners, moved the humble men who were to found Quakerism, and the practical visionaries who were to inspire democracy with its best peculiar hopes and ideals.

The time had come when British freedom might be secured, if skilled hands would boldly snatch for it ; but it was by no means the inevitable outcome. The course which the world has since taken depended upon this ;—that the one English Parliament which sat protected for the moment by the Scottish pikes and by the union of the whole people against the Government, should throw aside long traditions of isolated respectability and be ready to foment and lead the revolutionary forces of the land. But how should five hundred members, collected by the hazard of unorganised elections, have courage, skill or union for such proceedings ? This Parliament, it cannot be doubted, would have run a higher course than its predecessors in constitutional votes and high sounding declarations, only in the end to have fallen in deeper ruin, had not the leadership of Lords, Commons and country together, been seized by a band of

self-elected tribunes, who had the courage and talent to execute
plans formed in the council chamber of intimate family friendship.
During the eleven years' tyranny, though the existence of a party
had not been notified by any organisation or any public action, a
group of friends, containing several of the richest peers and highest
commoners in England, had formed the habit of living together for
months under one roof to watch and discuss events. This home
conspiracy, the true origin of our party system, was hatched far from
London in deer parks and on garden terraces ; its chief members
were Pym, Hampden and St. John ; the great Earl of Bedford ;
the hot Puritan Lord Saye and Sele ; Lord Mandeville, heir to the
Earldom of Manchester ; and his wife's father the Earl of Warwick,
colonist and sailor, whose jolly yarns, smelling of the Spanish main,
made the persecuted preachers, with whom he filled his hospitable
house, laugh like pluralists at their Bishop's table.

When the session of the Short Parliament had revealed, and its
dissolution aggravated, the mutinous temper of the country, these
careful watchmen saw that the time for action had come. On the
eve of the Second Bishops' War, seven English peers signed a letter
to the Scottish rebels, in which they recognised a common cause,
promised all constitutional aid, but deprecated invasion and refused
to give help in arms.[1] Such a document, even if no verbal message
of more treasonable import was sent with it, was not a really serious
discouragement to the plan of invading the northern counties.
Again, when the Scots had crossed the Tweed, and Charles was
hesitating at York, Pym organised petitions for a Parliament, both
from Peers and people. When the general election was taking
place, he went a riding tour with Hampden through the towns of
England urging men to choose known Puritans, and forming in
distant counties those ties of personal connection and mutual agreement which leaders must have in hand before a great agitation in
the provinces can be organised from the capital. So, when the Long
Parliament assembled, this small group of Lords and commoners
were already recognised not only as the successors of their friend
Eliot in the informal leadership of the Commons, but as the authors
of a policy outside its walls which came as near to technical treason
as any word or deed of Strafford.

Yet these innovators were revolutionaries only in their means.
In the ends which they sought, they wished to be conservative,
although they evoked force to preserve what they conceived to be
the old Constitution. In November, 1640, they did not contemplate
the expedient by which the two Houses, a year later, themselves
assumed administrative power. They did not recognise that they
would soon be forced to transfer the sovereignty of England from

[1] Bedford, Essex, Warwick, Saye, Mandeville, Savile and Brooke (see G., ix.,
pp. 178, 179).

the King to his subjects. They only intended by the punishment
of the greatest men in the land so to illustrate the power, and by a
series of new laws so to define the rights, of Parliament, that no
Privy Council would ever again find the courage or the legal pretext
to govern Church and State contrary to the will of the Houses and
the Protestant feeling of the nation.

When in November the gates of the Tower closed upon Strafford, Flight of
a sense of their own security and omnipotence inspired the Commons, Finch and
for two months, in the work of general retribution ; while despair and Winde-
panic spread among their destined victims. The impeachments Arrest of
avenged in the person of the highest delinquents each of the various Laud
kinds of wrong which England had so long endured. Windebank,
the Secretary of State who had done most to give a Catholic bias to
our policy at home and abroad, fled to France, and was there reconciled, before he died, to the Church whose interests he had so well
promoted.[1] Finch, the Judge who at Hampden's Ship Money trial
had first roused Englishmen to their senses by pronouncing that
their property was not their own but the King's, escaped to Holland, the first of the long series of political refugees, who in rapid
mutations of Cavalier and Roundhead, Tory and Whig, were for
fifty years seen daily by the inhabitants of the Hague pacing the
avenues with the restless strides of hunger, and misery, and hope.
But the predecessor in exile of Charles II. and of Shaftesbury,
found Holland already inhabited by the humbler exiles not of State
but of Church. Brownists and Anabaptists from our country had
thriven in Amsterdam and were shrewd or kindly enough to supply
this new flight of unfortunates with a comfortable home and an
English table. In the following August Evelyn found Finch and a
whole household of Cavaliers living *en pension* in the houses of these
strange bedfellows.[2] Laud himself, too old and brave to fly, was
carried to the Tower, where he lay unfeared and unregarded, till
four years later his enemies did all that could be done to vindicate
his policy to mankind, by illustrating in his execution the malignant
spirit that always haunted and sometimes possessed the temple of
English Puritanism.

Thus the chiefs of the old Court party, who had so long silenced
every voice in England but their own, were for ever broken and
scattered, many months before the King's later Cavalier friends had
divided their fortunes from those of Warwick and Pym. The
Queen and a few swashbucklers were left, for a while, alone against
all England. Men who had curried favour with the Privy Council
by exacting Ship Money from their neighbours and had now to

---

[1] He had in May, 1640, joined the Queen in her appeal to the Pope for men and
money to subdue England (G., ix., p. 135). Such were the men and women to
whom Charles I. committed our interests.

[2] Evelyn's *Diary*, August, 1641.

earn the mercy of Parliament, spoke and voted for Pym's measures in the House, and some of these even drew sword in the Civil War faithfully to their new allegiance.[1] For in the winter of 1640 a new world had come into being.

London, the workshop of the revolution

The change was first and most clearly seen in the City. No royal police, no municipal despots fettered the early revolt of the capital. Self-governing London was in a state of uncontrolled freedom the moment that her citizens ceased to fear Lambeth and Whitehall. She had been restrained from without, rather by moral than physical force. Merely by ceasing to obey the Court and Bishops she had already, before the day of Strafford's arrest, become a free republic of political thought and writing, the workshop of the English revolution. The episcopal censorship, in the hands of academic pedants such as in all ages hate intellectual vigour of any class but their own, had long stifled the growth of mind. But now the time had come for free interchange of ideas. Pamphlets on religion and government were daily piled on the stalls, and daily disappeared down streets and through doorways, each on its mysterious mission, making creeds, wars, systems, men. In courtyard, chamber and pulpit sermons were delivered day and night to excited and interpolating audiences, like speeches in some well-contested election. The old Gothic churches, in which the City was then so rich, saw many a strange scene that Christmas ; in some the congregation raised psalms to drown the Prayer-book service ; in nearly all they carried back the communion-table into the nave. But besides these busy reformers of the Church, a score of sects, seeming to spring in as many days out of the earth and numbering many thousand Londoners, scorned the " steeple house " and met in the largest rooms they could find, no longer as thieves by night, but daily visited by inquiring multitudes.

Onwards for many years from these first days of November, 1640, London was great and wonderful as Paris in 1789. The centre of revolution, the curb of the neighbouring Court, and the rude protector of the neighbouring Parliament, it produced in fierce intellectual ferment a new world of thought and action, to guide the coming centuries. But the likeness to the Paris of 1789 marks the difference. Our English theorists spoke for the most part of religion, Church government and individual conscience ; and the London mob was not the wreckage of a ruined society, drifting into the capital on the search for bread to eat and finding only victims to slay, but was largely composed of and wholly guided by prosperous shop-keepers and apprentices, many of them descended from gentle families.[2] The popular passion to which our Parliamentary leaders

---

[1] Hutchinson, pp. 127, 128, case of Sir John Gell. Clar., p. 73.

[2] See p. 16 above. Yet a large proportion of the followers in the " prentice " mobs probably consisted of the slum dwellers from the " liberties " outside the city proper. See note p. 42 above. But these had no social end of their own to serve and simply became a political force in the hands of their betters.

trusted, had for motive not hunger but religion. The mob howled under the doors not of bakers but of Bishops. The hatred of Catholicism, the rumour of papist massacre often as wild as the silliest story that ever gulled Marat's Paris, the wiser fear of real army plots and possible Cavalier conquest, these were the furies that drove the blind multitude to battle on behalf of nobler men and higher projects than any of which they themselves were aware.

In this atmosphere the Scots Commissioners, whose treaty busi- The Scots Commissioners in London ness had been moved from Ripon to London, and who had taken care to come up well supplied with preachers and theologians, soon conceived the new hope that England would adopt the ecclesiastical system of their country. The guests of the City, visited by the greatest Peers, consulted beforehand on every move by the organisers of agitation, preaching on Sundays to a great audience on the merits of Scottish religion and the demerits of " his little grace of Canterbury," they were for a few all-important weeks the favourites of the town. " Gramercy, good Scot," was the refrain of popular street ballads. For the English were not ungrateful to the army which had first opened the house of their bondage and which still secured the continued session of Parliament by occupying Northumberland. " No fear yet of raising the Parliament, so long as the lads about Newcastle sit still," Baillie wrote back to his Scottish countrymen. The same idea was openly expressed in debate by some members of the House of Commons. The invaders' friendship was retained by occasional doles towards their daily allowance, while their presence on this side the Border was prolonged by the unwillingness of the House to pay the full indemnity. Its extravagant amount was to some members a real reason, to others a welcome excuse, for delay. The financial demands of the Scots Commissioners and the rude persistence with which they now claimed the abolition of Episcopacy in England, had by the end of February lost them all favour with one section of the English patriots.

For while Strafford still gazed from the Tower window, sick with Question of Episcopacy, Nov., 1640- Feb., 1641 the plethora of intellect cut off from knowledge and of energy withheld from action ; while his Irish enemies, eager to bear witness against him, were still tossing along the coast of Wales ; the men who were agreed to compass his destruction were already dividing on another issue. During the long preparations for the great trial, the City and the House of Commons were agitating the question of the future—were Bishops to be reformed or abolished ? In the country, where men impatiently scanned their letters for the news that his head was off, Church settlement did not begin seriously to attract study or to divide opinion till many eventful months had intervened. But where the voice of inquiry and debate arose round the London bookstalls, where members with bent head and knit brows paced Westminster Hall between the scaffoldings erected against the day of the Earl's impeachment, the learned argument ran high on apostolic succession and the usage of the primitive Church. But other influences had more weight than that interminable and uncertain antiquarian controversy, in the decision which each of the future leaders of England now made for or against the retention of a modified Episcopate.

Unpopularity of the Bishops almost universal   Of the various groups which it was Pym's art to unite for action, the strongest in wealth and numbers, to which he himself belonged, made objection to Episcopacy on purely practical grounds. The great body of Englishmen had neither sympathy with the Sectarian's demand for religious freedom, nor interest in the Presbyterian system advocated by their own doctors and by their Scottish allies, but they were convinced that the abolition of Episcopacy was now the only means of securing for ever the Protestant character of the State Church to which they intended that all men should still be forced to belong. They were true successors of the men who defended Elizabeth's system against Catholic and Presbyterian attacks. The political and religious action of the Bishops since the death of the Queen had altered their view, not of the State Church, but of the Bishop's office. Laud had revived Anti-episcopalianism in England, not now as an ecclesiastical ideal, but as a political and religious necessity. In 1640 it required an effort of memory or imagination to picture a Bench of truly Protestant Bishops. The prospect of ever again obtaining such a Bench was small, since the appointments at that time lay, not with Parliament, but with the obstinate man who was the husband of Henrietta Maria, the patron of Windebank, and the friend of Laud. The Bishops were hated not only by the City mob but by the whole body of gentry, on whose political, social and religious feelings they had so long trampled. Episcopacy had defenders in the Long Parliament, but the Bishops themselves had none. In a speech delivered in defence of their office, the Cavalier Digby declared himself " so inflamed with the sense of them," that he was ready to cry out " Down with them ! Down with them ! even unto the ground." Falkland, who followed on the same side, admitted that some of them " had laboured to bring in an English Popery ". Pym differed from Digby and Falkland, because he believed that nothing short of the abolition of the office itself would be more than a temporary safeguard against a revival of Catholicism in the bosom of the English Church.

The Prayer-book more popular than the Bishops   It is probable that the moderate Cavaliers would not long have posed as defenders of men whom they detested, had not the fate of another institution, which they loved more heartily, been involved in the fate of the Episcopate. The proscription of the Prayer-book service was eventually the ruin of the Puritans. The intolerant and offensive zeal with which they pursued it, is explained but not excused by two considerations. First, the Prayer-book had become under Laud's *régime* associated in practice with ritualism. Secondly, no one beside the Sectarians contemplated the permission of any system of Nonconformity and therefore all who conscientiously desired for themselves a different service from the Prayer-book, were forced to prohibit its use to others. It soon became apparent how difficult it was to supply a good alternative service every Sunday in every church. Country gentlemen and their wives who had supported Pym and the Puritan cause, were often disgusted when they had to listen in their own parish to " a very strange service, and in such a tone that most people do nothing but laugh at it ".[1] The Puritans were no more able than the Anglicans to take over the whole machinery of religious life in England.

The resolution to abolish Episcopacy " with all its roots and branches," that is, with all those upper ranks of clergy whose office and tradition were inextricably associated with a Catholic conception of the Church, was the policy that bound together men who differed in a hundred different ways as to the proper form of Church settlement. And if the views of those who wrote and spoke were divergent, the views of those who thought and kept silence were vague. " I can tell you, sirs, what I would not have ; though I cannot, what I would," answered Mr. Cromwell, to the bewilderment and scandal of two Episcopalian members who had asked what system he proposed to substitute for theirs.[2] But to Milton, whose ecstatic vision of his regenerated country, moved him at last to descend in the stately measure of his poet's prose among the assemblies of common and secular spirits, it seemed, as he wrote his immortal pamphlet, *Of Reformation in England,* that only libertines dreading the correction of their sins had reason to fear the establishment of Presbyterian discipline. The gods laughed, and gave him to drink the bitter cup of his ideals realised. On a lower scale of intelligence and feeling, thousands were uncertain as Cromwell and changeable as Milton.

{marginal note: No scheme of reform agreed upon}

If, then, it be remembered that comparatively few persons were Erastian, Presbyterian, or Independent with any consistency, it is safe to distinguish the main features of the three rival schemes. They had indeed one common element, besides a sternly Protestant faith and worship ; all three proposed to introduce democracy into the Church. The priest was to be subjected to some measure of election and control by the people. This change would require a high spiritual level throughout the country, and a democracy of intellect such as the Presbyterian system had found or fostered in Scotland. Could the English villagers be raised to the same height ? If not, Puritanism would again give place to the old Church establishment, more compatible with squirearchy and more suited to a population whose mass lacked intelligence and enthusiasm.

{marginal note: Three Puritan schemes of Church government}

---

[1] Verney, ii., p. 258.   [2] Sir P. Warwick's *Memoirs* (ed. 1703), p. 177.

Erastian   1. The scheme adopted by Pym and the Parliamentary majority which he came to command, was that of a Puritan State Church, not tolerating dissent either of Anglicans or of Anabaptists, but controlled by Parliamentary Lay Commissioners in the place of the Bishops. Such was the anti-clerical system planned out by the representatives of England. Laud himself had not been more Erastian.[1]

Presby-   2. The "true blue" Presbyterian scheme, recommended as
terian   infallible by the Scottish people and by a few English divines, though it also would have established a democratic ecclesiastical organisation in each village, would have unified all under a system of clerical synods and Church councils, and would rigorously have enforced the orthodoxy of Geneva. This scheme was rejected by the Long Parliament in 1641-42, and was only adopted in 1643 as the necessary price of the Scottish alliance in an hour of deadly peril. The Parliamentary majority of Puritan Erastians only consented to become Puritan clericals in the middle campaign of the war.

Sec-   3. But the scheme most characteristic of England herself and of
tarian   her future history, was now put forward in London by the Sectarians, who demanded not only a congregational system, but liberty of worship and belief. Here lay the true road of Puritan development in England ; here was the only possible solution of Anglican and Puritan rivalry ; here, too, lay the road towards free-thought.

The Sectarians had read the secret of the future, but the present was for their rivals. As yet there was hardly a man in the House of Commons who would have risen in his seat to aver in clear language that toleration ought to be allowed outside the Established Church. The supporters of a Puritan State Church were for the moment the standard-bearers of freedom. Patriots, led by Pym, rallied to support this system, careless of its basis in theory and ignorant of its meaning in practice. Of these men thousands were soon to join the sects ; thousands more were to return to the Anglican worship. The Puritan State Church was the improvised fighting organisation of Protestant religion and constitutional liberty. It fought, conquered, and dissolved again into its component parts.

Root-and-   On 11th December, 1640, " a world of honest citizens in their
Branch   best apparel " came to the doors of the House of Commons with
Petition,
Dec.,   a petition, signed with 15,000 names, for the abolition of Episcopacy
1640   " with all its roots and branches ". The well-dressed crowd waiting in Westminster Hall was the first official announcement of a new platform in Church policy, known from that day as Root-and-Branch. It was also the first sign that the City intended to play a part in politics as third to King and Parliament. The reception of the citizens showed that Pym's friends in the House welcomed their interference and relied on popular demonstrations. Although

------

[1] G., ix., pp. 407, 408. Shaw, *passim.*

on this first occasion the petitioners came " in a very modest way,"
their coming was the prelude to rougher work in Palace Yard.

Two months later, the Commons got so far as to debate whether Debate
they should refer this terrible petition to a committee; it lay on on the
their floor like an apple of discord that all would fain let lie un- Feb.,
touched. This first debate was a friendly exchange of opinion 1641
between men still acting together like brothers in a struggle for law,
liberty and life; but on whichever side each leader spoke about
the treatment of the petition, on that side he afterwards fought in
the Civil War. Yet there was much even in Church affairs on
which the whole House was agreed. All vied in abusing the existing
Bishops; the future Cavaliers were eager to reduce their coercive
power and to make them serve, though by what means none could
tell, as instruments no longer of King but of Parliament. The
revived mediæval theories of the priestly office, the legal and social
pretensions of the Laudian clergy, were more than the Church laymen of that day could swallow. A ceremonial interpretation of the
Prayer-book was odious to the great majority of its defenders. The
whole House was at one in requiring that the table in Saint Margaret's,
Westminster, where they attended service, should be moved down
for their use to the body of the church. And so, when the Root-and-
Branch Petition was debated, nothing was heard about the Catholic
Faith or the Apostolic Succession; but men spoke out their dread of
Presbyterian discipline, of alterations in the Prayer-book and of
popular interference in religious questions.

It was significant that Digby protested not only against the Affinities
matter but against the manner of the petition; he deplored " ir- in
regular and tumultuous assemblies of people, be it for never so good and re-
an end ". He clung fast to the old ideal of Eliot, by which Parlia- ligious
ment was regarded as a thing apart, acting on behalf of the people, opinion
but not with them. Much as Digby, Falkland and Hyde loved the
law and hated Strafford, none of them had ever shown such bitter
hostility to the Court as the Puritan leaders; none of them had
shared in those family gatherings where the deliverance of England
had been planned; or had taken part in those mysterious activities
which led to the summons of the Long Parliament and to the election
of so stout-hearted an assembly. When Hampden and Saye were
resisting the levy of Ship Money, Hyde was a busy practising lawyer
known and favoured at Court, and Falkland was discoursing with
poets and divines in his rustic academy at Great Tew. Affinities
appeared between religious and political opinions too subtle for
analysis, but demonstrated by innumerable particular examples to
be general laws. The Catholics and Ritualists were the friends of
despotism; the Protestant Churchmen were staunch for legal rights,
but dreaded popular support; the Puritans alone would go all lengths
in the defence of political liberty.

The debate on the petition was the first, but it was also for many
months the last, held by the prudent Commons on the religious
differences that threatened to divide them. The Scottish Commissioners, now in full cry after a Presbyterian settlement for both
countries, were with difficulty persuaded by friendly Peers to cease
their clamour for a while, in order that English patriots might unite
to secure their own laws, lives and liberties, by putting Strafford
out of the world. Not revenge but fear drove the Parliamentary
leaders to strain the law and convulse the State in order to bring a
fallen minister to the block. Although they did not foresee the
future step by step, they had a just premonition that this one man
might yet find means to undo them all. If Strafford had escaped
to join the King during the Civil War he might have led the Western
Cavaliers to the sack of London, hung up King Pym in front of the
Banqueting House, relegated Falkland and Hyde to the pursuit of
philosophy and law, driven 100,000 refugees across the Atlantic
and established here, over the remnants of the English race, a
continental despotism based on pike and musket.

The Commons having determined that he ought to die, had
little doubt that he could be found guilty before the law of technical
treason. They supposed that his impeachment would be carried
through, much as other political trials had always been, and were
long afterwards, conducted. But on this occasion they reckoned
without the judges. The Lords were not, like the Commons, a party
in the State. Bedford and his Puritan friends were the most active
political group in the Upper Chamber, but their intrigues did not
induce the Peers as a body to adhere consistently to either side.
The Lords, having instead of a policy a sense of dignity and tradition,
determined to do justice to the case on its legal merits. Such
pedantry, thought the Commons, was ridiculous in politics and
treacherous in a time of crisis. But the previous action of the Peers
in ordering the arrest of Strafford at the moment when the balance
of power was still in their hands, and their subsequent passage of
the Bill of Attainder that took away his life, show that their impartiality as judges at his impeachment was genuine and not the
cloak of subtle partisanship.

Impeach-
ment of
Strafford,
March-
April,
1641
The case for the impeachment was opened in Westminster Hall
on the 23rd of March by Pym and the other managers for the Commons, in the presence of the rest of the Lower House, the accused
and his counsel, his judges the Peers in their robes of State, the
King seated unofficially behind a lattice and a world of onlookers,
many of whom paid large sums for admission. The charges were
of two kinds—acts of tyranny in his own government of Ireland
and advices to the King tending to the overthrow of the laws and
liberties of England. The actions in Ireland that were proved
against him illustrated his arbitrary temper and his contempt for

the letter of the law.   But none of these charges, even if it had been possible to prove what he had said in council and in closet, would have brought him under the laws of treason, framed to defend the power and person of the King.   Pym, therefore, ingeniously tried to show that he had endangered the royal dignity and life, because those lands where the ruler was " free and absolved from all rules of government," as Strafford had said that he wished Charles to be, were lands " frequent in combustions, full of massacres and the tragical ends of Princes ".   These words of the bold Commoner fell on that hushed audience with a thrill like the voice of prophecy and were heard by Charles himself trembling with anger behind his lattice ; in eight years' time that very hall was to witness if the words were true.   But carrying the argument into a yet broader plane, Pym showed that to destroy the customs of the land and the liberties of the subject was in itself treason against the State which the King represented and that treason against the whole Common-wealth was indeed the highest treason of all.   The argument, true and noble in spirit, was false and dangerous in letter.   It was good reason why a new law should be passed to punish Strafford, but nothing could be good reason why existing laws should be strained to bear meanings which their words did not express.   Day after day the Lords heard evidence and arguments on both sides with exasperating fairness, till at last, at a flagrant instance of imparti-ality that boded ill for the verdict, the patience of the accusers gave way.   Several hundred members of the Commons, who sat crowding the high scaffolding reared up to the roof on either side, rose with loud shouts to depart ; from floor to rafters all was welter and tumult in the vast hall, there was a roar of confused inquiries, cries and counter cries, while in the midst rose the proud face of Strafford lit with the smile of victory.

But the Commons had only shifted the battle from the field of justice to the field of legislation.   An ancient custom of the Con-stitution, much used by the Parliament-loving tyranny of the Tudors, allowed King, Lords and Commons to pass, like any other Bill, an Act of Attainder to put any subject to death without trial.   It was the last safeguard of the State, and now, if ever, was the moment for its just employment.   So thought the more violent of the Commons led by Sir Arthur Hazlerigg and Henry Marten, the first English republican.   For once they carried their fellow-members with them against the advice of Pym and Hampden.   These two clung so fondly to the high theories on which they were conducting the impeachment that they failed to see how completely it had broken down.   But after the Bill had been read a first time, the leaders whom the House ordinarily preferred to Marten and Hazlerigg, came in to the new policy and finally carried the Attainder up to the Lords.

Bill of
Attainder
against
Strafford,
April,
1641

No one knew what treatment the Bill would receive from this handful of noblemen, sensitive to every passing gust of sentiment and of rumour. Some chance event of the hour would decide the Earl's fate among his peers. At present they were plainly under the influence of ill-humour with the Commons for the scene in Westminster Hall and of natural pity for fallen greatness. Even Bedford was against the death penalty; though Essex now took his stand on the side of Parliament and told Hyde that "Stone dead hath no fellow". In the last week of April and the first of May the tide was rapidly turned by outside events, which showed the moderates that their own lives and liberties were at stake.

Henrietta Maria Henrietta Maria, who after the death of Buckingham had gained her husband's affections once for all, was allowed to carry on a policy of her own supplementary to that of the State. Her independent action began with the Scottish troubles, when she raised money from the English Catholics and appealed to the Pope for military aid. But her efforts became touched with frenzy when the Long Parliament renewed the persecution of her co-religionists, the inevitable consequence of the favours which they had so long and so openly enjoyed. As soon as power had shifted from Whitehall to Westminster, districts which had for years omitted to compile the official tale of recusants, or had reported only two or three noted papists in each parish, produced alarming lists of scores and of hundreds who abstained from the State worship. The priests dived into their old recesses behind panel and chimney, pursued by the terror of the Penal Laws, once more an unsheathed weapon in the hands of Protestant magistrates. Against such proceedings Henrietta Maria would have welcomed an alliance with the Grand Turk himself. She bribed the House of Orange, by giving in marriage her daughter Mary to the Dutch Prince William. She again implored the Pope to rescue his suffering people. She appealed to Richelieu; but the politic Cardinal refused to allow the daughter of France even to visit her native country. Foiled for the moment in foreign intrigue, she found an instrument to her hand in England. The army lying at York was growing daily more hostile to Parliament. The officers had been from the first the pick of English Royalism. Of the men, the Puritans deserted soonest, or were the most quickly dismissed. All ranks were offended at the comparative favour shown by the Houses to the Scots and by the money chests passing by to Newcastle and never stopping at York. The officers agreed to march on London, release Strafford and dissolve Parliament. One of the chief conspirators was the dissolute and unprincipled Goring. It is uncertain how far the plot was intended **The Army Plot, March-May, 1641** only to restore the shaken balance of the Constitution. But it is certain that it was regarded by all England as a 5th of November conspiracy to destroy Protestants and Parliaments together.

Wherever the Queen's hand was detected, plain men saw only one issue, Protestant against Catholic, liberty against servitude.

The Army Plot brought Strafford to the scaffold. The Court could keep no secret; the officers in Yorkshire openly displayed their sympathies; and the air was soon charged with rumour and suspicion. The last stage was reached when Pym, on the 5th of May, gave the House details which Goring had basely betrayed to the Parliamentary leaders a month before. All over England, the thought of Strafford still alive, and about to be placed at the head of a military force, raged in men's blood beyond the medicine of words. The City closed its shops in panic, and masters and men, set free from business, came day after day to threaten the lives of the "Straffordians," as they called the recalcitrant Lords, and the fifty-nine who had voted against the Attainder in the Commons. It was then a grave breach of privilege to publish division lists, but the unpopular names had on this occasion been posted by some treacherous member.

The Lords, not unmoved perhaps by these demonstrations, and themselves profoundly alarmed at the intended military violence to Parliament, united with the Commons in a series of self-protecting measures, which diverged far from the line of constitutional propriety. They sent up to the King a Bill to prevent the dissolution of the present Parliament without its own consent and the Peers took upon themselves to issue administrative ordinances to protect the kingdom. The members of both Houses bound themselves together by oath, in a "Protestation" to defend the privileges of Parliament and the Protestant religion. To crown all, on Saturday, 8th May, the Bill of Attainder passed the Lords. *The Lords pass the Bill, 8th May*

The King's assent, as all men knew, could only be extorted by force. During the night after Strafford's Attainder had been accepted by the Upper House, a mob surrounded Whitehall. The voice of wrath, terrible in numbers, heard there once before in distant unregarded warning from round the pillory of Prynne, now shook the frail walls of the old timbered Palace. The courtiers confessed themselves to the Queen's priests and marked on staircases and at passage-turnings where men could make a stand. But the outlook from the windows took away all desire of a battle, from those who thought how many women were in the upper chambers. Far away in houses along Strand and Holborn, Lords and Commons lay with uneasy consciences, listening through bedroom windows to the rise and fall of the distant roar. Dawn broke upon the pitiless siege, and all day long fresh congregations came up hot from Sabbath gospellings in the City churches. Charles was in agony; he consulted the Judges and Bishops, who were divided in opinion. At nine on Sunday evening he gave way. Noise had conquered, as when the Bastille fell. Three days later 200,000 persons witnessed on Tower Hill the death of "Black Tom the Tyrant". *Execution of Strafford, 12th May*

He served England well, for he dignified her history. He showed that the cause of tyranny did not fail among us, first of all great nations, because among us it lacked princely intellect or royal valour.

St. Stephen's Chapel

Between the Strangers' Entrance of the present House of Commons and the Central Lobby, men quicken their pace to run the gauntlet of two opposing rows of marble statesmen, who still harangue and gesticulate unappeased across the narrow floor, though Falkland, with head bent sadly over the sword which he would never stain with English blood, protests for his part that the less now said about the past the sooner a bad business will be forgotten. Few linger in this passage to realise that it represents in situation and dimensions St. Stephen's Chapel, the old House of Commons, on whose vaulted foundations it was rebuilt after the fire of 1834. Pent in that narrow measure was the whole wisdom and wrath of the Long Parliament. Westminster Hall, together with a small lobby lying between it and the Chamber, was used by members for those anxious consultations which precede and direct action in the House. Where the modern Parliament buildings stretch out on piles into the Thames, was then nothing except a small garden with its wall and water stairs. Over these Cavalier and Roundhead looked out from a large Gothic window behind the Speaker's back, across to the green Lambeth fields and the barges on the gay river carrying their friends to the City or their enemies to the Tower. At the other end of the long room, facing the chair, was a wooden gallery, reached from below by a rude ladder near the door : this primitive means of ascent was one day obstructively monopolised by an honourable member, till Speaker Lenthall called to him " not to sit upon the ladder as if he were going to be hanged : at which many of the House laughed ". Overhead, the pointed arches of St. Stephen's Chapel were hidden from sight by a flat roof, which reverberated English eloquence from the days of Wentworth and Eliot to those of Canning and Peel. Along the length of the room, seats rose on either side in tiers. The chance shape of the chapel helped in later years to keep English politicians divided into two parties, one on each side of the House. Already the few courtiers and the many Episcopalians usually sat on the north side, and the Root-and-Branch men on the south, but this general rule had certainly some, perhaps many, exceptions. The seats near the Speaker's chair were already reserved by custom for " Privy Councillors and men of distinction," [1] but the chiefs of the parties did not

---

[1] Verney's *Notes of the Long Parliament* (Camden Soc., 1845), p. 156. In January, 1642, a member of no distinction " to the great scandal of the House " did " seat and place himself near the Speaker's chair " in place of his betters ; and there giving vent to his political feelings, " cried ' Baw ! ' to the great terror and affrightment of the Speaker and of the members of the House of Commons, and contrary to his duty, and the trust reposed in him by his country ". He appears to have been a Cavalier member protesting against the proceedings of Parliament with regard to the militia.

occupy that position. Pym and Hampden sat inseparable near the
foot of the ladder. Opposite, also near the bar, sat the no less
inseparable Hyde and Falkland.

One effect of the smallness of the room was to discourage that
full attendance which the Parliaments of James and Charles I.
sometimes tried to enforce by fine. The crowded benches, on which
Sir Ralph Verney could sometimes find no elbow-room to take his
journal of the events he witnessed, were less attractive to many who
had never before visited the capital than were the theatres across
the water and the bowling-alleys of the City gardens. Party
organisation only grew up after Strafford's death, when equal division
arose within the walls of the House and it had to be decided by
counting heads which party should proscribe and banish the other.
But even in that last struggle which drove the Cavaliers, so barely
outnumbered, at last to yield the House and fly to the tented field,
there was no systematic " whipping ". In the division on the Grand
Remonstrance itself, only 307 members voted out of some 500.
The less contentious Attainder of Strafford had passed by 204 to 59.
The number who usually voted on an important division was scarcely
more than half the assembly. Since " pairing " was not then a
custom, these small divisions, in a time of intense public excitement,
show that many members waited to see which party would be victorious, and that many cared little for great questions of State.
Probably not more than half had been chosen on any definite political
understanding with their constituents. An ordinary member, once
he had taken his seat, was irresponsible and independent as no
politician is to-day. Those who had elected him never heard how
he voted, or whether he voted at all ; and he was under no obligation,
real or implied, to act with any of his colleagues. The steps taken
by Pym and Hampden to rectify these conditions were important
and novel. Their riding tour through England at the October
elections secured that at least a large proportion of members were
carefully chosen and impressed with a sense of allegiance to a cause.
In the House the leaders secured that this chosen band should act
as a party and find means to recruit its numbers from the timorous
and the indifferent.[1]

The sittings began at eight or nine in the morning. At noon
the hungry members—especially, as Falkland laughingly complained, the lukewarm defenders of Episcopacy—" ran forth for

*Thin
divisions
and party
manage-
ment*

*Parlia-
mentary
customs*

---

[1] Important political conversations, in which the statesmen of this Parliament tried to win each other over, were sometimes held walking up and down
the churchyard round the Abbey, or " riding together in the fields betweenWest-
minster and Chelsea ". Pym, Hampden and their friends kept common table
at Pym's lodgings behind Westminster Hall. Here they held their longer consultations, and " invited " thither those of whose conversion they had any
hope ; they often " importuned " Hyde to dine with them (Clar., *Life*, i., pp.
936, 937).

12

their dinners " to the neighbouring taverns, leaving the Speaker to starve in the Chair, and a handful of patriots, who had swallowed some bread and cheese in the hall, to push through in an hour business that would have taken days if properly discussed. Several times the House sat on after dusk. Debates, sometimes taking the form of a scuffle for the candles, were held to decide whether lights should be placed upon the clerk's table. Even when these symbols of permanent session flickered in the middle of the room, the note-takers along the benches must have put up their tablets in despair, unless, like the imperturbable pedant Sir Simon D'Ewes, they boldly spread out their writing materials on the table itself. Disorder and breach of privilege were punished rather at the will of the majority than by the ruling of the chair ; a few days of confinement in the Tower was the usual form of suspension.

Star Chamber and High Commission abolished, 1641
The unanimity of the Commons did not end at once with the life of Strafford. Constitutional changes, which it would have been useless to put on paper before he had been removed from the world of action, were formulated during the summer, in laws passed without debate by the Houses and signed without thought by the King.[1] The means of unparliamentary revenue—Ship Money, Forests, Knighthood, Tonnage and Poundage—were made illegal beyond further dispute. Another Act destroyed the Star Chamber and its kindred courts of Wales and the North. Thus were extinguished the judicial powers of the Privy Council, by the terror of which its administrative sovereignty could alone be maintained in a rebellious age. With the sovereignty of the Council fell the State system of the Tudors. Their Church system fell at another stroke, which ended the Court of High Commission, the coercive power of the Bishops as derived from the Crown. When next the tyranny of Anglicanism over men's souls and bodies revived, it was armed not by the King but by Parliament (1661). The work of this summer was never undone. It became the basis of the Restoration Settlement and even the Second Stuart despotism of 1683-88 had to find other forms than those which had been ready to the hand of Charles I.

But all these reforms, though final, were only negative. They deprived Crown and Council of sovereignty, but they did not transfer it to Lords and Commons. They left the King dependent on Parliament, and Parliament on the King. Government could only be carried on if both parties were willing to work the two-handed machine together. But since in 1641 there was no suitable William of Orange in whose favour Charles could be deposed, the constitu-

---

[1] The Bill perpetuating the present Parliament till it chose to dissolve itself had received his indifferent assent when he gave way on the greater issue of Strafford's execution.

tional compromise was only a constitutional deadlock. In 1642 men were forced to choose between the complete sovereignty of the Crown and the complete sovereignty of Parliament, though few wished for either one or the other. When at last even men like D'Ewes and Falkland found that the choice had to be made, each made it according to his religious sympathies, for that generation had also to choose whether the Anglican or the Puritan worship should be proscribed. Before England could become a land of settled government, two things were required—the doctrine of religious toleration and a King who could be trusted.

For several months after Strafford's execution, Charles was ready to make almost any concession demanded by Parliament, and to entertain almost any plan of violence suggested by his wife. In the morning he could plot with Catholic agents and army officers ; in the evening he could sign, with a glow of virtuous constitutional pride, laws destructive of monarchical power in England. With the same light-hearted magnanimity does the spendthrift sign every paper brought him by the Jew, whom he sometimes intends honourably to pay, sometimes justifiably to kill. Charles's double-dealing, the despair alike of his friends and foes, was that of a stupid and selfish, not of a clever and treacherous man. Even his plans of violence were not mutually consistent. All the summer he was in close correspondence with the Pope's agent Rossetti and the Catholic world ; while in the same months he was preparing to cast away the last shred of Laud's Scottish reformation, for which he had ruined the monarchy, in the hope of winning the hearts and using the swords of the best Pope-haters in Europe. He appears to have thought that the disciples of John Knox, and of Parsons the Jesuit, would forget old quarrels and sink individual interests, in order to share the privilege of serving Charles Stuart. *Charles's double-dealing*

Thus, while he signed bill after bill, he failed to win the confidence even of Episcopalian members, because he could not dissipate the rumour of the now chronic Army Plot and because he declared his purpose to visit Edinburgh in person. The Scottish Commissioners, already grown impatient with their English friends in proportion as they had at first been too sanguine, were negotiating an alliance with their native King, whose duplicity they had not yet fathomed. The visit paid by Charles I. to his northern kingdom was to the English what the flight of Louis XVI. was to the French. But the person of a King was still sacred, and no one of the Londoners who clamoured round his coach, imploring him to turn back, dared to lay hand upon the reins. *The King's visit to Scotland, Aug., 1641*

The departure of the King, for a while stopped the Root-and-Branch Bill, and united the two parties for the last time in a sense of danger still common to both. Lords and Commons issued ordinances for the security of the stores at Hull, the Tower, and *Parliament still united* other strong places of the kingdom. This illegal assumption of administrative power by the Houses, in which Falkland and Culpepper took a share, and which even the law-ridden Hyde did not oppose, proves that the moderate Episcopalians would have fought for Parliament if the King had raised his standard in August, 1641. They broke the Constitution in that very way which six months later they reprobated as treason. Yet even now they gave their support to the ordinances only as a temporary measure of defence during the Scottish journey ; they never grasped, like Pym and the Puritans, the necessity for a permanent settlement of sovereign power on the House of Commons. On the constitutional issue, if they made fewer mistakes than Pym, they had less courage in supplying the needs of the present and less foresight in distinguishing the hopes of the future.

Root-and-Branch Bill and division of parties, Aug.-Nov., 1641 The King was absent in Scotland from the middle of August to the latter end of November. During those three months the Episcopalians became Royalists. The Root-and-Branch Bill for the abolition of Episcopacy had been introduced in the summer, in the first instance by a small body of enthusiasts, including Oliver Cromwell. But it was soon adopted as the platform of Pym and the working majority in the House, themselves neither Presbyterians nor Sectaries. The occasion of this great party move, that moulded the future of English religion and politics, was the refusal of the Lords to exclude the Bishops from the Upper House ; but its cause was the need to take religion out of the hands of royal nominees, under whose guidance the Church was becoming an academy of absolutist doctrine and of Catholic sentiment. If Charles had been a Protestant in the sense in which Falkland was a Protestant, the proposal to abolish Bishops would never have obtained more than fifty votes in the House of Commons. The Bill, as amended in the Lower House, was not framed on any Presbyterian model. It proposed to give all ecclesiastical jurisdiction to a committee of nine laymen nominated by Parliament. No cleric was to be allowed a place on the committee. This thoroughly English proposal pleased many of the best Puritans, adverse to the rule of clergymen whose doctrines they approved but whose persons they despised ; and it even won the support of Episcopalians like Selden, who loved neither presbyter nor priest.[1] But Erastianism, however useful as an expedient in revolution, would scarcely have afforded a permanent settlement.

Proposal to alter the Prayer-book The question of Church government involved the question of Church worship, to which Englishmen were less indifferent. The alliance of Pym's partisans with the Root-and-Branch men involved them, before they were well aware, in an attack upon the Prayer-book. When at the close of the summer session soon after Charles's

---

[1] G., ix., pp. 407, 408. Shaw *passim.*

arrival in Scotland, ordinances were being passed with apparent unanimity to suppress ritualism and to move the tables down into the naves, a member suggested changes in the Service itself. The Prayers were at once defended with an affectionate warmth which no one had expressed for the Bishops. The question, not decided before the Houses adjourned on 9th September, was the thought which members carried away with them on their month of well-earned holiday, and digested as they sat far from party strife in the cool atmosphere of the drowsy old parish church, or followed the dogs through the stubble for the last of many pleasant seasons with the old game nets or the new shot-gun.

When the Houses reassembled for the autumn session, many who had swelled Pym's majority in the summer could no longer be found by their friends. The smallness of the average division alarmed the popular leaders.[1] Still more disquieting was the changed political allegiance of the moderate Episcopalians. Their fear of Pym's " godly thorough reformation " of the Church, had at least outgrown their fear of Charles's muddled proceedings in Scotland. Men who had voted for the disloyal military precautions on the King's departure in August, looked forward to his return in November as to their own deliverance. But before he arrived, news came from oversea which divided the two factions, as it would a few months before have united them.

Land spoliation, social inequality and religious persecution, which had so long been the lot of the Irish Catholics, at length, when the strong hand of Strafford was withdrawn, produced the inevitable explosion. The general uprising of a half-barbarous people, maddened by the loss of tribal lands and rights, and led by an upper class more civilised indeed but goaded to frenzy by religious persecution, could not but result in terrible atrocities. Some four or five thousand Protestants perished by massacre, and a still greater number from cold, hunger and ill-treatment.[2] Rumour, crossing the channel, told tales yet more ghastly than the truth. While England was celebrating the memory of Guy Fawkes, she learnt that the Catholics of Ireland had massacred the Protestants. All Englishmen, equally ignorant of Ireland, were agreed that the task which Cromwell long afterwards accomplished must be set about at once. Both parties concurred to raise an army of reconquest and revenge, and to pay for it by the assignment of two and a half million acres of Irish land to the State's creditors. But while Pym dared not for his neck allow men to be enlisted except by officers nominated by Parliament, the Episcopalians already saw with alarm how easily their opponents could create praying regiments, to

The Irish Rebellion, Oct.-Nov., 1641

---

[1] Forster's *Grand Remonstrance*, pp. 163, 164 (ed. 1860).

[2] G., x., pp. 43-69.

> Decide all controversy by
> Infallible artillery ;
> And prove their doctrine orthodox
> By Apostolic blows and knocks.   (*Hudibras*, i., l. 197.)

On this vital question of the command of the Irish army, the follow-ers of Hyde and Falkland voted Royalist.

The Grand Remon-strance, Nov., 1641   The Parliamentarians, shaken in their hold on the House and dreading the imminent return of Charles to head his new partisans, could still hope to appeal to the country, where Protestants in their rage and terror attributed the Irish St. Bartholomew to the Queen and her husband, and regarded it as the rehearsal for a like tragedy in England. An appeal to the people was made in the Grand Remonstrance, a long history of the wrongs endured by the nation at the hand of its present King, followed by suggestions of reform. Chief among these stands the far-seeing proposal of Pym, that ministers must be " such as the Parliament may have cause to confide in " (secs. 197, 198). The Remonstrance, like the strife which it focussed, is at least as much constitutional as ecclesiastical. But not the least significant part of it is found in those clauses where the members declare their purpose to effect great changes in the Church, and desire that a synod of English and foreign divines be summoned to discuss the bases for the " intended reformation " (secs. 182-87). The appeal to forces had come ; the defenders of Parliament called to their aid the living Puritan spirit, and the defenders of Anglicanism conjured with the magic name of King.

The Grand Remonstrance was passed in committee clause by clause, carried on 22nd November by eleven votes, and ordered to be printed and published. The result of that close division decided that Parliament should remain in the hands of the faction that was still ready to defend its claims. So much was achieved in a fortnight of set debates, ending in scenes of wild passion, that nearly stained the sacred floor with blood. In that fortnight the House of Commons ceased for ever to be a party, and became the battle-ground of parties.[1]

Charles's return   On 25th November Charles arrived home from Scotland. The shrewd nation, whom he had intended to yoke with the Catholics to the chariot of his fortunes, had taken all and given nothing. His failure was eagerly used by the Episcopalians to do duty for his innocence. Feeling against him so far subsided on the day of his return, that he was cheered in the London streets, on his way to feast with the Royalist Lord Mayor. But if on that evening the Crown was again within his reach, he had long ago bound his own hands by the Act depriving himself of power to dissolve the present

---

[1] Forster's *Grand Remonstrance*, *passim*. The famous document is printed in G. (*Const. Docs.*), pp. 202-32.

Parliament. Before Christmas he had taken measures to restore
" King Pym " in the hearts of his fellow-countrymen.

Though on the two questions of the hour—the Church and the Faction-
army—Charles had the letter of the law, and half the Lords and fights at
Commons on his side, he chose as his champions at this fearful $\frac{\text{Westmin-}}{\text{ster.}}$
crisis the officers of Strafford's regiments, lately disbanded in York- " Cava-
shire and now waiting for commissions in Ireland, and the portion- liers "and
less younger sons who daily drifted into Whitehall with lean purses heads,"
and long swords—that vulture portion of the upper class which Dec.,
regards the solid parts of the community as its prey, and is in re- 1641
turn justly feared and despised. These first " cavaliers," whose
nickname was a few months later shared by more honourable men,
came all too welcome to the luckless King. He found in them
much-needed guardians of his Palace against the outrageous mob
that had forced him to kill Strafford. But he tried also to throw
the terror of them over the City, by naming their debauched and
ruffianly chief Lunsford to the command of the Tower itself. After
it had done his cause untold harm, Charles abandoned the plan.
Lunsford was withdrawn from the Tower, and had to content
himself with leading out his companions to angry parle with the
" roundhead " apprentices near the Houses of Parliament. On
27th December a dozen officers chased the mob out of Westminster
Hall at the sword's point, not sparing to draw plebian blood. More
frequently, the citizens held both Palace Yards, and made roaring
lanes down which Lords, Commons, and as many Bishops as dared
run the gauntlet, passed under rude inspection to their duties. The
Commons, at Pym's advice, refused point blank " to dishearten
the people ". After that turbulent but cheerless Christmas, it was
impossible for citizens to resume business under the shadow of
imminent massacre. Shops were shut, and men of both parties
furnished themselves privately with arms for self-protection. But
to organise the public defence was the legal right of the King alone.
Would some strange event make over the moral right to his foes ?

On 3rd January (1641-42) the Attorney-General rose in the Attemp-
House of Lords on behalf of the King to impeach five members of $\frac{\text{ted im-}}{\text{peach-}}$
the House of Commons—Pym, Hampden, Hazlerigg, Holles and ment of
Strode—on charges of high treason. The Lords did not conceal the Five
their amazement and horror. The part they had chosen, now as $\frac{\text{Members,}}{\text{3rd Jan.,}}$
during the struggle for Strafford's life, was to defend the letter of 1642
the law and the peace of the land. Now, as then, they were rapidly
becoming Royalist ; but now the impeachment of the five members,
as then the Army Plot, drove them back to the other side. An
impeachment brought before them by the King as accuser was
unconstitutional ; [1] and the opening, under any form, of a bloody

---

[1] Stephen, i., p. 160. Bristol had been unconstitutionally impeached by the
King in 1626. But at least his arrest had been left to the Peers.

proscription was exactly what they were determined to prevent
Their Lordships, who had perfected the political art of doing nothing in particular, as their favourite refuge in these stormy times,
declined to order the arrest until they had inquired whether the
Attorney-General was acting according to law. Digby, the Episcopalian whom Charles had just raised to the Upper House and so
removed from the wiser neighbourhood of Hyde and Falkland,
rose from his seat and hastened out, muttering that the King had
been ill advised. Yet he himself had been the King's adviser, and
again that evening he joined the Queen in giving the worst counsel
that Charles ever received.

The impeachment of the members on the 3rd had been a blow
to legality and peace ; but the attempt to arrest them on the 4th
was more certainly illegal and incomparably more violent. It was
an infringement of the undoubted right, dearly cherished by the
Peers, to order or withhold the arrest of impeached persons ; and
the method of its execution was a threat, on the least sign of resistance, to massacre the Commons in their House.

Prepara-
tions for
their
arrest

All morning the " Cavaliers " gathered at the Palace by command, scenting prey ; the stir at Whitehall was viewed with apprehension by Fiennes, the member for Puritan Banbury, strolling
warily at the dinner hour. But while the Commons were still
ignorant of his purpose, Charles continued to debate it with the
Queen. It was three in the afternoon before his long-expected
figure was seen on the staircase, descending among an excited crowd
of 400 gentlemen in arms. Calling on all " faithful subjects and
soldiers " to follow, he stepped into a coach. Surrounded and
hampered by the sea of " red-coats," the carriage moved at a foot's
pace from Whitehall to Westminster, far outstripped on the short
journey by flying rumour. A Frenchman arrived panting at the
door of the House. Fiennes stepped out to him and at once carried
back to the Speaker his news of the approaching procession. The
Commons, who had known for two hours, by a message from the
Queen's ill-chosen confidante, Lady Carlisle, what such a procession
would mean, sent off the five members by water to the City. Then
came a cry and scuffle of frightened tradesmen closing their booths
in Westminster Hall ; the noise of an armed multitude entering
confusedly with shouts heralding the approach of its chief ; a rush
of steps and clank of swords across the great hall and up the stairs
into the lobby ; last of all, as the door of the House of Commons
itself was flung open, a King's voice, bidding his followers stand

Charles
enters the
House,
4th Jan.

outside on pain of death. Then Charles, with the young Elector
Palatine behind him, entered the room. He passed to the Speaker's
chair between rows of silent, standing members. From that point
of vantage he soon satisfied himself that his " birds were flown,"
and after no discourteous language walked back as he had come,

while the cry " Privilege, privilege," rose behind him as he went. All this time the door had been, with insolent suggestion, held open from without, displaying a crowd in the lobby armed to the teeth, cocking pistols and uttering wanton threats of slaughter.

Pym had known how to wait; he knew now how to strike. Lords, Commons and City entered that week into the triple alliance which fought the Civil War. A Committee of the Commons sat for safety within the walls of London. The King's friends were for several days ashamed to open their mouths. The majority of the Lords voted the illegal ordinances, which a week before or six months later they would have opposed. For the need to defend Parliament from massacre was no longer regarded as a bad excuse to prepare rebellion, but as a stern reality. The train-bands of London, the only effective regiments at that moment in the kingdom, were called out on a war footing. Four thousand armed squires and freeholders, from the Thames valley and the wooded hills of Buckinghamshire, rode in to protect their Hampden. The Mariners of the Royal Navy marched up to the Guild Hall, where the Commons sat in committee, cheering for the sailor Earl of Warwick, and offering the King's stores to defend the Parliament. On the 10th of January Charles and his swordsmen fled from Whitehall, resigning the capital and its neighbourhood to his enemies; on the 11th the Commons returned to Westminster in gala barges, with high military and civic pomp by land and water.

The City protects Parliament

Flight of the King, 10th Jan.

For eight months both sides slowly prepared a civilian nation for war; the King by Commissions of Array; the two Houses by unconstitutional militia ordinances. Gradually the Royalists in both Houses summoned courage to protest; but they were too late to oppose. The scene of Royalist resistance had shifted to York. There Hyde had joined Charles, and was busily composing specious and persuasive proclamations which showed the King as the defender of the " known laws of the land " and the " never-enough-commended Constitution." One by one, members took the North Road with their servants and horses, till a great majority of the Peers and a respectable minority of the Commons were with the King. But because the attempt on the Five Members had caused the Lords in their corporate capacity to set the seal of their approval on rebellion, the true Parliament of England was found in the 300 Commoners and the thirty Peers who remained at the seat of government to organise war.[1]

Preparations for war, Jan.-Aug.,1642

---

[1] Mr. Firth (*Cromwell*, p. 69) calculates that thirty Peers supported Parliament, eighty the King, and twenty remained neutral, while 300 of the Lower House were for Parliament, 175 for the King.

CHAPTER VIII

THE CIVIL WAR, 1642-46

To Thee, dear God of Mercy, both appeal,
Who straightway sound the call to arms :   Thou know'st ;
And that black spot in each embattled host,
Spring of the blood-stream, later wilt reveal.
Now is it red artillery and white steel ;
Till on a day will ring the victor's boast,
That 'tis Thy chosen towers uppermost,
Where Thy rejected grovels under heel.—GEORGE MEREDITH.

Probable
outcome
of a royal
victory

THE First Civil War is the decisive event in English history.
The defeat of the King's armies alone enabled Parliamentary
institutions to triumph.

For if Charles had won, those who could keep alive resistance
to Anglican and royal absolutism must have sailed for America.
The men who formed the strength of the anti-monarchical and the
Puritan part of the community, were always contemplating emigration. England sent enough of these elements to found a new
world ; but if the war had gone differently, she would have sent
out enough to ruin herself. The most adventurous merchants,
the most skilled artisans, the Lords and gentlemen who took counsel
for the liberties of their country, the ploughmen who saw visions,
the tinkers who dreamed dreams, were perpetually thinking of New
England, whither twenty thousand Puritans had already gone.
The Roundhead armies were raised by men of the merchant class,
and were led by landed gentlemen of the type of Cromwell, who
were not, like the Cavaliers, deeply attached to the soil, who regarded their estates merely as assets in the money market, who
had here no rest for the spirit or home for the heart, who so long
as they were sojourners upon earth, lived " in Mesheck which
they say signifies Prolonging ; in Kedar which signifieth Black-
ness ".[1] Such men would have emigrated rather than live under
the military despotism of an Anglican King. Thus defeat in the
field would have ruined for ever the cause of Parliament and would
have driven the Puritans out of England. Freedom in politics and
religion would never have been evolved by the balance of parties,
for one party would have left the land. Without its leadership,
the mass of Englishmen, indifferent as they showed themselves to

---

[1] Carl.'s *Crom.*, Letter ii., *anno* 1638. Cromwell twice meditated emigration ;
once under Laud when he sold his land ; and again when the Grand Remonstrance was in danger of rejection by the Commons. On the subject of Puritan
and Cavalier Emigration. see Appendix A. below.

the result of the Civil War, would never again have risen in revolt against a royal Church and a royal State. The current of European thought and practice, running hard towards despotism, would have caught England into the stream. America, strengthened by the influx of all who could change their country but not their religion, might perhaps have proved unconquerable and gone on her way alone. But England would then have become a mere outlying portion of the State system of Europe, had she not, by the campaign of Naseby, acquired her independent position between the old world and the new, and planted freedom in the deep fruitful soil of antiquity. The flowers of genius and the fruits of life that have since flourished upon that tree, could not have shown their heads under the shadow of tyranny, nor could they have so quickly bloomed to perfection in the thin soil of a newer land.

The great issue was decided in a war waged by two small minorities. When Edgehill was fought, not half the nation, nor half even of the gentry, had been induced to support the war whether for King or Parliament.[1] Except in London, there was no rush to arms. The tale of foot was on both sides filled up with pressed men. But since the two factions divided between them all the leaders and all the sources of power and law, the peaceful majority could only look on in despair, unled, unauthorised, and without a policy. There was indeed no middle party : every man was a little for the King or a little for the Parliament ; though few were willing to be sequestrated for the sake of the one, or plundered for the sake of the other. The utmost that such men of peace could attempt was to keep the war from their own doors, by short-lived " County Treaties," which preserved neutrality in Yorkshire, Cheshire and other shires for a few uneasy weeks.

Most of the nation adverse to war

As the war dragged on, neutrals were everywhere forced to abandon their neutrality by the particular attention they received from both parties. In the opinion of the Roundhead Committees, " Neuters deserved neither respect nor protection from Church or Commonwealth " ; preachers directed against them the curse which the Angel of the Lord pronounced against " Merosh," and every passing troop made itself the instrument of God's exceeding wrath. Nothing but avowed adherence to the Parliament could secure a man's house against plunder in Middlesex and Kent, or save his horses from requisition by the Cambridge Committee in the better disciplined Eastern Association. Within the Cavalier lines, where Goring and Rupert rode, neutrals had no hope, for even Royalist

Treat- ment of neutrals

[1] The small size of the armies in October, 1642, and the immense difficulty in recruiting even by help of the press-gang, prove that as Clarendon wrote (p. 347) : " It fared in those counties as in all other parts of the kingdom that the number of those who desired to sit still was greater than of those who de- sired to engage in either party."

houses were lucky to escape the visits of Captain Ferryfarm and Quartermaster Burndorp.[1] And while the neutral was most frequently plundered, he was also liable to be most heavily taxed. By the severe assessment of those who would not take up arms, County Committees ingeniously contrived to recruit at once their credit and their cavalry. Before the end of the war all the gentry and most of the yeomen and merchants had declared themselves, each on the side which he most favoured or most feared.

Conduct of the various classes : the labourers

But the hired labourer in the field remained neutral to the end. In a few villages he enlisted under Puritan influence ; in many he followed his landlord to war ; in all he was the victim of the press-gang. But he had not the inducement of his wealthier neighbours to barter his allegiance for protection, for his allegiance could not command so high a price. When he took up clubs, it was to save his goods from the soldiers of both parties ; and when at last he realised that the presence of the New Model Army was a security against plunder, he joyfully hailed, even in the Cavalier districts of the West, the march of victors who brought peace to the cottage. As Cornwall was not an English La Vendée, so there was no rural district even in the East where the tocsin could have brought out the countryside from their beds, to resist the armies or to arrest the flight of the King.

The gentlemen

For it was not, like the French Revolution, a war of classes. No class stood to win or lose property or privilege, until under the Commonwealth the gentry were rallied to the fallen throne by a sense of their own diminished importance. But during the first Civil War a large minority of the gentry in every shire headed the Parliamentary cause and almost alone officered its numerous armies. The most devotedly Royalist were the largest owners of land : the Catholic Earl of Worcester, whose munificence alone saved Charles from bankruptcy in June ; the Earl of Derby, who possessed more truly than either Parliament or King the allegiance of one-half of Lancashire ; and many others of less name who maintained in their great country houses an almost feudal state, and in their lofty isolation scented with quicker alarm than their neighbours the first breath of coming democracy, these were the most conspicuous adherents of the Crown. Among the Roundheads were found many at least of the smaller squires, led by those who had acquired influence in the country rather by public service than by broad acres or ancient name, who had none of the sympathies of a *noblesse*, who had lived among yeomen and townspeople, feeding fat cattle, hearing long sermons, judging rustic causes, and who had finally been sent up to represent their neighbours in Parliament.

---

[1] The names given by the Cavalier soldier Lacy to the Royalist officers in his play, *The Old Troop*, *vide* Lacy's *Dramatic Works*, 1875.

The tenant-farmer was in no position to avow any political or Farmers
religious faith but that of his landlord. But the yeomen free- and
holders, partly from a desire to show their independence as in- yeomen
dividuals and their cohesion as a proud and honourable class, were
solid for the " good Parliament " in East Anglia and the Midland
counties ; but in districts beyond Severn, where Puritanism was
only known by evil report as the new religion of the cockneys, they
were the backbone of the royal cause.

The towns were the strength of the Roundheads, although in Towns-
every town there was a Cavalier party, and in many, especially in men
cathedral cities, it prevailed. The part usually played by the
tradesmen was attributed by Baxter to that " correspondency with
London " which had long cultivated their general intelligence and
their Puritanism, and which Pym had lately been at pains to increase
in a political direction. But it was only in Lancashire that the war
degenerated into that feud between the urban and rural populations, which had done so much to ruin the development of Germany,
Flanders and Spain. In most districts, gentlemen of the shire like
Hampden, Cromwell or Hutchinson, with their local knowledge
of town and country alike, acted as a link between the citizens in
the market-town and the yeomen on isolated farmsteads, combined
under their own leadership forces that had no other point of union,
and therewith captured the county town, the militia, and the stores,
before the neutrals could protest or the enemy unite.

While most men sat still, some hoping that war would not begin,
others raking dim family traditions of St. Albans and Barnet for a
hint how war was to be begun, the fate of a whole city or district
was often decided by the energy of one man. For the local forces
were nowhere unequally matched, except in East Anglia and
Middlesex, and in the counties along the Welsh and Scottish borders.
Indeed, in the heart of the Eastern Association itself the Royalist
party was only kept from arming by the ubiquitous activity of
Cromwell ; to that officer the Parliament's Commission in his
pocket seemed from the beginning warrant enough to disarm any
of his neighbours whom old acquaintance taught him to suspect.
But it needed two pitched battles between the local forces in the
West, before the genius of Sir Ralph Hopton could do for the King
in Cornwall and Devon what Cromwell did bloodlessly for Parliament in Suffolk and Cambridge.

It was, on the whole, a war of North and West against South A war of
and East.[1] But the North never felt that it was engaged in a death principle
struggle with the South, nor were East and West roused to battle
by conscious intention to subdue one another. In every shire there
were two parties, of which the weaker only waited opportunity

[1] See map of England at end of book. Places mentioned in this chapter are
marked there.

to join hands with an invading force from the other side of England. For in motive it was a war not of classes or of districts, but of ideas. Hence there was a nobler speculative enthusiasm among the chiefs and their followers, but less readiness to fight among the masses of the population, than in other contests that have torn great nations. The French Revolution was a war of two societies ; the American Civil War was a war of two regions ; but the Great Rebellion was a war of two parties.

Humane character of the war   This war, as compared to nearly all that preceded it and to nearly all that during two centuries followed it, was eminently humane. There was much plunder, sometimes accompanied by arson. But no part of England was burnt to a desert, like all Germany of that day ; towns were not reduced to half their size ; villages did not disappear wholesale. Indeed, the population was not even noticeably diminished. Economic progress, though checked for perhaps a decade or more, yet received no such injury as was caused by contemporary events in Ireland and on the Continent. Cases of cruelty and treachery were proved, and more were charged, against both sides. But plunder was the only crime that was general, and even plunder was very exceptional in the later Roundhead armies. A civilian nation in arms relaxed the rules of war so as to save combatants from unnecessary bloodshed, and disregarded military customs so as to save noncombatants from vilest outrage.[1] There were many reasons why the contest was,

Why it was humane   by comparison, humane. Two minorities were fighting under critical inspection for the favour of all England, and when rivals duel they take care not to wound their mistress. Classes, professions, neighbourhoods and families were so divided in this war of ideas, that there was usually found, among the spoilers or conquerors of the hour, some one who was bound by affection or interest to save the persons of the conquered and the properties of the spoiled. Again, the combatants were of one race and one nation. And lastly, the English were thoroughly civilian in habits and temperament. Wherever these conditions were absent, the war was more cruel. The worst deeds were done by those Cavaliers who rode under professional soldiers, trained in the German military rules of storm and plunder ; and by those Roundheads who came across Welsh pikemen in the hour of battle, and Irish camp-followers in the hour of victory. Contemporary war in Ireland and in Scotland was not humane at all.

---

[1] The troops were often given " storm-money " in addition to their pay, instead of the plunder they would have obtained if the places stormed had been given to sack according to continental rules of war (Firth's *C. A.*, pp. 193, 194. G. (C. W.), ii. p. 97). In the matter of sack, the Cavalier armies sinned most often. They sacked Birmingham (1643), Leicester (1645), without massacre ; Bolton (1644) was sacked by Rupert with massacre, but this was cried out against as exceptional, and was largely due to the local feud of Catholics and Puritans in Lancashire. The New Model sometimes sacked castles and houses taken by storm, as Sherborne and Basing.

It may perhaps be asked why this war of religion was not distinguished by the cruelty which is the hall-mark of other such contests. But it was not a war between two definite creeds. The mass of both parties were Protestant. And where Catholic met Puritan, the furies of Alva were unloosed in the streets of Bolton, and retaliated in the chambers of Basing.

Neither was it a war between two fierce fanaticisms. The Cavaliers were fighting to prevent the excess of religion; their enemies sometimes called them " Baalists," but more often " atheists "; and many were kept from joining their noisy camps by the marked discouragements offered to any outward form of piety.[1] The Roundheads indeed were enthusiasts, but they were enthusiasts for Calvinism, the religion of self-restraint. As their armies became more Calvinist, they refrained more and more from plunder. When the Puritans triumphed, they declined to bring their conquered enemies to the scaffold by scores; in granting terms of surrender, the fanatics showed themselves more merciful than the politicians. Last of all, from the heart of the Puritan sects sprang the religion of the Quakers, in which many a war-worn soldier of the Commonwealth closed his visionary eyes.

In the eight months that intervened between the attempt on the five members and the opening of the Edgehill campaign, Charles, at York, for the first and last time in his life behaved with prudence. To every one of his slender band of followers was assigned a suitable task. The Queen was sent out of England to tout for money and arms among her relations in France and Holland. Prince Rupert was summoned from fighting for the lost heritage of his brother in the Palatinate to teach others to fight for the lost heritage of his uncle in England. Constitutional Hyde was employed to indite manifestoes, in which the King appeared as the guardian and his enemies as the destroyers of law. Charles himself refused, at the cost of military efficiency, to arrest by illegal warrants the Fairfaxes and other suspected gentry of Yorkshire. Fair words, for once not belied by foul deeds, won for the King the favour of many moderates.[2] They noted the contrast with the contemporary proceedings of the two Houses, who were vigorously preparing for war,

Wise conduct of Charles at York, Jan.-Sep., 1642

---

[1] " They that maintain," wrote Chillingworth, " the King's righteous cause with the hazard of their lives and fortunes, but by their oaths and curses, by their drunkenness and debauchery, by their irreligion and profaneness, fight more powerfully against their party than by all other means they do or can fight for it, are not, I fear, very well acquainted with any part of the Bible " (*Chillingworth's Works* (1820), iii., p. 14).

[2] The " Oxford Crowns," coined by Charles in 1642, 1643, bore the inscription RELIG PROT LEG AND LIBER PAR, " The Protestant religion, the laws of England, the liberties of Parliament " (Hawkin's *English Silver Coins* (1841), p. 165. See also *B. M. Handbook, Coins of Great Britain*, H. A. Grueber (1899), plates xxvi., xxvii.).

crushing the legal voice of opposition in the home counties, and prematurely threatening to seize the estates " of the malignant and disaffected party in the kingdom ".

The in-
stinct of
loyalty
Men had been willing to resist the King's encroachments on their properties and laws ; but when the standard was raised, when the word came round to ride to battle, the case seemed different. Something deeper, if less rational, was touched by the call to arms —the claim of ultimate authority. Obedience to the King was still in the age of Pym, as the worship of the Saints had still been in the age of Latimer, an instinct inborn in every child of the race at that stage of its evolution, wrapped in a thousand mysterious associations with a remote and still unbroken past, transmitted from father to son through thirty generations, since the Kings of the Heptarchy had crushed their rebel thanes in ages which, though long forgotten, still had their influence on ideas unconsciously inherited. No other picture of war then lurked in the mind's eye of the Englishman than that of following the King's banner to Hastings, to Crecy or to Flodden. He had been taught no other connection between religion and public duty but the old text, then painted upon the walls of so many manor houses—" Fear God, honour the King ". Those two duties could not have been divided in men's minds, except by the new Puritan faith. What a task had Pym !—to replace the old-world ideals and associations of kingship by some stronger emotion which had yet taken no form, and had yet no history or tradition. That would require all the progressive impulse of a great race at the zenith of its energy. Without the Puritan religion it could not, in that age at least, have been accomplished.

Mighty still was the name and office of King. Shakespeare, child of a day of which the aftershine still glowed in the West, had known no symbol of the public weal grander than this of royalty. And to many the world seemed still the same as in the noontide of Elizabeth. " I cannot contain myself," wrote Cornish Sir Bevil, grandson of the Grenvile who had fought the *Revenge* for his Queen through that famous summer night, " I cannot contain myself when the King of England's standard waves in the field upon so just an occasion." Sir Edmund Verney had grown old and sad since as a young man in Prince Charles's train he struck the priest in Madrid ; [1] the standard-bearer of a master whose every action he disapproved, Verney loved the Bible and Parliament well, but he loved honour more. " I have eaten the King's bread," he de-clared, " and served him near thirty years, and will not do so base a thing as to forsake him ; and choose rather to lose my life—which I am sure I shall do—to preserve and defend those things which are against my conscience to preserve and defend ; for I will deal

[1] See p. 105 above.   Verney, i., pp. 82, 83.

freely with you "—(he was speaking to Hyde)—" I have no reverence for Bishops, for whom this quarrel subsists." [1]

Much as they differed one from another in politics and in character, all the Royalists of England took arms, not as clients but as freemen, not to recover at the expense of the nation odious and forfeited privileges of their own, but to risk their all for a King. Therefore they have become for all ages the type of pure loyalty ; therefore, even in the horrid hour of fratricide, their worthiest champions were respected by their foes. " My affections to you," wrote Sir William Waller to Sir Ralph Hopton on the eve of battle, " are so unchangeable that hostility itself cannot violate my friendship. We are both upon the stage, and we must act the parts assigned us in this tragedy. Let us do it in a way of honour and without personal animosities."

There was little of this feeling exchanged between the debauchees and the hypocrites that disgraced their respective parties. Among the first to take arms for the King and Bishops were the ale-house rabble of Western towns, led by roystering gentlemen whom no decent householder would allow his son to follow to the wars, or his wife to admit to quarters for a single night. " Almost all these drunkards," as their neighbours observed with satisfaction, " were quickly killed, so that scarce a man of them came home again and survived the war." [2]

Yet while the elements, good and bad, of which Charles's armies were afterwards composed, were slowly beginning to bestir themselves in local affairs for the control of castles, stores and militia regiments, no central army gathered round his own person so long as he depended on the hard-headed and peace-loving Cavaliers of Yorkshire. At Nottingham on the 22nd of August it was a slender band that greeted the erection of the royal standard with a cheery shout of " God save King Charles and hang up the Roundheads ". In September, without arms, money or munitions, they moved off to try their fortune in the West, caparisoned rather like strolling players than like a King and the prime of his nobility going forth to war.

The standard raised at Nottingham, 22nd Aug., 1642

Essex had already taken the field with a well-appointed army. The Houses would have been no better able than the King to raise the country at this early stage, had not London, containing ten times the population and more than ten times the ready money of any other city in England, supplied recruits by the thousand, war loans to any quantity and at any moment, and the best weapons that England or the Continent could furnish for money down.

Initial advantage of Parliament

While both sides had to create an army and to learn the art of war on land, a fine navy, whose sailors only needed regular pay and

The navy deserts the King

---

[1] Clar., *Life*, bk. ii., pt. ii., p. 954.   [2] Baxter, *Life* (ed. 1696), p. 42.

13

humane treatment to make it once more the finest in the world, was ready to the hand of Parliament. The royal men-of-war which had defeated the Armada, had been maintained at fair nominal strength by the Ship Money despotism. But it was a common saying among seafaring men, that the galleys were preferable to the King of England's service. Unpaid, unfed, unclothed, his sailors continually deserted to foreign flags. The year after Felton had brought Buckingham's naval administration to an end, a despairing admiral declared that, unless great changes were made, Charles would " lose the love and loyalty of his sailors ".[1] When the Civil War broke out the prophecy was fulfilled to the letter.

Moreover, the professional traditions of the service, which Hawkins had created and Drake had led to glory, were interwoven with the rough breezy Puritanism of those who go down to the sea in ships. In James's reign, the King, the Prince, and the favourite who had sought the friendship of the cruel idolators of Spain, had never been forgiven by the forecastle hands. They had tried to lynch Buckingham, and they still pined for leaders with the old hatred of Popery and the old cunning in war. By his sympathy with these traditions, the sailor Earl of Warwick had won all their hearts. When he was appointed admiral by the Houses, the few captains who refused to obey the Earl were haled before him by their own mutinous crews. Along all the coasts of England one small warship alone remained true to the royal service. The wholesale defection of the navy was a fit reward to the Government that had deserted the Elizabethan tradition, and refused sympathy in the hour of deadliest need to Protestantism oversea. The gain to Parliament was immense. Some approach to regularity in their pay kept the delighted sailors enthusiastic Roundheads throughout the struggle, when a Royalist blockade of the Thames would have sealed the fate of London and of Parliamentary institutions. The " foreign mart for implements of war " was almost closed to the King by the hostile activity of his own ships round the few second-class ports over which his flag still waved. His prestige among foreign nations and English merchants passed over to the men who wielded the whole external power of the island. The Customs revenues became a fruitful source of income to Parliament. Commerce, the life-blood of London, was little diminished during a war of which scarce an echo was heard at sea. From the naval bases of the Thames and Portsmouth, the fleets supplied all the military needs of Plymouth and Hull, impregnable garrisons in the enemy's territory, which in the hour of danger prevented the advance of West and North on London.[2]

[1] Oppenheim, p. 235.
[2] Oppenheim, pp. 184-301, for treatment of navy by James and Charles I.

Some thirty Peers retained their seats at Westminster, half Essex
of them because in August Parliament seemed certain to win ; but
the other half, like Essex, Warwick, Brooke and Mandeville, now
Earl of Manchester, because, though deeply jealous of the encroaching power of the Lower House, they remained faithful to
the common cause of political liberty and Puritan religion.   These
few Lords, by their social position and personal character, made rebellion respectable.   When men stopped on the brink of treason
to look round for company, Essex " broke the ice," and " by his
very name commanded thousands " all over England into the service
of Parliament.   In London itself he was specially popular.   His
quiet Puritan manners, formed in long retirement from the court
of princes who had so grossly insulted his honour as a man and a
husband ; [1] his brief words ; his tobacco-pipe from which the dignity
of office could not part him, won the hearts of the citizens, many
of whom sent each his favourite apprentice, with a pocketful of
money and a scriptural blessing, to follow Essex through the war.
The formula of rebellion in these early months was the oath " to
live and die with the Earl of Essex ".   But the good Earl was only
a figure-head, not a motive power.   He belongs to that type of
man, faithful and honourable, who is put at the head of armies
when a civil war begins, but has to be removed before it can end.
He shrank unconsciously from beating up the royal camp, and this
political instinct was not counteracted by the promptings of an
active military genius.   In the last week of August and the first
fortnight of September, Essex delayed to march on Nottingham at
the head of a regular force, against which Charles had then nothing
to oppose save a few thousand horsemen without discipline, and
a few hundred pikemen without pikes.

The royal army was saved by moving in time to a happier re- Charles
cruiting-ground.   The remote shires bordering on Wales had lived moves
through the long accumulative discontent of the rest of England into the
with the policy of James and Charles, in plain, homely loyalty to Sep., 1642
the name of two Kings whose actual doings scarcely reached them
in report.   The last twelve months had been full of peril for isolated
Puritans in Salop, Hereford and Worcestershire.   " Every drunken
sot that met any of them in the streets, would tell them ' we shall
take an order with the Puritans ere long.' " [2]   Murderous riots
against them had preluded the outbreak of war.   When, three weeks
too late, Essex arrived in pursuit of Charles on the banks of Severn,
his Londoners found themselves in a country where they had little
in common with the natives.   Old and New England looked each
other in the face with some disapproval and more astonishment.
Sergeant Nehemiah Wharton, writing to his friends in the capital,
describes the choral service in Hereford Cathedral on the first Sunday

---

[1] See p. 93 above.   [2] Baxter, *Life* (ed. 1696), p. 42.

morning in October : " The pipes played and the puppets sang so
sweetly that some of our soldiers could not forbear from dancing
in the holy choir ; whereat the Baalists were sore displeased ".
On the way back through the streets it was the turn of the cockneys
to be shocked. The shops were open and men were at work, " to whom
we give some plain exhortations ". The army chaplain preached
" two famous sermons which much affected the poor inhabitants,
who, wondering, said they never heard the like before ; and I believe
them ".[1]

Edgehill,
23rd Oct.,
1642

By this time the King was at the head of several thousand foot,
many of them from the hills of Wales ; and the hard-riding Englishmen whom Rupert was training in the usages of war, were no
longer inferior in numbers to the town-bred cavalry whom the
Parliament officers were teaching the rudiments of horsemanship.
The royal army turned East and headed a race for London. On
the top of Edgehill ridge, far-seen from Shakespeare's Avon, Charles
turned to face his pursuers. In the plain below a drawn battle was
fought, which proved that both armies were too badly organised
and disciplined to receive or obey commands on the field ; that
Rupert's cavalry could not at present be resisted ; but that some
regiments of London foot, and a few troops of country horse, who
were distinguished for their piety, had in them the making of fine
soldiers. Cromwell, who stood through the thickest of the fight,
formed a notion as to the proper method of recruiting cuirassiers,
recommended it vainly to Hampden for the reform of the main army,
and returned to his local work in the East determined there to carry
it out for himself.

But to one tender and gallant knight the Civil War had ceased
already. Struck through by the Puritan sword that he would
himself so gladly have wielded, the body of the King's standard-
bearer lay under Edgehill between the lines of midnight watchfires,
unclaimed by the two armies, as they crouched silent after their
day of wrath. Formed on that noble type of character—the Puritan
Cavalier—which had flourished for two generations and was now
to fall extinct, Sir Edmund Verney lay slain, like the oak fallen
first among its fellows, though all will soon be crashing in the gale
that lays the forest low. When our civil storms at length subsided,
the ground was cleared indeed : public life in the age of Whig and
Tory was no longer adorned by men like this, honourable almost
to excess, shunning power and despising gain, Puritan in thought
and practice, but laying no restraint upon others, and pitiful of all
woes but their own.

Since the King's army had not been routed under Edgehill, he
was able to continue his advance through the Midlands. On 29th
October he entered Oxford, fixed there his staff, his arsenal and his

---

[1] *Archæologia*, xxxv., for the sergeant's journal, a most remarkable document.

Court, and so determined the strategical character of the whole Royalist
war. The Royalist headquarters were now a fortified out-post far head-
in advance of the three bases of their recruiting strength—the at quarters
North, the Welsh border, and the South-west. Not sixty miles Oxford
of road divided the Oxford quadrangles, swarming with play-actors
and peeresses, Jesuits and Privy Councillors, from the London
Artillery-Garden where officers from Sweden and Holland put the
City apprentices through their drill under the eyes of their masters
and sweethearts. The Thames valley, thus become the seat of the
central war, was kept in perpetual alarum by the passage of rival
armies, which were never strong enough to lay siege to the earth-
works now hastily flung up to enclose and protect the old walls and
new suburbs of Oxford and London. Sometimes Hampden and his
troopers pounced down from his wooded Chilterns on to the plain
below ; or Essex wound in slow pomp of horse, foot and artillery
over the uplands south of Thames. More often Rupert, issuing from
the fortress of Magdalen College at the Bridge-head, where he was
quartered with the hardest riders of the army, could be seen by the
first light of morning high on Shotover Hill, galloping towards
glory and plunder afar.

But the struggle in the Thames valley was decided by other Turnham
wars and other warriors in distant North and South. For it was Green,
early proved by experience that London could not be overpowered Nov.,
by a frontal attack. When in November Charles advanced to 1642
take it by a *coup de main* from Oxford, the commercial world mustered for the week at Turnham Green a well drilled and brilliantly
equipped army of militia, over 20,000 strong. So small was the
chance that this weighty shield could be broken through by the
light field-army of the King, that Milton wrote a jesting sonnet
" When the assault was intended to the City " ; he would have
been in no mood to trifle with such a prospect, if he had really
expected the fate of Magdeburg to befall the island capital, where
freedom had found her strong place of refuge.

After the bloodless repulse from Turnham Green, the last im- The
portant operation of 1642, the Cavalier stragetists went about by triple ad-
more scientific approaches to the same objective—London. By the vance on
plan of campaign on which they founded their operations in 1643 1643-44
and 1644, three forces were to advance concentrically, each from
a different base, corresponding to the three districts where armies
were most easily enlisted and equipped for the King. The Earl of
Newcastle, with the men of the Northern counties, was to pierce
through the hostile Eastern Association and appear on the Essex
shore of the Thames. Hopton was to lead the men of Devon and
Cornwall to the opposite bank, unmuzzling the Royalist half of
Kent on the way. If the rebel merchants had not the sense to
surrender as soon as they found the Thames navigation cut off

below the wharfs, the King could lead the Oxford army, recruited in Wales and the middle West, to join Newcastle and Hopton in a united attack on the starving and isolated capital. The plan was sure of success if the three districts of England which were strongest in local feeling as well as in loyalty—the North, the middle West and the South-West—would put love of King before love of home, and march hundreds of miles into the land of " foreigners," to whose welfare they were indifferent rather than hostile.

Until June, 1645, the Roundhead leaders had not, like their opponents, any clear conception of their own strategical objects. They sent out their armies through the length and breadth of England, often on useless and sometimes on disastrous errands, like a pugilist who sends his slow heavy blows astray and sometimes overreaches and falls. To whom are we to attribute the superior strategy of the Cavaliers ? It is impossible to know which of the generals and nephews who frowned at each other across the King's council board, sharing military authority by the most whimsical arrangements, and securing favour in irregular alternation, was the real father of a plan worthy of Wallenstein or Gustavus. Perhaps it was Rupert's. By tireless work and fierce infectious valour he had in a few weeks produced, out of a mob of grooms and hunts-men, a cavalry fit to charge and conquer, and he knew also how to sketch in theory the plan of a whole campaign. But he lacked the arts that lie between cavalry leadership and strategy, the arts of conducting the campaign which has been sketched, and of fighting a battle of all arms together. It was here that the Cavaliers failed. The jealousies of their generals, which did not prevent the forma-tion of the grand design, gravely impeded its execution.

Oxford during the war   Indeed, no military virtue except dashing valour was stimulated by the atmosphere of Oxford. A gentleman who had no pay but plunder, and no discipline but honour, could not be called to account if he chose to spend one month in the field and one at Court ; if he volunteered on a forage with Rupert because the lady was cruel or the husband inquisitive, and came galloping back in mid campaign. Fashionable women, the despair of army reformers in every age, held sway in the college rooms, disturbing Aristotle's reign over the spiders of three centuries, and making gaol delivery of the Lares and Penates of celibate learning. Plays were written and acted, sonnets dedicated and admired, satires laughed over and avenged ; fashions in dress and manners came in and went out, gallants kept assignations at nightfall, and swordsmen brushed the morning's dew from the meadows of Thames and Cherwell. To be as different as possible from the ascetics and hypocrites, with whom they had at last come to death-grips, seemed more than ever the duty of a Court which had been, from the days of Queen Elizabeth, the centre of corruption and good taste.

Above all, political intrigue in its most personal form raged Parties at Oxford as fiercely as if the Royalists had already nothing to at Oxford do but to divide up England among themselves. There were as many parties as there were men and women. All Protestants were against the Queen and her Catholics, who had secured commissions in the army in full proportion to their large numbers, great wealth and devoted loyalty ; and among the Catholics themselves their own obscure divisions only multiplied under stress of war. All the civilians in Oxford were against the professional soldiers. But among the civilians, the courtiers taunted the solemn Privy Coun- cillors with turning loyal at the eleventh hour ; and among the Privy Councillors, constitutional Hyde and Falkland were opposed by Digby, who had recommended the arrest of the five members. Among the soldiers, the old and official were plagued by the licensed impertinence of the young ; and among the youths, the good soldier Rupert was at deadly feud with Goring and Wilmot, whose drunken bestiality prepared and solaced defeat. Amid such clamorous confusion of counsels, the man whose business it was to control them had no one person in whom he confided, and no one plan on which he had determined. During the war Charles pursued simul- taneously a dozen secret intrigues and public policies, opposed in spirit one to another, and none carried through to the end.

But on the whole the constitutional elements inevitably lost ground. Hyde got the Cavalier members summoned to a Parlia- ment at Oxford, but no Parliament could flourish in that uncon- genial soil. The English and Rhenish soldiers, who cared equally little about English law, gradually encroached on the counsels of the Crown ; and the most favoured rivals with whom the various military cliques had to contend, were not the constitutional states- men, but the ultra-royalist Digby and the Catholic Queen.

If the dilatoriness of Essex had thrown away the initial advan- Greater tage which the power to raise loans from the City merchants had financial resources given to Parliament, the resources on which those and all later of Parlia- loans were secured outlasted the wealth at the disposal of the King ; ment and, after three years of balanced power, gave the Roundhead armies for the second time a superiority, of which the New Model was more quick to make use (1645). These resources were of a regular nature, and increased as the war went on. The Houses, fighting in the King's name, used against him the revenues which he had enjoyed, as well as the taxes which they had the power to levy in their own right. They collected the rents of all the royal estates within their lines ; and the port duties, under Parliamentary manipulation, gave a largely increased return. Much of the indirect taxation came out of the pockets of upland Cavaliers, obliged to pay enhanced prices for goods that could only reach them taxed from Roundhead warehouses,

Still larger sums were realised by the adoption of new financial methods. No widening of the basis of taxation had been attempted for the last fifty years by Parliaments more anxious to control than to supply their sovereign. Now that Parliament was itself the executive, experiments leading from mediæval to modern finance were introduced by the ready statesmanship of Pym. An Excise on the sale, first of drink and victuals, and finally of most articles in common demand, was established on the newest principles of the Dutch statists, and levied in the first instance at the sword's point. The English, who would never willingly have consented to its first introduction, submitted to its retention as an established part of the national finance under the restored monarchy, but did not cease to nurse a suspicion of the name Excise that broke out into madness under Walpole.[1]

Direct taxation also was reformed. The old method of levying a subsidy, nominally an *ad valorem* charge on lands and moveables, had declined under Elizabeth into a fixed charge on each district in England, amounting to £70,000 in all, and not increasing with the increasing wealth of the country. This had seemed to the Commons good enough for the King's needs. But when the war began, they ordered a New Assessment of all England to be made monthly ; the total amount required every month was fixed by Parliament with reference to the momentary exigencies of the campaign, and the rating of each individual proprietor was made the business of the County Committees, which, before the New Model, were the chief instruments of all military and financial business. The New Assessment was not only more profitable in results but more fair in incidence than the old, even if the Committees seldom neglected to be as hard as possible on neutrals and suspected Royalists. Like the Excise, the New Assessment was continued by the statesmen of the Restoration, and was developed into the Property and Land Tax which paid for our great wars with France.[2]

The successful levy of taxes so odious that Strafford never dared to suggest them during the despotism, or Charles to impose them on his own West in time of war, shows how complete was the military occupation of the East by Parliament. It suggests also that many, who cared little for the results of the war provided it came to an end, were so accustomed to think of the Commons and not the King as the rightful imposers of taxation, that they paid

---

[1] Strafford, who understood better than his contemporaries the evil effects of port duties, had wished to forestall Walpole by taking steps in Ireland towards " an excise, which although it be heathen Greek in England, yet certainly would be more beneficial to the Crown, and less felt by the subject, than where the impositions are laid upon the foreign vent of commodities inward and outward " (1633, G., viii., p. 39).

[2] Dowell, i., pp. 150-59 ; ii., pp. 1-14, 47-51, 61, 68, 79, 128, 129.

the Assessment and the Excise with a mechanical indifference, which
they had not shown when the Royal Commissioners came round for
the Ship Money.

The classes and the district put under contribution by Parlia- Financial
ment were not only comparatively willing but fairly able to pay ; disad-
for much of their wealth was in ready money. Within the Royalist of the
lines the case was different. Charles had no commercial centres King
where he could negotiate loans, even if he could have offered the
security of taxation. He had to fight the war on plunder and free
gifts. The Cavaliers offered their own wealth to the King and
their neighbour's goods to themselves. But in spite of this liberal
disposition, the average Royalist had in 1642 little ready money,
in proportion to the sum for which he was forced to compound his
estate in 1646 : he could not realise his wealth because it was in
land. There were only two things which he could offer to the King
—his plate and one year's rent.

Plate was indeed a larger part of the national assets than it is The melt-
to-day. In the generation preceding the establishment of banks in ing of
England, the savings of all classes brightened the shelves, or were plate
served up with the beef and ale. For 150 years silver plate had
been accumulating undisturbed by war, during a period when the
art of the silversmith was as exquisite as it was widely spread.
Every cobbler in London, wrote Sir Philip Warwick, drank out
of his silver beaker, " so rife were silver vessels among all conditions ".
In 1642 one of the noblest arts of the European Renaissance disappeared down the King's melting furnaces ; just as the mediæval
saints from the church niches, and the purple robes of Pilate in the
windows, came clinking down under the Puritan hammer on to the
heads of laughing mobs.[1]

Even before the fighting began, gentle families who had helped
the King were not only eating off pewter, but were hard pressed to
purchase the ordinary necessaries of life. And as the war went on,
the rent which the Cavalier could collect off his estate to share
with his master became smaller every year. The rise in wages, the
unwillingness to take farms, the constant plunder and arson, brought
down many rentals in Cheshire and Gloucestershire to one-half.[2]

The foremost to share their wealth with the King were his Catholic The
subjects. The loyalty of the gentlemen of the old religion, naturally Catholics
cool during the dozen years' persecution after the Gunpowder Plot, Crown
and the

[1] But the Cavaliers were not the only people who melted down their plate for
the war. Thus in *Hudibras,* canto ii. :—

> " Did Saints for this bring in their plate ?
> And crowd as if they came too late ?
>
> .   .   .   .
>
> And into pikes and musqueteers
> Stampt beakers, cups and porringers ? "

[2] G. (*C. W.*), iii., p. 196. Verney, ii., pp. 88-90.

warmed to James when he relieved them against the will of his Parliaments, and had now become with most an instinct and a passion, whatever reservations might lurk in the subtle brains that guided the Jesuit intrigue. During the wars and rebellions of the next hundred years, the Stuart, whether crowned King or wandering outlaw, could count on the swords and rentals of the Catholics, at times when Churchmen would only send him messages and drink him healths. In 1642 a quarter of a century had passed away since the legal penalties and fines had been regularly inflicted on the recusants, and it was for this reason that they were both willing and able to save Charles from financial ruin. Protestant fears were so far well grounded, that the Catholics were a rich community. The Earl of Worcester, reputed the greatest monied man in England, had an annual rental of £24,000. He gave it almost wholesale to the King.

Such were the royal resources. But they were not regular and they were certain to diminish.

Private armies and loca-wars

Owing to the poverty of Charles, and the bad organisation of the Roundheads before their New Model reforms, most regiments on either side consisted of private companies and troops, and many campaigns of private sieges and wars. At a time when about 140,000 men were under arms in England, it was seldom that either party brought more than 9,000 to 15,000 into line of battle. Marston Moor was the only occasion on which as many as 20,000 men were fighting on one side, and that was because the Parliamentary generals had united three separate armies on the field. The great majority of the combatants were engaged in small local wars, which seldom had influence on the main result, at any rate after 1642. Gentlemen who never took part in larger operations, except for a few days while Rupert or Essex passed through their country on the road to bigger game, were eager to wage war on each other, at the head of their servants or tenantry, strengthened by a few soldiers wandering from the colours in search of higher pay.

The garri-son system

England was at that date full of Plantagenet castles, still in good repair as dwelling houses, though their battlements now peered over the mossy roofs of outhouses and the waving tops of trees, whose age told how many generations had gone by since the inhabitants last expected the approach of besiegers. These veteran strongholds which had seen our Kings go forth to Normandy, and the palaces of red brick whose mullioned windows recalled the peace of Elizabeth and her successor, were alike put into a state of defence, and supplied with 50 to 300 men apiece. The garrison system proved the ruin of the King. As the means to provision and pay his armies in the field diminished, regiments that had better have been dismissed at once, were left behind at free quarters, each with a district assigned for its maintenance. Living in garrison, they ate up the country-side; and, so long as there was anything left to plunder, would not shift to ground where they were really needed. " I'll fight," says Tom Tell-Troath when he turns Cavalier in Lacy's play, " partly for love, partly for mine own ends. I'll fight bravely for a battle or two, then beg an old house to make a garrison of, grow rich, consequently a coward, and then, let the dog bite the bear, or the bear the dog, I'll make my own peace."

Some regiments in the field were raised and officered by private persons, but paid by King or Parliament to serve in the main army. Others were both raised and paid at the expense of the Colonel, and went on whatever service he chose. Of the soldiers in receipt of public money, some were paid by special local contributions, others out of the general taxes; some were paid by the King or Parliament direct, others by the Committee of the County, or of the Associated Counties. Many were not paid at all. Some were engaged permanently, others for single expeditions. _{Methods of levying the armies}

The appearance of the men was as motley as the methods of levying them were various. On both sides a regiment would be dressed in red or blue, white or green, each according to the taste of the man who had raised it. The colour of his servants' livery was often selected. At last, under the unifying influence of the New Model organisation, red began to predominate, apparently because red had been the favourite colour in the Eastern Association. To distinguish themselves from the Cavaliers, many of the Roundhead officers and some of the men appeared from first to last in orange scarfs. But friend or foe were more usually distinguished through the smoke drifts of the mêlée by challenging for the password— " God with us," or " Have at you for the King,"—and by badges specially assumed on the day of battle. At Newbury the Roundheads wore green twigs, like the assailants of Dunsinane; at Marston, white handkerchiefs or pieces of paper in their hats; at some onslaughts of towns, the " forlorn hope " quaintly left their shirts hanging out behind, for the better guidance of their own supports through the night.[1] The innumerable flags, without which no army in that age thought of taking the field, were often of fanciful design. The armorial bearings of the Colonel, the crest of the town, an emblem or a motto, a political cartoon of Bishops, or of the little dog Pym biting the lion's tail, rejoiced the hearts of the troop when it marched out, and of its captors when it laid down its arms.[2] _{Uniforms, badges and flags}

The military art which English amateurs had now to master in the school of experience, was propounded to them by books on Swedish tactics, and by officers flocking home from various schools of war on the Maas, the Danube and the Rhine. Dutch and German horse usually charged in columns, deep in inverse proportion to _{Cavalry}

---

[1] Hence a night attack was called a " camisado "—shirt-fight.
[2] Firth's *C. A.*, pp. 45, 175, 232, 234, and chap. ii. *passim*.

the discipline and courage of the troop. The squadrons riding up
in phalanx to exchange sneaking pistol-shots and fly, with whose
cowardly attitudes the artists of the Thirty Years' War have loaded
so much canvas in the picture galleries of the Continent, are the type
of our Roundhead cavalry before the rise of the Ironsides. But the
Swedish horse, taught by their great Gustavus, fought in line three
deep, never halted to fire, reserved their pistols and carbines for the
mêlée, and charged straight in with flourished steel. Rupert perhaps found it all the easier to train his chivalry after this improved
pattern, because in 1642 few of them had any firearms to let off.
As Charles filled his war-chest with plate from the cupboards of
loyal squires, so he was fain to fill his armoury with trophies off
their walls. When the firearms seized from the militia had gone
half the round of the musketeers, the horsemen had to be contented
with old corselets, headpieces and swords, some of which may have
been taken down on the night of the Armada beacons.[1] Yet no
more than this was required for a charge home.

The private in the cavalry seldom came from the ranks of hired
agricultural labour. A trooper involved an outlay of capital.
Sometimes he had invested the savings of his own farm or shop in
a horse and armour, speculating on a return in the shape of plunder
or religious liberty. Sometimes he had been equipped by his landlord, or by subscription among the " young men and maids " of
the neighbouring Puritan town.[2] His pay, when he got it, was three
times that of his poor brother of the foot.

Infantry   The infantry were more than half of them pressed men, generally
from the lowest classes. The cavalry, socially, physically and in-
tellectually superior, " pillaged and wounded " the linesmen on
their own side when the war began,[3] and instructed them in new
policies and new religions when it drew to a close. It was seldom
thought worth while to sink good men and money in improving
the foot, before the invention of the bayonet enabled them to make
better resistance to the horse. A regiment of foot contained only
half as many pikes as muskets ; but the former was still accounted
the more honourable weapon. If a gentleman volunteered to fight
on foot, he trailed " the puissant pike." In a combat between
infantry, the musketeers were ranged on the two flanks ; when
they had delivered their shot, if possible into the enemy's pikemen,
the men of each successive rank wheeled round and formed up
again in the rear of the long column, to reload while the others kept
up the fire in turn. But the victory was finally decided " at push
of pike " in the centre. If cavalry appeared while the regiment
was drawn up in this order, all was lost. Only when, like the London
train-bands at Newbury, they had time to from square with the

---

[1] Clar., p. 305.   Carl's *Crom.*, Letter xiii.
[3] *Archæologia*, xxxv., p. 321.

musketeers kneeling under shelter of the long pikes, could the best infantry in the world hope to drive off a charge of horse.

The comparative value of horse and foot would have been re- **Relative** versed, if England had then been, as she is now, a country chequered **value of** with hedgerows. But the enclosure of land that marked the agri- **horse and** cultural change in the Tudor times had stopped far short of com- **foot** pletion. Midland English scenery was coppice, moor and waste, alternating with broad naked plough-field, like that of continental lands to-day. When Rupert swept across the battle-fields of Edge-hill, Marston Moor and Naseby, they were as open as the field of Waterloo; a single hedge is a marked feature in the maps of con-temporary historians. Whenever armies met in enclosed fields like those of Newbury, or orchards like those round Worcester, all de-pended on the courage with which the pikes and musketeers con-tended for each mound and hedge; but on open ground the infantry of the time were helpless. The proportion of foot to horse employed in the field armies was not more than two to one. Yet for all pur-poses of siege, occupation, storm, and warfare in broken country, infantry were essential; Charles lost the North because the foot were destroyed at Marston and the South because they were de-stroyed at Naseby. The horse escaped from both fields, but could not alone carry on the war.[1]

Under such general conditions, the conflict, for which the com-batants had only taken position in the autumn of 1642, began in earnest before the next spring.

In the first year of war, when only well-known statesmen or **Cavalier** professional soldiers had any claim to high command, the rebels **success,** lost two chiefs, who rivalled Essex in political and social position **1643** and surpassed him in military daring. The death of Lord Brooke in March, 1643, by a bullet from the beleaguered Cathedral of Lichfield, and of Hampden in June on Chalgrove Field, left Parlia-ment perforce content with Essex, Waller and Manchester, until men of no political fame or previous military experience had time to force their way to the front by sheer talent for war. But it seemed likely that all would be lost before time and chance revealed the great soldiers. The Roundheads, who by holding the towns had at first seemed to hold the country, lost their grip on North, West and Midlands by a series of disasters so rapid that in August, 1643, the preparations for the advance of the three Cavalier armies on London seemed almost complete. One by one the Roundhead organisations of counties associated for miliatry defence, were dissolved, and each shire was either governed by its own separate Committee or overrun by the Cavaliers. Cromwell's Eastern Association alone remained, henceforth known as " The Associated

[1] See Firth's *C. A. passim* for preceding paragraphs about horse and foot.

Counties," *par excellence*. On the break up of the Midland Association, Royalist armies and garrisons were everywhere intruded, neutralising central England. But in North and West their successes were more striking and more complete.

The war in the North, 1643   The seat of the struggle for Northern England was South Yorkshire. In the East Riding, the great military depot of Hull, the first town to close its gates on Charles, was still held from the sea, and communicated across the Humber with Cromwell in North Lincoln. In the West Riding, above the steep valleys of Calder and Aire, a population, leavened by refugees from Flanders and Holland, dwelt in stone-roofed cottages on the moors, exposed to every wind, praying and weaving cloth, which they sent on packhorses across the grey hills to the Puritan towns of Halifax, Bradford and Leeds. But between rebel Hull and the rebel clothing district lay the garden of loyalty—the agricultural plain encircling the Cathedral City of York. This balance of local power was upset by armies coming from afar.

From Ripon to the Border, Northern England was Cavalier, and between the departure of the Scots in 1641 and their return in 1644, was free to show its colours. Industrialism, Wesleyanism and Presbyterianism had not yet arisen in Durham and Northumberland, nor the Quaker influence in Cumberland. Probably half the population was Catholic, and all still lived and moved in bygone ideals and memories enshrined in the Border ballads. The actual life of the Borderer was more sordid but scarcely less exciting than in the old days of the Scottish wars. Moss-troopers descending from the head-waters of Redesdale and Tyne " into the low countries, carried away horses and cattle," and were hung sometimes by scores together at Newcastle and Hexham. Private disputes, with a great part of the population, were still decided not by law but by single combat.[1] In such an old world society the Marquis of Newcastle enlisted for the King's service fighters of the right Border breed, moormen who won their hay at Lammastide with sword ever ready to hand. With his " Northern Papist Army," containing " Newcastle's White Coats," perhaps the best foot regiment raised in the war, the Marquis plunged among the balanced forces of South Yorkshire, overran the clothing district, chased out the Fairfaxes (the old Lord, Ferdinand, and his son Sir Thomas), and shut them up within the walls of Hull. The gallant father and son now held no foot of ground outside the sea stronghold, but they retained in the hour of defeat the affections of the Yorkshire Puritans and the confidence of Parliamentary soldiers throughout all England.

East Anglia invaded   In Midsummer, 1643, Newcastle led his Northerners into the Associated Counties, through which lay his road to the rendezvous on the banks of the Thames. But as soon as he entered Lincoln-

[1] *Harl. Misc.*, iii., pp. 283, 284 (*Survey of Newcastle, etc.*, 1649).

shire, he found himself confronted with the small beginnings of great things.

When Cromwell had returned from Edgehill to resume his local Cromwell work, he produced in miniature every part of that system that was afterwards copied on the larger scale of the New Model Army. As the agent of the Associated Counties Committee, which owed the survival of its organisation to his energy alone, he secured comparatively regular pay for the soldiers—the prime condition of all other reforms. As the leader of the Puritan laity in East Anglia, he personally attracted into his service men to whom religion was not only the cry of party but the passion of life. As Colonel of his regiment, he would not suffer the Presbyterian orthodox to apply dogmatic tests to any soldier of Puritan temperament, and he insisted that his men should observe a discipline unknown alike to their enemies, who made licence a proof of loyalty, and to their fellow-Roundheads, among whom psalmody was but the shibboleth of common men, living as common men live. In Cromwell's strange regiment, plunder, drunkenness, wenching, even swearing, were abolished by penalties ; but these penalties only enforced the public and private opinion of the soldiers, for otherwise such rules would have been as impotent as they proved when the victorious army attempted to impose them on the civil population. These horsemen were freeholders or sons of freeholders. Many of them rode their own horses, in which they took a special interest. They learnt from Cromwell, as easily as the gallant Cavaliers learnt from Rupert, to fight in line, to reserve their fire, and to charge home sword in hand. They learnt also what the younger man never taught his impatient and ill-disciplined squadrons, to halt when the foe scattered, to face about when he pursued, and to wheel to the support of other troops when the day was still in doubt. Rupert could only lead, Oliver could handle, cavalry, and he who could handle cavalry could win the war.

The war was won, because the pick of East Anglian yeomen, uncompromisingly hostile to royal power in the State and to any form of enforced orthodoxy in the Church, volunteered to serve together in a few troops of horse, under a man who commanded their confidence for every reason—political, religious, military and personal. Victory would probably not have fallen to Parliament, and would certainly not have fallen to the Independents, if Cromwell had really, as poets sing, spent his early manhood " in his private garden," " reservéd and austere ". On the contrary, when war broke out, he had already for long been the man best loved and hated on the banks of Ouse and Cam. Love of justice, that soon turned to hot anger in his working brain, had made him the people's champion in days when it was dangerous to be popular. The property of the poor and the land of the community were then often seized by " enclosers," sometimes to enlarge their own parks, sometimes for real economic improvements, but always without just compensation. The right of the rich man to seize whatever common land he coveted, was a maxim on which the Star Chamber and the great Parliamentary Lords were agreed. But Cromwell had stood out on behalf of classes so poor and so numerous that the " sacredness of property " was not held to apply to what they possessed. On three several occasions, with loss and danger to himself, he pleaded for those who had no other to plead for them.[1]

These services he made dearer to the middle and lower class by a rough, kindly directness in speech, and a fraternal sympathy in manner. When the outbreak of war turned him into the leader and friend of a cavalry formed by voluntary enlistment among these neighbours of his, he retained a " familiar rustic carriage with his soldiers," and was as full of vivacity and humour " as another man is when he hath drunken a cup of wine too much ". In religious conversation the same qualities, playing on the surface of deepest faith and doubt, prolonged melancholy, and rare outbursts of joy, won him the hearts of many who laughed at the frigid, omniscient superiority of the Presbyterian clerics.

It was for these reasons that, when Newcastle entered the Associated Counties, he found himself opposed by a remarkable kind of cavalry.

Cavalier advance from the North checked, Aug., 1643

The Parliamentary men in London, terrified at Newcastle's advance and pleased at the amount Cromwell had done with scanty material, as attested in July in a calvalry skirmish near Gainsborough, saw that they ought at once to raise a main army for service in East and North. They sent down Manchester into the Associated Counties to raise there, with the help of Cromwell's local knowledge, an army of 10,000 foot and 5,000 horse, to be paid out of the national taxation. But before the end of harvest enabled the force to be raised, Newcastle had already turned back. The slight resistance that Cromwell's regiments had offered had been enough to discourage the Northerners, who had not begun with any strong desire to march far from their homes. The officers on whom Newcastle most depended, refused to advance on London, so long as the garrison of Hull was left behind ready to pounce out on their estates. To besiege this fortress, Newcastle returned to Yorkshire before the end of August. But Manchester and Cromwell soon advanced north with their newly raised force, secured the hold of the Associated Counties on Lincolnshire by another cavalry action known as " Winceby-fight " (October, 1643), and joined hands with the Fairfaxes across the Humber. These operations not only made Hull as safe as London, but prepared

---

[1] For the details of Cromwell's championship of common rights in 1630, 1637 and 1640, see Firth's *Crom.*, pp. 31-34. For the Star Chamber and enclosures for deer parks, see *Court and Times of Charles I.*, ii., pp. 60, 61, 181, 182.

the way for the recovery of the North in the following year. On
this line, the Cavalier march on the Thames had failed, owing to
Hull, Cromwell, and the purely local character of Newcastle's force.

The Western war of 1643 has the same story as the Northern, The ad-
except that there was no Cromwell. Hopton and his Cornishmen vance
overran Devon, Wilts and Dorset as Newcastle and his Northum- West,
brians overran Yorkshire. Taunton fell like Halifax ; Bristol and 1643
Exeter like Leeds and Sheffield. But Plymouth, like Hull, was
maintained by the fleet ; and so long as the garrison of Plymouth
threatened their homes, the gallant men of Cornwall and Devon
refused to pursue their unbroken career of victory into Hampshire
and Kent. Therefore, the farthest point of their success was
Roundway Down, outside Devizes, where they helped the cavalry
from Oxford to cut Waller's army to pieces (13th July).

On the third line of advance through the Midlands, the force The ad-
in Wales similarly refused to march till Gloucester fell. The royal vance
strategists saw that, before their three-fold attack on London could the Mid-
take place, the three local armies who were to carry out this great lands,
plan must first be satisfied by the capture of the Roundhead for- 1643
tresses at their own doors—Hull, Plymouth and Gloucester. So
the King in person sat down before Gloucester (10th August).

The siege was regarded by his followers as a brief, unnecessary Parlia-
delay in the course of a victory no longer doubtful. The renegade ment at
Lords, who in the middle of August deserted the sinking fortunes 1643
of Parliament and appeared in the Oxford quadrangles to court the
pardon of the fashionable world, were awarded the contemptuous
reception of men who have changed sides too late to affect the
balance of fortune. In the capital Pym and his committee-men
were struggling in deep waters. They could not prevent Parliament from debating terms that amounted to surrender. On one
day the mob filled Palace Yard to demonstrate against this betrayal
of the public cause (7th August) ; but on the two following days
women, and men disguised as women, battered at the doors of the
House of Commons, with shouts of " Peace, Peace," " Give us that
dog Pym," and were only dispersed when the cavalry rode in among
them with drawn swords. The perpetual defeats, the monthly assessments almost amounting to wholesale confiscation of property, the
dislocation of internal trade, made all Londoners frantic to obtain
peace—some by victory, some by compromise, some by surrender.
While such was the divided feeling of the capital, it is likely that
if Gloucester had fallen the provinces would have rallied to the
side that seemed able to end the war, and the advance on London
would have been resumed with every chance of success.

Such at least was the opinion at Westminster. Every hazard
must be run to relieve Gloucester, for its fall would involve the
fall of London. A last appeal for the " good old cause " was

14

The
prentices
march to
relieve
Glou-
cester made, and not made in vain. The peace party, finding compromise
impracticable, was not yet in the mood for capitulation. The
Gloucester crusade was preached to the great City wild with religious
zeal. Every shop was closed by order, and the London prentices
marched out in their train-bands. Hitherto only a small number
of the famous City militia had been employed at any distance, for
in their absence London's trade, the sinews of the war, must languish.
Their campaign at Turnham Green had been a few days' holiday.
But now they were to follow Essex across England. If Parliament
was to be saved, he must bring them back soon, and bring them
back victorious.

Meanwhile, in Gloucester the Puritan minority, having overawed
their less zealous fellow-townsmen, were valiantly conducting an almost desperate defence. The end was only delayed because Charles
was hampered at this crisis of his fate by want of munitions and
engines of war, the result of want of money and of sea communication. When it was known that the prentices were coming to the
relief of Gloucester, the infantry and guns were left in the trenches
to press the siege, and Rupert was sent with the cavalry to prevent
the passage of the Cotswold Hills. The Royalist horse swept that
upland cloth district of its thousand flocks, as they had already on
less occasion swept many other sheep runs in the West, winning for
the King's cause the hostility of loyal populations. The citizen
soldiers had therefore to advance without provisions over an open
plateau, where the agricultural land was " all champion," that is,
unenclosed by hedges, and where consequently they were subject
Relief of
Glou-
cester,
5th Sep.,
1643 to fierce attacks from Rupert's cavalry. But Essex had troops of
all arms, including on this occasion an infantry, who were not rascals
gathered by the press-gang, but " citizens of good account ". Arrived
at last on the steep edge of the Cotswolds above Cheltenham, they
saw across the plain the roofs and towers of Gloucester in the morning light, and the long columns of besiegers winding away from their
burning camp.[1]

First
battle of
Newbury,
20th Sep.,
1643 The object of the great march had been achieved, but it remained for Essex to bring the citizen army home. The Cavaliers,
in full force, blocked his retreat at Newbury. Already short of
food, he must cut his way through, or surrender in a few days.
As the fields round this town were much enclosed, a fierce soldiers'-
battle was fought in the lanes and ditches at push of pike all day
long, until the enemy could be detected only by the flash of his musket
through the darkened hedge. Then both sides flung themselves
down to sleep among the slain, each regiment in the ground it held.
Not to have conquered meant destruction for the Roundheads.
Their generals waited uneasily for dawn. But if Essex was short

---

[1] Clar. pp. 421-27 (and p. 965, *Life*, iii.)   G. (*C. W.*), i., pp. 184-86, 202-6.
King's Pamphlets, B.M., 126, E. 69.

of bread, Charles was short of powder. At dawn the royal army had disappeared. On the 25th of September, scarcely five weeks after they had marched out, the prentices returned to their sweethearts in triumphant array.

On the heaths and under the hedgerows of Newbury many chiefs of the Cavaliers, and sons of grand old houses lay cut off in their prime. Among the hundreds slain whom memory has long forgotten, one is mourned by imagination still. Falkland, who could not endure to see England wasted year after year in endless war, to be crushed at last under the tyranny of rebel and Puritan, nor yet to witness the triumph of despotism with the cause he had chosen but never loved, adopted the dress and manners of Hamlet in his melancholy, and sought death every day beneath the walls of Gloucester. At last at Newbury he rode alone into a Roundhead regiment, not to slay but to be slain. Hyde lived on, to bear for thirty years the weight of miseries which Falkland had refused any longer to share ; and raised to the memory of the friend who had gone so long before him, a lasting monument of English prose.[1]

But on the side of Parliament the noblest men desired the completest victory. Cromwell was no more than Falkland a stranger to doubt and melancholy, but they were not the lords of his soul ; and it was not his own death that he sought amid the enemy's ranks.

The Parliament men were the nationalist party—a fact by which they gained many adherents against the King, who was always in correspondence with Dutch, Danes, French, Pope and Catholic Irish, for military aid which his detractors could always announce to be coming, but which never came. The King was defeated by these phantom armies which he himself invoked. Yet his nationalist enemies, in the hour of their extreme need, sought one foreign alliance and secured it with decisive results. During the Gloucester campaign the Parliament had come to terms with " their brethren of Scotland ". The Scots were then looked on as foreigners, and by no one more than by the opponents of the House of Stuart. The Puritan Parliament had refused to be led by James I. into a union of the two kingdoms. In later years Cromwell declared that England had better be conquered by her own Royalists than by the Scottish Puritans. Yet, again and again, fear of despotism drove the patriots to restrain their natural sentiments and to hail the Scots as fellow-countrymen, until the repeated process had so far altered public sentiment that the Whigs under Queen Anne carried the Act of Union.

The Scottish alliance and the Covenant, Aug.-Sep., 1643

The English subjects of the House of Stuart had first observed the real political and religious character of the Scottish nation at the time of the Bishops' Wars (1639-40). In the early months of

[1] Clar., pp. 430-44.

the Long Parliament the Scots had been popular, so long as danger, novelty, gratitude and mutual ignorance continued to combine the two peoples. Security and closer acquaintance soon brought about a coldness, which lasted from the paying off of the Scottish army of occupation, until the late summer of 1643. In that season of peril, Puritans on both sides of the Tweed saw that if they were to survive severally, they must unite once more. In return for the military assistance of Scotland, the English Parliamentarians bound themselves by a Solemn League and Covenant to maintain the Church in Scotland as now established, and to reform religion in England " according to the word of God " and " the example of the best reformed Churches ". How far they hereby gave up their own liberty will appear in the sequel. But it may be observed that during the first year of war they had preferred to run great risks rather than put themselves again under any form of obligation to " their brethren of Scotland ".

Death of Pym, Dec., 1643

Pym's last work was done. He had formed a compact English party, prepared to fight for the sovereignty of Parliament and the Puritan religion. He had guided that party through the disastrous summer of 1643, when the presence of a capable and trusted leader had been needed to ward off destruction. In the autumn, he prepared by the Scottish alliance for offensive operations which should turn the scale at the opening of the next year. In December he died, and was buried with State honours in the Abbey of the Kings. For his colleagues knew that it was he who had saved Parliament. But they did not know that he had saved it to be the mother of Parliaments, and to be the origin of many liberties more free than that Puritan liberty for which he had caused the sword to be drawn, though surely of none more deeply loved or more bravely won.

Scots again invade England, Jan., 1644

In January the Scottish army entered Northumberland. In the spring they forced their way into South Yorkshire, where their arrival created a revolution as sudden as that caused by the incursion of the northern Cavaliers twelve months before. As Fairfax had then been shut up in Hull, Newcastle in his turn was besieged in York. The all-important question whether Manchester and Cromwell could be spared to join the Scots in the reduction of the North, depended on the opening of the campaign in the South, where the Royalists were preparing to advance into the Home Counties. Their prospects seemed good, until, owing to the indiscipline of their colonels, which increased as the war went on, they were drawn into battle at a tactical disadvantage near Cheriton in Hampshire (29th March), and there received a check from Waller, which en-

Siege of York, May-June, 1644

couraged Parliament to send their East Anglian forces north of the Humber. The Scottish and Yorkshire armies were therefore joined in the trenches before York by the army of the Eastern Association under Manchester and his great lieutenant. But the men who next summer broke day by day into castles and walled cities and rejoiced greatly when they went up against the breach, had not yet mastered the arts of siege and storm. Again and again they were hurled back from those mediæval battlements of York, of which one long curtain still looks out over the river gate, towards the meadows where the Roundheads planted their cannon in vain.

Meanwhile, Rupert, at the height of his reputation, was coming to the rescue, with an army very different from the prentices who had raised the siege of Gloucester. Half his forces were cavalry. For as he passed northwards through the West, men of spirit who could still anywhere find horses, swords and pistols, flocked in from dull garrisons, and from households that had long been neutral, each gentleman burning for the honour to be one of Rupert's Cavaliers. His route led him through the scene of the Lancashire war, where, isolated from the strategic, religious, and social conditions of the larger conflict, the Puritan clothing towns were holding down the rural districts and their Catholic inhabitants. Rupert's passage *Rupert in* brought momentary deliverance and revenge to the papist squires. *Lanca-* According to the law of storm that was the rule of war on the Con- *shire,* tinent, but not the custom of war in England, except where the *May-June* contest lay between a Catholic and Protestant population, the Cavaliers massacred the defenders of Bolton and indulged themselves at the expense of the inhabitants in the worst horrors of sack. Followed by the curses and prophecies of the Bible readers of Lancashire, they rode off over the low mountain passes by Skipton and entered the plain of York.[1]

Rupert outmanœuvred his formidable enemies and succeeded *Marston* in relieving the city without a battle. The besiegers struck camp. *Moor, 2nd* But, as might be expected, the all-victorious general of three-and- *July,* twenty followed up their retreat, and offered them the battle which *1644* they so much desired on the moor by Long Marston, eight miles west of York. Never before or after did either King or Parliament put such numerous forces into one field. The Roundheads brought into line three armies—those of Scotland, of North England, and of East Anglia. Together they numbered 20,000 foot and 7,000 horse. Rupert and Newcastle had 11,000 foot and about 7,000 spendid cavalry, who, until that fatal summer evening, could boast themselves invincible. Yet Rupert himself had listened with respect to strange tales from those who had met the East Anglian troopers in their own country. " Is Cromwell there ? " he asked, as he viewed the Roundhead line. After the battle, with the loving familiarity which one good soldier often assumes with the person of another, he bestowed on his conqueror the immortal nickname of " Ironsides ".

[1] Chetham Soc., *Civil War in Lancs.*, pp. 188-98 and *passim ;* and *Lancashire Lieutenancy*, ii., *passim.*

The sun was falling low, the Puritans had struck up the evening psalm, Rupert had retired to supper, and Newcastle to his coach to smoke, when suddenly the three Roundhead armies rolled down off the high corn lands where they stood, on to the moor, where the strength of monarchy in England had been gathered to a head and exposed at one stroke to ruin. On the Royalist left, Goring drove Fairfax's horse off the field. In the centre, the Yorkshire foot gave way. With them went half the ten regiments of Scots ; but the rest stood firm in the rout. Shoulder to shoulder still, each man grasped his pike, the ancient weapons of Scotland that the descendants of the men of Bannockburn and Flodden, else little skilled in modern war, well knew how to use. Not in vain they stayed to die for Christ's Crown and Covenant, for their stand decided the fate of the two kingdoms.

Far on their left wing, beyond the tide of routed foot, Cromwell was leading 2,500 of his own horse, followed by 800 ill-mounted Scots. Both sides were well accustomed to charge home ; only after long hacking of swords on armour, man to man, were Rupert's cavalry driven from the field. Wheeling round to the relief of the Scottish pikemen, Cromwell, by a series of well-planned charges, cleared the moor, as the last glimmer of daylight followed the sunken sun. The Border Whitecoats fiercely rejected quarter from the Scots and died to a man, as though it had been some old day of pride between Douglas and Percy. When dawn came up again after the short summer night, thrilling the weary victors with exultation, the yet unuttered thought then first, perhaps, had birth among some whom Cromwell had enlisted, that God had called them not merely to be troopers for Parliament in their own fen country, but to deliver England from kings, and themselves from all priests and all Churches.

Rupert, gathering 6,000 horse, escaped out of Yorkshire by the Western dales. The rest of the army had dissolved. York surrendered. England north of Trent was recovered at a stroke.[1]

The surrender at Lostwithiel, 2nd Sep., 1644   Although a large proportion of the upper classes had by this time been compelled to choose sides, the want of enthusiasm which the bulk of the population had shown in the first year of the war, developed during the third year into hatred of the rival taskmasters. The assessments which maintained the army of Parliament, the plunderings on which Cavalier troops and garrisons subsisted, as they grew ever more oppressive, alienated the good-will of all save the strongest partisans. In such a state of feeling, victory, and with victory the loyalty lavished on the peace-bringer, can be snatched by a comparatively small body of able men who love their cause the more as the enthusiasm of others declines. But in the

[1] For the numbers, value and position of the various troops at Marston Moor, see Mr. Firth's article, *R. H. S.*, 1898, pp. 17-18.

summer of 1644 there were not enough of such men in Southern England. Neither Essex nor his troops had the spirit of those who had turned the day at Marston. After the great news came from the North, instead of seizing the moment to destroy the royal forces, he sought to overrun the royal territories. He led his men into Cornwall, the one part of the West where the population would still turn out to defend King and County. His means of subsistence and his communications with London were soon cut off. Seeking to re-establish them by sea, he marched his hungry troops towards the long tidal creek of Fowey, whose reaches of sheltering woodland were well known to merchants homeward-bound, as a safe refuge from the storms and pirates of the Channel. On the moors above, and among the steep lanes sloping down to the water side, Charles and his Cornishmen established a circle of posts round the rebel army. Essex himself escaped by taking ship to London ; his cavalry had broken through the line of blockade at Lostwithiel, and ridden off by night ; but his foot were starved into the surrender of their arms and munitions. If the disaster had befallen him twelve months before at Newbury—as it so nearly did—the balance of war might then have been decided. It was now only restored.

The unavailing efforts made by Parliament to prevent the *Need for* catastrophe had served to show the weakness of their military system. *reorgan-* Waller had been called on to save Essex. His utmost endeavours *isation apparent* had failed to raise a mobile force. The men pressed for his service by the various County Committees ran off as soon as they had seen the bottom of his war-chest. Hundreds of soldiers wandered about from shire to shire, from regiment to regiment, from Roundheads to Cavaliers, and back from Cavaliers to Roundheads, in search of more regular pay or greater licence to plunder. The system of short enlistments, effected through the agency of County Committees or private individuals, had broken down. The failure to relieve Essex was the crisis which forced on the remedy of the disease. It was Waller who first told the Houses that they could not win, until they had a standing army " merely of their own ". In the winter this suggestion of a New Model was pushed through by Cromwell. It was his first and last appearance as a Parliamentary leader on the floor of the House, but none of England's lords of debate ever produced in one session more decisive results.

In all effective movements of army reform, the adoption of a *Army re-* new organisation goes with the employment of a new type of man. *form and religious* And because the New Model turned on a question of men, it also *differ-* raised and decided the question of religion. For the men who *ences* made the best privates and the officers who were best fitted to carry out the proposed reorganisation, claimed a liberty of worship which their less efficient comrades, led by the clergy and the peace party, were unwilling to grant. The split among the Puritans on the question of toleration was as old as the reign of Elizabeth. First the Brownists and the Mennonites, then the Independents and the Baptists, had declared against the existence of a State Church and in favour of freedom of thought and worship. In England the Bishops had persecuted them to the death, and the official Puritans had refused to receive them in Massachusetts. But these men, who alone among their contemporaries deserve the name of Free Churchmen, had multiplied by hundreds a week, from the moment that the meeting of the Long Parliament had abolished the power of the old Church without setting up the new. England was for a few years alive with many things other than the orthodox religions.

The official Puritans were driven frantic with rage by this mutiny on board the good ship *Reformation*, just as she was coming into harbour. Yet even among the State Churchmen who were agreed not to tolerate dissent, there was grave difference of opinion as to what it was that they ought to force upon the nation. In 1641 Pym and his majority had deliberately rejected the Presbyterian scheme and voted for an Erastian State Church governed by Parliamentary Commissioners. The disappointed Presbyterians had denounced the Parliamentarians as lawyers and worldly-wisemen, " extraordinarily affrighted to come under the yoke of ecclesiastical discipline ". But since the beginning of the war the clerical party had recovered ground. The Westminster Assembly of Divines, summoned to give Parliament specialist advice on the true methods of Reformation, had been a strong influence in favour of professional theology and the clerical element. The Covenant, swallowed in 1643 as the price of Scottish military alliance, bound Parliament morally, though not verbally, to establish the Presbyterian system which it had once rejected. For the Scots at least interpreted the promise made by their allies, to follow " the example of the best reformed Churches," to mean clerical synods and the discipline of Geneva. Therefore, from the taking of the Covenant, history applies the name " Presbyterian " to the majority of the House of Commons, and to the English party that supported a Puritan State Church, although two-thirds of its members would have been regarded by all true followers of Knox as rank Erastians.

Military career of Independents endangered Thus in the autumn of 1644, though nothing had yet been decided by the two Houses, there was a clear intention of erecting a Presbyterian form of Church government, without any inside or outside place left either for Anglican or Independent. The tendency of the hour at Westminster reacted in the camps and garrisons of Parliament. On County Committees the Presbyterians applied the test of orthodoxy to candidates for the public service, while the Independents could only press the claims of their friends on the poorer plea of efficiency. In the Eastern Association alone could the sectarians get fair promotion, and there even their strength lay not in numbers but in ability and character. The clergy and officials were in most places combined against them. Cromwell and the Hutchinsons saw day by day, in field and garrison, how the common cause was being wrecked by the imbecile pedantry of the orthodox. At the crisis of a siege, some gunner who had stayed away from Church, or spoken against tithes and steeple-houses, would be put under arrest; or some Anabaptist corporal, who had been caught preaching, would be sent home to his farm. If next morning the gun was less well pointed, or if a dozen of the best troopers went off after the corporal, it in no way troubled the Presbyterian clergy and their maintainers, who had learnt to comfort themselves for want of success by talking wise nonsense about an " accommodation with his Majesty ".

And so, if the Independent chiefs failed to carry Parliament with them in the winter session of 1644-45, the next spring would probably see the dismissal of the soldiers of all ranks who were most able and most willing to finish the war. The majority of the House of Commons held a middle position ; Presbyterian though it now was in name, it still hated Scottish orthodoxy as much as English heresy, and clerical rule as much as sectarian toleration. The members hoped, as soon as the war was over, to gratify the keen sense of their own virtue and importance by persecuting sectaries through their own Commissioners ; but they had no wish that the black-coated tribe, whom they themselves had rescued from poverty and persecution under Laud, should in the hour of danger weed the fighting regiments of all the best men. Since the war began, the House of Commons, like all assemblies of simple-minded country-men to whom the disposal of great wealth and power is suddenly committed, had grown to exceed in worldly wisdom. From Speaker Lenthall downwards, many of the degenerate successors of Eliot, Hampden and Pym, dipped their hands in bribes, and in the rich spoil of their enemies that should have gone to relieve the over-burdened public. Such men were determined not to risk the sweets of power for the pleasure of persecuting the sects ; they knew that unless they commissioned Cromwell to beat Charles, they would too late regret their folly at the foot of the gallows or in the hold of the emigrant ship. To escape the vengeance of the Cavaliers and the interference of the Scots, they armed the sectaries, intending however, to throw them over as soon as they had finished the war.

The New Model debates were ushered in by a personal attack on Manchester. Since Essex had returned wholly discredited from Cornwall, Manchester was the chief representative of the old school of society, politics, religion and war, which had begun but which could not end the Great Rebellion. At the second battle of Newbury at the close of the last campaign (October, 1644), the unwillingness

Attitude of the Commons

Cromwell attacks Manchester in Parliament, Nov.-Dec., 1644

of Manchester to fight had prevented the decisive victory which the activity of his lieutenants had prepared. Cromwell, therefore, rose in his seat to accuse his superior of backwardness to fight, deriving from unwillingness to defeat the King. The Scots supported the Earl, and demanded the dismissal of " the darling of the sectaries ". The few Lords who still represented their order at Westminster were Presbyterian, and were further alienated by the disrespect which Cromwell openly expressed for rank and social position ; the fellow judged soldiers only by their service, and was ready to accept on his merits any " plain russet-coated captain, who knows what he fights for and loves what he knows ". Their Lordships felt that the air around them, especially in the neighbourhood of this man, was becoming tainted with a spirit dangerous to hereditary pretensions. The Commons, on the other hand, were doubtfully inclining to the side of the best soldier. A rupture between Lords and Commons, between Scotland and England was imminent. Cromwell saw that to crush Manchester on such terms would be a Pyrrhic victory. He therefore withdrew the charges just as they were on the point of success. But they had done their work. The personal attack was only dropped on the tacit understanding that a real measure of Army Reform should be passed, in which the Independent chiefs should have a secure footing. To this the Lords sullenly consented.

The Self-Denying Ordinance and New Model, Dec., 1644-March, 1645

A Self-Denying Ordinance, by which members of either House were to resign all military commands (without however being precluded from reappointment), was chosen as the most complete and the least offensive method of getting rid of all the old gang. The younger Fairfax combined the reputation which he had won in the North as a dashing soldier with that of a politician who had committed himself to neither section : he was made commander-in-chief. The post of lieutenant-general, which involved the command of the horse, was left open till the moment was ripe for the appointment of his friend Cromwell. As the right of promotion was at the same time vested wholly in the commander-in-chief, the position of sectarian soldiers in an army so commanded was safe enough.

Not less important than the selection of generals was the formation of the New Model Army which they were to command. A great standing army paid by Parliament itself, and absolutely under the control of one commander, was substituted for various local forces. The remaining soldiers who had not yet deserted the standards of Waller, Essex and Manchester were merged into this unit, and 8,000 fresh men were raised by the press-gang. The New Model, thus constituted, contained 22,000 out of some 80,000 men who were fighting for Parliament in the year 1645. Financial arrangements were made by which more regular pay was secured, as the first condition of more regular discipline. Success in the central campaign of the war would not in the coming year depend on the personal jealousies and whims, the religious intolerance and the political apathy of local magnates and County Committees, nor on the unwilling adhesion of vagabond soldiers to a cause that appealed neither to their hearts nor their pockets.

Yet for all these immediate improvements, more than half the infantry of the New Model, in the first year of its formation, were pressed men. And not half of its total force were Independents. A whole regiment of foot mutinied when their sectarian colonel was moved to speak a few words to their condition. But preaching officers found more willing audiences among the cavalry. The old troopers of the Eastern Association, who formed the greater part of the horse in the New Model, had enlisted to win themselves civil and religious freedom, and they had in them a spirit which soon leavened the whole army. Two years afterwards, when the other Parliamentary forces were disbanded, the New Model remained as the instrument of the Independents and the Republicans. *Change not complete*

Thus in the year 1645, when Presbyterianism was first officially announced as the State religion, its real power received at that very moment a blow which prevented it from ever obtaining force in England.[1]

The Spring was spent in getting the new army under weigh. In the summer it fairly entered into the war under conditions at last favourable to a decisive issue. At last the civilian English, who had begun the war like landsmen rigging out a ship, had learnt, in their own favourite school of experience and practical necessity, how to evolve a perfect fighting machine, which was soon to show itself superior to the professional warriors of Europe. But in 1645 the change had only begun. As yet but a fourth part of the forces in the sevice of Parliament had regular pay, good discipline, good organisation and fine generals. But the other side had no such force at all. The Cavaliers, though they might at one time have hoped to carry London at a rush and so end the war, could never have created such a machine as the New Model. They had not the money with which to buy discipline, nor the public spirit with which to effect reorganisation. They had loyalty, courage and private ambition, but not the sense of commonweal, which caused Lords and Commons, English and Scots, Presbyterians and Independents, Cromwell and Manchester, to sink private ambitions and quarrels until victory was secured, and to compromise differences far more grave than those which divided Digby and Rupert. *Roundheads and Cavaliers: new prospects*

At the beginning of the war there had been little to choose between the two sides in the matter of plunder and ill discipline. But the Royalists, for want of money and self-restraint, had become

[1] For the preceding paragraphs, see Barclay, Gooch, Shaw, Hutchinson *passim* Firth's *Crom.*, pp. 112-23, and *C. A.*, pp. 30-36, 55, 56, 318, 319. G. (*C. W.*), ii., pp. 23, 58-59, 82-84, 177-96.

steadily worse ; the Puritans, especially those of the New Model, were becoming rapidly better.

> Those under the King's commanders (Clarendon observed with stern regret) grew insensibly into all 'the licence, disorder and impiety with which they had reproached the rebels ; and they again, into great discipline, diligence, and sobriety ; which begat courage and resolution in them, and notable dexterity in achievements and enterprises. Insomuch as one side seemed to fight for monarchy, with the weapons of confusion, and the other to destroy the King and Government, with all the principles and regularity of monarchy.[1]

Naseby,
14th
June,
1645
In the summer of 1645 even the superiority in plan of campaign went over to the Roundheads. Hitherto the Cavaliers had had the advantage of a general plan of advance on London. London was their objective. To take it would end the war. The Roundheads had no such objective. To take Oxford would be to capture an outpost. Essex, Waller and Manchester had wandered about aimlessly enough, sometimes as far as Cornwall. But the generals of the New Model saw that their true objective was the King's army in the field. If that were once defeated, all his garrisons could soon be taken, and all his recruiting-grounds overrun. The strategy that led to Naseby was no more based on geographical considerations than was Nelson's hunt for Villeneuve and his " fleet in being " through all the waters of the world. During the first few weeks, indeed, the politicians of Westminster directed the movements of the New Model, as they had done those of Essex, in accordance with the old territorial ideas of strategy. But in June, frightened by the unimpeded activity of the King's troops, they at length gave their commander-in-chief the complete military freedom that he and his successor ever afterwards enjoyed. Fairfax at once sought out Charles, who was wandering about in the Midlands uncertain whether he dared march north to effect a junction with the victorious Montrose ; the New Model came upon the King in the rolling uplands of Northamptonshire, between Market Harborough and Naseby. Superior in numbers, in cavalry, and in leadership of cavalry, the Roundheads scattered one wing of the Royalist horse, while the other, under Rupert, went far in wild pursuit. The deserted foot stood firm for awhile against a fierce onslaught from all sides, until Fairfax and Cromwell themselves led the way into the thick of the pikes. All the King's infantry and all his munitions of war were taken.

The result surprised many Cavaliers and many Roundheads ; for it had been well known that the infantry of the New Model were mostly raw recruits, of whom the best were supposed to have deserted from the royal standards. Yet the event had been in less doubt than the sway of battle on Marston Moor, and had been

---

[1] Clar., p. 444.

more confidently expected in the breast of one who knew the veterans
of the cavalry :—

> When I saw the enemy (wrote Cromwell) draw up and march in gallant
> order towards us, and we a company of poor, ignorant men, to seek how to
> order our battle : the General having commanded me to order all the horse,
> I could not, riding alone about my business, but smile out to God in praises,
> in assurance of victory, because God would, by things that are not, bring to
> naught things that are. Of which I had great assurance, and God did it.[1]

Though he had lost everything else, Charles had brought off his Charles's
cavalry strangely intact from the field. And he still had a force of position
all arms engaged, under Goring, in the plunder of friend and foe after
in the South-west. He ought never to have separated from that Naseby
army, and now his last hope was to unite his remaining troops.
But the false strategy of retaining the area of occupation undimin-
ished had taken such a hold on his mind, that he carried the survivors of Naseby to the Welsh border, and even refused to call
into the field the scores of petty garrisons with which his generals
had saddled the country at a time when foot soldiers had been
plenty. He thus condemned himself and his large body-guard of
horse to a year of futile wanderings, which declined by insensible
steps into the flittings of a fugitive.

Trusting the Scots to watch the King's movements, Fairfax Langport,
carried the New Model into the South-west to deal with the last 10th
royal army. He came upon Goring in a strong position at Lang- July,
port. The Cavaliers were drawn up on the crest of a steep hill, 1645
covered by the marshes of the Yeo, across which ran a deep, narrow
ford. If Goring had kept his guns, he could not have been driven
out of the position, but with the plunderer's instinct he sent off his
train to safety in Bridgewater. The fire of the Roundhead artillery
was able to cover the passage of the ford for about six hundred
horse. They struggled up the hill by a deep lane into the middle
of Goring's position, and charged. After a brief struggle the army
in battle array turned and fled before them. The infantry were
overtaken and surrendered. The victors broke out aloud into
prophecies and raptures : it seemed to them that God had put
fear into the hearts of their enemies, causing the strong men to
throw away the spear, and the men of war to fly before a troop.
Clearly the Lord had chosen them as His instruments for some high
purpose. The idea of a special call, which inspired them when the
war was over to such strange political activity, took strong hold
on the cavalry that day. But the panic really signified the utter
demoralisation to which a long course of plunder, and despair of
winning the war, had brought the once gallant Cavaliers.

The King's last field army was no more. The horse took refuge Siege
beyond the Exe and the Tamar, where their enemies wisely left them operations of
the New
Model

[1]Carl.'s *Crom.*, App. Q.

alone for six months, till they had plundered the very Cornish out
of their loyalty. The New Model turned back to North and East.
At last the time had come for them to reduce piecemeal the garrisons and territories of the King. They soon discovered that
they had a special call to siege operations. Though they might
have found difficulty in conducting the year-long approach to
scientific fortresses like Breda, no army in the world could have
reduced a greater number of walled towns and a larger tale of
castles and manors in a less number of weeks. Before the walls of
a city like Bristol or Winchester their method was a summons, foaowed
if necessary by battery ; then as soon as the breach aplleared,
another summons, which the governor, under pressure from the
burghers, generally accepted ; if he did not, the stormers burst
in before the next morning's light. For the siege of a manor house,
it was generally enough to blow in the gate by a petard, or to storm
the parish church, whose tower often commanded the patron's
roof at a few yard's distance. Though Langport was the only
battle of the war in which the result had been largely affected by
field artillery, the excellent siege-train which Parliament purchased
for the New Model shortened the war by many months.[1]

**The Cava-
liers
ready for
peace**
During these operations the Cavaliers were seldom in a mood
to throw away their lives in useless resistance, or the Roundheads
to refuse them terms of safety and honour. Even at Basing House
(14th October, 1645), after a bloody assault, more than half the garrison, who had deliberately chosen death, were spared ; although,
as the defenders of Basing were Catholics, both sides showed an
animosity that was quite exceptional at that stage of the war.[2]
The Protestant Cavaliers desired peace. Rupert, who if he was a
bad constitutionalist was a good soldier, and was becoming a good
Englishman, had as early as July, 1645, advised the King to capitulate. He spoke the sense of the party which he had taught to
fight, the gallant gentlemen who were now everywhere surrendering
their manor houses at the second summons, or sorrowfully paying
off their soldiers with good wishes and old campaigning jokes. For
the fierce Royalist sentiment which nothing could appease after
the sequestrations, the King's execution, and the rule of the major-
generals, did not yet exist in the minds of the gentry. Most of
them had not yet suffered sequestration, and hoped to escape it ;
at least they could save their estates from further ruin in war by
placing them under the orderly protection of the New Model. And
at this moment there was no popular sympathy among the masses
**The Club-
men**
to give their Royalism an atmosphere in which to thrive. The Club-
men, as the infuriated peasants of Somerset and Devon were called,
who turned out to defend their cattle against both parties, did most

[1] Firth's *C. A.*, pp. 164, 170, 177. Sprigge *passim.*
[2] *Civil War in Hampshire* (1882), pp. 234-46.

harm to the stragglers of Goring ; under the firm and equitable treatment of Fairfax and Cromwell, they soon learnt to welcome an army that paid its way. In Dorset, Wilts and Hants the Club-men were more under the influence of the Cavalier gentry, because the royal troops no longer infested those districts.[1] But everywhere Englishmen were ready to accept peace from the men who held it in their hand.

At the same time nationalist feeling was more than ever alienated from the King, whose captured infantry turned out to be Welshmen, whose only hope lay in the conquest of English-speaking Scotland by Celtic tribesmen under Montrose and whose letters arranging for the importation of Danish, French and native Irish armies, one after the other fell into the hands of Parliament during the last year of the war. The Cavaliers themselves had no wish to fight with such allies. The Roundheads outraged humanity, but not popular sentiment, when they refused quarter to Irish Catholics found in arms in England. The brute instincts of the natural man, which the Puritan warrior thought that he had tamed within his breast, were often aroused in special forms by the very religious principles which restrained him from indulging the greed, cruelty and lust of the ordinary soldier. The victors of Naseby massacred 100 Irish women whom they found among the baggage, and gashed the faces of the English harlots. The Roundheads found it their duty and pleasure to slay any Catholic priest who fell into their hands, and when they scented a witch, they were sometimes capable of putting a woman up against the nearest wall and blowing out her brains without trial or law.[2] But women whose nationality, character, or dealings with Satan did not render them suspect, had nothing to fear ; non-combatants welcomed the arrival of the New Model ; and its chiefs granted such easy conditions to the vanquished that the laying-down of arms assumed almost a friendly character.

When at last Fairfax turned to the reduction of Devon and Cornwall, the ex-Royalist population helped him to secure what was left of the Cavalier bands. The poor fellows for the most part had no ambition but to get safe home, whither they were sent off, each with a present of twenty shillings in his pocket. On 20th June Oxford capitulated on generous terms, by which Fairfax and Crom-well saved many Royalist grandees from the revenge of more malignant foes.[3]

Reduc-
tion of
Cornwall,
Jan.-
March,
and fall of
Oxford,
June,
1646

---

[1] Clar., pp. 556-59. *Civil War in Hampshire*, pp. 216-20. G. (*C. W.*), ii., pp. 264, 265, 273, 305, 313.

[2] G. (*C. W.*), ii. p. 364. *King's Pamphlets*, 126, E. 69, for the witch of New-bury.

[3] G. (*C. W.*), iii., pp. 58-69, 79-81, 108, 109. Firth's *Crom.*, pp. 139, 140. Clar., pp. 582-85. For Oxford terms, see Sprigge, pp. 260-83.

Thus, in little more than a year, all that soldiers can do to lay the foundations of peace by victory, justice and mercy, had been done by the New Model. The spirit of Puritan warfare could not do more than this, it could not effect a settlement where all the conditions of a settlement were wanting. But it had secured for ever that monarchy in England should not be a despotism. Our island had been cut free from the political history of the continent. No King should ever triumph here by the sword. When royalty was restored, it was restored by the restoration of Parliament. And because under a Parliamentary rule, however intolerant it may be for awhile, every religious and political party has hope of asserting sooner or later its place in the national life, there never has been that exodus of freemen from England, that abandonment of the hope of liberty, which must have followed the armed victory of Charles I.

When the Civil War was brought to an end under the command of Fairfax, Cromwell was not yet " our chief of men," but it was due to him that the Civil War had been won. And so. in our own day, men have agreed to let his statue stand on guard outside the doors of the Parliament which he saved, holding the Bible and the sword, the two instruments by which that salvation was wrought. English freedom had been won by wisdom, by valour, and by chance.

CHAPTER IX

PARLIAMENT, ARMY AND KING, 1646-49

—by industrious valour climb
To ruin the great work of time,
    And cast the Kingdoms old,
    Into another mould.—(*Ode to Cromwell*), MARVELL.

THE government of civilised nations, especially of England, has Strange
often been the government of custom, opposed alike to brute condi-
force and to rational reform.   A civilised nation rides safe above national
the two enemies of custom, Constraint or Necessity on the one life,
hand, and Free Will upon the other ; it detests both the Tyrant 1646-60
and the Innovator.   The most successful politicians are men of
talent who hold by the common ways of thought.   But between
the end of the First Civil War and the Restoration, the governors
of England were men of a different type ; they desired to pursue
ends not customary, and they held power by no prescriptive right.
The rule of Kings was dead, and Parliament failed to establish its
new claim to obedience.   As a vacuum was thus left in sovereignty,
strange things rushed in.   Toleration, Republicanism, abolition of
tithes and State Church, Universal Suffrage, the " Career open to
talents," the rule of the Saints—ideas opposed by the King, Parliament and nation—were advocated by the men who grasped supreme
power ; while underneath the tumult, the Quakers, in the same spirit
of change and novelty, though by far other means, won many to
new ways of thought and life.   It seemed that we were to be
governed by the Free Will and rational choice of the few strongest
men, who by a rare coincidence happened also to be the few most
active thinkers.

But Free Will had to share the throne that she had usurped
from custom, with her own arch foe Necessity.   The prime need of
man to avert social chaos and utter destruction, continually rose to
thwart each attempt to establish the ideals.   The rival claims of
Necessity and Free Will give an appearance of double dealing to
the actions of all who have been pushed off the middle path of use
and wont.   In the mind of Cromwell we see this constant war between Need and Principle, but it raged in every town and village
of the island that he held coerced.   Poor lazy custom seemed trampled
dead in the dust of that fierce strife.

This joint rule and mutual antagonism of the two primeval
forces so seldom present in the government of civilised nations,
appeared again in the French Revolution.   But Free Will then
was the will not of the few but of the great majority.   So there,
15

after horrible convulsions, Necessity was subdued, and Free Will established a new *régime*, somewhat according to her own thought and fancy. In France the old custom was really trampled dead.

But in England the ideals that grew up in the minds of the victors of Naseby, and had their day of power, were utterly swept away again, when it had been proved that a few enthusiasts could not evoke a settlement either out of brute force or out of their own divided counsels of perfection. The English thereupon went back to many of the old ways, and the spirit of custom resumed its reign. Only, in restored custom, Parliament loomed larger than before.

Intolerance of the victorious Parliament That Parliamentary sovereignty did not at once succeed to royal sovereignty, that room was left for a while to the enthusiasts and breakers of custom, was due to the want of constructive statesmanship among the members of the Long Parliament. Pym and Hampden had known how to organise the struggle, but not how to settle and conciliate. Now even Pym and Hampden were gone. The second-rate politicians who succeeded them, murmured at the liberal terms of surrender so often conceded by their soldiers to bring the war to an end. They did not understand that if the sovereignty of the two Houses was to become the settled principle of England's Government, they must not only hold together all who had fought for the " good old cause," but must render life tolerable to their defeated foes.

The Cavaliers had surrendered in a spirit open to conciliation. Two things were requisite—to allow some form of toleration for the Prayer-book service, and to leave untouched all their property that had escaped the ravages of war. If these two things had been done, the Cavaliers would certainly not have risen in revolt, and perhaps if the King had refused to come to terms, one of his family would sooner or later have accepted the new position of constitutional monarch. But the idea of granting religious toleration and financial immunity at the end of a fierce civil contest, was not considered to be in the region of practical politics. Such a course was dreamed of here and there by a theorist. But serious statesmen and men of the world knew better.

Anglicanism proscribed All true professors agreed that the Prayer-book had in these latter days become the most abominable idol in the land, " and that it was high time therefore to remove this brazen serpent and grind it to powder ". As the first result of conquest, some 2,000 Anglican clergy were expelled from their livings, each with a small pension. The Prayer-book service was forbidden by law, as the Conventicles had been under the High Commission. The quarrel between squire and parson, which Laud had created, was soon adjusted by the busy zeal of the Puritans. Common sufferings gave the gentry an entirely new attachment to the Anglican clergy. The rites which they administered obtained in the eyes of the English upper class a new set of political associations which has never since been lost.

Parliament could not resist the temptation to solve its financial difficulties by laying the burden of the war on the estates of the conquered. Besides those excepted from pardon, all who had assisted the King were forced to compound for their " delinquency " by huge fines, varying from half to a tenth of the value of their estates. The actual amount of land that changed ownership was not large, apart from the Church and Crown lands, but months and years after the last shot had been fired, Royalist gentry were still cutting down their trees, mortgaging their estates and sending up their wives to soften the Roundhead Committee-men in London, with meed of bribes and tears for the lords of the hour. It was a time not to be forgotten by these poor men and women. Fear and poverty reigned in many homes where party feeling would otherwise soon have died out. Com-pounding of Cava-lier estates

In one respect the Parliament men chose well. They were not shedders of blood. In a mean spirit of revenge they had brought the old man Laud to the block, after a trial that made as little show of legal justice as any in the century (January, 1645). But after that bad deed they stayed their hands.

Though bitter complaints were made of particular cases of injustice and hardship, scarcely a voice was raised against the treatment of the Cavaliers as a general policy. The victims themselves felt resentment but not surprise. Common-sense and public opinion regarded such a policy as the inevitable logic of war. Posterity should not perhaps find it hard to forgive these men because they took the course always so obvious to victors in occupation and did not see the bitter feuds and the terrible reaction that they were preparing for the future. But they can be less easily excused for not seeing the actualities of the present. The persecution of the Cavaliers was a natural error ; but the persecution of the Independents was an egregious folly. The members of the Long Parliament were too proud to recognise that at that instant they held their supreme power in fee from the crusaders of the New Model. They could not realise that if the Puritan party was going to trample on the interests and the conscience of all Cavaliers, it must be held together by toleration within its own borders. They could not even see that if they wished to suppress the Independents of the army, they must at least divide the ordinary soldier from the sectarian enthusiast by a prompt settlement of material interests common to the whole force. They proposed to disband the bulk of the New Model without the payment of its arrears, and at the same time to institute that vigorous persecution of Nonconformists which they had been careful to postpone so long as Baptists were needed to stem the tide of battle, and Seekers to find their way up the breach. Ill-treatment of the army, 1646-47

Such ingratitude and blindness require to be explained. It must be remembered that the Commons, at the time they were deprived by death of their great leaders, had become possessed of the sole authority to issue commands in England ; confused by this height to which they had suddenly been raised, they made the quite illogical deduction that any commands that they chose to issue would be obeyed. Their orthodox Presbyterian platform was indeed supported by the City mob and the City magistrates, whose alliance had hitherto sufficed to see them safe through every danger. The new leaders of Parliament, men like Stapleton and Waller, whose military careers had been cut short by the Self-Denying Ordinance, could not avoid a personal jealousy of the New Model soldiers, that warped all sense of justice and even of expediency. But the most rational motive for their conduct was the wish to appear as the friends of order. It was time to show that there were limits to innovation. So they sought to conciliate the moderate Cavaliers, the common sober citizens, and the King with whom they were in treaty, not indeed by tolerating the Prayer-book, but by persecuting the sects.

They established the Presbyterian system of Church government, so far as it could be set up by paper decrees. At last they consented to borrow the system of Synods, Classes, Lay Elders and Church Discipline from their insistent Scottish allies. But in spite of this great surrender of English Puritanism, the new establishment would be wholly dependent on the votes of the Houses,—" a lame Erastian Presbytery ".

Bills to suppress sectarianism, Sep.-Dec., 1646 This newborn Church, the child of political treaty by military need, claimed full powers over the conscience of every English subject. In September, 1646, while the King's flag still waved from his last fortresses in Wales, the House of Commons ventured to read without a division, bills by which Unitarians and free-thinking heretics could be put to death, and Baptists and other sectaries imprisoned for life, solely on account of their dogmatic opinions ; in December they voted that no laymen should be permitted to preach or expound the Scriptures. A prospect of intolerable dreariness was opening for the speculative and religious life of England. Even Milton's invective was not too bitter to describe a tyranny equally crushing to the exercise of brain and spirit, sacrificing all to a foreign system which in England had the merits neither of the best Anglican nor of the best Puritan religion.

Soldiers ordered to disband unpaid, 27th May, 1647 As a preliminary to the effective persecution of the sects, the Houses ordered the New Model to disband—but without its arrears of pay. The soldiers hesitated, petitioned and remained in camp. Instead of paying them off, while they were still ready to go home on receipt of their wages, the Parliamentary leaders, in the spring of 1647, entered on a great political and military intrigue. They determined to coerce the New Model, in the name of the King, and in part alliance with the Royalists. Charles had fled to the Scots, but had been given up on the payment of money due to them, and was lying, in the power of Parliament, at Holmby in Northampton-shire. The New Model was not the only force in the pay of Parlia-ment. Many garrisons and regiments, largely consisting of old Cavaliers, were kept undisbanded in the West, on purpose for the new service. The City Militia, freshly weeded of all Independents, was to hold the South of England ; while the Scots and another English army were to advance from the North. The train of ar-tillery at Oxford and the King at Holmby were to be brought up to London.[1] But the Independent chiefs, against whom the Par-liament men were plotting, combined a double portion of their ad-versaries' astuteness with a straightforwardness of purpose and a genius for action that was all their own.

Cromwell had for months honestly striven to keep the peace. From his seat in the House, and from his quarters in the camp at Newmarket, he had urged Parliament to pay the soldiers, and the soldiers to obey Parliament. He had been willing to disband the army, at the risk of the religious freedom for which he most cared, because he fully understood that the country could only be settled by peaceful and constitutional means. " What we gain in a free way," he said, " is better than twice as much in a forced way, and will be more truly ours and our posterity's." The mutiny of officers and men had been stirred up by others. He was the last to put himself at its head ; but once he had decided, he became the fore-most in action. On 31st May he despatched Joyce on a high errand. The Cornet was to forestall the Parliamentary agents sent down that day to seize the artillery at Oxford ; he was then to go on to Holmby House, similarly to secure the King from removal to London.[2] Unless the soldiers were willing to surrender both their just pay and their liberty of conscience, they could not have delayed action against Parliament another twenty-four hours. *Crom-well's action*

When Joyce presented himself at Holmby, Charles had for some months been playing at negotiation with Parliament. But he was no less agreeable to try a hand with the army. At sight of the Cornet's " well-written " warrant of 500 troopers, he changed his plan of rising to the throne on the shoulders of the Presbyterians, and accepted the same help from the Independents. In either case he would kick away the ladder. Besides, his new friends were more courteous, did not interfere with his private devotions, and seemed less zealous enemies of the Prayer-book. The poor gentle-man, to whom all men were the same, did not see that these kindly *Holmby House, 3rd-4th June, 1647*

---

[1] *Mystery of two Juntoes (Select Tracts on the Civil War*, 1815, ii.). G. (*C. W.*), iii., p. 265. Firth's *Crom.*, p. 162.
[2] Not, however, to carry him off, as Joyce did—into the midst of the army at Newmarket (*Clarke Papers*, xxvi.-xxxi.).

titans, sprung of old earth, had pent in their breast tumultuous fires and floods, of which Presbyterian pedantry was void.

By the refusal to part with the guns and by the seizure of the King, the soldiers conveyed a warning, well calculated to bring the members to reason without actually violating their sanctity as representatives. Two months of negotiation followed. The army drew nearer to London. The Houses, to avoid the presence, yielded to the approach of military force. Enraged at the surrender of the Houses to the army, the City prentices broke in upon the debates, held the Speaker down in the chair, and forced the members to vote at dictation of the mob things which they would have voted freely but for fear of the sword (26th July). At that news the army marched on London. Many of both Houses, including the two Speakers, Manchester and Lenthall, were so disgusted by the weak violence of their Presbyterian friends that they came out to join the advancing force. With the officials of both Chambers in their camp, the soldiers had about as much legal right as the City, and moral right had been theirs throughout. The English capital has had a fortune almost peculiar to itself, in that its streets and environs have never been the scene of warfare in time of civic revolution : when the army arrived, the City Militia dared not fight, and Hyde Park was occupied without a battle. Eleven Parliamentary chiefs were expelled from their seats. On these terms the leaderless Presbyterian majority was permitted to resume power on sufferance. The army retired and all seemed as before.

Military occupation of London, 6th Aug., 1647

Yet in fact all was lost. The Roundheads were now irreparably at feud, not only with their opponents, but with each other. For many years to come a general election for a new Parliament would but confound confusion. And the existing assembly had failed to settle the constitution, or even to maintain its own freedom against City and Camp. Now if Parliament had not been able to reconstitute the English polity on the basis of general consent, no other power self-chosen from among the fragments of the Roundhead party could possibly succeed in that task. Law had given place to force, and agreement to coercion. Henceforth, the history of the Interregnum is a series of experiments in political theory and political necessity, interesting and noble, but foredoomed to failure. "Whatever we get by a treaty will be firm and durable, it will be conveyed to posterity"; "that which you have by force I look upon it as nothing": so Cromwell had said on 16th July, deprecating the march on London. A fortnight later the violence of the City mob compelled him to lead that march. For the next eleven years he strove to put his own prophecy behind him, in order to retain hope under the burden of gigantic tasks. Desperate of all rational expectation, he could only keep repeating to himself and to others, that his God would not allow so great a work to perish.

All hope of a settlement lost

When the brave and the clear-sighted dull their vision with spiritual drugs, it is because the pain of sight which they cannot endure is intense beyond the apprehension of posterity.

But however fatal the use of force may have proved, the soldiers had been compelled to defend themselves against the basest in-gratitude. Like cheating hucksters, the men whom they had saved denied them all things, material and spiritual, for which they and their dead comrades had risked their lives in the field. In defending themselves from gallows and prison, the Independents defended freedom of thought in England. The liberty which was proclaimed in Milton's *Areopagitica* (1644), in Jeremy Taylor's *Liberty of Prophecying* (1647), and in all that should spring from them and every other new source of light, had been foredoomed to destruction in the scheme of Presbyterian intolerance. It is easy to say that such a scheme could never have been maintained in England; it was not maintained, because men were found who did not allow it to be set up. *The army in the right*

Parliament when it defied the army, probably calculated that some Presbyterian feeling would show itself in the ranks. In the New Model, at its formation two years before, there had been zealots among the cavalry who were generally sectaries; but in the in-fantry, ordinary men were serving by impressment or for the sake of hire. The pikemen and musqueteers were many of them Puritans, but unlearned in the quarrel that divided their party, and some-what prejudiced by vague Presbyterian talk against " antinomians and blasphemers ". The private soldiers might easily have been led into the stricter way, if the orthodox chaplains had stayed with the regiments, and if Parliament had paid the men their arrears. But the Presbyterian clergy had hurried back from the hardships of campaign to secure the tithes and rectories from which the Angli-cans were being turned out. By the time of Naseby, the soldiers seldom heard a sermon except from latitudinarian clergy like Hugh Peters, or from the very captains and colonels who had led them to victory. The influence of these latter over their men was naturally very great. Until the period of active war ended at Worcester (1651), the officers were nearly all gentlemen by birth; and already in June, 1647, three-quarters were Independents.[1] Thus professional feeling, comradeship in victory, and above all the refusal of Parlia-ment to meet their just financial claims, rallied the ordinary soldiers to the side of the theorists. The zeal of the cavalry was contagious throughout the camp, and their arguments for liberty in Church and State appealed straight to plain men unlearned in theological sophistry. *Conver-sion of the army by the Inde-pendents*

The improvement in quality, and the change in political opinions

---

[1] In that month only 167 officers had gone over to Parliament, followed by a few hundreds of men (Firth's *C. A.*, p. 319).

Change in
the char-
acter of
the in-
fantry

of the infantry of the New Model, received fresh impetus from the events of 1647. Volunteers of a higher type came forward in good plenty. Impressment became rare, and after 1651 ceased altogether. The victories of Preston and Worcester, the conquest of Ireland and Scotland, victories not so much of Parliament as of the army and its chiefs, enhanced the professional pride and religious enthusiasm of all ranks and of all arms. The infantry became what the cavalry had always been. After Dunbar Oliver declared " it would do you good to see and hear our *poor foot* go up and down making their boast of God ". When all other forces had been disbanded, and when the soldiers of the New Model had become the favourites, and in some sense the masters, of the State, the profession of pikemen and musqueteers attracted men of good position and character, especially those who held advanced religious and political views. These views also gained by the dismissal of those Presbyterian officers who had taken the side of Parliament in June, 1647. Thus it came about that all arms of the service gradually approximated to the political, religious and military type that had once been peculiar to certain regiments of cavalry and to certain officers of foot.[1]

Birth of
English
Demo-
cratic
opinion

During the two years when this transformation was most actively in progress (1647-48), the modern conception of democracy was evolved by the most active minds in the army, and adopted by the elected agents of the rank and file. This movement was greatly stimulated by their victory over Parliament in August, 1647. When that event made it clear that the soldiers would have the last word in any proposed settlement, they determined that the first word also should come from the camp ; and they had a word to say which would not come from any other quarter. They produced in forms of English thought and speech the democratic ideas which seemed to perish with them, until, after a century and a half, Frenchmen made these same aspirations the common heritage of all the white races of the world.

" Career
open to
talents "

Two analogous but distinct parts of the democratic idea can be detected in the demands of the soldiers as clearly as in the propaganda of the French Revolution. The first is what we now call equality of opportunity, or " the career open to talents". The actual elevation of new men at that moment called for some such theoretical explanation, parallel on the secular plane to the Rule of the Saints. The country gentlemen, yeomen and craftsmen who composed the officers and sergeants of the omnipotent army, finding the House of Peers bitterly hostile to their power, naturally asked,

---

[1] Firth's *C. A.*, pp. 37, 38, 46, 47, 319. G. (*C. W.*), ii., pp. 319-26. Baxter, *Life* (ed. 1696), p. 51. Carl.'s *Crom.*, Letter cxl.
     As early as the Preston Campaign, 1648, the best Royalist leaders wished to avoid fighting in enclosed ground because they feared the superiority of Cromwell's " firemen   Carl.'s *Crom.*, Letters lxiii.-vi.).

" what were the Lords of England but William the Conqueror's Colonels ? or the Barons but his Majors ? or the Knights but his Captains ? " [1] They declared that they would set themselves and their heirs free from the usurped superiority of the Norman race, who had now lost the power of the sword, their only title to rule over the English.[2] King and Lords must go. Individual merit should be the sole road to greatness.

But they also forestalled the second principle of democracy, *Universal suffrage* that all the inhabitants of a land ought to share in the framing of the laws. Every man born in England, the poor man, " the meanest man in the kingdom," had a right to elect his rulers. To support this claim, which really lay in the needs of the future, they pleaded the laws of an imaginary past. " Before the Conquest," they said, all Englishmen had a voice in the Government ; it was " the old birthright " of Englishmen—" our inheritances which have been lost ". Translated out of English into the larger utterance of humanity, this plea of a lost birthright becomes Rousseau's Rights of Man. Colonel Rainborough had already taken this step into a wider atmosphere. He looked not so much to the supposed national customs of the remote past, as to an eternal and universal right. " The poorest he that is in England," he told his fellow-officers in council, " hath a life to live as the greatest he. And therefore, truly, Sir, I think it's clear that every man that is to live under a Government ought first by his own consent to put himself under that Government." He appealed straight to the " law of God " and " the law of Nature," to prove that every man ought to have " the choice of those who are to make the laws for him to live under ". On surer ground, he then pleaded that the continual oppression of the poor by the rich could only be remedied by an equal franchise.[3]

These ideals could be realised by Republicanism, Universal Suffrage and Religious Toleration. Such were the demands of Lilburne and the Political Levellers,[4] who from 1647 to 1649 dominated *The Levellers in the army*

---

[1] Baxter, *Life* (ed. 1696), p. 51.

[2] *Harl. Misc.*, vi., pp. 36-42 ; viii., pp. 95, 102 ; ix., 90-94. *Clarke Papers*, i., pp. 235, 318, 368, 401.

[3] *Clarke Papers*, i., pp. 235, 300, 301, 305, 309, 311, 353.

[4] The Social Levellers, comparatively unimportant in the history of forces in this period, have their place in the history of thought throughout the ages. Winstanley founded English Communism, and the idea of restoring the land to the people (Gooch, pp. 206-26. *Clarke Papers*, ii., pp. 215-24. *The Social Problem in the Days of the Commonwealth ;* and *Single Tax Review*, 15th July, 1902, articles by L. H. Berens). Winstanley in his pamphlet (1652), *The Law of Freedom in a Platform* (programme), says : " Before they are suffered to plant the waste land for a livelihood, they must pay rent to their brethren for it. Well this is a burden the creation groans under." " I have an equal share in the earth which is now redeemed as my brother, by the law of Righteousness."

In the *New Law of Righteousness* (1649) he writes : " And this is the beginning of particular interest, buying and selling the Earth from one particular hand to another, saying, ' This is mine,' . . . as if the Earth were made for a few and not for all men." " All the men and women in England are all children of this opinion in the ranks. Deceived by their own omnipotence of an hour, they did not see that Republicanism and Universal Suffrage, unlike Religious Toleration, could only be attained by the active consent and participation of the majority. But the majority did not wish for these changes ; the first use it would make of that Universal Suffrage would be either to restore the old system, or to plunge England into a new strife of parties where all sight of the new ideals would be hopelessly lost. Yet it is to the credit of these men that they desired, though in vain, to abdicate in favour of the people. It was not their wish, but their fate, to become, for a while a new " *noblesse* of the sword," in place of the " Conqueror's barons ".

Cromwell well understood that the true method of progress is to realise the best which can obtain general consent, rather than to establish the very best by force. Together with his son-in-law, Commissary-General Ireton, he undertook a hard double task, to restrain the army and to bring Charles to terms.

Land ; and the Earth is the Lord's, not particular men's who claim a proper interest in it above others.'' In the same pamphlet appears his practical sugges-tion : " If the rich still hold fast to this property of Mine and Thine, let them labour their own land with their own hands. And let the common people that say ' The Earth is ours, not mine,' let them labour together upon the commons.''

The " Diggers," as the score of Social Levellers called themselves, who began digging and ploughing the soil on the common, St. George's Hill, Surrey, on com-munistic principles, were led by Winstanley, and were interrupted by the neigh-bouring gentry and parsons (1649). They had a song, " *Stand up now, Diggers All*," almost certainly by Winstanley, of which the following verses describe the social condition of England :—

> " The gentry are all round, stand up now, stand up now,
> The gentry are all round, stand up now.
> The gentry are all round, on each side they are found,
> Their wisdom's so profound, to cheat us of our ground.
> Stand up now, stand up now.
> " The clergy they come in, stand up now, stand up now,
> The clergy they come in, stand up now.
> The clergy they come in, and say it is a sin
> That we should now begin, our freedom for to win,
> Stand up now, Diggers all.''

Their principles were, however, Tolstoian and Quakerish ; they were opposed to physical force.

> " To conquer them by love, come in now, come in now,
> To conquer them by love, come in now.
> To conquer them by love, as it does you behove,
> For He is King above ; no power is like to love.
> Glory here, Diggers all.''

The Diggers warned the Regicide Government that the political revolution would not stand its ground unless it was based on a social revolution. " We know that England cannot be a free Commonwealth unless all the poor Commons have a free use and benefit of the land.'' They rightly said that the " Lords of the Manors '' were really in the " Cavalier '' interest. Winstanley knew that he would very probably fail. A verse of his prophesies the Restoration :—

> " In thee O England is the Law arising up to shine,
> If thou receive and practise it, the crown it will be thine,
> If thou reject and still remain a froward son to be,
> Another land will it receive, and take the crown from thee.''
> —*Clarke Papers*, ii., pp. 215-24.

At a series of formal debates held at headquarters in Putney, The de- the elected Agents of the army laid their proposed democratic bates at Constitution before the generals, and demanded that it should at Putney, Oct.- once be put in force. Cromwell and Ireton withstood the demand, Nov., and declared that the army had no power to legislate. They con- 1647 sented, however, to argue across the table with the " buff-coats " and the radical colonels, as to the real nature of the " contract " on which society was based. They urged the law of the land against the " law of Nature ". Ireton pleaded that Republicanism and Universal Suffrage were never to be desired, Cromwell that they could not at present be obtained.

" How do we know," he asked the eager assembly, " if whilst we are disputing these things, another company of men shall gather together, and they shall put out a paper as plausible perhaps as this ? "

. . . .

" And not only another, and another, but many of this kind. And if so, what do you think the consequence would be ? Would it not be confusion ? Would it not be utter confusion ? " [1]

The two Generals had for their part tried to solve the problem The by coming to terms with the King. The treaty known as the Heads Generals of the Proposals, which Cromwell and Ireton laid before Charles, negotiate with would have afforded a noble and permanent settlement. It would Charles, have been the settlement of 1689 with a larger flavour of democracy July-Sep., 1647 and of Puritanism. The protection of Cavaliers' estates from ruinous sequestration, the retention of the Episcopate shorn of all coercive power, and the use of the Prayer-book in Church by those who wished, stood to reconcile one-half of England ; while religious toleration for all, equal electoral districts, large security for the control of royal power by Parliament, should have satisfied the democrats, if they had been wise enough to approach their ends by sure, slow steps from generation to generation. The scheme was wrecked by its very merits. It was drawn up to conciliate all parties ; but it came too late ; all parties were now inflamed, and it displeased all alike.

Even if parties had been reasonable, there was one person who Flight to must have marred it all. Charles was only playing with the men Caris- who had gone beyond anything he could hope, in offering restoration brooke, 15th to himself, amnesty to his followers, and a fair position to his Church. Nov., On 15th November he fled from Hampton Court to Carisbrooke 1647 Castle in the Isle of Wight. From that retreat he spent the winter and spring in summoning Scots, Presbyterians and Royalists to rise and destroy the sects.

The negotiation had only served to alienate the army from the two Generals. Their treachery was exposed by John Lilburne, the friend of the people. The " Grandees," it was said, were bartering

---

[1] *Clarke Papers*, i., pp. 237, 226-418, lxvi.

the hardly recovered heritage of England, re-establishing the fallen power of Kings, Lords and Prelates.

Deserted by both King and army, Cromwell saw that his treaty was a failure, and concluded that it had been a sin. At the summons of the false wizard of Carisbrooke, by whose wiles he had allowed himself to be ensnared, the war clouds were scudding up again from Wales and Scotland, from Essex and Kent, from land and sea. Once more all lives were to be put to the hazard ; once more the land was to be filled with blood, this time without a hope that any true settlement could follow the victory of either faction. A noble rage filled the soul of the man who had striven so hard to make sure the footing of peace. On the 1st of May, 1648, Cromwell attended a prayer-meeting of the army leaders in Windsor Castle. Tears of sorrow and disappointment stood in their eyes, as they agreed that the troubles rising on them were the punishment of God for their late negotiations with the King; while many declared unrebuked their resolution " if ever the Lord brought us back again in peace," " to call Charles Stuart, that man of blood, to an account for the blood he had shed ". In such fierce exaltation the military saints again rode forth to war, carrying with them their chiefs, made captive to their doctrines against reason and against will, by the force of fate and the irretrievable event.

The prayer-meeting at Windsor, 1st May, 1648

The Second Civil War, May-Aug., 1648

The Second Civil War was a strange combination of oppressed Cavaliers with that very Presbyterian party whose stupid refusal to give truce to their religion and estates had brought them into the frame of mind for this revolt. What sort of agreement among themselves the two most intolerant factions supposed that they could make, after they had finished hanging the sectarians, was a subject on which every man was for once allowed to think what he liked, provided nothing at all was said. The only rallying-cry permitted was " God save the King ". Half the Presbyterian gentry and merchants who had organised the Great Rebellion had already become Royalist, although not till 1660 were they fain to become Anglican and Cavalier. The process of evolution was graduated for them by a stubborn belief that they could convert Charles into a Presbyterian King. But the other half of the Presbyterians cared just enough for the " good old cause " to sit still and sullen, watching the sectaries again deliver them from the common foe. Such, on the whole, was the attitude of the Commons. But the select body to whom they delegated their executive functions, was more heartily on the side of the Independents ; the Derby House Committee [1] acted with saving vigour, as if Pym were still among them, and Rupert again at the gates.

[1] So called from holding its sessions at Derby House. In January, 1648, it had succeeded to the powers of the old Committee of Both Kingdoms which had fought the First Civil War—the Scots Commissioners being sent home (G. (*C. W.*) iv. pp. 51, 52).

" God save the King " was the cry that suited the various English and Scottish factions that had sworn to extirpate the New Model. It was a good cry, for it was becoming popular. Out of the welter of confused issues, out of the dim negotiations and intrigues of which the truth has now been revealed by historical research, but was then lost in flying rumours, one fact rose clear to the mind of the common sentimental man—the captivity of the King. For the first time since the fighting had stopped, the ballad-monger and the ale-house politician found a theme which every one could understand. One of the great *motifs* of the drama of popular English history—the sufferings of King Charles—was already beginning to play upon men's emotions. A popular atmosphere, in which Cavalier feeling could revive and flourish, was being created. The democrats, as they rode to battle, knew more of the needs and rights than of the mind and character of the people, and utterly refused to respect a wave of sentimentality, which on their home-coming they converted by the great deed into a national tradition of pity, strong as the Englishman's pride in Magna Carta or wrath at Gunpowder Plot.

But the Second Civil War was, even more markedly than the First, not waged by the people at large. Presbyterian soldiers in charge of places of strength declared for the King. Cavaliers of good family rode fast and far to reinforce the revolted garrisons, or to raise the country-side. But except the New Model, no one stirred to put them down ; except the men of Kent and Essex, no one ventured to join their ranks. The people of England looked on in bewildered neutrality. Fairfax in Kent and Essex, Cromwell in Wales dashed down upon the gathering revolt (May-June). The Cavalier horsemen scattered and vanished ; the revolted garrisons were shut up in close siege. But a fourth part of the fighting navy had declared for the King, the Scots army was on its way, and the issue still hung as uncertain as the minds of men.

The promptitude of the New Model sufficed to prevent the English Royalists from organising a campaign with a regular head-quarters. It had been the wise policy of the conquerors in the First Civil War to dismantle captured fortresses by blowing a gap in the walls. The object was not to wreak revenge or devastation, but to save the expense of garrisoning every place which, if left derelict in a defensible condition, might again be occupied by Cavaliers. This foresight now had its reward. The Second Civil War might have gone better for the King if there had been many garrisons to revolt, or many castles in a state to make resistance. For Colchester alone kept Fairfax' great army before its walls, and the siege of Pembroke delayed Cromwell six long weeks, when every day was a fresh danger to the State.

Cromwell was scarcely set free from before Pembroke when England was invaded by a large Scottish army, under leaders from

Preston,
17th-19th
Aug.,1648

both sides of the Border, who, while claiming the Presbyterian alliance, scarcely tried to conceal their Cavalier sympathies. They passed southward by the route that lies between the Yorkshire hills and the coast of Lancashire. If these Scots were not crushed before they debouched into the Midland plain, their strength would be a nucleus for local revolt, sufficient to alter the whole character of the war in England. Gathering his veterans in the Yorkshire valleys, Cromwell dropped down from a pass of the Pennine Range on to the centre of the Royalists' line of march where it straggled south-wards through Preston. In a running fight of three days he over-took and captured all their infantry, as, driven by panic, they splashed along the soaking roads ; their horse was scattered north and south in fugitive parties, of whom few stole safely back to Scotland.

At that terrible stroke the war fell dead. Colchester at once surrendered to Fairfax. But the friendly feeling that marked the close of the First Civil War had now given way to exasperation and revenge. Cromwell divided the rank and file of the Scots prisoners into two classes—the pressed men, whom he sent home, and the volunteers, whom he shipped across to the Barbadoes. The soldiers who had defended Colchester were sent by Fairfax to a similar fate, and two Cavalier officers, Lucas and Lisle, were shot by court martial. Transportation was an advance on the practice of Queen Elizabeth, who hanged her poorer subjects by the hundred after the suppression of the revolt in the North ; but it was a decline from the merciful conduct of these same victors two years before. The transporta-tions of 1648 became the unhappy precedent followed by all our Governments in times of rebellion, as late as the year 1715.

The last
negotia-
tion,
Sep., 1648

Freed from the fear of an armed Cavalier Restoration, Lords and Commons again made haste to cheat the men by whom they had again been saved, and pushed forward for the last time the negotiations with the King. Charles, still at Carisbrooke, pretended to make concession to the Presbyterians—" merely in order to my escape "—as he confided to his friends. The Penal Laws against heretics, passed by the two Houses in May last, had given the soldiers fair warning what to expect from a Presbyterian monarchy ; when they heard of a new treaty between King and Parliament that might render them in very fact subject to the power of such laws, they determined to be rid both of Parliament and King. They no longer showed the moderation that marked their first dispute with the

Pride's
Purge,
6th-7th
Dec.,
1648

Houses (1647). Officers and men had come home from the war in a fierce mood, prepared to commit any violence. Colonel Pride and his musqueteers, stationed at the door of the Commons, ex-cluded some hundred members and carried off nearly fifty more to prison. On the 4th of January, 1649, the Rump that remained, not one hundred strong, passed this resolution :—

That the people are, under God, the original of all just power : that the Commons of England, in Parliament assembled, being chosen by and representing the people, have the supreme power in this nation ; that whatsoever is enacted or declared for law by the Commons in Parliament assembled, hath the force of law, and all the people of this nation are concluded thereby, although the consent of the King or House of Peers be not had thereunto.

In logical accordance with these new principles, it was voted a few weeks later that the House of Lords was " useless and dangerous, and ought to be abolished ". The King disappeared from the constitution by a yet more signal and symbolic act. " We will cut off his head," said Cromwell, " with the crown upon it."

Abolition of the House of Lords, 6th Feb., 1649

By the " dark lantern of the spirit " Cromwell saw that the Providences of God, the preordained victories in Essex, Wales and Lancashire, pointed the road to a deed for which there was no human law. He did not, like many of his colleagues, think a Republic necessary to civil and religious freedom ; he had long striven to preserve monarchy ; but once persuaded of the practical necessity and Divine sanction of a new order, he led the revolution, and carries through all time the responsibility which he then accepted without fear and bore without remorse.

The Commons appointed a Commission to try Charles Stuart. Unless the theoretic declaration of the omnipotence of the Lower House held good by " the law of Nature," this Commission had no legal power. Furthermore, Charles had committed no legal crime. Law and pity would both plead on his side. His own outward dignity and patience made his appeal to pity and to law the most effective appeal in that sort that is recorded in the history of England. Law and pity were known of old to Englishmen ; the ideas ranged against these two powerful pleaders were new and strange. The sovereignty of the people and the equality of man with man in the scales of justice, were first ushered into the world of English politics by this deed. Against them stood the old-world ideals, as Charles proclaimed them from the scaffold with his dying breath :—

For the people (he said, as he looked out into eternity) truly I desire their liberty and freedom as much as anybody whatsoever ; but I must tell you, their liberty and freedom consists in having government, those laws by which their lives and their goods may be most their own. It is not their having a share in the government ; that is nothing appertaining to them. A subject and a sovereign are clear different things.

That, indeed, was the issue. Those who sought to substitute a better theory of government for that proclaimed by Charles as his legacy to England did not pause to consider that the people, for whose new-born sovereignty they struck, was heart and soul against the deed. By the side of this objection, the charge that they acted " by no law " shrinks to insignificance. They were striving to make a new law of democracy, and could not be expected to effect this by observing the old laws. But their fault lay in this, that the new law by which they condemned Charles, while it claimed to derive from the people of England, did not, save in theory, derive from that source at all. When the bleeding head was held up, the shout of the soldiers was drowned in the groan of the vast multitude.

If there was any chance that the establishment of a more democratic form of government could gradually win the support of the people at large, that chance was thrown away by the execution of the King. The deed was done against the wish of many even of the Independents and Republicans ; it outraged beyond hope of reconciliation the two parties in the State who were strong in numbers and in conservative tradition, the Presbyterians and the Cavaliers ; and it alienated the great mass of men who had no party at all. Thus the Republicans, at the outset of their career, made it impossible for themselves ever to appeal in free election to the people whom they had called to sovereignty. Their own fall, involving the fall of democracy and of religious toleration, became therefore necessary to the re-establishment of Parliamentary rule. The worship of birth, of pageantry, of title ; the aristocratic claim to administrative power ; the excessive influence of the large landowner and of inherited wealth ; the mean admiration of mean things, which became so powerful in English society after the Restoration—all these gained a fresh life and popularity by the deed that was meant to strike them dead for ever.

It is much easier to show that the execution was a mistake and a crime (and it was certainly both) than to show what else should have been done. Any other course, if considered in the light of the actual circumstances, seems open to the gravest objection. It is not possible to say with certainty that if Charles' life had been spared Cromwell could have succeeded in averting anarchy and the disruption of the empire until opinion was again ripe for government by consent.

> This was that memorable hour
> Which first assured the forcéd power :—

that was the verdict on the King's execution privately passed by Cromwell's secretary, Andrew Marvell, a man of the world if a poet ever was such, who in the same poem wrote the lines we all still quote in praise of Charles' conduct on the scaffold. The situation at the end of 1648 was this—that any sort of government by consent had been rendered impossible for years to come, mainly by the untrustworthy character of the King, and by the intolerant action of Parliament after the victory won for it by the Army. Cromwell, in the Heads of the Proposals, had advocated a real settlement by consent, only to have it rejected by King, Parliament and Army alike. The situation had thereby been rendered impossible, through no fault of his. But he was not the man therefore to return to his private gardens and let the world go to ruin. He took upon his massive shoulders the load of obloquy inherent in a situation created chiefly by the faults of others. Those Herculean shoulders are broad enough to bear also the blame for a deed preeminently his own, inscribed like a gigantic note of interrogation across the page of English history.

CHAPTER X

THE REVOLUTIONARY GOVERNMENTS, 1649-60

> But thou, the War's and Fortune's son,
> March indefatigably on ;
>   And for the last effect
>   Still keep the sword erect :
> Besides the force it has to fright
> The spirits of the shady night,
>   The same arts that did gain
>   A power, must it maintain.
>   —(*Ode to Cromwell*), MARVELL.

The new Government and the Levellers ALL Revolutionists, the moment they undertake the actual responsibilities of government, become in some sort conservative. Robespierre guillotined the Anarchists. The first administrative act of the Regicides was to silence the Levellers. By the mere act of acquiring sovereignty the Independent chiefs arrayed against themselves that very party whose insistence on first principles had driven them to the brink of regicide and usurpation. John Lilburne, having thrust Cromwell over the precipice, himself stopped short, and called mankind to witness what a falling off was there. For many months his pamphlets were more dangerous to Government than even the loud wail of Royalism over the murdered King ; for Democracy, to which the Levellers appealed, was still the active spirit of the hour, and was the only spirit by which disaffection could be conjured in the ranks of the New Model. Throughout the year 1649 England's spokesman was " Freeborn John," and her heroes were the democratic mutineers of the army. In April one of these soldiers was executed in front of St. Paul's door ; his corpse was followed to the grave by a countless multitude of London's citizens, who had strangely decked their respectable hats with the green ribbon of the Levellers. In May three regiments mutinied at Salisbury. The infection seemed likely to spread ; and if the army revolted the new State would fall. Fairfax, who had lost all political position by neutrality during the great events of the winter, consented to serve though not to support the Republic. Seconded by Cromwell, he chased down the mutineers in a brief campaign in the valley of the upper Thames, and captured them by a midnight attack on Burford.

Campaign against the mutineers, May, 1649

John Lilburne Meanwhile, the rage against military despotism that was common to Cavaliers, Presbyterians, Levellers and ordinary Englishmen, was concentrated in the defence of John Lilburne's remarkable personality. Many who cared little for his democratic theories saw that individual liberty was in danger. The press was gagged, the pulpits silenced on political topics, by the very men who two years before had saved liberty of thought. Lilburne stood for the property and freedom of the individual. Himself a *political* leveller, he disowned the communistic theories of the *social* levellers who were demanding the restoration of the land to the people. He thus retained the sympathy of the proprietary classes. Within two months of the King's execution " Freeborn John " was standing before the Council of State, refusing to take off his hat in the presence of a company of gentlemen who, as he observed, had no more legal authority than he had himself. Then, affecting to perceive for the first time some members of Parliament at the board, he ostentatiously uncovered in their honour. Removed for a moment into the adjoining room, he heard through the door the voice of Cromwell raised loud in anger, " I tell you, Sir, you have no other way to deal with these men but to break them, or they will break you ". In August, twenty file of musqueteers, sent to take Lilburne alive, shrank back in fear from the formidable presence, and yet more formidable language, of the prophet of England's liberties. His sacred person seemed fenced about by the Majesty of the People. When in October the great pamphleteer was at last brought into court, he bullied the Judges as he had bullied the Councillors and the musqueteers. It required a Jeffreys to put down a Lilburne, and Jeffreys was not yet old enough to scold anybody except his nurse. At this famous trial, the prisoner at the bar ruled that it lay with the jury alone to decide whether his writings had contravened the law. He had written that the Government was a tyranny and a usurpation, and to write thus had been made treason by an Act of the Republican Parliament. The issue in law was clear, but it was freely left to the decision of the jury by the brow-beaten Judges. A verdict of acquittal, boldly defying the new law and the new Government, called forth " such a loud and unanimous shout as is believed was never heard in Guild Hall, which lasted for about half an hour without intermission ; which made the Judges for fear turn pale and hang down their heads ". Such a demonstration in the presence of a tribunal backed by the political power of Government, had been a thing unknown in England in the time of the Tudor and Stuart Kings.

His first trial, Oct., 1649

In 1652 the Rump passed a special Act banishing Lilburne on pain of death. Next year he was home again, declaring that the law which banished him had been beyond the powers of Parliament. That Parliament had then ceased to exist, but Cromwell and the Barebone senators were no more willing than the Rump to have Lilburne always on their flank. He was at once put on trial for his life. The excitement was again intense. Six thousand spectators attended his second trial. " Tickets were thrown about," inscribed with the well-known refrain of popular protection :—

His second trial, 1653

And what, shall then honest John Lilbourn die ?
Three score thousand will know the reason why.

Nor was this held to be an idle threat. Soldiers were massed to prevent the outbreak. But when Lilburne was again acquitted in the face of the evidence, the very soldiers beat their drums and blew their trumpets, and the public rejoicings displayed a triumph at the judicial defeat of a detested Government, analogous to that which followed the acquittal of the Seven Bishops and of Hone the Radical.[1]

Lilburne's two trials had established that juries were judges of law as well as of fact, and could even set aside an unpopular law by their verdict. An increase in the political freedom and judicial power of the subject had been won under Governments apparently more despotic than their predecessors. Nothing shows more clearly how deep was the change registered by the First Civil War in the attitude of the subject towards the Government. That attitude was but little affected by the Restoration.

Position of the new Government, 1649 That Lilburne could make Cromwell look ridiculous was due to the illogical position of the usurpers. When in the name of the people they had seized power, they found not only the active champions of democracy, but the people itself—whatever definition be given to that term—bitterly hostile to their rule. Yet they could not retire from the false position. Their enemies were still so divided among themselves that the fall of the Regicides would have been followed, not by a Restoration, not by Parliamentary Government, but by a state of anarchy that would have destroyed all political landmarks. It might have ended in economic and social chaos from which feudalism itself might have reared its head. But England was held together by force, till after twelve years her factions and her people were all agreed to accept one particular form of free Government.

This gaoler's work, which necessity imposed on the idealists, was only part of a larger duty. To prevent anarchy in England was not enough ; they had also to prevent the disruption of the British Empire. Scotland and Ireland, and half the Colonies across the Atlantic, had proclaimed another Government. The mastery of the sea was challenged : a fourth part of the war ships had revolted to the new King ; and privateers harbouring in the Royalist Scilly and Channel Islands, and in the Isle of Man, preyed upon English commerce almost at the mouth of our ports. So unlikely did it seem that England, divided against herself, would be able to recover her lost heritage, that the City merchants, instead of lending more money for the reconquest of Ireland, betted twenty to one that Cromwell would never even set sail. The sovereigns of Europe refused to recognise a Government whose

[1] *State Trials*, 1649-1653. Stephen, i., pp. 365-68. Thurloe, i., pp. 367, 441.

principles they abhorred and whose power they as yet despised. Our ambassadors were murdered,[1] our merchants were robbed, our goods were everywhere seized on the open sea. It seemed in 1649 that one of two things must happen. Either the British power would be dissolved into its component parts, and the advance of our race, so far as it depended on political union, would be checked in either hemisphere ; or else the King would reconquer his father's throne by the sword and by foreign aid, and would build up the British Empire again as a regal despotism. Cromwell prevented both the disruption of the British Empire and its reunion by Cavalier conquest. It is this supreme consideration that takes the sting of irony from the failure of so much heroic effort, spent in enterprises so often ill-conceived : that renders not vain in the eye of history the truceless war of plague-stricken and hungry men spearing each other on the islands of the Irish bogs ; the smoke of Blake's cannoneers hanging in the sunlight of the Spanish seas ; and the fury of the radical saints as they scatter their fellow-Puritans over the edge of the Lowland moor, or come thundering in upon the flight through the tumultuous streets of Worcester. *Cromwell's task*

The task of recovering the Empire would have been impossible if the enemies of the English Government had combined. But the events of the last decade had divided Catholics and Protestants in Ireland, and the followers of Argyle and Montrose in Scotland, by blood feuds more bitter even than the memory of the English wars which set enmity between the City Presbyterian and the Western Cavalier. A common devotion could be simulated, just so long as its object was an unknown quantity. For a few months after his father's death the young King, flitting shadow-like between the Channel Islands and the Dutch port towns, seemed all things to all men. It was the boast of the Irish Catholics that he had asked and received the support of the Pope ; of the English and Scottish Cavaliers that he knelt to receive the communion by the rites for which his father had died ; of the Scots that they would manufacture him into a Covenanted King. *Charles Stuart and his friends*

It was well for his chance of reigning at Holyrood or Whitehall that he never elected to go in person to Ireland, but left to faithful servants the task of uniting its distracted factions. Ormond, the Lord-Lieutenant, used the first revulsion of feeling caused by the regicide, to combine the Irish who had perpetrated the rebellion of 1641 with the English and Scottish colonists who had suffered by it, and with the troops who had from time to time been sent over for its suppression. These combined forces held all Ireland, except Londonderry and the capital, and threatened England with an Irish invasion. Dublin itself would have fallen but for the victory won almost under its walls by the Republican commander *Cromwell in Ireland Aug., 1649- May, 1650*

---

[1] Dorislaus in Holland, and Ascham in Spain, by exiled Cavaliers.

Jones, when the first regiments from England arrived to his relief. A few days later (15th August, 1649) Cromwell himself landed. His own first success, when the *élite* of Ormond's army was cruelly put to the sword in the steep streets of Drogheda, broke up the unnatural alliance which Ormond had engineered. Everywhere the Protestant soldiers and colonists went over to Cromwell. The Catholics put themselves under the military rule of their prelates, and began to transfer even their political allegiance to the Papal Nuncio. Before the end of the war Ormond found himself in the Celtic camp, the plenipotentiary of a foreign prince, rather than the lieutenant of a beloved sovereign. In ten months Cromwell, hailed as liberator in each Protestant colony, conquered eastern Ireland. Leaving his subordinates to reduce the more purely native West by long guerilla warfare, he himself hurried back to England to protect her from other foes.[1]

Montrose hanged, 21st May, 1650 If Charles was to go to Scotland, it would best have pleased him to appear at the head, not of the Presbyterians but of the Scottish Cavaliers. But since the overthrow at Preston, was their strength any longer sufficient to carry the King and his fortunes ? Montrose, whose life was held cheap both by himself and his master, was sent first to make the experiment. In the spring of 1650 he again raised the Royal Standard in the Highlands, in defiance of the Kirk party. But the hold of the Presbyterians was surer now than it had been five years back in the days of his triumphs. His chance now was small at best ; but even before he had time to put it to the touch, Charles deserted him and came to terms with Argyle and the Covenant. This hastened the end. Montrose was seized and hanged. His enemies may have had a right to put out of their way the man whose life endangered their State. But the insults with which they pursued their noble victim to the last, are one out of many instances of the ferocious character of Scottish politics in that century.

A Covenanted King A month later Charles was received by the slayers of Montrose. At Aberdeen he saw the dissevered hand of the man who had died for him, nailed on the town gate. As his sense of humour was more highly developed than any of his other qualities, he had taken the two Covenants, promising, with less trouble than his father would have felt in altering a single sentence of the Liturgy, to establish Presbyterianism in Scotland and in England. But if he ever reached Whitehall by way of Holyrood, it was certain that he would enter it with the same feelings towards Presbytery as those which his grandfather had brought from the same school. The unlucky effect of the Kirk discipline on the mind of James I.

---

[1] For the Cromwellian settlement of Ireland see p. 264 below ; here I only treat the conquest as a first step in the recovery of the British Empire by the Republicans.

had not been taken to heart by the taskmasters of Charles II. The Don Juan of Jersey was not permitted in his northern kingdom to " walk in the fields " on the Sabbath, or to indulge in " promiscuous dancing ". He partook of the sober vanity of golf in the company of staid persons. He was made to bewail the sins of his father, and the idolatries of his mother in solemn and public fasts. On one of these occasions, in which, after the chastisement of Dunbar, the whole nation had been called on to join in their King's lamentations, the victim was heard to remark : " I think I ought to repent too that ever I was born ". [1]

A month after Charles had landed in Scotland Cromwell was in arms at the gate. He tried to persuade the Kirk party that they were ruining their own cause. More clearly than they, he saw that the fate of their Kirk was involved in the common fate of Puritanism in Great Britain. He seems to have taken the measure of the Scottish clergy : " I beseech you," he wrote, " in the bowels of Christ, think it possible you may be mistaken ". But he was baffled in negotiation and strategy alike. His " army of heretics and blasphemers " was penned up between the sea and the trackless Lammermuirs, on whose edge the Covenanted army lay unassailable. But the Scots descended too soon from their post of vantage, and were broken to ruin in the famous sunrise of Dunbar.[2]

Cromwell in Scotland, July, 1650

Dunbar, 3rd Sep., 1650

After the destruction of its army, the Kirk party could no longer maintain its exclusiveness. All Cavaliers who would submit to the idle form of " repentance," were readmitted to share in the defence of Scotland ; and Charles obtained some political freedom in return for unabated religious hypocrisy. Cromwell, who had occupied Edinburgh as a result of Dunbar, was unable to force his way much farther. The new combination of unreconciled enemies, so long as it sat still, could prevent his advance ; but if it moved it would fall to pieces. To dissolve what he could not break, Cromwell left the road to England open. Charles, accompanied by his most devoted followers, started in the race for London. Presbyterian Argyle, jealous of the Cavaliers, refused to accompany the uncovenanted leaders across the border. Charles marched onwards by the Lancashire route, down which four Royalist invasions of England have passed in procession to their ruin (1648, 1651, 1715, 1745). Cromwell raced back through Yorkshire to head off the invaders. The militia of the Western shires turned out at the summons of Parliament ; while Charles obtained few recruits, although the Earl of Derby himself tried to raise Lancashire. Englishmen disliked the Government much, but they disliked the Scots more. The Presbyterians would not join an army

---

[1] Airy, pp. 57-65.

[2] See Carl.'s *Crom.* for the most poetical and vivid, and Firth's *Crom.*, pp. 280-84 (and map), for the most accurate, account of the greatest feat of Puritan warfare.

in which the Cavalier nobility was supreme, nor the Anglicans and Catholics die for a King who still with his lips proclaimed the Covenant.   The prey was hunted down and surrounded in Worcester

city.   After fierce fighting on both sides of the Severn, the Royalists were driven in from east and west.   When the battle rolled into the town, the slaughter and rout ended in a general surrender.   The cavalry alone fled out by the northern gate, but few even of the horsemen escaped the man-hunt that raged next week through the country-side.   Worcester streets were foul with carnage ; and the vast Cathedral served as a loose-box, in whose aisles and neglected chapels wandered and reposed in various attitudes of dejection several thousand prisoners of all ranks, creeds and parties in the two kingdoms.   Among the few who escaped, pursued by proclamations and rewards for capture, was a dark-haired young man " above two yards' high ".   Passed on, a solitary fugitive, from one Catholic house to another, Charles reached the coast and disappeared, bequeathing to the Cavaliers another great national legend, of the loyalty of subjects and the escape of a King.

Scotland was now speedily reduced.   The " crowning mercy " of Worcester put an end, during Cromwell's lifetime, to all movements of revolt in Great Britain.   But they would have been kindled once more, if the Empire of the sea and of the Colonies had not at the same time been recovered.   In the Second Civil War, out of forty-one ships in commission, eleven had revolted from Parliament, though several of them had soon voluntarily returned to their allegiance (1648).   The complaints of the mutineers had referred, not to bad food and bad pay as they would have done at any other period between the days of Drake and Nelson, but to the treatment of the King and to the practice of putting army officers in command of ships.   The fanatic Rainborough was specially and personally detested by the Presbyterian sailors.   But three-quarters of the fighting navy was actively loyal to the Independents, and some at least of the seamen had concurred in the army petition for " justice " on the " grand author of our troubles ".   Though Rainborough was removed, the Republicans continued to put landsmen in command of ships and fleets.   But the colonels of the Commonwealth army were better able to learn the craft of war at sea than the courtiers who, both before and after the interregnum, begged or bought naval commands from the Stuart Kings.   Indeed, the element thus imported of military discipline and tactical skill in close combat, was of great value in developing the traditions of the fighting navy as distinct from the merchant service.[1]   Blake had, perhaps, made voyages early in life as a Bridgewater merchant, but his training in war had been the renowned defence of the inland city of Taunton.

[1] Oppenheim, pp. 248-50, 306.   Mahan, *Sea Power*, pp. 125-30.   Corbett, i., pp. 154, 181-94, and p. 354 below.

After the execution of the King, this good soldier, who was to become so great a sailor, was put in command of the fleet on active service.

Meanwhile, the revolted ships had been reorganised in the Dutch ports under the command of Prince Rupert. If possible with less experience of the sea than his rival, Rupert proved as heroic and resourceful in piracy as Blake in admiralty. The English Presbyterian sailors in Holland were replaced and overawed by the refugee Royalists, and the Cavalier party invested the wreck of its fortunes in a fleet which was expected to bring in a good percentage at the expense of regicide commerce.[1] In 1650 Blake chased Rupert round the shores of the Iberian Peninsula, teaching Portugal and warning Spain that Kings could not with impunity harbour the foes of the English Commonwealth. It was by these operations against the Cavalier fleet, which had chanced to take refuge among the Catholic states of the Western Mediterranean, that England was drawn to send her fleet into that sea, and to influence the politics of Europe by acquiring Mediterranean power.[2] Rupert then fled across the Atlantic. The islands of the English and Irish Channels were reduced to submission, and the Republicans following the Prince across the ocean, by a mere display of power, brought back Virginia and the Barbadoes to the English allegiance (1651-52). Rupert's last ship, without consort or harbour, wandered forlorn upon the waters.

Rupert and Blake. Recovery of the ocean and the Colonies, 1650-52

The reconquest of the Empire, thus happily completed by Blake in his first three years of naval warfare, had forced Republican England to increase her martial strength at sea out of all proportion to her commerce. In 1649-51 the navy had been doubled by the addition of forty-one new ships of war. Charles I., though he had neglected the crews, had kept up the numbers of the fleet; but the Commonwealth had now far surpassed his efforts not only in the treatment and quality of the sailors, but even in the numerical strength of the ships.[3] If this great maritime force had been used solely to preserve peace, prestige and commerce, England might have known rapid economic recovery and such political reconciliation as prosperity can give to a divided State. Unfortunately, the abnormal size of the fleet at their command tempted the rulers in their pride, first to match themselves with the yet unchallenged strength of Holland and then to take advantage of the weakness of Spain. In consequence of the Dutch and Spanish wars, foreign nations, who had just learnt from Blake to respect the regicide flag of St. George, again fell foul of our commerce, and the period of England's great naval strength was not a period of commercial welfare. At home the

Naval power and its temptations

---

[1] Warburton's *Rupert*, iii., pp. 256-64.
[2] Corbett, i., pp. 199, 200 and 110-33. James I.'s expedition against Algiers in 1621 had failed.
[3] Oppenheim, pp. 302-7.

taxation necessary for war, collected by arbitrary power, was injurious alike to the wealth and to the freedom of the subject ; above all, it was made to fall severely on the Cavaliers, whose property the warrior Republic came to use as a reserve fund. Thus the Dutch and Spanish wars helped to bring about the fall of the Commonwealth.[1]

The Navigation Act, 1651

In the middle of the seventeenth century it might have been predicted that the abnormal share of the Dutch skippers in the carrying trade of England and her Colonies could in no case last another fifty years. An eminent economic historian of our own day doubts whether this natural development of English as against Dutch shipping was in fact very greatly accelerated by the Navigation Act of 1651, although contemporaries attributed to the action of this law the marked expansion of English commerce between the Restoration and the Treaty of Utrecht.[2] But whether the Rump really conferred, or only seemed to confer, great benefits on our shipping by the passage of the Act, the Dutch War of 1651-54 was an evil in itself, and did not arise as an inevitable consequence of the Navigation Laws. The Dutch Government had protested against those laws, but was prepared to submit to their operation, partly because they could not be completely enforced. War would not have broken out if the Rump had desired peace. Foreign affairs were now for the first time in the hands of Parliament men, who were more sensitive than kings and courtiers to the aspirations and prejudices of the commercial world : they held that wars ought to be made not to help dynasties but to help commerce, and that a sea war with Holland was therefore required. The usual quarrel arose over the right of search and the traditional claim of the English, that all ships should salute their flag in " the British seas ". These claims were rudely enforced by the simple and ignorant sailors, who hated all foreigners, and now for the first time felt themselves strong enough to pay off old scores against the Dutch. The Parliament men knew that the war was disliked by the soldiers of all ranks from Cromwell downwards, but they hoped that it would be popular in the city, as it certainly was in the fleet. But the burden of taxation and the capture of merchant ships soon turned opinion strongly against the war, and still more strongly against the Government.

The Dutch War, 1651-54

---

[1] Oppenheim, pp. 302-7, 368-70. Cunningham, pp. 178, 179, 186-90.

[2] Cunningham, pp. 479, 603, 209-13. The policy of the Navigation Laws of 1651 was not new; their principles had been adopted as early as the reign of Richard II., and frequent attempts had been made to enforce them by the Stuart Kings. It was not found possible to enforce the provisions of the Act of 1651 at all regularly. That Act " prohibited the introduction into any territory of the Commonwealth of produce of any country in Asia, Africa or America, except in vessels owned by Englishmen or by the inhabitants of English Colonies and manned by crews of which more than one-half were of English nationality. Imports from any part of Europe might be brought in only in English vessels, or in vessels the owners of which belonged to that nation in which the goods were manufactured or produced."

The prosperity and stability that had seemed in its grasp after Worcester, again passed away.

But much as the English suffered, their enemies suffered more. The two war fleets were nearly equal, but the merchant navy of Holland was larger and therefore less well protected. Holland, as the Dutch complained, presented to the attacks of her adversary a mountain of gold, England a mountain of iron. It was calculated that seven-eighths of the inhabitants of Holland lived by industry or commerce. And the bulk of her industry and commerce depended on the transit of great fleets along the British Channel, as they passed out into the open sea, bound for Africa and Ceylon, Smyrna and Venice, the Spice Islands, China and Japan. Never yet, since the beggars of the sea, with the good-will of all true English mariners, had founded the Dutch State upon the barren shore, had navies hostile to Holland inhabited our ports and controlled the narrow Channel through which lay her daily passage to the ocean. She was now at the height of her wealth and power, but she could not survive on her own resources, when the possession of the Channel was successfully disputed. Starvation reigned in the most civilised region on the surface of the globe. Mobs of hungry workmen roamed out over the country, while grass grew in the streets of Amsterdam. The masts of whole fleets were seen idly rocking on the Zuyder Zee, like a decaying forest of innumerable trees; while amid other sights and sounds, in the still unbroken quiet of the empires and anarchies of the far and farthest East, the Dutch settlers searched the sky-line morning by morning in vain for the gleam of expected sails. Holland could still defy Spain and France when her land was under the waves, but could not make head against the men who took from her the command of the sea. She yielded to the starvation that followed the partial and hard-won victory of Blake over Tromp in the grandest sea war that the world had known. So a treaty of peace gave to the English Commonwealth the barren honours of a conflict to which it had in fact sacrificed its last chance of political stability.[1]

Peace with Holland, April, 1654

But before the Dutch peace a change had taken place in the Government of England. The recovery of Great and Greater Britain, and its unnecessary sequel, the war with Holland, had been the common achievement of all who had consented to the King's death. But this party was itself divided into at least two sections. The three or four score members still regularly attending the House of Commons had brought about the Dutch war, and were so anxious to prolong their own power, that they foresaw more clearly than others the dangers of holding a general election.

Army, Parliament and Council, 1649-53

[1] Mahan, *Sea Power*, pp. 37, 38. G. (*C. & P.*), ii., *passim.*

The soldiers, on the other hand, disliked the Dutch war; clamoured for more reforms in Church and State; were tired of the oligarchy of lawyers in the Parliament House; and failed to perceive that when they had removed this last pale shadow of representative Government, they would still be unable to appeal, as they wished, to the suffrages of an alienated and divided nation. Between the army and the Parliament stood the Council of State. It was composed of the best men of both parties. Here Vane and Cromwell, with forty others, members of Parliament and officers together, worked side by side in the Government of Britain. The bribery and favouritism that so often marked the proceedings of the Rump could not be charged against the Council of State, whose republican virtue was the wonder of unfriendly foreign envoys. Legislation, and the power of extraordinary justice, and therefore the direction of general policy, lay with the House of Commons; but the administrative work of the Council had sufficed to save the State.[1]

The Army demands a new Parliament, 1653

As soon as the State was saved, the inevitable quarrel came to a head. The soldiers clamoured for a dissolution, and were only held in check by Cromwell. Now, as six years before, he strove to the last for union between the army and the civil power, well knowing the dangers of the course down which he was again fated to be pushed as leader. The Rump replied to the agitation of the army by introducing a Bill to perpetuate its own existence and the almost unlimited powers of its members, and even to provide that they should in effect choose the men who were to sit in future Parliaments. Cromwell, who was still for compromise, extracted over night (19th April) from Vane and other leaders of Parliament a promise that the Bill should not be pushed on the next day. But when morning came, the rank and file of the House, who were more corrupt than their own leaders in the Council of State, and had therefore more reason to fear an inquiry into their past conduct, proceeded to hurry through the Bill for their own perpetuation, before Cromwell should hear what they were about. Fairfax was to be made general in his place, to head a reaction against the fanatics and the military chiefs. Vane sat still, and made no attempt actively to redeem his promise of the night before. Cromwell was surprised by the news in his lodgings at Whitehall. In his plain morning dress, but with a body of soldiers behind him, he hastened to Westminster by the road down which Charles, with another troop of armed men, had passed to the arrest of the Five Members. Hot with newly-roused passion against the promise-breakers, and stirred to his military manner by the need for instant action to prevent the conspiracy, he used against the only representatives of legal power in England, words and gestures that would have suited better if he had surprised Lilburne presiding over a meeting of mutineers in camp. The man who had saved Parliamentary government in our country, compared the mace to a jester's staff, and with hat on head stamped up and down the middle of the floor, drove out the members with twenty file of musqueteers, and locked behind himself the magic doors, which close at the touch of force, but which force cannot reopen.[1] *Cromwell dissolves the Rump, 20th April, 1653*

At first men were delighted when they heard what "brave Oliver" had done. But his popularity, which was only a reflex of the universal hatred for the Rump, did not outlast the nine days' wonder. Now that the way was cleared for the free democratic election which the army had sought over the bodies of so many Governments, all that Cromwell would do was to summon an assembly of choice spirits from the Independent congregations, selected partly by their fellow-worshippers and partly by the officers themselves. This nominated Parliament, which has been posthumously nicknamed after the name of one of its members, Praise-God Barebone, was guided in its decisions by a minority, more well-intentioned than politic, who attended with a regularity that gave them the control of the House. Chosen from the Nonconformist congregations, these men proposed to abolish tithe and patronage, and to set up a voluntary Church system. An equally sweeping measure to abolish the Chancery Court was proposed, but had not been thought out in any practical form, for the lawyers were not taken into the counsels of the just. The proprietary classes were gravely alarmed. Cromwell, who under the short-lived influence of Major-General Harrison, had, in his opening speech to the Assembly, gone into exaltations and prophecies at the approaching rule of the Saints, lost all enthusiasm when he perceived how few Saints were as politic as he was himself, and was well pleased when the moderates rose early one morning and, before the others knew what they were about, voted an abdication of their powers. *The Barebone Parliament, July-Dec., 1653*

But it is easy to laugh too much at the Barebone Parliament. Tithe when it was paid in kind, and the Chancery Court then and for long generations to come, caused widespread misery and injustice. Neither is it self-evident that patronage is the best method of choosing clergymen. And in other respects this Assembly was on the path of true reforms, to which there was even then no practical objection. They provided for the proper care of lunatics and for the relief of imprisoned debtors. And they showed the secular and anticlerical leanings of advanced Puritans by passing an Act which established Civil Marriage before a Justice of the Peace, according to the usage

---

[1] *E. H. R.*, viii., pp. 526-34. G. (*C. & P.*), chap. xxv. Firth's *Crom.*, pp. 315-25. But see also remarks in Morley's *Cromwell*, pp. 346-49.

now prevailing on the continent. This could scarcely have been the Act of an Assembly of religious bigots.[1]

Cromwell becomes Protector, Dec., 1653 After the failure of the Nominated House, the officers took upon themselves to draw up the " Instrument of Government "—the Constitution under which Cromwell began his rule as Protector, with powers carefully divided between himself, a perpetual Council and an occasional Parliament. Thus the general election, which men had expected as the immediate sequel of the expulsion of the Rump, was only permitted after the new Constitution had been established.

Unlike the Barebone Assembly, the elected Parliaments of the Protectorate in some sort represented public opinion, at any rate of the middle class. The Cavalier gentry were indeed excluded from election, but the Cavaliers were a small community, whose wrongs already excited indignation, but whose policy could not yet obtain support. Men upheld the Puritan rule from 1653 to 1658, for the reason that they upheld the Cavalier rule from 1660 to 1666, because their first desire was peace and settled government ; only they thought the government ought to be settled at the outset by themselves and not by the soldiers. The representatives of the nation refused to endorse the new Constitution, not because it kept the King from his own, but because it had been drawn up by the red-coats. It was not the Cavaliers, but the civilians and the Republicans who between them wrecked the scheme of a constitutional Protectorate. In the same way, although there was no popular movement of Anglican revival, the Puritan supremacy became odious when the rule of the Saints, to which the army had once put a stop when it appeared as the rule of the Presbyterian clergy, took new shape in the rule of the Major-Generals. People found that the warrior saint was no more to be endured than the priest, because if he was more tolerant he was also more powerful.

First Parliament of the Protectorate, Sep., 1654-Jan., 1655 At the polling for the first Parliament of the Protectorate, candidates who had sat in the Barebone Assembly were generally defeated, and the conservative Puritans were sent up in force. Oliver asked them to ratify the Instrument of Government. He was willing that they should alter it in " circumstantials," but they saw need for alteration in " fundamentals ". They sat to defend the rights of the nation against the army, and in pursuit of this end they were naturally drawn on to claim for themselves the sovereign powers of the Long Parliament. Rejecting two " fundamentals " of the Instrument, they threatened to revive religious persecution, and to take the control of the armed force out of the hands of Council and Protector.

---

[1] G. (*C. & P.*), ii., p. 242. H. A. Glass, *The Barbone Parliament*, 1899, pp. 99-101, for the full text of the Act. It was done partly to facilitate registration. Some Puritans were uncommonly clerical, but some, without being the less zealously religious, were strongly secular and anticlerical, as this Act, an indefinite number of centuries in advance of its age, bears witness. Such civil marriages actually took place, as parish registers show.

Oliver was determined to save England from religious intolerance and from the omnipotence of an irresponsible Assembly. The members were determined to save her from despotism and military rule. He would not suffer England again to tread the weary round of Long Parliament tyranny ; they would not suffer her to be ruled by the sole will of a Puritan Strafford. He knew that war and anarchy would raise their heads if, while factions were still so divided, he resigned to an Assembly the power of the sword. They knew that as long as he retained it, constitutional government was a farce. Both were right. There was no escape from the situation which the Long Parliament had created when it refused to reconcile parties after the first Civil War. Until there was again a united body of national opinion, there was no real sanction for the powers either of irresponsible assembly or of military dictator.

Oliver dissolved the Parliament, intending however still to rule by the laws of the land, and by the Instrument of Government. But, in a few months, Cavalier conspiracies of rebellion and assassination drove him for awhile into another course. He divided England into military districts, each under the special charge of a Major-General. The Justices of Peace were sternly held to the performance of disagreeable duties by these military overseers. While the fear of an immediate rising lasted, scores of Cavalier gentlemen were put under arrest, by way of precaution. But even after the first panic was over, race-meetings, cock-fights and bear-baitings were prohibited, partly on political grounds, as likely to be made the scene of seditious assemblies, and partly for the moral welfare of the community. Unnecessary public-houses were suppressed in large numbers. Rogues and jolly companions ; wandering minstrels, bear-wards and Tom Goodfellows ; tipsy loquacious veterans, babbling of Rupert and Goring ; and the broken regiments of stage-players whose occupation was now gone ; all the nondescript population that lived on society in olden times and repayed it in full by making it merry England, were swept up before the military censors, and if they failed to show their respectability and means of livelihood, were sent to prison or to banishment. These proceedings were not only unjust but illegal. Thus, the rule of the Saints in its latest stage was not a clerical, but a military and magisterial inquisition, conducted partly " to discourage and discountenance all profaneness and ungodliness," but partly also " for the preservation of the peace of the Commonwealth," " breaking the designs of the enemies thereof ". [1]

To maintain the system of military police and to conduct the Spanish war, special taxes, known as " decimations," were exacted

The Major-Generals, Aug. 1655

Special taxation of Cavaliers, 1655

---

[1] In another aspect, the rule of the Major-Generals was an isolated attempt to set up an efficient system of police, and so to diminish the shameful number of highway robberies and other crimes which disgraced England until the establishment of a civilian police in the nineteenth century.

from all men of estate who had formerly been Cavaliers. Oliver, aggravated by the plots of their faction, and forgetting his old principles of individual justice and national solidarity, persuaded himself that the Cavaliers had an interest hostile to that of the nation, and might be treated as a class apart. It was a grave falling off. In the days when the small estates of ex-Royalist squires had been sold up by the Rump to pay for the Dutch war, he had seen with pity and indignation the threadbare rustic coats and bewildered glances of the " poor men " " driven, like flocks of sheep, by forty in a morning to the confiscation of goods and estates ; without any man being able to give a reason why two of them had deserved to forfeit a shilling ". [1]   Now he himself repeated the very injustice which he had censured in the Long Parliament.

The special taxation of the Cavaliers was not only unjust but impolitic. At the stage which social and economic development had then reached, the gentry were the class most firmly planted in the land and institutions of the country.[2] Parliaments and Protectors might harry and fine and dragoon them for a season, but not root them up from the ancient soil where they grew. The poor gentlemen had now very little following, but if ever the day came when Royalism should prove the only road back to civilian and settled government, these men whom Cromwell was filling with hatred of all that he most desired to perpetuate in England, would again be the ruling class in the State. It was because of the treatment meted out first by Parliament and then by Protector to the general body of rural Cavaliers, that Puritanism was allowed no religious or civil status in England at the Restoration.

Second Parliament of the Protectorate. First session, Sep., 1656-June, 1657
The second Parliament of the Protector met in a state of grave discontent. The cry was " no swordsmen ". But Oliver himself was already sickened by methods contrary to his really generous nature. The rule of the Major-Generals was stopped. The Commons showed a very proper spirit in throwing out a finance bill for the continued " decimation " of Cavaliers. But the impression made was never to be effaced.

The new Parliament before long produced a new Constitution known as the Humble Petition and Advice. It further exalted the powers of the Protector over his Council, for the majority of the Commons wished to revive the civil power in the person of Oliver. They made common cause with him against his soldiers. They looked for his help to restore the ancient civil Constitution. They would even have made him King but for the opposition of the army ; and they actually succeeded in creating a House of Lords.

Second session, Jan.-Feb., 1658
Oliver had secured the Parliamentary recognition of his powers, which four years back he had sought in vain. At last he seemed

[1] Carl.'s *Crom.*, Speech III.   G. (*C. & P.*), ii., pp. 141, 142.
[2] See Appendix A. as to the small quantity of Cavalier emigration, 1645-1660.

nearing the port of constitutional government. The incoming tide
of regret for all the old things which he had helped to destroy had
been strangely turned in his favour. But that regret was less universally felt in the Puritan party on which his system rested, than
in the nation at large. The unquiet spirit of Lilburne, who had
been carried to his grave by his latest friends the Quakers, was still
ranging for revenge. In the second session of the second Parliament, owing to the calling up of so many supporters of Government
to the new House of Lords, the Republicans could no longer be outvoted. They opposed Oliver in the Commons, while in City and
country they intrigued for his overthrow with Levellers and Cavaliers.
To render the State secure from a conspiracy of which the House
of Commons was the centre, the Protector dissolved his second
Parliament. He himself had now only seven months more to live.[1]

From the beginning to the end of his public career in England
and Scotland alike, it was Cromwell's first object to maintain a
united Puritan party in affairs both of Church and State. Yet in
the end Holles and Harrison, Lilburne and Ludlow, scarcely hated
Charles Stuart worse than they hated him. As Protector, he had
quarrelled with two Puritan Parliaments, even after a hundred duly
elected members had in each case been turned back at the door.
But the union which he failed to secure in politics he accomplished
in religion. The wisdom and justice of his ecclesiastical system
vindicated itself in the end to all Puritans. Milton and Baxter,
Hugh Peters and George Fox, were alike constrained to praise the
tolerant and conservative guardian of the interests of the Lord's
people. He succeeded in reconciling all, because, while he put down
persecution, he maintained endowments. The Protectorate meant
to one party defence from the blasphemy laws of orthodox Parliaments, to another safety from the spoliation of Barebone Assemblies.
The country-side swarmed with enthusiasts denouncing a " hireling
priesthood " to applauding audiences of tithe-payers ; but as long
as Oliver lived, the parson knew that he would still be able to venture
into the fields of the retired corporal, and humbly carry off his lawful
sheaves, at risk of nothing worse than ironical inquiries where he was
at Worcester fight, and whether he had read Matthew xxiii. 13. But
the old soldier and his co-religionists on their side were not ungrateful
to the chief who had won for them the liberty to worship God in
conventicles, and to rebuke the parson ; while the Quaker, when he
was periodically delivered from gaol by colonels and magistrates still
fuming with rage, divined that they were acting not by their own
light, but through the power of the Lord's servant, Oliver Cromwell.

Success of Oliver's ecclesiastical polity among all Puritans

---

[1] Professor Firth thinks that if he had lived he would, very soon after Sept.,
1858, have been able to accept the Kingship. Opinion was rapidly maturing in
that direction, even in the army. *Last Years of Protectorate*, ii., pp. 278-9.

17

The endowed parsons represented the three largest sects—Presbyterian, Independent and Baptist—into which Puritan religion was in those years divided. But around the consumers of tithe, were scattered innumerable free congregations, either supporting their own ministers, or dispensing with ministers altogether. Provided the Prayer-book was not used, any form of Protestant worship was openly practised. Cromwell's was in fact a congregational system, partly endowed and partly unendowed. Scandal and anarchy were prevented by his Commissions of Triers and Ejectors, whose business it was to weed the Established Church of disorderly and unlearned servants. They exercised their power so honestly and tolerantly that the inquisition won the applause of all parties, and kept up the education and usefulness of the endowed clergy to a level which there is no reason to think inferior to the level reached under Laud.[1]

Rapid spread of unorthodox sects   Under these conditions of free competition, the unorthodox gained fast on the orthodox forms of doctrine and worship. Now was proved how little hold Presbyterianism had over the English Puritan mind. Now were formed the free religious communities in which the Nonconformist spirit survived through the Restoration period, and took its final shape in English society. Now was shown what Laudism and Presbyterianism had repressed, the wealth of imagination, the depth of emotion, the vigour and variety of intellect that were to be found among the poor. The thousands that were awakened to the use of their minds by Bunyan and Fox, were too near the prime needs of body and spirit to be interested in theologies and Church systems.[2] To the poor also the Gospel was preached, sometimes in crude and coarse forms : but in one form at least that was as pure as it was simple, and as hostile to the degrading superstitions as to the indifferent ethical practice of the more respectable churches. The rise of the Quakers was rendered possible, because Cromwell prevented the annihilating persecution which would have fallen on such a sect at its first appearance under any other *régime ;* and because this was the period of religious and intellectual stirring among the English common people. By the time of the Restoration, the Society of Friends was sufficiently well-rooted to survive any increase of persecution.

George Fox   The ideas of Quakerism came from many sources, foreign and English, but the formation of the Friends' Society was due to one man. George Fox, the weaver's son, apprentice to a shoemaker and dealer in wool, had little book-learning beyond the Bible ; but he

---

[1] Firth's *Crom.*, pp. 357-60. G. (*C. & P.*), ii., pp. 320-26.

[2] " Your word-divinity darkens knowledge. You talk of a body of Divinity, and of Anatomysing Divinity. O, fine language ! But when it comes to trial, it is but a husk without the kernel, words without life. The spirit is in the hearts of the people whom you despise and tread under foot " (Winstanley, *New Law of Righteousness*, see p. 233 above, note).

had as a young man acquired first-hand knowledge of varieties of religious experience, by walking through the Midlands to seek out and converse with " professors " of Puritanism in all its forms. Thus trained, he was better suited to found a new religion that should satisfy the desires of the soul, than if the academic study of Hooker and Calvin had accustomed him to regard the organisation of Churches and the details of dogma as matters of spiritual importance. His views, which he drew from obscure corners of his own country, had come from distant lands and ages. He gathered up, certainly from the General Baptists, perhaps also indirectly from the Family of Love and the Diggers, ideas which had in the course of long generations travelled to England from Silesia and far Germany, by way of the Mennonite communities of Holland. These ideas, of which perhaps he did not understand the full intellectual bearing so well as Winstanley, or some of his own followers, he alone was able to impress upon a large portion of mankind, by the fire of his living genius. He had an overwhelming, perhaps an hypnotic, power and presence, like one of the ancient prophets. To hear Fox preach once in the churchyard as he passed through the town, or to spend an evening with him by the fireside, often was enough to change a persecutor into an enthusiast, to emancipate a man from the intellectual habits and social customs of a lifetime. The views to which he converted the common people of his day were not those of the religious revivals which for 300 years have constantly recurred in lower English society. The religion which he did so much to spread was a mystical and Christian free-thought. The success of such a movement, which, before the founder died in 1691, counted its followers by tens of thousands, is witness to the intellectual richness of the soil in which such seed could spring up to so plentiful a harvest. His followers were largely recruited from the various sects, and from the individual enthusiasts belonging to no community, who abounded in Cromwell's England. Unorthodoxy running almost to pantheism, as in the case of Winstanley, then often went with all the signs of intense religious exaltation.

The Episcopalian and Presbyterian training tended to fix the mind far from such thoughts and feelings ; and the rule of Bishop or Presbyter would have prevented by force the free teaching of such blasphemies. But under Cromwell the Quakers enjoyed through the action of the central government the opportunity to teach their doctrines in public; and this right would have been allowed without any qualification, if they had not abused it by peculiar and disorderly methods of propaganda. It was their custom to enter into churches at service time, and denounce the parson to his parishioners as a " dead dog," a hireling receiver of tithes, and a preacher of superstitions as false as those which enslaved the spirits of the heathen. The strange words often brought sudden conviction

Methods of Quaker propaganda

to a few men and women in corners of the church, but stirred the rest there and then to a murderous rush against the man who insulted them. The cheerfulness with which on such occasions the Quaker stretched out his arms and neck to the kicks and blows, gave to his offensive tactics of propaganda partial justification and complete success. Where Fox himself went, people were converted by scores and sometimes by hundreds at a time. And these conversions were not the mere passing swell of a vulgar ecstasy and remorse. Those whom the Society of Friends took into the bonds of its close but free community, seldom chose to return out into the world.

Quaker doctrine

Quakerism corrected the worst faults of those Puritan sects out of whose midst it grew. It was not for nothing that Fox had spent so many years studying " professors ". Instead of the military spirit, he proclaimed the wickedness of all war. Instead of the reliance on force, he enjoined martyrdom. Instead of the suppression of vice, the influence of example. In place of the religion of gloom and reprobation, he opened the inner well-springs of constant joy. In place of the hell waiting the sinner in the next world, he taught men to unfold the heaven that each carried hidden within himself on earth. From the Bible which the Puritan had made the sole authority, he appealed, not back to the Church, but forward to the individual. The doctrine of " inner light "—that inspiration comes from within each man, not from without—was the centre of his system. The individual interpretation of the Bible had long been preparing the way for this idea. The " inner light " was at once the outcome and the countercheck of the Puritan Bible-worship.

Quaker practices

On the whole, Quakerism was more a development than a reaction from the spirit of the sects. The Quaker's objection to gaiety of dress and luxury of life, though not so cheerless and morose as that of the Puritan " professor," was yet more severe. The democratic scorn of the pomp and circumstance of worldly authority, then widely felt among the sectarians, was stereotyped by the Quakers in their well-known rules of speech and behaviour. Above all, the religious appeal to the mind and spirit was made more simple and direct than ever ; not only was there no ordinary service or ritual, but the rites of Baptism and of the Lord's Supper were disused, and the special priesthood was abolished. Every man and every woman, Fox declared, was a priest. In thus rejecting the organisation by which other Christian bodies maintain their numbers when the spirit has fled, the Quakers, when the missionary zeal of the first two generations was over, lost the power of propagating their religion, but on the other hand did not lose their spiritual intensity and freedom.

Protectors and enemies of the Quakers

The usurper and the restored monarch were both personally favourable to them ; Oliver from enthusiasm, Charles II. from indifference. Charles's first act at his Restoration was to save the Quakers from Puritan rage in his American colonies. But in England Cromwell's protection was the most effective ; the severest persecution on this side of the Atlantic, " the great and general imprisonment of Friends," was at the hands of the Anglicans, subsequent to the abortive Rising of the Fifth Monarchy men in 1660.

The Presbyterians hated Quakerism because it threatened to take away their tithes ; the Baptists because it actually took away their congregations ; and the Episcopalians because it was further removed than any other sect from the ideas of ritual and Church government. But most of all the Quakers were hated by the magistrates and officers, who could extort no sign of outward respect, and by the ordinary man who could not get the small change of politeness, without which he will refuse to take the most precious gifts. The hatred with which the Friends were at first regarded, the rules, in themselves absurd, which they observed in order to escape the contagion of worldliness and the stifling influence of conventionality, drew them into so close a communion with each other for purposes of intermarriage and habits of life, that they resembled in this as in many other ways some mystical sect of the East. The founder, in whom ecstasy and common-sense, violence and peacefulness were strangely blended, tamed the frenzy of his first disciples by the discipline of silent worship and by his own invincible power to calm as well as stir the soul ; he saw prevalent before he died that quietness of manner and spirit which thenceforth was regarded as the truest symbol of the inner light and of the blessedness that it gives.[1]

At the time of Restoration of Charles II. there were as many as 60,000 Friends in England, drawn principally from the trading and yeomen classes. The persecution which they had to endure at the hands of the Cavalier Parliaments put a check on their propaganda ; their leaders were kept in prison for years together, and many thousands emigrated to America, especially to their own colony of Pennsylvania. When at length under William III. the period of permanent toleration set in, their propagandist fervour had spent itself, and the Quaker body passed into its " quietist " era. *Limit of toleration under Protectorate*

Oliver's ecclesiastical system, though it did lasting work in sheltering the infancy of the Nonconformist sects and the Society of Friends, was based on a principle which ensured its own downfall. Its toleration was limited to Puritanism. Cromwell himself would have wished to tolerate the use of the Prayer-book, but the majority of those on whom he depended had made up their minds otherwise. Even he, as his political and financial methods made the hatred of

[1] Fox's *Journal, passim.* Barclay, *passim.* Gooch, pp. 270-82. G. (*C. & P.*), ii., pp. 19-24 ; iii., pp. 106-11, 210-16. Westcott's *Social Aspects of Christianity.* Miss Stephen's *Quaker Strongholds.* Braithwaite's *Beginnings of Quakerism.* Sir Alfred Lyall pointed out to me the similarity of the early Quakers to an Eastern sect.

the Cavaliers more bitter and their conspiracies more frequent, thought it necessary to prevent them from gathering in powerful religious assemblies. They were not systematically dragooned and spied upon, and the public exercise of their religion was often winked at, though it was often interrupted.[1]

Under the Protectorate the majority of religious people in England were Puritans of one sort or another.[2] There was no popular movement on behalf of the Prayer-book. But whereas the adhesion of the landed gentry to the new order of things was necessary for its permanence, a large proportion of that small but important class was being driven into sympathy with Anglicanism by social, political and financial oppression. And even if the bulk of the religious people of England were Puritan, the bulk of the non-religious were now as heartily against the Puritans as they had formerly been against Laud. The rule of the Major-Generals, the closing of the theatres, the frequent interference with sports, the occasional punishment of vice, the arbitrary arrests, imprisonments and banishments, the effacement of the old leaders of society, the ubiquity of soldier and saint, and the Englishman's latent sense of humour, were all secretly preparing an incredible resurrection of things killed and buried.

Puritanism threw away its best chance in England, because all its parties—even the democrats—assumed as an axiom that no one who was not a Puritan was to share in the Government. With this idea they had gone into the war ; with this idea they had tried to settle the nation in the first hour of victory ; and with this idea Cromwell ruled. Even in the minds of those who thought religious toleration right in itself, the prohibition of the Prayer-book worship followed as a deduction from this axiom of political exclusiveness, just as in later years the yet more cruel enforcement of the Conventicle and Five Mile Acts followed as a deduction from the axiom that no Puritan should sit in Parliament or serve on a Corporation.

Condition of the Catholics
If the Roman Catholics had reason to regret the personal rule of the Stuart Kings, they were at least better off in the hands of the Independent chiefs than in the hands either of Presbyterian or of Cavalier Parliaments. The recusancy Acts had been repealed in 1650, and though the Catholics were not allowed publicly to exercise their religion, they were not otherwise molested under the Protectorate.

Return of the Jews
It was natural that during the decade when Old Testament sympathies and theoretical religious toleration inspired the governors of England, the Jews who had been expelled in the day of mediæval Catholicism should find the road of return opened to them by the enemies of the Inquisition. Indeed the popular prejudice against

---

[1] *Clarke Papers*, iii., pp. 130-31.   Firth's *Crom.*, p. 361.
[2] G. (*C. & P.*), ii. pp. 323-24.

which Oliver had in this matter to contend was due to commercial jealousy rather than to any other feeling.

In spite of so many disturbing influences, the years 1640-60 represent one of our great periods of educational enthusiasm and improvement. In the fifty years from 1601-51 as many schools were founded as had been founded in a century of Tudor rule. The movement reached its climax under the Puritans. The same utilitarian social enthusiasm, which had been only too pronounced in the Barebone Assembly, took more practical forms in the educational policy of Parliament and Protector. The national duty of education was eagerly taken up by the Long Parliament in 1641, and though war caused them to abandon their design of a complete system, donations from the confiscated Church lands were continually made for the maintenance of schools and schoolmasters. Treasury grants in aid of education were frequent in the period of Puritan rule. The expulsion of the Episcopalian dons from Oxford and Cambridge was an unfortunate result of the system then prevalent in both parties of mixing up learning with religion and politics, but the zeal of the new Government, and the abilities of the men whom they substituted for the old, led to results the excellence of which even Clarendon had to acknowledge. It is difficult to say whether the Universities were best under the restrictive system of Laud, or under that of the Parliamentary Commissioners ; but the schools of England certainly benefited by the Great Rebellion.[1] *(marginal note: Educational progress)*

After Cromwell returned from Ireland in the spring of 1650, Ireton, Ludlow and Fleetwood completed her subjugation in two years of guerilla war. When the Tories took refuge in the oozy isles of the bogland, and defied pursuit, the English hunters sent the unsubstantial hounds of famine down the watery ways to throttle them in their last lair. All Ireland was devastated of food : its last defenders lay down to die unseen among their hills and wailing rose faint in many a secret place with only the birds of the air to hear it. Others came out to die in battle in yelling hordes. The Puritans themselves drooped with starvation and disease as they plied the pike, wearily now and in grim silence. They rose victorious over the horrors of that war by the discipline and self-restraint which they brought from the English field ; but they left their human kindness in their own country. Like all the English who touched that fatal shore, they were degraded towards the level of the bands that had wasted Germany for the woeful Thirty Years. When Ireland at last lay dead at their feet, one-third of her inhabitants had perished by the sword, pestilence or famine.[2] *(marginal note: Last stages of the war in Ireland, 1650-52)*

[1] E. H. R., xv., pp. 58-72. Firth's Crom., pp. 353-57. Visitation of Oxford (Camden Soc., 1881).

[2] The Tories were " irregular bands who robbed and massacred without being enlisted in any regular force ''. Major Morgan describes himself and his colleagues as engaged in the destruction of three kinds of beasts : " The first is the wolf, on

Then followed the settlement.

When at the dissolution of the mediæval system of polity on the continent, England saw France and Spain arise as nations, and set themselves against each other and against herself, her governors felt the need that Ireland should be occupied in force. From Henry VIII. to Cromwell three methods of holding the country were tried in succession, each more potent as a means of military occupation, but more unjust and fatal as a political settlement, than that which it superseded.

The Tudor system in Ireland
First, under the early Tudors an attempt was made to rule the tribes of half-savage Irish by English military governors, respecting their traditions and their interests as those of the sole inhabitants, but leading them by peace and order to more civilised forms of life. If this plan had been carried out, Ireland would have prospered. But England had then neither the money, nor the soldiers, nor the trained service of proconsuls requisite to confer Imperial Government on foreign provinces ; and at that moment the Reformation came to divide the rulers from the ruled.

System under the early Stuarts
Experience under Elizabeth showed that the English hold on Ireland could only be maintained by large classes settled there for economic reasons. This second plan, attempted under James I., was worse for the natives, because it involved dispossession from whole districts, and the creation of a new interest hostile to their own, which the Government was thenceforth bound to consult. Ulster (1610), and some smaller colonies in the South, were planted. But except in those places where a large English or Scottish population was settled thickly, the land was left to the old possessors, and Celtic society was not disturbed. Under the early Stuarts, Catholic Ireland was still alive, though fettered by Penal Laws and caged in by Protestant colonies.

The Cromwellian Settlement of Ireland, 1652-56
The rebellion of 1641 showed that these colonies were insufficient barriers. The settlers had usurped the land and the political and religious rights of the Irish, enough to exasperate, but not enough to suppress. All agreed that after the reconquest they must somehow be strengthened. But instead of increasing the colonies by clearing the Irish from whole new districts, a third policy was now introduced, of leaving the poorer Irish everywhere on the soil, and giving the landlord-rights in three-quarters of the island to English immigrants. This policy, announced by Parliament in 1642 as the

whom we lay five pounds ahead and ten pounds if a bitch. The second beast is a priest, on whose head we lay ten pounds. The third beast is a Tory, on whose head, if he be a public Tory, we lay twenty pounds ; and forty shillings on a private Tory."

	£	s.	d.
Paid for taking Wolves	3,847	5	0
„ „ „ Tories and wood kernes .	2,149	7	4
„ „ „ Popish Priests . . .	756	3	3

E. H. R., xiv., pp. 108, 703, and see Ludlow, *passim.*

security for the Irish war loan, and adopted by the Rump in the Act of Settlement of 1652, was approved and executed by Cromwell. Ultimately the worst of the three policies, it was at the time the most practical. It held down the old inhabitants and secured the island against the invasion of Catholic powers. It lasted two centuries and a half. But it deprived the Celtic nation of its natural leaders by destroying the Catholic upper class.

The new landowners themselves came to little good. Some of them were the capitalist " adventurers," who had found the money for the Irish wars ; others, the officers of the conquering army. But the scheme of settlement had further provided for a great middle class of Puritan yeomen, consisting of the private soldiers who had won their lands with their own swords. As the Holy Land was divided among the conquering tribes by lot, so by lot the counties and districts were assigned to each regiment, company and troop. But the accumulative and squirearchical trend of English society was too strong even among those democratic bands. The officers bought up cheap their men's reversionary claims, and out of these they formed for themselves great estates, while the poor silly soldiers went off with a little ready money in their pockets. Those few who remained to be yeomen, too thinly scattered among an alien population, yet dissevered by social caste from the Protestant squires, found the loneliness of their position intolerable, and in a few generations became merged with their Catholic neighbours by marriage, feeling and religion. The larger landowners, utterly dissevered from the native farmers, became like the *noblesse* of the continent, a class foredoomed soon or late, by violence or by purchase, to be swept off the land, as clean as a silk cloth is swept off a deal table. Ulster, the older garrison that had roots in the lower and middle class of town and country, has survived. But Cromwell's landlords will soon be a memory of the past.

The failure of the Protector's plan would have been less complete if his free-trade policy had been continued after his death. He did all that could be done for the Protestants of Ireland, regarding them, as he regarded all Englishmen the world over, as citizens of one State. The Tory and Whig politicians of later days, regarding them as a dependent class to be sacrificed to English economic jealousy, ruined Protestant and Catholic together by prohibiting their most important trades. But they maintained Oliver's land settlement with little change, as the only means then known of preserving the English Protestant State from continual danger of attack by its foreign and domestic foes.[1]

Oliver made both Scotland and Ireland part of the British Empire, but by very different means. In Ireland, his conquest was Crom-
wellian
Settle-
ment of
Scotland

---

[1] Cunningham, pp. 120-24. G. (*C. & P.*), chap. xliv. Firth's *Crom.*, chap. xiii. ; *C. A.*, pp. 202-8. *E. H. R.*, xiv., pp. 700-34. *Joshua* xiv-xix.

the prelude to the destruction of a class, the slavery of a race, and the proscription of a creed ; in Scotland, it was a friendly occupation, to protect the common Puritan interest until such time as its Scottish leaders should " think it possible they might be mistaken ". The Kirk was left untouched, save that it could no longer govern the State, and no longer enforce its fundamental doctrine of persecution. The Scots were treated on an equality, and invited to a fraternity with their English brethren. Free trade with England gave them a solid advantage, while representation in the Parliament at Westminster, if it did them little benefit, at least proclaimed in principle that Great Britain had been formed. Nor was the Union all that Scotland lost when Charles Stuart returned. Within her own borders, the utilitarian and democratic soldiery conferred great but short-lived benefits on the population. Vassalage, servitude and hereditary jurisdictions, which still disgraced a country essentially popular in spirit, were done away. The subjugation of the Highlands, that first condition of Scotland's progress, which she was too poor ever to have fulfilled for herself, was carried out by the English regiments as never before, and never again till after Culloden field. The Great Britain of the Hanoverian *régime* was already established by Oliver, in all save the one thing needful for its permanence, the consent of the two peoples. Therefore, his Scottish reforms died with him. A long course of troubles, and the slow education of a century, were needed before the same settlement of religion and politics, commerce and public order, society and law, was again step by step erected for Scotland, under the less heroic but more persuasive influence of the Whigs.

Puritan
nationalism
In the comity of great nations, England was then both weak and vulnerable. The English, while they were still a small people compared to the French and the Spaniards, and a poor people compared to the Dutch, already had an Empire beyond the ocean to protect. Whenever the English were divided against themselves, as in the reign of Elizabeth, as again from 1640 to 1715, their scattered territories were exposed to foreign invaders, in part alliance with some domestic faction. It was the danger of invasion that drove our ancestors, in an age when all their natural tendencies were peculiarly peaceful and insular, unwillingly to wage wars beyond the sea, and to attain a new position in the world by broken steps of Protestant foreign policy under Elizabeth, under Cromwell, under William and Anne. The trade rivalry was with Holland ; but the danger of military conquest came always from the Catholic and absolutist power of Spain or of France. For this reason English nationalism appealed more strongly to the Puritans and to the Whigs, and became in them an overbearing imperialism ; while in the Cavaliers and Tories it remained a passive provincial exclusiveness.

Cromwell held, with his secretary, that God had revealed himself " as His manner is, first to His Englishmen ".[1] The Protector's mind could never logically separate this idealised patriotism from his Protestant and Free Church sympathies. He outstripped even Puritan sentiment in his championship of England's quarrel with the Catholic world, and injured shipping and finance by the pertinacity of his commercial and colonial wars. As general, he recovered the Empire ; as Protector, he held it together and made the great powers bid for its friendship ; but the defect of his qualities and of the machine by which he had accomplished this task, caused him, when all was done, to drag his still bleeding country into a war with Spain.

Between the outbreak of the Civil War and the end of the Protectorate, the navy had, as we have seen, been doubled in numbers and more than doubled in fighting power. The Puritans, inspired by their aggressive nationalism, and supplied by revolutionary finance, had both the will and the means to maintain the British fleet as the greatest in the world. But the authors of this root principle of modern English policy, which happily survived their own downfall, had failed to comprehend its noblest and most necessary condition. To them an invincible navy was not a permanent insurance for peace, but a perpetual stimulous to war. Men were so little accustomed to the possession of a great fighting force actually afloat, that they could not bear to see it sail idly protecting our commerce and enforcing our diplomacy ; they itched to use it in battle. Just as the fleets, which had been trained in the recovery of the Empire for the regicides, had then been turned by the Parliament against the Dutch ; so the yet greater fleets which had brought Holland to its knees, were used by the Protector against Spain. " Providence," said Oliver at his Council board (20th July, 1654), " seemed to lead us " to the attack on the Spanish Indies—

Having 160 ships swimming ; most of Europe our enemies except Holland, and that would be well considered also : we think our best consideration had to keep up this reputation and improve it for some good, and not lay them up by the walls. . . . This design would cost little more than laying by the ships, and that with hope of great profit.[2]

The raid to which Providence so plainly pointed (on the great island of San Domingo, then known as Hispaniola), proved the one military fiasco of Oliver's life. Despising the enemy, the author of the New Model made preparations worthy of Buckingham. The worst soldiers of the various regiments, hastily drafted together, augmented by recruits taken off the streets, and improperly equipped for the tropics, were sent to San Domingo to sicken with dysentery and to run away before a charge of half-breed cowboys armed with

Origin of the war with Spain

San Domingo and Jamaica, April-May, 1655

---

[1] Milton's *Areopagitica.*   [2] *Clarke Papers*, iii., p. 207.

cattle-lances. Jamaica, whither they sailed to retrieve their disgrace, being thinly peopled by Spaniards, surrendered without resistance. Oliver would have been willing to retire with the disgrace and the spoil of the West Indian raid, but the incensed statesmen of Madrid declared regular war in every part of the globe. He was therefore constrained to accept the alliance of the Catholic, but as yet tolerant, power of France.

The English in the Mediterranean   The expedition to San Domingo, and the Atlantic and Oceanic war with Spain to which it led, were the more to be regretted because Oliver had already discovered a more profitable use for the English naval power. Immediately after the Dutch war, our ships, which had some years back passed through the Straits of Gibraltar in pursuit of Rupert, were again sent under Blake to police the Mediterranean, and by their presence there to terrify the Catholic powers on the French, Spanish and Italian coasts into accordance with the wishes of Oliver. Thus the idea of the Mediterranean fleet, the true method by which England can make her will felt abroad, was first discovered by the great Protector. The Christian powers of Europe respected Blake and his master ; and next year the Bey of Tunis saw his ships destroyed beneath the guns of his stronghold (1655). When the Spanish war broke out, the energies of England were again turned principally to the Ocean ; yet even so, the Protector still maintained a British fleet permanently stationed in the Mediterranean.[1]

The great Spanish war colours the history of the last three years of the Protectorate in several different ways.

Battle of Dunkirk, June, 1658   As a Protestant war it was useless, because it had no distinctive object. It was the ill-luck of the Reformed religion on the continent, that the period when England was governed by a man willing and able to play the part of Gustavus, was the period when Spain and Austria had ceased, and France had not begun, to attack the old established liberties of Protestant populations. With scornful joy Puritan sailors sank galleons flaunting the pennons of the Virgin and the names of the Saints, and it was a good sight for our French allies when the red-coats scrambled up the sliding sand-dunes of Dunkirk and drove before them the embattled hosts of the Idolators, " our strongest soldiers and officers clubbing them down ". But no Protestant worshipped God more freely for all this glorious bloodshed. The armed diplomacy by which Oliver bettered the lot of a few Waldensians in their Alps (1655) was, in his day, a more effective means than a grand war, to extend England's protection over the Protestant communities of the world.

The Jamaica planters   As a colonial war, the struggle with Spain succeeded where it seemed to fail. In Jamaica, seized by his men on their repulse from San Domingo, Cromwell found scope for a work peculiarly his own. By efforts often disappointed, but never abandoned, he artificially

---

[1] Corbett, chaps. xvi., xvii., xviii.

planted the island with Englishmen. More than the Irish land settlement, our West Indian Empire was the result of his personal wishes and efforts. But it was fortunate that his Jamaica planters did not come from the place whence he first attempted to procure emigrants : with more zeal than the statesmen of his era for the spread of the English race, but with no more knowledge of the true conditions for its eventual success, he tried to divert the further expansion of New England from Delaware Bay to his new land of promise in the summer seas, and vainly sought to persuade the Northern colonists " to remove themselves or such numbers of them as shall be thought convenient, out of those parts where they now are, to Jamaica ". So little was the Anglo-Saxon plantation of the North American continent due to the deliberate action of statesmen, or to any man's foreknowledge of the vast destinies, that Charles I. gave the New World to the Puritans by attempting to suppress them in the Old ; while Cromwell, in his greater eagerness to spread the Gospel and the British race, attempted a State policy of removal, which, if it had been carried through, would have ruined or at least retarded the expansion of the English-speaking races on the mainland of America.[1]

As a commercial war, the breach with Spain proved a bad investment. The justifying cause of the attack on San Domingo had been that the Spaniard claimed and exercised the right to seize our ships anywhere in the West Indian seas, even if they were only trading with our own Colonies. Our quarrel on this issue was a just one whenever we chose to take it up, but at that moment English finance and commerce required a period of retrenchment and recovery after fifteen years of almost continual war. In his anxiety to protect British shipping from Spain in the Caribbean Sea, Oliver exposed it to injury from all nations in all quarters of the globe. Much of our great trade with European Spain fell permanently into the hands of neutrals. Everywhere our merchant ships were preyed upon by enemies who took advantage of the Spanish war to wreak their hatred on a Commonwealth feared by all but loved by none. In the Western counties, merchants were half-ruined by the Spanish frigates waiting off Land's End. In London, monied men cursed the war and turned their backs on the Protectorate.[2] *The war injurious to commerce*

As a naval war it was altogether glorious, and in one respect useful. As a sequel to the Civil and Dutch wars, the Spanish war gave our seamen a long period of active work, and thereby permanently fixed the new traditions and institutions of the service that now first became truly professional. For nearly twenty years the ships were constantly at sea ; the officers and men had continual employment from the State. The professional feeling and experience *The war develops naval tradition*

[1] Thurloe, iv., pp. 130, 634 ; v., p. 510. *Clarke Papers*, iii., p. 205. *Memoirs of Sir W. Penn*, ii., pp. 585-89. [2] Corbett, i., chaps. xvi., xvii., xviii.

that now first separated them in habits and in ways of thought from both merchant crews and landsmen, stood the country in good stead when " Oliver's captains " fought the great sea wars of the restored monarchy. And only by the help of this splendid service could our commerce have survived the number of enemies whom Oliver's policy aroused in his own day. Under him the Turkish pirates could not reappear in the Channel ; and the old haunt of the Christian buccaneers of Dunkirk, so long the terror of our Eastern ports, was occupied by red-coats. The Mediterranean was policed by our ships. In the Canaries the Spanish galleons could find no

Blake destroys Spanish fleet at Santa Cruz, 20th April, 1657

safety even in the guarded waters of Santa Cruz ; for like the man who five generations later lost his arm in that twice-famous harbour, Blake could trust his gunners and his captains so well, that he initiated the English tactics of silencing shore batteries from the sea, and destroying fleets who had sought shelter under their protection. Thus, though commerce suffered, the navy flourished ; and the pride of the English in England and the respect shown her by the rest of the world, was remembered in after days when the commercial distress had been long forgotten.[1]

Financial difficulties become acute, 1658

By the end of the Protectorate, the prosperity and therewith the security of the Puritan rule had at length been undermined by continuous war. The merchants were at last alienated by their loss at sea, as the landowners had long been alienated by their loss of broad acres and social influence. On both classes the pressure of war taxation fell so heavily as to cause a reduction in the standard of living. The maintenance of a great army and a great navy together, and a perpetual state of war, was much more than England could then afford. The price of a military empire was becoming as embarrassing to the governors as it was unendurable to the governed. In the last years of the Protectorate, the navy itself began to decline from want of money. Yet the united service, always under the Cromwellian *régime* the first charge on the treasury, had long been involving the country in debts with which even confiscations and arbitrary taxes were unable to cope. The financial problem, which the Puritan statesmen trained in the easy school of revolutionary finance had never learnt to regard with proper reverence, was rising to take its revenge on the party, when the death of Oliver destroyed the political stability of their system, and gave the speed of panic to a reaction that economic causes had done much to set on foot.[2]

---

[1] In laying due stress on the financial and commercial distress of the period consequent on the Dutch and Spanish wars, it must always be admitted that the tradition of this distress did not survive in the national memory. Thus Swift in arguing for the fleet as against the army was able to say in *The Conduct of the Allies :* " The usurpers had almost continual war with Spain or Holland ; but managing it by their fleets, they increased very much the riches of the kingdom, instead of exhausting them ".

[2] Oppenheim, pp. 303, 304, 342, 355, 368-70. Corbett *passim*. G. (*C. & P.*), chaps. xlv.-xlviii., and Firth's *Crom.*, chaps. xviii., xix. *Cf.* Gardiner's *Cromwell's*

On the 3rd of September, 1658, the anniversary of Dunbar and of Worcester, Oliver went to his rest. " Let us all," he had once said, " be not careful what men will make of these actings. They, will they, nill they, shall fulfil the good pleasure of God, and we shall serve our generations. Our rest we expect elsewhere : that will be durable." [1]

Death of Oliver, 3rd Sep., 1658

The trust in God that had been his strength had also been his bane. In all that he did of good and of evil in the three kingdoms, it was too much his way to trust that the Lord would support him in everything that he undertook. What he judged to be necessary for the present, that he thought to be predestined for the future. His victories seemed to him, not the result of the means which he employed, but proofs that his policy was also the will of Heaven. It was from Ireland that he wrote to the Speaker—

> Sir, what can be said of these things ? Is it the arm of the flesh that hath done these things ? Is it the wisdom and counsel, or strength of men ? It is the Lord only. God will curse that man and his house that dares to think otherwise. Sir, you see the work is done by a Divine leading. God gets into the hearts of men, and persuades them to come under you.[2]

Hence, it was easy for him to think that the Irish themselves would be converted by " assiduous preaching," when their priests had been removed to penal settlements. In England and Scotland he made, though in a less degree, the same mistake of trusting God to reconcile public opinion.

Yet in England and Scotland, at least, he had no obvious alternative. Early in his political career, he had striven hard for conciliation and consent. But he soon found that there was no general consent to be had in England to any plan, either Royalist, Presbyterian or Independent. There was no active agreement of public opinion between 1641 and 1660 ; and no human being who ever lived could have made a permanent settlement out of the situation left by King and Parliament in 1648. In that general wreck of powers and parties, Oliver saved the British Empire from partition, the civil liberties of England from Royalist reconquest, the Free Churches and free-thinkers from destruction by those of the narrow way. Those deeds outlived him, and the lovers of England, of civil liberty, and of free-thought will for ever be grateful for such benefits, though all else for which he fought perished with him.

Oliver's permanent achievements

But to value men solely by uncertain calculations of their achievement, is to disinherit the human race. If some who have done great things were only men with better opportunities or more of common talent than the rest, others, like Cromwell as his comrades knew

His character

Place in History, pp. 97-101, with Firth's *Crom.*, pp. 434-36. Seeley's *Growth of British Policy*, vol. ii., pp. 1-107. And *cf.* Cunningham, pp. 178-93, and *Macmillan's Mag.*, November, 1902, pp. 72-80, with Beer's *Cromwell's Policy in its Economic Aspects (Pol. Sci. Quarterly*, vol. xvi.-xvii. and reprint).

[1] Firth's *Crom.*, p. 253. [2] Carl.'s *Crom.*, Letter cxvi.

him and as modern learning has let us know him again, show to what height the plant Man can sometimes grow. In the agony of war, in the interminable crisis of revolutionary state-craft, he kept his noblest qualities of mind untired. He was always fresh from nature, open to new spiritual desires and human joys. In the hardest years of his last solitary struggle against unyielding destiny, a meeting with George Fox could move him first to tears, and on another occasion very seasonably to laughter.[1] He sought always, and often with deep questioning, what was right and noble in every choice of action. He could not bear the stiff and dry : in all human relations, his tenderness, his humour, his fellowship were always striving to burst through. For while he aspired to heaven, he had his roots deep in earth.

Richard Cromwell's fall, May, 1659 More than a year and a half passed between the death of Oliver (September, 1658) and the Restoration of Charles II. (May, 1660). In that period, England fell into the power of generals, who like the generals of old Rome, made and unmade Governments at their will. It did not take them long to dispose of the New Protector, Oliver's eldest surviving son, " Tumbledown Dick " as he was called. One Constitution after another was set up and overthrown by the soldiers.

Oliver had ruled by civil power. Starting from the Instrument of Government, he had striven ever more earnestly, if not successfully, towards constitutional growth. But the generals had no dealings with the classes and parties whom their great predecessor had courted. Lawyers and judges, merchants and gentry, Presbyterians and Republicans were nothing to the soldiers, each striving to realise by force his own personal ambition, or some visionary reign of Christ. In its last stage the military rule contained no power of evolution or principle of settlement.

Oliver had protected property and civil peace. Strong govern-

---

" Many more words I (*Fox*) had with him (*Cromwell*), but people coming in, I drew a little back ; and as I was turning, he caught me by the hand, and with tears in his eyes, said, ' Come again to my house, for if thou and I were but an hour a day together, we should be nearer one another ' " (1654). " Whereupon I rode to his coach-side ; and some of his life-guards would have put me away, but he forbade them. So I rode by with him. . . . When we arrived at James's Park gate, I left him ; and at parting he desired me to come to his house. Next day, one of his wife's maids, whose name was Mary Saunders, came to me at my lodging, and told me her master (*Cromwell*) came to her, and said he would tell her some good news. When she asked him what it was, he told her, George Fox was come to town. She replied that was good news indeed (for she had received truth) . . . The power of the Lord God arose in me, and I was moved in it to bid him (*Cromwell*) lay down his crown at the feet of Jesus. Several times I spake to him to the same effect. Now I was standing by the table and he came and sat upon the table's side by me, and said he would be as high as I was ; and so continued speaking against the light of Christ Jesus ; and went away in a light manner " (1656), George Fox's *Journal* (ed. 1901, i., pp. 210, 332, 333).

ment by an omnipotent army had been a bad, but not the worst conceivable, form of polity. England now seemed a victim to a worse fate, the weak but violent rule of soldiers, united indeed against civilians, but divided against themselves. Skirmishes between the regiments of rival chiefs, between cavalry and infantry, between veterans and recruits, had already begun. In addition to this, a general civil war between the militia and civilians on the one hand, and the regular soldiers on the other, was on the very point of breaking out when it was prevented by the " happy Restoration ". There were several reasons why the great change took place without war : one part of the soldiers, Monk's army of occupation in Scotland, joined the party of the civilians ; the troops quartered in England were divided under different chieftains and into different factions ; many even of Lambert's section of the army shrank from plunging the country into blood, in order to establish they knew not what ; the officers had lost the love and confidence of the men by trading on their financial necessities,[1] while the King promised a full payment of arrears ; and last but not least, Monk was a strong, patriotic and unselfish man. He occupied London and declared for a " free Parliament ". The assembly freely elected under his protection called back Charles II. Though their own disbandment was certain to follow on a Restoration, the veterans yielded at the last moment to the general voice, and consented to take part in the reception of Charles into London. For, soldiers as they were, they were the very pick of Englishmen ; and fanatics if they were, they loved their country hardly less than their God. Of all that they had done for England's welfare and liberty, nothing is more to their credit than that they voluntarily laid down their power when they perceived that they had begun to abuse it.

Monk declares for a " free Parliament," March, 1660

No one will ever know how far the great reaction in sentiment was caused by Puritan supremacy, or by military rule under Cromwell, or how far it sprang up after his death to avoid permanent anarchy and immediate civil war. This only is certain, that the Restoration of Charles was necessary as the only form of government on which all parties could agree. After twenty years of national division, a consensus of opinion came about for this one act of recalling Parliament and King together, because the alternative was a new civil war without an aim. But when once the Restoration had been agreed upon in fear and doubt, a chord in men's minds snapped with long tension and sudden relief, and all, save the very few, rushed delirious into old memories and new desires. The joy of men just escaped from a fearful danger, gave electric force to the reviving passion for all that was old.

[1] Firth's *C. A.*, pp. 202-8. See p. 278 below, note. For the history of 1658-60, see Firth's *Crom.*, pp. 445-49, and Julian Corbett's *Monk*, though the effect attributed to the Portuguese incident in pp. 179-82 in the latter book is very doubtful.

Landing
of Charles
II., 25th
May, 1660 On the 25th of May the English world stood crowded on Dover beach, to see what kind of angel was this deliverer for whom they had sent. A man stepped out of the boat, whose thick, sensuous lips, dark hair and face of a type more common in Southern Europe, confessed an origin and temperament in every way the opposite to those of the English squire who had grown up among the Puritans of Huntingdon. The Mayor of Dover put the English Bible into the strange hand. He of the thick lips declared that " it was the thing that he loved above all things in the world ". The worthy Mayor was enchanted at so honest an answer, for he did not perceive that the comic spirit had landed on our coast. The wittiest company of comedians that history records had come to tread the stage for a while, as little appreciated on the whole by the English people as were the great tragedians who had played their piece and were departing, undismayed by the howling and the fury, wrapped in the dignity of self-dependent virtue, Republicans without fear, without repentance, without hope.

CHAPTER XI

THE RESTORATION EPOCH, 1660-78.

Change, the strongest son of Life.—GEORGE MEREDITH.

ON the 29th of May the King entered his capital. The new Government at once took up all its functions. Monk recommended to the King for Privy Councillors a long list of Presbyterians, which struck a momentary terror into Charles ; but the lord of the army had no ambition to be Mayor of the Palace, and acquiesced when the King selected from his Roundhead nominees only Ashley Cooper and one or two more. Charles put the real power of the Council into the hands of an inner circle, where old Cavaliers of the exile, like Ormond and Secretary Nicholas, deliberated under the presidency of Chancellor Hyde. Monk, created Duke of Albemarle, became a great Lord and courtier often in the highest employment, but gradually dropped out of the more intimate counsels of his sovereign. He was regarded to the day of his death (1670) as a great and honourable man, the father of his King and of his country.[1]

The royal Government established

Though secure in the affections of the people, the Government was not completely safe until in the autumn of 1660 the old army had received its just arrears of pay and been disbanded. Charles and Hyde did what Parliament might wisely have done in 1647 ; they paid on the nail, and the red terror walked soberly off to set up trade with the money in its pocket.[2]

The army disbanded

In Scotland there was no more resistance to the change than in England. North of the Tweed, the Restoration meant the restoration of national independence ; for a while it was regarded as a minor matter that the Presbyterian form of Church government was replaced by the Episcopalian, and that the men at the head of the State " were almost perpetually drunk ".[3] It seemed better to be ruled by Scottish drunkards than by the soberest men from England ; and if they were Episcopalians, their predecessors had been Sectaries. As symbol of the establishment of the Cavalier order of things, the great Presbyterian chieftain, Argyle, was duly executed.

Restoration in Scotland

[1] Airy, p. 111. Julian Corbett, *Monk*, pp. 192-221.
[2] The only Cromwellians not disbanded were the Coldstreams and part of the garrisons of Dunkirk and Tangier ; others were sent to fight for our allies the Portuguese against Spain (*R. H. S.*, xvii., pp. 106-10).
[3] Burnet, i., p. 220.

The two Restorations, 1660 and 1661 There were two Restorations in England. First, in 1660 were restored Parliament and King, the non-military state, and the dominance of the hereditary upper class; secondly, in 1661 was restored the persecuting Anglican Church. The first Restoration was made by the Presbyterians, the second by the Cavaliers; the first by the Convention Parliament, the second by the Cavalier Parliament. The political and social restoration fixed its roots permanently in the character and institutions of the English. The religious restoration, though substantially modified in 1689, has formed the religious and political character of the various strata of our society on lines fixed indeed, but very different from the uniform national religion contemplated either by the men of 1640 or by the men of 1661.

The Convention Parliament, April-Dec., 1660 The first, the largest, and the most lasting of the two Restorations, was the work of the free Parliament elected under Monk's protection in the turbulent spring of 1660. It was by the letter of the law no true Parliament, because the King did not summon it; on the contrary, it summoned the King. Hence, it is known as the Convention Parliament.

The social restoration, 1660 This assembly in nine months restored not only the political rule of Parliament and King, but the social rule of the upper class. In every town and village the Republicans and Democrats, who had so long governed by their self-granted charter of the " career open to talents," sought refuge in private life; while Lords and gentlemen, lawyers and parsons, and all the old world of hereditary caste and ancient custom, everywhere resumed the functions from which their Royalist or Presbyterian opinions had so long debarred the great majority. From this social restoration proceeding in every corner of England, the Cavaliers derived strength out of all proportion to what was gained by their Presbyterian allies.

The year 1660 was the triumph of Presbyterian over Sectary, of Constitutionalist over Republican, of the hereditary social order over the democratic ideal. It was these things, rather than the still dissembled triumph of Anglican over Puritan, that were symbolised in the execution done upon the bodies of the regicides, dead and alive, whereby England repudiated the one great digression of her history, and vainly sought to wipe out from the just calculation of her worth, the deeds that her sons had done without her commission, but in her name for ever. It was by the order of the Convention Parliament that the bodies of Cromwell, Bradshaw and Ireton were dug up, dragged on sledges to Tyburn, hanged in sight of the people till sunset, and buried at the gallows' foot. There, if anywhere at this hour, is " Imperial Caesar, dead and turned to clay ". Over him the English pass, day after day and generation after generation, and no longer fear priest, presbyter or King.[1]

[1] Mr. Firth (*Crom.*, p. 452) calculates that it is " where Connaught Square now stands, a yard or two beneath the street ".

So too it was by the sentence of Cavalier and Presbyterian Execu-
judges sitting together, that a dozen of the regicides suffered death. tion of
The gallows and butchery were set up in Charing Cross, in sight of the Regi-
cides,
the place before Whitehall where the scaffold had been dressed for 1660
Charles ; as the hangman cut the king-killers to pieces, their heads
and hearts were shown reeking to the people, whose shouts testified
that on this occasion they felt neither pity nor respect. Hugh
Peters had scarcely the strength to face so terrible a scene, and
came staggering on to the scaffold. But Cook the lawyer, Harrison
and the other soldiers and politicians proved worthy of their cause
and of that hour. And none died better than Sir Harry Vane (1662),
proclaiming the principles of liberty to the last ; like Peters, he had,
though no regicide, been marked for death by party vengeance.
Others fled oversea, dogged by the assassins sent after them by the
House of Stuart. Ludlow found refuge among the kindly Repub- Ludlow at
licans on the shore of Lake Geneva, where alone in Europe the Geneva
deeds in which he had played a part were not then regarded with
execration. There, in sight of the mountains as stern as his own
soul, he lived in silence for thirty years, and there by the Lake of
Calvin and of Rousseau he died, the last of the English Republicans.
Once, when the old man heard how William had delivered England,
he returned to serve the country that he loved, but even in that
year of public salvation, he was again expelled with universal horror
by Whigs and Tories, to whom his half-forgotten name suggested,
not new hopes for mankind, but an old tale of crime and tyranny
told them by their fathers. No stronger proof could be given that
the ideas of which he was the last representative had perished when
his comrades died upon the scaffold.

The regicides served a national purpose as scape-goats for other Act of In-
rebels. Their blood sealed up the past. The best opportunity that demnity.
The Land
informers and terrorists ever had in our island was fortunately Settle-
disallowed. Since the Restoration had been absolutely one of consent, ment,
and not in the least degree one of conquest, since it had been initiated 1660
by the Presbyterians under no constraint from the Cavaliers, the
Convention Parliament, consisting for the most part of men of
Roundhead families, took measures for the personal safety and even
for the financial interests of the Roundhead partisans. Here they
were supported by the wise state-craft of Charles and Hyde, who
were determined to associate the rule of the restored House of
Stuart with the sense of universal security for person and goods.
A combination of courtiers and old Parliamentarians was strong
enough to disregard the outcries of the Cavaliers, who complained
that the Act of Indemnity and Oblivion meant Indemnity for the
King's enemies and Oblivion for the King's friends. Royalists who
had suffered exile and direct confiscation of estates, recovered what
they had lost. But a far greater number, in order to pay to the

usurping Governments the heavy fines by which they had " compounded for delinquency," had been forced to sell portions of their land in a fallen market : and these obtained no compensation. As to the purchasers who continued in possession of such estates, it is not known what element in religion and politics was most strongly represented in that fortunate class ; but probably most of them had been Presbyterians, who were now about to turn Anglican for convenience, and perhaps some day to become Whig by conviction.

Members of the Independent and Republican party must upon the whole have fared less well. For it was principally they who had shown confidence in the Regicide Government by investing money in the purchase of Church and Crown lands, which were at the Restoration resumed without compensation to the purchasers. This unlucky class largely consisted of the officers of Cromwell's army. Like all others who had bought up the spoils of Church and Crown, the officers sank back to the social status whence they had striven so hard to rise. The Independent aristocracy was ruined. But in Ireland—on condition of turning Anglican—it became the landlord caste.[1]

Settlement of religion postponed in 1660 The Convention Parliament settled everything except religion. On this subject alone the dominant parties were divided. There was much discussion of " Bishop Usher's model," the compromise by which twenty years before that good man had proposed to reconcile incensed factions, on the basis of alterations in the Prayerbook, and limitations of the episcopal power by a council of Presbyters. The King chose chaplains from among the Presbyterian divines, and might probably have supported their comprehension in the National Church, if they had consented to outbid Episcopalians for his favour by an offer of toleration to Catholics. But the Lord Chancellor Hyde was even more bitter in his Anglicanism now, than when as plain member for Saltash Borough he had quarrelled with Pym over the Root-and-Branch ; Hyde saw the Cavaliers gaining strength every day as the social restoration proceeded, and laboured to put off the ecclesiastical settlement until after a new general election.

Error of the Presbyterians The Presbyterians did not foresee that a restoration in religion would follow from the restoration in society and politics. They did not know that in re-establishing squirearchy they were setting up a persecuting Anglicanism ; for the squires whom they remembered had been haters of parsons and Bishops. Nor did they suspect that in realising at last their cherished ideal of a monarch controlled by a free Parliament, they were laying firmer than Laud the foundations of an Anglican State Church ; for their recollections

---

[1] Many of the officers had, with little consideration for the interests of their men, bought up from the rank and file their " debentures," or claims on the Church and Crown lands allotted them in December, 1647, for the security of deferred pay (Firth's *C. A.*, pp. 202-8). At the Restoration they lost these lands.

of a free Parliament recalled groups of angry gentlemen shouting approval while Eliot demanded the suppression of Arminians, or while Pym declared that Prelacy had been tried and found wanting. Absorbed in hatred of the sects, the orthodox Puritans did not consider that the class for whom they were now forging power, was led by men whose religion and estates they had themselves proscribed at the close of the first Civil War,—men who for their part had not forgiven the rule of the Long Parliament, because it had been followed by the rule of the Major-Generals. The Presbyterians little suspected that in a year's time their own Church would be swept out of England for ever, while the sectaries, whom they thought to be slain by the stroke which slew the Republicans, would inherit and carry on the Puritan work.

The few divines and politicians who in 1660 represented the Presbyterian cause, were leaders without an army. The great host which had fought for England's liberties under the banner of the Puritan State Church, had now dissolved again into its component parts—the gentry to a Protestant type of the Anglican faith, the middle and lower classes to sectarianism or to religious indifference. Thanks to Cromwell, the future of the Puritan faith lay with the sects, of which Presbyterianism itself was to become one.

But the sects succeeded to this inheritance only on condition of becoming civilian. Military Republicanism, the form in which they had first secured their right to exist, was put down for ever in January, 1661. In that month the rising of the Fifth Monarchy Men gave Government the opportunity to kill off the few score of veterans who had not accepted the new order of things. The " lion sprawled its last," when after a fierce encounter the maddest of the soldiers were shot down or disarmed by the children of this world in an ale-house near Cripplegate. The panic created by this last venture of the men of war caused a furious persecution of the pacific Quakers, who were haled to prison by thousands. It also helped the return of violent reactionaries at the polling that immediately followed for the famous Cavalier Parliament. *Rising of the Fifth Monarchy Men, Jan., 1661*

The new members were " of loyal families, but young men for the most part, which being told the King he replied that was no great fault, for he would keep them till they got beards ". Charles was as good as his word. Well knowing that his people would never again give him such a Parliament, he kept it for eighteen years. These men, by the first acts of their lewd and insolent youth, gave to English religious life its perennial character, basing it on the cleavage of party and of class ; when they came to years of ambition they secured and perpetuated as custom of the country the control of the House of Commons over the direction of affairs ; and when they passed the threshold of middle age, they evolved among themselves the two national factions which the deeds of their own early *The Cavalier Parliament, 1661-May, 1661-Jan., 1679* youth had prepared, and suffered change, in all but name, from a cavalier to a Whig and Tory Parliament of the right English breed.

Character of the new English polity

The Second Restoration (1661) was politically the child of the First (1660). In May, 1661, the Cavalier squires were masters of the State, by right of election to a free Parliament, not by foreign arms or by civil war. If under the Protectorate, or during the Anarchy after Cromwell's death, any one of the dozen plots for a rising, backed by Spanish or French invasion, had placed the King's partisans in power by force of arms, their triumph could only have been rendered secure by assimilating the English monarchy and the English military system to those of the Continent. Brought back by victorious soldiers, Charles would have been absolute and militarist. But events had given his friends almost all their desire, by means of a Parliament and in despite of unconquered battalions. So the Cavaliers in 1661 were no less favourable to Parliamentary power and to local independence, no less hostile to a standing army, than the Presbyterians in 1660. But one thing of their own they added to the work of the Convention Parliament—the destruction of Puritanism. On these principles the most loyal of Parliaments built up a new political system.

No standing army

There was to be no standing army. Not the least beneficial result of Oliver's rule was that the party most favourable to Kingly power henceforth was least favourable to the instrument by which Kingly power is maintained ; no loyalist captain of militia could see a company of regulars straggling friendlessly from their bad quarters in one public-house to their grudging welcome in the next, without twinges of bitter memory and jealous fear. The rising of the Fifth Monarchy Men gave Charles the excuse to keep some hundreds of Household Guards, which he strove not without success to develop into a small army. But the Cavalier Parliament watched its every increase with alarm. Only at rare intervals, when the Houses were preparing for war, was it put on a footing to repel invasion, and on those occasions the 10,000 red-coats on Blackheath soon caused more genuine panic than the 100,000 blue-coats over the water. To resist foreign conquest, the county militia was the normal provision ; to resist a rising of London City, no force was provided at all.

Financial dependence of the Crown on Parliament

There was to be no financial independence on the part of the Crown. In the utmost intoxication of loyalty the Cavalier Parliament never consented to fix upon Charles a permanent revenue sufficient to defray the ordinary expenses of Government. On his return to England £1,200,000 a year had been settled upon him in perpetuity, but in effect not half this sum was derived from the sources assigned.[1] On little more than half a million a year, a Sully or a Frederic the Great would have found it difficult to carry on the machine of English Government. Charles was therefore compelled throughout his reign, even in time of peace, to sell the control of his policy either to the English Parliament or to the French King, except on those occasions when by some masterpiece of cunning he obtained money under false pretences from one or both of the purchasers. But never once did he venture to tread the path that had led his father to ruin, to levy unparliamentary taxes that would free him directly from all control. The excise and the new assessment of the land tax—those revolutionary expedients which Pym had introduced to fight the war—were soon found by the Cavaliers to be indispensable as the basis of the new national finance. Since the land tax fell largely on the squires, they had more interest in keeping down taxation than the nobility of continental countries where the peasants paid the " taille ".[2] The Parliament men had therefore personal as well as public motives to keep the Government close, to inquire into accounts during the Dutch wars, and to be scandalised when the money that came out of their own estates was spent by the Court on pleasures in which they were seldom invited to take a share. The supposed expensive character of the King's domestic arrangements put enmity between Court and Parliament, at a time when Puritan scruples were as much out of fashion in one as in the other. Yet modern investigation of the Royal accounts has revealed that there was no truth in the general belief that a large part of the national revenue was poured into the lap of the King's mistresses.[3]

There was to be no more pride of clergy. The Church passed out of the hands of King and into the hands of Parliament. The Court of High Commission was not revived. The Bishops who had formerly been allowed to persecute by favour of the King in despite of the House of Commons, were now allowed to persecute by favour of the House of Commons in despite of the King. Owing to this change in the nature of her dependence, the Church was less insolent than in the time of Laud. Laud's attempt to revive the mediæval pretensions of the priest in society had not been a success. Made wiser by the sectarian and radical interregnum, the parson was careful never again to set himself up against the squire, while the squire vowed he would never again fall foul of the parson.[4]

Dependence of the Church on Parliament

---

[1] *Owens College Historical Essays*, 1902, pp. 399-401. *Beginnings of the National Debt and Calendar of Treasury Books*, by W. A. Shaw. And see App. E. below.

[2] It is none the less true that as the Expenses of Government increased from the Restoration onwards, the two Houses of Landowners unduly shifted the burden of taxation off the land, beginning from the day when they put on to the Excise the redemption of the Feudal Dues, 1660.

[3] Shaw, *Calendar of Treasury Books*, 1660-7, p. xxvi.

[4] G. (*C. W.*), iii., pp. 136, 137.

No *droit*
adminis-
tratif

There was to be no more *droit administratif*. The abolition of the Star Chamber held good ; and the Privy Council, even in the exercise of its remaining functions, was no longer an irresponsible organ of the King's will. The result of the Civil Wars had rendered it impotent to override either the political decrees of the Commons, or the administrative indolence of local authorities. It soon found that it could not set aside statutes by proclamation ; and it no longer attempted to enforce the Poor Law on recalcitrant magistrates and parishes with the strict inquisition that had been so beneficent in the days of Charles I.[1] Critics of Government policy can hardly be said to have had any liberty of person or speech guaranteed to them under the old Tudor and Stuart *régime*, except in the case of defined privileges, uncertainly enjoyed, within the walls of Parliament ; but after the Restoration men no longer talked in whispers. The principles of the Habeas Corpus Act of 1679 were already to some extent recognised in 1661, although, owing to occasional violations by Clarendon and Danby, they still needed to be fenced round by stricter legislation. The law of the land judged impartially all cases between officials and private citizens, and there was no longer a prerogative law and a special court to which Government could, as in other lands and in earlier times, appeal.

How England appeared to the French Ambassador

" This Government has a monarchical appearance because there is a King, but at bottom it is very far from being a monarchy." So in 1664 wrote De Cominges, the French Ambassador in England, to Louis XIV. The emissary of returning civilisation, sent over to an island so long cut off by unmentionable deeds from the knowledge of polite communities, rendered his master in these early years of the restored kingship an account of our uncouth institutions, which informed and prepared the French Foreign Office for its subsequent astute interference in English politics. "The members of Parliament," wrote De Cominges, " are not only allowed to speak their mind freely, but also to do a number of surprising, extraordinary things, and even to call the highest people to the Bar ". Power and energy dwelt in the Commons, who, when summoned to hear the King's speech, " rushed tumultuously into the Upper House, as the mob does in the hall of audience at the Paris Parliament, when the ushers have called ". Indeed, to the suave courtier of the Louvre, the whole of this mad country seemed to whirl in a "tumultuous rush ". In spite of the Clarendon Code, the capital was buzzing with the strangest sectaries—*Kakers*, Anabaptists and *millénaires*. Persons of all ranks publicly discussed affairs of State. The Thames boatmen " want the *mylords* to talk " about politics as they row them to Westminster stairs. Riots were of such frequent occurrence, and the Government was so powerless to suppress them, that even the punctilious Ambassador, whose special business it was to maintain the dignity and

---

[1] See pp. 18, 19, 23, 24 above, and Appendix B below.

precedence of the French Crown, consented to the periodical breaking
of his windows as custom of the country. All was free, vigorous,
barbaric life. England, emancipated by the Great Rebellion, was
" rushing tumultuously," in a manner very different from the ordered
march of the dragooned and priest-ridden civilisation of the Grand
Monarch. That the day would ever come when France herself would
" rush tumultuously," never occurred either to Louis or to his
servant.[1]

By the Restoration settlement the landowners bore rule in The
England, as against Puritan and soldier, Bishop and King. The Clarendon
Cavalier squires, however loyal they might be in profession or even passed,
in feeling, were so enchanted by the sweets of power tasted during 1661-65
the early years of their Parliament, that they set themselves steadily
to maintain and enlarge their own supremacy, and to enforce upon
all other classes the type of religion and politics with which it was
now associated. This was the policy afterwards known as Toryism ;
till the rise of the Whigs fifteen years later there was no one to oppose
Tory supremacy, except the King and the Catholics of the Palace.
By the " Clarendon Code " the squires closed the ranks of their class,
imposing on all the shibboleths of Anglicanism, which few, at any
rate of the upper ranks of society, ventured to refuse.

In the first five years of its hot youth the Cavalier Parliament
passed the great Code, called in history after the name of Chancellor
Hyde, now Earl of Clarendon—those Penal Laws which broke for
ever the pretensions of Puritanism to political supremacy, reduced
the quantity and purified the quality of its religious influence, confined its social sphere to the middle and lower classes, and created
the division of England into Church and Dissent.

By the Corporation Act (1661) the membership of the municipal
bodies who ruled the towns and usually controlled the elections of
their Parliamentary representatives, was confined to those who would
receive the Communion by the rites of the Church of England.

By the Act of Uniformity (1662) 2,000 Puritan clergy were
expelled from livings in the Established Church, for refusing to
assert their " unfeigned consent and assent " to everything in the
Prayer-book.

By the Conventicle Act (1664) attendance at meetings for religious rites, other than those of the Established Church, was punished
by imprisonment for the first and second offence, and transportation
for the third, on pain of death if the criminal returned.

By the Five Mile Act (1665) no clergyman or schoolmaster was
to come within five miles of a city or corporate town, unless he
declared that he would not " at any time endeavour any alteration

---

[1] *A French Ambassador at the Court of Charles II.*, Jusserand, 1892, pp., 99,
100, 104, 115, 144, 146.

of Government either in Church or State ". As the Puritan congregations were principally seated in the towns, the great body of dissenters were hereby cut off from even private education or domestic encouragement in their faith. The Act must have hastened the great decline in the numbers of Puritanism and the consequent decay of religious zeal in England, which was so evident when the century closed. And perhaps it had a worse effect upon educational progress than anything the Puritans ever did.

The Clarendon Code enforced
These terrible laws were not left suspended, a mere threat to restrain activity of propaganda, as the yet more terrible laws against Catholics had been suspended by the action of Charles I. Under his son, Parliament had power to insist that the statutes which it framed should be executed without Royal mercy or Court favour. Until the Revolution of 1689, with a few brief intervals, the Clarendone Code was vigorously enforced. Its execution was entrusted to the Justices of Peace, and of that body the most violent members became, by a natural process of selection, the principal agents of violent laws. In each county a few magistrates, who were filled with the bitterest rancour against their late oppressors, made revenge the chief duty of their office. Under their patronage there was room for an increase in the numbers, enterprise and professional spirit of the tribe of paid informers, who, when the party strife stirred up by this persecution took new unhappy forms, only needed the example of Oates to rise from audacity to genius of conception, to transfer their activity into a new political atmosphere, and to trim with each shrieking blast in the hurricane of rage and fear. Some magistrates spent a good part of their lives surprising midnight conventicles ; trapping teachers and clergymen who had strayed out of bounds ; crowding the plague-stricken gaols with hundreds of priests and prophets, and thousands of men and women ; creating day by day the martyrology of dissent, and the political tradition that has handed down through long generations of English Puritans an attitude of vigilant criticism and protest towards the powers that rule society and the State.

Alteration in character of Presbyterianism
Thus the Presbyterian Church was hurled down into the common clay of other sects, and compounded therewith under the heel of the Cavaliers. In politics, the distinction of Presbyterian from Sectary disappears ; and even in religion, the Presbyterian's distinguishing mark of orthodoxy gave way after a generation of company with the heretics ; at the beginning of the eighteenth century the Unitarian movement made its home in what had once been the most dogmatic of all the Protestant faiths. Presbyterianism, in the old sense of the word, was dead. Indeed, except to a few divines, that word had never in England meant more than an artificial organisation of Puritanism with a view to capturing the Established Church. When that attempt was finally abandoned, Puritanism took the free congregational forms more natural to its English genius.

The fundamental cause of the Anglican triumph was economic Social causes of the Code
and social. The Church systems of Presbyterian and Independent
had this in common, that they were both democratic. Presbyterianism required an atmosphere of comparative equality among the
congregation, and an eldership chosen from the middle class. This
was uncongenial to the semi-feudal life of the English village. In the
economic and social history of England the squire was still in the
ascendant, the yeoman freeholder was about to decline, and the
agricultural labourer could not, like the Scottish peasant, rise to the
height of the argument of human equality, and attain through a
democratic Church to self-reliance and self-respect. The complete
failure of the Presbyterian, and the part failure of the congregational
system in the English village, perpetuated the aristocratic rule of the
squire and his dependents, which did so much to depress English
rural life and to drive so many of the best men to the more liberal
atmosphere of the towns.

The permanent result of the Clarendon Code was to prepare the Social effects of the Code
way for a most important feature of modern times, " the strict and
remarkable influence of class on religious observance in England ".[1]
The Puritan gentry, unwilling to forfeit their political rights and
social status, hastened to conform to the established religion ; the
local chiefs of the Whig party were afterwards drawn from the
numerous families up and down the country who had chosen this
unheroic course. These men never again attempted either to destroy
or to secede from the Anglican Church, but only to restrain her
power of persecuting their political supporters. But in the middle
and lower classes, although many conformed solely to avoid ruin,
there was found a large body, led by a devoted band of ministers,
that refused to abandon the Puritan worship. Though some crossed
the seas, the majority remained to endure for long years the bitterest
persecution. If Charles I. had triumphed sword in hand, they could
only have escaped by flight to America from an Anglican absolutism
really and finally established. But absolutism had fallen, and their
faith in Parliamentary institutions was not destroyed by the elections
of 1661. They confidently waited the day when some ambitious
statesman, playing for power at Westminster, would voice their
grievances and bid for their support. Persecution under a Cavalier
Parliament was, so long as it lasted, more thorough than persecution
under the vexed and straitened monarchy of Charles I. ; the Bishops,
with their Church Courts and officers, had not harried Nonconformists
with half the regularity which the squires were able to ensure, by
use of the more formidable machine of local administration and
national justice. The present under Clarendon was worse than the
past under Laud. But the future was now full of hope. For under

---

[1] Chas. Booth, *Life and Labour in London : Religious Influences*, vol. vii.,
p. 47.

the new *régime* it was only a matter of time before an oppressed but influential section of the community could make its weight felt in the even balance of a free party system.

Dissent was strong among the merchants and shopkeepers; indeed the injury done to trade by the ruin and terror spread among them under the Clarendon Code, became a stock argument for Toleration. If Presbyterianism was strongest among the richer merchants, other forms of dissent were rife in the lower-middle and working classes. The secular and anti-Puritan reaction in the higher ranks was less marked among small traders and workmen. The Quakers endured their martyrdom or fled to America; and the books which Bunyan wrote in Bedford gaol represented religion to thousands of the poor. Thus the Church of England, while she enfolded all the genuine piety of the Protestant upper class, and the unnumbered host of indifferents of all classes who had their statutable Church duties to fulfil, put outside her borders the largest sections of religious enthusiasts.

Puritanism leaves its mark on the laity   Yet Puritanism left deep marks on the laity of the Established Church. In the reign of Charles II. the whole people, Whigs and Tories, were passionately Protestant. The altar was again moved to the East; but the ritual movement of Laud made but little further progress. To the devout Englishman, much as he might love the Prayer-book service and hate the Dissenters, the core of religion was the life of family prayer and Bible study, which the Puritans had for a hundred years struggled not in vain to make the custom of the land. The self-restrained and melancholy strength of individual purpose which armed the English to surpass all nations in economic and industrial enterprise, the struggle towards purity, the deep and continuous affections which freed and ennobled family life, these habits of body and mind were not wholly cast aside by the people, whatever might be the case with their governors at Whitehall.[1] The defects of the Puritans survived with their qualities, and their sad Sabbath became the Englishman's Sunday. Even when the passions of the hour and the policy of the State were united to restore all things Anglican, the people did not choose to make the very small effort that would then have sufficed to recover their day of pleasure and recreation, but continued to offer up to an ascetic ideal the weekly sacrifice of joys deliberately forgone.

Meanwhile, in the ancient churches where Presbyterian and Baptist had lately debated knotty points of regeneration before bewildered audiences of rustics, the restored clergy preached week after week, and year after year against rebels and Dissenters. Their

---

[1] See a most interesting opinion as to the Puritan influence on industrial development and family life, in Professor Marshall's *Principles of Economics* (ed. 1891), pp. 34-36.

frequent and unanswered denunciations at length sank some way
into the English mind. Yet on the benches close under the pulpit,
where the families of yeomen sat with decent pride, and in most
parts of the town congregations, there were many who while they
listened with half-approval, were still half-Puritan at heart. Without the help of these Churchmen the Whig party could not have
been formed at a time when active Dissenters enjoyed but few
political rights.

But in the upper class the proportion of these conformists with
Puritan tendencies was not large, and the number of actual Dissenters was negligible. The Clarendon Code and the tyranny of
social custom left no place for a Puritan squire. The type of manorhouse religion which had supplied England with Eliots, Hampdens
and Cromwells, was not seen again until the time when the Evan-
gelicals raised up within the borders of the Church herself another
Puritan gentry to rule India and to free the slave.

The desertion of the whole upper class, and the legal prohibition
of Nonconformist schools and colleges, injured the natural development of Puritan thought, by divorcing it from many sources of
culture which had been open to it in the days of Milton. But,
if the Clarendon Code forcibly cut off the Puritans from learning
and literature, it drove them into a situation where their moral
service to the country was enhanced. A large body of the most
conscientious and enthusiastic men became political critics and
social reformers by profession, for their own wrongs sharpened their
sensibility to the wrongs of others, and their own position never
permitted them to fall into the sleep of those to whom the world is
an easy bed.

The division of the religious world into Church and Dissent *Free-*
made freedom of thought a possibility for the future. The English *thought*
could not be argued into toleration by their reason, but they could *saved by*
be forced into it by their feuds. In a country where the proportion *the*
of really devout persons is so large and their spontaneous activity *Church*
so great, it would have been dangerous if all the principal forces *and*
of religion had been accumulated in one State Church. If the zeal *Dissent*
of the Anglicans who enforced the Clarendon Code had been united
to the zeal of the Presbyterians who passed the Blasphemy Laws,
English popular religion would have become hardly less intolerant
and far less assailable than the hierarchy which Voltaire undermined ;
for in England no Voltaire could have attacked Christianity with
any chance of political success. Fortunately, a settlement was made
under which the persecutors would rage unceasingly against each
other. The rivalry of Church and Dissent forced both sides to over-
look, to tolerate, and sometimes even to court, any third party.
The Dissenters needed deliverance from oppressive laws too much
to inquire whether Shaftesbury or Charles Fox were in a state of

grace ; the Church made no attempt to invigilate over the proceedings of the Royal Society, and could not effectually silence
Hobbes, when Lords of the Council were plotting with mob leaders
to marshal against her the rallied forces of fanaticism ; nor, in an
age of milder measures, could she long oppose herself to Darwin,
in the midst of another flood of political Dissent. Thus the laws
of the Cavalier Parliament, which were meant to dragoon all England into one religion, have helped to secure freedom for a hundred
religions, and a thousand ways of thought.

Growth
of indiff-
erence
and of
rational-
ism

If, however, the new era had wrought nothing more than a
political and social redistribution of the old religious forces that
had met upon Naseby Field, intellectual freedom could not have
been secured solely by the mechanical division of Dissenters from
Churchmen. But a new spirit was abroad. Secular feeling was
now sometimes to be found in the provinces, while in the capital
it was already a fashion and almost a creed. Among the politicians
of Westminster, the statesmen and courtiers of Whitehall, and the
wits who set the tone in the coffee-houses where all met on common
ground, the reaction against the Puritans took the form, not of
Anglican devotionalism, but of indifference to religion. Of all the
statesmen who guided the fortunes of the new era, scarcely one was
highly religious, except Clarendon, whose ideas dated from before
the deluge ; and perhaps half were suspected of greater or less degrees of infidelity. Buckingham and Rochester, Halifax and Temple,
Sidney, Essex and Peterborough lightly bore imputations of a kind
which in an earlier age would have been enough to destroy the
political career of Pym, Hampden or Falkland. And it is well told
that Shaftesbury, who in old days had sat a keen-eyed politician
among the Barebone Saints, replied to a fair inquirer, " Madam,
wise men are of but one religion ".—Which one was that ?—" Madam,
wise men never tell."

The
Royal
Society

Much of this fashionable scepticism was mere froth, and for the
most part foul, left by the spent waves of strange events and terrible
emotions now moaning at low tide far out at sea. But the deep
had cast up its treasures also. The secular reaction among the
libertines of life and politics at the capital would not have outlasted the generation that had suffered under Oliver, if it had not
become joined to the more solid and respectable influence of a
scientific movement springing up in the same time and place. The
Royal Society was Royal in more than name. It was closely allied,
not indeed with the politics, but with the social life of the Court.
Charles I. had extended an intelligent patronage to art, but in an
age too soon, when English painters were inferior and the English
art public small ; the Puritans had sold away his Titians and
Vandykes for money down. Charles II. extended an intelligent
patronage to science when the time was ripe ; bigotry could never

exile nor years efface the native achievements of Newtonian discovery; while the idea of the rule of law in the universe slowly
penetrated downwards from class to class, remoulding by unopposed
and unsuspected influence the unconscious forms of thought, and
even of religion itself.

In the Restoration era the common people still firmly believed Persecu-
in the presence of witchcraft. On one occasion at the Exeter tion of
Assizes the clamour of the populace for the condemnation of two declines
old women was so terrible that an outbreak was expected if the
thirst for blood had not been gratified. But the movement no
longer found leaders among either the dominant clergy or the
governing class. The witch-hunt had been set on foot by James
I. himself, backed by a credulous Parliament, Magistracy and
Bench. The sport had reached its height during the Civil War
under the Presbyterian rule, but had been mitigated under that
of the Independents. Now the Puritan influence was reduced,
and the restored Anglican clergy showed much less of the abominable zeal that " would not suffer a witch to live " ; while men of the
professional and official classes were rapidly getting rid of the grosser
superstitions which their ancestors had handed down unchallenged
from the ages of barbarism. No longer in the reign of Charles II.,
as in the reign of his grandfather, would a high law-officer of the
Crown soberly discuss over the supper-table whether the best way
to cure disease among horses were to burn one of them alive, or to
roast its heart on a spit in the presence of a witch.[1] The Judges
on Circuit, who in previous reigns had thrown the weight of magistracy and learning on to the side of panic and superstition, now
sometimes laboured to obtain acquittals by exposing the flimsy
evidence, such as in former times had passed muster with courts
where every soul present believed in witchcraft. But the task
required caution as well as skill. For if once the country jurymen
detected a London sceptic on the bench, they would cry, " ' This
Judge hath no religion, for he doth not believe in witches,' and
so, to show they have some, hang the poor wretches ". Under
these conditions, without controversy and almost without notice,
the persecution of witches died out of England—and its death was
the first triumph of the humanising spirit of Rationalism.[2]

Thus the English Protestant world, which had long ago ceased The idea
to expect miracles from God, gradually ceased to expect them from of law in
the devil. The principles of Descartes now first began to get a hold the Union English thought, and gentlemen like Roger North, who had verse
studied his philosophy at Cambridge, began to " aim at a system of
nature upon the Cartesian or rather mechanical principles, believing

---

[1] P. 44 above, note. *Camden Misc.*, x., p. 69.
[2] Lecky's *Rationalism*, i. (ed. 1866), pp. 108-37. *Life of Lord Keeper Guilford*,
sects. 191, 192, and of *Roger North*, sects. 163, 164.

all the common phenomena of nature might be resolved into them ".[1]
The influence of the new spirit was felt even in religious circles.
Though the rural clergy continued to urge their fanatical crusade
against fanatics, some of the great divines of the capital, who
preached in the classic temples which Wren constructed on the site
of the old Gothic Churches, proclaimed the principles of Toleration,
while some waged war on the immorality of Court and stage, and
others began to appropriate the idea that divine power was mani-
fested through unbreakable law, and was best argued by the evidence
of design.   It has been well said of Tillotson that " after the orgies
of the Saints and the orgies of the sinners, he made sanity acceptable to a whole generation ".[2]   The same Rationalism which was
driving some Presbyterians to deny the Trinity, was driving some
leaders of the Church of England to inaugurate the ideas and spirit
that were to dominate the eighteenth century.   The conception
that regular law was the guiding principle of all things, began to
affect speculation, literature and politics.

The history of the years 1661 to 1678, though crowded with a
sequence of famous events and a mob of brilliant men, is yet so
lacking in unity and so barren of decisive result, that it has most
significance when regarded as prologue to the revolutionary strife
of parties and religions which raged in this island from 1678 to 1689,
and decided the future of England and of Europe.   The ministry
of Clarendon and the Cabal, the Dutch wars and the Triple Alliance,
the Dover Treaty and the Test Act, the conversion of James and
the marriage of Mary, Danby's tenure of office and Shaftesbury's
commencement of opposition—these were events which served only
to neutralise each other and to create a state of tension such as men
can seldom endure without breaking at last into madness.

The
Cavaliers
of the
Restora-
tion

The history of this period, which is essentially one of intrigue,
was conditioned by the moral atmosphere of Whitehall.   The
difference between the old Cavalier Court and the new was apparent
from the very first moment of the Restoration.   On the very night
of the Happy Return, the restored wanderer showed his gratitude
to heaven by taking Barbara Villiers for the ruler of himself and
his Court.   Except Clarendon and a few of the older men, no party
at Whitehall resented on moral grounds her spendid and outrageous
domination, or the presence of whole suites of ladies with whom
she shared the King's favours.   The Puritans, in revenge for the
civil disabilities which they had legally imposed on all Anglicans,
found themselves excluded for ever from the governing class, and
from fashionable Society ; and as a result of the similar disabilities
which they had practically imposed on all except rigidly moral

[1] Roger North's *Autobiography*, sects. 21, 26.
[2] Dowden, *Puritan and Anglican*, p. 336.

persons or hypocrites, they saw Society and government given over for one generation at least to open profligacy. But Restoration vice was not merely a reaction against the rule of the censorious ; it was also due to the folly of successive Puritan Governments, in striking the homes of the Cavaliers with fiscal penalties. The resulting poverty had prevented the resumption of the old manner of life when the war was over. The family life of the rural gentry, that had produced generation after generation of Verneys, Hydes and Hampdens, had now for twenty years been broken up ; its traditions were therefore unknown to the younger generation. While his sisters had been living in a corner of the sacked manorhouse under the charge of the steward, the heir had been seeking bread for his mouth among the bullies and sharpers of low life in Dutch port towns, or sponging on the vicious nobility of France and Spain. If youth and obscurity had enabled him to remain at home, without parents or without money, he was often brought up among the grooms, with no instruction in morals and dignity of conduct beyond salt stories of Puritan hypocrisy, in which the defeated veterans found solace and revenge. Whether spent at home or abroad, his youth had been necessarily divorced from the education, religion and morals of his own land. It is not then surprising that when at the Restoration " debauchery was loyalty, gravity rebellion," there were many loyal courtiers and few grave. Outside the Court it is probable, though there is less evidence on the subject, that a temporary decline in morals took place throughout the upper class.

The man who presided over the Court was destined in the last years of his life to prove himself one of the greatest politicians who ever succeeded in the struggle for power in England. But it was only when driven to defend himself against dangers incurred by the intriguing but lazy policy of the first fifteen years of his reign, that Charles at the last bestirred himself to use his true political ability ; and even then, half his art was to prevent his adversaries from discovering till too late that he had any political ability at all. The consideration that constantly overruled all his other plans, was how to avoid business ; till at last the day came when he had to consider how to avoid the loss of his kingly prerogatives. " It was resolved generally by others," said one who knew him well, " whom he should have in his arms, as well as whom he should have in his councils. Of a man who was so capable of choosing, he chose as seldom as any man that ever lived." His love had " as little mixture of the seraphic part as ever man had ".[1] But of all his mistresses only one or two at a time presided over the Court and enjoyed control over affairs of State. Throughout the early years of the reign none of them seriously challenged the political rights of

Character and Court of Charles II.

---

[1] Halifax, *Character of Charles II.*

Barbara Villiers, Countess of Castlemaine. But it was necessary to introduce a Queen, not indeed to preside in any real sense over Castlemaine's Court, but for purposes of State to bear legitimate children. Catherine of Braganza, an unfortunate little woman from a Portuguese cloister, was brought over, married and held up to ridicule by her husband, who compelled her in spite of tears and fainting fits to employ the Castlemaine as her own lady of the bed-chamber. But she had her revenge : she failed to fulfil the purpose for which she had been made Queen, and so laid up for her husband an old age of the thing he most hated—business. The game of dark intrigue, in which the great forces of English Protestantism and continental Catholicism fought for England through all the next generation, turned on the fact that Charles's wife bore him no children, so that his brother James Duke of York remained heir to the throne.

Marriage treaty with Portugal negotiated, 1661-62 A shrewd combination of English designs on the trade of tropical Empires, with French designs on the sovereignty of European Provinces, had sent our statesmen to seek this unlucky Queen in a nunnery of Portugal. France had brought the era of her Cardinals to a victorious close by the treaty of the Pyrenees (1659), which ended her twenty-five years' war with the Spanish Crown, and left her a short breathing space of peace before her career of aggrandisement under Louis XIV. The one danger to the policy of France was that in this breathing space her ally Portugal might be over-whelmed. In time of war France had easily protected the House of Braganza in its secession from the Empire of the Philips ; but who would now save the rebel kingdom from the retarded vengeance of Spain ? Louis XIV. saw the man for his purpose in the King of England looking for a wife. The first and least nefarious use of French influence and gold in the counsels of Charles, was the nego-tiation of the Anglo-Portuguese marriage treaty by Louis. The bargain proved a good one for England. A little money and a few troops sufficed to preserve Portugal independent, without seriously embroiling us with Spain. In return, we obtained an alliance which remained a nearly constant condition of politics for more than a century and a half ; in days when we had many enemies, the Portuguese trade and harbours remained open to our manufactures and ships of war, and proved in our later wars with Louis XIV. and Napoleon a basis secured upon the sea for operations against the continental armies of France. The Portuguese also conceded to us, as Catherine's dowry, two colonial possessions, Tangier and Bombay. In the outpost of Christendom, among the barren moun-tains round Tangier, the King kept up regiments of foot whose existence was regarded as a menace by Parliament and nation, and who finally were indeed brought home to practise on the peasant followers of Monmouth cruelties learnt in long warfare with the

Moors.[1] The occupation of Tangier as a naval base was the sign that the Restoration Government would continue Cromwell's policy of sending our ships into the Mediterranean.[2] Not less valuable was the trading island of Bombay. Bombay, Madras, and the station on the Hoogli, together formed for us the three points of the triangle whence the East Indian Company was one day to advance over the length and breadth of India.

As a set-off to its new responsibilities and burdens at Tangier, Government broke up Cromwell's Dunkirk garrison and sold the place—not indeed back to Spain, but on to France, the broker of the marriage treaty. The sale, though unpopular among the City merchants, aroused no general agitation at the time, for the Restoration Government was still popular and prosperous.[3]

Sale of Dunkirk, 1662

The four years of peace and retrenchment that ensued on the fall of Cromwellian imperialism were naturally a period of commercial recovery and enterprise ; this movement was fostered by the interest which Prince Rupert and the Duke of York took in merchant adventure along Hudson's Bay and the Guinea coast. The patronage extended to the most pushing commercial explorers by the prominent men at Court recalled the reign of Elizabeth ; while the state of private warfare in time of public peace which in those days had existed between the English and Spanish merchants, was renewed between the English and the Dutch. The Dutch seized the ships of our African and East Indian Companies, and stirred up the native populations to drive us from their lands. The English landed a force and seized the New Netherland colony in America (1664), which they rechristened New Jersey and New York. The merchants of both nations grew tired of peace on such terms ; Charles and his brother hated the Republican Government of Holland, which kept their relatives of the House of Orange from enjoying monarchical power ; and the Republican Government hoped by successful maritime warfare to outbid the military faction by which the Orange pretensions were upheld. Thus both Governments, and both peoples, were responsible for the official declaration of war between England and Holland in March, 1665.

[1] It is curious to remark that " Kirke's Lambs " (the Second or Queen's) was originally composed in large part of the old Cromwellian regiments who had beaten the Spaniards in Flanders (*R. H. S.*, xvii., p. 108. *Hist. Records of British Army* (1837), *2nd Foot*, p. 2). Some old sergeant may have served both at Dunkirk and at Sedgemoor. If so, he had seen great changes in the " tone " of the regiment, though not in its fighting qualities. The bad character of the soldiers when they returned from Tangier on its abandonment in 1683, had been particularly developed by the character of the last governor, Kirke (see, besides Macaulay, Corbett, chaps. xxiv., xxv.).

[2] Commercially Tangier was valueless. But before our occupation of Gibraltar (1704) it would perhaps have been dangerous to allow any other power to occupy Tangier, and so close the entrance to the Mediterranean, to the command of which we now aspired (see Corbett, ii., pp. 7-10, 110-13, and for the expert contemporary opinions of Mr. Love and Sir W. Temple, see Grey, viii., pp. 14, 15, 18, 19).   [3] Burnett, i., pp. 303-4, note by Mr. Airy.

The
second
Dutch
war,
1665-67
The second Dutch war (1665-67) resembled the first in the size and character of the combatants. It was another battle of giants. If the victory of England was less decisive than in Blake's war, this was due to administrative corruption and shortage of war supplies for political reasons on shore, rather than to any falling off in fighting quality at sea. The great battle of the Four Days, as its name suggests, was a marvel of physical endurance and courage in both fleets, and was famous, especially on the English side, for the discipline, regularity and skill with which the whole line executed the orders of the Admirals. The Dutch Captains were perhaps the better sailors, and they often surpassed in deeds of daring. But they were less trained to common action, and if some excelled, some few fell short of their duty. The reason of this difference is not far to seek. The traditions of the Dutch navy were developed almost entirely out of the merchant service, those of the English by a combination of maritime and military ideas. In the second Dutch war " Oliver's Captains " were sent to sea again.

Three
classes
of naval
officers
There were in fact three elements among the Captains of the Restoration navy. First, ignorant and incompetent young men of fashion who had begged or bought commissions at Whitehall. Secondly, the " tarpaulins," or old sea-dogs, who lived and died at sea, and knew the management of a ship in all weathers and on every coast. These two classes were mutually exclusive. But there was a third class, whose existence has sometimes been overlooked in history, perhaps because it is merged with the tarpaulins at one end and the favourites at the other. This third class consisted of men who had seen military service on land, but who adapted themselves to sea warfare, and helped the tarpaulins to fight the battles and evolve the traditions of the English navy.[1]

King,
Parliament and
the war
The cause of our less marked success in the second Dutch war, was the want of one political authority controlling all departments of the executive, and commanding all sources of taxation. England was richer in 1665 than in 1654, but she was no longer a milch cow for the purposes of Government. Complete accord between Parliament and King was the condition of effectual war supply under the political system established at the Restoration, and although King and Parliament were equally anxious to humble the enemy, they fell out with each other in the course of the struggle, for reasons of temperament rather than of policy. Charles was lazy and spendthrift ; the Commons were interfering and suspicious. These faults aggravated one another. The more lazy and spendthrift the Commons found Charles to be, the more interfering and suspicious they themselves became ; they voted money in large sums, but voted it too late, after long debates and recriminations. Many of the sources of taxation, especially the King's fixed revenues, were

---

[1] Mahan, *Sea Power*, pp. 125-30. Corbett, i., pp. 181-94.

bringing in scarcely half what was estimated ; this fact, not then fully realised, added to the difficulties of an incompetent War Ministry, and to the rage of a suspicious Assembly. Charles, whenever there was not money enough to go round, preferred that his seamen rather than his mistresses should lack ; and the Commons again could only mark their disapproval of this choice by further delaying their vote of supply, to call for inquiry and appropriation at the very crisis of the war.[1]

The result was understood and deplored by a few excellent public servants, who in spite of the inefficiency of their colleagues in the Admiralty, in spite of their own low standard in handling public money, and in spite of the disheartening political conditions, did not a little to reform naval institutions in the course of this extraordinary reign. Pepys, who was the best judge of the matter in the country, declared that the personal interest taken by the King and the Duke of York in naval affairs had restored the strength of the fleet, which the Protectorate in its last years of bankruptcy had allowed to decline once more. But Pepys also attributed the ill-success of the war itself to the habits of the royal brothers. They " mind their pleasures and nothing else," so that " we must be beaten ". When pressing letters arrived from the dockyards or the fighting fleets, Charles might be out walking at four and a half miles an hour, or idling in bed, in the tennis-court, in the dissection-room, with Lady Castlemaine, or in any retreat but the council chamber. If at last he was caught and brought into council, he played with his dogs and let the others talk unheeded. The war administration fell out of gear, and precious days and weeks slipped idly by at Chatham and Portsmouth, while Charles " employed his lips about the Court," or the officials of the Exchequer waited for the money to come in.

When the head of the administration would only work by fits and starts, when the war-chest was tardily filled and dishonestly emptied, contracts could not be executed, and the sailors' wages got twenty to fifty months in arrear. Towards the end of the war the unpaid crews ran riot in London streets. In June, 1667, as the negotiations for peace were far advanced, Government laid up the ships, for want of money to keep the men on board. De Ruyter sailed up the Thames and burnt a portion of the fleet where it lay in the Medway. An attack on London was expected, the city militia were under arms, and men sent their families and money out of town for safety. The plague and the fire had lately taught them to expect portentous calamities as natural and likely events. It was everywhere said that the Court had sold England to the papists, that a French army was about to land, and the general

The Dutch in the Medway, June, 1667

---

[1] *Owens College Historical Essays*, Shaw, pp. 392-401. Pepys, 31st Dec., 1666 7th Jan., 24th April, 1667.

massacre of Protestants to begin at last. Thus fear betrayed the real thought of the nation, that it was not the Protestant Dutch who were the worst enemy. In that hour of panic and disgrace, patriotism was less strong than mutual distrust and indignation with Government. Many of the brave men who had fought the battle of the Four Days and burnt the Dutch shipping in " Flie harbour " the year before, refused to stir a finger to save our ships from destruction in the Medway, until their tickets of arrears were cashed by the Admiralty officials. From the decks of the victorious Dutch vessels English deserters were heard talking in their mother-tongue, shouting messages to their friends on shore, and boasting that whereas in the King's service they had fought for tickets, in the Dutch service they fought for dollars.[1]

The Treaty of Breda, 3rd July, 1667

There was nothing to be done but to conclude the peace. The English plenipotentiaries at Breda ceded the still outstanding points of dispute. The treaty was a compromise, more disgraceful to the English than to the Dutch, because of the events that had hastened its signature, but not on account of its terms. We acquired from Holland Delaware, New Jersey and New York. These additions to our Empire were not at the time regarded as outweighing the cession of Poleroon, because Europeans had not then learnt by the experience of centuries the immensely superior value of white men's territory over tropical stations. But, in the light of subsequent events, we can see that in the history of British settlement in the United States, the Breda Treaty takes the next place to the planting of Virginia and the landing of the Pilgrim Fathers ; for now, joining the Puritans of New England to the Royalist slave-owners of the South, stretched a third group of English Colonies. These " Middle Colonies " were inhabited partly by the Dutch population, soon reconciled to the new flag by the tact and statesmanship of Governor Nicolls, who refused to establish British race ascendancy or to interfere with the Dutch language and institutions ; they were also rapidly filled up by fresh floods of immigrants from Old and New England, and from the Protestant populations of the Continent. In the twenty years of Puritan supremacy at home, as many persons perhaps had returned from New to Old England as had gone out from Old to New. At the Restoration, individual clergy and Republican leaders took refuge in the Northern Colonies, but with no large number of followers. Under a Parliamentary system the mass of Puritans elected to stay in England, for they could still hope to win toleration in the end. But since that hope, though not eventually disappointed, was long deferred, the Clarendon Code soon began to drive away many, especially Quakers, to the new Middle Colonies. At the same

The Middle Colonies

---

[1] Pepys, 31st Oct., 1665 ; 8th and 19th Dec., 1666 : 14th-17th June, 1667. *E. H. R.*, xii., pp. 17-66, 679-710 (J. R. Tanner).

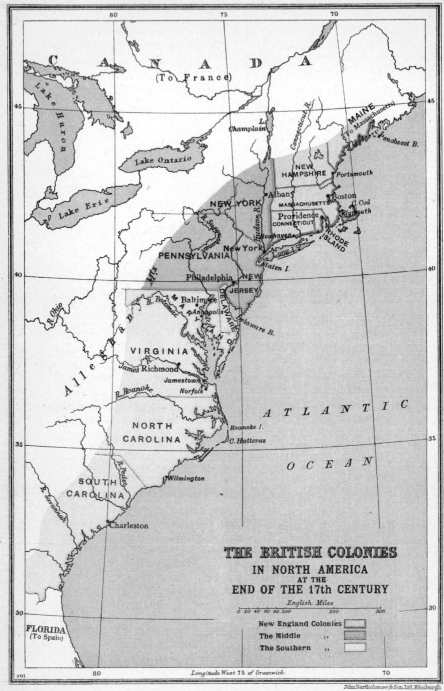

THE BRITISH COLONIES
IN NORTH AMERICA
AT THE
END OF THE 17th CENTURY

English Miles

0 20 40 60 80 100   200   300

New England Colonies	
The Middle	,,
The Southern	,,

Methuen & Co., Ltd., 36 Essex Street, London, W.C.2.

John Bartholomew & Son, Ltd., Edinburgh.

time, the Northern Colonies bred so fast that they sent down south a stream of Puritan emigrants of the old school to live among the Quakers and the Dutch. These regions became the asylum of different races and religions, English Quakers, New England Puritans, Scottish Presbyterians, and continental victims of the revived Catholic reaction. Sheltered behind the warlike sea-front of Delaware, New Jersey and New York, the Quakers of Pennsylvania could dwell at peace with white men, and traffic on brotherly terms with the Red Indians of the woods. In religious character these four Middle Colonies resembled the tolerant Rhode Island of Roger Williams, rather than the persecuting Massachusetts of Cotton Mather; for in communities containing, besides English-speaking Puritans, Swedes, Dutch, Finns, Huguenots, Palatines, Scots and Quakers, Toleration rather than Puritan citizenship necessarily became the basis of political rights. But subject to this beneficent alteration, the prevailing temper of the Middle Colonies resembled the Puritan democracy of the North; while Maryland and Carolina, though they also attracted by religious toleration a large variety of races and creeds, were doomed by their soil and climate to join the social and political civilisation of the slave states.[1]

In the middle of the war, the Plague and the Fire of London had occurred. The Fire was an unique event; the Plague was merely the last, and not perhaps the worst, of a series of outbreaks covering three centuries. Between the campaigns of Crecy and Poitiers, the Black Death had first swept over Europe from some obscure and terrible source in the Far East, with the ubiquity and violence usual to the incoming of a new disease. The obscurest hamlet had little chance of escape. It is thought not improbable that half the countrymen of Boccaccio and of Froissart, half the subjects of Edward III., perished within three years. The Black Death remained in the soil of England, and became known as " The Plague ". It never again swept the whole country at one time, but it perpetually broke out in different localities. In London under the Lancastrian and Tudor Kings it was for long periods together endemic and nearly continual; under the Stuarts it came in rare but violent outbursts, as though the Death itself were in the spasmodic agonies of dissolution. For after 1665 England knew it no more. *The Plague in England, 1347-1665*

The rejoicing in London for the accession of James I. had been cut short by an outbreak of the Plague that carried off 30,000 persons; the accession of Charles I. was the signal for another no less destructive, attended by horrors at least equal to those of the great plague described by Defoe. In 1636 a slighter attack occurred. *The Plague of London, June-Dec., 1665*

[1] Goldwin Smith's *United States* (1893), pp. 48-63. J. Winsor's *History of America*, vol. iii. *C. M. H.*, vii., pp. 38-58. See also App. D, p. 437 below.

Then followed thirty years of comparative immunity, during which other events took place calculated to make men forget in their talk the plague horrors that their fathers and grandfathers had endured. So when the last outbreak came in 1665, although it did not destroy a much larger proportion of the Londoners than some of its predecessors had done, it struck the imagination more, for it came in an age of greater civilisation, comfort and security, when such calamities were less remembered and less expected, and it was followed close, as though at the Divine command, by another catastrophe to which there was no parallel in the most ancient records of London.

The Fire of London, 2nd-7th Sept., 1666

The Great Fire raged for five days and destroyed the whole City proper between the Tower and the Temple ; yet it probably did not unroof more than half the population of the capital. The " Liberties " beyond the walls were only in part touched, and these contained by far the greatest portion of the inhabitants. London had been increasing with immense rapidity in the last sixty years. It was about 40,000 short of half a million ; about fifteen times the size of the second city in the Kingdom. In all other cities of England the townsfolk still lived within breath of the country, under conditions of what we should now call country-town life.[1]

The slums round London

In London alone the conditions of great-city life were growing up, n many respects in a peculiarly odious form. The poor were crowded out of the City into the slum districts of the " Liberties " beyond—St. Giles's, Cripplegate, Whitechapel, Stepney, Westminster, Lambeth—where they multiplied exceedingly in spite of an enormous death-rate among infants. In earlier centuries the constant presence of the Plague—the " Poor Man's Plague," as it was sometimes called—had helped to relieve Society of the proletariat, carrying off as its first victims the starving, the unemployed and the unemployable. Now that the Plague had ceased to be continuous, the numbers of the London poor made them a terrible force. This force had first made itself felt during the gathering of that revolution which overthrew Laud and Charles I. ; and Shaftesbury, with the utmost deliberation, organised it during the Popish Plot to begin a second revolution in the State.

The housing and the general condition of the poor in London were so little improved by the building alterations consequent on the Fire, that although the Plague never returned, the average death-rate scarcely decreased.[2] For only a small part of the " Liberties "

[1] See p. 42 above.
[2] Annual averages of deaths in London (Creighton, in *Social England*, iv., p. 470) :—

1653-1665 including year of the Great Plague	19,946
1666-1678	17,990
1679-1691	22,237

But some allowance must be made for increase of population.

was burnt, and that part was rebuilt much after the old fashion.
In 1722 Defoe declared that " they were still in the same condition
as they were before ". Finally, in 1780, the inhabitants of these
districts, under Lord George Gordon, burst out into a last diabolic
orgy of anti-popish rage, in which they far surpassed the barbarism
of Shaftesbury's " brisk boys."

The seat and origin of the Plague had always been in these Changes
slum districts outside the City. Now as these districts were not due to
burnt down and rebuilt on improved principles, it is certain that the Fire
the rebuilding of London after the Fire was not the reason why the
Plague disappeared from England.[1] The portion of London that
was changed by the Fire was the residential and business quarter
in the heart of the City itself, the great commercial houses where
the merchants with their orderly and well-fed households lived,
worked and slept. These pleasant palaces of commerce had gardens
behind and courtyards within, but still presented lath and plaster
walls to the narrow and crooked streets, and the old English gables
sometimes protruded so far that the prentices in their garrets could
shake hands across the way. Only in the few places where the
racing Fire met brick walls, was it forced to linger and to fight.
The merchants took the opportunity to rebuild their houses of better
material, and in a more wholesome if less picturesque relation to
the street. Eighty-nine churches, including the old Gothic St.
Paul's, had perished ; if they were to perish at all, no better year
could have been chosen for their destruction, for Christopher Wren
was beginning to be known at Court. The Court was a good patron
to him, but the Fire was the best patron ever man had.

The Plague and the Fire affected the atmosphere of politics for Political
twenty years to come. The Rationalism setting in among the effect of
educated had not yet conquered the middle and lower classes. Plague
They regarded the Plague, the Fire, and the Dutch in the Med- and Fire
way as a triple manifestation of God's anger against their governors.
It could not escape notice that the prophets who had gone through
the plague-stricken streets crying, " Yet forty days and London
shall be destroyed," had only erred in their reckoning by one year.
To the popular mind the Fire was the vengeance of God, but none
the less the work of the French. Louis XIV. was in a state of
passive alliance with Holland against us, and though the French
did nothing effectual by sea or land, they were regarded by our
people as the more dangerous enemy of the two. For they were
" Papists ". Catholicism was the power secreted behind the English throne, and of this fact the nation had somehow become dimly
aware. When the Fire broke out (accidentally, as there is no doubt

---

[1] Creighton, *Hist. of Epidemics*, i., pp. 202, 651-80 ; ii., pp. 34-43. Defoe,
Journal of the Plague Year (ed. 1835), p. 344. Clar., *Life*, p. 1186. Cunningham,
pp. 314-17.

at all) the rage of suspicion was turned in a significant direction. The papists were said to be throwing " fire-balls " into the houses. Catholics and Frenchmen who appeared in the streets were seized by the mob, and roughly handed over to the authorities, but according to a good tradition of the English rioters of this epoch, not one of them was murdered. A general massacre of Protestants by French help was expected to follow on the Fire which the Papists had kindled. Here we have the symptoms and ideas revived ten years later at the Popish Plot. It was largely the Plague and Fire that unsettled men's reason, made their imaginations foul, and charged the political air with thunder. Indeed, after the two catastrophes that had really befallen the capital, what events were too enormous, too terrible to expect ? If these strange misfortunes had not occurred, half Oates' stories would never have been believed by a nation of whom even Charles I. had said, " they are a sober people ".

Thus the Puritan feeling revived on a wave of popular superstition and political discontent. After the Dutch had been in the Medway, men everywhere began to " reflect upon Oliver," " what brave things he did, and made all the neighbour princes fear him ". Even playgoers, returning from Ben Jonson's *Bartholomew Fair*, admitted that " the business of abusing the Puritans begins to grow stale and of no use, they being the people that at last will be found wisest ". Another decade was to pass before this revived feeling was organised by Shaftesbury into the Whig Party. At present men accepted the fall of the chief minister as a sop, not as a satisfaction.[1]

Fall of Clarendon, 1667   Clarendon's position was so exalted as to attract the jealousy of all, so isolated as to enlist the sympathies of none. The marriage of his daughter Anne Hyde with James Duke of York (1660) had raised him above his fellow-subjects, as the father-in-law of the prospective King. His interest in the succession of James laid him open to unjust suspicions for his part in the unsuccessful Portuguese marriage, and the changes of British territory that had accompanied it.

> Three sights to be seen
> Dunkirk, Tangier and a barren Queen,

had been written up against his door by the mob that broke his windows when the Dutch were in the Medway. The disasters of the fleet were more justly attributed to him, for while he scarcely bestirred himself to see that the money voted was properly spent, he had embroiled Charles with the Commons by refusing to let them supervise the expenditure themselves. To the people at large he was the type of much bad government and the cause of many calamities. To resurgent Puritanism he was the chief per-

[1] Clar., *Life*, pp. 1185-87. Pepys, 12th July, 1667 ; 4th Sept., 1668.

secutor. To the regiment of women, wits and panders at Court, he was the Cavalier of the old school, who upheld the solemn manners and proprieties of an earlier age ; without the protection of a sense of humour, he was a prey to the mimicry of Buckingham who by the help of the fire-shovel and bellows for the mace and great seal used to imitate the Chancellor's strut, to the uncontrolled delight of a master more grateful for the amusement of an hour than for the devotion of a lifetime. To the Commons he was the representative of royal prerogative, which no one expected the lazy King of his own initiative to defend ; it was Clarendon who had resisted the claim of Parliament to examine accounts and to appropriate supplies, as " an introduction to a Commonwealth, not fit for a monarchy ". But to Charles he was the leader of the factious Parliament ; it was Clarendon who had incited the Houses to resist the King, whenever he attempted to ease the lot of his Catholic and Noncomformist subjects. By representing King against Parliament in matters of money, and Parliament against King in matters of religion, Clarendon incurred the hostility of both, and fell between the two stools on which it was his constitutional theory that every minister should sit. Yet though he clung with the honesty of an earlier age to his political principles of Anglican intolerance and royal prerogative, he was too ready to sacrifice his dignity as a man in order to retain his office as a Chancellor. In his sly and curious method of defending his daughter's honour when James hesitated to acknowledge her as wife, in his dealings with the Queen, in his love of splendid living and of high place, he recalls the sordid side of Coke or Bacon. It had been his fate to live too many years among mean men. Clarendon had lost the nobility of Hyde. But when, again in exile, he was thrown back on the resources of his own virtue and intellect, and again set himself, an old and broken man, to complete the great literary work of his life, he seemed once more to enter the pure presence of the friend who had deserted him on the field of Newbury, of whose love he had once been worthy and was again worthy at the end.[1]

Since the attack on Clarendon had come from Parliament and from country, Charles gained credit for yielding to the wishes of his subjects. Yet it was the King and not the Houses who gained by the change. Charles could now choose ministers of his own liking, to pursue his own policy, so far at least as they could avoid the inquisition of Parliament. He could intrigue with the great officers of State for the Toleration of Dissenters and Catholics.

The Privy Council, by whose advice the Tudors had ruled the

The situation after Clarendon's fall

---

[1] The King compelled him to resign the Great Seal, August, 1667. Parliament impeached him, he fled and was banished, November, 1667-April, 1668. He remained in exile till his death at Rouen in 1674.

land, still retained important executive functions, but had ceased
to be the consultative oracle of the Crown. The existence of an
inner circle of the more important ministers had long been officially
recognised, and was often spoken of as the " Cabal ". The Cabal
of the seventeenth century was a step towards the Cabinet of the
eighteenth. But it was formed and held together solely by the
King. Its members were not responsible for one another's actions,
or dependent on the support of Parliament. The theory of ministerial responsibility was still the same in the days of Clifford,
Arlington and Buckingham as it had been in the days of Finch,
Laud and Strafford. So long as the King wished to retain their
services, their ministry could not be brought to an end by the vote
of the Commons, except by some direct form of personal attack.
Parliament drove Clarendon from office only by the threat of impeachment, and his successors only by passage of a Test Act (1673)
which legally disqualified some of them for service under the Crown.

The Cabal, 1670-1673   The most famous of Cabals, which soon succeeded to the powers
vacated by Clarendon, was entirely the King's choice, and its mem-
bers, though in principle less devoted to the royal prerogative,
were in policy more opposed to Parliament than the fallen minister
himself. Clifford, Ashley, Buckingham, Arlington and Lauderdale,
whose names by a strange coincidence spelt " Cabal," were all of
them perfectly unscrupulous as to means. But some of them
adhered to principles in choosing their ends. Clifford was passionately Roman Catholic. Anthony Ashley Cooper, afterwards first
Earl of Shaftesbury, was a sceptic who believed in civil liberty and
religious Toleration for all Protestants ; through all changes of
Government, through all the shifting arts of his criminal career,
Ashley followed those two public ends, and his own personal ambition. Sometimes the servant, sometimes the enemy of Cromwell
and of Charles II., he was always the servant of civil freedom and
the enemy of a persecuting State Church. Buckingham, who slew
in duel the man whose wife he had seduced, was the friend and
patron of the Independents, whose religious views he sometimes
embraced. Arlington inclined to Catholicism. Scottish Lauderdale had no principle ; he was a Covenanter at heart, a Prelatist
and persecutor in act. Thus there was not one sound Anglican in
all the Cabal.

**Parlia-
ment
reinforces
persecu-
tion, 1670**   In this congenial company, hiding the thought of his own heart
and the object that for him underlay the design, Charles laboured
to break down the Anglican monopoly. He spoke to Presbyterians
of Comprehension within the Church, to Independents of Toleration
without. Neither did he by any means exclude the Catholics from
hope of the royal mercy. The intrigue provoked a fierce and
effectual demonstration. In 1670 the members of the Cavalier
Parliament met in a rage. It was not to weaken the policy of the

Clarendon Code that they had overthrown Clarendon. They renewed the expiring Conventicle Act by large majorities. Yet already
there was a sign of a new era in thought and politics ; for the first
time in the history of an English Parliament, the debating talent
in both Houses was displayed on behalf of the theory and practice
of Toleration. The cause of Puritanism had become the cause of
the sceptics, humanitarians and moderates, and the day was slowly
coming round when sceptical, humane and moderate men would
look big. A new platform of Toleration for Puritans had been
brought into existence in the Cabinet closetings of the King and
his unscrupulous ministry at Whitehall. But so long as the new-
born party of Dissent was still wrapped in the swaddling-clothes of
Royal prerogative, it could not make appeal to its natural and ultimate sources of strength in the country at large. Charles and his
ministers knew that a general election in 1670 would produce a
strong Protestant Parliament, with a touch of old Roundhead
feeling against the Court, prepared indeed to tolerate and even
to encourage Dissent, but determined to pursue the Catholics with
the sharpest edge of the law. It was significant that after some
hesitation the King decided to continue the life of the Cavalier
Parliament that thwarted his designs, rather than exchange it for
an Assembly dominated by the well-wishers of Puritanism, with
whose interest he was to outward appearance allied.

For in fact, ever since 1662, his intrigue for the temporary
Toleration of Dissent had been the by-play of his plot for the permanent restoration of Catholicism. The secret motive of Charles's
actions, lay in his design to erect a Second Stuart Despotism, based
on Catholicism and the presence of French troops in England,—
if it could be done safely and without too much trouble. It was
not indeed in his character to carry through such a design, and he
soon relinquished it, but the consequences of his aberration were
lasting.

The plan of the Second or Catholic Stuart Despotism was long **Plan of**
thought to have been due to the personal insanity of James II. **the**
for he alone put it in force ; but Charles originated the idea, and **Stuart**
second
though he afterwards abandoned it, he handed it on to his less able **Despot-**
brother. It was based on Catholicism, Toleration, a standing **ism**
army and the French alliance. Herein it differed from the First
Despotism of Laud's and Strafford's master, who had been hostile
both to Popery and Toleration.

The King's intention as regards the Anglican and Roman **Catholi-**
Catholic Churches is known to us from the records of his negotia- **cism**
tions with the Pope in 1662-63 and with the Pope and Louis XIV.
in 1669-72.[1] Charles II. offered these two foreign powers to alter

---

[1] Ranke, iii., pp. 397-400, 493-95, 518. *Home and Foreign Review*, i., pp.
153-55, 158-61, *Secret Hist. of Charles II.* (by Lord Acton). The accepted theory

the doctrines of the Church of England into those held by the Church of Rome ; and to make a similar change of ritual, except for the retention of communion in both kinds and some English hymns to be interspersed with the Mass. The State Church thus remodelled was to preserve a considerable independence under the Papal Suzerainty, not unlike the position of the Gallican Church for which Louis XIV. was then contending with the Pope.

Tolera
tion

The analogy of France was also before the King's eyes in the matter of Toleration. France was still, nominally, the land of the Edict of Nantes. For a few years longer she was still distinguished among the States of Europe as a place where the rights of Dissent were acknowledged in theory, though her practice was beginning to be very different. In the past at any rate, the royal power and the Catholic power had grown up by the alliance of the House of Bourbon with the principle of Toleration : and now the happy result had been reached that the tolerated were too weak to insist upon their privileges. The recent history of his own realm also pointed the would-be despot of England in the same direction. Since the days of Laud and Charles I., Cromwell had shown that Toleration of sectaries was not only practicable, but even useful in keeping turbulent elements in the community content under a military despotism. Charles II. was ready, as a temporary means to a greater end, to relieve the Puritans from the laws on which Bishops and Parliaments insisted. He would thus make the Dissen-ters vassals of the Crown, and grant them terms ; but he would not, by dissolving the Cavalier Parliament, allow their friends to get possession of the House of Commons, and thence grant terms to him.

French
help

The forced conversion of the Anglican Church to communion with Rome, by an alliance of the Crown with the factions most hostile to Popery and tyranny, was too uncertain a venture in politics to be accomplished without the backing of military force.

of Charles II.'s relations with France has been challenged by Mr. W. A. Shaw in his admirable work in the *Calendars of Treasury Books*, 1904-13. He tells us that " so-called histories are one and all false throughout ". According to Mr. Shaw, Charles could not have meant to change his religion under the protection of French troops, and the clause to that effect in the Secret Treaty of Dover was " never taken seriously by Charles," because his financial position was so des-perate that the plan could not have succeeded. It is true that Mr. Shaw has brought out, in his own admirable manner, the straits to which Charles was reduced by the wholly inadequate Parliamentary supply from 1660 onwards. But the flaw in Mr. Shaw's argument appears to me to be this : the Treaty of Dover was obviously not the result of financial calculations on the part of Charles, for it involved the second Dutch War which, as Mr. Shaw himself has shown, was bound to lead to bankruptcy and did so. Is it not probable that Charles was chiefly guided not by financial but rather by religious and political considera-tions in making the secret treaty ?   His offer to Louis to change religion in 1670 is in a straight line with the offer which he made to the Pope in 1662 to reconcile England to Rome. It is true that he shrank from carrying out the religious part of the Treaty of Dover because he found it too dangerous and Parliament too Protestant. But that does not prove that he had never seriously meant it.

Charles looked to France, because France was the only State willing and able to supply him with gold pieces and trained veterans for his purpose, and also because he himself, the son and companion in exile of Henrietta Maria, was half a Frenchman by birth, sympathy and training. With skill and good-nature that deceived all who saw him so lightly tread the boards, he could act the part of the happy English King, proud to preside over the sects and factions of a living body politic ; but in his southern heart he pined to sit on the throne among a submissive and well ordered people. Small wonder! For even the Cavalier Parliament had thwarted his religious policy and scandalously starved his administration by refusing adequate supply. The eccentric English plan of dividing power between Crown and Parliament was leading to anarchy. Catholicism and despotism, in their natural alliance against all liberty of action and thought, were in these years regarded as the ideal polity, in Italy, in Austria, in Spain, in many of the German states, but most pre-eminently in France. In 1670 this system in Church and State was everywhere triumphant, and till the Marlborough wars revealed the power of England to the world, was held to be the secret of strength. In these years Louis took the rising sun for his emblem, and *Nec pluribus impar* for his motto. The prevailing literature of the world was French Catholic ; military glory and diplomatic success belonged to France ; the ideal of a Government, of a society, of a Court, was looked for nowhere but at Versailles. Each petty ruler of Germany and Italy, whether his troops were purchased to fight for or against the Grand Monarch, worshipped the type of perfection which he held up before the eyes of all Europe.

In England too the monarch adored ; but the people looked askance. Republican Ludlow, when he fled to Switzerland at the Restoration, had " loathed " as he passed through France

to see such number of idle drones, who in ridiculous habits wherein they place a great part of their religion, are to be seen in every part, eating the bread of the credulous multitude, and leaving them to be distinguished from the inhabitants of other countries by thin cheeks, canvas clothing and wooden shoes.[1]

This notion of " Popery and wooden shoes," the cant term for the French polity, was almost as familiar to Ludlow's English enemies as to his English friends. From the English Restoration down to the French Revolution, " Popery and wooden shoes " was the leading political idea common to all Britons, Tory as well as Whig. Whoever would know the feeling that inspired the terror of the English Popish Plot, the expulsion of James II., the Marlborough wars, hatred for and in a less degree the wars which the Pelhams and the elder Pitt the *ancien* waged against France in three continents, should look with care at *régime* of France

[1] Ludlow, ii., p. 298.

Hogarth's picture of *Calais Gate* in the National Gallery. Though nearly a hundred years had gone by, Hogarth only repeated on canvas the very words of Ludlow. That was how the English people thought of France under her old *régime*.

The passion of mingled fear and contempt of France had continually appeared in the votes of the Cavalier Parliament, and in the actions of the mob in London streets, ever since the accession of Charles. When, after being eight years on the throne, he entered on his great scheme, without regard to the existence of this passion, he put the fortunes of the House of Stuart a second time at stake.

The English Catholics

The great majority of the English Catholics would never willingly have consented to take part in the King's plot. For two good reasons they prayed to be left at peace ; they had not yet recovered from great losses, and they had still much to lose. Catholicism, now nearly extinguished in the classes of field labour and of trade, was the religion of landowners and their households, who had many of the good things of life still left them to enjoy. But the Civil Wars had been to them a terrible lesson not to appeal to force. It has been calculated that one-third of the gentry who had died in arms for the King were Catholics. Their castles had been sacked, their priests slain, their estates confiscated. If they no longer numbered, as before the Civil Wars, some of the wealthiest subjects in the land, like the old Earl of Worcester or the owner of Basing House ; if many ate off pewter whose fathers had been served on plate, it was because they had ventured to rise for an Anglican King, who had half the statute book in his favour and half the nation on his side. If, therefore, they could now have made themselves heard by his Catholic son, they would not have urged him to a forlorn hope against the fundamental laws and the whole people of England. But there was no way in which they could make themselves heard either by the King, by the public, or even by one another. The Catholic squires were not, like the Anglican squires and the dissenting tradesmen, the ultimate judges of the policy of their own party. They had no representatives and no centres. They lived in rural mansions, far from the world and from each other, prevented by the laws of their country from taking part in her public life, and by the custom of their Church from framing a religious policy for themselves. Even the secular clergy, who on the whole joined in the desire of their flocks for peace, had been ousted from the control of English Catholic policy. The Jesuits, victorious in the struggles that had divided the persecuted Church in the days of the Gunpowder Plot, still acted for the English Catholics whom they did not represent ; and had now won the ear of the royal brothers, who might otherwise have been good Catholics and better Papists, without ceasing to be good Englishmen.

This same division between the pacific and the intriguing, the Quarrel secular and the Jesuit parties, held good all over Catholic Europe. between The Jesuits had ceased to be the militia of the Pope, and had at- the Pope and the tached themselves to the rising fortune of France.[1] Their enemies, Jesuits therefore, found some support with the Pope, who was hostile to the liberties of the Gallican Church, the foreign policy of Louis, and the independence of the Jesuit Society. The Pope, though he by no means wished Toleration to be extended into new spheres, no longer aspired to attack prescriptive and legal rights of established Protestant communities. But the Jesuits retained the crusading spirit of their founder so well, that for two generations after the Treaties of Westphalia (1648), which had been supposed to end the wars of religion, Europe was kept in a state of unrest by fresh intrigues for the extension of Catholic ascendancy by force. They used the arms and gold of Louis of France as they had once used the arms and gold of Philip of Spain. To the Jesuits and the Grand Monarch, not to the Pope or the House of Hapsburg, was due the aggression of Catholicism against Holland and on the Rhine, the scheme of the Catholic Stuart Despotism, and the Revocation of the Edict of Nantes.[2]

Charles II. had first applied to the Pope. In 1662-63 he had Abortive propounded to the Vatican his scheme for the conversion of the negotia- Anglican Church to the Roman doctrine and ritual. He seems to tion of Charles have met with little encouragement. The Pope, probably, was no with the more willing to concede to Charles an Anglican claim to half inde- Pope, 1662-63 pendence, than he was to concede the Gallican claim to Louis ; nor did he wish to be embroiled once more with the terrible English Parliament. The Jesuits still dealt with England in the spirit of Parsons, but the relentless zeal of the Pope who excommunicated Elizabeth no longer inspired the counsels of the Vatican.[3]

It was not till six years after this abortive negotiation with the The Pope that Charles applied to the French for help in his Catholic Triple Plot. For six years he had been forced to bow to the alliance of his Alliance, Jan.-Apr. Anglican minister with his Anglican Parliament ; the Dutch war 1668 occupied as much of his attention as he chose to give to public affairs ; in that war France was England's enemy, and when it came to an end, our first action was to combine with Holland against Louis. The Triple Alliance of England, Holland and Sweden, to check the advance of the French armies in the Low Countries and on the Rhine, showed that Holland had changed the policy of a hundred years, and gone round from the side of France to that

---

[1] That is the French Jesuits and their allies the Jesuits in England. The Jesuits in Rome were loyal to the Pope.

[2] The House of Hapsburg, in Silesia and Hungary, persecuted Protestants, but not in so novel or so atrocious a manner as Louis XIV. and the Jesuits in France.

[3] Ranke, iii., pp. 397-400. *Home and Foreign Review*, i., pp. 153-55.

of Spain. It was no longer in the interest of her own safety, as in
the days of Henry IV. and the Cardinals, to divide up the Spanish
Netherlands between France and herself, but rather to preserve
them as a buffer state. Holland's new policy, which finally
triumphed at Blenheim, Ramillies and Utrecht, she could only hope
to carry out by the help of England. For though Spain had once
been formidable as an enemy, she was now almost useless as an ally.
The Triple Alliance made Europe suppose for a few months that
England was already prepared to assume the required part. And
indeed if our foreign policy had been directed either by the prejudices
of the squires in the House of Commons, or by the wisdom of Sir
William Temple in diplomatic circles, the career of Louis' ambition
might have been checked at the outset, and Europe would have
been spared an age of blood and destruction. But the Triple
Alliance was no more than a forecast of the policy resumed with
steadier purpose after the coming of William to the English throne.
For while the ministers who had succeeded Clarendon regarded the
anti-French Treaty as an easy high-road back to popular esteem,
while Temple saw in it the security for European peace and English
interests, Charles only consented to it in order to make France the
mortal enemy of the Dutch, and to induce her to put a high price
on the English alliance which he was now in a position to offer her
for sale.

Charles resumes his Catholic designs, 1669
In April, 1668, while the Swedish plenipotentiaries were putting
their names to the Treaty of the Triple Alliance, Charles was trying
to form a secret understanding with the French Ambassador.
Louis, sore at the curb which the Triple Alliance placed on his
claims at the peace of Aix-la-Chapelle (April-May, 1668), hesitated
before trusting himself to a King who must certainly be deceiving
one side or the other. At this stage, perhaps, Charles had not
decided to tack his old religious design on to his new dealings with
France ; for the Catholic-minded Arlington still hotly opposed
the French connection. But early in the year 1669 the face of
things had changed. James, Duke of York, had thrown in his
political fortunes with the Catholic intriguers of the Court over
which he was one day to preside ; and Charles himself had disclosed to Clifford and Arlington, in strict confidence, that he adhered
to the Roman faith, and was seeking means to put himself in a
position to abjure the political ties that bound him to the Protestants. For until the King of England and his brother James would
separate themselves from the heretical worship, the Catholic Church
would not permit them to participate by stealth in her sacraments.[1]

Under these conditions the alliance with France was sought out
again for a new and larger purpose. With Clifford and Arlington

[1] Ranke, vi., pp. 37, 38. James took the final step probably not earlier than
the year 1672 ; Charles only on his deathbed in 1685.

the King entered on the great intrigue, of which the other members of the Cabal were to be the dupes and the English nation the victim.

The Franco-Catholic policy of the Second Stuart Despotism *Charles's* was the result of the marriage long ago of the first Charles with *sister* Henrietta Maria of France. In exile, in Catholic countries, after the death of her Protestant husband, the Queen had sought by every means of persuasion and even of unkindness to convert her children to her own faith. Young Charles alone had been shielded from her efforts by his dead father's strict command, by Clarendon's care, and by his own impatience of his mother's control in anything. She did not convert him. But she had given him her French Catholic blood which in good time worked its own. effect ; and she left him his sister Henrietta, Duchess of Orleans, whom he tenderly loved, a devout Catholic.

This lady now became the principal agent in the secret of the King's reign. In 1669 and 1670 she induced her brother to make with Louis the secret Treaty of Dover, by which England and France joined to partition Holland, and Louis promised money and soldiers to Charles to enable him to declare his own conversion to Catholicism, with a view to establishing that religion in England.[1] Thus the lady of whom nothing but what was gentle was ever reported, obedient to the training of confessors who had made her think such deeds to be works of mercy, set on parties, churches and nations to slay each other and be slain, and then herself passed suddenly into the Court of death.[2]

The secret Treaty of Dover, signed in May, 1670, by the English Catholic ministers, was covered next year by a sham Treaty of Dover, solemnly negotiated for the benefit of the Protestant members of the Cabal who were not in the real secret. The sham Treaty was nearly the same as the real Treaty, except that Catholicism was not mentioned. England was to be subsidised by France, and the Dutch State was to be destroyed. The Catholic ministers affected to hesitate, but Buckingham and Ashley were all impatience. Charles laughed to himself as he fooled Ashley, and in the spirit of the jest raised him to be Earl of Shaftesbury (1672) and Lord Chancellor ; but the man who made a fool of Shaftesbury was running risks for the future.

In March, 1672, the Treaties had effect, and war with Holland *Third* was duly proclaimed. But the King postponed his declaration of *Dutch* *war, 1672* Catholicism ; Louis did not press him, preferring to destroy Holland

---

[1] Lingard xi., Appendix for terms of the secret Treaty. For its intention, see Clarke's *Life of James II.*, i., p. 442, " for the setting of the Catholic religion in his Kingdoms ". Lord Acton, *H. and F. R*, i., pp. 169-74 ; Ranke, iii., pp. 495-504 : *Athenæum*, Ap. 1st, 1905. And see note on p. 304 above on Mr. Shaw's views.

[2] The Treaty was signed 22nd May (O.S.), 1670. Before the end of June Henrietta was dead.

while he could, rather than to stake his ripe plans on the doubtful chance of converting England. Charles and the Cabal, who had fraudulently obtained war supplies from the Commons by pretending to adhere to the Triple Alliance, and money from the national creditors by the stop on the Exchequer, began the war on slender means without asking leave of Parliament. They hoped to make the enterprise popular after it had begun, by raising the cry to avenge the Medway and the Amboyna massacre. As long ago as 1623 the Dutch traders in the Spice Islands had massacred the English in Amboyna, and retribution had never been fully exacted. The English had left the islands to the Dutch and concentrated their own trading operations on the mainland of Hindustan. The Dutch were still our chief rivals in world trade and maritime supremacy. Commercial greed and national pride might have answered to that appeal if we had been fighting alone against Holland. But in this " destruction of Carthage," of which Shaftesbury in his new Chancellor's robes boasted to the unresponsive Commons, France clearly played the part of Rome. The French alliance made the Dutch war suspect. Already it was rumoured that the heir to the throne was a Papist ; Popish schemes were scented in every act of Government.[1]

If the English ministry had refused to join in the partition of Holland, Louis would never have dared to attack the Republic, for his commerce would have been swept off the seas. Now the French and English fleets sailed together against the Dutch, but together scarcely obtained more advantage than the English alone had obtained in former wars. The Dutch nation once more was terrible when at bay for its life. Neither on land were the great traditions forgotten. The river-dykes were opened and the un-rivalled host of 100,000 French soldiers whom Louvois had prepared for his master's purpose, were checked by the waters as the Spanish spearmen had been checked before. Young William of Orange was called from his private gardens to save his fatherland. The De Witts were moved out of the path of his ambition by the murderous frenzy of the mob. The quasi-monarchical government of the Stadt-holderate was revived in his person. He soon showed that he was

Revolution in Holland, 1672 able to fill the ancestral place, and to make Holland once more the capital of the liberties of Europe. In 1673 his diplomacy brought to the rescue of his country the great Catholic powers of Austria and Spain. The Pope's hostility to Louis and to the Gallican Church rendered possible this strange alliance against the Jesuit power. Thus already was sketched out the great coalition which after forty years brought Louis to his knees. But England had not yet joined its ranks.

[1] For the commercial rivalry with Holland in the Indies, see *The East India Trade in the Seventeenth Century*, Shafaat Ahmad Khan, 1923.

Holland was less obnoxious to Charles when the Republican Government had been overthrown, and his kinsman of the House of Orange restored. The revolution that established the Stadt-holderate prepared the way for peace with the English Court. But the power that actually insisted on the peace of 1674 was not the Crown but the Parliament.

The history of the Cavalier Parliament that sat from 1661 to 1678 is the history of a House of Commons elected in a frenzy of loyalty, rising by a series of struggles with the King, to acquire a control of his accounts, a negative voice in the selection of his ministers, and the power of veto on his policy at home and abroad. Clarendon's ideal of a loyal Parliament and a gracious King working together, each within the limits allotted by the Constitution, the one initiating legislation, the other free to administrate, was shown once more, as Pym had long ago perceived, to be a dream. Clarendon's two co-ordinate powers were perpetually coming into contact, either of rude hostility or of corrupt union ; and on one of these occasions he himself was crushed between them. Government was reduced to anarchy by the constant friction ; no policy could be carried on for many months together without reversal. England would soon be again compelled, as in the days of Charles I., to choose between an absolutism or the sovereign power of Parliament. Charles II., with his usual cleverness, had seen, when he made the Treaty of Dover, that unless the King got help from abroad, the sovereignty was more likely to pass on to Parliament than back to the Crown. The Civil War had reversed the relation of Whitehall and Westminster. The members now feared nothing from Court, but the courtiers feared much from Parliament. Government no longer dared invade the privilege of the House, or lock up the more outspoken members in the Tower. When Sir John Coventry alluded to the King's pleasures in open Parliament, Charles could find no means to revenge the royal honour on his subject, save to permit a band of rascals to wait for him by night in the Haymarket and slit his nose. The House replied by banishing the offenders for life, and making the slitting of all noses felony without benefit of clergy ; and Charles could do nothing to protect his servants. The *droit administratif* had been weakened in England by the Civil War, or rather was in some sort passing over to the Commons, who were well able to avenge themselves on their enemies. The King's effective weapon of defence was not force but corruption.

On the eve of the Restoration the Republican philosopher Harrington is reputed to have said :—

Let the King come in and call a Parliament of the greatest Cavaliers in England, so they be men of estates, and let them sit but seven years, and they will all turn Commonwealth's men.[1]

[1] Hallam (1884), ii., p. 355 note.

If indeed Harrington said, " Let them sit but seven years," he showed peculiar shrewdness. For it was the long life of the Cavalier Parliament that enhanced the claims of its members to political sovereignty. The royal power lost as well as gained by Charles's unwillingness to force a dissolution. In the short Parliaments and infrequent sessions of old Tudor and Stuart Kings, the squires came up each time unknown and unknowing to the capital, to transact the business of their localities, to criticise the policy of the Crown, perhaps to impeach a minister, to vote or refuse money, and to return to their rural pursuits. They had no time to acquire the habits of administration or of corruption. The Puritans who had cheered Eliot and locked the doors against Black Rod, were " countrymen," without acquaintance at Court, or ambition to share in a Government which it was then their sole duty to intimidate. When, therefore, the great revolutionary statesmen of 1642 seized all administrative power for the House of Commons, its blunders were a measure of its inexperience. And just as the Roundhead Long Parliament (1640-60) gradually turned one set of members into professional politicians, so the Cavalier Long Parliament (1660-78) had the same effect upon another set. In the course of nineteen sessions, the members became habitual residents in London. Their persons and prices were well known at Whitehall. Neither George III., nor Walpole, nor even Danby was the first to protect the position of ministers by purchase of votes in the House. The system was introduced during the struggle over the accounts of the Dutch war of 1665-68, by the statesmen of the new style. Clarendon indeed saw with anger and disdain the country members thronging Whitehall stairs, and going off with pensions and places to vote against their conscience. The contemporary of Laud and Hampden denounced such intimacy between legislative and executive as " contrary to all former order," well remembering the sharp line, as of caste, that used when he was young to divide the well-ordered Court from the pure and patriotic Parliaments.[1]

When the antediluvian Chancellor had fallen, the Cabal made free use of the system of corruption. But what with his soldiers, his sailors and his mistresses, the King had little money left for his faithful Commons ; the number of places was limited, and the number of members was large. Even when some two hundred had been " taken off," as the word then was for corrupting members, a majority was not secure.[2] Those who could get nothing, invigilated unceasingly over the accounts, and clamoured of Popery. And there were two things which even gold could not buy in that House—friendship towards the Catholic religion and towards the French Crown.

The Court corrupts members

Limitations to the system

---

[1] Clar., pp. 1121-22. Burnet, i., p. 486 ; ii., pp. 80-81.
[2] Burnet, i., p. 486, ii. p. 79 and notes.

When the Cavalier Parliament met for its twelfth session in Jealousy March, 1673, all that men knew fell far short of the truth, that against Charles was bound in treaty with Louis to put down Protestantism Catholicism, in England by French military force. But the visible indications 1673 of danger loomed all the more big and black, because what lurked behind them was unseen. The unnatural alliance with France to destroy the Protestant State of Holland, the presence of a standing army under officers whose religion was suspect, the ill-concealed Romanism of the Duke of York, who commanded our fleets, and of Clifford, who controlled our counsels, the abeyance of the Penal Laws throughout the country and the " flaunting of Papists " at Court, all combined to create a panic which for a few weeks overcame the desire of pensioners to earn their reward, of Dissenters to enjoy the Declaration of Indulgence, and of Anglicans to persecute Dissent.

The alleged royal power to dispense with the execution of the laws against Catholics and Dissenters had been exercised by Declaration in 1662, and again with better hope in 1672 when there was no longer a Clarendon to interfere. The prisons were opened, the preachers and congregations assembled, and thousands of the best men in England enjoyed another short respite from ruin. Yet fear of Catholicism was stronger than personal interest. In March, 1673, the Dissenters in the country, and their friends in Parliament, denounced the Declaration of Indulgence as a cloak for bringing in Popery. While the Puritans thus rejected the royal mercy and the Catholic alliance, the Anglicans showed a zeal against the Roman religion that left no hope that any large section of High Churchmen would favour reunion when the King's plot came to light. That plot was now vanishing into air. Charles began to see that his foreign education had led him to misconstrue the psychology of both sections of English Protestantism. Anglicans and Puritans united to unmask the hidden Catholics at Court and in the army, and to expel them from the service. The famous Test Act of 1673, Test Act the black charter of English Protestantism, forbade any one who and Dissolution would not take the sacrament by the rites of the Church of England of the to hold civil or military office under the Crown. The Bill was in Cabal, part the result of an intrigue within the Cabal against itself. 1673 Arlington, who though Catholic at heart was ready to take the Test, and Shaftesbury, who began to sniff Popery under the royal methods of Toleration, combined to forward the bill which would drive the scrupulous Clifford from office. They succeeded, and the Cabal was dissolved. The religion of Clifford, and of James, Duke of York, was unmasked. Rupert, the good Protestant and hater of Frenchmen, succeeded James in the Admiralty of that great fleet from whose guns he had once fled, a much daring pirate, through so many waters.

Meanwhile, the Nonconformists, who supported the Test Act·

though it excluded the more scrupulous of their number from the service of the Crown, were rewarded by a prospect of Parliamentary and Protestant Toleration. So great was the fear of Popery, that a Bill for the " Ease of Protestant Dissenters " was passed through the Cavalier House of Commons, and only stopped in the Lords by the inveterate malignity of the bishops. Change was in the air, and Shaftesbury from his seat on the wool-sack darted his cunning eyes on the shifting scene. Before another year had passed, he was out of office and at the head of the Opposition.

Peace with Holland, 1674

Thus in the month of March, 1673, fell the domestic policy of Charles and the Cabal. In the winter session following, their foreign policy was reversed. The Commons forced the Crown to make peace with Holland, by refusing supplies for an army which they expected soon to be used against themselves.

The work of Parliament in 1673-74 had been to destroy every piece of the artificial structure on which the King balanced his French Catholic plot. The Dissenters had refused the royal Toleration, the High Churchmen had proclaimed their loathing and fear of communion with Rome, the Cabal had dissolved into its component parts, the Catholic ministers and officers had been driven from their posts, and the French alliance itself was no more.

Charles II. learns wisdom

Charles learnt the lesson of 1673. The lacuna of his foreign education was filled up. Henceforth, though in politics he had not one English feeling of his own, he understood admirably how much and how little could be done with the national sentiment, and could play some tunes upon that pipe with the right Tudor touch. Not even in the last triumphant year of his reign, when the Whig chiefs had perished in exile and on the scaffold, when England lay at his feet in self-chosen abasement, did he forget the lesson he had learnt. He never again used Catholicism either as a means or as an end in his politics. But he had roused suspicions which could not be allayed, and launched a French Catholic intrigue in this country which was not stopped by his own defection. His brother could learn nothing. In 1674 James stepped into the place of Charles as the prime agent and patron of the Jesuit plot.

Alliance of Charles with Anglicanism, 1674-78. Danby

Charles politically abandoned Catholicism, but not absolutism. He would have preferred to found a Catholic monarchy on the French model ; he was perforce content to reign as a professing Protestant, but he could still aspire to free himself from the inquisition of Tory squires in Parliament, and from the lowering face of Dissent in the country. The man for his new purpose was the Yorkshire cavalier, Sir Thomas Osborne, whom he made Earl of Danby and first minister of the Crown. From the failure of Charles's Catholic Plot to the coming of Oates, in that confused interval of four years that divided the King's crime from its punishment, Danby ruled England, like the younger Pitt, by reconciling the

lately divorced affections of Parliament and King. Appealing to
the old Cavalier prinicples of intolerant Anglicanism and royal
prerogative, he built up in the last years of this old Parliament the
new Tory party, by the aid of wholesale bribery out of the public
revenue, and distribution of the spoils of office on lines of strict party
tests. In hot opposition on the floor of both Houses, Shaftesbury
and Sacheverell were building up the Whig party on the principles
of Toleration and Parliamentary supremacy ; but at present they
had little money for distribution among their followers except such
as came from the French Ambassador, who was forced to enter into
strange friendships during this confusion of politics.

The peculiar strength of Danby's position, so far as Charles Danby
allowed him to have his way in the matter, was hostility to France. hostile to
Danby wished to make the Tory party a nationalist party, in spite France.
of the royal brothers. He carried through the marriage of James's of
daughter Mary to William of Orange, thereby strengthening the William
reversionary claim of Europe's Protestant champion on the English and Mary,
throne, and pledging the House of Stuart to friendship with Holland. 1677
Indeed, from 1674 onwards, Louis' diplomacy could aim at little
more than to keep England neutral, while his armies devoured the
Low Countries and the Rhine. Over here, Parliament and people
clamoured for war. Danby, at a public banquet, gave the indecent
toast, " Confusion of all that were not for a war with France " ; [1]
the Tory minister hoped to efface in a continental struggle with the
Jesuit power the accumulated suspicions that divided the nation
from the throne. To Charles himself the pretence of a war policy,
in which he had no intention really to engage, was useful. On this
pretext, he could obtain as large an army as he wished, and then use
it to establish an absolute monarchy in alliance with Cavalier sentiment. Thus the same danger of a standing army, which threatened
Louis, was no less terrible to the friends of civil and religious liberty
in England. So long as the English monarch adhered to the principles of absolutism, it was impossible for the Whigs to be a war
party. Until 1688 they could bark against France, but never bite.
They could cry a note louder than Danby about Popery and wooden
shoes, but they could not vote supplies.[2]

If the Cavalier members were delighted to be given their head The Non-
against France, they were even more delighted to have the Puritans Resisting
once more at bay. All thought of " Ease for Protestant Dissenters " Bill, 1675
vanished from their minds when the fear of Popery receded, and
from the King's mind when he abandoned his hopes for a Catholic
ascendancy. Danby cried on the pack. The Clarendon Code was
set in full vigour, and a Non-Resisting Bill was introduced. It was
a Test of political opinion drawn up so as to exclude from either

---

[1] Burnet, ii., p. 128.
[2] Airy, pp. 210-219 on foreign politics, 1677-78.

House of Parliament all but the high-flying Anglicans and Cavaliers : no one was to sit as a legislator until he had sworn to alter nothing in Church or State. The future Whig party would thus have been excluded by law from political life. The Tories, fearing the result of the next election, determined by this means forever to prevent a free appeal from being made to the people. The iniquitous measure was fought by the Opposition with the energy of men who see the whole future to be at stake. But its passage into law was prevented only by a timely quarrel between the two Houses. Violence and faction were becoming the order of the day.

Shaftesbury tries to force a dissolution The hopes of Shaftesbury and the new Country Party, thus schooled to desperation and revenge, lay in the constituencies. In the present Parliament they were a powerless though vociferous minority. But they justly calculated that the yeomen and townspeople were eager to reverse the electoral decision of 1661. All the politics of Europe turned on the question whether Charles could be forced to dissolve. William of Orange was Danby's partisan, hoping that England would declare immediate war ; while Louis, anxious to see civil discord arise in England before she broke the chain at which she was tugging to fly at the throat of France, supported the movement for a general election, and filled the hands of many Whig members with gold.[1] In February, 1677, Shaftesbury made a false move. In his rage to see the King's will stand alone between his party and the power that an election would bring to them, he made a strained interpretation of an obsolete statute enjoining annual Parliaments, and accordingly moved in the Lords that the present Parliament was no longer a lawful Assembly. For this offence he was committed to the Tower by his Peers, and remained there a whole year.

Prospects of the Country Party, 1678 When he came out the fortunes of his party seemed at a low ebb. Since their attack on the existence of the present Parliament, the leaders had been as unpopular at Westminster as at Whitehall. The men in office, by the system of spoils for the victors, had bought up the Pensionary Parliament, as it was often called, and every means had now been tried in vain for its dissolution. If it had lasted seventeen years it might last twenty-seven. Meanwhile, the cruel laws cruelly enforced were " extirpating dissent " ; in ten years' time an appeal to the electors might be too late. Trade was again prosperous, and the country, after a sort, contented. The King had armed forces on foot in England, Scotland, Tangier and in foreign service on the Continent. An Anglican monarchy, backed by an efficient army, by the whole Church, and a large proportion of the squires, seemed to be fastening its chains on England, by the wisely directed violence of Danby's faction. The only hope for

[1] Shaftesbury, Russell and probably Sacheverell were above taking bribes ; not so Algernon Sidney, and many of the rank and file (*First Whig*, pp. 24-26).

religious and civil liberty in England was that the " French and Popish counsels " of the Court would be detected in spite of Danby's vigilance. The history of the Secret Treaty of Dover might at any moment come to light. Even now Charles, who openly left 10,000 English troops in French pay, secretly took gold from the French Ambassador as the price of this favourable neutrality. In still more dreadful secret, on the 24th of April, 1678, the English Jesuits held their provincial Congregation in the rooms of the heir to the throne, in St. James's Palace. If Shaftesbury could have laid his hand on some one of the innumerable mysteries of the backstairs, of which two or three have been revealed to posterity, he could therewith have blasted Danby and created another revolution. The Dissenters, at death-grips with their fate, were prepared to save themselves by desperate measures ; the well-organised Parliamentary opposition was mad with the rage of a baffled and ill-used faction ; in the mind of the common man, twelve years of misgovernment, disaster and betrayal had still to be revenged, and the long tension of a chronic fear in the Protestant mind had not yet found relief in frenzy.

The truths that would have saved the Whigs remained hid, but a liar came to their deliverance. In the autumn of 1678, Titus Oates deposed that the Jesuit Congregation had met on the 24th of April in the White Horse Tavern and taken counsel to murder the King. The position of Shaftesbury and his followers was not one in which they could afford to look a gift horse in the mouth.

CHAPTER XII

THE REIGNS OF TERROR, 1678-85

Must hate and death return ?—SHELLEY.

Titus
Oates

TITUS OATES, whose father had been a Baptist and Chaplain to one of Oliver's regiments, at an early age became a clergyman in the restored Anglican Church, and in 1677 was reconciled to Rome. He belonged really to the mendicant order of scoundrels who flourished as bullies and spies under the patronage of the more respectable Churches. The informers of the Restoration epoch, used first by the Anglicans against the Dissenters, then by the Whigs against the Catholics, and again by the Tories and Catholics against the Whigs, cannot claim Oates as their Founder ; but it was he who made their sordid trade imaginative and magnificent, attacked the highest persons in the State, and let loose over England the revolutionary passions of the decisive decade in her history.

In youth he had been guilty of false witness against the innocent, and of other crimes scarcely less foul. His conversion to Rome was prompted by the hope of gaining reward, either as an agent of Catholic intrigue, or, if chance offered, as the betrayer of his patrons. During his residence in the English Jesuit Colleges, first at Valladolid in Spain (1677) and then at St. Omers in the Low Countries (1678), the loathsome and unpopular novice gleaned from the talk of his associates that King Charles was now held to stand in the way of the conversion of England which he had once undertaken ; that high hopes were fixed on the survival and succession of James, and on the aid of the French King ; that much passed through the hands of the Duke's busy secretary Coleman and of Louis' confessor, Père La Chaise. He learnt in particular that the Jesuit Congregation or " consult " in England was held on 24th April, 1678, but unfortunately he did not learn that it was held in the rooms of the heir to the throne.

Two months after that secret meeting had taken place in St. James's Palace, Oates was expelled from the Flemish College, as he was always sooner or later expelled from every society into which he thrust himself. He returned to London, penniless, but with raw material that could be manufactured for the market. He sought help in the Protestant section of Grub Street, joined himself to a miserable fanatic scribbler named Tonge,[1] and drew up with him, in a copious manuscript of eighty-one sections, the

---

[1] Whether before or after his residence in the Jesuit Colleges is uncertain (Pollock, pp. 9 10).

imaginary details of a plot ; lists of the conspirators were added, including several score of the English Jesuits and their friends, and a few Catholic nobles and others who were not of that faction. Oates deposed that he had discovered, during his residence among the Jesuits, " a hellish plot " to fire the City, raise the Catholics in Ireland, conquer England by French and Irish arms, massacre every Protestant who refused to recant, and murder the King according to arrangements made at the Congregation of 24th April. At that famous " consult " Oates asserted himself to have been present.[1]

This tale the informers laid before the King and ministry ; they also lodged a copy of the declaration with a good and fearless magistrate, Sir Edmund Berry Godfrey, that he might publish it if the Court strove to " stifle the Plot ".[2] But the Court did no such thing. The monstrous fiction did not seem absurd to a generation that had well in memory the true tale of the Gunpowder Plot, and a distorted version of the Irish massacre of 1641, and had seen the City totally destroyed by a fire falsely attributed to the Catholics. In very fact a King was on the throne who had signed treaties to convert England by French arms ; and the cruel and unprovoked extirpation of the peaceful Protestants of France was yet to take place. In such an age the tale told by Oates was not deemed impossible. And since Councils of State and Courts of Law were accustomed, for want of a professional detective force, to use the evidence of low-class informers whom no one expected to tell an ungarnished tale, the inquiry was not abandoned, even after the shrewd King had twice caught Oates lying in his answers before the Privy Council. Though Court and ministry had every reason to avoid a fierce Protestant agitation, they did not dismiss the matter as absurd. After each examination, on three consecutive nights, Oates ranged the City with warrants from the Council against the Jesuits whom he had named. As the result of his information, Danby had Coleman arrested and his papers seized ; a box was discovered behind his chimney containing treasonable correspondence with the Papal Nuncio and the French King's confessor, Père La Chaise. Drawing his bow at a venture Oates had brought down a royal quarry. The movement for the exclusion of James from the throne originated from these written proofs of his secretary's treason.

The discovery of Coleman's letters saved Oates from the immediate exposure that threatened him, and created a disposition, for a while almost universal, to believe in the rest of the plot. A

Marginal notes: Oates before the Council, 28th-30th Sep., 1678

Coleman's papers seized, 30th Sep.

---

[1] *State Trials*, vi., pp. 1433-72, for the eighty-one heads of the charges.

[2] The use Godfrey made of the information was, however, to warn Coleman. Though politically a stout Protestant, Godfrey had a personal feeling for many of the Catholic intriguers.

fortnight later, on the murder of the magistrate with whom he had deposed his evidence before going to Court, the creed of the plot became a raging panic.   On 17th October the corpse of Sir Edmund Berry Godfrey, whose disappearance had for some days been the talk of the town, was found in a ditch under Primrose Hill beyond Marylebone, with marks of strangulation on the neck and breast, and his sword thrust through the heart.[1]   When the news was

Panic after the murder of Godfrey, Oct. passed round the coffee-houses and workshops of the City, multitudes flocked out across the fields to the scene ; the concourse was still greater when the corpse made State entry into London.   There Godfrey was laid out in the open street, in dumb appeal to his fellow-Protestants, who for two whole days defiled before him with clenched hands and oaths of vengeance.   At last he was attended to the grave by a train of a thousand nobles, gentlemen and clergy (1st Nov.).   When they reached his parish church, a bishop preached vengeance to this notable congregation from the text : " Died Abner as a fool dieth ? " while the countless multitude outside swayed and hummed with passion and with fear.   The Whigs, it is said, inaugurated these fierce pageants.   Cæsar's funeral rites roused no such ecstasy, for the Romans who cried for vengeance in the Forum had no thought that Brutus meditated a massacre of all the Quirites.   But terror of death took hold of the 500,000 inhabitants of London.   It was thought that the execution of the plot which Oates had detailed had already begun, and that Godfrey had been the first victim.   Night after night each householder lay down half-expecting to be awakened by the alarm of fire or massacre.   The cheerful tramp of the train-bands echoing down the frosty streets as he lay awake, seemed to him the only reason why that mad Christmas passed in safety.   When his prentices came in from patrol duty at dawn, he rose and prayed that all the household might be preserved that day from sudden death.   The women carried daggers or pistols ; and for the men, enterprising Whig tradesmen invented the " Protestant flail," a hard-striking weapon, small enough to " lurk perdue " in the capacious cross pockets of the long coats then in fashion.

The Whigs fan the flame This terror, very genuine among the common people, lasted " not for a few weeks or months only but for a great while together ". It was not ignorance alone that prolonged the panic.   A large number of the cleverest men, who should soonest have come to their senses, were busy fanning the flame.   The Whigs knew that so long as the terror lasted they had power.   Their artifices now seem grotesque enough.   One of the most acute Whig lawyers sent a special message to town to have the billets of wood moved to the back of his house, where the " fireballs of the Jesuits " could not reach them.   Some went to their business clad in silk armour, warranted t᾽ turn pistol bullets.   The " Protestant flails " proved

---

[1] See **Appendix C, Who Killed Sir Edmund Berry Godfrey ?**

needless against papist assassins, but in elections and street fights
were brought into action against the Tory partisans.[1]

But it was above all by the votes of the House of Commons that Last
the triumphant party excited the terrors of the multitude. On session
21st October the Cavalier Parliament met for its last session. That of the
week, when men were thronging to view the corpse of the murdered Parl.,
magistrate, the panic caught hold in the House even on Danby's 21st Oct.-
pensioners. If any member doubted the plot, to utter his thought 1678
would have been to brand himself as a concealed papist, and to
run risk of figuring in Oates' next edition. The leaders of the
Whig minority became leaders of the House. A resolution was
carried without one dissentient voice in either chamber that

> there has been, and still is, a damnable and hellish Plot contrived and carried
> on by Popish recusants, for the assassinating and murdering the King, and
> for subverting the Government and rooting out and destroying the Protestant
> religion.

As the Court and ministry were suspect, committees of Lords and
of Commons, presided over by Whig politicians, took over the
examination of prisoners, witnesses and documents. Charles, who
alone of Englishmen was in a position to avow his disbelief in the
plot against his own life, was compelled by the addresses of Parliament to call out the militia, enforce the Penal Laws, fill the prisons
with hundreds of Catholics, plant cannon round Whitehall, and
issue a proclamation commanding all Popish recusants to depart
ten miles from London. Guards were placed in those ancient
vaults where Fawkes had once stood to his post beside the faggots.
The Test Act of 1673 had excluded Catholics from service under
the Crown ; this winter they were excluded from sitting in either
House of Parliament by an Act which remained in force till the
days of O'Connell and Wellington.

To all these measures, arising out of a belief in the plot and in Cole-
Godfrey's murder by the Papists, there was no opposition. But man's
the proposals arising out of the examination of Coleman's letters James im-
divided the two parties. Oates had not dared to bring charges plicated
against the heir to the throne. But now the letters and confessions
of the Duke's secretary [2] implicated his master in treasonable designs
hatched with foreign powers against the Church of which he was
soon to be the head and protector. Coleman had destroyed most of
his own later correspondence, but the Houses were in possession
of his letters for the year 1675. Those letters contained a correspondence with Père La Chaise about a plan for the complete overthrow of Protestantism, to be begun by putting the Catholics on an

---

[1] North's *Examen*, pp. 201-5, 572, 573. *Life of Lord Keeper Guilford*, sec. 70.
Burnet, ii., pp. 164, 165. *First Whig*, pp. 138-39, note. Pollock, pp. 84, 103, 104.
[2] I speak of Coleman as the Duke of York's secretary, because that was still
his business and position in reality. It had once been his office in name also, but
it had latterly been thought prudent to call him secretary only to the Duchess.

21

equal footing with Anglicans. To accomplish this, Louis is asked
to give a sum of money that will enable Charles to govern without
Parliament, and hand over to James the chief influence in the State.
Finally Coleman writes thus to the French King's confessor :—

The real Popish Plot

We have a mighty work upon our hands, no less than the conversion of three
kingdoms, and by that the subduing of a pestilent heresy, which has domi-
neered over a great part of this northern world a long time ; there was never
such hopes of success since the death of Queen Mary as now in our days, when
God has given us a prince who is become (may I say a miracle) zealous of being
the author and instrument of so glorious a work. . . . That which we rely
upon most, next to God Almighty's providence and the favour of my master
the Duke, is the mighty mind of his most Christian Majesty (*Louis*), whose
generous soul inclines him to great undertakings, which being managed by
your Reverence's exemplary piety and Prudence, will certainly make him
look upon this as most suitable to himself and becoming his power and thoughts.
So I hope you will pardon me if I be very troublesome to you on this occasion,
from which I expect the greatest help we can hope.

Well-informed French Catholic onlookers did not deny that Coleman had been detected in treason.[1]

Sacheverell first suggests Exclusion 4th Nov., 1678

The unfortunate secretary, when examined before a Committee
of the Commons, confessed that his master knew and approved his
correspondence. The Whig leaders at once began their attack on
James. On 2nd November Shaftesbury, Halifax and Essex in the
Lords, and two days later Lord Russell in the Commons, moved that
the Duke of York should be withdrawn from the King's presence and
councils. Russell's motion gave rise to a long debate, analogous to
the debate on Root-and-Branch in February, 1641, which had foreshadowed the impending division of men still united by a common
peril. The future Tories spoke of the reverence due to royalty,
the future Whigs of the danger to the Protestant religion. Towards the close of the debate, William Sacheverell, the brain of his
party in the House of Commons, rose to ask " the Gentlemen of
the Long Robe " " whether the King and Parliament may not dispose of the succession of the Crown ? " No one present had the
courage to speak after him on that issue. But before many months
were out, his proposal to change the succession had been adopted
as the policy distinctive of the Whigs. For it was soon clear that
the motion of Russell and Shaftesbury was a false and dangerous
step, unless they were prepared to exclude from the throne the
revengeful man whom they thus insulted. Indeed, the safety not
only of the Whigs but of all England was involved. Sacheverell's
plan was the one measure of precaution which Parliament ought to
have adopted in that crisis. It alone involved no cruelty to the

---

[1] Coleman's letters, George Treby's *Collection*, 1681, pp. 116-18. Pollock, pp.
44, 45, note. So strongly does Ranke feel the guilt and importance of Coleman's
letters that he even says " it cannot be affirmed that all they (*Oates and his colleagues*) alleged was mere invention ". Ranke thinks that in consequence of the
state of things revealed by the letters, the question of Exclusion " from a kind of
necessity came to the front " (iv., pp. 60-64).

great body of Catholics, while it alone could secure the Protestant
religion.   The Exclusion policy, associated as it was for the next
ten years with a sequence of errors, crimes and catastrophes scarcely
equalled in the history of English parties, was nevertheless adopted
as a national necessity at the Revolution of 1688.[1]

The Whig party—as it came to be called in the heat of the The Whig
Exclusion struggle—was a combination of part of the aristocracy Party
with the middle class to wrest political power from the Crown, and
to force the squirearchy and the bishops to grant toleration to
dissent.   To obtain these ends the Whigs played upon the popular
fear of Catholicism, which they themselves shared.

A party with this platform was perhaps a natural outcome of Shaftes-
the social, religious and political institutions of the day ; but its bury
actual formation was the work of Shaftesbury.   As courtier and
Cabal minister, Ashley had intrigued against Parliament in the
cause of Toleration ; but the King, with his Secret Treaty of Dover,
had delved a yard below his mine.   Driven from office in 1673, the
Earl of Shaftesbury, as he had now become, sought revenge at the
head of a small clique of great nobles, including Buckingham and
Halifax, who opposed Danby in the House of Lords.   He was the
first of these nobles to perceive, that if they sought to break down

[1] Grey, vi., pp. 121-49.   Events showed that the Whigs in no way exaggerated
the degree to which James was undesirable as a King.   But events also showed
that they greatly exaggerated the force, numbers and violence of the Catholic
population as a whole.   The fear of an immediate rising of the Popish recusants
was of course ridiculous, but we only know that after the events of 1678 and 1688.
The error was certainly no worse than the error of Pitt and the reactionaries of
1794, in supposing that there was danger of a Jacobin revolution in England.   In
those days, when there were no statistics, and when large numbers of people concealed their religious opinions in order to avoid persecution, there was great uncertainty at the back of men's minds as to the real stability of Protestantism.
Sir Thomas Meres, speaking in the House of Commons (Grey, vi., p. 138) on
Lord Russell's motion of 4th November, thus puts the case as it appeared to
many of his contemporaries : " We changed religion pretty well in Henry VIII.'s
time, and Edw. VI., and in Queen Mary's time all the clergy turned Popish
except an hundred and sixty.   About forty years ago the Church was at its
height ; and then we had changes in the late times of rebellion, and now we have
a Church of England again if we can keep it.   We are a mutable people, and the
Papists number is great.   We see an army of 20,000 men listed in the Plot ;
I am really afraid that when such a day comes, that two-thirds of the nation will
stand neuters, and so about one-third part will engage for the Protestant religion."
Except for Oates' lie about the Army of 20,000 men, these arguments are not
absurd, although they proved to be a miscalculation.   Coleman thought exactly
the same as Meres, and had said so in his letters, which were then occupying the
attention of the House.   This miscalculation accounts both for the activity of
the Jesuit intriguers, and for the absurd terror of the Protestants during that
winter.   As the Whigs thought that Meres' analysis was very probably correct,
it would have been criminal in them to allow James to succeed to the throne.
And although the calculation was incorrect, James's succession proved dangerous
and mischievous to a degree which the Tories had wholly failed to foresee.   Thus
both Whig and Tory leaders made a miscalculation, and it is easy to forgive them
for that ; but it is hard to forgive them for the violence and criminality of their
political methods.

Anglican intolerance and royal supremacy, they must demean themselves to agitate, and to organise those classes who would elect the next House of Commons—the townspeople with their dissenting sympathies; the yeomen with their dislike of parsons and hatred of Catholics; and the Roundhead elements among the gentlemen in the existing House of Commons, and in the Courts of Law. This union of peers and people was the essence of the Whig party. The Earl wooed the City of London as John Pym had done before, but with even more pains and success. He moved his town house from the fashionable quarter near his old friends at Whitehall, to Aldersgate in the heart of the merchant world. One of the common sights of the city was the jolting of the great noble's coach through the narrow streets, amid the shouts of a bodyguard armed with clubs and flails, and decked with green ribbons; while at the carriage window appeared, beneath the spreading brim of a round felt hat, a face wasted with disease, but

> Politic as tho' one eye
> Upon the other seemed to spy.

When he arrived at Westminster, his daily task was to unite the opposition in both Chambers in a course of action pre-arranged by himself. To his enemies in Lords and Commons he seemed the "fairy fiend that haunted and deluded both". Thus, if he lured his party to ruin, he first brought it into existence.[1]

The Whig Lords He was a master of debate, when the debates in the Upper House rivalled those of the Lower House in importance, and surpassed them in art, wit and intellectual power. The Peers of that generation formed a small assembly of some of the cleverest men our island has ever produced. In such a House the bishops were little able to defend themselves, and the poor men got no more mercy from Buckingham and Shaftesbury than they themselves showed to the Dissenters. King Charles often came in, partly to hear the sport, and partly to overawe the Opposition. He used to stand listening and joking by the fire, incognito, but plainly visible to all. He was known in the pamphlets of the day as "the fireside". The proud Whigs, who were not for nothing called the King's Peers, would turn undismayed towards the stranger by the chimney, and attack his measures and his Government with polished sarcasm. Charles, who declared it was as good as a play, would join sometimes in the laugh against himself. In a country where men love to be led by their superiors in rank and fortune, such aristocrats were in some respects better fitted than Pym and Cromwell to lead a great attack on regal power. They were high enough to bend for popular favour, without seeming to the gentry to lose caste. More witty, less scrupulous and less Puritan than

Ranke, iv., pp. 12, 166, 167. Traill's *Shaftesbury*, p. 129.

their fathers, these Peers had succeeded to the traditions of the Essexes and Bedfords of 1640 who had called Laud and Strafford to account. In the Lower House, though Sacheverell was the first in counsel and debate, Lords Cavendish and Russell, heirs to the titles of Devonshire and Bedford, were the official leaders whom the party loved to put forward.[1]

Yet there were also many gentry in the Whig ranks. These, and the nobles who led them, all conformed to the Anglican Church ; some were free-thinkers ; others indifferentists ; few were Puritans. But they led the yeomen, merchants and shopkeepers who were pro-avowed Dissenters, and the still greater number of those classes who had no objection to attend the Anglican service, but who were Puritan in general sentiment. Most of the lawyers were Whigs, for the Roundhead leaders of the profession, retaining their position and practice under the Act of Indemnity, had influenced the rising generation against the Court.[2] The whole of this formidable party aimed, not at overthrowing the Church, but at forcing her to tolerate dissent. Since the religious forces in the country were now organised from London by managers who had no personal attachment to any faith, but considerable breadth of intellectual grasp, the fanatics, when rallied under the Whig name, were taught to lisp the word Toleration, of which Pym hated the very sound, and of which Cromwell had only half understood the meaning. In politics the party aimed at depriving the Court of its administrative freedom, and subjecting the King's will to that of ministers chosen from the Whig nobles, and from those gentry who best represented the middle class electorate.

The Whig democracy and the Whig programme

In the winter and spring of 1678-79, the Popish Terror detached the Cavaliers from the Court. For six months there was no movement among the squires against the Whig efforts to snatch all power into the hands of Parliament. But the King, left alone with a small knot of unpopular counsellors, refused to yield. He only bowed to the storm so far as to sign the death-warrants of Oates' victims, while he told his friends that Oates was lying.[3] He refused to surrender the militia to the Houses ; he refused to be guided by the advice of Whig councillors ; above all he refused to take part in changing the succession. The question of the government of England on Charles's death became the test question on which the command of the present situation was felt to turn. The Whigs adopted Sacheverell's Exclusion policy. But when they came to decide the further question, who was to take the place of James, they would not adopt the cause of the legitimate next heirs, English Mary and Dutch William, because William had courted

Exclusion and Divorce schemes

---

[1] Christie, ii., pp. 206, 380. Marvell, i., p. 516. Burnet, ii., p. 83 note. Airy, p. 236.
[2] *Examen*, p. 513.   [3] Ailesbury, p. 96.

the friendship of Danby. In looking for a man to preside over the whole English race, the Whigs sought one who would be the puppet of their own faction. This was their error and their crime, which they were bitterly to expiate. In the winter of 1678-79 they had not yet fixed their choice on the bastard Monmouth, but were still strong for a divorce. Indeed, as late as October, 1680, long after Monmouth's claims had been advanced, Shaftesbury was prepared to throw him over, if the King would take a Protestant wife. For if Charles married again, had a child, and died before it came of age, a Protector would be needed during the minority. Shaftesbury might well hope to win that post, and make the Whigs supreme.[1]

Attack on the Queen Nov., 1678

So on 24th November, 1678, Oates, in flat contradiction to his original evidence, swore personal knowledge of a plot, in which the Queen and her physician Sir George Wakeman had conspired to poison the King. Whether or not Oates was directly suborned by Shaftesbury, the leader and his faction took up the wild tale with greed and clamour. If noise enough were made, they did not think that Charles would stake his Crown rather than put away a woman he had already so grossly injured. But their scheme failed, because he had still a certain standard of honour ; and because he knew that his whole system of government, for which he cared a great deal, was involved in the defence of his wife, for whom he hardly cared at all. The Whig estimate of Charles was as great an error as the Tory estimate of James.

The Green Ribbon Club

If the King held fast to the weapon of executive government, the Whigs were the first in the field, with a party organisation. Since their strength lay in the people, they invented the art of digging channels for the streams of popular opinion. All over England elections were arranged, petitions and demonstrations set on foot, political literature handed round, in print and manuscript, by agents sent down from the headquarters, the Green Ribbon Club. That Club occupied the King's Head Tavern at the west side of Chancery Lane End, opposite to Inner Temple ; it was named after the new party colours that had succeeded to " Presbyterian true blue ". Before the Club was founded in 1675, no party in England ever had a local habitation, beyond such as was afforded by the private hospitality of individual chiefs. Certainly no party ever before showed such organising power as the Green Ribbon men. When a display of force was needed, Southwark and Wapping were called out by the Club, like the Faubourg St. Antoine by the Jacobins. Although in the streets of London the mob might only massacre priests in effigy, the work of the Green Ribbon was no child's play, and resembled that of the Jacobin Club in many of its functions. Its missionaries were sent out to form the opinion of

---

[1] Christie, ii., pp. 379-81. Mr. Pollock (pp. 228-31) takes a different view of Shaftesbury's motive. in this matter from that which I have advanced.

the country ; at its private debates, policy was discussed and Parliamentary eloquence rehearsed ; in its upper rooms, motions for the next day's session in either House were drawn up and the proposers assigned. Shaftesbury was President of the Green Ribbon ; but it had not the lofty and aristocratic atmosphere of Brooks's in the time of Fox and Grey. Besides Lords and Commons from Westminster, the list of its members included City Aldermen like Bethel, Roundhead veterans like Romsey, professional plotters like Ferguson, hired poets like Shadwell, and pamphleteers like Blount. Young lawyers, who went to Hobbes for their religion, but to Harrington for their politics, came in at evening from their chambers over the way ; young men of estate, just come up to town, were brought round to the Club, to be won for the Whig cause by a word in confidence from the President, or a reminiscence of life at St. Omers from the favourite member. Oates, secure in his promise of a Bishopric from the party, and already enjoying " an influence more than episcopal," was driven down by the first nobles in the land, to carry elections by lifting up at the hustings the light of his hideous countenance. In the rooms of the Green Ribbon Shaftesbury discussed the latest version of the plot with the cloud of witnesses suddenly arisen from the slums and gaols ; Cavendish was argued over to support the Exclusion Bill ; politicians debated with Dissenting ministers the rival advantages of Toleration and Comprehension ; and Monmouth was lured by toasts and flatteries to his fate. Of the thousands who to-day are hurrying into the City by the site of Temple Bar, intent on such different errands and engrossed in thoughts so alien to those dead passions of their ancestors, scarcely one knows of the old inn, which there faced the street ; or imagines how at nightfall the Lords and gentlemen, perjurers and patriots, spies, lawyers, saints, atheists and poets, leaving their perruques inside, swaggered out of the reeking wine-room, pipe in hand, on to the long balconies, to chaff in cant terms the *mobile vulgus* packed in the street below, to lead the groan at the name of James, and the cheer when Monmouth or Oates was seen among them, or when the waxen Pope was emptied from his throne on to the bonfire.[1]

The Cavalier Parliament became the instrument of the Whigs for driving the plot home. When Bedloe, the witness who hunted in leash with Oates, complained at the bar of the House that he had " many great men his enemies," the Speaker told him that " he had the House for his friend ".[2] Nor did the Tory squires show less Protestant zeal against the standing army and against the dealings of the Court with France. These two questions of the day, never

Parliament, Nov.-Dec., 1678

---

[1] *First Whig*, pp. 74-93, 197-203. This decade of turbulent faction, enriched our language with the word " mob,"—generally written in full as *mobile vulgus* in Shaftesbury's day, then sometimes as " mobily," turning about the time of the Revolution into " mob ".

[2] 18th November, 1678, Grey, vi., p. 210. *State Trials*, ix., pp. 654-59.

out of men's minds since the last Dutch war, were raised by strange events in the winter of 1678, at the moment when every suspicion was inflamed by the Popish Terror.

Parliament in terror of the army

A standing army was equally unpopular with both parties. Even at the height of Danby's supremacy, Parliament had demanded either its disbandment or an immediate war with France. In April, 1678, the servant riding behind the coach of Sir John Coventry, who had formerly suffered in his own person for the privileges of Parliament, had his head broken by an ill-disciplined company and its captain. At the word "soldiers" the House was all agog. One after another the angry members leapt to their feet, crying : "These men are raised for an imaginary war " ; " these red-coats may fight against Magna Charta " ; "drums ought not to be beat here, nor red-coats to be about the Parliament, *in terrorem populi* ". Such was their sensitiveness even in normal times. When, six months after this incident, the terror of the plot broke out, the army, which if it had been in the control of Parliament, would have removed all fear of a Catholic revolution, being in the King's hands was itself an additional cause of panic. Nor were these fears as idle as Oates' tale. The King had a force in Scotland, estimated at 20,000 men, specially raised by Lauderdale "to march into England upon call ". There were troops in Tangier, Ireland and England. Worst of all, 10,000 British subjects, pressed for the French service in Flanders, won his battles for Louis, but were always "within summons " of England ; many Catholic officers, driven from the home army by the Test Act of 1673, were now in command of these hard-fighting regiments. Even the forces in the British islands were rightly or wrongly believed by the House to contain a heavy proportion of Papists and Irish both among the officers and in the ranks. Therefore, one of the few sensible measures of protection against the Popish Plot which Parliament demanded, was the disbandment of the regular army. "Popery and slavery," Shaftesbury told the Lords, "like two sisters go hand in hand ". The Tory squires were at present as little enamoured of the one as of the other.[1]

Betrayal and fall of Danby, Dec., 1678

The question of the army was intimately connected with the question of France. In the spring of the year, when troops had at Danby's instance been voted and raised for a war against Louis, why had no such war been begun ? At the height of the Popish Terror the answer came out. Charles had, in March, 1678, negotiated a secret treaty with Louis in return for a yearly pension of £300,000 in French gold. In that transaction Danby had been an unwilling agent. In order to retain office, he had consented to do the bidding of his master, and sell our policy for the time being to the King whom

---

[1] Grey, v., pp. 285-88 ; vi., pp. 268-70. Marvell, pp. 508, 515. Burnet, ii., pp. 124, 125 and notes. *Parl. Hist.*, iv. p. 1116

it was his chief object to thwart. Louis, who knew Danby to be the
foe of France, betrayed to the Whigs the transaction which made
him appear her friend. The agent in the betrayal of the Tory
minister was Montague, the English representative at Paris. Louis
paid him 50,000 livres to publish the instructions which he had
received from Danby for this infamous sale of British interests;
Charles had written on the manuscript : " I approve of this letter,
C. R.". In collusion with the French Ambassador Barillon, and the
Whig chiefs, Montague on 19th December gave these letters to the
Speaker, who read them aloud from the chair. When the reading
was ended, there was an interval of silence and astonishment. Then
the Whig orators leapt to their feet. " This agrees well with Coleman's letters," they cried. Coleman's letters had shown that the
payment of French money to Charles was to be the first step to the
overthrow of Protestantism in England. And now the King himself,
the intended victim of another Popish Plot, was detected as a willing
participant in the first half of Coleman's scheme. Henceforth a
Protestant people could put confidence in no one inside the Palace
walls. The party in total opposition to Court alone seemed to offer
a chance of security to the nation. The prestige of the Whigs again
rose by as much as it had risen a month before, on the day when the
corpse of Godfrey was discovered ; though if the truth had been
known, they, more than the disgraced minister, were Barillon's
pensioners and confidants. A pretence was made in public speaking
to shield the real traitor, Charles, in order to crush the instrument
Danby under the full weight of the charge. The responsibility of Cavalier
ministers was established at Danby's expense, and his Tory plea Parlia-
that it had been his duty to obey the King was rejected. His im- dissolved,
peachment was voted, and his head was in great danger if the Jan., 1679
Houses. sat another month. He therefore persuaded Charles to
dissolve the Cavalier Parliament, nearly eighteen years after it had
first met. At last the Whigs had forced the King's hand.[1]

During these last wild weeks of the old Royalist Parliament, The trials
and on through the wilder sessions and prorogations of the three of the
Whig Parliaments that followed, the Law Courts in Westminster Plot,
Hall and Old Bailey beheld a series of historic and terrible scenes. 1678-81
One traitor and a score of innocent men were done to death by false
swearing, amid shouts of triumph in the crowded court and at the
foot of Tyburn shambles, while half a dozen more were saved by the
resolution of Judge and jury in the face of such a storm as few
tribunals have ever dared to defy. The various trials of the Popish
Plot differed one from another both in criminality of the participants
and in result to the accused.

[1] Grey, vi., pp. 347-49. Burnet, ii., pp. 182, 183 notes, pp. 187, 188. Pollock,
pp. 179-81. In later years Danby fraudulently substituted " writ by my order.
C.R.," in place of the less decisive original, " I approve of this letter '

Convic-
tion of
Coleman,
27th
Nov.,
1678

The first trial for the plot proper was that of the Duke's secretary, Coleman. His letters, read in court, showed him guilty of treason in trying "to subvert the Protestant religion as it is by law established," "by the aid and assistance of foreign powers". "Mr. Coleman," said Lord Chief Justice Scroggs, "your own papers are enough to condemn you." But Oates and Bedloe added a false accusation that he had conspired to assassinate the King. After sentence had been passed, Coleman, though still denying his guilt, confessed that the court had allowed him "all the fairplay imaginable". He was an enthusiast who had staked his life in the cause of his religion, and lost.

Convic-
tion of
innocent
men

A few weeks later the blood of the innocent began to flow. First Oates and his accomplices swore away the lives of a batch of Jesuits for the imaginary plot against the King's person (17th Dec.). Next three innocent men were convicted for the murder of Godfrey, chiefly on the evidence of Prance, who was perhaps not lying when he claimed to have had a share in the deed himself (5th February, 1679).[1]

In June another batch of Jesuits, and the Catholic lawyer Langhorn, were convicted for the assassination plot, although sixteen witnesses came over from St. Omers and bore evidence that Oates was with them at the seminary on 24th April, the day when he claimed to have been present at the famous "consult" in the Strand. But mob, judges and jury attached no weight to the oaths of Jesuits, for all believed them to hold the casuistic doctrine that it was pardonable to lie in the interest of the Church.

Acquittal
of Wake-
man, 18th
July,
1679

In July came the first acquittals. Three Benedictines were on trial, together with the Queen's physician, Sir George Wakeman, who was charged with conspiracy to poison the King. It was in effect the Queen's trial also. The divorce policy of the Whigs was at stake. A witness from the Privy Council came into court, and, referring to the whole Council for the truth of his statement, exposed Oates as a liar. "My Lord," cried Wakeman in an ecstasy of sudden hope, "this is a Protestant witness too." Oates prevaricated, then lost his head and abused the Privy Council. But the bully had his match on the Bench. "You have taken a great confidence," said Scroggs, "I know not by what authority, to say anything of anybody." For the first time the Whig champion was put to silence. Then Scroggs, after he had abused the Popish religion in terms more scurrilous than were usual even from his mouth, felt safe in instructing the jury that they might disbelieve the evidence for the prosecution. Oates was still in a state of collapse, but Bedloe's croak was heard: "My Lord, my evidence is not rightly summed up." "I know not," said Scroggs,

[1] Stephen, i., p. 393. Pollock, pp. 117-166. But see also Lang's *Valet's Tragedy*, chap. iii. See Appendix C. below.

" by what authority this man speaks." And so, to the rage of the spectators, the prisoners were acquitted. It was a memorable triumph of the respect for law and public authority which alone can overcome the natural instincts prompting mobs in every age and in every civilisation to lynch those of whose guilt they are convinced. The courts had in some cases been deceived into unjust convictions. But that was a less evil than if the law had been dictated by the popular will, or had given place to massacre.

The acquittal of Wakeman and his friends was long regarded as a perversion of justice by the influence of the throne. The Whigs still led through London streets, in their Pope-burning pageants, the figure of the Queen's physician with a bottle of poison in his hand. But their worst fury was let loose on Scroggs. A foul-mouthed and drunken voluptuary, like so many able men of that day, he was no difficult mark to hit. But the arrows aimed at him were somewhat broad in the head. Oates undertook to prove that he had danced naked. He was libelled, he was assaulted, he was impeached. It was said even by Tories that his motive for treating Wakeman fairly had been the desire to stand well at Court. But whatever the motives, this coarse and courageous Judge and gallant jury had saved many other lives besides the four at stake that day. Wakeman's acquittal stemmed the flood. During the next year, not only were Gascoigne and Castlemaine acquitted, but the number of persons brought to trial fell off in the most marked degree.[1]

Scroggs and the Whig party

The Catholics took courage and tried to turn the tables on their assassins. Through the agency of the infamous Mrs. Cellier, the personal friends of the Duke of York found an instrument in Dangerfield, an inhabitant of Newgate prison, took him out, gave him money, and set him to spy on the Whigs. He soon produced a Presbyterian plot. But in the hour of peril he deserted to the safer ranks of the Protestant perjurers. The fraud of the " Meal Tub Plot " was exposed, and the exposure renewed the popular belief in the criminality of Catholics.[2]

The Meal Tub Plot, Oct., 1679

The credibility of Oates was not yet denied on all points, even by his political opponents. More than a year after the rejection of his evidence against Wakeman, the Tory Lords, who had thrown out the second Exclusion Bill, accepted his testimony against one of the most honourable of their own number, and sent Lord Stafford to death (Dec., 1680). Even as late as the summer of 1681, after the fall of the Whigs had removed all pressure on the Government to shed more blood, Plunket, the Catholic Archbishop of Dublin, was found guilty, and was left to execution by the unscrupulous King, who had from beginning to end let his friends know that he " believed not one word of what was called Oates' Plot ".[3]

---

[1] *State Trials, sub. loc. First Whig*, p. 104. Pollock, pp. 354-58.
[2] *State Trials*, vii., pp. 1043-68. Pollock, pp. 204-213.
[3] Ailesbury, i., p. 96.

Unscru-
pulous-
ness of
men of all
creeds
and
parties

Plunket was the last victim of the Popish Terror. Times had changed, and several of the witnesses who had formerly supported Oates were brought into court to swear away the lives of Shaftesbury and their old employers. Either, therefore, the Tories still thought these men trustworthy witnesses ; or, as is more probable, they cared no more than Shaftesbury, and no more than the patrons of the Meal Tub Plot, how they contrived the death of enemies of whose general turpitude they were convinced. The Whig, Tory and Catholic politicians, and the King, all proved to be rogues. Despairing historians turn for honesty to the famous Trimmer : Halifax indeed voted " Not Guilty " in Stafford's trial, because he had the sense to believe that the Catholic gentry had " not put off the man in general, nor the Englishman in particular " ; but such was his fear and hatred of the Jesuits that he told Sir William Temple " the plot must be handled as if it were true, whether it were so or no," and wrote to Henry Savile that " the notoriety of the fact is evidence enough of the plot ".[1]

When the well-informed expressed an almost universal opinion, it cannot be imputed as a crime to the ignorant that they shared it with more complete sincerity. But the conduct of the mob was most horrible. At the trial of Langhorn they assaulted the witnesses for the defence outside the doors of the Old Bailey, beat one of them within an inch of his life, and apparently prevented the others from ever reaching the box. When prisoners could put no compulsion on witnesses to attend, such demonstrations were, to say the least, a serious discouragement to volunteers.[2]

The innocent Catholics were injured to some degree by conditions peculiar to their trials—the unscrupulous zeal of the politicians, the prejudice of the mob, the abusive harangues of the Judges against their religion—but they were injured far more by the unscientific treatment of evidence common to all the trials of that and every previous age. Under the system of justice established under the House of Plantagenet, every man's life had been at the mercy of common rumour ; that system had been reformed, but still every man's life was at the mercy of two false witnesses. One witness was thought as good as another, provided he had taken the oath, to which every one in court, except the swearers themselves, attached a superstitious reverence. Critical analysis of evidence was not understood by any one. The Catholic prisoners were no more able than the Judge or the Counsel for the prosecution, to point out reasons why the evidence against them should be disbelieved. As we read the State Trials with modern eyes, we see them losing one chance after another of establishing their innocence.[3]   In that

---

[1] Temple, *Works* (1770), ii., p. 506. Foxcroft, *Life of Halifax*, i., p. 163; ii., p. 318.   [2] *State Trials*, vii., p. 463.

[3] Thus why did not Langhorn, himself a lawyer, ask the hostess of the White Horse Tavern who had really visited her house on 24th April, 1678 ? (*State Trials*, vii., p. 464).

generation there were only two admitted tests of incredibility in a witness—a previous conviction for perjury, or flat contradiction by some other witness on points raised by the trial on hand. These common rules were adhered to in perfect good faith in the case of the Catholic prisoners, except that once the rebutting evidence was most unjustly disregarded because it was given by Jesuits. On this system Stafford was condemned and Wakeman acquitted.

When such was the conception of evidence, the innocent were frequently convicted, not in political cases alone. The injustice of the trials for witchcraft, wherein hundreds of the generation previous had perished, has been revealed to posterity solely by the accident of a change in our religious beliefs. And there can be no reasonable doubt that at the common Assizes, mute, inglorious Staffords perished in the ordinary course for murders and robberies which they had never committed. Informers of the lowest type were encouraged to do for society the needful work now done by trustworthy detectives ; as they ran no risk of exposure before courts ignorant of the rules of evidence, there is grave reason to fear that the informer was, as often as not, a perjurer as well.

Besides this supreme disadvantage, there were many others besetting any accused person, which Catholics suffered in common with Protestants. In a century when the State perpetually feared, and several times suffered, overthrow, the Courts of Law were citadels against treason, rather than asylums for innocence. The Judges, as Bacon had put it, were " lions under the throne ". For the political prisoner, whether guilty on the charge or not, was known to be, in general, the King's enemy. The judicial theory was only expressed in an exaggerated form by the Mayor of Hastings, who said, when retailing the alarming news of Wakeman's acquittal, that if he had not been guilty, he never would have been put on his trial.[1] Therefore, no counsel was allowed for the prisoner ; his witnesses could not be compelled to attend, and were not permitted to take the oath ; and he did not know until he came into court of what he was about to be accused. Yet, severe as were these conditions under which the victims of the Popish Plot were tried, they were less severe than the procedure under which Guy Fawkes and Raleigh had been condemned. For the Puritan Revolution had enlarged the liberty of the accused subject against the prosecuting Government, as the trials of John Lilburne had shown in Cromwell's time. Questions of law as well as of fact were now left to the Jury, who were free to acquit without fear of consequences ; the witnesses for the prosecution were now always brought into court and made to look on the prisoner as they spoke ; witnesses for the defence might at least be summoned to appear ; and the accused might no longer be interpellated by the King's Counsel, entangled in a rigorous

[1] Ailesbury, i., p. 31.

inquisition, and forced to give evidence against himself. Slowly, through blood and tears, justice and freedom had been advancing. And if, as we may reasonably suppose, the eventual exposure of Oates' perjuries produced a profound effect on the readiness of ordinary courts to accept evidence, and helped forward the legislation by which special advantages were conceded to prisoners in trials for treason (1696), the innocent Catholics did not shed their blood wholly in vain, as did thousands of innocent persons who without pity and without record had for countless ages perished with undeserved ignominy under the hangman's hands.[1]

Whig triumph at the elections, Feb., 1679

The incidents of each trial connected with the Popish Plot, eagerly watched and construed according to the needs of the hour by all the rival factions of the State, affected public opinion from day to day in the long three years' struggle for power between the Whig party and Charles II. If the King and Danby had hoped by dissolving the Cavalier Parliament to gain anything more than time, they were soon undeceived. At the elections of February, 1679, the Whigs swept the country. The organising powers of the Green Ribbon Club gave to this General Election the character, which such contests have ever since retained, of a victory won by a disciplined party on a national issue. The historical origin of the House of Commons in local selection of fit men to speak for their neighbours, was now but little reflected in the proceedings of the candidates nominated by their respective parties. With this step forward in the sense of national unity, essential to any land before a monarchical can be replaced by a Parliamentary government, came attendant evils. As the power of the House of Commons over the executive increased, men were ready to invest fortunes in the acquisition of seats, which in the days of Eliot and Hampden had been posts of danger, but were now stepping-stones to honour and emolument. Bedfordshire cost the Whigs £6,000, roughly equivalent to £60,000 in our own day. The price of votes was higher than ever before ; the electors, who when they last exercised the franchise, eighteen years back, had been content to be made drunk now claimed also to be carried to the poll at the candidate's expense.

Temporary abeyance of Royalist sentiment

But the principal reason of the Whig success was the panic of the country, and the temporary abeyance of Cavalier and Tory sentiment. At the Restoration, Anglican and Catholic gentry, who had shared the command of regiments at Naseby and waited together on the Committee of Sequestration, were bound to one another by personal feeling, on the continuance of which the Jesuits had counted too much. These common memories were now forgotten. When Dissenting ministers appeared in defiance of the

[1] Stephen, i., pp. 325, 326, 333-35, 358, 366, 367, 374, 396-402, 414-16, 426, 427.   Pollock, pp. 266-68, 286-303.

law, and stirred the voters to fury against the Catholics and the Court, the parsons and the country gentlemen let them be, and made little effort to resist the consequent Whig success at the polls. For the Tory squire owned Abbey lands, and the Tory parson collected parish tithes, which in the undying memory of the Roman Church were still her rightful property. Thus the class and the profession whose members were least ardently Protestant, and who much preferred, man for man, a Catholic gentleman to a Dissenting shopkeeper, were most bound by self-interest to oppose any movement to restore the Roman Catholic religion. Whenever, therefore, it was believed that the Court was meditating such an attempt, as in the spring of 1679 and the autumn of 1688, the Tories would not move a finger to suppress the Puritans or to help the King.

But this abnormal state of politics could never last long. In 1679, and again in 1688, it lasted for a few months together. But whereas in 1688 those months were employed to effect a settlement of our polity which has been proof against time and chance, in 1679 the golden opportunity was let slip. For when the Whig Parliament met in March, the Protestant leaders, who had the whole nation behind them, and could have passed almost any measure to which they had agreed to give their united support, began a quarrel over policy which was soon aggravated into a fierce personal contest between two self-willed statesmen.

The dispute between the Earls of Shaftesbury and Halifax at first concerned rather the nature than the extent of the revolution which both thought necessary for the State. Shaftesbury had adopted Sacheverell's scheme of excluding James from the throne. Halifax wished to keep him as nominal King, but to " limit " his power by law, handing over to Parliament his executive functions. If this plan of Limitations had been carried into effect, it would virtually have turned England into a republic, governed by two co-ordinate and rival Polish Diets, the Lords and Commons. No worse arrangement could have been devised than to charge two debating assemblies with the direct executive authority, instead of vesting it in ministers serving the King but responsible to Parliament. The Whigs indeed objected to this scheme of government not because they thought it would work ill, but because they feared it would never be allowed to work at all : James would not submit to it, and it could therefore only lead, on his brother's death, to a civil war in which the Whigs would appear as Roundheads, fighting against the name and office of King. It is indeed hard to say whether Exclusion or Limitations was most likely to end in an appeal to arms. But Shaftesbury's proposal, abstractly considered, was nearer than that of Halifax to the lines of future constitutional development ; for Shaftesbury urged the absolute necessity for England to have a Protestant monarch, who could be

Quarrel of Shaftesbury and Halifax

Exclusion or Limitations

trusted to exercise the functions of royalty in a constitutional spirit. His bad choice of such a King soon compromised his Exclusion policy. But in March, 1679, Monmouth's candidature was not yet very prominent, and it is possible that at that date the Exclusion scheme was as likely to be generally accepted as Halifax's Limitations. Both were fraught with great dangers. But to devise a scheme that was not fraught with great dangers would have passed the wit of man.

First Whig Parliament meets March, 1679

Such were the two proposals canvassed at Westminster at the meeting of the first Whig Parliament. The representatives of the great Whig houses at first favoured the Limitations proposed by Halifax. But when Shaftesbury and he quarrelled, and men had to choose which of the two leaders to follow, Russell and Cavendish enlisted, as men of uncertain opinions and strong party spirit always do, under the most hard-fighting captain. The dividing currents were too strong for any one remaining in politics to take up ground exactly of his own choosing. A conscientious and ineffectual man like Temple would soon retire. Halifax, the "Trimmer," was fast becoming a courtier. Shaftesbury before long carried the party over to Exclusion. But when the first Exclusion Bill was introduced in May, 1679, its principle was still opposed by several prominent Whigs who next year took charge of the second Bill themselves.

First Exclusion Bill, May, 1679

The moment when any well-framed scheme for Exclusion, Regency or Limitation could have been put through without a civil war was rapidly passing away. While the enemies of the Court were dividing, its friends were beginning to unite. It was the object of Charles to gain time. By consummate political ability he gained two years, and in those two years the reaction had gathered head. By making many concessions he avoided any surrender. With imperturbable joviality he spent his days fishing and sauntering, as if nothing were amiss. His natural easiness and good-nature helped him to play without effort the subtlest of political games. By never losing his temper he at last enjoyed his revenge.

Temple's Privy Council, April-July, 1679

His first move, in the spring of 1679, was suggested by a scheme of Sir William Temple. That excellent man, who held it a statesman's business to be a scholar in his own profession, had by long study and thought discovered the true interest of Britain at home and abroad. But though well able to serve her in the cool atmosphere of diplomacy, the author of the Triple Alliance was utterly unfitted to leave the impress of his wisdom on our warring domestic factions. Just before he retired in despair to the congenial refuge of his books and his garden at Sheen, he persuaded both parties to adopt a plan whereby the King and his subjects could carry on the Government together. On Temple's advice Charles altered the composition of the Privy Council, and revived its powers, which had been gradually passing over to the smaller Cabinet. He made thirty of his principal friends and enemies into the new Privy Councillors, and promised to take no action except by their corporate advice. This body was to stand as an umpire between ministers and Parliament, and between Tory and Whig. It was expected to represent a moderating third party, but in fact it was only important because it was composed of the most prominent partisans of both sides. The Whig Lords took their seats beside their deadliest foes, and their leader Shaftesbury consented to be President of the Council ; but, meanwhile, they continued to push on their agitation in Parliament and country with unabated violence. Charles, on his side, was equally disloyal to the spirit of Temple's compromise ; he never took the new Privy Council seriously, except as a means of gaining time. " God's fish ! " he said to his friend Bruce, " they have put a set of men about me, but they shall know nothing, and this keep to yourself." [1] He formed his resolutions after the meetings were over, in private conversation, sometimes with Halifax or Temple, and sometimes with Lauderdale, though hatred of Lauderdale was the one point on which all the others were united. The end of Temple's Privy Council as a real organ of Government came when, against its advice, Charles prorogued and then dissolved the first Whig Parliament, in order to prevent the passage of the Exclusion Bill. Shaftesbury, blind with rage, cried out that he would have the lives of the men who had counselled the prorogation. Among these was Halifax. Already the statesmen were playing for each other's heads.

First Whig Parliament prorogued (May), dissolved (July), 1679

Though the times were growing tragic, comedy put her healing touch on everything that passed. The iron age of politics was the golden age of wit. Charles was specially jovial and friendly to the Whig Lords whenever he had secretly resolved on some crushing stroke, such as to prorogue or dissolve their Parliament. The Act of Habeas Corpus itself, the one great measure which he had given them time to enact, had only passed the Upper Chamber because the tellers in jest had counted a fat Lord as ten, and had failed to rectify their figures.[2] It was the best joke ever made in England. Individual liberty would have been at an end during the ten years of violence that followed, if persons obnoxious to Government had not possessed the new machinery for availing themselves of the Englishman's old right of a speedy trial or release. The fat Lord's vote secured that even James II. could not imprison his subjects at pleasure.

Habeas Corpus Act, May, 1679

In the summer of 1679 the star of Monmouth rose. The son of Lucy Walters, one of Charles's mistresses in the early days of exile, he had been treated since the Restoration as a favourite, but never as a legitimate, scion of the Royal House. He was a weak,

Monmouth

---

[1] Airy, p. 240.　　　[2] Burnet, ii., p. 264 and note 1.　Airy, p. 239.

bad, and beautiful young man. Though popular, good-natured
and charming as his reputed father, he had once, in a drunken
frolic, helped to murder a watchman, while the unoffending
wretch had begged for mercy on his knees.[1] Monmouth was, perhaps, too light to be accounted criminal. He was born to be the
tool of others.

The opportunity for those others had now come. The violence
and corruption of Lauderdale's government of Scotland had put all
that kingdom in smouldering discontent, and the dragonades of
Claverhouse had set one corner actually ablaze. The Whigs of the
South-west were up in arms, under the old terrible banner of Christ's
Crown and Covenant, and had scattered their persecutors at Drum-
clog. Shaftesbury's followers, mindful by what means the King had
been forced to consult Parliament in 1640, began an agitation in
England on behalf of their Scottish brethren. The popular feeling
was so strong against the use of English troops to suppress the
Covenanters, that Charles would not have dared to order his army
to march north, if he had not bought leave from Shaftesbury by
sending Monmouth as commander-in-chief. Charles was playing
Bothwell a dangerous hand. Monmouth conquered the rebels at Bothwell
Brig, Brig, won by his clemency the heart of Scotland, and returned to
22nd Court, possessing the love and commanding the armies of the two
June, kingdoms. At this unlucky moment Charles fell ill. His death
1679 was hourly expected. The Whigs prepared to keep James out of
the kingdom by use of the royal forces which chance had put into
the hands of their champion. James was an exile in Brussels,
whither Charles had compelled him to retire, that the fear and
hatred of him might be allayed by his absence. The Tories were
scattered, without a leader and without a cause ; the Whigs were
armed, led, united ; the great majority of Englishmen sat still in
Danger- dull terror of what the next hour would bring. James was sum-
ous moned back by the " Triumvirate," Halifax, Essex and Sunderland,
illness of with his brother's consent to his brother's death-bed ; he crossed the
Charles, sea and travelled to Windsor in disguise. He might well have
22nd expected to find, in halls hung with black, the last of the panic-
Aug., stricken courtiers debating whether to hold the castle against
1679 Monmouth's Guards, or fly to unfurl the standard in the West ;
but he was greeted instead by a cheerful convalescent, expressing
well-feigned brotherly surprise at the exile's unexpected return.
Charles had recovered, and England breathed again.

The accident by which the Whigs had so nearly won all had
turned to their loss. England had had a fright, and those who
had frightened her must pay. A few days of terrible anxiety had
burnt it on the minds of men that the Whig plans meant civil war,

[1] Marvell, i., pp. 195, 416.

and that the King stood between his subjects and a sea of troubles.
Charles began almost to be popular with those who care more for
peace than for politics, while the Tories saw in the supremacy of
Monmouth and his faction, from which they had escaped by a hair's
breadth, a danger to their interests more immediate than the secret
intrigue of the terrified and proscribed Catholics, who were crowding
the gaols in every shire. If the Tories had not yet arrived at regarding James as their party leader, they already turned their utmost efforts against his rival. They were further alarmed and disgusted by the language of the Nonconformists, who poured out the
vials of long pent wrath through pamphlets and broadsides, avenging
eighteen years of martyrdom on the general reader. As the censorship of the press had fallen into abeyance on the sudden dissolution
of the last Parliament, great masses of literature went out to spread
the passions of both parties among the common people. The Tory
pamphleteer, Roger L'Estrange, retaliated ferociously on the Nonconformists, and in his weekly *Observator* called on the Church to
defend herself. The clergy mounted the pulpits and ranted against
fanatics. The word was passed round that " forty-one " had come
again : the Church was in danger.

Encouraged by these symptoms, Charles ordered Monmouth to
lay down the military command with which he had threatened the
public peace. With most one-sided impartiality he exiled both
the claimants. Monmouth, whose advantage it was to show his
handsome face among the shouting crowds, was ordered off to
Holland ; while James, whose presence at home kept the magistrates
in perpetual fear of an uprising of the Protestants, was in his own
best interest sent off to Scotland, till the pamphleteers had impressed upon the mind of the English Tories an unreal picture of
the mild, long-suffering exile. *Monmouth and James exiled, Sep., 1679*

Meanwhile, the general election was taking place. In spite of
the efforts of the parsons and the rural Cavaliers, the counties
were held solid for the Whig interest by the yeomen, and only the
results in some of the smaller boroughs represented the fact that
the King again had a party. Charles saw forces in the far distance
gathering for his relief, but he knew that for many months the
siege would be close. Therefore, he must risk everything to gain
time. Sure in his own mind of this, he prorogued the newly elected
Parliament, against the moderating advice of Halifax, Essex and
Sunderland. The support and counsel of the Triumvirate were
thought to be his only hope. But when at last he was at grips
with fate, he relied on no judgment but his own. For a whole
year, during which he refused to allow the triumphantly elected
Whigs to assemble at Westminster, they battered like madmen
against the closed portals of the Constitution. Infuriated by the
Prorogation policy, which even Halifax condemned, the Opposition
Second Whig Parliament prorogued, Oct., 1679- Oct., 1680

resorted to methods of such violence as must either beat down resistance or recoil on those who use it.

Pope-burning procession, 17th Nov., 1679

The custom of symbolical processions and public masquerades, which, coming down unbroken from mediæval times, still gladdened the jolly festivals of the English, and the ruder ceremonies with which Guy Fawkes was yearly committed to the flames, together suggested to the genius of Whiggery a superb and costly pageant of hate and fear. On Queen Elizabeth's Accession Day, as soon as the early November twilight had closed upon the City, a splendid torchlight procession of Cardinals and Jesuits, allegorical and political personages, wound slowly through the expectant streets. A bellman, chanting dolefully at intervals " Remember Justice Godfrey," was followed by the effigy of the murdered magistrate, in his familiar camlet coat. The Londoners had often looked on that well-loved figure in life, and once in death. A Jesuit riding on a white horse held the body upright before him ; in that fashion all believed him to have been carried from the scene of his murder to the ditch on Primrose Hill. In the glare of torches, the glamour and the press of men, the scene was infernal, appalling. The City population was strained to the highest pitch of emotional excitement. At ten o'clock, when the Pope and his courtiers arrived beneath the balconies of the Green Ribbon, where the Whig aristocracy awaited their arrival, the chanting of a triumphant Protestant pæan beneath the statue of Elizabeth, looking down on the scene from Temple Bar, preceded the final conflagrations :—

> Your Popish Plot, and Smithfield threat,
> We do not fear at all ;
> For lo, beneath Queen Bess's feet
> You fall, you fall, you fall.

By midnight the vast mob was so highly wrought that many supposed the proceedings had been designed to end in a revolution before the dawn.[1]

Monmouth's return, Nov., 1679

November had not gone out when another spectacle kept Londoners from their beds. Monmouth, returning from Holland against the King's orders, made entry, while lines of bonfires roared in the streets, and the steeples rocked at midnight. Next year he made his progress through the West (1680) ; won the ill-starred love of the yeomen and weavers of Somerset ; and assembled the Whig gentry at hunts and race meetings, as much suspect to Government as the similar gatherings of Cavalier sportsmen had been under Cromwell. He struck the baton sinister from his arms, claiming legitimacy. The story was put about by the Whig understrappers that a certain Black Box contained the contract of marriage between his mother Lucy Walters and the King. But if

[1] *First Whig*, chap. vi.

real investigation had been made into a subject so obscure, the world would perhaps have discovered with surprise that so far from being a legitimate Prince, he was not even a royal bastard. It is by no means certain that his father was not Robert Sidney, a paramour of his mother's, whom he himself closely resembled.[1] The official policy of the Whigs was still Divorce, in spite of Wakeman's acquittal. In their party songs they still taught the people to sing :—

> Then down with James, and set up Charles
> On good Queen Bess's side ;
> That all true Commons, Lords and Earls
> May wish him a fruitful bride.[2]

But the pathetic and fatuous devotion of the common people to Monmouth, and the fact that the wretched creature had broken all ties at Court and become the puppet of their faction, at last attracted these unprincipled statesmen to support his candidature in all but name.

Meanwhile, pressure was brought on Charles to call the elected Parliament together. The first of a series of petitions to this effect was carried up to him by seventeen Whig Peers (Dec. 1679), headed by brave old Prince Rupert. Rupert's religion had not been affected by the atmosphere of the Restoration Court. Still as stout a Protestant as he had first become at his mother's knee and in the old Rhenish wars of his early youth, he had since grown, during his long residence in England, to be a good Englishman and a good Parliamentarian. The Lords' example was followed, and monster petitions came up from the towns and shires. All over the country the names were collected by house-to-house canvassing of " agitants and sub-agitants," often, as the Tories averred, by fraudulent methods. But the conduct of these " petitioners " who would constrain the King's free choice was " abhorred " by the rising Cavalier sentiment, which was embodied in the following February in counter-addresses of " abhorrence ". But in the course of the year 1680 the names of Abhorrer and Petitioner were changed for those of Tory and Whig. England owes her greatest party names to Titus Oates. He used to croak " Tory " at any man who dared to question the plot, and his admirers took up the word. And as soon as one side thus called its opponents after the Catholic bandits who waylaid the Saxon settlers among the Irish bogs, it was an obvious retort to hurl back the name of the Covenanted " Whigs " who murdered Bishops on the Scottish moors.

It was now war to the knife. On the 26th of June, 1680, Shaftesbury, accompanied by Russell, Cavendish, Oates and a great company, entered Westminster Hall, to present James to the Grand Jury as a Popish Recusant ; and to indict as a " common nuisance " the

Petitioners and Abhorrers : Whigs and Tories

Essex, Sunderland, and Madam Carwell desert to the Whigs, 1680

---

[1] Clarke, *James II.*, i., p. 492. Airy, p. 33.   [2] *First Whig*, p. 106.

Louise de Querouaille, Duchess of Portsmouth, the King's Popish mistress. Chief Justice Scroggs, who had gone too far in saving Catholic prisoners to hope for pardon if the Whigs ever came to power, dismissed the Grand Jury before they could find a true bill. But the demonstration was not without effect. Madam Carwell, as the English called De Querouaille, was thoroughly frightened. She and her master Louis, who, since she had succeeded to Lady Castlemaine's political influence, regarded her as his most influential agent, began to expect the victory and to fear the vengeance of the Whigs. Carwell entered into an agreement with them, that, in return for a sum of money and the abandonment of all proceedings against her, she would win over Charles to accept Exclusion and any successor whom Shaftesbury should name. Her desertion carried with it that of Sunderland, always seeking a quiet place on the strongest side, while Essex, who was at heart a Whig, at length passed over to the innermost counsels of the Opposition. Thus two of the Triumvirate had deserted the King. But when the rats left the ship, Halifax once more came on board. Since Charles had, against his advice, prorogued the newly elected Parliament, he had been living in seclusion. But when the Houses at last met in October, 1680, he came out again to defend the inheritance of James, whose person and policy he detested, rather than subject himself and his country to Shaftesbury's factious rule.

The second Whig Parliament had all the characteristics of a revolutionary assembly, except power to execute its violent will. Headed by Russell, and accompanied by the Lord Mayor and Aldermen, the Commons " with a mighty shout " carried the Exclusion Bill into the Upper Chamber. There the battle was fought out. The Lords held the balance of the Constitution, and no one knew how they would decide. Charles and his faithful Commons watched the debate hour by hour in painful anxiety. Monmouth felt constrained by piety to speak for the Bill, as necessary to stop the plots against his father's life ; " the kiss of Judas," Charles was heard to exclaim. Halifax, at bay against all the famous orators of the House, in fifteen debating speeches of consummate ability, carried the waverers against the combined efforts of Shaftesbury, Essex and Sunderland. The Bill, instead of naming the Princess Mary to replace her father James, was purposely worded by Monmouth's friends so as to leave the succession uncertain ; and thus the friends of William of Orange, who all through this period had his agents and correspondents among the English politicians, were lost to the Whig cause. The Bill was rejected by 63 to 30.

Then the Commons broke loose in rage. Every day some person was attacked or some violent resolution passed. Halifax was impeached on " common fame " that he had dissolved the last

The Second Whig Parliament, Oct., 1680-Jan., 1681

Second Exclusion Bill rejected by the Lords, Nov., 1680

Parliament. " Had not that Parliament been dissolved," said one
member, " Sir George Wakeman had not been saved, nor the King's
evidence reproached." " I would rather have Halifax's head," cried
another, " than any Popish Lord's in the Tower " ; yet the meaner
prey was all that they could secure.   Scroggs and North were
impeached for their conduct on the Bench.   Private Tories throughout the country were wrongfully arrested by the Speaker's warrant.
One member was expelled the House for having promoted an
address of " abhorrence," and another for having " proclaimed the
Popish Plot no plot of the Papists ".   It was in vain that he denied
the words and assured the Speaker, " I ever did and ever shall
believe this to be a Popish Plot, as sure as you are in the Chair ".
Finally, a Bill for a Protestant Association, to put the civil and
military power into the hands of the Duke of Monmouth, was
introduced.   But with Lords and King against them, the Commons
could effect nothing for all their fury.[1]

One sacrifice was made by the upper powers to divert their wrath. Trial of
Viscount Stafford, the most venerable of those five " Popish Lords Stafford,
in the Tower," who had been lodged there in consequence of the 30th
first depositions made by Oates, was singled out to be impeached Nov.-7th
by the Commons before his Peers.   As in the trial of Strafford forty 1680
years before, the scaffoldings for the spectators of the great event
had been set up in Westminster Hall, " to the shortening the promenade of the lawyers and the severe oppression of the shops," which
ordinarily occupied its floor.   For seven days the wooden galleries
were crowded up to the roof with ambassadors, great ladies, and
row above row of Commons ; while the judging Lords, the witnesses, the counsel, the prisoner and the executioner beside him
with the axe, held the floor below.   Charles could be seen in one
gallery ; and in another Madam Carwell dispensing smiles and
sweetmeats among a crowd of gallant politicians, who six months
ago had entered the same Hall to indict her as a " common
nuisance ".   Before this audience Oates and Tuberville performed.
As usual, what was sworn against the prisoner was believed,
because it was not, as in Wakeman's trial, rebutted by counter-
evidence.   Some Peers were biassed by a desire to conciliate the
Whigs for the rejection of the Exclusion Bill, and as the Plot was
still widely credited in Tory circles, they were able to vote for his
death with the comfortable belief that his guilt was proved.   The
good old Lord's last words were disbelieved by the mob on Tower
Hill, and when his white head was held up to their gaze, it was
greeted with yells of delight.[2]

[1] Grey, vii., pp. 384, 385 ; viii., pp. 22-24.
[2] Clarke, *James II.*, i., p. 640. *State Trials*, vii., 1294-1559. *First Whig*,
pp. 140, 141. *Examen*, p. 217. Pollock, pp. 367-70 and note 5, p. 870. Lord
Acton also rejected the more pleasant story of the popular remorse at Stafford's
death-scene.

The
Third
Whig
(or Ox-
ford)
Parlia-
ment,
21st-28th
March,
1681

On the 10th of January Charles prorogued Parliament, and after a few days dissolved it. The new elections took place amid scenes of great enthusiasm on both sides. But again the Whig gentlemen, in spite of the frantic efforts of the majority of their own class, were returned by the freeholders of the towns and counties. It was mooted among the chiefs of the party, whether, if the King dissolved this Parliament as he had dissolved its predecessors, they should continue to sit in defiance of the law. Charles, knowing that such a revolutionary assembly would be protected by the train-bands and the Pope-burning population of the capital, called the Houses together at Oxford. The Whig members could not bring up with them the London mob, but they rode into the loyal city with bands of retainers, heavily laden with swords and pistols, and gay with blue streamers bearing the legend " No Popery, No Slavery ". John Locke, the intimate friend of Shaftesbury, was commissioned to find lodgings for his patron. Most of the Ex-clusionist Lords took up their quarters together in Balliol, where the governing body, in return for a high rent, allowed their college to be made the Whig citadel. No less war-like was the guise of the squires of Oxfordshire, who accompanied Charles in military order to the gate of the City, crying at his coach window " The devil hang up all Roundheads ". The militia of the county joined in the ominous demonstration. The King lodged in Christ Church, where he was surrounded by his own Lifeguards, and had at hand those of the undergraduates who had not been rusticated to make room for Court and Parliament. The bells of the city rang and the undergraduates cheered in honour of " Charles the Great," and at night bonfires blazed along the streets, loyally fed with faggots, " rumps " and " cropt ears ". The Whigs could scarcely raise a cheer from town or gown, but they came up strong and insolent. So the blue and red ribboners vapoured against each other in the streets and quadrangles.[1]

The third Whig Parliament was composed of much the same elements as the last two, but almost every member of the majority was on this occasion pledged to his constituents to accept nothing short of Exclusion. Charles therefore cheerfully offered an alter-native which he would have been most unwilling to concede. He proposed, with regard to the succession, that James should be banished, and William or Mary of Orange made regent to govern in his name. But this excellent plan, far superior to Halifax's first scheme of Limitations, was not really the policy of the Court party, who eagerly expected its rejection. They were not disappointed. Shaftesbury interpellated the King, openly requiring him to recog-

[1] London Gazette, 14-17th March, 1680(1). Christie, ii., pp. 391-401. College Histories, Balliol, H. W. Davies (1899), pp. 162-63. Wood's Life and Times, ii., pp. 524-27.

nise Monmouth as his successor. The regency proposal was rejected by the Commons. " God be praised," wrote one of the courtiers, " God hath blinded them."

For the Whigs felt certain that the want of money would leave Charles no choice but surrender, unless indeed he was prepared to begin a war, with his exchequer as empty as his father's before Edgehill. The last Parliament had refused supply, and declared that all merchants who should lend money to the King should answer for it to the Houses. The King's soldiers, sailors, and civil officers were unpaid and mutinous ; his cannon were unmounted, his magazines empty ; his own table was with difficulty replenished. It seemed that in a few weeks Government must capitulate, or else anarchy would usher in Civil War. But the Whigs calculated without Louis. They naturally supposed that the Grand Monarch was still on their side, as he had been three months back. He had given money not only to members of Parliament, but to influential Presbyterian preachers and City magnates. But in fact, though he had eagerly stirred up the Houses to put the King into difficulties, he had no desire to establish the supremacy of statesmen who would keep terms with France only until the day when they had acquired power. On the other hand, Charles, from the day when he should break Parliament and establish absolute rule, must become financially dependent on France. With the utmost precautions for secrecy, the English King met the French Ambassador in the Queen's bedroom ; standing between the bed and the wall, they negotiated a verbal treaty. Since the betrayal of Danby's letter, Charles had had enough of signing documents. He would not even give receipts for the gold. Louis, however, had all the security he wanted in the slender nature of Charles's unparliamentary income. So, when the King faced the Commons at Oxford, he had a promise of three years' supply from the French King, and they did not know it. This is the key to his action and to theirs.[1]

Louis finances Charles, March, 1681

The Whigs, unconscious of the trap that had been laid for them, were in high spirits. They too thought that " forty-one " was come again. Cartoons of pulling down the King, and doggerel catches such as

Halloo ! the Hunt's begun
Like Father, like Son !

were popular among the lower class of scribblers and partisans who had been brought from London. Rash men like College, " the Protestant joiner," ate, sang and even slept with the perjured informers of the Popish Plot, who noted what they saw and heard in Whig company, and prepared to bite the hands that fed them.[2]

[1] Airy, pp. 253-55. Burnet, ii., p. 286, note 2. Christie, ii., p. 403.
[2] *State Trials*, viii., pp. 595-602. *First Whig*, p. 145. *Examen*, pp. 100-2.

The
Third Ex-
clusion
Bill

Meanwhile, the leaders in the Commons hurried through the Exclusion Bill. The University buildings had been made ready for the use of Parliament. The Commons sat in Convocation House, and the Lords in the Geometry School; the rest of the Schools were given up to the various Parliamentary Committees. The quadrangle was alive every morning with the buzz of politicians and grandees. On the eighth day of the session the King appeared suddenly in the House of Lords. He had come in a sedan chair, closely followed by another, of which the drawn curtains presumably concealed some attendant Lord. The Commons, hastily summoned to the Upper House expecting to hear the King announce his surrender, came rushing tumultuously across the quadrangle, crowded up a steep and winding staircase, jostled through a narrow door, and passed down some steps into the body of the hall. Charles with a gay face watched his enemies defile. At length they stood there, as many as could fight their way in, below the throne, panting,

Scene at
the Dis-
solution,
28th
March,
1681

a close-headed mob. The King was in the robes of State—the real contents of the second sedan. In those robes alone could he dissolve Parliament. He spoke the fatal words and left the room, while the Commons trooped back the way they had come, with " dreadful faces " and " loud sighs ". The secret had been kept so well that the Whigs had no plan of action. A couple of hours' warning might have served to organise resistance, as it had served to save the Five Members. But now Shaftesbury in vain sent his messengers round the town to induce the Parliament men to stay together. A panic seized the undisciplined and braggart host that had ridden into Oxford. They believed that if they stayed Charles would send his guards to " pull them out by the ears ". The price of horses doubled, as in a city about to be entered by a victorious foe. The roads to Banbury, Witney and Shotover were thick with men, in coaches and on horseback, flying for their lives, each to his far country home.[1]

The Whigs never came together again in force till William of Orange summoned the Convention. Their party had no medium except Parliament. But there indeed they had an almost unfair advantage. At three successive elections they had defeated the Church and squirearchy at the polls. Owing to the peculiar constitution of the House of Commons, this result was inevitable whenever the middle classes were led by a competent minority of Lords and gentlemen; a disproportionately large majority of the seats belonged to the boroughs, and even in the counties the franchise

---

[1] Airy, pp. 254-57. *Examen*, pp. 104, 105. Ailesbury, i., pp. 56, 57. Woods, *Life and Times*, ii., pp. 524-31. I have studied on the spot, and with the kind assistance of Mr. Madan, the question of the locality of this remarkable scene. There does not appear good reason to suppose that the Lords had adjourned from the Geometry Schools, where they certainly met on the first day of session. There is no record of any such change, which could hardly have escaped notice in some document or other.

was the privilege of the independent freeholding classes, and not of the tenant-farmer and agricultural labourer who would have been compelled to obey the landlord. Therefore, after the lesson of the years 1679-81, the Cavalier party adopted notions of royal prerogative, which had been much in abeyance during the long years of the Cavalier Parliament. It is significant that Filmer's works in defence of the absolute authority of Kings, though written before the Restoration, were not published till twenty years after it, when their popularity was such as would have astonished its author if he had still been alive. The Tories made themselves the theoretical champions and the political agents of despotism, carried on in the interest of their Church and class, because the Whigs had used the House of Commons at the dictation of other classes and in the interest of other Churches. The Tories ceased to be Parliamentarians and became Courtiers. This aberration, which, but for James II.'s madness, would have enslaved England, took the theoretic form of the doctrine of "non-resistance". Men who turned purple with rage when the Dissenters asked them for Toleration, and when the yeomen outvoted them at the polls, knew so little of their own high temper that they vowed that if Nero were hereditary King of England, they would let him take their lands, their tithes, their laws, their very lives, without raising a hand against him. The Universities of Oxford and Cambridge, and the Anglican clergy throughout the land, regularly proclaimed these astonishing doctrines. The Court was crowded with gentlemen, divines, grand juries and corporations, bearing to the throne Addresses of such fulsome loyalty that one of the ministers in disgust declared that the Whig Petitioners only spat in the King's face, but the Addressers spat in his mouth. Yet even Charles seemed too mild a monarch for subjects in this mood. His popularity waned before that of his brother, whose health was now everywhere drunk with the loud "Huzzah," the cry of the Tory partisans. The "tantivy parsons" made it a test of loyalty to rejoice in the prospect of a Catholic successor; they preached with fury against Dissenters, but thought it indecent to speak against the religion of the heir to the throne.[1]

The Tories on the side of despotism, 1681-86

Popularity of James with the Party, 1681

These excesses on the part of the upper class were rendered possible by a change in sentiment lower in the scale of society, where men began to dread the close prospect of a civil war, and the old unhappy round of rebellion ending in Major-Generals. Yet the ministers of the Crown knew that the Tory temper among the townspeople and middle class was not yet universal and violent, as it became two years later after the Rye House Plot. Every means, therefore, was taken to crush the Whig party before it could rally from the panic of its flight from Oxford, and to goad its leaders to violence that now would certainly lead to their ruin. When

[1] Airy, ii., p. 259. Burnet, ii., pp. 290, 302. *Examen*, p. 617.

Proscrip-
tion of
Whigs
in the
public
service,
1681

Parliament was not sitting, the ministers had complete executive freedom ; and the full executive power was then a truly formidable weapon of party warfare. The favourite minister after Sunderland's secession was Hyde, whose very name was indicative of his exalted views of royal power. Great changes were made in the magistracy and militia of every shire. The Justices of Peace who had zealously hunted Catholics, were replaced by men who would zealously hunt Dissenters. This process was assisted by the seizure, among Shaftesbury's other papers, of two lists of local magnates prepared for his own use ; one of " worthy men " ; the other of " men worthy," in the opinion of the Whigs, to be hanged. To turn " worthy men " off the bench, and to put " men worthy " in their place was a task of which Charles could appreciate the full humour.

Persecu-
tion of
Dissenters

With the militia and magistracy in its hands, the Tory party enforced the Clarendon Code with the utmost cruelty and rigour. The gaols were again crowded with the bolder of the Nonconformists, and the Parish Churches with the more timorous. The persecution was probably as fierce as any which the Catholics had ever endured, and more fierce than that which the Anglican laity had suffered under the Long Parliament. Such religious persecution is the strongest provocation to rebellion that the subject can undergo.

Trials of
College,
(Aug.),
and
Shaftes-
bury,
(Nov.),
1681

The Whig politicians, no less than their Noncomformist followers, were put in fear for their own persons. The first blood shed was that of College, an understrapper of the Green Ribbon Club ; he was found guilty of treason, amid yells of delight in the courthouse of Oxford, on the evidence of his own friends, the quondam witnesses of the Popish Plot. The same men were ready to swear against the Whig chief himself, and the Tories had no scruple whatever in hiring their service. But Shaftesbury could not legally be tried outside London ; and there no jury would convict him. The rejoicings by which the City celebrated his acquittal occasioned the last Whig demonstration of this period. The courtiers consoled themselves by reading Dryden's *Medal*, the successor to his *Absalom and Achitophel*.

Election
of Tory
Sheriffs
for Lon-
don, June-
July,
1682

Provoked by the result of Shaftesbury's trial, the Royalists began their attack on the self-government of London. The election of two Tory sheriffs was carried against the majority by a mixture of fraud and violence.[1] As the sheriffs appointed the juries, and the juries could dispose of the life and liberty of every man obnoxious to the Court, the Whig leaders feared a general proscription and, in an evil hour, determined to appeal to arms.

In the autumn months following the election of the Tory sheriffs, two separate schemes of violence were formed by the leading mem-

[1] *Examen*, pp. 597-617.   Burnet, ii., pp. 335-37.   Airy, p. 263.

bers of the Green Ribbon and their friends. Shaftesbury and a The In-
Council of Six, consisting of Monmouth, Essex, Russell, Sidney, surrec-
Hampden and Howard discussed a general Insurrection; while tion and Assassin-
their subordinates, with the help of two old Cromwellians, Rumbold ation
and Rumsey, planned an assault upon the persons of Charles and Plots,
James. The official heads of the Insurrection, with the possible Aug.-Oct.,
exception of Shaftesbury, were not actively engaged in the Assassina- 1682.
tion Plot. But it is by no means certain that they were ignorant
of a scheme, hatched in the Green Ribbon Club, where many of
them resorted, by their own agents, who lived with them on terms
of intimacy, and at a time when the larger scheme of Insurrection
was common talk among both sections of plotters. The attack
on the King's coach and lifeguards, though it alienated the sympathies of the bulk of the English middle class, was by no means
outside the moral latitude of the politicians of that age; it was
not so basely murderous as the plots formerly approved by Clarendon
and the royal brothers against the regicides; and it was the same,
in all except time and place, as the plot which James II. afterwards
approved against the life of William III.[1] Of Shaftesbury and the
Council of Six, Russell and Essex are the only two whose characters
afford the least presumption that they would have stood boldly
out against such a design.

But whatever their relation may have been to the Assassination
Plot, the chiefs soon found that their own scheme of Insurrection,
if less criminal, was no less rash. The very conditions that goaded
them on to violence: their own growing unpopularity; their adversaries' control of the executive, and of the military force throughout the three kingdoms; the absence of any legal machinery to
reassemble the hosts that had fled from Oxford, indicated how
different was their position from that of the armed Lords and
Commons of 1642. The Whigs had no authority and no strength
except when Parliament was sitting. The real analogy to their
present position was that of Sir John Eliot and his friends in 1629.
Even Monmouth, in his second Western tour (Sep., 1682), perceived
that, though the people of Cheshire shouted for him, they were
not ready to rise in arms. On the 30th of September London itself
passed into the hands of the Tories, in the persons of the incoming
Mayor and Sheriffs. That night Shaftesbury left his house in
Aldersgate Street, and hid in the slums of the City that had once
been his own. Yet even now he fell foul of Monmouth and Russell Confused
when they refused to begin the Insurrection at once. All was wrang- counsels of the
ling, intrigue and confusion among the conspirators. No one knew Whig chiefs

---

[1] G. (*C. & P.*), ii., p. 453; iii., pp. 166, 167. In 1683 Archbishop Sancroft received and forwarded to the Council of State a letter from a Tory spy, offering to
assassinate Sir W. Waller (Christie, ii., p. 454 and note). No doubt Sancroft disapproved, but the fact that such an offer was made at all to the Primate shows
how much matters were viewed in that age.

in what name war was to be raised. Many were still for Monmouth ; yet Monmouth's closest friend, Russell, had been in close communication with William of Orange when he had visisted England in the previous summer. Essex and Sidney were for an aristocratic Republic, like old Rome ; but Rumbold and the veterans looked for a democratic Commonwealth, like that over which they themselves had kept the armed watch for Cromwell. But all sections were united in suspicion of Shaftesbury, who, racked by pain and failing health, was working with fevered energy on the flank of his own partisans, neither reposing nor receiving confidence. Some said that he had thrown over the cause of his protégé, and would declare for a Republic ; that he was pushing the Assassination in order to divide his party for ever from monarchy and from Monmouth. Thus the ranks of both the conspiracies were filled with suspicious, intriguing men, of whom not a few were only waiting for the time to betray their comrades. There was little here of the self-sacrifice and mutual confidence that are needed for desperate undertakings. Those who drew their inspiration from the models of the ancient world, should have known that it was not by such a company that Tarquin was expelled or Cæsar murdered.

Flight of Shaftesbury, Nov., 1682　　The customary papal pageant on Queen Elizabeth's Accession Day (17th Nov.), which according to one plan was to be the signal for the Insurrection, was prohibited by Government ; the waxen courtiers of the Pope were carried off under arrest, to the vast entertainment of the mob, which a year before would have torn the interfering officers to pieces. Fearing for his safety, Shaftesbury fled oversea. His departure relieved, but did not reunite, his partisans. Both plots were postponed till the spring. Then both were again resumed. The Insurrection indeed still hung fire, but the day when Charles should return from Newmarket was selected for

The Rye House Plot, April, 1683　　the Assassination. The place was Rumbold's Rye House, commanding the road. An accident alone prevented the King's journey. But Ferguson the plotter afterwards declared that he and Rumbold would in any case have prevented the blow from being struck ; according to his own account, Ferguson had only remained in the counsels of the plot at Monmouth's special request, in order to prevent the murder of Charles and James, on which Shaftesbury had set his heart. It is impossible to say how far, if at all, the plotter spoke the truth ; but it is highly probable that the scheme would in any case have been betrayed by one or other of the two score rascals who would have been necessary for its accomplishment.[1]

The Plots betrayed, June, 1683　　In June both plots were betrayed to Government. Instantly there was keen competition among both Lords and Commons for

---

[1] *Ferguson the Plotter* (1887), *passim*. Ferguson's own account will be found in Appendix I. to that biography. See also *First Whig*, pp. 88, 89, 154-58, and *State Trials, sub loc.*

the honour of being employed as evidence for the Crown. Half a dozen of the Assassination conspirators came forward and swore away several of their comrades' lives. The popular fury even in the towns was turned against the Whigs, and particularly against the Green Ribbon Club, where the plots had been hatched. Its two long balconies now looked down upon Temple Bar, forlorn and empty, like the Hall of the Jacobins when the Terror went out of fashion ; those of its members who were not under arrest, would have had their neighbours forget that ever they had been seen near its noisy doors.

Meanwhile, the President of the Club, the founder and ruiner of the Whig party, had died a miserable refugee in Holland—the land whose very existence he had striven ten years before to sacrifice to his own ambition, and whose chief he had but lately sought to disinherit ; the land which he had always regarded as a mere counter in English politics, not seeing—as Temple, Halifax and even Danby had seen—that it was the natural and indispensable ally of the religion and liberties of England. In Holland Shaftesbury died, " after having cast some very deep sighs ". The hatred of the English Court was let loose in indecent outrages on their dead enemy. In allusion to the painful disease against which he had struggled for long years, an abscess which required to be drained by a tap fixed in his body, the name given by the Tories to the factious Earl was " The Polish Noble, Count Tapski ". After his death, Dryden's *Albion and Albianus*, produced for the delectation of the royal brothers and their servile Court, was set on the stage with a huge picture of

Death of Shaftesbury, Jan., 1683

a man with a long, lean, pale face, with fiend's wings, and snakes twisted round his body, accompanied by several fanatical rebellious heads, who suck poison from him, which runs out of a tap in his side.[1]

The other chiefs of the Whigs were not suffered to die in their beds. Even in the high circle of the Council of Six, Government could find a traitor for its purpose. Lord Howard, dragged trembling and crying from his hiding-place behind a chimney, offered to disclose all. Russell and Sidney were convicted and executed for the Insurrection Plot, chiefly upon his evidence. While the miserable man was telling his story against Russell, the news came into court that Essex had cut his throat in the Tower. The trials of Russell and Sidney were conducted before packed juries, and the law perhaps was strained to obtain their conviction. Yet there is little doubt that they had actually plotted the Insurrection. Sidney delivered from the scaffold a speech breathing the contemptuous fortitude with which the *boni* of old Rome, men no less rapacious and unscrupulous than himself, regarded the tyrant and the mob, when in the hour of Imperial victory they were called upon to die.

Execution of Russell (July), and Sidney (Dec.), 1683

[1] Christie, ii., p. 437. Wilkins' *Political Ballads*, i., p. 250.

Russell, with a gentle courtesy that disarmed even the revengeful passions of that hour, refused to purchase the life that was so sweet to him by a declaration that subjects may not resist their sovereign. Soon people forgot his cruel pursuit of Lord Stafford's life, and his plots of Insurrection ; and remembered only how Lady Russell had sat below him in court to take the notes for his defence, and how he had chosen death rather than deny the principles of freedom. Thus these two men, on whom all eyes were turned in the days of the blackest ruin and shame that ever befel the cause of freedom in England, showed to the world, in spite of the guilt and violence with which they themselves had helped to associate that cause, that liberty is a religion for which men who most enjoy life and love and power, can cheerfully lay down all these, because without liberty they are nothing.

Such is the legend that was rightly handed down to remote generations of Whigs as the most instructive lesson of their great defeat. The party had fallen because its leaders had been ill-advised, selfish and violent in the methods they chose ; but not because they lacked faith in its principles of Parliamentary government and religious Toleration, or because those principles were unsuited, like those of the regicides who had suffered twenty years before, to the social conditions of the age and the temper of the English people. And therefore the new party did not perish on the scaffold with Sidney and Russell.

Local self-government abolished, 1683-84

It now remained to be seen what the Tories and the Monarchy would make of England. Their first step was to destroy local self-government. The charters of many of the principal cities were challenged and declared forfeit on frivolous grounds by Chief Justice Jeffreys ; while numbers of other towns, great and small, hastened to prevent the confiscation by the voluntary surrender of their privileges. The King restored the charters in new forms, which put the municipalities into the hands of his own nominees. No such thing had ever happened before in England. While the Hapsburg and the Valois monarchs had been setting their own Commissioners to rule in the free cities of Spain and France, the Tudors had continued to respect the mediæval privileges of our towns. It was no part even of Stafford's policy of " thorough," that the power of the sovereign should be extended to municipal affairs, or to the nomination of members of Parliament. But now the towns would be governed, and the borough members chosen, by the King's party alone. Local government and Parliamentary independence, which had been secured afresh at the Restoration, were suddenly brought to an end, and the last strongholds of independent political opinion were in the King's hands.

No protest was made while the most ancient liberties of Eng- Free
land were surrendered. The Tories approved ; and no Whig could speech
raise his voice in speech or writing without imminent danger of pressed
being brought up for sedition or libel, and ruined by packed juries
and new Judges who had been put in the place of predecessors not
sufficiently servile. The censorship could not be re-established till
1685, when Parliament met again, but meanwhile there was no more
freedom of the press than in the days of Laud. Whig pamphlets
only appeared by stealth, and words uttered in private and in public
were more guarded than in the days of the Star Chamber.

The second Stuart despotism had come into being. It was Nature
based, as Charles had designed in 1670, on a standing army and on of the
the financial help of France. Yet he had realised only half the despotism
ideas of the Dover Treaty. For the supreme power which he enjoyed was connected, not with Roman Catholicism and the purchase of Nonconformist support, but with Anglicanism and ferocious
persecution of Dissent. The King had bought the Tories at a
price. If Charles's successor would continue to pay that price, to
extirpate the Nonconformists and depress the Catholics, the despotism wielded in the interest of the squires might be confirmed
by time and become the established constitution of the realm. But
if an attempt were made to convert it into a Catholic despotism,
there would be hope for England yet.

Charles had earned his rest. For the last two years of his life Last
he again sauntered free from care ; he was more than ever tired of years of
business, and glad to leave the administration to his solemn brother II., 1683-
and his wrangling ministers. James, restored to office in defiance 1685
of the Test Act, had the strongest party among the courtiers, headed
by Hyde, now Earl of Rochester ; they feared that if a Parliament,
however loyal, were summoned, it would lead to a war with France,
and so open the floodgates of Protestant feeling. They therefore
made common cause with the French Ambassador, Barillon, and
with Madam Carwell ; that lady had once more come back with
her attendant Sunderland to the Tory camp. This combination
persuaded Charles to violate the Act of 1641, by leaving Parliament
in abeyance for more than three years. Against them was Halifax,
as hostile as ever to France ; he urged that no harm could possibly
come of a Parliament chosen after the remodelling of the corporations, and that a vote of supply would render Government independent of Louis, and able to check his rapid advance in Luxemburg
and on the Rhine. But the French Ambassador and the French Death of
mistress kept the King of England true to his foreign allegiance. Charles
In February, 1685, Charles was again taken ill. His splendid Feb.,
constitution, which for forty years he had been constantly ruining 1685

23

by excess and repairing by athletics, at last gave way. At his death-bed, Rome no longer denied him the rites which he had never dared to earn before by publicly declaring his faith. He died, after receiving the sacrament from the old priest who had saved him in the flight from Worcester. A fitting epitaph over this King can only be spoken by the one among his subjects who matched him in wit. Halifax saved his throne, but in return had the humour to leave to posterity a *Character of Charles II*. Its last words are these, " Let his Royal ashes then lie soft upon him, and cover him from harsh and unkind censures ; which though they should not be unjust, can never clear themselves from being indecent ".

CHAPTER XIII

JAMES II., 1685-88

What struggling confusion, as the issue slowly draws on ; and the doubtful hour, with pain and blind struggle, brings forth its certainty, never to be abolished !—*French Revolution*, CARLYLE.

THE powers wielded by the Tudor Kings, who changed religion in England, were in some important respects less than those to which James II. succeeded. They had chosen the rural magistrates ; he also chose the town corporations. They had appointed their own ministers ; his friends selected the House of Commons. They had named the officers of the militia ; he had besides a regular army of his own. And this despotic organism was animated, if not by the love of the whole people, at least by the partisan devotion of the omnipotent Tories. Whigs and Dissenters were everywhere trying to efface themselves from the notice of the laws, the magistrates and the juries—now become the mere instruments of party vengeance.

Position of James on his accession

If Elizabeth, or even Charles I., had come into such a heritage, despotism might perhaps have been established upon a permanent footing. But James owed his extraordinary position to a personal misunderstanding. As Duke of York he had worshipped God in private, and had said little in public about his religion ; it was not yet known that the Jesuits had held their congregation under his roof. Churchmen therefore believed that he would always treat his creed as a private matter. It was on this supposition that they had placed a Popish Prince on the throne, and armed him with greater powers than had been enjoyed by his Protestant predecessors. But the illusion was not confined to one side. James also had been deceived as to the character of the Church which had chosen him for her protector. For five years her clergy had directed all their controversial powers against the Nonconformists, regarding it as disloyal to decry the faith of the heir to the throne : how much more, then, would they favour Catholicism when it was the religion of the King himself. So at least James must have argued. He supposed that High Churchmen were half Catholics, who would allow their Church to be assimilated to Rome by a process of evolution like that contemplated by the Papal emissaries in the days of Charles I., and by Charles II. himself at the Treaty of Dover. Here James was wrong. The High Churchmen who followed Sancroft had even less call than the High Churchmen who followed Laud, to ally themselves with the old religion. For whereas the Arminians of 1630 had depended, for power to keep down the Puritans, on the King and the Catholic squires, the Tantivy parsons could now depend for that purpose on the Parliament and the Protestant squires. The devoted Anglican now felt a broader basis than the throne underpropping his creed.

Cruel religious persecution

One bad passion still united Church and King. The accession of James was the signal for yet more cruel treatment of Protestant Nonconformists. In England they were imprisoned, fined and ruined ; in Scotland men were shot and women drowned. In this persecution James was following the desire of his heart ; it was only when the breach with Episcopacy drove him to dissemble, that he took into his mouth Penn's noble doctrine of universal Toleration. Nothing but the quarrel of Bishops and King saved the Nonconformists from extirpation.

Punishment of Oates, May, 1685

The fate of one eminent champion of the Nonconformists is regarded with mingled feelings. Titus Oates, brought to trial for perjury, could not legally be condemned to death for an offence of that nature. But he was sentenced to be flogged twice through the streets of London, in a manner which the Judges probably intended to be fatal. The grotesque man survived his horrible and famous punishment, and lived to enjoy in obscurity a small pension, with which the Whigs at the Revolution thought necessary, in accordance with the invariable rule of their party managers,[1] to reward one who had been faithful to them. If each sin deserves its punishment, and if it is the task of justice to turn earth into a well-regulated hell, Oates deserved more than his 3,000 stripes. But his scarcely legal sentence became the precedent for similar cruel floggings for political offences of a very different character from his, until the bad custom ended with the bad reign.

A packed Parliament, May, 1685

During his brother's last years, James had prevented the summons of Parliament. But he had now a double use for the Tory nominees misrepresenting the constituencies of England, whom he called together in May, 1685. He wished them to fix on him a large revenue for life ; and to relieve the Catholics from the Penal Laws. They gratified his wishes in the first respect ; but before he had time to come to grips with them on the Catholic question, Monmouth landed in the West.

Expeditions of Argyle (May-June) and Monmouth (June-July), 1685

No stroke of chance could have rendered successful the double attack of the Whig exiles on the throne of James. Argyle's expedition in the Highlands was little more than the hunt, capture and execution of a chief who knew how to die. Monmouth's levy of the South-West acquired for a few weeks the character of a regular campaign. Landing at Lyme Regis with a few followers (11th

---

[1] " The Tories are not noted to stick so fast to their friends as the others " (the Whigs), (1710, *Wentworth*, p. 156). The solidarity of the Whig party was one of its attractions to neophytes.

June), he gathered round him the peasants of Dorset and Somerset
as he advanced across country to the west coast. At Taunton,
where the Puritan inhabitants were rendered desperate by religious
persecution, he was proclaimed King. At Bridgewater he fixed
his headquarters, whither, after a futile advance on Bristol, he
retreated again. He had now little hope. The royal forces were
gathering fast, nominally under command of Lord Feversham, but
really under the care of John Churchill, a rising courtier, who had
served his military apprenticeship under Turenne. They were encamped a few miles from Bridgewater, on the flat wastes of Sedgemoor reclaimed from the neighbouring ocean. There on the 5th
of July the Royalists were carousing in joyful expectation of an
easy rebel hunt. Yet Monmouth's rustic army very nearly performed that most difficult of military operations, a night surprise.
Even when the alarm had been given and they were exposed to
the fire of the regulars over a ditch which they could not cross, Battle of
they stood their ground in the midnight battle till their powder was Sedge-
spent, with the veteran constancy of religious zeal. By the early moor, 6th
glint of summer dawn, their chief, who had fled betimes on to the 1685
hills that border Sedgemoor, saw his too loyal subjects break at
last in rout across the distant plain.[1]

This rising of the peasantry of Somerset is a remarkable and Social
puzzling phenomenon in social history. We have no evidence that signifi-
any such *levée en masse* of the lower orders of a country-side took the Rising
place in the period of the great Civil War, not even in East Anglia,
where Cromwell enlisted his famous troops of horse.[2] For in those
earlier days an intelligent and devoted Puritanism had taken hold
of the mass of the people only in the towns. Taunton was no less
devoted to the " good old cause " when Blake defended her against
the Cavaliers, than when forty years on she welcomed Monmouth ;
but the readiness of the rural population to turn out and die for
their faith was a new thing in Somerset, and in England.

For these peasant followers of Monmouth, the dark Puritan
faith glowed in all the colours of personal romance ; they loved
the young man more than they loved their lives. Of Monmouth,
as of Napoleon, tales were told at nightfall beneath the thatch,
and his return was still expected long after he was dead. As the
march of the man from Elba through the valleys of Dauphiné,
so the march of King Monmouth through the lanes of Somerset
is to the historian full of social as well as political significance. The
record of this brief campaign is as the lifting of a curtain ; behind
it we can see for a moment into the old peasant life, since passed

[1] The account of the campaign by Macaulay should be read with that by Lord
Wolseley (*Life of Marlborough*, chaps. xxxvii.-ix.), whose remarks on the military
aspects of the battle have authority.
[2] Possibly the rising of the Cornishmen for Charles I. partook of this character ;
but there the movement was organised by the gentry.

away into the streets and factories, suffering city change. In that one glance we see, not rustic torpor, but faith, idealism, vigour, love of liberty and scorn of death. Were the yeomen and farm servants in other parts of England like these men of Somerset, or were they everywhere else of a lower type ? The curtain falls ; and knowledge is hidden for ever.

One thing is certain, that only in an age when the class of free-hold yeomen formed a large proportion of the population, and employed a part at least of the hired labour, could any district have thus risen in arms against the will of the squires. The land of England was not then owned by the few.

The Bloody Assize, Sep., 1685 The revenge taken by James upon his subjects went far beyond expectation and precedent. It was perhaps natural that 800 rebels should be sent to forced labour in the Barbadoes. The Crom-wellians in 1648, and the House of Hanover in 1715, committed the like cruelty. Transportation was the fate which the common rebel might customarily expect if taken in arms. But death had for fifty years past been regarded as the punishment proper for the leaders alone, when James II. reverted to the more barbarous methods of Elizabeth and the mediæval kings. Not content with the long tale of military executions by Kirke and Feversham in the days immediately following the battle, he allowed over 300 of the peasants to be hanged by Jeffreys in the Bloody Assize. He also allowed one woman, Alice Lisle, to be beheaded for exercising common charity to fugitives who had implored food and shelter ; and another, Elizabeth Gaunt, to be burned alive for saving one of the conspira-tors of the Rye House Plot. In the spirit of the hour, Cornish, one of the most influential and honourable of the Whig merchants of London so bitterly hated by the Court, was singled out and murdered on a false charge of treason. These horrors appealed the more forcibly to the imagination of all, because the highways and public places in town and country were elaborately desecrated with the corpses and hewn quarters of the well-loved dead ; because Jeffreys on the bench of justice shouted, swore and laughed over his victims ; and because the sufferers were religious men who went to the gallows and butchery glorifying God. The analogy of the Marian persecution was the first thing to strike a generation brought up on Foxe's *Book of Martyrs*. The horror excited among the Tories themselves is the best comment on the conduct of Jeffreys and his master. The Bloody Assize did not shake James's throne, but it lent to the opposition, provoked by his subsequent action, the character and the enthusiasm of outraged humanity in revolt. When Jeffreys, in his last dreadful days on earth, was sheltered by the walls of the Tower from a nation of men seeking to kill him with their own hands, he was hiding not from the Whig mob but from the human race.

One rebel, at least, richly deserved his fate. Monmouth, after begging his life on his knees and with abject tears before the King himself, suffered death at the hands of Jack Ketch, the executioner who flourished in this heyday of his profession, of which he became the eponymous hero. Execution of Monmouth, July, 1685

The Western Rebellion produced great and immediate effects on the course of English history. The removal of Monmouth reconciled the House of Orange to the Whigs, for their Exclusion scheme could no longer be carried out in favour of the bastard against the legitimate claims of William and Mary; the way was cleared for the acceptance by all English Protestants of William as their only champion. And the demand for a champion was soon created, as a direct consequence of Sedgemoor. For the subjection of the rebel West by the regular army made James believe that he could Romanise England in a shorter time, and by more arbitrary methods, than those which he seems to have contemplated in the first months of his reign. Consequences of the Western Rebellion

The root of all his errors in method was the complete reliance placed by him on his soldiers. Monmouth's rebellion enabled him to become a military despot. The regulars in England were raised from 6,000 to nearly 30,000. A great camp of 13,000 was formed on Hounslow Heath to overawe the capital. Such a host of red-coats had not been seen together since Charles, on the day of his Restoration, had timidly reviewed the last of the old and terrible army. But these were a different sort of soldiers. The lowest of the people, they were subjected to what we should now regard as the laxest discipline. In the neighbourhood of Sedgemoor, some regiments, encouraged by commanders who were not all as humane as Churchill, had shown fierce cruelty. In the neighbourhood of London, robberies and murders were plentifully laid at their door. Reports were readily believed against them, for civilians of all parties hated the camp at Hounslow, rightly regarding it as a menace to their liberties and their religion. But it escaped the notice of James, that though the soldiers were ready to fight against the liberties, they were not ready to fight against the religion of England. They were not indeed religious men. But hatred of Popery had sunk so deep into the nation, that the classes most removed from the influence of religion were, in a negative sense, fervent Protestants. A wooden chapel was set up within the lines, and horse, foot and dragoons were encouraged to attend the Mass. Priests went to and fro among the tents. But the Protestant soldiers refused to be converted. Indeed, now that they were collected in great camps, they were better able to see that, in spite of alarming rumours, the King had not yet had time to introduce enough of his own religion to put the Protestant soldiers in a minority; they were therefore the more bold to encourage each other in the James and his army faith.[1] The faith of the British army was no longer that which Milton held, but that which inspired Kirke. It consisted of a profound belief that papists deserved to be hanged scarcely less than rebels.

But meanwhile in Ireland, James was forming a really Catholic army, under the orders of his Popish Lord-Lieutenant, Talbot, Earl of Tyrconnel. On these soldiers, regarded by his other subjects as foreigners and serfs, he was ready to depend, in the last resort, for the coercion of the English Protestants.

Tory ministers replaced by Jacobites and Catholics, 1685-87 Thus magnificently but perilously armed, James proceeded to Catholicise England. In October, 1685, Halifax was dismissed from the Government for opposing the breach of the Test Act. And the High Tories soon found their position in office as precarious as that of the Trimmer. A tribe of Jacobite statesmen, some devout Catholics like Father Petre, some self-seeking scoundrels like Jeffreys and Sunderland, saw that the time had come to overthrow their Tory colleagues and reign supreme. The hunt had first begun when, at the opening of Parliament, the highest Court in the kingdom had resounded with scorn and outrage poured by Chief Justice Jeffreys on Francis North, Lord Guildford, the Tory Keeper of the Great Seal, under colour of reversing some of his Chancery decrees. Guilford was harried to his grave, and Jeffreys, returning from the Bloody Assize, was made Lord Chancellor in his place. A like intrigue soon led to a like change in the Palace and at the Council-board, where Sunderland pursued Rochester with animosity less noisy but scarcely less venomous. The advice of the Tory minister was seldom taken after the autumn of 1685, and in January, 1687, Rochester was at length driven from office as a direct consequence of his refusal to change his religion. Roman Catholicism, which was a bar to service under the Crown by law, was rapidly becoming a condition of it in practice. Sunderland, though he did not announce his conversion till the summer of 1688, early showed that he had an open mind on the great controversy ; he, therefore, with Jeffreys, the Jesuit Petre and some Catholic Lords, remained as the counsellors who cheered James on to his ruin.

James quarrels with and prorogues Parliament, Nov., 1685 In the winter of 1685 a second session was held of the Parliament which Monmouth had interrupted. The House of Commons was little better than a nominated Assembly, but the members had been selected on the assumption that a high Tory would serve the King's ends. In the second session this had ceased to be the case. A great standing army, largely officered by Catholics, was now in existence, and the Houses, in real alarm, wished the army reduced in accordance with custom, and the Catholic officers dismissed in accordance with law. The King, on the other hand, wished the officers' position to be legalised by the repeal of the Test Act. If

---

[1] Burnet, iii., pp. 163, 164, 286. Wolseley, chap. xli. Macaulay, chap. vi.

this Lords and Commons refused to be assistant. James, therefore, prorogued Parliament, and proceeded on his three years' course, in defiance of those laws which he had in vain attempted to have changed.

Now that the Catholic propaganda was publicly revived, and that heavy rewards were offered for apostasy, the Church of England was forced to look once more to her defences on the side which she had so long left exposed. But James ordered her controversialists to be silent. One of them, named Sharpe, continued to preach to his parishioners on the errors of Rome. The King called on his Bishop, Compton of London, to suspend him. Compton neglected to obey. James formed a Court of High Commission, of which Sunderland and Jeffreys were the leading spirits. This tribunal suspended the bishop from his functions. The High Commission was illegal, for the law which had abolished its predecessor had forbidden the creation of any similar authority. Meanwhile, vacant Bishoprics were either left empty, or filled by men who were Roman Catholics in feeling ; one of these, Parker, the new Bishop of Oxford, was expected, as the King wrote, to " bring round his clergy ". Thus, in the revolutions of time, a Catholic King made use of the ecclesiastical powers which the Tudors had appropriated from the papal armoury, in order to carry back to the papal allegiance the Anglican Church which had rashly chosen him as her defender. *Court of High Commission, July, 1686*

But the chief efforts of the King were directed to filling up the civil and military offices with Catholics. Since the Test Act could not be repealed, he declared that his prerogative enabled him to dispense with its provisions ; he dismissed the Judges who refused their assent to this doctrine, and so obtained the famous decision in the case of Hales (June, 1686) in favour of the dispensing power. Roman Catholics were then freely placed upon the bench of magistrates ; the whole government of the country was passing into their hands. A hundred years earlier such a policy might well have succeeded, but now it was difficult to find men for the posts. The Catholic gentry, who by family tradition and personal experience well knew their countrymen, were many of them unwilling to become instruments for the folly of the Jesuits. A Catholic middle-class hardly existed. The King, therefore, had to seek alliance with some section of his Protestant subjects, in order to fill up the corporations, and to pack a new Parliament, as hostile to the Church interest as the last Parliament had been devoted. *Magistracy and army put into Catholic hands, 1686-87*

Never in English politics was there a *volte-face* so immediate and so complete as when James sought the alliance of Dissent. But he could not wade back through all the blood he had shed. The bulk of the Nonconformists refused the hand of their bitterest persecutor, the more readily as the Church, awakened by peril to remorse, was beginning to offer them friendship and Toleration. *James seeks the alliance o Dissent, 1687*

Suddenly all parties were talking Toleration. The eccentric doctrine of the Whig statesmen and philosophers, that all Protestants should be allowed the public exercise of their religion, was proclaimed in rivalry by both Tories and Jacobites.[1] The King offered the Dissenters instant release by an Act of royal absolutism ; the Church offered them the distant prospect of legal and Parliamentary Toleration.

The Fellows of Magdalen, 1687

The full fury of the tyrant now fell on the Anglican Church. As her leaders had refused to lend her influence on behalf of his Catholic propaganda, he determined instead to seize her property for that purpose. In those days the Universities belonged to the Establishment. The King illegally converted two Oxford Colleges into Popish seminaries, turning the Fellows of Magdalen adrift on the world to make room for Catholic successors. The attack on freehold property roused against the King all those conservative instincts which Burke long afterwards aroused against the French Revolution. The parson had now real reason to fear that his tithes and his vicarage, and the squire that his abbey lands, would be taken from him without compensation and without law. The priests and monks were already gathering round the spoil, and were singled out to general observation by their fantastic costumes, which in that generation were known to the English only from prints of foreign countries and of Smithfield fires.

William Penn

James had at his side no good counsellor, and only one good man. William Penn would have been ungrateful if he had not been a Jacobite. The House of Stuart had saved the Quakers from complete destruction at the hands of the Anglicans in England, and of the Puritans in America. Nevertheless, the Friends had, since the Restoration, endured terrible sufferings, with a cheerful indifference that did far more than Rye House Plots and Monmouth rebellions to render the persecuting laws odious, and to prepare the era of Toleration. As these sufferings had been inflicted by the Cavalier Parliament and by the Episcopalian party, Penn felt no affection for Parliament or Established Church. But he hoped to persuade the King to extend Toleration to the Quakers and to all other men.[2] Largely at Penn's instigation, though certainly not in Penn's spirit, James issued the two Declarations of Indulgence.

[1] How much the Tories really hated the idea of Toleration, is shown by some of their writers, who taunt the Whigs with the word even as late as the trial of the Seven Bishops.

<blockquote>" From freedom of conscience, and Whig Toleration,
For ever, good Heaven, deliver us ! "</blockquote>

sings an anti-Jacobite Tory poet, summer 1688 (Wilkins' *Political Ballads*, i., p. 256).

[2] Penn was working, consciously and enthusiastically, for universal freedom of religion, to which all other parties were being pushed by the mere force of events and the needs of the hour. He approached Toleration by a different road, both of philosophic theory and of political action. Thus when he is accused, most justly,

These Declarations, by an Act of royal authority which Charles The two
II. had exercised in 1672 and had been forced to abandon as illegal, Declara-
gave freedom of worship to Dissenters and Catholics, and suspended tions of Indulg-
all laws by which they were debarred from civil and military office. ence,
James's first Declaration was in April, 1687. The prisons were Apr., 1687, and
opened to thousands of the best men in England, and everywhere Apr.,1688
public worship was freely resumed by congregations who have
never since been forced to close their doors. Penn had not become a courtier for nothing ; the year 1687 dates the beginning
of religious freedom in England. The Nonconformists could not
but be grateful, and many of them wavered in their allegiance to
the national cause. But twelve months later the Second Declaration of Indulgence brought the struggle of King and nation to a
crisis. The first gratitude of the Dissenters for release from prison
had had time to cool, and the question had become one rather of
Tests for office than of Toleration for worship. The Second Declaration, while repeating the provisions of the First, differed from it
in boasting of the appointment of Catholics to civil and military
command ; and in that light the Second Declaration was read by
all. James ordered the clergy to publish it from their pulpits.
Unless the whole profession stood together in their refusal, individual delinquents would be ejected by the High Commission,
as the Fellows of Magdalen had been ejected. Fortunately, the
whole Church, and indeed the whole nation, was now united.
Encouraged by Nonconformist sympathy, seven Bishops undertook to petition James against the Declaration ; by so doing they
concentrated on themselves the vengeance of the King, which could
crush Fellows and parsons, and even individual Bishops, but not
perhaps seven of them headed by the Primate. He instituted
proceedings against them for seditious libel. If the King had not
been stirred almost to madness, he would have stopped the prosecution of the petitioners, when he heard that the whole population
of London, the headquarters of Whiggery and Dissent, had given Birth of a
the fathers of the Church on their way to the Tower the same fierce Prince (10th
ovation as their grandfathers had given to Prynne in the pillory. June) and trial of

of indifference to the English Constitution as usually defined, it must be remem- Seven
bered that to him the fundamental laws of England meant the property and free- Bishops
dom of the individual, which had been unconstitutionally violated by Penal Laws (29th-
and Clarendon Codes. He thought it was *ultra vires* for Church or Parliament to 30th
coerce the conscience of man. " Nothing," he wrote, " is more unreasonable than June),
to sacrifice the Liberty and Property of any man (being his Natural and Civil 1688
rights) for religion. . . . Religion under any modification is no part of old English
Government " (*England's Present Interest Considered*). This is true English talk,
as much as the Bill of Rights itself.

The same *a priori* view of the right to Toleration in religion is found in Burnet,
who says (v., pp. 108, 109 ; vi., p. 189) : " I have long looked on liberty of conscience as one of the rights of human nature, antecedent to society ". In this view
of Toleration, the much-abused Whig Churchman was as far ahead of his contemporaries as the equally hated Tory Quaker.

But at last, almost beyond hope, a son had been born to him by his second wife Mary of Modena. Thinking that heaven was working for his cause, he ordered the prosecution to proceed. So the Seven Bishops were tried and acquitted, and the army cheered on Hounslow Heath.

William, England, and Europe

The birth, which had encouraged James to proceed, showed the English that they must act. Passive resistance had been the hope of many, so long as the next heirs to the throne were Mary and Anne, the Protestant daughters of James by Anne Hyde. But with the birth of a male heir, son of the Italian princess, the prospect opened out of a long succession of Jesuit-loving and foreign-hearted Kings. Mary, whose peaceful succession to her father was now impossible, had for husband William of Orange, Stadtholder of Holland, armed champion of the Protestants of Europe, and leader of the papal enemies to the French and Jesuit power. Thus the struggle for the English throne became the pivot of European politics, at one of those rare crises which from time to time decide the trend of civilisation.

Revocation of the Edict of Nantes, 1685

The English were ignorant of the details of foreign affairs, but they knew that an attempt to extinguish the Protestant communities of Western Europe was being made with every prospect of success. They could not be persuaded that James and his Jesuits were overthrowing the English Constitution merely in order to establish religious Toleration, when they saw what Louis and his Jesuits were doing in France. Ominously, in the year of the Bloody Assize, many thousand Huguenots took refuge on our shores, and during the three years of James's reign, stories of sickening cruelty done abroad were told by the sufferers themselves to hundreds of thousands of English men and women. The view of the Catholic character, which the exposure of Oates had shaken, was reconfirmed by the indisputable presence in our land of a population driven forth from its own, by one of the most barbarous and unprovoked persecutions in all time.

Under Louis XIV. the Huguenots were the most industrious part of the French nation, corresponding socially to the Puritan Nonconformists in England ; but they were less formidable, and no longer took part in political life. As harmless and retiring as the English Catholic squires, they were more fortunate in that they had no intriguers at Court to embroil the good name of their religion with their fellow-countrymen. There was no political cause for the Revocation of the Edict of Nantes, such as there was for the Clarendon Code and for the Popish Terror. On this innocent population a whole army, as cruel as the regiments of Claverhouse and Kirke, was let loose, with orders to convert the recalcitrant. Robbery, torture and the insult of women were the portion of households distinguished among the surrounding Catholics for morality, industry and education. The Bishops incited and often accompanied the soldiers ;[1] there was no escape, save by conversion, from unbearable bodily anguish. The neophytes were taken by their executioners from the torture to the communion. Finally, the Edict of Nantes was revoked, at the instigation of the French clergy and Jesuits, by the ungrateful grandson of Henry of Navarre. By an excess of cruelty the Protestants were forbidden to emigrate ; the roads and ports were watched against the families flying by night. They must stop and worship idols, while their children were torn from them and educated by priests and nuns. The bulk of the Protestant population disappeared for ever out of France ; in the course of time 400,000 effected their escape, settling in large numbers in England, Brandenburg and Holland, and inciting those powerful States to the crusade of self-defence against the civilising influences of the Grand Monarch. The fate of those who failed or neglected to escape was terrible. The hearts of many women were broken in unrecorded martyrdom, in nunneries where they lay entombed for life. The men who were sent to die of hardship among common criminals in the galleys had perhaps the easiest lot. Thousands of men and women, who refused to abjure their faith, were crowded into damp and loathsome prisons and pestiferous " hospitals," where, assailed with stripes, ill-usage and insult, and exposed to the company of diseased and criminal wretches, they suffered things as horrible as depraved ingenuity could invent. " Touched with so many marvels," cried Bossuet in a celestial rapture, " let our hearts go out to the piety of Louis. Let us raise praises to heaven and say, . . . ' Heresy is no more. God alone could have done so marvellous a thing. King of heaven, preserve the King of the earth, it is the prayer of the churches ; it is the prayer of the Bishops.' "[2] So spoke the clergy of France by the mouth of one who is held up as a model of Catholic virtue, humanity and moderation. Is it strange that, in spite of the innocent life of the ordinary English Catholic, our ancestors nurtured prejudice against the Catholic faith, and determined to exclude its professors from office ?

Such was French religion, now threatening to overrun in arms the shores of the Lakes of Geneva and Neuchâtel, the Rhineland and the cities of Holland. James would hold England in leash while the Protestants of these lands succumbed to the armies of the great persecutor. But it was the predestined task of William, and of Marlborough after him, to free England and lead her into the war, to show that the monster power of Louis had feet of clay, {.sidenote: Danger of Protestantism, 1685-88}

---

[1] *Etudes sur la Révocation*, Puaux et Sabatier, p. 81 and notes.
[2] Bossuet, *Oraison funèbres* (ed. 1874), p. 219, (*Michelle Tellier*).   *Hist. Univ.*, Lavisse et Rambaud, vi., pp. 281-302.   *Hist. de la Reformation Fr.*, F. Puaux, livre xxxviii., caps. i.-viii.   Félice, *Hist. des Prot. de France*, livres iii. iv.   Puaux et Sabatier, *Etudes sur la Révocation* (1886), proves up to the hilt the responsibility of the French clergy and Jesuits.

and to destroy the prestige of all that order of society and government.

William combines with the Catholic enemies of France

In consequence of the Revocation of the Edict of Nantes, the European struggle from 1688 to 1713 was as much a war of religion as the last part of the Thirty Years' War. The populations threatened by French conquest, England, Holland, the Rhenish Protestants and the Huguenot refugees, were, like the soldiers of Gustavus, fighting for their religion. But just as Gustavus had, at the critical moment of the struggle against the persecuting power of Spain and Austria (1630), been assisted by Catholic France, and by the Pope, so now at the critical moment of the struggle with the persecuting power of France, William was assisted by the Pope and by Catholic Austria and Spain. In the year 1688 the Austrian armies were already marching to defend German interests on the upper Rhine ; the Spaniards were still more closely allied to William though they were not yet actually at war with France ; and the Pope's secretary of State was in the secret of the conspiracy that launched the Protestant Armada against our shores. Innocent XI. himself urged all faithful Catholics to aid the heretics and the Holy See against their common enemies, the French Jesuits and the Gallican Church. For the temporal, and to some extent the spiritual authority of the Bishop of Rome has always depended on the balance of power in Europe and in Italy.[1]

Meanwhile, the Protestant State of Brandenburg-Prussia, lately established by its Great Elector as one of the powers of Europe, joined Holland in defence of common religious interests on the lower Rhine. Thus a league against France of both religions was forming fast ; but in order to succeed, the allies must have England as paymaster and protagonist. And to attain that end it was their common interest to effect the necessary revolution within the English state.

William's English policy. Burnet and Penn

For some time after the execution of Monmouth, William's attitude on our domestic questions remained uncertain. As Mary had not then ceased to be heir to the throne, her father, James, playing on her husband's well-known love of Toleration, tried to persuade the pair to endorse his policy and to pursue it when he was gone. If William had fallen into the well-laid trap he would have been lost. But he seldom made mistakes from want of accurate information about the internal affairs of foreign countries. He was besieged with contradictory advice on English politics by two equally zealous champions of Toleration—Penn, generally regarded as commissioned by James ; and Burnet, commissioned by himself. Though Burnet was forward and loquacious, and William as reserved as his famous ancestor, they had much in common ; the exiled

---

[1] Ranke, *Hist. Eng.*, iv., pp. 373-84 ; v., pp. 4-9, and *Popes* (ed. 1847), ii., pp. 276, 277.

Broad Church divine was an Anglican in the same spirit in which William was a Calvinist ; both were primarily Toleration men and Protestants. The Prince, luckily for his future, came to the conclusion that Burnet knew more than Penn about the real state of England.[1] He publicly replied to his father-in-law, that he hoped to see the Penal Laws reduced, and freedom of conscience secured for Catholics, as well as freedom of public worship for Protestant Dissenters ; but that he would not support the abrogation of those Tests which excluded members of the Church of Rome from office. This famous manifesto against persecution and in favour of Tests was translated into several languages, and was widely circulated in England. It prepared the way for the great combinations of 1688. The Pope and the anti-Jesuit section of the Church all over Europe, and the peaceable English Catholics, were satisfied with an offer which would save them from reprisals for the Jesuit policy. The Dissenters learnt that they would secure Toleration. The Church was assured that the dykes which penned out the Roman flood would again be repaired. Thenceforth, William's agents were in active concert with Whigs, Tories and Trimmers. Before the news of the Second Declaration of Indulgence had reached Holland, he had agreed to the principle of an armed expedition to England (April, 1688). The birth of the Prince of Wales and the trial of the Seven Bishops induced the conspirators to act at once. On the day the Bishops were acquitted, the written invitation demanded by William was signed by Shrewsbury, Devonshire, Danby, Lumley, Russell, Sidney and Compton, Bishop of London. These men were risking their lives in legitimate rebellion against a King whose measures they had openly opposed. But the great conspiracy was extended among scores of courtiers and army officers, who still crowded into the Palace to offer expressions of service and devotion to the man whom they had marked for doom. At the head of these traitors was Churchill. To him, foremost among Englishmen, the success of the Revolution was due.

Though secure of the good-will of both parties, William refused to sail without a Dutch force, large enough to protect him against the fate of Monmouth, and to mask James's great army so that the counties of England could be free to rise in revolt. His military and naval preparations for the attempt went on throughout the hot months of the year. The rumour of an impending attack on Holland by England and France after the manner of 1672, made his jealous countrymen unwontedly eager to forward whatever warlike preparations he advised for their defence ; and the same

William declares for Toleration and Tests, 1687

The invitation signed, 30th June, 1688

Louis, James and the Dutch, Aug.-Oct., 1688

---

[1] Ranke, iv., pp. 389-94. On the value of Burnet's history, see the admirable critique of Ranke, vol. vi., where also the value of the various portions of Clarke's *Life of James II.* is estimated. See pp. 362-3 above, note, for the views of Burnet and Penn on Toleration.

rumour screened from friend and foe the real destination of these armaments. In August, Louis took alarm and warned James. All would have been frustrated, if the infatuated man had accepted the French alliance, or if Louis had taken on himself to throw his troops into the Spanish Netherlands, and threaten the safety of Holland. But instead of that, Louis in September declared war upon the Empire and sent his forces on to the middle Rhine, so giving William two months in which to cross the Channel, before winter set in. Freed from immediate, but by no means from prospective, fear of French invasion, the Dutch gave their consent to the desperate bid for their own national security. Without that voluntary consent, the ruler of a free nation could not have carried off her fleets and armies to the rescue of England.

Struggle between Sunderland and Petre, Aug.-Oct. James's refusal of French help in August had been largely due to the advice of Sunderland, who had lately turned Catholic. There will always be dispute as to what this entirely selfish counsellor intended to bring about by dividing his master from Louis. It is not impossible that his object was to stave off the threatened revolution by a return to an English and Parliamentary policy ; and this reading of Sunderland's motives is quite consistent with the fact that he was communicating with the Prince of Orange, in order that his head might be safe even if, in spite of his efforts, the revolution took place. In the last fortnight of September Sunderland persuaded James, who was at last thoroughly frightened, to make large concessions and to hold out promise of a Parliament from which Roman Catholics should be excluded. But the concessions came too late, and were too obviously the result of the stir in the dockyards of Holland. Meanwhile, the French and Jesuit clique had broken with Sunderland ; Petre well knew that the summons of a Protestant Parliament must lead to his own downfall, even if it saved the head of his slippery convert, and kept off the Dutch invasion. So in the last days of October, when William was already embarked, Petre had his way and Sunderland was dismissed from office. These vacillations in the presence of danger lost the advantages both of French interference and of genuine concession.

Vacillations of James's policy Owing to James's management, the Prince left Holland without fear of the French army, and crossed the sea without fear of the French navy ; the concessions had encouraged all willing but timid rebels, by revealing that Government had more reason to expect defeat than in 1685 ; and yet, since the King was governing by Petre's counsels when William landed, the Bishops could not be induced to issue a manifesto against resistance, such as would have puzzled and restrained the conscientious Tories.

The "Pretended Prince of Wales" To secure the alliance of that large and important class, the statesmen who had signed the invitation persuaded William to come to England with a falsehood in the forefront of his appeal to the nation. It was everywhere put about by politicians, and generally believed by the populace, that the new Prince of Wales was not really the Queen's son. James had indeed neglected to summon thoroughly satisfactory witnesses to the birth, and some excuse can be made for a nation in the agonies of its fate grasping too blindly at a belief which smoothed the way to the union of parties. Conscientious men and women can be named who genuinely believed that James had practised a fraud. But it is not likely that all the responsible persons who used the story had examined it, or that the patrons of Oates, on their sudden return to politics and power, cared very much whether or not the Prince of Wales were indeed a Pretender.

Every political and military combination of the last three years *William* on either side of the British Channel, had worked as by magic in *lands at* favour of this almost impossible enterprise. And now, even the *Torbay,* *5th Nov.,* winds kept William clear of the English fleet, and landed him in *1688* Torbay on the very day of the year when the nation was wont to celebrate its deliverance from the Gunpowder Plot. The landing of the Prince with a force that could not instantly be overpowered, among a people so well prepared to receive him, made it certain that a free Parliament must be called. But whether that Parliament was to be called under the auspices of James or of William, it was still in the power of James to decide. Fortunately, while he was as strongly determined as his father never to be a constitutional King, and never to give up the interests of his religion, he had not his father's patience to play off armed enemies against each other by deceptive promises and intrigues. His refusal to summon a free Parliament on William's landing led to the long-premeditated desertion of Churchill, Kirke and other officers; the consequent demoralisation of the whole army; the rising of the civilian population all over England; and the unresisted advance of William on London. The Irish troops on this side of St. George's Channel, on whom alone he could depend, were too few to do anything but exasperate the people and alienate their companions in arms.[1] Within a month of the landing at Torbay, James was, from a military point of view, as much at his rival's mercy as Richard II. had been at the mercy of Bolingbroke, or Charles I. at the mercy of Cromwell. Yet even then he could still have prevented his own deposition, if he had accepted the terms which William was forced to offer. For Tory principles, and indeed Tory interests, would not have allowed him to be deposed if he had not himself abdicated

---

[1] The famous Revolution song, *Lillibulero*, whose author was said to have " sung James out of Three Kingdoms," turns entirely on Tyrconnel and the Catholic Irish who are to " cut de Englishman's troate ". It has less than no merit as literature. The merit lay in the tune. (Wilkins' *Political Ballads*, i., pp. 275-77.)

24

the throne. If he had consented to remain in England as constitutional monarch, we could not have obtained that union of parties, and that strong monarchical administration on behalf of national and Parliamentary ideals, on which depended the future progress of England and the immediate salvation of Europe. The battle of Blenheim could not have been fought, nor the House of Hanover called in, if James had not sent his family out of the kingdom, and himself followed to appeal to the national enemy to restore him by force of arms. He was lodged at St. Germains as the French candidate for the English throne.

James refuses compromise and flies to France, Dec., 1688

CHAPTER XIV

WILLIAM AND MARY

For therein stands the office of a King,
His honour, virtue, merit, and chief praise,
That for the public all this weight he bears.—MILTON.

THE days that followed the flight of James saw even greater confusion in England than the months which preceded the Restoration or those which ushered in the Civil War. Then there had been too many claimants to legal authority ; now there was no legal authority at all. Travellers were searched upon the roads The by no warrant save that of public safety ; villages were held by Inter-regnum. mounted men, the town gates by militia, in no name save that of Danger of the Protestant religion. The gentry and middle classes were up in anarchy arms, expectant of the unknown, while mobs were sacking Catholic chapels and mansions, as the first rite in a saturnalia of thieves. A great English army, legally disbanded by James as his last royal act, stood in distracted and angry regiments, on the worst of terms with the civil population, and distrusting as Catholics or as Williamites even those officers who had not deserted them. A smaller force of Irish Catholics were drifting about in search of safety, terror-struck but inspiring terror, starting midnight alarms a hundred miles off by the mere rumour of their march. Englishmen were drawn out as for war, armed, excited, in the grip of panic, ready to plunge the sword into one another at a word. Order and set purpose were found only upon those western roads converging on the capital, where warriors drawn from all the chief Protestant races of Europe, side by side with a few regiments of red-coats and an enormous staff of Lords and gentlemen, moved under the flag of William of Orange. But that Prince possessed and claimed no right to issue commands outside his own camp. If, before some one authority was established to confine the course of this drifting chaos, the inevitable quarrels were to break out between Tories and Whigs, Dissenters and Churchmen, English and foreigners, the whole land would instantly fall a prey to civil war, as aimless and confused as that strife of multitudinous factions which Cromwell's The tyranny had once been called on to avert. Therefore, the Lords Prince in-vited to and an informal Assembly of the old Commoners of Charles II.'s undertake Parliaments, hastily convened in London in December, 1688, the ad-unanimously voted the civil and military administration into the ministra-tion, Dec., hands of the Prince of Orange. For if they had hesitated, England 1688 would have been in flames at the New Year.

The Convention offers the Crown to William and Mary, Feb., 1689

Under the provisional government of the Prince, the Estates of the Realm were summoned, free and orderly polling took place, and a Convention, elected like an ordinary Parliament, was held forthwith. There the Tory party vainly strove to prevent the inevitable solution of the problem on Whig principles; first a regency in James's name, then the sovereignty of Mary alone as hereditary monarch, were discussed and rejected. For William refused to become regent, and Mary refused to reign by herself. The Whig majority was firm, and the Tory minority dared not be obstinate with anarchy and invasion at the gates. The same needs which had forced the Tories to give William the temporary administration in December, compelled them in February to make him the permanent and legal sovereign. William and Mary were proclaimed together (13th Feb.), and the administration was conferred on the husband during his life.

Like the proclamation of the Commonwealth forty years back, the proclamation of William and Mary was dictated by the necessities of the moment. But it chanced that, on this latter occasion, the necessities of the moment coincided with the strongest tendencies of the age and the best possibilities of the future. It was needful to a lasting and happy settlement, that the Tories should surrender their principles and the Whigs forgo their vengeance. Yet so fierce was party passion, that nothing short of the need to preserve society would have compelled the Tories to abandon hereditary right and religious persecution, and the Whigs to let their dead sleep without the atonement of blood. They both learnt their lesson, but could not forgive their Dutch schoolmaster.

Declaration of Right (1688) and Bill of Rights (1689)

Tories as well as Whigs were now, both in retrospect and in prospect, jealous of the prerogative power. By the Declaration of Right and the Bill of Rights the tenure of the Crown was made strictly conditional. All the outstanding disputes between King and subjects were decided against the King before the new monarchs were invested with their shorn authority. By this beneficent Revolution, the liberty of the subject and the power of Parliament were finally secured against the power of the Crown.

William III.'s position in England

The tradition of ages was snapped. In the eyes of no section of his subjects did William succeed to the majesty that had hedged the ancient Kings of England. While few felt affection for his person, none felt reverence for his office. Tories and Whigs agreed to think of him as temporary caretaker for the English people. Loyalty to him was binding as a patriotic duty, not as an inalienable allegiance. In return for such loyalty, William was expected to do whatever was required of him by every greedy nobleman who had tried to rob him of his heritage in favour of Monmouth, or had betrayed James at the eleventh hour; in case of refusal, a personal grievance had arisen to justify communications with the exiled Court of St. Germains.

William never attempted, as his predecessors would have done, fraudulently to resume the prerogatives which he had signed away at his accession. He preserved the compact. But he acquired considerable power over the internal, and yet more over the external policy of England, by playing off the two parties against each other. By means of an admirable outsider's understanding of English politics and politicians, he left the imprint of his personal will on our foreign policy, even while he introduced a new era of constitutional monarchy and party government.

The rule of England by the contests of the two parties now began in earnest, no longer complicated by a struggle for supremacy between Parliament and King. The Tories no longer tried to carry out their ecclesiastical and social ideals by making themselves the instruments of the Crown, but struggled against the Whigs to possess the Crown as their instrument. From the flight of James to the accession of George III., there was no doubt as to the limitations of the power of the Crown, but grave doubt as to who would wear it ; and on that largely depended the question whether Whigs or Tories should be Mayors of the Palace. No one ever knew who would be on the throne in five years' time—whether Mary or William, Anne or some Hanoverian Prince, or the Pretender turned Protestant. This uncertainty made it hard for English statesmen to cease to be knaves. Ministers and ex-ministers, Tories and Whigs, admirals and generals, regardless of the fidelity they had sworn to the reigning monarch, corresponded with St. Germains as well as Hanover, so that their fortunes should in all events be secure.

Long uncertainty as to the Succession

But short of foreign conquest, there would never be absolute monarchy again. A restoration, other than by French bayonets, could only be a restoration of the Clarendon Code and high Parliamentary Toryism. But as the balance of parties was kept by William and Anne, party strife came to impregnate all English life. Party spirit was the spirit of the age. Its coarse, free, vigorous breath kept the nation heartily alive. It pervaded the worlds of high society, commerce, and even of scholarship ; it inspired literature, religion, finance ; it guided diplomacy and war. It was the motive power of our great achievements : it founded the Bank and the National Debt ; it carried through the re-coinage ; it evoked the genius of Swift ; it effected the union of England and Scotland ; it won the wars of Marlborough and it made the peace of Utrecht.

Party spirit, 1688-1714

At last the time had come when English Protestants were ready to let one another worship God. All their parties were exhausted with fifty years of revolution, bloodshed and terror, culminating in the recent narrow escape of their common religion. Like dogs that have been flogged off each other, Anglican and Puritan lay down and snarled. The best characteristic product of Restoration society had been the sceptical Whig Lords and philosophers, who had

The Toleration Act, 1689

prescribed for the State the unpopular regimen of Toleration. First the Dissenters, because they were hopeless of supremacy and crushed by persecution, had allowed their powerful friends to inscribe Toleration on the party banner. And now in the year 1689 the political situation compelled the Church to follow. For William, a Calvinist and a Latitudinarian, though he was ready to attend the communion of the Establishment, would not consent to reign unless freedom of worship were conceded to the Puritans ; the pledge of legal and Parliamentary Toleration made to the Dissenters by the Bishops themselves in the hour of peril under James, could not be broken without shame to the Church and danger to the State ; and the Catholic invasion impending from France preserved among English Protestants some sense of common interest. Yet even under these favourable conditions, Toleration was introduced as a practical necessity, not as an accepted principle. By the Toleration Act of 1689, no Nonconformist minister might exercise his functions unless he subscribed thirty-four out of the Thirty-nine Articles ; but the Quakers, who had no ministers and no politics, were allowed to meet on less severe conditions. The result of this curious and illogical compromise was to relieve all sects except the Unitarians and the Catholics. Yet even those strange bed-fellows in misfortune were not in practice left to the rigour of the laws. William, the ally of Spain, of Austria and of the Pope, was the sworn protector of the English Catholics. The remarkable fact that no papist had lost his life in the months of Revolution was due to the exertions of William, to the comparatively humane character of the English mobs and clergy when contrasted with the French, and to the peaceful conduct of the Catholic gentry, who gratefully sought and acknowledged the clemency of the Prince of Orange. For the same reasons, when the new *régime* had been fully established, the Penal Laws were laxly enforced on this side of the Irish Channel. Mass was said regularly in private houses ; there were many well-known Catholic chapels and some monasteries ; the priests conciliated opinion by passing about in disguise, but were seldom hunted and imprisoned. Periodic outbursts of Pro-testant zeal took the form of fresh Penal Laws that were not en-forced. Thus Catholics and Unitarians, though denied the exercise of public worship, were saved from cruel persecution, owing to William's temperament, England's European alliances, and the spirit of humanitarianism, rationalism and indifferentism now per-vading high places and infecting public opinion.[1]

The Tories prevent religious equality, 1689

This grudging and partial step towards religious tolerance was not accompanied by any legislative advance towards religious equality. Within certain limits, it was no longer criminal to preach and to pray. But the Test and Corporation Acts, which kept

[1] Lecky, i., pp. 349-63.

Dissenters as well as Catholics out of civil and military office, were preserved by the Tories against the wish of the Whigs and in spite of the efforts of the King. Nonconformists continued for many generations to be shut out of national administration and local government. Sometimes, indeed, Dissenting merchants took the sacrament to qualify for municipal office. But except for this practice, known as " occasional conformity," which highly incensed the bitter jealousy of the Tories, the Church maintained her social and political monopoly intact. Every member of the governing class had to remain within her communion. In return for this immense advantage secured to her by the State, it was just and necessary that statesmen should interfere in her government enough to check tendencies dangerous to the public peace, and to the new religious concordat. A very great majority of the clergy, known as the High Church party,[1] who completely dominated the Lower House of Convocation, were only half loyal to the reigning sovereigns, and were wild with hatred of Dissent. Government was able to set bounds to their disturbing influence, by putting the small but able minority of Low Churchmen and Latitudinarians in possession of the Bishoprics and chief places of the Church.

This process was effected with rapidity, owing to a remarkable The Non-secession that took place in the first three years of William and Jurors Mary. Five of the " Seven Bishops " honourably adhered to their old doctrines of non-resistance and hereditary right, refused to swear allegiance to the usurper, and together with four hundred of the most advanced High Churchmen were deprived by Act of Parliament.[2] These Non-Jurors long maintained a private Church dear to the Anglican Jacobites. Their exodus left the field open for the elevation of men like Tillotson and Burnet, as overseers of a flock that hated them. The appointment of Latitudinarian Bishops was the chief grievance of the Tories against William. But it was only thus that the religious peace could be kept in England against the outcries of the country parsons and the intrigues of the High Church party, which was in that age distinguished, not by ritualistic practices, but by the desire to go back on the Act of Toleration.

The Tories had prevented religious equality for the future ; Whig the Whigs tried to exact political revenge for the past. They Corporation Bill, hoped to see the shambles set up as in 1661 ; they hoped that exile Jan., 1690 and confiscation would be the lot of those by whose agency so many hundreds of Whigs had been hanged, beheaded, flogged, fined,

[1] The terms High and Low Church first came in at the beginning of Anne's reign, but the distinction existed as strongly under William.
[2] William characteristically wished to let the Non-Jurors stop in the Church, in return for admission of Dissenters to civil and military office. But the Whigs and Tories in Parliament agreed to have two persecutions rather than none (1689), (Mac., chap. xi. Burnet, iv., pp. 12-16).

imprisoned and exiled. They refused to pass the Act of Indemnity repeatedly demanded by William, and pushed forward the new Corporation Bill in a form to exclude from municipal office for seven years all who had been concerned in the surrender of the town charters to Charles II. The Bill was not more unjust than the existing Corporation Act excluding Dissenters from office, but owing to the strength of the Tory party it was more inexpedient. The Whigs revived a slumbering feud in time of utmost peril to the State, when France and Ireland threatened invasion of our distracted land. William was not to be thus trifled with. He was King of the English, not King of the Whigs. Reviving the part of Charles II. rather than of Monmouth, he came down suddenly to the House of Lords and dismissed the Convention Parliament with the same dramatic circumstances with which the merry monarch had routed the Whig members at Oxford. Like Charles, William watched the " faces an ell long " of those who had thought to disturb his kingdom with impunity. But unlike Charles he appealed at once to the country and to the moderate Tories. A Tory majority was returned to the new Parliament, which thankfully buried the past by accepting the Act of Grace presented to it by William, and voted him supplies for the reconquest of Ireland.

Dissolution, 27th Jan. New Tory Parliament helps William, March-May, 1690 Ireland

The scheme of land proprietorship by which Cromwell had hoped to make the Protestants of Ireland strong enough to defend themselves, had failed from its inherent faults of principle.[1] The middle class of Protestant yeomen, who were to have been the backbone of the settlement, had been too few from the first, because the officers bought up the farms allotted to their soldiers to swell their own estates ; it dwindled still further because the aristocratic pride of the gentry, who held themselves aloof from the other classes, had driven the smaller Protestant freeholders to live and to marry among the Catholic population. A severe blow had been struck at all the Protestant settlers together, when the Cavalier Parliament, at the instigation of the graziers of England, had deliberately ruined Irish cattle-breeding, by forbidding the export of cattle to England and her Colonies. Thus weakened by their own social and economic divisions, the English in Ireland were unable to resist the blows struck by James II. at their interest. He had placed the civil and military power in the hands of the Catholics, not intending to destroy, but only to subordinate or to convert the English settlers. But when his throne fell, the native population rose in his name and settled Ireland according to their own ideas. When in 1689 James arrived in Dublin, to head the Celtic insurrection, with arms and officers supplied him by Louis, he could do little to defend the interests of his English subjects, or to prevent the wholesale resumption of the land from the Saxon usurpers. The Protestants

[1] See pp. 264-67 above.

were driven to bay behind the walls of Londonderry. Though they **Relief of** could defend the place against storm, they were only relieved by **London-** **derry,** the English ships breaking the boom in the Foyle at the very last **28th July,** moment, when they could no longer hold out against starvation. **1689**

The racial war for the possession of the island involved the fate **William** of England and of Europe. Before Britain could send her armies **goes in** **person to** to fight France on the continent, she had first to secure her own **Ireland,** shores. The Protestants of England, France, Holland, Germany **June,** **1690** and Scandinavia poured over under their deliverer to strike down Louis XIV. in Ireland. All who rejoice that the Protestant communities of Europe maintained their freedom against Louis and destroyed the prestige of his system on the fields of Blenheim and Ramillies, must read with thankfulness the story of that initial passage of the Boyne, which first gave stability to the Revolution **The** settlement. When it was known in England that the Irish army **Boyne,** **1st July,** had been scattered in rout, our politicians calculated that a restora- **1690** tion would be a matter of years rather than of months, and each man trimmed his policy to suit.

Yet the deliverance of Europe was turned, on the scene where **Treaty of** it was enacted, into a terrible oppression. The final surrender at **Limerick,** **October,** Limerick of Sarsfield and the last Irish army, to the generals whom **1691** William had left behind him, was the enslavement of a race. William made as much and as little effort to save the Catholics of Ireland as James had made to save the Protestants.[1] But the two forces on which his power depended were set against all mercy and all justice ; the Protestants in Ireland and the Parliament in England were bent on complete spoliation and cruel persecution. The English Parliament, which had become by the Revolution settlement the ultimate authority on Irish questions in place of the King, enabled at the same time the Irish Protestants to crush the Irish Catholics, and the English clothiers to ruin the Irish Protestants. England, while she made every Catholic her deadly enemy by enforcing the Penal Laws, prevented the growth of a large Protestant population by stopping the export of Irish cloth, in the interest of her own West- **Ruin of** country clothiers (1698). And in order that every curse known in **Ireland** England should flourish in Ireland without the accompanying **com-** **pleted by** blessings, the Anglicans, numbering about one-third of the Irish **bad laws** Protestants, were permitted not only to keep all the spoils of Church and State for themselves, but even to prevent the exercise of Nonconformist worship. The Toleration Act was not extended to Ireland. The Presbyterians who had manned the walls of Londonderry, though they might now kick the papists into the gutter, were not themselves allowed to worship God. The net result of this economic and religious jealousy was that over 20,000 of the best Protestant stock in the world left Ulster, and the American backwoods were

[1] Ranke, .v., p. 542 ; v., pp. 215-19.

peopled with dour Scotsmen, who had even less reason than the descendants of the Pilgrim Fathers to love the English State.

With the murdered cloth industry perished the last hope of Ireland. Even in the ten distracted years that followed the Revolution, it had given promise of employing a vastly increased Protestant population, and of bringing the Catholics into industrial relation with the English world. But, as it was, the laws had abolished all the old forms of secular life for the native Irish, destroyed their upper class, deprived them of lands and employments, schools and universities, and prevented the growth of new interests in place of the old ; the peasants had nothing left to render bondage endurable but memories and religion kept alive by the priests, to extirpate whose influence these frantic statutes had been passed. Under a legal code that left them no choice except to be disloyal and priest-ridden, the native population multiplied and took real possession of the soil, of which they had in the eye of the law been deprived ; while the landowners soon dwindled to a small caste of noblesse, living on the plunder of the land and divorced from the soil and its inhabitants.[1]

Killie-crankie, 27th July, 1689

Scotland in the first year of the Revolution had been more happily settled on a natonal and Presbyterian basis. Another invasion of the Lowlands by clans hostile to the reviving fortunes of the house of Argyle, flickered out more quickly than the similar undertaking of Montrose in 1644-45, owing to the death of Claverhouse at the very moment when the red-coats broke before the claymores at Killiecrankie. Deprived of the only warrior with authority enough to lead and unite their jealous chieftains, the barbarians retired to their valleys before the year was out. No attempt to bring the Highlands within the pale of civilisation and law was made until 1746, but a cordon of forts and troops was established to protect the Lowlands, and the chiefs were kept quiet by gifts of money from their new sovereign, whom they were on these terms content to acknowledge (1691). One small clan, inhabiting the valley of Glencoe, was late in taking the oath of allegiance. The opportunity was seized by their Scottish enemies as an excuse to perpetrate a massacre among the mists, by wiles as basely treacherous as those wherewith, under brighter skies, rulers of the blood of Medici or Borgia lured their guests to death. In Glencoe it was the guests who rewarded hospitality by midnight slaughter. The story makes it clear that the cruelties done upon the Covenanters by the statesmen of the Restoration and by the soldiers of Claverhouse, resulted not from the greater wickedness of one party, but from the general state of political civilisation in

Glencoe. 1692

[1] Cunningham, pp. 370-79. Lecky (ed. 1878), ii., pp. 220, 221 and *passim*. Froude, *English in Ireland*, book ii.

Scotland. Yet even in Scotland, where the age of barbarism was at last coming to an end, the breach of hospitality and the deliberate slaughter of women and children aroused universal horror. William, though ignorant of the base means that were to be employed, had in general terms consented to the " extirpation " of the clan of barbarian robbers. The man who gave this evil order, the man who failed to bring the murderers of the De Witts to justice, was the same man who, by Cæsarean clemency in the midst of traitors and assassins, introduced the new *régime* of humanity and toleration into English government.

The establishment of his authority over the British Isles enabled William, in the third year of his reign, to lead the British troops across the sea. The war of the League of Augsburg saw Dutch, Austrians, Spaniards, Savoyards and Germans fighting Louis along all the frontiers of France. But the result of the struggle turned chiefly on those seven campaigns in defence of the Spanish Netherlands, wherein William trained our army to surpass on the field those of all the other nations whom he led to battle, moulding with his own hand the splendid instrument that he bequeathed to Marlborough. If we remember the want of skill, leadership and organisation with which our civilian ancestors invariably began great military operations after any long interval of peace,—if we recall the expeditions of Buckingham, the opening of our own civil wars, and even in a more military age the opening of our wars against the French Revolution,—then, such defeats as we suffered at Steinkirk (1692) and Landen (1693) will appear necessary and not inglorious preludes to the great victories of the next reign. The result of William's seven campaigns was all that he could have hoped, with treason and division at home, and unwillingness and jealousy among his allies. The Spanish Netherlands were successfully guarded against Louis. If Namur was lost in 1691, it was retaken in 1695. But the real outcome of the war was that the Revolution settlement in England passed safely through the fire. Twice an invasion of England, concerted by Louis with the Jacobites, was attempted and failed. On both occasions the Tories and Whigs rallied to the defence of the King, and the property of Non-Jurors was in some danger from mobs who usually attacked Nonconformists.

The importance of the first invasion scheme was naval. In 1690, when William was reducing Ireland, the French fleet, after a victorious encounter with the English and Dutch off Beachy Head, had held the Channel and even landed a regiment of French troops in Devonshire for a few hours. In 1692 preparations were made to send across a great army. The plan, which had much the same chance of success as those of Philip II. and Napoleon I., was frustrated by the same means. The French fleet was defeated on the open sea, chased into the harbours of Cherbourg and La Hogue,

[Side notes:] War of the League of Augsburg, 1688-97

English in the Netherlands, 1691-97

First Invasion Scheme, La Hogue, May, 1692

and burnt as it lay in port. At La Hogue the conflagration took place under the eyes of James II. and the army of invasion. From this battle dates a change in the maritime conditions of the struggle against Louis XIV. During the rest of the wars of William and Marlborough, the English and Dutch fleets held the sea. . Until the peace of Utrecht the ocean was a safe pathway for the military operations of the allies, and French commerce was annihilated. As Louis had chosen to engage himself in land wars on his Flemish, Rhenish, Alpine and Pyrenean frontiers, he could no longer afford to repair the losses of La Hogue, and the waste of time and weather. William and Marlborough revived the policy of Cromwell in maintaining a British fleet to command the Mediterranean, a policy which had for a while been neglected by Charles II. and his brother, when the want of money involved in their autocratic policy had compelled them to abandon Tangier (1683), and to become the vassals of France.[1]

On the land frontiers, where evenly matched armies marched and counter-marched under wary generals, the victory in the war of the League of Augsburg would be to that Prince who could last raise money from his impoverished subjects. In the contest of endurance between the credit of France and the credit of England, the genius and policy of the Whig financiers affected the fortunes of all Europe.

William and the Whigs. Cabinet government

For the conduct of the war fell more and more upon the Whigs. Experience gradually taught the first of our post-revolutionary monarchs, to obtain unity in the public service by selecting his ministers from one of the two parties ; and to prefer that one which at the time had the majority, to carry ministerial measures through Parliament.[2] Now in time of war the Whigs were preferred both by the electors and by the King. They were more irreconcilably hostile to James, and to French ideals of Church and State. And, in spite of the incident of the dissolution of 1690, the Tories became ever more unfriendly to William. They could never heartily accept the change of dynasty, in which they had acquiesced to the destruction of their own political monopoly. Their hereditary allegiance, which they could not render to James and his son, seemed due only to his Protestant daughters. Mary

[1] Corbett, chaps. xxv.-xxx., and p. 313.
[2] This principle of closer connection between the executive and legislative, unknown to Charles II., and not laid down in the terms of the Revolution settlement, was adopted as of practical utility, rather than granted as of constitutional right. In this limited sense William originated Cabinet government. But he did not govern solely by the advice of his Cabinet. Often in home affairs and nearly always in foreign affairs he acted without the advice of his ministers and sometimes against their wishes. Again, he often consulted, on questions of the highest policy, men who were not in the Cabinet of the day and who were detested by the House of Commons, as Dutch Bentinck, and the repentant renegade Sunderland. Neither ministers nor Parliament could complain of his practice in these respects, for it was strictly constitutional. It was not prohibited by the Bill of Rights or by custom.

reconciled them to the present, and Anne to the future. So when Death of
Mary unexpectedly died of smallpox, their hostility to the Dutch Mary,
King became more marked. Dec.,
1694

But owing to the same pitiful misfortune, William and the war The Marl-
party received one great accession of strength. On her sister's boroughs
death, Anne was reconciled by her political advisers to the widowed and Anne
King, whom she was almost certain to survive and now almost recon-
certain to succeed. Sarah Churchill controlled the will of the William,
Princess, and her husband's great fortunes were staked on those of 1695
Anne. John Churchill, nominally a Tory but really a political
eclectic, had brought about the complete and bloodless triumph
of William's invasion. In return, the new King had made him
Earl of Marlborough, and left him authority and patronage in the
army, which he was well able to use both for his own and his country's
benefit. He had, however, while Mary stood between Anne and
the succession, intrigued with St. Germains, betrayed military
secrets to France, and tried to manipulate English jealousy of the
Dutch favourites into a treasonable movement, ostensibly in favour
of James, but probably in the real hope of benefiting Anne. On
the unexpected death of the Queen, this group, which may almost
be said to have held the balance of power, went over to William
and the war party. Thus early was formed the union of the Whig
party with Anne, the Marlboroughs and their friend Godolphin ; it
continued intermittently, until in the next reign it had destroyed
the power of Louis.

The great achievement of the Whig ministers was the institution Bank of
of the modern system of finance with which England has since fought England
all her great wars of European security and colonial expansion. The and
National
Bank of England was established in connection with the National Debt,
Debt, against the opposition of the Tories, who were jealous of the 1694.
Re-coin-
monied interest. A regular method of Government borrowing was age, 1696
thus set up, which enabled a King who could not tax his subjects at
will, to outlast in resources a despot whose subjects had but little
left for him to take.[1]

The yet more difficult task of a re-coinage was carried through
in danger and difficulty, at a time of war and general depression,
by the same set of statesmen who formed the Bank.

The Whig leaders of the rising generation, Somers and Montague,
in close consultation with the Whig philosophers, Newton and
Locke, effected these great measures, which they had devised by
their own science and wisdom, and carried through by the strength
of party spirit in the City and the House of Commons. Under
this new leadership, the wisdom of the Whigs saved the State which
had so often been shaken by their folly.

[1] See Appendix E below.

The
Whigs
even more
Protec-
tionist
than the
Tories
Yet these great financiers were behind those of the opposite party in one important respect. A false theory of the Balance of Trade, common to both sides, was held in a more extreme form by the Whigs than by their opponents. Burnet declared that " we lost every year a million of money by our trade " to France. This state of opinion was partly due to the dependence of the Whigs on the trading interest, which believed in monopoly and high protection ; while the Tories were the Landed interest, which so long as it had its Corn Bounties was suspicious of trade, and indifferent to the means by which men generally supposed that it could be fostered. But besides this ignorant multitude of squires, the Tory party contained economic thinkers like Dudley North, Child and Davenant, who were already tending towards free-trade theory. There was also another reason for the difference in economic creeds. It was the traditional policy of the Whigs to stop commerce with France, as a measure of antagonism to the great Catholic monarchy ; while the Tories, as Bolingbroke afterwards expressed it, thought that " when once our people have felt the sweet of carrying on a trade with France, under reasonable regulations, the artifices of Whiggism will have less effect amongst them ". In 1678 the Whigs had employed their first Parliamentary supremacy to pass an Act absolutely prohibiting the French trade ; under the Tory reaction commerce was resumed, but in 1689 the trade was again prohibited, as a measure natural to a time of war.[1]

Second
Invasion
Scheme,
and As-
sassina-
tion Plot,
1696
At the elections of 1695 the Tories, who had already lost the confidence of the King, proved to have lost the confidence of the country. And in the following year Whig power and popularity was confirmed by the second invasion scheme of Louis. With the recapture of Namur the slow tide of war had turned against bankrupt France ; as a last snatch after departing victory, Louis prepared another army to invade England. To clear the way for the landing of the French, the Jacobites laid a plot to murder the King in his coach, curiously similar in its details to the Rye House Plot. It was detected only just in time. A deep, though transient, emotion of loyalty and gratitude to William burst out in all classes. The triumph of the Whigs who served him was complete, but it was short-lived.

Treaty of
Ryswick,
Sep., 1697
Next year the war was brought to an end. As regards Europe, the Treaty of Ryswick was little more than a cessation of arms ; for though Louis gave up Luxemburg and Lorraine, the general balance of power had not been finally decided. But as regards England, the contest had been decisive of much ; the King of England was at last acknowledged at Versailles. The ship of the Revolution had come safe to port, with the fortunes of William on board.

---

[1] W. J. Ashley, *Surveys Historic and Economic* (1900), pp. 268-303. Bol. iv., pp. 153, 196-97. Burnet, vi., pp. 156-58. See also p. 425 below.

The most dangerous years of his life were now behind, but the most vexatious and humiliating were yet to come. Louis had granted the terms of Ryswick only because he saw looming in the immediate future the contest between the French and Austrian candidates for the succession of the Spanish Empire. That contest would be decided by the attitude of England, Holland and Spain. If the fateful hour when Charles II. of Spain died had found all Europe still at war with France, and Spain herself still in armed alliance with the Austrian Emperor, then by no possibility could a Prince of the House of Bourbon have been placed in possession either of the Netherlands, or of any other part of the vast inheritance. Louis, therefore, had hastened to make peace. William, thankful as he was for the secure and honourable position which he obtained by the treaty, knew that a greater struggle on a new issue was at hand, unless it could be averted by previous arrangement. The King of France, aware that his country had been ruined by the last two wars, was equally anxious to avoid another breach. Twice in three years (1698-1700) Louis and William formed a secret agreement, against the death of Charles II., for the Partition of the Spanish dominions in a manner least calculated to disturb the balance of power.

But meanwhile the English people, taking it for granted that foreign affairs were well settled, were revelling in a holiday of domestic faction. Strengthened by the elections of 1698, the Tories and the Independent Whigs broke loose from the bonds of loyalty to the Government which the war had imposed upon them. The Whig ministers did not dare to call their own party to heel.[1] In the sessions that followed the peace, the most important debates emanated from the action of private members and from the general opinion of the House. The ministry merely tried to avoid the blows. In spite of the protests of William, who knew that another war could be prevented only by war-like preparations, the Commons cut down the army to 7,000 men (1698-99) ; for hatred of red-coats was an old English principle, that appealed to both sides of the House. In particular, William's Dutch guards, for whom he felt a love which was an offence to his English subjects, were sent back across the sea. The King was also deeply hurt when the grants of forfeited Irish land made by him to his Dutch servants were cancelled by Act of Parliament (1700). Yet there was something to be said from the English point of view for both these decisions.

[1] The House of Commons then had an independent will of its own ; the majority was in the highest degree jealous of the ministers, who were invidiously known as " placemen ". So little did men foresee the present form of the English Constitution, that a Place Bill actually passed the House of Commons in this reign, to prevent " placemen " from sitting in the Lower Chamber at all. In the long interregnum between Royal autocracy and Cabinet autocracy, the House of Commons was always free and often showed itself both irresponsible and tyran nical.

A Tory
Parlia-
ment,
Jan.-
Nov.,
1701

At the elections of January, 1701, the Tories were returned in strength enough to take party vengeance on the Whig ministers themselves. When the first Partition Treaty came to light, it was made an excuse to impeach Somers and Montague (March, 1701). These ministers, having aroused more jealousy than gratitude by the success with which they had guided the nation through the perils of the last war, were now in danger because they had consented to the wise efforts of William to prevent the next; charges of peculation were also trumped up to strengthen the case against Montague, the financial saviour of England.[1]

Anti-
monarchi-
cal spirit
of the age

In the four years intervening between the wars of William and the wars of Marlborough, the English people and the English Constitution of that day were seen in their most free and characteristic mood, at their worst and at their best. The action of the Tory House of Commons, though in some respects very unwise, showed that their party, under the growing influence of the moderate Harley, was wedded to Parliamentary life and the Revolution settlement;[2] that England was not becoming militarist or forgetful of her own domestic traditions in the course of the continental struggle; and that the new prestige and functions acquired by the Whig House of Commons, session after session, during the war, were to become permanent in our national life, whatever party was in fashion. Since the House of Commons had waged and won the war, had found supplies and instituted the new financial policy, its functions had multiplied and its prestige had increased in all quarters. The old power of the Crown over commercial affairs had passed to the Commons; English and Irish clothiers, Old and New East India Companies, came no longer begging and bribing to Whitehall, but to Westminster, where the fateful tariffs and bounties, that made and ruined merchants, were sold for money or for political support.[3] Even Ireland, the garrison of prerogative power ever since the days of Strafford, had at last been brought under direct cognisance of the House. And again, it was in accordance with the anti-monarchical spirit of the age that the House refused to renew the Licensing Act, and so finally freed the English press from the action of the Censor.

Freedom
of the
Press,
1695

But though the House of Commons feared neither King nor Cabinet, there was still one power that could call it to account. It was never for more than three years together independent of public opinion, as it afterwards became in the days of Wilkes and North. Many boroughs were rotten, but not yet rotten enough to

---

[1] *Parl. Hist.*, v., pp. 1258-1315.

[2] This was proved when the Tories introduced and passed, with the hearty concurrence of the Whigs, the Act of Settlement of 1701, securing the Crown to the House of Hanover, in case William and Anne should both die without leaving children. Mr. Feiling's *History of the Tory Party* is very good on this period.

[3] Cunningham, i., pp. 403-10. This control of Parliament over the course of trade was made clear in 1678 when the Whigs prohibited the trade with France.

prevent the sense of the upper and middle classes from making itself felt at the frequent elections held under the Triennial Act.[1] Behind the evenly balanced parties of this period, there always stood, cudgel in hand, the independent electors, imbued in this generation with a remarkable instinct both for home and foreign affairs, and well able to keep both parties in order, with alternate blows.

As one of the periodic waves of High Church feeling against Dissenters and Toleration had now set in, it is probable that the Tory Saturnalia of 1701 would have been allowed to proceed to great lengths in the first years of the century if another European crisis had not suddenly threatened the independence and commerce of Great Britain. In November, 1701, the electorate, again appealed to by William as the last act of his life, cut short the Parliamentary revels, and insisted that the whole energies of the country should be turned to meet the danger from abroad. The French troops were in occupation of the Spanish Empire.

The War of the Spanish Succession (1701-1713) is the only example in history of a struggle between the principal powers of Europe for the possession of a great Western Empire, unable to defend itself and scarcely consulted as to its own fate. Yet only a hundred years before the Spanish Empire had been the terror, and almost the ruin, of those who now fought over its division. *The Spanish Succession*

Spain had already begun the long penance for her crimes. The expulsion of the Jews and Moors had been followed by the decadence of the Christians ; clericalism had led to the impotence of the great Catholic power ; the attempt to monopolise the riches of the world by preventing exchange, had ended in economic ruin ; despotism and centralisation had led to the collapse of the central authority. Yet the multifarious possessions in both hemispheres held together under the tyranny of Spain, had not yet been torn from her, though she was equally unable to resist external attack or to suppress domestic insurrection. For thirty years past her Empire had been defended from foreign annexation by leagues of powerful allies, and from internal disruption by the inertia of her subjects. If the spirit of Van Arteveldt, of Mazzini, or of Bolivar, had been stirring in that dead time, Flanders, Italy and America could with ease have thrown off their effete Castilian governors. Portugal alone had rebelled, and Portugal was again an independent State. And now Charles II. of Spain was dying without heir. The Partition Treaties arranged by Louis and William broke down. The first Treaty (1698) was annulled by the death of the Electoral Prince of Bavaria, the neutral heir who had been named as more *The Partition Treaties, 1698-1700*

Death
and Tes-
tament of
Charles
II., Nov.,
1700

acceptable than the Austrian or French candidates.[1] The second Treaty, which divided up the inheritance, failed because neither Spain nor Austria would consent to any Partition. Charles II., in his will, offered the whole Empire to Philip, the cadet of the House of Bourbon, if his grandfather Louis XIV. would support him in possession by French arms. If Louis refused, the whole Empire was to go to the Austrian candidate, the Archduke Charles, the cadet of the House of Hapsburg. On the death of Charles II., Louis, knowing that, if he refused, Austria would accept the offer, and that neither Holland nor England would fight to enforce Partition for the benefit of France, threw over the Treaty he had made with William, and accepted the whole inheritance for his grandson—now Philip V. of Spain (Nov., 1700). In Philip's name the French troops took possession of all the fortresses of the Spanish Netherlands up to the borders of Holland, and poured unresisted over the Alps, to guard for him the plains of Milan and of Naples against the Austrian. In a few weeks Louis had come peaceably into occupation of whole countries for whose outlying posts he had waged three long and ruinous wars. In the spring of 1701 he was in a position from which nothing could dislodge him but the prolonged efforts of a coalition stronger than the League of Augsburg. Of such a coalition there appeared no prospect. The Dutch and English peoples viewed the change with complacency,

[1] GENEALOGICAL KEY TO THE PROBLEM OF THE SPANISH SUCCESSION

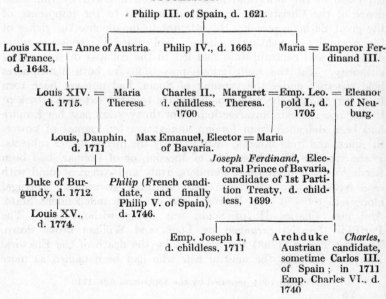

Philip III. of Spain, d. 1621.

Louis XIII. = Anne of Austria.   Philip IV., d. 1665   Maria = Emperor Fer-
of France,   dinand III.
d. 1643.

Louis XIV. = Maria   Charles II.,   Margaret = Emp. Leo. = Eleanor
d. 1715.   Theresa.   d. childless.   Theresa.   pold I., d.   of Neu-
                             1700   1705   burg.

Louis, Dauphin,   Max Emanuel, Elector = Maria
d. 1711   of Bavaria.

                              Joseph Ferdinand, Elec-
                              toral Prince of Bavaria,
Duke of Bur-   *Philip* (French candi-   candidate of 1st Parti-
gundy, d. 1712.   date, and finally   tion Treaty, d. child-
                    Philip V. of Spain),   less, 1699.
Louis XV.,   d. 1746.
d. 1774.

                    Emp. Joseph I.,   Archduke   *Charles*,
                    d. childless, 1711   Austrian   candidate,
                                          sometime Carlos III.
                                          of Spain; in 1711
                                          Emp. Charles VI., d.
                                          1740

fondly hoping that Louis would soon withdraw the French troops Louis in
from the Spanish dominions, and sever his connection with Philip V. occupa-
The Tory squires were rejoiced to hear that Louis had vexed William tion of the
by tearing up his precious Treaties of Partition. The new King of Spanish
Spain was acknowledged by England and by Holland. So long as domin-
the maritime powers remained neutral the French could easily ions, 1701
ward off sulky Austria, who could not reach the Netherlands, and
who vainly attempted in 1701 the task of recovering Italy with her
own armies. The work of William's life seemed undone.

But Louis himself came to the rescue of his enemies, and aroused
against France the old hatreds and the old alliance. While Charles
was dying, Louis had trod carefully. But when the prize seemed
to him secure, his natural instincts of pride and insolence awoke
too soon for his fortunes. By a series of violent acts he showed
Europe that he was still the same Grand Monarch who had burned
the Palatinate, dragooned the Pope, and revoked the Edict of
Nantes, but now twice as strong and therefore twice as dangerous as
he had ever been before.

He seized the Barrier towns [1] of the Netherlands from the Mistakes
Dutch : Holland saw that she must again fight for her life. He of Louis, 1701
declared that Philip was not incapacitated from the French success-
sion : Europe was again overshadowed by the phantom of a Universal Monarchy. He proclaimed that France would be treated as
the most favoured nation in trade with the Spanish-American
Colonies : England and Holland saw that they would be excluded
from the riches of the new world, which were no longer to be used
only by effete Spain, but also by France herself, the one rival whom
the maritime powers had to fear in the world across the ocean.

Louis had been encouraged to commit these premature acts of Agitation
violence by the spectacle of Parliamentary England baiting her for war begins in
King, and by the belief that the Tories were able and willing to the
keep peace at any price. But when it was realised in England that country,
Louis intended to exploit the Spanish Empire as an appanage of Apr.-June,
France, an agitation for war arose outside the doors of the Tory 1701
House of Commons. The majority within were angry at being disturbed in the more attractive programme of impeaching the Whig
statesmen, and when the famous " Kentish Petition " called on them
to adopt a different attitude in the face of foreign danger, they
imprisoned the gentlemen who brought it, for breach of privilege.
It was the first battle in the long war between the House of
Commons and the public, with which the annals of the next hundred years are so full. But the Tories were not really indifferent
to the danger of the country in face of Louis' aggression, and

---

[1] Fortresses which the Dutch had been allowed to garrison in Spanish territory,
as a safeguard against French invasion of Holland through the ill-defended
dominions of Spain.

Grand Alliance formed, 7th Sep., 1701
gradually came round to give assent to a new war. Thus armed by England, William went abroad and formed the Grand Alliance which was destined at length to reduce " the exorbitant power of France ".

Louis acknowledges the Pretender, 17th Sep., 1701
But the Tories, still in a majority in a Parliament only six months old, were less likely than the Whigs to show zeal in waging war, especially on the Continent. While war loans and war contracts enriched Whig monied men, war taxes were to the disadvantage of Tory squires. It was the policy of their party to confine our operations as much as possible to the sea. But again Louis cleared the last obstacle from the path of his enemies. Standing by the death-bed of James II. among the English exiles, who adored him as their patron and champion, his heart swelled with that private generosity and pity which in him took the place of generosity and pity for nations. Against the advice of his ministers, he proclaimed James's son, the Pretender, to be King of England.

Elections of Nov., 1701
William, like a victorious race-horse that is to die at the goal, rose to one last effort while breath was still in his body. He hastened over for the last time to England and dissolved the new Parliament. Indignation against Louis was for the moment almost universal. The elections took place amid scenes of warlike enthusiasm ; the Whigs were much strengthened, and the Tories pledged to vigorous prosecution of the war.

Death of William, 8th March, 1702
During the winter that closed the eventful year 1701, Europe was ringing with preparations for the greatest war the world had ever seen. With the spring, the armies everywhere shook themselves and began to move on the Meuse, the Rhine, the Danube and the Po. But William was dead. The fierce clear light that had so long flickered in the frail lamp of his body was at last extinguished. But the great machine he had set in motion rolled irresistibly on. In charge of it, in Flanders, appeared the man whom he had chosen for that place ; because, though he knew his treasons, he understood his motives and had detected his genius. Marlborough was going to the war.

Outside his own people and his own country of Holland, William never sought the love of contemporaries or of posterity, and he has not obtained it ; but he sought their welfare and freedom, and these he achieved. His Calvinism was the garb in which his age and country dressed the temper of a Stoic, who serves God for duty, not for joy or fear. He scorned to be popular. He scorned to be cruel. His wisdom was indefatigable. His patience was like the patience of the gods.

CHAPTER XV

THE REIGN OF ANNE, 1702-14

While strength upholds the free.—BOWEN.

WHEN Charles II. landed at Dover, it had been decided Protes-
beyond all future appeal that the Puritans were not to rule tantism
and Par-
the State, and that England was not to be a republic ; but when liament-
William marched from Torbay, it was decided no less irrevocably ary
that the Catholics were not to rule the State, and that England was govern-
ment
not to be a despotism. Under Queen Anne the supremacy of the secure
Protestants was never once threatened by the Catholics, nor the
liberties of the subject by the monarch ; and even if on her death
Bolingbroke had restored the Pretender, that prince would have
been bound to the High Churchmen and Tories as helplessly as
George I. was bound to the Latitudinarians and Whigs. But the
Revolution, like the Restoration, had drawn with it some by-
consequences, which many of those who supported its main provisions did not intend to become permanent. These accidents of
the Revolution were Toleration for Dissenters, the growth of a
monied interest in close alliance with Government, a system of
national credit, and a standing army. All these were necessary
conditions of the great land war with France, into which the events
of 1688 had plunged the nation. While William lived to protect
the Dissenters, and while the country was daily threatened with
conquest by France, the Tories, who were quite as patriotic as the
Whigs, though in a different way, curbed their party passions and
made no serious effort to overthrow the new domestic system. But
in 1702 their opportunity seemed to have arrived. A High Church
Queen ascended the throne ; and if the danger to Europe was greater
than before, now that the French infantry were garrisoning the
towns of Flanders and Italy, the danger to England was less obvious Tolera-
than ten years before, when they had been crowding the ports of tion and
embarkation along the Norman coast. The Tories felt encouraged financial
system
by the new monarch, and justified by the new situation, in beginning insecure
a reactionary movement against that part of the Revolution settlement which concerned the treatment of the Dissenters and of the
commercial classes. This policy encouraged among its advocates a
readiness to confine our operations against France chiefly to naval
warfare, an indifference to the fate of Holland and the other States
of Europe, and no " very settled resolutions " on the question of the
Hanoverian succession.[1] The Whigs, on the other hand, in their

---

[1] Bolingbroke's *Letter to Sir W. Windham* (ed. 1753), p. 22.

zeal for Toleration and for the monied men, would be at any pains to secure the success, but at none to secure the termination, of a war whose continuance was, under a Tory monarch, the only safeguard of the domestic interests under their charge.

The country gets the best of both parties

It was the good fortune of England, in this glorious reign, to get all that was good out of both parties, when a few turns of chance would, as often happens, have given her all that was worst. When Anne died (1714), the Whigs had, by a vigorous war on land, restored the safety of the States of Europe, broken for ever the prestige of the persecuting Catholic despotism of France, established in its place that of the tolerant Protestant constitutionalism of England, and thereby prepared the way for the intellectual and political downfall of the *ancien régime* on the Continent ; they had passed the Union with Scotland ; they had secured the Hanoverian succession ; and in doing these things they had rendered secure for the future the monied interest and the Toleration of Dissent. These great achievements, the starting-point of European and English development in the coming centuries, were party measures taken to defend certain classes of the island community. The Tories, on their side, though they failed permanently to secure their other objects, garnered for us by a lasting peace the fruits of the Whig war. Their Treaty of Utrecht (1713) was a measure to promote the interests of their party, just as the campaign of Ramillies, the Union with Scotland, and the bringing over of George I., were designed to protect the other. Thus out of the contests of two factions was snatched the welfare both of England and of Europe.

The Age of Anne

This game of rise and fall, played out for the dozen years of Anne's reign by the chiefs of a small people scarcely more numerous than the inhabitants of London at the present day, decided the trend of European civilisation. But in order to understand the turns and chances of this game, it is necessary first to appreciate the forces, interests and principles which had in recent years taken possession of the Whig and Tory parties respectively, as a result of the reign of William and the French wars.

Whig party under Anne : its composition

The Whig party, in the reign of Anne, was, as its adversaries loved to observe, "patched up of heterogeneous, inconsistent parts " : [1] a small majority of the House of Lords, where the balance was held by the Whig Bishops of William's creation ; the officers and veterans of the army ; the trading classes, especially the great monied men of the City and the Bank, who financed and therefore advised the Revolution Government ; the yeomen in the southern, eastern and south-western shires ; the whole body of Dissenters ; and the " several gradations of free-thinkers "—more talked of in this than

[1] Swift, *Examiner*, No. 35.

in the succeeding reigns—Latitudinarian Bishops, Quakers, Unitarians, deistic philosophers, and blasphemous libertine aristocrats of the type of Wharton. These classes were bound together by common fear of the Tory reaction, which, as press, pulpit, and coffee-house loudly proclaimed in the opening years of the century, had marked them for common overthrow and persecution. They were united not only by a common fear but by a set of principles, intelligently and heartily understood by all classes of Whigs, except perhaps by the soldiers, whose affections, like those of Corporal Trim, were centred on the persons of William and Marlborough, and who were Whigs only because the Whigs were the war party. The principles that bound the rest of the coalition together were the doctrines of Locke, confirmed and enlarged by experience. They are stated by Swift under three principal heads, as follows :—

> 1. They do not think the prerogative to be yet sufficiently limited ; and have therefore taken care (as a particular mark of their veneration for the illustrious House of Hanover) to clip it still closer against the next reign.

This jealousy of the powers of the Crown was indeed always the central point of Whig theory ; but it had also been the Tory practice under William. On the accession of Anne the old state of things was restored. For while the Tories could lead, the Whig ministers had to drive the Queen. In the middle of her reign the Tories could point to Anne as another Royal Martyr in the hands of the army, the fanatics and the Parliament. *Its principles*

> 2. As to religion (continues Swift) their universal, undisputed maxim is that it ought to make no distinction at all among Protestants. . . . Union in discipline and doctrine, the offensive sin of schism, the notion of a Church and hierarchy, they laugh at as foppery, cant and priestcraft. They see no necessity at all that there should be a national faith ; and what we usually call by that name, they only style the *religion of the magistrate*.

This is a perfectly fair account of Whig principles, if it be borne in mind that no attack on the emoluments or position of the Church was suggested, but only a partial and gradual admission of some of the Dissenters to civil office, and a defence of their right to educate their own children.[1]

> 3. Swift adds " another acknowledged maxim in that party, and, in my opinion, as dangerous to the Constitution as any I have mentioned ; I mean, that of preferring, on all occasions, the monied interest before the landed ".[2] This meant that the Whig ministers under Anne continued the financial system that Montague had begun under William, basing the policy of the country on public borrowing. It was therefore necessary for Government to retain the good-will and consult the wishes of the capitalists of the City,

---

[1] See the statement of the Whig majority in the House of Lords on the Occasional Conformity Bill, 1702, where not even complete civil equality is claimed for Dissenters (*Parl. Hist.*, vi., pp. 76-91).

[2] Swift, *Examiner*. No. 35.

organised in the Bank of England, undeterred by the fact that many of them were Presbyterians. The Whigs perceived the true lines on which British power and wealth could be developed in the coming century.

The Tories claimed to represent the more solid interests in the nation, because in their opinion no interest was solid but that of the landowners. Their party consisted of most of the country gentlemen and nine-tenths of the country clergy, together with the large classes wholly dependent on the manor house, such as family servants, tenant-farmers and their employees. The agricultural labourers, then the vast majority of the English nation, had no voice in politics ; but as they trooped off meekly to the parish church, and as there was then no social agitation on foot against squire or farmer, it may be presumed that all except those employed by the yeomanry could count as Tories at a pinch. Both parties could, at favourable seasons, excite to riot the rabble of the large and small towns. In the reign of Anne the Tories succeeded in this more often, in spite of the advantage possessed by the Whigs as the war party ; for there were more Dissenting than Catholic chapels at hand to be sacked.

The Tory party desired not to overthrow but to modify the Revolution settlement. They wished not to raise the Catholics, but to depress the Dissenters ; not to restore absolutism, but to extend squirearchy. It was their ambition to monopolise power for the landowning class.

We supposed (wrote Bolingbroke to Windham) the Tory party to be the bulk of the landed interest, and to have no contrary influence blended into its composition. . . . We supposed the Whigs to be the remains of a party, formed against the ill-designs of the Court under King Charles II., nursed up into strength and applied to contrary uses by King William III., and yet still so weak as to lean on the Presbyterians, on the bank and other corporations, on the Dutch and other allies. . . . The view, therefore, of those amongst us who thought in this manner, was to improve the Queen's favour to break the body of the Whigs, to render their supports useless to them, and to fill the employments of the kingdom, down to the meanest, with Tories. We imagined such measures, joined to the advantages of our numbers and our property, would secure us against all attempts during her reign ; and that we should soon be too considerable not to make our terms in all events which might happen afterwards : concerning which, to speak truly, I think few or none of us had very settled resolutions.[1]

The spirit of the Tory party was the jealousy of the old world against the new ; the wish to restrain the growth of new classes and new ideas. But there was one bit of old England that was on the side of the Whigs. The great days of the yeomen were over. Doomed economically to a slow extinction, they were only able to maintain their political influence against the neighbouring squires

[1] Bolingbroke's *Letter to Sir W. Windham* (ed. 1753), p. 22.

by alliance with the more flourishing classes of the Whig union—
the Lords, the monied men and the shopkeepers. It would appear
that the Tory creed did not regard the small freeholder as one of
those " possessors of the soil," who, according to Swift, " are the
best judges of what is for the advantage of the kingdom " ; for
Tory legislation under Anne excluded the yeoman, as well as the
mere merchant, from the right of sitting in the House of Commons.[1]
In the same spirit, the legislation of former reigns had excluded all
freeholders of under a hundred pounds a year from killing game
even on their own lands.[2] Game preserving had, all through the
seventeenth century, been increasing the antagonism of the squire
to his yeoman neighbour, the only person on the country-side who
was not at his mercy. The jealousy even of the good Sir Roger de
Coverley is half-aroused against the

> " yeoman of about an hundred pounds a year " who " would be a good man if
> he did not destroy so many partridges ". " He is just within the game act, and
> qualified to kill an hare or a pheasant : he knocks down a dinner with his gun
> twice or thrice a week ; and by that means lives much cheaper than those
> who have not so good an estate as himself."

Thus the game laws passed by the gentry had robbed the poorer
yeomen of an important part of their means of livelihood, because,
in the eyes of these defenders of property, the private inheritance
of a poor man was as little sacred as the common lands and rights
of the village. The greater eagerness about game preserving which
marks the legislation of the seventeenth century was partly due to
the shot-gun, which had come into general use since the reign of
James I., had largely displaced hawking, and had caused a more
rapid destruction of birds. In William III.'s reign, the grouse and
blackcock were first mentioned in the game laws ; and about this
time it gradually became the custom to " shoot flying ".[3]

The class jealousy of the squires was directed not only downward The
against the yeomen but upwards against the Lords. Squire Western squires
declared that he would not try to marry his daughter to one of the Lords
great fortunes of the kingdom, for " most o' such great estates be in
the hands of lords, and I heate the very name of themmum ". A
Whig Peer—(half the lay Peers and more than half the Bishops
were Whigs)—was independent of county opinion ; he lived a great
part of the year in his town mansion ; he liked the company of the
great political, literary and mercantile world of the capital, with
which his rural neighbours were unfamiliar ; at election time he
came down in his coach to help the handful of Whig gentry to

---

[1] Swift, *Letter to Pope*, 10th January, 1720-21. *Stats. of Realm*, 9 Anne V.
[2] *Stats. of Realm*, 22-23 C. II., xxv. ; 4 W. and M., xxiii.
[3] *Gentleman's Recreation*, 1685, p. 125. *Spectator*, No. 122. *Stats. of Realm*,
4 and 5 W. and M., xxiii., sec. 9. See p. 8 above. Addison's Tory Foxhunter says
the game law is the " one good law passed since King William's accession to the
throne " (*Freeholder*, No. 22).

organise and encourage the yeomen, Dissenters, and small townsmen. This social offence was the more resented because the lordly offender was beyond the reach of resentment. To add insult to injury, he was often of no better family than the neighbours over whom he took precedence. A great part of the Lords of either party were, like Somers and Montague, Harley and St. John, Churchill and Godolphin, "new men" raised to the peerage for service done. They had attained their rank in the State, and their leadership in their respective parties, by talent, not by birth. But at a time when the forces of democracy were still too weak to stand by themselves, such leaders were of even greater importance to the Whig than to the Tory side.

The parsons and the soldiers

Another class for whom squire and parson felt a natural dislike was the army officer. Many men acquired riches, popularity and sometimes insolence, as the heroes of two long wars with France. The praises of William and Marlborough were always on their lips, together with other language scarcely more palatable to a Tory parson. Swift describes how he encountered a red-coat

sitting in a coffee-house near two gentlemen, who were engaged in some discourse that savoured of learning. This officer thought fit to interpose, and professing to deliver the sentiments of his fraternity, as well as his own (and probably he did so of too many among them), turned to the clergyman and spoke in the following manner : "D——n me, doctor, say what you will, the army is the only school for gentlemen. Do you think my Lord Marlborough beat the French with Greek and Latin ? D——n me, a scholar when he comes into good company, what is he but an ass ? D——n me, I would be glad by G——d to see any of your scholars, with his nouns and his verbs, his philosophy and trigonometry, what a figure he would make at a siege, or blockade, or rencountering. D——n me " (*Essay on Modern Education*).

The army men were not all like this hero of Swift's, nor were all the squires like Addison's Foxhunter ; but neither were they all like Corporal Trim or Sir Roger de Coverley.

Tory crusade against Dissenters

But, most of all, the spleen of the Tories was roused by their old enemies the Dissenters, and by the Dissenters' new allies, the free-thinkers. To extirpate these heresies by legislative interference was the avowed object of the Tories, who, as Swift confessed,

cannot agree that the truth of the gospel and the piety and wisdom of its preachers are a sufficient support, in an evil age, against infidelity, faction and vice, without the assistance of secular power. . . . I believe they venture to go a little further, and think that, upon some occasions, they want a little enlargement of assistance from the secular power against atheists, deists, socinians and other heretics (*Public Spirit of the Whigs*).

Thus spoke the pious author of the *Tale of a Tub ;* his most religious leader, Bolingbroke, wrote that the intention of the Tory party was not to distress the consciences of the existing generation of Nonconformists, but to prevent any fresh generation from being brought up in error.[1] For this purpose they passed the Schism Act (1714), to prevent the Nonconformists from educating their own children. These sentiments among the literary and political chiefs of the party interpreted an amount of frenzied prejudice on the part of the rank and file such as it is hard for our generation to realise. The press poured out on the Nonconformists, as hypocrites, rebels and regicides, invectives which in that generation had neither truth nor excuse. The Quakers, who were now driven for shelter under the Whig banner, were held up to execration as the vilest and most licentious of mankind.[2] Addison's Tory publican " had not time to go to church himself, but . . . had headed a mob at the pulling down of two or three meeting-houses," while his patron, the Foxhunter,

had learned a great deal of politics, but not one word of religion, from the parson of his parish ; and, indeed, he had scarce any other notion of religion, but that it consisted in hating Presbyterians.

To sum up in the words of Lecky :—

The facility with which this atrocious Act (*the Schism Act of* 1714) was carried, abundantly shows the danger in which religious liberty was placed in the latter years of the reign of Queen Anne. There can indeed be little doubt that had Tory ascendancy been but a little prolonged, the Toleration Act would have been repealed.[3]

The same fierce spirit was turned against the Low Churchmen, who were regarded as traitors in the camp, and, what was worse, traitors in command. " There is scarce a Presbyterian in the whole county," says the Foxhunter, " except the Bishop." [4] Their orders were, however, little obeyed. The most pronounced Episcopalians were distinguished by their insolence to the Bishops, who, ever since Tillotson held the See of Canterbury (1691-94), had been fairly hunted by their flocks. The hatred felt for Bishop Burnet in no way abated with time, and in the reign of Anne and her successor it was equalled by the violence of the Lower House of Convocation against the Latitudinarian controversialist, Hoadley. The Low Churchmen, as this small band of town clergy were called in their own day, would in our time be better described as Broad. In fact, they had little in common with the modern evangelical, except friendliness to the Dissenters. It is not perhaps necessary to commiserate the lot of these excellent men, since their real crime was that they annexed the loaves and fishes ; but those few of them who were sensitive to abuse had much to endure. The fact that the majority of the Bishops spoke and voted in the Lords against the measures of persecution urged on behalf of the Church,

[margin note: Tories and the Low Churchmen]

---

[1] *Letter to Sir W. Windham* (ed. 1753), pp. 22-25. See also *Wentworth*, p. 389, where also it is confessed without shame that the object of the Schism Act is to extirpate Dissent in the coming generation.
[2] See Ned Ward's popular *Hudibras Redivivus*, cantos xv.-xvii., and *passim.* Prints and Drawing, B.M., 1417, 1418, 1502, 1509, 1536.
[3] Lecky, i., p. 120. *Freeholder*, Nos. 22, 37, 47.   [4] *Freeholder*, No. 22.

was one of the chief causes why the Occasional Conformity and the Schism Acts could not be passed until the end of the Queen's reign, and were repealed under her successor.

Tories and the religious refugees

The same spirit of persecution was turned, though in a milder form, against the Calvinistic and Lutheran refugees. Those who choose to go into exile for their faith are generally superior in mind and character to those who stay behind, and it was the good fortune of England that such men were now coming to her shores by the thousand. As soon as they were naturalised here, their vote was certain for the Whigs and the war party. The Whig Lords made great personal efforts to settle them in England, in Ireland and in America. But the improvement of our silk trade by the French Huguenots failed greatly to impress squires who held that " trade would be the ruin of the English nation " ; [1] the Tories made capital out of the popular clamour raised against the Palatine refugees, whom the Whig ministry welcomed in 1709. England, it was said, was being turned into a Holland, a mercantile republic, based on religious tolerance and foreign immigration. Finally, in 1711, the Tories passed a Bill to prevent the naturalisation of foreign Protestants, which was fortunately thrown out by the Lords. [2]

Tories and the monied interest

The Tory belief that England was being turned into another Holland was inspired, not only by the toleration extended to domestic sects and foreign immigrants, but also by the growing importance of the " monied interest ".

> Let any man (wrote Swift) observe the equipages in this town, he shall find the greater number of those, who make a figure, to be a species of men quite different from any that were ever known before the Revolution ; consisting either of generals and colonels, or of those whose whole fortunes lie in funds and stocks (*Examiner*, 13).

These monied men were exerting influence through two channels. In the first place, they bought up constituencies, contesting by wholesale bribery the territorial influence and intimidation which was the strength of the Tory gentlemen in the small boroughs. Secondly, they exacted terms from the Government, whose war policy they financed through the agency of the Bank and National Debt. Since they were mostly Dissenters or Low Churchmen, their war loans were practically conditional on the abeyance of persecuting legislation, as Marlborough and Godolphin discovered very early in the reign of Anne. " Must our laws," wrote Swift, " from henceforth pass the Bank and East Indian Company, or have their royal assent before they are in force ? "   Some merchants throve on contracts for the armies in the field and the ships at sea ;

---

[1] *Freeholder*, No. 22.
[2] Lecky, i., pp. 52, 233-40.   Stanhope, ii., pp. 209, 210.   Wyon's *Queen Anne*, ii., pp. 157, 158.   *Parl. Hist.*, vi., pp. 999-1000.   *Wentworth*, p. 96.   Swift, *Examiner*, No. 21, and *Sentiments of a Church of England Man*.

few of them felt the war taxation as severely as the squires. The landowners complained that, under the existing financial system, land paid more than its share, and that the money went to support wars which benefited only the mercantile class. The Tory leaders, when they came into full power towards the close of the reign, hastened to make a peace which freed Government from bondage to capitalists, and passed a law preventing any merchant or soldier, who did not draw at least three hundred pounds a year from land, from sitting in the House of Commons (1711). Bolingbroke, if his party had remained longer in power, would have relieved land, and burdened industry with more taxation, and would perhaps have withdrawn the trading privileges of some of the Whig companies, or remodelled them on a Tory basis. If the Pretender had been restored, it was generally feared in the City that Government would not satisfy the National Creditors.[1]

Such were the various projects of religious, social and political reaction, all tending to prolong artificially the old monopoly of power by one class against the new forces of the time. This scheme of domestic policy was assisted by the favour of the Queen, tempered, in her case, by a desire to keep the peace among her subjects and to beat Louis to his knees. But the new Tory platform was weakened, because it still stood in theory on those absolutist doctrines on which the first Tory platform had been reared at the time of the Exclusion Bill. Passive obedience and non-resistance were still an essential part of Church of England teaching, ratified by the Lower House of Convocation in 1705 in opposition to Hoadley, and taken up as the war-cry of the squires in the Sacheverell controversy five years later. The position of zealots for passive obedience who upheld the Revolution settlement, was so clearly illogical,[2] that the appeal of the Tories to the plain man was made under a great disadvantage; their protestations of loyalty to the Hanoverian succession were coldly uttered and incredulously received. So long as the doctrine of passive obedience was in being, the Whigs were able to argue, in perfect good faith, that the restoration of the Pretender would be the restoration of absolutism; although probably his return would have involved no more than religious persecution, squirearchy, and perhaps the repudiation of the National Debt.

But the influence that most affected the fortunes of the Tories and their scheme of domestic reform, was the course of foreign affairs. There were only two English statesmen of the first rank

Tories and passive obedience

---

[1] *Examiner*, Nos. 13, 35, 37. *Letter to Sir W. Windham* (ed. 1753), pp. 20-22, 25-29. *Spectator*, No. 3. Lecky, i., pp. 247-51.

[2] " For my part," says the Tory Foxhunter, in 1716, " I and my father before me have always been for passive obedience, and shall be always for opposing a prince who makes use of Ministers that are of another opinion " (*Freeholder*, No. 22).

who regarded home affairs as subsidiary in importance to foreign, but these two—Marlborough and Godolphin—when the reign opened, held the balance between parties, and, secure in the Queen's favour, possessed the keys of office.

War
of the
Spanish
Succes-
sion,
1701-13
The war of the Spanish Succession (1701-13) was the last and decisive stage of the struggle of European liberty against Louis XIV. At the outset, the Allies had less apparent chance of success than in any of the former wars. For Louis was now the man in possession of the Spanish Empire. In the fatal spring of 1701 his troops had become masters of provinces for whose frontier strongholds he had been striving all his life with varying fortunes. His grandson, Philip V. of Spain, called in French garrisons to guard the Netherlands and Italy ; and French troops would be welcomed in Spain itself the moment that an attack was threatened there against Bourbon interests. To crown this tremendous edifice of power an alliance with Bavaria enabled Louis, in 1703, to penetrate into the very heart of Germany.

Four
seats of
war
The war of the League of Augsburg (1688-97) included four distinct wars on land—those on the Flemish, the Rhenish, the Alpine, and the Pyrenean frontiers of France. The war of the Spanish Succession included the same four wars, but the seat of each had been removed by Louis far into the enemy's country, from the borders of France to those of Holland ; from the valley of the Rhine to that of the Danube ; from the Alps to the valley of the Po ; from the Pyrenees to the coast-line of Spain, the border of the British power. Thus the Allies had again to undertake the same four wars, no longer as wars of defence but as wars of recovery. The whole of the Latin peoples were united under the Bourbon despotism ; Amsterdam and Vienna were no longer divided by buffer States from the attack of French armies. Napoleon's scheme of conquest was greater than that of Louis only by its extension into Prussia and Russia, and was in many points of detail and method a close imitation. Indeed the balance of power in 1704 is curiously comparable to that a hundred years later, though the results of Austerlitz and of Blenheim were different.

Task be-
fore the
Allies
It did not seem likely that Austria, Holland, England, and a few of the small and mercenary States of the German Empire, would defeat France, Spain, Savoy and Bavaria so signally as to drive Louis' troops out of the Spanish Empire. It was even doubtful whether they could save Holland and Austria from destruction. For William was dead. The coalition, which in former years he alone had kept together by his European reputation and his knowledge of Europe, by his tact, his genius, and his sole devotion to the common cause, had only just been able to defend the Spanish

Empire; how should it now, without him, recover that Empire, by the divided counsels of ignorant English parties and selfish continental princes? The despotism of Louis seemed on the point of becoming at last the "universal monarchy," whose slow approach statesmen had been watching with alarm for thirty years.

But chance had raised up a new deliverer. At her accession, Anne had not yet discovered that she disliked her old favourite Sarah, Countess of Marlborough, the companion of her filial disobedience at the Revolution, and of her clouded fortunes under William. Sarah's husband, therefore, was allowed by the Queen to guide her policy and lead her armies. Without his wife's help, it would have been worse than useless for Marlborough to remind Anne that William, in the last years of his reign, had marked him out to succeed to the headship of the coalition. The late King had perceived in Marlborough qualities even more suited than his own for the final stage of the struggle. Indeed, in a few years, the new chief acquired a knowledge of Europe only second to that of his predecessor, and a European reputation that gave to him at Vienna, Berlin and the Hague an influence never before surpassed. His word was always given for the course dictated by the common interest, which would otherwise have escaped the notice of the crowd of mean princes whom he led and flattered. Marlborough was superior to William in tact; his manners were winning, and his personal beauty and presence the most attractive of any to be found among the crowd of gentlemen who had whispered their way to fortune in the Court of Charles II.; a certain indifference to his own dignity, which was partly common-sense and partly meanness, enabled him to flatter with the more unction a prince who would not send his troops to a campaign, or a general who would not lead them to the attack. More than once, when he saw his long-prepared plans countermanded on the field of battle by Dutch burgomasters, he showed a patience surpassing the almost invincible patience of William. The Englishman also was of iron, but he had set his features not in a frown but in a smile. Above all, if in the highest realms of state-craft and diplomacy he fell below William, he surpassed him in far greater measure as a winner of battles and a taker of towns.

At home, Marlborough stood firm in the Queen's favour, which, together with his own nominal Toryism, kept the Tories from openly thwarting his policy in the early years of the war, until the Whigs were strong enough to be his sole support. Godolphin, knit to the fortunes of the Marlboroughs by the marriage of his only son to one of their daughters, presided over the Treasury, and found without a murmur the money for the great plans which he himself helped to form. Never, even by Chatham, was British gold better spent. Not only the victories of our own armies on the Danube and in Flanders,

[marginal notes: The Marlboroughs; Comparison of Marlborough with William; Godolphin finances the Alliance]

but the no less decisive victories of the Austrians in Italy, were
largely paid out of the pockets of English squires who, when they
discovered what had happened, cried out that they had been robbed.

**Outcome
of the
war**

In three out of the four seats of war, Marlborough became master
of the event. The French were driven out of Germany (1704), out
of Italy (1706), and out of the Netherlands (1706-8). But it was
not found possible to dislodge the Bourbons from Spain. The
Peninsular War of 1702-13, though memorable for the exploits of
Peterborough, is important chiefly as the pivot of naval operations.

**Naval
side of
the war**

The naval side of the war was not dignified by great battles, but
by great results. In the reign of Anne, the overwhelming character of our naval supremacy in modern times was first established
as against both France and Holland ; and in the reign of Anne, the
Mediterranean became the principal and permanent arena for the
activity of our fleets.

Owing to the expense of his land wars, the French King could
seldom in this period afford to put his ships to sea. Holland, similarly preoccupied and exhausted in the anxious defence of her land
frontier, failed to supply her due proportion of ships to the allied
fleet, and trusted her naval defence to Great Britain, more than in
the last war. Little complaint was made over here of this part of
the failure of the Dutch to fulfil their obligations as Allies, for both
our parties wished the British fleet to be superior to that of any other
nation. When peace was restored, Holland was no longer the rival,
but the dependant, of British naval supremacy. Thus, by means of
a close alliance, we destroyed the naval power which had defied
Blake, Monk and Rupert. Our fleet grew, and no one complained
of the burden. The Tories wished England to wage war as a mere
auxiliary on land, but as a principal at sea ; while the Whigs wished
her to take the lead on both elements.

Marlborough, with his broader vision of European politics, saw
not only that a large fleet was necessary, but that it should be
stationed in Mediterranean waters, as a means of making British
influence felt in the capitals of Europe. This policy was originated
by Cromwell ; revived by William ; but enlarged and fixed by
Marlborough. It has remained ever since, through all other changes,
long after the policy of his Danube and Netherland campaignings
had served its day and been discarded. Our operations in Spain
(1702-13), involving a necessity to supply and to connect our two
bases of Lisbon and Barcelona ; the recovery of Italy (1706) ; and
the attack on Toulon (1707), kept the British fleet as active in those
waters as in the days of Nelson. The capture of Gibraltar (1704)
and of Port Mahon in Minorca (1708) were the results of Marlborough's
Mediterranean policy, and the security for its continuance in after
years.

The employment of the fleet round the coasts of Spain drew it away from operations against French and Spanish Colonies. Indeed, the support that we gave, after 1703, to the pretensions of the Archduke Charles to the Spanish throne made it impossible for us to filch for ourselves the territories he thereby claimed in South and Central America and in the West Indies. But the policy of Marlborough won us prizes in colder latitudes worth more to us than all the lands near the Equator. Nova Scotia, Newfoundland and Hudson's Bay—long in dispute between the British and French colonials, were finally ceded to us at the peace, as a result partly of Blenheim, partly of our supremacy at sea.[1]

In 1701 Austria began in Italy the war of the Spanish Succession. Eugene, with great skill, introduced the Imperial forces over the Eastern Alps, and maintained them in the plain of the Po, face to face with the larger armies of France. The next year saw the struggle joined by England and Holland, and extended to Flanders, the Rhine, and the coasts of Spain. *Opening of the war*

In March, 1702, Anne met the Houses, and made known her intention of waging war on a grand scale both by land and sea. The announcement, awaited with uncertainty, caused intense relief to the princes of the Grand Alliance, who might otherwise never have taken the field, and to the English Parliament, which consisted of Whigs and moderate Tories chosen in the last reign as an expression of the popular demand for war. Rochester expostulated in the Privy Council against the continuance of the late King's policy, but the other Tory ministers fell into line behind Marlborough and Godolphin. War was declared in May, at London and at the Hague, and Marlborough crossed the sea with a British army containing many who had been trained in William's wars for the great services which they were about to perform.

The French had already pushed into Dutch territory, and were encamped on both banks of the lower Maas. But the Anglo-Dutch armies, under their new chief, crossed the river and forced the enemy to retreat upon the lines of the Dyle and its tributaries.[2] There they remained, strongly entrenched, for over three years, covering the Flemish towns. This campaign of 1702 established the European reputation of Marlborough, and justified the Queen in raising him that winter to a Dukedom. It had put heart into the Grand Alliance ; and if the rout of the French armies in the Netherlands was postponed till the year of Ramillies, this was due to the repeated refusals of the Dutch Field Deputies to allow their troops to be taken into a decisive action. These gentlemen were the counterpart in position, and the opposite in spirit, to the *Flanders, 1702 and 1703*

---

[1] Corbett, chaps. xxx.-xxxiii., especially vol. ii., pp. 313-15. *Influence of Sea Power*, Mahan, chap. v.
[2] See map opposite p. 411 below.

Representatives in Mission who plagued the generals of the French Republic ninety years later. Their object was to put Marlborough's genius to their own uses, and to render the territories of Holland safe at a smaller expenditure of their costly armies than would have been necessary under a less brilliant captain. Again and again they prevented him from fighting a decisive action.

Spain and Portugal, 1702 and 1703 — In August, 1702, the British fleet under Sir George Rooke, with a detachment of troops under the Duke of Ormond, failed in an attack on Cadiz as disgracefully as their predecessors in the days of Buckingham. Three months later, by a feat of arms as brilliant as any in the annals of our united service, they stormed the forts and broke the boom of Vigo Bay, where lay the treasure galleons from the West Indies with a score of French and Spanish warships. The memory of that night, on which the great fleet was burnt to the water's edge in spite of the efforts of the English sailors to save their prizes, was handed down among generations of seafaring men, who loved to spin yarns about the twenty millions of pieces of eight, and devise means to fetch up the fabled treasure from the bottom of Vigo Bay.

This fierce proof of what sea-power means, encouraged the King of Portugal to declare his true sympathies, to defy the House of Bourbon, and to trust his kingdom's defence to the English ships and the soldiers whom they brought to defend his frontier. In 1703 he broke off his alliance with Louis, and signed Mr. Methuen's famous Treaty, by which the old system of alliance between Portugal and Britain, initiated at the marriage of Charles II., was renewed for another and a longer lease of life. In war, Lisbon became the English place of arms for the conquest of Spain. The accession of Portugal lured on the Allies to attempt to place the Austrian Arch-

1703, the Allies' change of policy — duke Charles on the throne of Madrid, as Carlos III. The original object of the Grand Alliance of 1701, which had been to leave Philip crowned in a kingdom shorn of its external dependencies, was abandoned in favour of the *ignis fatuus* of " no peace without Spain ".

General election, July, 1702 — Meanwhile, much was taking place at home. In spite of the protests of the Duchess, who was more of a Whig than her husband was a Tory, the Queen had remodelled the ministry on a Tory basis, as a preliminary to the dissolution of William's old Parliament. The general election had the opposite result from that of the former year, and the Tories came in with a large majority. So great was the power of the Crown that the mere fact of Anne's accession had caused, not only a change of ministry, but the acceptance of that change by the votes of the nation. Between the years 1702 and 1715 there were six general elections ; three were won by the Tories and three by the Whigs ; but in every case the decision was in favour of the existing ministry and the influence of the Crown. This result was in part due to the great number of

officers in the civil service—Lords-Lieutenant, Sheriffs, Justices of The
the Peace, tax-gatherers, and coastguards—all of whom, " down to influence
the meanest," as Bolingbroke boasted, were liable to be changed Crown
with a change of ministry. Many lost their places, but more,
probably, changed their politics for fear of dismissal, and courted
the powers of the day at election time, when, alike in their official
and their private capacity, they had many opportunities of in-
fluencing the poll. Hence the significance of the fact that in 1702,
1710 and 1714-15, the change of ministers took place before
and not after the general election, and was the cause, not the effect,
of the electoral decision. In 1702 the power of the Crown, which
could make and unmake ministers at will, was further strengthened
by the reviving tide of loyalty that gathered round a Queen whose
heart, as she boasted to the delight of the Tories, was " entirely
English ".

The new Tory Parliament hastened to trample on the memory The new
of the Dutch King. It was voted that Marlborough had " signally Parlia-
retrieved the ancient honour and glory of the English nation ". An Oct.,
inquiry into the alleged peculation of William's Whig ministers 1702
was held at great length, but with little success. Vexatious and
only half-honest in purpose, it was useful in effect ; for such charges,
brought almost as a matter of course against ex-ministers by the
opposite party, kept the public service more pure, especially in its
higher branches, than if there had been no fear of investigation.
The passions of Church and Dissent, the hatred between Whig and
Tory, prevented that corrupt understanding between two parties,
which arises when politicians are divided by nothing more fundamental than rivalry for the spoils. At the end of the reign the Tories
failed to bring home to Marlborough any serious charge of peculation,
but no one knows what use the gallant miser would have made of
his command of the army, if he had not had before his eyes the almost
certain prospect of his worst enemies sitting some day in committee
on his accounts.

The attack on the Dissenters, which occupied the Tories through- Occasion-
out the reign, was opened with a Bill to prevent " Occasional Con- al Conformity ". It punished with ruinous penalties any man who, having Bill, 1702
qualified for State or municipal office by taking the sacrament in
Church, afterwards attended a place of Nonconformist worship.
Occasional Conformity had been defended on religious grounds, by
Baxter and other moderate Presbyterians whose differences from
the Establishment were not deep ; as a means of obtaining office,
it was perhaps less worthy of praise, but legislators who had made
the sacrament a State test had no right to call the practice indecent.
In 1702 the persecuting Bill was passed by a large majority of the
Commons, to be lost in the Upper House, in spite of the influence
of the Queen and her ministers. But Marlborough soon learned

that if his war measures were to be carried through, he must fall into line on this point with the City and the Whigs. The high Tory chiefs in the Council—first Rochester, and, when he had been dismissed (1703), Nottingham—obstructed a vigorous war policy, and urged the reasoning, afterwards so formidable in the hands of Swift, that British interests did not call for our interference as principals on the Continent. But unless it was a British interest that the French should occupy Vienna, it was becoming necessary to interfere as principals more decidedly than ever. In 1703 the French armies pushed through Bavaria to the Austrian frontiers. That winter the Duke secretly planned his great march on the Danube, which alone could save the Empire and the Grand Alliance from disruption. This march, he knew, would make an irreparable breach between himself and the Tories. If he failed, they would impeach him ; even if he succeeded, he must thenceforth depend on the opposite party. The Duchess brought him overtures from her friends of the Whig Junto. So in the session of 1703-4 he allowed his influence to be used secretly against the Occasional Conformity Bill of the year, while he voted for it in person. It was defeated in the Lords more signally than twelve months back.

Occasional Conformity Bill, Dec., 1703

Turningpoint of the war, 1703-4 The turning-point of the war of the Spanish Succession was the attempt of Louis, in 1703-4, to break up the Grand Alliance at one blow by the capture of Vienna. This plan, almost successful in 1703, ended in the next year on the field of Blenheim, not merely in repulse, but in disaster that affected the conditions of the struggle in all the other seats of war.

The attempt on Vienna, 1703 It began with nothing less than the Napoleonic design of a combined advance on Vienna, down the Danube from Bavaria, and over the Alps from Italy. In May, 1703, Villars, the most capable of the French Marshals, led an army past the feeble watch on the Rhine maintained by German princes in the lines of Stolhofen, crossed the Black Forest, and joined the forces of the Elector of Bavaria on the banks of the Danube. War had not been carried on by combinations and marches of this sort since the days of Gustavus. The scheme was indeed too gigantic ; for if, in the summer of 1703, the Franco-Bavarian armies had been content to hold on straight down the Danube, without waiting for Vendôme to join them from Italy, Vienna must have fallen. But the Elector of Bavaria, whom the French had bribed to desert the cause of Germany by the offer of the Austrian Tyrol, marched into those mountains, partly to secure his new territories, and partly to join hands with Vendôme as he came up the Brenner from Italy. The Tyrolese, whose loyalty to the House of Austria then, as in the days of Andreas Hofer, partook of the nature of mountain freedom, drove back the new lord whom France had set over them, in such a plight that he refused to accompany Villars a step further towards Vienna that year.

Neither did Vendôme reach the top of the Brenner Pass. Italy, Savoy after close on two centuries of slavery to the Spaniards and the joins the Jesuits, still contained one Italian State. The Duke of Savoy Allies, Victor Amadeus II., the persecutor of the Vaudois, would have had 1703 little sympathy with the liberalism of his descendants, but he was at least a good Italian, in so far that he maintained the political independence of Savoy against Spain, Austria and France. By perpetually changing sides in the wars of Louis XIV., he had kept up in those regions a balance of power which gave importance to his small State. In pursuance of this policy, he now deserted his too-powerful French ally at the very crisis of the war. Vendôme, who had got as far as Trent only to find that the Bavarians had retired to the Danube, hurried back when Savoy rose on his communications. The territories of Victor Amadeus were occupied by the French, and his fortress besieged. Thus, at the end of 1703, Italy and Bavaria were still French ground, but the doom of Vienna had been averted for a year.

In 1704 the French would resume their march down the Danube, Prospects this time without aid from Italy, but with the no less formidable for the aid of the Hungarian Protestants under Ragotzi. Maddened by year 1704 religious persecution, to which the recent expulsion of the Turks by the Austrians had subjected them, the Magyar horsemen were swarming over the Emperor's dominions ; a truceless war of creeds and races was raging, from castle heights among the beech-clad Transylvanian mountains, almost to the gates of Vienna, where sat Eugene, struggling with the ineradicable evils of the Austrian War Office. Without men or money to save the Empire, he had at least the winter months in which to solicit help from some other quarter of Europe.

England and Holland alone could send aid sufficient ; but if The plot any man had openly suggested in either country to send the national of Eugene and Marl- army to the Danube, popular indignation would at once have put borough, a stop to the scheme. There was hope only in one man. Perhaps 1703-4 Marlborough could, if he dared, cheat the two nations into saving the Empire and the Alliance. Fortunately his view of the situation was so broad that he could see from London what no one else could see except at Vienna. He entered into a plot with Eugene to steal the English and Dutch armies. There were two other accomplices, to whom part of the scheme was revealed : Heinsius, William's old servant, who helped to deceive the Dutch, and Godolphin, who undertook the management of the Queen and Cabinet. Early in 1704 the Emperor sent a letter to Anne, begging for help. By means of this letter Marlborough obtained an instruction from the Cabinet to concert with Holland measures for the safety of Vienna

(April) : nothing was said or intended about the British troops, but vague instructions are the opportunity of the determined man. He had next to cheat the Dutch. Crossing to Holland, he there announced that he would begin the year with a campaign on the Moselle. By the help of Heinsius, the Dutch were induced to grant him for this purpose a large army of foreign troops in their pay, on the understanding that they were not taken further away from Holland than that region. When, however, he had reached the Moselle with the Anglo-Dutch forces, he threw off the mask, fled up the Rhine to Mainz, and then struck across Germany. The Tories swore they would have his head ; the Dutch made a virtue of necessity and accepted the *fait accompli*. The consternation among the French Marshals was great. Where would Marlborough strike—on the Moselle, in Alsace, or on the upper Rhine ? The French armies, that should have been half-way to Vienna, were kept on the west bank of the Rhine in dreadful expectation. By the end of June it was known throughout Europe that the red-coats had appeared in the distant plains of Bavaria.

The march on the Danube, May-June, 1704

On their way to the Danube, the Anglo-Dutch forces had been joined by a German army under Prince Louis of Baden. To establish themselves in Bavarian territory it was necessary to capture Donauwerth, protected by the heights of the Schellenberg, behind whose trenches lay an army of French and Bavarians. Marlborough and Louis of Baden held command on alternate days. Early on a morning that was his to use, the Duke ordered the assault of the Schellenberg. It was carried after a desperate fight, in which the allies lost over five thousand men. Bavaria was now theirs. All the open towns fell to the victors, who laid waste the country in order to coerce or punish its ruler. Marlborough's fame was spread over the world. " I must tell you," so Shrewsbury wrote to him from Rome, " that in this holy, ignorant city they have an idea of you as of a Tamerlane ; and had I a picture of old Colonel Birch with his whiskers, I could put it off for yours ; and change it for one done by Raphael ".[1]

The Schellenberg stormed, July 2nd, 1704

But France was preparing to recover all. The great army under Marshal Tallard, who succeeded this year to the more competent Villars, at last crossed the Rhine and entered Bavaria. Eugene, who had been left to guard the lines of Stolhofen, hastened back eastward with part of his forces by a parallel line to Tallard, and was joined by Marlborough near Donauwerth. Louis of Baden was induced to undertake the siege of Ingoldstadt, and so to leave the two great generals unhampered at the supreme moment of their lives. The united armies of Tallard and the Elector of Bavaria were also north of the Danube, only ten miles away to the west. On the 12th of August (N.S.), Marlborough and Eugene rode out

[1] Coxe, i., p. 268.

to Dapfheim, climbed the church tower, and saw the Franco-Bavarian army taking up camp between Blenheim and Lutzingen. They determined to join battle next day, before the spade could render the new position impregnable.

That night 36,000 men from Denmark, Prussia, Holland, Austria, Hanover and Hesse, and 9,000 Englishmen, were camped round Dapfheim village, knowing that at break of day they would be led to a memorable attack.[1] That evening, at Marly, the Grand Monarch feasted two persons whom it pleased him to call " the King and Queen of England," at a " sumptuous repast with new services of porcelain and glass, on tables of white marble without cloths ". " At nightfall, drums, trumpets, cymbals and hautbois announced that the fireworks were about to begin." The triumphal

The eve of Blenheim

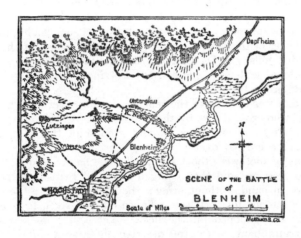

SCENE OF THE BATTLE of BLENHEIM

Scale of Miles

arch was magnificently illuminated. " After supper the King and Queen of England returned to St. Germains." But till midnight the gardens were thronged with delighted courtiers.[2]

About the time that the last revellers by the Seine were slinking to their beds, the English trumpets woke the sleepers by the Danube. Early in the morning Tallard learned that the Allies had broken camp at two o'clock ; but he was deceived by a rumour of the country that they were retreating to the north. While he was writing home this welcome news, a light morning mist hid from his view the defile, two miles in front of the French position, where the wooded hills came close down to the river, or he would have seen the armies of Marlborough and Eugene wending towards him

The battle of Blenheim 13th Aug. (N.S.), 1704

---

[1] Coxe, i., pp. 289, 292, notes. The enemy were a few thousand more, about 56,000.

[2] *Journal du Marquis de Dangeau*, 12th August, 1704.

in nine long columns. At seven the mist cleared, and the French saw their enemies debouching into the plain before them. Wooded hills on the left, the Danube on the right, and the marshes of the Nebel stream in front, protected the position of the Franco-Bavarian armies. But they were badly disposed ; most of the cavalry, and only nine battalions of infantry, were stretched along the centre ; while the foot were massed in the villages of Oberglau and Lutzingen to the west, and Blenheim on the Danube bank. The line of battle was five miles long ; it was afternoon before Eugene had led his men to their northern positions.

At one o'clock the attack on the villages commenced. Cutts, the fighting man of William's old army, nicknamed the Salamander for his valour where fire was hottest on the breach, and known to posterity as the subject of the most brutal of all Swift's satires, directed the English attack against the fortified front of Blenheim. Again and again they were driven back from the stockades, defended by the flower of the French army. Far to northward, at the foot of the wooded hills, the Danes and Prussians under Eugene struggled all afternoon, with slow success, for Lutzingen and the posts held by the Bavarian troops.

The day was decided in the centre. Under cover of some British infantry, who crossed first by the bridges at Unterglau, Marlborough passed his cavalry over the marshy ground of the Nebel. Some waded, some crossed over planks and fascines. The enemy's nine battalions of foot were too few ; his horse charged too late to prevent the crossing, and then charged ill. The British cavalry came on, sword in hand, without firing ; the French, who in the last war had been famous for their sole reliance on cold steel, halted to fire, wavered, and galloped off the field.[1] The centre was swept away in one triumphant roar ; the deserted infantry were ridden over and cut down ; Tallard was taken and lodged in Marlborough's coach ; the cavalry were chased far beyond Hochstadt or herded towards the south, and driven over the steep river-bank, where hundreds found refuge or death in the wilderness of marshy shore and reedy island, divided by the broad, deep currents of the Danube.

In that storm of flight the messengers were lost who should have carried timely orders of retreat to the defenders of Blenheim ; consequently they made no efforts to withdraw from the angle of the Danube that shut them in until the British infantry, coming up victorious from the central battle, had closed the trap upon the village. Lord Orkney stormed into it from the rear, cheering on his red-coats at the high stone wall of the churchyard, but was stormed out again. Thinking that the French were about to make a desperate sally to cut their way out through his tired troops, he

Dangeau, 29th August, 1704.

beat a parley, and the handsome young Brigadier Denonville surrendered with the two nearest battalions. Orkney learned from his prisoners that there were 10,000 men still under arms in the village. This staggered him, for he knew that no further assault could be made, either by his own men, who had broken the French centre, or by Cutts' men on the further side of the village, who had all been repulsed five times that day. Blenheim could probably hold out till nightfall, when some of its occupants might perhaps escape : at least they could sell their lives very dear. With admirable presence of mind, Orkney swaggered to Denonville, and sent him back into the village with an English aide-de-camp to demand the capitulation of his superior, Blansac. Instead of addressing Blansac, Denonville rode up to the troops themselves, and exhorted them to surrender. Before the officers could drag him away, his words had taken the heart out of all the soldiers, except those of the Regiment of Navarre. Discouraged by the attitude of his troops, Blansac consented to come out of the village and see the real state of things for himself. Orkney showed him that the rest of the army had indeed fled, and by dint of " a little gasconade " induced him to sign a capitulation. The Regiment of Navarre, with tears of rage, burnt the colours and buried the arms which they were not accustomed to yield to the foe.[1]

For a full week after his sun had set for ever on the banks of the Danube, Louis hunted and prayed, disturbed by no news worse than that the English fleet had put some men ashore at Gibraltar, who had climbed the rock and taken the castle. " It is impossible to imagine how careless the Spaniards are," said the courtiers. It was only on the morning of the 21st that " the King going to Mass told us that he had sad news of the army of Mons. Tallard." Letters from prisoners taken at Blenheim had been forwarded to Versailles by the Imperialists in the lines of Stolhofen. The evidence left no room for hope or doubt. But no one could " understand how twenty-six French battalions could have surrendered as prisoners of war ". It was not the sort of news one brought to Versailles.[2]

Gibraltar taken, 3rd Aug., 1704

All Bavaria fell at once to the Allies. The wrecks of the enemy's force, reduced by 40,000 men, never halted till they reached the Rhine ; for the rest of the war that river again became the scene of uneventful operations between the French and Imperial troops. When the news reached England, every one went mad with joy, except the politicians. The Tory House of Commons, in its Address to the Throne, invidiously coupled the victory of Blenheim in the same sentence with the naval action of doubtful result fought by

Consequences of Blenheim

[1] Compare St. Simon's narrative (iv. pp. 125-28, 140, ed. 1885), based on that of Blansac, with Lord Orkney's letter (*E. H. R.*, xix., pp. 309, 310). They tally to a remarkable degree.

[2] *Dangeau*, 14th-21st August. St. Simon, iv., pp. 130-32.

Sir George Rooke off Malaga.[1] The Tories used all forms of detraction to render Blenheim less popular ; such another success, they declared, won by Marlborough, and " the Constitution of England would be ruined " ; on the other hand, " it was true a great many men were killed and taken, but that to the French King is no more than to take a bucket of water out of a river ". Marlborough, who never showed a mean jealousy for fame, was at last nettled. " This vile, enormous faction of theirs," he wrote, " vexes me." And again, in a finer spirit : " I will endeavour to leave a good name behind me in countries that have hardly any blessing but that of not knowing the detested names of Whig and Tory ".[2]

Whatever name Marlborough has left behind on the Continent, he had in fact opened for many nations the way to the blessings of freedom, for he had destroyed on one famous field the glamour and prestige of despotism in Church and State. If the battle of Blenheim had been won by Louis, no Voltaire could have made his system look ridiculous, no Rousseau could have made it seem irrational. Marlborough himself knew that his victories were opening the way to a new order in France. On one occasion he seriously proposed to Godolphin that, when the Queen could dictate peace, she should " insist upon putting the French Government upon their being governed by the Three Estates ".[3]

The "tack" winter, 1704 In the winter session of 1704-5, the high Tories tried to force the Occasional Conformity Bill through the Lords by " tacking " it to the financial measures of the year, but the " tack " was defeated in the Commons by the efforts of the ministerial Tories under Harley and St. John. The Bill came up as usual, to be thrown out in the Lords, and this time Marlborough and Godolphin voted openly against the measure which they had supported only two years before. At the general election next spring, the influence of the Crown and of the victor of Blenheim was used in favour of the Whig candidates against all " tackers," to whom, as Marleborough expressed it, " no quarter " was to be given at the polls.[4]

Whig victory at the elections, 1705 The Whigs secured a small majority in the new House over the Tory party thus divided against itself. Using the lever of their predominance in both Houses, and aided by the sleepless insistence of Sarah on their behalf with her husband and with the Queen, the Whigs in the next three years forced a way for their leaders,

---

[1] The consequence of this unwise comparison was that Rooke, the hero of Vigo Bay and Gibraltar, was next year removed from the command of the fleet and succeeded by Sir Cloudesley Shovel, perhaps as good a sailor, but certainly a better Whig.

[2] *Parl. Hist.*, vi., p. 357. Coxe, i., pp. 340-43, 404.

[3] Marlborough to Godolphin, 7th June, 1709. *Coxe Papers*, B.M., xxviii., 9105.

[4] Coxe, i., pp. 381-404. Stanhope, i., p. 195.

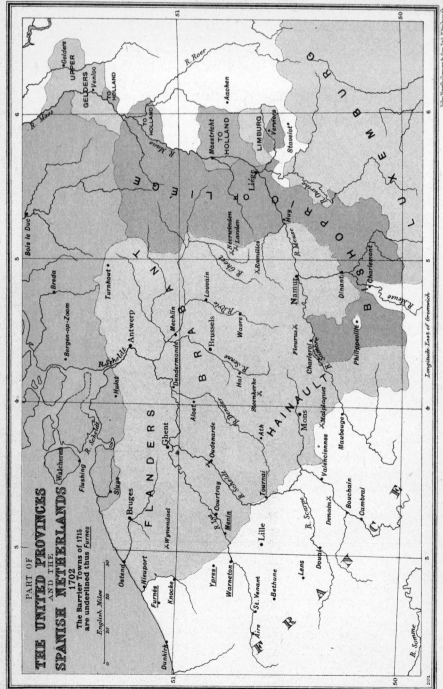

PART OF
THE UNITED PROVINCES
AND THE
SPANISH NETHERLANDS
1702

The Barrier Towns of 1715
are underlined thus Furnes

English Miles
0   10   20   30

FLANDERS

BRABANT

HAINAULT

LIMBURG

LUXEMBURG

FRANCE

Dunkirk
Ostend
Nieuport
Knocke
Furnes
Bruges
Sluys
Flushing
Walcheren
Hulst
Warneton
Ypres
Menin
Courtray
Ghent
Oudenarde
Alost
Ath
Tournai
Lille
Bethune
St. Venant
Aire
Lens
Douay
Denain
Valenciennes
Maubeuge
Bouchain
Cambrai
Mons
Malplaquet
Charleroi
Fleurus
Hal
Steenkerke
Waure
Brussels
Mechlin
Louvain
Dendermonde
Antwerp
Turnhout
Bergen-op-Zoom
Breda
Bois le Duc
Namur
Philippeville
Charlemont
Dinant
Huy
Ramillies
Landen
Neerwinden
Liège
Maestricht TO HOLLAND
Aachen
Verviers
Stavelot
TO HOLLAND
GELDERS
UPPER
Venloo
Gelders

R. Somme
R. Scarpe
R. Lys
R. Scheldt
R. Dendre
R. Dyle
R. Senne
R. Sambre
R. Meuse
R. Ghete
R. Maas
R. Roer
R. Ourthe

Longitude East of Greenwich

John Bartholomew & Son, Ltd. Edinburgh

Methuen & Co. Ltd. 36 Essex Street, London W.C.2.

one by one, into the ministry. Anne, whose political ideal was a mixed Cabinet with a predominance of moderate Tories, resisted each step to a pure Whig Government. But she kept no Court, like Charles II., to aid and abet her resistance ; her husband was a fool, and she had no one about her person except her ministers and their friends. Sometimes Godolphin would fain have taken her side, but, as Wharton put it, the Whigs " had the Lord Treasurer's head in a bag ". The league to coerce the Queen's wishes had to be joined by all her servants, except only two. Harley and St. John retained office, making constant and fulsome asseverations of fidelity to the Marlborough interest, which did not impose upon Godolphin. They would, he perceived, renew relations with the high Tory party, as soon as they had won for themselves the confidence which the Queen was gradually withdrawing from all her other ministers. But the coalition of Marlborough and the Whigs with Harley and St. John, served the Queen and country well while it lasted ; it recovered Italy and Flanders, and carried through the difficult negotiations resulting in the Union of Great Britain.

The Scottish Parliament, by the Act of Security (1704), had refused to accept the Hanoverian Succession. The danger of a Stuart reigning in Holyrood in time of war made the Union of the two Crowns and the two Parliaments appear as a necessary measure of self-defence to most Englishmen, though the high Tories outside the Cabinet looked askance at an Act that secured the Scottish Presbyterian Church. Scotland, where public feeling was against the Union, had the whip-hand of English politicians, who could not afford to see the negotiations fail. Good financial terms and Free Trade with England were therefore granted to North Britain, at a moment when racial and commercial jealousy in the south of the island dared not make itself heard, for fear of breaking off the Treaty.

Union with Scotland, 1707

Meanwhile, the whole nature of the war was altered by the events of 1706. The timidity of the Dutch Field Deputies prevented Marlborough from doing anything in 1705, except to drive back the French from their carefully constructed lines on the sources of the Gheet. But he could not dislodge them from the line of the Dyle without a battle. Marlborough, in despair of ever being allowed to use the large bodies of troops which the Dutch paraded under his command, designed to cross the Alps in 1706, and repeat on the banks of the Po his exploits on the Danube. But a lethargy seemed to have fallen on the Alliance. He could induce neither Prussia, Denmark nor Hanover to send their troops to Italy. It seemed that the Duke of Savoy must be left to his fate, for Austria could not supply Eugene with men or money to relieve Turin ; when it had fallen, the French supremacy in Italy would be secure.

Prospects for the year 1706

Marlborough took the field this year with the belief that nothing

Ramillies (23rd May), and Conquest of the Netherlands, 1706

would be accomplished. But the Dutch had instructed their Deputies to leave him a freer hand, and Villeroi, the worst and most favoured of Louis' Marshals, gave him the battle he desired on the field of Ramillies. The French were routed with the loss of 15,000 men, but the panic that fell upon them, and most strongly upon their incompetent general, was out of all proportion to their defeat. Brabant and half Flanders were evacuated without a blow. " We have done in four days," wrote Marlborough, " what we should have thought ourselves happy if we could have been sure of it in four years." Even when Vendôme superseded Villeroi, he found " every one ready to take off their hats when they name the name of Marlborough ".[1] Before the year was out, Louvain, Brussels, Antwerp, Ghent, Bruges, Ostend, Menin, Oudenarde and many smaller places were in the hands of the Allies. The French occupation of the Netherlands was brought to an end almost as quickly as it had come into being five years before.

Battle of Turin (7th Sept.), and Conquest of Italy, 1706

The news of Ramillies put fresh heart into the Alliance. The King of Prussia and the German Princes listened to Marlborough's urgent petitions, and at last sent their troops over the Alps.[2] With armies thus provided by English diplomacy and paid by English gold, Eugene, in an admirable campaign, relieved Turin, defeating the French under its walls, so that they evacuated Italy as rapidly as they had evacuated Bavaria and the Netherlands. Savoy recovered its independence, and the Austrians won Naples and Milan.

Toulon Expedition, 1707

In 1707 the Allies crossed the Alps into France, and attacked Toulon, in conjunction with the English fleet. The plan was Marlborough's ; the money came from the British treasury ; the real object was to secure England's Mediterranean supremacy by destroying the French arsenal. In such an enterprise the Austrians showed little zeal ; Eugene let his military opportunities slip by, and soon retreated into Italy. Thenceforth the war in those parts resolved itself into a watch on the top of the Alpine passes. The war on the side of Italy, and the war along the Rhine, both went to sleep. The interest was confined to Spain, and to the Netherland frontier of France.

War in Spain, 1705-10

After 1706 Louis was no longer the man in possession of the Spanish Empire. Italy and the Netherlands had been recovered ; it only remained to drive the Bourbons from Madrid. This was attempted in two ways : directly, by the occupation of Spain itself ; and indirectly by penetrating the French frontier from the base of Flanders, and so dictating terms to Louis. The conquest of Spain could be seriously undertaken after the romantic capture of Barcelona, accomplished by Peterborough in contravention of all the maxims of siege-craft (1705). This town was the capital of the Province of Catalonia—then, as now, the thorn in the side of the

[1] Stanhope, i., p. 247. Coxe, i., p. 38.　　　　　[2] Coxe, ii. pp. 36, 82.

Spanish monarchy. The Catalans rallied round Peterborough, and accepted Charles III., in order to recover their *fueros*, or provincial liberties, which Philip V. denied to them; in Valencia also there w as apopular feeling for Charles. The real strength of the Allies lay in the 15,000 guerillas of Catalonia and Valencia, who held the east coast in the most effective manner. From these two provinces on one side of the Peninsula, and Portugal on the other, with the British fleet and its base at Gibraltar to keep up the communications, it was possible to set about the reduction of Spain. In 1706 the English and Portuguese entered Madrid. But the task of policing the territory and subduing the spirit of the Spanish people, which proved too vast for the armies of Napoleon, was not to be achieved by a few thousand soldiers, who marched about, merely fighting battles and taking towns. Before long Philip recovered Madrid, and the marchings of the English and Portuguese were temporarily brought to an end by their total rout at Almanza (1707). A few years later the marchings were resumed; in September, 1710, Madrid was again occupied; but in December the capitulation of Stanhope's army at Brihuega brought the war to an end. The Whig formula of " no peace without Spain " would mean " no peace till Doomsday ".

On the side of the Netherlands, the task of capturing the fortresses Oudenwent on more slowly after 1706. The victory of Oudenarde led arde and to the siege and capture of Lille, the greatest of the French strong-Lille, holds on that frontier. France was exhausted and famine-stricken. 1708 Her armies had lost hope and courage. The barrier of fortresses between Marlborough and Paris was growing thinner every year. In the early months of 1709 the Grand Monarch, as a suppliant, begged terms of the Allies, offering almost everything, that it was in his power to give.

The chances of peace at this most favourable moment, were Triumph compromised by further changes that had recently occurred in of the English politics. In the year 1708 the last step was taken, and Whigs the Whigs at length obtained complete control of the Government. 1708 Godolphin discovered what he had long suspected, that Harley treacherously used his position as minister to win the Queen's confidence away from his colleagues, and to insinuate a rival favourite to the Duchess of Marlborough—one Abigail Hill, become by marriage Mrs. Masham. Originally a *protégée* of the Duchess, she supplanted " Mrs. Freeman " in the love of " Mrs. Morley," [1] and used her influence for the High Church and Harley, against the Whigs and Marlborough. In February, 1708, the General and Treasurer, by the threat of their own resignation, forced the Queen to dismiss Harley; but it was impossible to get rid of

---

[1] The names of endearment used by Sarah and Anne in their private correspondence.

Mrs. Masham, or to remove Anne's bitter resentment against all her remaining ministers. Thus, in the year 1708 the principle of party unanimity within the Cabinet was finally established, in spite of the wishes of the Crown. In the general election that summer, the ministers had their power confirmed at the polls. When, early in 1709, the negotiations for peace were opened in Holland, the Whigs seemed to have Louis and the Tories at their feet, with Anne, Marlborough and Godolphin, as the half-unwilling instruments of their supremacy. In the pride of newly acquired power, they were not in the mood to take a wise and broad view of Europe's need for peace. The one fear that haunted their triumph was that a Tory reaction might quickly follow if the war came to an end.

Louis' offers rejected, May-June, 1709   Louis offered the whole of Spain and its dependencies, Strassburg, and the best of the French fortresses along the Netherlands frontier. If William had been alive to receive such proposals, he would have known how to coerce the Allies into closing with Louis' offer, as he had done at the time of the Treaty of Ryswick. But Marlborough, though he could make the Princes of Europe wage war, had not skill to make them accept peace. The terms were rejected ; Louis was told that he must lend his own armies to expel his grandson from Spain, and that unless he succeeded in that odious task the Allies would be at liberty to renew the war against France. The excuse put forward for making an offer so absurd was that no trust could be reposed in Louis' good faith ; but the real reason was that no one knew how to expel Philip from Spain. The actual state of things in the Peninsula was not in accordance with the proposed basis of settlement.[1]

The prospect of reaching Paris   The guilt of all who protracted the war is greater or less, according as they had or had not expectation of ending it shortly in a more satisfactory manner. We do not know what the Whig leaders said to each other on this point in the private meetings of their Junto ; but there is negative evidence that they did not seriously and frequently question Marlborough about the possibility of an advance on Paris. In the military and political correspondence of the period, the word " Paris " hardly ever occurs in connection with the military prospects of the Allies,[2] and the invasion of France is only spoken of in vague terms. A letter of Godolphin's, in June, 1709, shows

---

[1] Torcy's *Memoirs, passim.* Articles four and thirty-seven of the Preliminaries of May were the point at issue. Marlborough thought that there were securities enough against Louis' playing false, without threatening him with a renewal of the war. Godolphin and the Whigs thought otherwise (Coxe, iii., pp. 40, 41).

[2] The on y case which I can recall is in Defoe's report to Godolphin of a letter rumoured to have been written by Lord Orkney to friends in Scotland, to the effect that, if Marlborough had sent 20,000 men to the frontier immediately after Oudenarde, " he could have gone to the gates of Paris with them " (*Hist. MSS. Com. Report*, viii., 1, p. 44).

him expecting that the war would go on for many years, and that we should gradually reduce France by the process of exhaustion.[1]

Marlborough, on the other hand, whether or not he expected to reach Paris, had the design of invading France, which he had urged on Eugene immediately after Oudenarde. Again, in June, 1709, he wrote to Godolphin : " There is no doubt a battle in the plains of Lens would put an end to this war ".[2] We may suppose that this hope of dictating terms at the end of another campaign, was one reason why he did nothing to force the Whigs and the Allies to accede to Louis' proposals. Yet, since he himself in the same week admitted great uncertainty as to the chances for the success of the invasion,[3] it is probable that he ought to have insisted upon peace. One reason of the poor part which he and Godolphin played this year, was that they were now wholly dependent on the Whigs, having no longer, after the dismissal of Harley, any hope of recovering favour either with the Tories or with the Queen.

The Dutch had followed the Whig lead in breaking off the negotia-tion, because they were offered a price. Ever since the beginning of the war, but most of all since the battle of Ramillies,[4] Marlborough, Godolphin and the Whigs had been in constant fear that the Dutch would make a separate peace with France. Louis had more than once approached the States of Holland with offers of a " Barrier," if they would conclude a separate treaty. As the only object for which they were waging war was to obtain territory and strong places in the Netherlands and France, sufficient to render them secure from French invasion in the future, there was every probability that they would some day accept these offers from Louis. Nothing remained for those of the Allies who wished the war to continue, except to buy the loyalty of the Dutch at a higher price ; this was what the Whigs did in 1709. The Barrier Treaty, signed between England and Holland, promised that Guelderland and the towns of Nieuport, Furnes, Ypres, Menin, Lille, Tournai, Condé, Valenciennes, Maubeuge, Charleroi, Namur, Hal, the castle of Ghent, and Dender-mond, should, at the peace, be placed permanently in the hands of the Dutch as a " Barrier " against France. They were to be allowed, not only to put garrisons in these places, but to levy taxes, and impose extra tariffs to the disadvantage of Austrian and English

Barrier Treaty, 1709

[1] " We shall be less able to support the war every year than another, but I believe we shall always be better able to do it than either our enemies or our neighbours " (to Marlborough, June $\frac{6}{17}$, 1709, *Coxe Papers*, B.M., xxviii.).

[2] 7th June, 1709. *Coxe Papers*, B.M., vol. xxviii. It is in this letter that he suggests reviving the Estates-General in France as part of the terms of peace to follow the " battle in the plains of Lens ".

[3] " It is impossible for me to express the apprehensions I have that we shall not find wherewithal to make the army subsist, especially if we enter France, so that it were to be wished the peace had been agreed " (to Godolphin, 13th June, 1709. *Coxe Papers*, B.M., vol. xxviii.).

[4] Godolphin to Marlborough, 17th May, 1706, and July $\frac{8}{19}$, 1708. *Coxe Papers*, B.M.

merchants, who bitterly complained.   In return, the Dutch promised
to send over troops to Great Britain to fight for the Hanoverian
Succession, if required.[1]   Secure of this immense accession of power
and wealth whenever the Whigs chose to make peace, the Dutch
followed them blindly in the policy of continuing the war.   Marlborough had long contemplated some way of binding the Dutch
to the war policy, but he considered the concessions of the Barrier
Treaty too large, and refused to join the Whig Ambassador, Townsend,
in signing it.   In the same spirit, unworthy of his great position, he
blamed the breaking off of the negotiations for peace, without doing
anything to prevent the rupture.   It was not by avoiding responsibility for the fall of Vienna and Turin that he had become the saviour
and guardian of Europe.

Renewal
of
hostili-
ties,
June,
1709

Holland and Austria, Marlborough, Godolphin and the Whigs
had all sinned against peace, and they were all to be punished by
events springing as direct consequences from their misconduct.   In
June, 1709, the negotiations at the Hague were broken off,[2] and
Louis, in desperate straits, deigned to take his subjects into his
confidence.   It was a new thing for the Grand Monarch to put
out a manifesto, recounting what sacrifices and humiliations he had
vainly offered to undergo as the price of peace, and appealing to
the patriotism of his people.   The spirit was roused which the
French have so often shown in defence of the sacred soil.   An immense army, more hungry and ill-clad than ever, but filled with
fresh ardour and justly reliant on their new commander Villars,
were drawn up in the trenches of Malplaquet, guarded on either
hand by deep forests.   Marlborough and Eugene, who had just
taken the great fortress of Tournai, confidently delivered an assault

Malpla-
quet,
11th
Sept.,
1709

on the face of this position.   Ninety thousand men of the various
nationalities belonging to the Grand Alliance, moved to the attack
against an equal number of Frenchmen ; twenty thousand of the
Allies had fallen, and nearly fifteen thousand of the defenders,
before Villars beat a slow and well-ordered retreat.   In spite of
the Field Deputies, the flower of the Dutch army, which they had
so often saved up when it might have been well spent, had at last
been thrown away in vain.   The heart was taken out of the war.
Mons fell to Marlborough in the winter, and Bethune, Aire and
St. Venant next year, but the allied armies were in no condition

---

[1] Swift's *Remarks on the Barrier Treaty*.   The object of the Whigs in offering
such high terms was not to obtain Dutch aid against the Pretender ; that could
have been obtained at a lower price, as was shown by the Barrier Treaties and
events of 1713 and 1715 (see map, p. 411).   The real object of the Whigs was to
bind the Dutch to the war.   This stands out clearly in the correspondence to the
time, but by far the best demonstration of it is to be found in Mr. R. Geikie's
analysis of the Barrier Treaty negotiations, unfortunately not yet published.
[2] They were temporarily renewed early in 1710 at Gertruydenberg, when Louis
made his last offer—Alsace.

to advance on Paris, until great political changes in England had
rendered such a movement impossible.

The Whigs miscalculated, if they thought that the periodic wave Trial of
of High Church fury would be kept back so long as the war con- Sache-
tinued ; and they hastened the event by a false step in home affairs. March,
Sole champions as they were of religious Toleration, they had little 1710
more conception than their opponents of the right of free speech in
politics, and had inherited from the Stuart despotism, which they
had overthrown, some bad notions of governmental prerogative.
At the advice of Godolphin, who had served James II., and who
still had hankerings after coercive methods, the Whigs impeached
Dr. Sacheverell before the House of Lords, for a sermon against
Revolution doctrines.   During the trial, the worship of the ridiculous
parson rose to a level with that of Charles the Martyr or the Seven
Bishops.   All the good and bad passions of Englishmen were aroused
against the prosecuting Government.   Even in their own London,
the Whigs could make no counter-demonstration against the frenzied
multitude who accompanied the Doctor's coach and the Queen's
sedan to the doors of Westminster Hall.   Inside, the scaffoldings
were again erected, as for a great historic scene ; Anne came day
after day, like Charles to the trial of Strafford ; and the Tory ladies
rose before seven each morning " to see and be seen at the trial,"
and importuned the " young lords " of their acquaintance to " make
a bustle to have their full number of tickets, eight apiece." [1]   The
eloquence of the Whig orators was chilled by the roaring of the
crowd outside the great doors ; at night, meeting-houses all over
London were sacked, and the ministers had to borrow the Queen's
bodyguard from St. James's to save the homes of Bishops and
Dissenters from similar destruction.

The light sentence passed upon the Doctor,—he was to be sus- Fall of
pended from preaching for three years,—showed that the Whigs the
were awed by the storm which they had provoked.   The Tories June-
and the Queen took heart.   The war was growing unpopular : Sept.,
the Barrier Treaty seemed to show that we were losing thousands 1710
of men every year in siege operations, to win an Empire for the
Dutch.   The name of Marlborough, who had foolishly asked the
Queen to make him Captain-General for life, aroused more jealousy
than enthusiasm among civilians.   In the summer of 1710, Anne,
at the instigation of Mrs. Masham, finally broke with Sarah, and
dismissed Godolphin and the Whigs from office.   They fell the
more easily, because they did not stand together : the Lords of the
Whig Junto [2] did not recognise either the General or the Treasurer

---

[1] *Wentworth*, pp. 112, 113.
[2] The Junto consisted of Somers, Wharton, Halifax (Montague), Orford
(Russell), and young Sunderland (Spencer).

27

as one of themselves, and Marlborough hoped to keep the military command even under a new ministry. A Cabinet was formed by Harley and St. John, and in September all was ready for a general election, with the influence of the Crown and its servants thrown into the Tory scale. Swift, who had come over from Ireland on ecclesiastical business, intending to return the moment it was done, found himself in the more congenial atmosphere of a political revolution. "Everything," he wrote to Stella, "is turning upside down. Every Whig in great office will, to a man, be infallibly put out; and we shall have such a winter as hath not been seen in England." [1] Indeed, since the winter of 1688, no change had taken place in public affairs so rapid and so complete.

Discipline of the Whig party, 1710-14

The result of the general election was to send back the Whigs in a hopeless minority. With Crown and people both against them, their case might almost seem as bad as it had been when Charles II. had dissolved the Oxford Parliament. But on this occasion the spirit of the rank and file was not broken, nor did the thoughts of the leaders run to desperate courses. The Lords of the Junto kept their heads and worked with cold calculation, first to stop the Peace, and when they had failed in that, to secure the Hanoverian Succession. The whole party moved under their orders like a regiment, forward or in flank movements, and sometimes right-about; at the end of five years they marched to complete and final victory.

The Tory party. Harley and St. John

Very different was the case of the Tories. The party of the landlords, larger and more homogeneous than the various classes who sought refuge under the Whig banner, was less disciplined and less intelligent. Harley and St. John lacked able lieutenants to stand between themselves and the swarm of ignorant and eager country gentlemen, who came up to London victorious from the polls and clamouring for vengeance on the Whigs. Vengeance was their one cry—they hardly knew for what; only they knew that 1681 had come again, and that rebels and fanatics were at last to meet their deserts. These stupid men found their leader in the most brilliant politician of the age; for St. John made himself the demagogue of squires. Harley, on the other hand, the nominal head of the Government, was suited to play the complementary part of moderate man; uncertain of what he ultimately wanted, yet cunning to obtain his immediate ends by deception, it was his business to keep the destined victims in play with fair words, while St. John hounded on the pack. Having begun public life as a Whig, Harley was able, at the time of the change of ministry, partly to separate the Junto from Marlborough and Godolphin by private promises that "a Whig game was intended at bottom". Coming of Nonconformist family, he was able to win some Presbyterian support at the elections

by assuring " their preachers that there shall be nothing this Parliament done against them, but their Toleration kept inviolable ".[1]
The one promise was as false as the other, but neither was altogether
without effect.

These two chiefs, so opposite in temperament and methods that Swift
they were sure to fall out in the end, in the first month of their
ministry attached to themselves a common friend.   Swift, who had
just written to Stella that Godolphin " received me with a great
deal of coldness, which has enraged me so, I am almost vowing
revenge," was in this humour asked to dine by Harley and flattered
to the top of his bent.   He became the constant boon companion
of the new ministers, who primed him over the bottle with facts
and arguments ; his pamphlets became the terror of the Whigs ;
he thought no more of returning to Ireland, but took lodgings
near town in the riverside village of Chelsea.   After his nights with
Harley and St. John, his walks home under the stars were made
perilous by the bands of " Mohocks," sons of Belial, rumoured to
be of the Whig persuasion, who were said to have vowed to slit
the parson's nose ; he sought safety in hiring a chair.[2]

Addison and Steele, less frequently and with more moderation, Pamphle-
wrote for the Whig party.   Before shorthand reporting enabled teering
the orator to address himself to all England, the pamphleteer and
literary man had to be enlisted at a high price by the politician.
They had also to be well protected.   No one in that age could write
freely on politics, if he was not sheltered behind one or other of the
great parties : for although there was no longer a political censorship, the freedom of the press was not in effect complete.   Government prosecutions for libel, and proceedings in either House of
Parliament, made it necessary even for Swift and Steele to publish
anonymously, and small fry had no quarter.   Early in 1714, while
Steele was being expelled from the Tory House of Commons for writing
The Crisis, the Whig House of Lords had fallen foul of the pamphlet
in which his great rival had answered him, had got the printer and
publisher in custody, and were only seeking evidence of authorship
to attack Swift himself.   Sometimes St. John had a dozen book-
sellers and publishers under arrest at the same time.   Swift used to
urge on his patrons to ruin his meanest Grub Street enemies.   " We
have the dog under prosecution," he once wrote to Stella, " but
Bolingbroke is not active enough ; but I hope to swinge him.   He
is a Scotch rogue, one Ridpath." [3]   The appearance of any important
pamphlet was a great event, talked of and heralded for weeks before ;
and the place where the politicians met to read and discuss it was

---

[1] *Wentworth*, p. 151.
[2] *Letters to Stella*, 9th September, 7th October, 1710, and 12th and 26th March,
1712.
[3] *Ibid.*, 24th October, 1711, and 28th October, 1712.

the " coffee-house," the centre of the vigorous politico-literary civilisation of the day.

Thus, in the last years of Queen Anne, " the town " became the theatre of a closely balanced party conflict, between tacticians as able and writers as gifted as any who ever struggled for power in Athens, Rome or Paris. Literary genius was then valued at its proper worth, but only because it consented to come down into the forum and hire itself out as a servant to political power.

Secret negotia-tions between England and France, Jan.-Aug., 1711

The Tories thought that they would not be secure in office until they had made peace. And if a Treaty were not signed before the Queen died, the House of Hanover might come in, recall the Whigs, and resume the war with the old vigour. By January, 1711, St. John was in close communication with Torcy, the Foreign Minister of Louis. For the next eight months these two carried on secret communications between London and Versailles, largely through the agency of the poet Prior. When the preliminaries of peace, assigning the disputed States in Europe and America to the various combatants, had been arranged between France and England, a conference was summoned for next year at Utrecht, where the other Allies were to be compelled to accept the terms dictated by the two principals.

Until August these negotiations with France were buried in absolute secrecy, and even then were only disclosed, owing to the ac-cidental detention of Prior by Custom-house officials on his way back from France. Swift himself had known nothing, and St. John had repeatedly denied to friend and foe that he was treating separately.[1] The proceedings had been concealed as carefully as Charles II.'s Treaty of Dover, though this time there was no crime to cloak.

St. John's action right in the two main principles

The two main principles of these negotiations—treating apart from the other Allies, and the abandonment of Spain—were necessary in order to obtain peace. The Allies were so obstinate, each for his own claims, that a conference at Utrecht might have sat for twenty years unless one of the Powers had previously agreed on the terms with Louis, and had come prepared to coerce the others into acceptance. William III., who best knew the needs of Europe and can hardly be accused of partiality for France, had made the Treaty of Ryswick in precisely this way, by preliminary private agreement with his great enemy. Whether the negotiations of the Tory minister need have been secret as well as separate, is another question. Certainly he need not have lied so often and so heartily as he did.

The abandonment of Spain was no less essential for peace. Philip could not be expelled. About the time that the negotiations were beginning, Stanhope's surrender at Brihuega put out the

---

[1] *Letters to Stella*, 24th August, 1711. Bol., i., pp. 66, 108, 123, 124, 141, 142. 172-74.

last hope in that quarter. In April, 1711, the death of the Emperor Joseph without children added another reason for leaving Spain to the House of Bourbon : Charles now became Emperor ;[1] he was in possession of Austria, Italy, the Netherlands, and if he were also to be King of Spain and the American Indies, he would revive the dreaded Hapsburg supremacy of Charles V.

But although the proceedings leading to the Treaty of Utrecht were right in their main principles, our negotiators approached the French in a spirit too friendly and even subservient. The Tories had so long been arguing that Holland was a more dangerous rival to us than France, that when they came into power they could not help acting as if it were true. Their political ideas, and the society in which they moved, made them glad to be rid of a degrading alliance with the tolerant and mercantile republic, and rendered them sensible to the flattery of the Grand Monarch and his courtiers. Prior and St. John, on their diplomatic visits to Versailles, accepted without hesitation the applause accorded to them as the saviours of France, and even Swift writes : " I took it very well of " the Spanish Ambassador, when he declared that " his master and the King of France were obliged to me more than to any man in Europe ".[2] *(margin: Attitude to France too subservient)*

Actuated by this spirit, the Tories withdrew military pressure from Louis. Early in 1711 they had sent an expedition against Quebec, and it had failed ; but Quebec might perhaps have been won nearer home. That year Marlborough made some progress, but could not march into France, partly because Eugene was engaged in the domestic affairs of the Empire. But in the spring of 1712, when Eugene came to the Netherlands with a large army, an advance might have been made that would have compelled Louis to yield all points still in dispute at Utrecht. Harley and St. John, however, had dismissed Marlborough from the command of the army (31st December, 1711), and they now withdrew the English troops from active operations (June, 1712). The Tory defence for deserting our Allies in the field was that nothing else would have made them accept the peace. It is hard to say whether or not this was true. In any case the Dutch and Austrians suffered defeat at Denain when the English troops had been withdrawn, and the Dutch soon afterwards signed the treaties. *(margin: English withdraw from the war, 1712)*

But the causes of the dismissal of Marlborough were domestic rather than international, and must be sought in the Parliamentary session of Christmas, 1711, when the Whigs made their great effort to prevent the peace. Every possible alliance at home and abroad was sought out and exploited by the Junto. The Dutch and Austrian envoys expostulated with the Queen : Eugene, though he *(margin: The crisis of the peace, Christmas, 1711)*

---

[1] See p. 386 above, note.
[2] *Letters to Stella*, 21st December, 1712.

came too late, was invited over to back their remonstrance. Marlborough was again brought to the front to declare that his victories
gave no security to Europe if Spain were left to the Bourbons. The
London mob, which had recovered from its fit of High Church zeal,
was to be stirred up by the traditional Whig methods ; preparations for a great Pope-burning procession were only frustrated by
the arrest of the waxen images by Government, on the eve of Queen
Bess's Accession Day. Above all, a coalition was formed with those
great Lords who, without being Whigs, were out of office and incensed against the ministers ; Somerset and Nottingham used their
influence with the Queen to induce her to change her servants. If a
new ministry could once be formed, no doubt was felt that, with the
influence of the Crown, the next elections could be " managed ".[1]
But while the Whigs could only hope for the Queen, they felt sure
of the House of Lords. Nottingham, the melancholy, dignified, religious leader of the High Churchmen, nicknamed " Dismal," made
an unprincipled bargain with the Whigs in the House of Lords, by
which he was to propose a motion for " no peace without Spain,"
and they were to let the Occasional Conformity Bill pass into law.
It was an odd affair. Nottingham, who had always before opposed
on high Tory grounds the vigorous prosecution of the war, now
moved to prevent the peace ; while in the disciplined Whig ranks
hardly a murmur was heard against the Occasional Conformity Bill.
The Dissenters were told that if the ministry fell the persecuting
Act could soon be repealed ; " Jack," as the Tory satirists put it,
had been induced to hang himself on the promise that he would
soon be cut down. The Bill went unresisted through the Lords,
where it had so often been lost. Meanwhile, on the 7th of December,
Nottingham's motion of " no peace without Spain " was carried by
sixty-two Peers to fifty-four. The ministerialists did not pretend
that with the Upper House against them they could go on with
the peace. Prior expected his friends to resign the next week,
and Swift told Harley that " I should have the advantage of him ;
for he would lose his head, and I should only be hanged, and so
carry my body entire to the grave ".[2]

31st Dec.,
1711,
creation
of Peers
and
dismissal
of Marl-
borough
But the two ministers were silently preparing a constitutional
coup d'etat. In spite of the influence of the Duchess of Somerset,
who threatened to be a new Sarah, the Queen was still on the side
of Harley and St. John. On the last day of December she created
twelve Tory Peers to carry the peace. The Whigs were beaten,
and knew it. Wharton could only jeer at the new jury of Lords,
asking them whether they intended to vote singly or by foreman.
On the same day that the patents were issued for the twelve Peers,

[1] *Letters to Stella*, 9th December, 1711.
[2] *Ibid.*, 8th and 15th December, 1711.

it was announced that Marlborough had been removed from the head of the British army.

Effective resistance to the peace was no longer possible in England ; and the defeat of the Dutch next summer as a conse- quence of the withdrawal of our troops, was soon followed by the submission of the statesmen of Holland.   On the 11th of April (N.S.), 1713, England, Holland and the minor powers signed the Treaty of Utrecht with France.   The Emperor Charles VI. thought that he saved his dignity by waging another year of unsuccessful war ; in 1714 he signed the Treaty of Rastadt, acquiescing in the terms arranged for him three years before by Torcy and St. John. *Treaties of Utrecht (1713) and Rastadt (1714)*

The Treaty of Utrecht was, except in minor points, a good settlement, and stood the test of time better than most diplomatic edifices.   As it did not leave great popular forces and aspirations out of account, like the treaties made on the fall of Napoleon, it gave to the polity of European states not only freedom, but stability for eighty years. *A sound settlement*

France was not dismembered.   If Marlborough's infantry had piled arms along the quays of Paris, the Allies would probably have taken back all the acquisitions of Louis and the Cardinals— Alsace, Franche Comté, and Artois.   But Louis was allowed at Utrecht to keep what he had won in the earlier years, before the bait of the Spanish Succession had lured him to his defeat.   Though his territories were left as great as in the time of William III., except for a few towns along the Netherland border, Europe was no longer afraid of him.   The prestige of France was gone and her fighting power exhausted.   Since she had been deprived of the rich recruiting grounds of Flanders and Italy, her own resources would not for a long time be again equal to the conquest of Europe.   She proved unable ever to renew her strength under the discredited system of society and government, once her glory, but now beginning to appear to philosophers as the cause of her misery and degradation.   It was not long before Montesquieu pointed to the constitutional government of England as the secret of prosperity and power. *France*

There was only one fear left from the French quarter.   If the sickly child who was to be Louis XV. were to die, Philip V. of Spain might disregard the provisions of Utrecht and claim also to become King of France.   In that case Europe would perhaps have to fight again to prevent the union of the two Crowns.   But it was better to run the risk of an uncertain event than to overset the balance of power by making the Emperor Charles VI. ruler of Spain.   So thought the English Tories, and they were right.

Holland was left secure from French aggression.   The danger that had sprung upon her so suddenly at the Treaty of Dover, and governed for forty years her whole domestic and foreign policy, *Holland* passed away at Utrecht. Not only was France exhausted, but the buffer State that lay between her and Holland was now occupied by Austria, instead of by the decadent power of Spain. Further, the Dutch were allowed to garrison a barrier of their own in the Austrian Netherlands, as formerly in the Spanish.[1] Holland had won her safety, but she had bought it at a price. The long struggle had exhausted her scarcely less than France ; and her economic strength being more artificial, could never be recovered when once it was lost. She has continued to be happy and prosperous, but after 1713 she was no longer one of the great powers.

Austria and the minor powers   Austria had contributed less than Holland to the armaments that had won the war, but she made greater acquisitions at the peace. Of these, she succeeded in preserving the Netherlands, Milan and the hegemony of Italian politics, until the revolutionary epoch. Savoy, Prussia and Portugal came off well at Utrecht, for the Tory jealousy of the Allies did not extend to monarchs of the second rank. The Catalans, however, were infamously betrayed : in spite of England's pledges, their *fueros* were not secured to them, and we stood by while Philip suppressed in a cruel war the aspirations which we ourselves had rekindled through the agency of Peterborough. For the Tories thought that none but English squires had a right to protect their liberties against a legitimate King.[2]

Great Britain   Great Britain was the power that gained most by the war and by the peace. In William's time, she had done little more than stand on her defence against Louis and the Jacobites ; William, rather than England, had been head of the League of Augsburg. But in the Marlborough wars, Britain held the Grand Alliance together ; she financed the other nations ; her fleet had almost a monopoly of the ocean ; her soldiers, for the first time since Agincourt, decided the fate of Europe on famous fields ; the great general of the Alliance was an Englishman ; and British ministers dictated the terms of peace. England was more powerful under Anne than under Elizabeth, for the maiden Queen had been content to prevent Philip from being the arbiter of Europe, and had never attempted herself to be the arbitress. But the glories of Anne offer a still more striking contrast to the shifty and despised international position of the Stuart Kings. The change was partly due to the rapid growth of our resources, but still more to the greater national unity consequent on the participation of the people in the policy of the Crown. Parliament had ceased to be the opposition and had become the government. England's civil troubles had for a hundred

---

[1] The Barrier Treaty of 1709 was torn up, but it was replaced by new treaties of 1713 and 1715. The towns that Holland obtained from the Tories were not so numerous and important as those which she had been promised by the Whigs, but they were sufficient. [They will be found marked upon the map of the Netherlands at p. 411.]

[2] Lecky, i., pp. 156, 157.

years handicapped her in the race between nations, but now that they were over, the effect of them had been to leave her supple and strong.   In the eighteenth century, a really national life and policy gave Britain advantage over the more populous but less vigorous dominions of Spain, Austria and France.

St. John took care to provide against the Whig argument that **British** he was selling our interests, as well as those of our Allies.   In **acquisi-** return for opposing the Austrian claim on Spain, Britain obtained **tions** very full compensation for herself.   We kept Gibraltar and Port **Utrecht** Mahon as the bases of our Mediterranean power ; according to the Whig proposals of 1709, these would have had to go back to our ally Charles, as King of Spain.   In America we acquired from France the outworks of Canada—the Hudson's Bay territory and Nova Scotia ; the French claim on Newfoundland was also abandoned, although the fishing rights off the coast were compromised.   And finally we obtained, by the Assiento Treaty with Philip, the sole right of supplying Spanish America with slaves.   The acquirement of a monopoly in the slave trade was approved by all parties as a sound piece of mercantile policy ; but the proposal to renew commerce with France by a reduction of tariffs on both sides, ran counter to the prevailing economic ideas of the merchant community, especially of the woollen industry and the East Indian merchants.   By the Methuen Treaty with Portugal, and the prohibitive duties against French wines, the course of trade had been deflected in one direction, and vested interests had been created which helped the Whigs to **June,** resist the Tory proposal to renew commerce with France.   They **1713,** succeeded in defeating the free-trade clauses of Utrecht, even in the **posals** Tory House of Commons.   St. John and Prior were unable to re- **to trade** establish the commercial intercourse, which, as they hoped, would **France** have softened the animosity against the French King, and have **defeated** created for party purposes a mercantile interest hostile to the Whigs.[1]

The stroke inflicted upon the Whigs by the dismissal of Marl- **Unpopu-** borough and the creation of the twelve Peers, proved irremediable **larity of** so long as the question of the day was that of peace or war.   The **Marl-** **borough,** country wanted peace, and the soldiers were no longer the favourites. **1712** The charges of peculation brought in Parliament against the late Commander-in-Chief served the Tory purposes for a while ;[2] Marlborough was hooted in the streets with cries of " stop thief " ; scores of vile scribblers abused him as an incompetent though fortunate

---

[1] See App. D, p. 437 below, for Mr. Meredith's remarks. Bol., iv., pp. 153, 196, 197.   *Parl. Hist.*, vi., pp. 1221-23. Burnet, vi., pp. 156-58. 161. Ashley, *Surveys Hist. and Ec.*, pp. 271-303.   Cunningham, pp. 458-62.   See p. 382 above, Addison represents his Tory Foxhunter as calling a man "one of the rump," "an old fanatical cur," because "he spoke twice in the Queen's time against taking off the duties upon French claret" (*Freeholder*, No. 22).

[2] A strict examination revealed that the great man had observed caution in filling his coffers, and had not gone beyond the custom of the service in that day (see p. 403 above).

general, a traitor, a coward, a Cromwell. Threatened with judicial proceedings, he retired to the Continent, where he was received with enthusiasm.

The Succession question saves the Whigs

It was only when the signature of the treaties in the spring of 1713 had rendered peace secure, that the Whigs were able to change the issue to one of immense advantage to themselves : the Queen was sinking to her grave, and the Hanoverian Succession was declared in danger. Although the question had not come to the front enough to cause the defeat of the ministers at the general election in the autumn, the minority came up next spring (1714) to the new Parliament in high spirits. For their chiefs had succeeded, by deputations and letters to Hanover, in convincing the Electress Sophia and her son George, that the Whig, not the Tory party was the friend. This impression had been created at the price of forfeiting all chance of a return to royal favour at present ; like Elizabeth, Anne could not forgive those who provided for her death and talked of the next reign. " I cannot bear," she had once told Marlborough, "to have any successor here though but for a week."[1] Furthermore, the daughter of James II. was inclined to look favourably on her brother's claim, if only he would turn Protestant. But the Whigs could no longer afford to humour her, as they had done in former years, when they were themselves in office and when there was no expectation of her immediate death. They now made motions in Parliament for putting a price on her brother's head, and proposed to bring over the Electoral Prince while she was alive, to look after the interests of his family (April, 1714). So little did they hope or fear from Anne, that on Princess Sophia's birthday in October, 1712, some of her party had lit a bonfire near St. James's Palace, and sung round it with drawn swords " Hanover, haste away over ".[2]

Fatal error of the Tories

The Tories fell into the trap. To secure themselves in the favour of Anne, they were cool in their protestations to the Court of Hanover. To enjoy the present, they shut their eyes to the future. When they saw what the Whigs were about, they should have outbidden them at the German Court, which would hardly have ventured to favour an unpopular opposition against the actual Government, if only those in office had shown the same zeal for the Protestant Succession. But the opposite course was the line of least resistance for Anne's ministers and for the party that upheld Sacheverell's doctrines, and down that course the Tories drifted

[1] *Conduct of the Duchess*, p. 153. See *E. H. R.*, i., pp. 470-506. A. W. Ward on *Electress Sophia*. *H. M. C. R.*, viii., 1, p. 52.

[2] *Wentworth*, p. 302. The ordinary version of the chorus ran thus :—

" Over, over, Hanover, over,
　　Haste and assist our queen and our State,
　　Haste over, Hanover, fast as you can over,
　　Put in your claims before 'tis too late."

Wilkins' *Political Ballads*, ii., p. 113.

throughout the years 1712 and 1713, without definitely intending
to become Jacobites, and without seeing the terrible danger towards
which they moved.   They themselves had, in 1701, passed the Act
of Settlement which fixed the Crown in the Hanoverian line, but they
now showed less than no zeal to implement it.   Early in 1714 they
suddenly became aware that, after a few months more of inactivity
on their part, the throne would be occupied by a new monarch,
filled with a prejudice, now ineradicable, against their whole party.
At the same time they recognised that their rivals were again in
favour with all good Protestants ; for while the Tories kept silence
about the Succession, the Whigs had been busy feeding the popular
mind with a mingled fear and contempt for " Perkin," as the
Pretender was called by their ballad-mongers.

> Whoe'er is in place I care not a fig,
>   Nor will I dispute between High Church and Low,
> 'Tis now no dispute between Tory and Whig,
>   But whether a Popish successor or no.[1]

Such was the Whig pose, and it carried the day.   " The generality,"
wrote one Tory Peer to another in March, 1714, " thinks of nothing
after the Queen, but the House of Hanover," " there is such an
aversion to Popery." [2]   Ruin stared the Tories in the face, for the
Electress and her son had at length come to regard them all as
enemies.   The perilous situation, once realised, was a touchstone
to reveal the opposite temperaments of the two Tory leaders, and
the long postponed quarrel between them burst at last into fury,
splitting the party from top to bottom.

St. John had been jealous of his colleague in office almost from Quarrel
the beginning.   In the spring of 1711, a half-mad Frenchman, of Oxford
Guiscard, had stabbed Harley at the Council board ; the victim Boling-
had, on his recovery, naturally become the favourite of Queen and broke
nation, and had been raised at once to the Earldom of Oxford.
It was more than a year later that St. John was moved up to the
Lords, and then, to his rage and mortification, only as Viscount
Bolingbroke.[3]   Yet it was solely owing to his energy that the
negotiations for the peace had been carried through.   He continued
for yet another year to chafe under the sluggish and secretive ways
of his senior colleague.   But when, in the winter of 1713-1714 he
perceived that the Fabian tactics which he despised and resented
were paving the way for the certain downfall of the whole party,
Bolingbroke thought the time had come to be rid of Oxford.

By this time Swift and the bulk of the party were for Bolingbroke,
since in his policy alone lay any hope of safety.   He soon won the

---

[1] Wilkins' *Political Ballads*, ii., p. 113.   [2] *Wentworth*, p. 361.
[3] Bol., ii., pp. 484, 485. " I own to you that I felt more indignation than ever
in my life I had done." " I remain clothed with so little of the Queen's favour
as she could contrive to bestow."

favour of Anne, who was beginning to find Oxford a careless servant. Mrs. Masham entered Bolingbroke's service, and was most pitilessly kept to her task as favourite ; when her son was dying, Swift stormed at her for nursing him instead of attending the Queen.[1] When the new Parliament met in February, Bolingbroke made a bid for the leadership by constituting himself the champion of the High Tory members and their " October Club ". For more than three years these men had been calling for severer legislation against the Dissenters, and for the reconstitution of the Civil Service and army on a High Tory or Jacobite basis. These measures, in deferring which Harley had had the support of many moderates, now seemed necessary if the party was to be saved from destruction on the Queen's death. If the Whig " supports," the Dissenters and monied men, were crushed, and if the High Tories were in complete control of every governmental force in the country, there would be good hope either of bringing back the Stuarts, or of dictating terms to the hostile House of Hanover. Which candidate for the throne Bolingbroke would select when the moment came, he would let the future decide. At present he was content if, before the Queen died, he could crush the Dissenters and place all civil and military posts, " down to the meanest," in the hands of High Tories and Jacobites.[2]

In May and June he hurried through the Schism Act, a large step towards the renewal of the Clarendon Code : its effect was to prohibit Dissenters from the education of children, even those of their own religion. It was openly avowed that the object was to extirpate Dissent in the next generation. The Bill rallied the Tories to Bolingbroke, who now declared war to the knife on all Whigs and moderates. On the 27th of July he induced the Queen to dismiss Oxford. Then at last he was free to take what measures he would. But Anne was sinking fast. It was a race against her death. In six weeks, he calculated, he could put the army and the State into the hands of men who could secure the Tory interest in the next reign, choose who was to be the new monarch, and dictate the terms

of his accession ; six weeks was all he asked, but he did not get six days. " The Earl of Oxford was removed on Tuesday," he wrote to Swift ; " the Queen died on Sunday. What a world is this ! And how does fortune banter us ! "[3]

During the week that the poor woman lay dying, her subjects had no time to think how good she had been, or to weep for her loss. Bolingbroke had forced all England to enter for a sweepstakes as to the date of her death. When the doctors reported her better, the stocks fell ; when she died, they rose. On the Sunday of her death

---

[1] *Letter to Mrs. Dingley*, 10th April, 1714.
[2] *Letters to Sir W. Windham* (ed. 1753), p. 22. See p. 392 above.
[3] And again : " Fortune turned rotten at the very moment it grew ripe " (*Letters to Swift*, 3rd August, 1714, and 24th June, 1727).

some Dissenters, who had come to pray together and prepare each other's minds for a long period of renewed persecution under a Catholic King and a Tory minister, burst out into a psalm of thanksgiving in their meeting-house when the news was told.[1] Bolingbroke, unprepared to resist, made a virtue of necessity, and joined with Shrewsbury, Somerset and Argyle to proclaim King George.[2]

So the principle of religious Toleration triumphed in England, Conclu-though many generations passed before it developed into that of sion religious equality. Under George I. the Whigs were strong enough to repeal the Schism and Occasional Conformity Acts, but they did not even attempt to abolish the Sacramental Test. Neither the parson nor the squire had really anything to fear from the statesmen whom they regarded as their enemies. Though persecution was warded off from Nonconformists and Freethinkers, the Church was not a penny the worse. Though the merchant classes remained high in favour with Government, though the nation continued to borrow from the monied men for her wars of Imperial expansion, yet squirearchy flourished in the eighteenth century as never perhaps before ; the yeomen disappeared, and the law by which the Tories had prohibited all except large landowners from sitting in the House of Commons (1711) was not repealed by their successors. For the arrival of the House of Hanover and the long rule of the Whigs that followed, was the triumph, not of Puritans or democrats, but of " moderate men," as they loved to call themselves. Indeed, a more democratic government would soon have been swept away by the forces of Toryism, which were really the most powerful principle in the economic society of that time. If England made no further political progress till after the Industrial Revolution, it was because she had, by sheer good fortune in the years 1688 and 1714, already advanced beyond the point guaranteed by her social structure and political education. Only cautious conservatism like that of Walpole could have staved off a violent reaction.

At a time when the Continent was falling a prey to despots, the English under the Stuarts had achieved their emancipation from monarchical tyranny by the act of the national will ; in an age of bigotry, their own divisions had forced them into religious Toleration against their real wish ; while personal liberty and some measure of free speech and writing had been brought about by the balance of two great parties. Never perhaps in any century have such rapid advances been made towards freedom. Whether in the sweat and anguish of that great battle and victory, the English lost

[1] Lecky, i., pp. 207, 258, 259.
[2] His mother, the Princess Sophia, died two months before the date when she would have become Queen of Great Britain.

certain finer spiritual qualities, whether the Whigs were inferior to the Puritans and the Tories to the Cavaliers, whether the value of life was greater among the contemporaries of Shakespeare than among those of Swift, it is profitable to inquire, provided we do not expect a final answer. The more honestly we attempt to compute the number and quality of the things wherein the value of life consists even in our own generation and at our own doors, the more complex and difficult does such a calculation appear. How much less then, shall we be able to pluck out the innumerable secrets of the past, count them, weigh them, and so find the total value of some dead century. Hundreds of untold stories may be no less noble and significant than the one story which, being famous in its own day, was enshrined in some superficial and imperfect record, whence now we drag it out and make it into history.

THE STUARTS

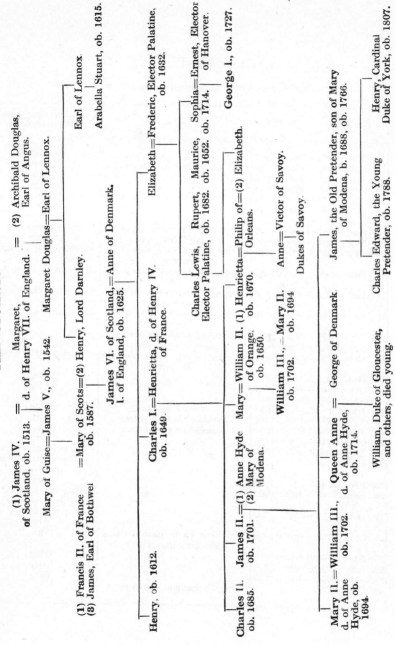

PARLIAMENTS, 1603-1715

Assemblies not legally summoned by the King are in italics

First Met	Dissolved.	Name.	Character of Majority in House of Commons.
1. Mar., 1604—Feb., 1611			Puritan
2. Apr., 1614—June, 1614		The Addled Parliament	Puritan
3. Jan., 1621—Jan., 1622			Puritan
4. Feb., 1624—Mar., 1625			Puritan
5. June, 1625—Aug., 1625		First Parliament of Charles I.	Puritan
6. Feb., 1626—June, 1626			Puritan
7. Mar., 1628—Mar., 1629			Puritan
8. Apr., 1640—May, 1640		Short Parliament	Puritan
9. Nov., 1640—*Apr.*, 1653		Long Parliament	Puritan
10. *July*, 1653—*Dec.*, 1653		*Barebone " Parliament"* nominated	Independent Puritan
11. *Sept.*, 1654—*Jan.*, 1655		*First Parliament of the Protectorate*	Anti-military Puritan
12. *Sept.*, 1656—*Feb.*, 1658		*Second Parliament of the Protectorate*	Anti-military Puritan
13. *Jan.*, 1659—*Apr.*, 1659		*Richard Cromwell's Parliament*	Anti-military Puritan
14. *May*, 1659—*Mar.*, 1660		*Restored Long Parliament*	
15. *Apr.*, 1660—Dec. 1660		*Convention Parliament*	Presbyterian-Royalist
16. May, 1661—Jan., 1679		Cavalier, Long, or Pensionary Parliament	Anglican-Cavalier
17. Mar., 1679—July, 1679			Whig
18. Oct., 1680—Jan., 1681 (elected Aug.-Sep., 1679)			Whig
19. Mar. 21—Mar. 28, 1681		Oxford Parliament	Whig
20. May, 1685—July, 1687		James II.'s Parliament	Tory
21. *Jan.*, 1689—Feb., 1690		*Convention Parliament*	Whig
22. Mar., 1690—Oct., 1695			Tory
23. Nov., 1695—July, 1698			Whig (Ministerial)
24. Dec., 1698—Dec., 1700			Malcontent, Whig and Tory
25. Feb., 1701—Nov., 1701			Tory
26. Dec., 1701—July, 1702			Whig or Moderate Tory ; for war
27. Oct., 1702—Apr. 1705			Tory ; but strong for war
28. Oct., 1705—Apr., 1708		The First Parliament of Great Britain (after 1707)	Whig
29. Nov., 1708—Sept., 1710			Whig
30. Nov., 1710—Aug., 1713			Tory
31. Feb., 1714—Jan., 1715			Tory
32. Mar., 1715.		First Parliament of George I.	Whig

APPENDIX A

THERE were indeed many ordinary Englishmen, and many Cavaliers, in Virginia and the Barbadoes, gone thither solely for economic reasons. But the Puritans in New England were more numerous and bred faster ; and, on account of geographical and climatic conditions, were engaged in the ordinary occupations of a white man's land, *e.g.*, fishing and corn growing ; the Virginians, on the other hand, who grew tobacco, had a system of indentured " servants," which from the outset prevented social equality, and in the following century gave place to negro slavery (*Economic History of Virginia*, Bruce, 1896, ii., pp. 572-73).

The Cavalier leaders in England, who largely consisted of those country gentlemen who were most attached to the soil, were less willing to emigrate than the Puritans. Thus, whereas the persecution of Puritanism (1620-40) sent many thousand Puritans to America, the persecution of Anglicanism and Royalism (1640-60) caused no corresponding exodus of Cavaliers ; a few only went out to Virginia. Those leaders of the Cavaliers who feared for their lives, took refuge in the towns of the Continent, waiting for better days. No permanent emigration was attempted by men whose habits and traditions did not incline them to start life afresh in a new country, with no attraction save the possible attainment of wealth by long and hard labour. No effort was made by the Cavaliers to find a new permanent abode for themselves in any part either of Europe or of the globe. The Anglicans felt they must live or die in England.

In the same way the large body of Catholics, though suffering severe intermittent persecution in England throughout the whole century, yet failed to make a success of their refuge colony, Maryland, which gradually lost its predominantly Catholic character. For the Catholics in England, even more than the Anglicans, were the non-industrial part of the population. They consisted almost entirely of country gentlemen and their retainers—the part of society least inclined to emigration.

In 1643 Massachusetts is calculated to have contained 15,000 inhabitants ; Connecticut 3,000 ; Plymouth 3,000 ; New Haven 2,500. These were the four principal confederated colonies, known as New England. In 1636 Rhode Island had also been founded by Roger Williams, as a refuge colony for unorthodox Puritans fleeing from the rigorous theocracy of the other colonies.

In 1648 Virginia is calculated to have contained 15,000 white men (of whom only 118 were Dissenters from the Anglican worship) and only 300 negroes.

For these calculations, see Justin Winsor's *History of America*, vol. iii., pp. 147, 148, 279, 312. Palfrey's *History of New England*, i., pp. 584, 585 and notes. For the latest historical views on early New England colonisation and society, see *The Founding of New England*, by James Truslow Adams. (Boston, 1921.)

The settlers in New England brought with them the habit of the large township or nucleated village characteristic of the eastern counties of old England whence they had migrated. But they left behind them the squire, or at least the idea of squirearchy. They submitted instead, for two generations, to the rule of the clergy and " church members," generally a small minority of the township and of the colony. After the Restoration of 1660, the battle of the untheocratic majority of the New Englanders was to some extent fought by the English Crown against the clerical theocracy. After the surrender of the Charter of Massachusetts at the end of Charles II.'s reign, the Revolution of 1689 restored the liberties of New as well as of Old England. But the renewed Charter of 1691 very properly provided for the liberty of the whole colonial community, and did not restore the political monopoly of a particular theological faction. " Thanks to England," writes Mr. Adams, " the final death-blow had legally been dealt to the theocracy, and the foundation laid for genuine self-government and religious toleration." The special importance of the affairs of early New England lay in this, that the New England township and its ideas of religion, politics and society spread ever westward, and, in gradually more diluted forms, extended across the whole vast continent. Fortunately the School had been a part of the original idea of the New England township.

APPENDIX B

THE POOR LAW AFTER THE RESTORATION

THE constant invigilation of the Privy Council over the local authorities did not revive at the Restoration. The regulation of prices in time of famine, and the rigorous enforcement of the Elizabethan Poor Law, by the supervision of the central power, had for ever come to an end. This class of Privy Council activity had not been made a political question, and resistance to it had not been connected with any set of opinions in Church and State. Therefore the decline of this function of the central government passed unnoticed in its own day. Yet one cause of its decline, probably, was that monarchical power in England was much diminished; and another, that society no longer lived in constant dread of the wandering bands of beggars. The Poor Laws had to some extent done their work in relieving the well-to-do from fear of a social revolution. As that fear declined, the interest in the condition of the poor declined also. One reason why the Poor Laws had not required vigorous enforcement under Long Parliament and Protector, was that high wages and regular employment had resulted from the state of war. During that period the custom, enjoined by the Poor Law, of employing able-bodied paupers out of parish stock set apart for the purpose, fell into disuse and was never revived. The other half of the Poor Law, the relief of the impotent poor out of the rates, had become and still continued the custom of the country, largely as a result of the vigour shown by the Privy Council under the early Stuarts.

After the Restoration, though the magistrates and the parishes supported their impotent poor, the heavy rates were paid grudgingly and on conditions. The parishes richer in ratable property or in common land, complained that undesirables came out of the poorer districts to squat on their commons, destroy their woods, and eventually claim poor relief from the community on which they had fastened. So in 1662 the Cavalier Parliament passed the Act of Settlement: this unfortunate measure enabled the authorities to prevent a labourer from moving into a parish, even if he had obtained employment within its bounds, if they feared that he might some day in the future come upon its poor-rate. The power granted by the Act was frequently and stupidly exercised by jealous rate-payers, the fluidity of labour was checked, and the working class deprived of personal and economic freedom for over a hundred and thirty years. It was the condition on which the upper and middle classes consented to fulfil their duty, that had now become traditional, of maintaining the impotent poor.[1]

[1] Leonard, pp. 132, 274-77, 296, 297. Cunningham, pp. 563, 570, 571. Adam Smith, *Wealth of Nations*, bk. i., latter part of chap. x.

APPENDIX C

WHO KILLED SIR EDMOND BERRY GODFREY?

UNLESS new evidence rather unexpectedly comes to light, the murderers of Godfrey will remain for ever undetected. I think the evidence (as stated by Mr. Pollock, *The Popish Plot*, pp. 100, 101 and note) precludes the theory of suicide, though Mr. Lang thinks there is still the shadow of doubt. The closest and most ingenious study of all the evidence as to the murder is to be found in Mr. Pollock's book. His theory is that Prance was really an accomplice, and told (roughly) the true story, but named the wrong men, wishing to shield the real murderers or instigators of the murder, the Jesuits about the person of James. The Rev. J. Gerard, S.J., author of *What was Gunpowder Plot?* has attacked Mr. Pollock as a romancer (see his pamphlet *The Popish Plot and its Newest Historian*). He has done much to clear the Jesuits of St. Omers of the implication of perjury in June, 1679, but on the larger issues he has said very little. Mr. Andrew Lang, however (*The Valet's Tragedy*, 1903, chap. iii.), has met Mr. Pollock in the face on the main issue. The student can form his own opinion on the debate. Nothing has been proved either way. I remark, however, that Mr. Pollock has laid too much stress on one particular motive which he has ascribed for the murder : there may have been any number of motives, personal or public, in an affair of which we know so little. Mr. Lang, on the other hand, has not explained why Prance was not flogged with his betters in 1685, and why he fled in company with the Jesuits in 1688. Until those facts are explained, Mr. Pollock's theories must at least be treated with respect.

APPENDIX D

COMMERCIAL AND COLONIAL POLICY OF THE RESTORATION ERA

THE best aspect of the policy of Charles II.'s reign, in which both Courtiers and Whigs had a share, was the encouragement of commercial interests and colonial expansion. The intelligent patronage extended by the King and Prince Rupert, by Clarendon and Shaftesbury to such enterprises as the Hudson's Bay Company, the planting of Pennsylvania and the Bahamas and the acquisition of New York ; and the wise treatment of our always difficult relations with stubborn Massachusetts (except indeed during the Tory reaction in the last years of the reign), all bear the same stamp of modern enlightenment as the Court patronage of the Royal Society. The Portuguese Treaty, the acquisition of Bombay, the wars with Holland, the Navigation and other restrictive laws indicated a growing consideration for the wishes and supposed interests of the mercantile class. But the time came when the Court's subservience to France for political and religious reasons ran counter to the sense of the mercantile community, who perceived that France was not only the political and religious enemy of England, but a commercial rival even more formidable than Holland.[1]

With regard to the restrictive economic policy of England in relation to foreign and colonial trade, Mr. Meredith writes : " There is no reason to doubt that the economic development of England was favoured by forcible entry into distant markets, by the iniquities of the Slave Trade, and in general by the exploitation of weaker nations. If the English had not forced an entry, the French, the Spanish, and the Dutch would have excluded them by force. Whether anything was gained by the attempts to monopolise these markets, and to secure them as well as the English market for English produce alone is more questionable. In particular the jealousy which wrecked the hope of a commercial treaty with France in 1713, was exaggerated and shortsighted " (see p. 425 above). After referring to the evil effects of the policy in Ireland, the American colonies and elsewhere, and to the gradual conversion of English statesmen to other views in the era of Adam Smith, Mr. Meredith adds : " The real problem is not whether the restrictive policy was beneficial, but whether sufficient national spirit to break up other nations' restrictions could have been generated without it. The promise of a monopoly is a simple and tangible gain, which the plain merchant can understand and fight for—or at least pay others to fight for. Neither his greed nor his patriotism will be so easily aroused by the proposal merely to reduce the foreigner to an equal position with himself, however probable it may be that by so doing he would satisfy at once a greater need and a larger patriotism."

[1] See Egerton, *Colonial Policy*, pp. 67-113. H. O. Meredith. *Economic History of England*, pp. 188-91.

APPENDIX E

FINANCE UNDER THE RESTORATION AND REVOLUTION
SETTLEMENTS

THE immense addition to national efficiency made by the National
Debt, the Bank of England, and more generally by the better relation
between King and Parliament caused by the Revolution Settlement,
are brought into very high relief by Mr. W. A. Shaw's revelation of
what had previously been the lamentable conditions of national
finance, as shown in his *Calendar of Treasury Books* for Charles II.'s
reign. Mr. Shaw shows that before Parliament obtained control
of policy in 1689, even the most loyal of Parliaments—the Cavalier
Parliament—had kept the King ludicrously short of money while
" there did not exist at the time in England any proper machinery
for anticipating revenue." This is so true that it is scarcely possible
seriously to blame Charles for the " stop on the Exchequer " in 1672.
" From the first day he set foot in England at the glorious and happy
Restoration his government was financially doomed." . . . " He
could not have escaped bankruptcy." Mr. Shaw has proved this
up to the hilt. Financially as well as politically the Restoration
settlement, giving Parliament control of the purse without control
over policy, was utterly unworkable. The Revolution settlement
was a financial necessity, to enable England to thrive in peace or
to conquer in war. For another part of Mr. Shaw's argument which
I am inclined to question, see p. 304 above note.

BIBLIOGRAPHY

The following lists have been compiled with the double purpose of assisting the general reader to books which he will care to read, and of pointing out to the student of the period some works where his studies can profitably commence. But see also notes to text above. In each of the following lists some books are recommended for both classes, others more specially to the student. The latter are distinguished thus—(st.).

I.—BOOKS FOR 1603-1660

(a) POLITICS AND WAR

MODERN

S. R. Gardiner. *History of England, 1603-42. Civil War. Commonwealth and Protectorate.* Together constitute the authority on the period for both general readers and students. See also Gardiner's *What Gunpowder Plot Was.* 1897. (st.) A conclusive answer to Father Gerard, S.J., *What was Gunpowder Plot ?* 1897. (st.)

S. R. Gardiner. *Cromwell's Place in History.* 1897.

✓S. R. Brett. *John Pym.* 1940.

✓G. M. Young. *Charles I. and Cromwell.* 1935.

✓John Buchan. *Oliver Cromwell.* 1934; and *Montrose.* 1928. Both excellent.

✓Maurice Ashley. *Oliver Cromwell.* 1937.

✓C. V. Wedgwood. *Strafford.* 1935.

✓C. H. Firth. *Oliver Cromwell.* (*Heroes of Nations Series.*) The highest authority on the subject.

C. H. Firth. *The Last Years of the Protectorate.* 1656-58. 2 vols.

Carlyle. *Historical Sketches (Reigns of James I. and Charles I.).* 1899. A posthumous work, less known than it deserves. Picturesque and philosophic descriptions of men and events. Not much historical authority.

Macaulay. Essays on *Hampden* and *Milton.*

D. Masson. *Life of Milton.* 6 vols. 1859-80 (new ed. 1881). (st.) Collection of data throwing much light on the period.

Lord Nugent. *Memorials of Hampden.* 1832. (st.)

H. D. Traill. *Strafford.* Julian Corbett. *Monk.* (*English Men of Action Series.*)

(Bacon). J. Spedding. *Letters and Life of Bacon.* 7 vols. (st.) Throws much light on the life of the period, and controverts Macaulay's Essay on *Bacon* (*q.v.*). For an impartial summing up, see R. W. Church's *Bacon* (1884). (*English Men of Letters Series.*)

H. A. Glass. *The Barbone Parliament.* 1899. (st.) Best monograph on subject.

John Foster. *Sir J. Eliot,* 1864. *Statesmen of the Commonwealth.* 1840. *Grand Remonstrance.* 1860. *Arrest of the Five Members.* 1860. Forster led the way, together with Carlyle, in the study of this period, and his works are still very readable monographs, and full of matter valuable to the student.

(Ireland.) Gardiner (*History, passim,* and *E. H. R.,* xiv., pp. 700-34) is the safest authority. Froude. *English in Ireland.* Prendergast. *Cromwellian Settlement.* (st.) J. T. Gilbert. *Confederation and War in Ireland.* (st.) 2 vols. 1882. Ludlow. *Memoirs.*

(Navy.) M . Oppenheim. *History of the Administration of the Royal Navy.* 1896. (st.) Julian Corbett. *England in the Mediterranean.* 1904. Vol. i.

(Civil War.) C. H. Firth. *Cromwell's Army.* 1902. The best book and the most learned authority on the military side of the war ; and throws much light on society, politics and religion. G. Godwin, *Civil War in Hants,* for details of a county war, and of Basing House. *Civil War of Lancashire* and *Lancashire Lord-Lieutenancy,* II. (Chetham Soc., 1844, 1859). (st.) Webb. *Civil War in Herefordshire.* 1879. (st.) R. W. Cotton. *Barnstaple during the Civil War.* (st.) C. R. Markham. *Life of Fairfax.* 1870, for the anti-Cromwellian view of military operations.

(439)

Carlyle. *Cromwell's Letters and Speeches.* The Letters and Speeches speak for themselves and are of the highest value ; as to Carlyle's running comment, he was the first modern who understood the character of Cromwell and the spiritual content of Puritanism. But he fails to understand the motives of all, whether Puritan or not, who opposed his hero. He shows, therefore, in this great poetical biography, a less catholic grasp of the whole period than even that shown in *Historical Sketches.* There is now an invaluable critical edition by Mrs. S. C. Lomas, 1904 ; the introduction by C. H. Firth is the best comment on Carlyle's book, and should be read by all intending to study either Carlyle or Cromwell.

Clarendon. *History of the Great Rebellion.* Full of noble writing, contemporary colour and valuable information, but full also of misrepresentations and misstatements. Fullest account of the inner counsels and quarrels of the Cavalier party. See Ranke, vi., pp. 1-29, and Firth, *E. H. R.,* xix., pp. 26-54, for analysis and estimate of its various parts. *Clarendon State Papers.* 1767. 3 vols. The documents used by him in composing his history.

Clarke Papers. (Camden Soc., 1891, 4, 9.) Introduction by C. H. Firth. Vol. i. Contains shorthand reports of debates of Cromwell, his officers and soldiers, on settlement of nation and political theory in 1647. These should be read by all who wish to know about the ideals of the interregnum.

Ludlow. *Memoirs.* 1894. Gives the strict Republican (anti-Cromwellian) point of view and type of character. Irish wars in detail. Valuable introduction by C. H. Firth.

Col. Hutchinson, Life of, by his Widow. Gives the point of view of the upperclass Independents, and is the most interesting personal story of all the memoirs of the period.

Bulstrode Whitelock. *Memorials.* 1860. *Swedish Embassy.* 1855, gives the point of view of a Puritan lawyer and constitutionalist, very much at sea under Cromwell and trying to serve his country in strange times.

Acts and Ordinances of the Interregnum. 1642-60. Edited by Firth and Rait. 2 vols. 1911. (st.)

S. R. Gardiner. *Constitutional Documents,* 1625-60. 1889. (st.) G. W. Prothero. *Statutes and Constitutional Documents,* 1559-1625. 1894. (st.) Selected documents with valuable introduction.

Court and Times of James I., and *Court and Times of Chas. I.,* 1848. (st.) Gossip of period, as it appeared to contemporaries, from day to day.

Rushworth. *Historical Collections.* 7 vols. (st.) For period 1618-48.

Thurloe. *State Papers.* 7 vols. (st.) For Republican period.

Cases in the Courts of Star Chamber and High Commission. (Camden Soc., 1886.) With introduction by S. R. Gardiner. (st.)

King's Pamphlets. Collection, British Museum. (st.)

Baillie's *Letters and Journals.* (Bannatyne Club, 1841.) For picturesque account of relations of Scottish and English Puritans, and Strafford's trial.

Sir Philip Warwick's *Memoirs.* Cavalier.

Verney. *Notes of the Long Parliament.* (Camden Soc., 1845) ; and for fuller reports, *The Journal of Sir Simonds D'Ewes.* Notestein. (Yale, 1923.)

Cromwell's Soldier's Catechism. Reprinted. (1900, Elliot Stock.) Tract for Roundhead army, illustrating Puritan attitude during the war. Nothing really to do with Cromwell.

Letters of Sergeant Nehemiah Wharton in Archæologia. XXXV. Journal-letters of a London prentice serving in Essex's army, to his master's family. Amusing and instructive as to character and condition of the first armies raised.

Lacy's play *The Old Troop.* Friendly satire on Cavalier soldiers by one who had served with them.

Sprigge. *Anglia Rediviva.* 1647. Semi-official history of operations of New Model, 1645-46. It contains a valuable map of Naseby. (st.)

Clement Walker. *Mystery of Two Juntoes* and *History of Independency.* Anti-Republican narrative of contemporary events, 1646-49. (st.)

A. Marvell. *Horatian Ode upon Cromwell's Return from Ireland.* This fine poem shows " how it struck a contemporary " (*Golden Treasury,* or *Marvell's Poems*).

John Walker. *Sufferings of the Clergy.* 1714. (st.) A biographical dictionary of many of the Anglican clergy persecuted, 1640-60. Not always reliable.

(b) RELIGION AND POLITICAL SPECULATION

MODERN

Lecky. *History of Rationalism.* Especially chap. i. on Witchcraft.

/E. Dowden. *Puritan and Anglican.* 1900. Essays and biographical studies.

J. N. Figgis. *Divine Right of Kings.* 1896.

Archbishop Laud Commemoration. 1895. Edited by W. E. Collins. Essays on Laud by Bishop Creighton and others.

L. A. Govett. *The King's Book of Sports.* 1890. (st.) Monograph on the subject.

W. A. Shaw. *History of English Church,* 1640-60. 1900. (st.) History of English Puritanism as an Established Church and its relations to Presbyterianism.

Neal. *History of the Puritans.* 5 vols. 1822. (st.)

G. P. Gooch. *English Democratic Ideas in the Seventeenth Century.* 1898. Should be read (together with *Clarke Papers,* vol. i.) by all who wish to understand the political and ecclesiastical ideas of the interregnum.

R. Barclay. *Inner Life of the Religious Societies of the Commonwealth.* 1876. (st.) For origins of the ideas of Quakerism and the most advanced sects.

Caroline Stephen. *Quaker Strongholds.* 1890.

✓ W. C. Braithwaite. *Beginnings of Quakerism.* 1912.

Hessey. *Bampton Lectures,* 1860. Lecs. vi., vii. on the origins of Sabbatarianism.

CONTEMPORARY

Laud's *Works (Library of Anglo-Catholic Theology).*

Ben Jonson's *Bartholomew Fair.* Butler's *Hudibras,* satires on Puritans.

Works of Andrewes, Chillingworth, Bunyan and Hobbes.

Fuller. *Church History.*

Baxter's *Life,* by himself. The early part gives a picture from inside of Puritanism before the Civil War. Later, the point of view of a moderate Presbyterian.

George Fox's *Journal.* One of the greatest spiritual autobiographies in the world.

Life of Thomas Ellwood, by his own hand. (Methuen, 1900.) A disciple of Fox. The early part gives an intimate and lifelike picture of a conversion to Quakerism—its ideals and the social sacrifices and family ruptures it involved.

Milton's *Prose Works,* especially *Areopagitica* and *Of Reformation in England.*

(c) SOCIAL

MODERN

Lady Verney. *Memoirs of the Verney Family.* 3 vols. 1892-94. Charmingly told story of the domestic life of a family actively engaged in politics and war under Charles I. and the Commonwealth. See also *Verney Papers.* (Camden Soc., 1853.) (st.)

College Life in the Time of James I., from *Diary of Sir Simon D'Ewes.* 1851.

Mark Pattison. *Casaubon, Life of,* and *E. H. R.,* xv., pp. 58-72, and books mentioned p. 15 above, note, for state of learning and the Universities.

D. H. Madden. *Diary of Master William Silence.* 1897. For sport, time of Shakespeare.

L. Einstein. *Italian Renaissance in England.* 1902.

J. A. Symonds. *Shakespere's Predecessors.* 1884.

CONTEMPORARY

Fynes Moryson. Itinerary (ed. 1617), and Fourth Part (ed. 1902, called *Shakespeare's Europe*), is the best of the books descriptive of English travel on the continent in the Elizabethan and early Jacobean period. See also books mentioned p. 6 above, note.

Lord Herbert of Cherbury's Autobiography. Illustrates very amusingly the customs of the upper classes in England and in France respectively, especially as to duelling.

W. Blundell. *Crosby Records.* *A Cavalier's Notebook.* (st.) Especially for condition of Catholics.

Stuart Tracts (Firth), 1903, and Arber's *Reprints*, and Percy's *Reliques* for specimens of popular prose, poems and ballads.

✓ Evelyn's *Diary.*

Diary of John Rous. (Camden Soc., 1856.) How things appeared from day to day to a country parson of some intelligence.

Journal of Nicholas Assheton. (Chetham Soc., 1848.) How things appeared from day to day to a country gentleman of little intelligence.

D'Ewes' *Autobiography.* 1845. 2 vols. *Diary of Walter Yonge.* (Camden Soc., 1847.) (st.) Typical Puritan gentlemen ; D'Ewes is more personal and intimate ; Yonge records the sort of daily news that reached and interested a Puritan Justice of Peace in Devonshire under James I. The interest in foreign affairs from a religious point of view is very marked.

Dorothy Osborne's Letters, rivals *Col. Hutchinson's Life* in personal interest, and light thrown on ordinary life of the period. See Macaulay's Essay on *Temple.*

Diary of the Duke of Stettin. R. H. S., 1892. How English customs struck a foreign visitor about the time of James I.'s accession.

Thomas Fuller. *Holy and Profane State.* Quaint descriptions of the various classes of the community.

Worcester County Records. Vol. i. (st.) Excerpts illustrating the ordinary business of courts and officials in an English county.

The Plays of the period illustrate most fully London life, as Ben Jonson's Comedies, Mayne's *City Match*, Chapman's *Eastward Ho !* Dekker's *Shoemaker's Holiday*, Beaumont and Fletcher's *Knight of the Burning Pestle.* But some represent the classes of country life, as Dekker and Ford's *Witch of Edmonton ;* and some the universities, as *Pilgrimage to* and *Return from Parnassus.* (Clarendon Press, 1886.)

II.—BOOKS FOR 1660-1714

(a) POLITICS AND WAR

MODERN

Macaulay. *History of England.* Essays on *Temple, Addison* and *War of Succession in Spain.*

Osmund Airy. *Charles II.*

✓ Arthur Bryant. *Charles II.*, and his *Samuel Pepys* (3 vols.).

David Ogg. *England in the Reign of Charles II.* (2 vols.). 1934.

✓ W. A. Shaw. *Calendar of State Papers, Treasury Books* from 1660 on. (1904-1913.)

Klopp (Onno). *Der Fall des Hauses Stuart.*

Feiling, K. *History of the Tory Party*, 1640-1714. (1924.) Specially good for ✓ the reigns of William and Anne and the rehabilitation of Harley.

John Pollock. *The Popish Plot.* 1903. For a brief notice of the controversies aroused by this interesting and scholarly book, see *The Popish Plot and its Newest Historian*, Rev. J. Gerard, S.J. ; *The Valet's Tragedy*, A. Lang, chap. iii. ; and Appendix C. above.

Clarke and Foxcroft. *Life of Bishop Burnet.* 1907.

Acton. *Secret History of Charles II.* No. 1., *Home and Foreign Review.* But see also A. Lang's *The Valet's Tragedy*, chap. viii.

Sir G. Sitwell. *The First Whig.* 1894 (unpublished). A most learned and entertaining description of Whig electioneering and party methods, *temp.* C. II.

Sir James Stephen. *History of Criminal Law in England.* (st.) Consult especially for his opinion of the various State Trials, *temp.* C. II.

W. P. Christie. *Life of Shaftesbury*, 1871. (st.) H. C. Foxcroft. *Life of Halifax.* 1898. (st.) Valuable letters and documents.

H. D. Traill. *Shaftesbury.* (*English Worthies Series.*) 1888. An appreciation of his importance in English political development.

O. Airy. *English Restoration and Louis XIV.* 1888. Best short text-book for 1660-78, especially for foreign affairs.

✔ Feiling, K. *British Foreign Policy, 1660-1672.* 1930.

F. W. Head. *The Fallen Stuarts.* 1901. (st.)

V. Barbour. *Henry Bennet, Earl of Arlington.* (1914.)

Viscount Wolseley. *Life of Marlborough.* 1894.

Ferguson the Plotter. 1887. (st.) For the Rye House Plot.

Lecky. *History of the Eighteenth Century.* Vol. i. The best book about the domestic history of Anne's Reign.

F. W. Wyon. *History of Great Britain under the reign of Queen Anne.* 1876. An excellent book and the fullest history of the reign.

W. Coxe. *Memoirs of Marlborough.*

Atkinson (C. T.) *Marlborough and the rise of the British Army.* 1921.

✔ G. N. Clark. *The Later Stuarts, 1660-1714.* 1934.

✔ G. M. Trevelyan. *England under Queen Anne.* 3 vols. 1930-1934.

Winston Churchill. *Marlborough and his Times, 1933-1938.*

✔ Stanhope. *Reign of Queen Anne.* 2 vols. Generally trustworthy and readable, but not exhaustive.

Churton Collins. *Bolingbroke.* 1886. A brilliant essay, and perhaps the best appreciation of Bolingbroke. Its view of his career and character should be contrasted with that of W. Sichell, *Bolingbroke,* 1901. (st.)

✔ Leslie Stephen. *Swift.* (*English Men of Letters Series.*)

r W. J. Ashley. *Surveys Historical and Economic.* 1900, pp. 268-303. *The Tory Origin of Free Trade.*

(Spain.) Col. A. Parnell. *History of War of Succession in Spain.* 1888. (st.), and *E. H. R.,* vi., pp. 97-151 (st.), exposing worthless nature of *Carleton's Memoirs.* W. Stebbing. *Peterborough.* (*English Men of Action Series.*) Stanhope's *Reign of Queen Anne,* and Macaulay's Essay on *War of Succession in Spain,* must be cautiously read in the light of Col. Parnell's discovery.

(Navy.) Capt. Mahan. *Influence of Sea Power upon History,* chaps. ii.-v. J. R. Tanner's Introduction to *Descriptive Catalogue of Pepysian MSS.,* 1903. (Navy Records Soc.) (st.) Pepys' *Diary. Social England,* v., pp. 377-88. Julian Corbett. *England in the Mediterranean.* 1904. Vol. ii.

ı William Law Mathieson. *Scotland and the Union, 1695-1707.* 1905.

CONTEMPORARY

Clarendon. *Life.* His own account of his ministry and fall. See Ranke, vi., pp. 24-29, for critical estimate of the book.

Pepys', Evelyn's and Narcissus Luttrell's *Diaries.*

Anchitel Grey. *Debates of the H. of C.,* 1667-94. 10 vols. 1769. (st.)

Burnet. *History of his Own Times.* Vols. i., ii., in ed. 1897, with O. Airy's critical notes, form an authority on the reign of Charles II. Vols. iii.-vi., ed. 1833. For a just estimate of the value of this much-disputed work, see Ranke, vi., pp. 45-87, and Mr. Airy's Preface, pp. v-ix.

Clarke. *Life of James II.* 1816. (st.) Only in early parts tantamount to James's own memoirs. See Ranke, vi., pp. 29-45, for critical estimate, and *Macpherson* Papers, vol. i. (st.)

Francis North's *Examen,* and Roger North's *Lives of the Norths.* (Bohn, ed. 1890.) Contemporary Tory view of events, and the Norths' views of persons, 1678-85. Full of colour ; throws great light on society of the time, especially the lawyers.

Clarendon (2nd Earl). *Correspondence and Diary.* (*Temp.* 1676 to Revolution.) 2 vols. (ed. 1828). (st.)

Marvell's *Works,* i. *Growth of Popery.* (st.) A fine pamphlet, which throws light on causes provocative of the formation of the Whig party.

Dryden. *Absalom and Achitophel,* the great political satire on Shaftesbury and the Exclusionists. *The Medal.* Satire on Shaftesbury at time of his acquittal. *Hind and Panther.* Satire in favour of Catholicism. (*Temp.* J. II.)

Sir W. Temple's *Memoirs.* (st.)

Memoirs of Thomas Bruce, Earl of Ailesbury. (Roxburgh Club, 1890.) A personal friend of C. II. during the Exclusion agitation.

J. Macpherson. *Original Papers*. 1775. (st.) Courts of St. Germains and Hanover, and relations of English statesmen to them.

Coxe Papers MSS., in B.M. (st.) for large masses of political correspondence (*temp.* Anne) still unprinted ; see also *Hist. MSS. Com. Report*, viii. (st.)

Conduct of the Duchess of Marlborough. By herself. 1743.

Marlborough's Despatches. (st.)

Lettres Historiques. (st.) Impartial. Till 1710 written by Dumont. Printed at the Hague. Excellent on the internal affairs of England, as well as European affairs.

Boyer's Annals. (st.) Whig.

Torcy. *Memoirs*. 1757. (st.) 2 vols., and *Bolingbroke's Letters*. 4 vols. 1798. (st.), together are the authorities for the secret negotiations which led to the Treaty of Utrecht. See also Torcy for the conferences of 1709-10.

Works of Swift, especially *Conduct of the Allies, Barrier Treaty, Public Spirit of the Whigs, Journal to Stella, Last Four Years of Queen Anne*.

Arbuthnot's *History of John Bull*. Tory satire on the foreign wars.

Works of Addison, and *Spectator, Tatler, Guardian*.

E. Ward. *Calves Head Club and Hudibras Redivivus*. Tory satires.

(b) RELIGION AND POLITICAL SPECULATION

Modern

✓Leslie Stephen. *History of Eighteeenth Century Thought*. *Hobbes*.

Lecky. *History of England*. Vol. i., chap. i.

H. Foxe Browne. *Locke*. 1876. 2 vols.

Basil Willey. *Seventeenth Century Background*. 1934.

M. R. Brailsford. *The Making of William Penn*. 1930.

Contemporary

Eikon Basilikê (then believed to be by Charles I.), and Butler's *Hudibras*. The two most popular works among the Anglicans.

Swift. *Tale of a Tub*. Defence of the Anglican position against Rome and Geneva.

Works of Locke, W. Penn, Jeremy Taylor, Hoadley (st.), third Lord Shaftesbury (st.)

Filmer's *Patriarcha*. Statement of the Tory political creed as accepted 1680-87, though written during Civil Wars.

History of the Quakers. W. Sewell. 1725.

(c) SOCIAL AND ECONOMIC

Modern

Macaulay. *History*. Chap. iii. should be compared with Sir G. Sitwell's *Old Country Life*, 1901 (unpublished), and Babington's *Mr. Macaulay's Character of the Clergy*, 1849. Lecky (*History of England*, chap. i., pp. 93-98, ed. 1892) appears to take Macaulay's view of the condition of the clergy.

J. Ashton. *Social Life in Reign of Anne*. 1882. 2 vols.

Memoirs of Sir John Reresby. Ed. A. Browning, 1936.

Contemporary

Pepys and Evelyn. *Diaries*.

Defoe. *London to Land's End*, and his works of fiction.

Hamilton. *Grammont's Memoirs* (for Court of Charles II.).

Comedies of period (Wycherley, Congreve, etc.), and Jeremy Collier's *Short View of the Immorality of the English Stage*.

Eachard. *Contempt of the Clergy*. Complaint of the poverty and low social status of the clergy, *temp.* C. II., perhaps exaggerated.

Works of Swift, Addison, Steele.

(Sport.) *Gentleman's Recreation*. 1686. With many interesting illustrations.

III.—BOOKS REFERRING TO BOTH THE PERIODS
(1603-1660 AND 1660-1714)

(a) GENERAL HISTORIES

Holdsworth (W. S.)   *History of English Law* (especially vol. v. on Coke).

Ranke.   *History of England principally in the Seventeenth Century.*   (Translation 1875.)   One of the great histories of our country, too much neglected.   The cause and growth of English parties in their wider aspect are luminously exposed, as also foreign relations.

Green.   *History of the English People* (*sub loc.*).   Its qualities as a general account of the period are too well known to need comment.

Hallam.   *Constitutional History of England* (*sub loc.*).   Excellent on the general history of parties and politics, as well as on the constitutional points which it treats at length.

Hume Brown.   *History of Scotland.*   vols. ii.-iii.

Andrew Lang.   *History of Scotland.*   vols. iii.-iv.

Lingard.   *History of England* (*sub loc.*).   A very readable history of the old school, told with candour and impartiality by a moderate Catholic.   But a good deal has been discovered since Lingard wrote in the first half of the nineteenth century.

Mathieson.   *Politics and religion in Scotland from 1550 to 1695.*   1902.   *Scotland and the Union.*   1905.

(Foreign policy and war).   Corbett.   *England in the Mediterranean.*   2 vols. 1904.   Seeley.   *Growth of British policy*, 2 vols., 1895, is *An Historical Essay* on the external relations of Britain and their connection with her political and religious development, from Elizabeth to William III.

H. E. Egerton.   *A Short History of British Colonial Policy.*

Bagwell, Richard.   *Ireland under the Stuarts.*   3 vols.   1909-1916.

(b) ECONOMIC AND SOCIAL

Alfred Marshall.   *Principles of Economics* (1891), chap. iii.

W. Cunningham.   *Growth of English Industry and Commerce.   Modern Times*, i., ed. 1903. (st.)   At present the highest authority on this subject which is, however, in a state much further removed from finality and certainty than the political history.   See also the old edition.

Thorold Rogers.   *Six Centuries of Work and Wages.*   1884. (st.)   *History of Agriculture and Prices.*   1866-87.   Vols. v., vi. (st.)   Largest collection of statistics, and much interesting comment.

W. A. Hewins.   *English Trade and Finance, chiefly in the Seventeenth Century.*   1892.   (*University Extension Series.*)

H. O. Meredith.   *Economic History of England.*   Bk. iii.

Lady Verney.   *Memoirs of the Verney Family.*   1899.

Pearsall Smith.   *The English Language.*   (Home Univ. Lib.)

Miss Leonard.   *Early History of English Poor Relief.*   1900. (st.)

A. H. Hamilton.   *Quarter Sessions from Elizabeth to Anne.*   1878. (st.) Illustrations of the ordinary business of quarter sessions.

G. Dowell.   *History of taxation in England.*   Ed. 1888. (st.)

Social England.   Vol. iv.   1895. (st.)   Articles and bibliographies on various aspects of English life, by well-informed writers.

Wallace Notestein.   *English Folk.*   1938.

Gladys Scott Thomson.   *Life in a Noble Household*, 1641-1700.   1937.   The Russell family and estates.

MacPherson's *Annals of Commerce.*   1805.

McCulloch's *Select Tracts on Commerce.*

(Population.)   Gregory King.   *Political Observations.*   1696.

(Health.)   C. Creighton.   *History of Epidemics.*   1891.   Defoe.   *Journal of the Plague Year.*

(Justice and Police.)   Sir James Stephen.   *History of Criminal Law in England.* 3 vols.   1883.   Melville Lee.   *A History of Police in England.*   1901.

(Army.)   J. W. Fortescue.   *History of the British Army.*

(c) WORKS OF REFERENCE AND ORIGINAL AUTHORITIES

The *Harleian Miscellany*, 1808, and *Somers' Tracts* are the two collections of pamphlets, etc., on all subjects, political, religious and social, most easily obtainable by, and most valuable to, general readers and students.

Reports of Historical MSS. Commission. For numerous collections of private and official letters, etc.

Statutes of Realm. (st.)   *Journals of House of Lords* and *House of Commons.* (st.) *Parliamentary History.* (st.)   *Calendar of State Papers.* (st.)

State Trials (Cobbett). Verbatim reports of the great State Trials of this period ; presents the most life-like picture of seventeenth century politics that we possess. See especially the trials in the reign of Charles II.

Dictionary of National Biography.

Sir W. Anson. *Law and Custom of the Constitution.* 1892.

INDEX

29